Legal History of the Color Line

The Rise and Triumph of the One-Drop Rule

Frank W. Sweet

Backintyme
Palm Coast, Florida, U.S.A.

Backintyme
30 Medford Drive
Palm Coast FL 32137-2504

386-446-4909
website: http://backintyme.com/publishing.htm
email: sales@backintyme.com

Printed in the United States of America
First Printing, July 2005

ISBN: 0-939479-23-0
Library of Congress Control Number: 2005905436

Dedicated to those courageous souls
who reject the madness,
check off "other,"
and write in "human."

Table of Contents

List of Figures

List of Tables

Acknowledgements

Foremost among those who provided encouragement and support are the former writers and editors of *Interracial Voice* magazine. Along with her advice, A.D. Powell provided stacks of newspaper clippings and other documents on the plight of those who do not fit comfortably on either side of the color line. The other members of the *Interracial Voice* team also helped my research, but I am particularly indebted to Charles Byrd, Javier Nelson, James Landrith, George Winkel, and Susanne Heine for their encouragement and support.

The moderators of the OneDropRule discussion group also have my gratitude. Barbara (Liana) Yanez, Tyrone (gemini072) Anderson, and Gordon (G-Man) Tapper have helped me to see the sometimes-subtle contrast between ethnic self-identity and biological ancestry. Among the group's members, John M. Hartley also stands out in my appreciation. Although our opinions often clashed, his uncompromising anti-racism often forced me to reconsider how best to express past events.

Mary Lee Sweet, my wife of 43 years, worked tirelessly researching court cases, writing case summaries, and proofreading the text. Most of all, she provided a patient and intelligent sounding board for ideas and arguments, without which this book would have been impossible.

The book's cover shows the scales of justice weighing a bicolor feather in the balance. The chains that suspend the scale tray are double helixes of DNA. This cover design was created by Jerry Forney of StoryTree Productions in Melbourne, Florida (http://www.storytreeonline.com).

Finally, many of the court cases were researched online using the remote access facilities of the George A. Smathers Libraries at the University of Florida in Gainesville.

About the Author

Frank W. Sweet earned a Ph.D. candidacy in history at the University of Florida in June 2003 and, at this writing, has completed all but his dissertation defense. He earned an M.A. in History from American Military University in 2001 and a B.E.E. from Cornell University in 1964. He is the author of eleven historical booklets and one trade paperback currently in print, and numerous published historical essays. He was a member of the editorial board of the magazine *Interracial Voice*, is a regular lecturer and panelist at historical conferences, and moderates an online discussion group on the history of U.S. racialism. His web site is at <http://backintyme.com/publishing.htm>. This book is his dissertation.

Mr. Sweet was born Francisco R. Valiente in 1939 Ponce, Puerto Rico, the son of a civil engineer father of Colombian and Mexican extraction and a schoolteacher mother of Puerto Rican and Spanish descent. He took the name Frank W. Sweet after his mother's remarriage to an officer in the U.S. Army Medical Corps who was based in Puerto Rico during World War II. A National Merit finalist from St. John's Preparatory School in Santurce, PR, he attended Cornell University on scholarships, and was awarded a Bachelor of Electrical Engineering in 1964. He married Mary Lee Howard (from North Carolina, of Irish extraction) in 1962 and joined IBM.

In 1972, he founded a software consulting practice. For 27 years, his firm served clients in England, France, Germany, Italy, Spain, Argentina, Venezuela, Brazil, and the United States. He served as the national chair of a professional association of database engineers, published nearly one hundred articles in the computer trade press, presented over a dozen papers at national conferences, and published six books on database and application design. He retired from consulting in 1999.

Chapter 1.
Introduction

In October of 2003, Miramax Film Corporation released *The Human Stain*, a movie starring Anthony Hopkins as a college professor named Coleman Silk. The character was born into a Black family but spent 50 years living as a White man. Some 237 published reviews of this film are available at a movie-survey web site.[1] Most reveal the above plot twist (a few do not reveal the "spoiler"). Of the former, virtually all describe Silk as a light-skinned Black man who pretended to be White.

- [Silk's] personal life is infected with cancer of a lie he has been living with for fifty years. – http://www.miramax.com/thehumanstain/

- Coleman Silk, a light-skinned black man able to pass for white in the segregationist pall of the 1940s. – Rob Vaux, *Flipside Movie Emporium*

- Silk, whom most people assume to be Jewish, is actually a very light-skinned African-American. – Craig Roush, *Kinopio's Movie Reviews*

---

[1] See URL <http:// rottentomatoes.com/m/TheHumanStain-1125977/reviews.php>.

- Setting aside the physical problems [Hopkins] of play-ing a light-skinned African-American with a Welsh burr in his voice... – James Rocchi, *Netflix*

- This Job-like tale of Coleman Silk (Anthony Hopkins), a black man who has spent his life posing as a Jew... – Peter Travers, *Rolling Stone*

- Coleman Silk is a black man who has passed for white for most of his adult life... – A. O. Scott, *New York Times*

- [Silk] is living a lie as a white Jewish intellectual with invented parentage when he was actually born into a light-skinned African-American family... – Andrew Sarris, *New York Observer*

- Anthony Hopkins is a bewildering choice to play a black man in "The Human Stain." Even a very, very fair-skinned black man, who has disguised his race... – Paul Povse, *State Journal-Register, Springfield IL*

- Silk is, as a matter of fact, an African American in dis-guise as a white upper-class intellectual. – Jeffrey Overstreet

- Coleman Silk, a light-skinned African-American who has passed himself off as a white Jew... – Austin O'Connor, *Lowell Sun*

- The professor is a light-skinned African-American who has been passing as white since he was in school. – Nell Minow, *Yahoo! Movies*

- The Human Stain, which stars Anthony Hopkins as a light-skinned African-American... – Marty Mapes, *Movie Habit*

- [Silk] is in fact an African-American who had decided early on to pass for Caucasian... – Harvey S. Karten, *Compuserve*

- While the 50-year lie lived by Silk may be understand-able in our racist culture... – Erica Abeel, *Film Journal International*

Page after page, many dozens of reviews say the same thing: Silk is "Black." Try as you might, you are unlikely to find even one that describes the character as "a White man with a trace of African ancestry." What is going on here is the American practice of labeling someone (and expecting a person to label himself) as "Black" if they have any African ancestry at all, no matter how distant or invisible. You could call it the idea of "invisible blackness."

The movie is fiction of course, but columnists are real people who earn a living writing for real readers. Those who lose touch with the popular culture of their readers see their columns dropped from publication. The public expects invisible-blackness rhetoric, so movie review columnists write invisible-blackness rhetoric: "a light-skinned Black man passing for White." Even scholars use the same rhetoric without noticing it.[2] They do this so unconsciously, so naturally, and so off-handedly, that most Americans do not see it until someone points it out to them. To someone from another country, it reminds of a building with an odd smell, to which its residents have become so accustomed that they no longer notice it.

* * * * *

This book traces the history of the idea of invisible blackness—the most extreme manifestation of America's one-drop rule—in three major sections: *Section I. America's Admixed Population, Section II. The Endogamous Color Line*, and *Section III. The One-Drop Rule*.[3] The one-drop rule (the idea of invisible

---

[2] A particularly instructive example can be found in Julia M. Klein, "'Human Stain' From Page to Screen: Self-Invention to Self-Revelation," *Chronicle of Higher Education*, October 31, 2003.

[3] Some people use the term "one-drop rule" as synonymous with Marvin Harris's term "hypodescent," [see Marvin Harris, *Patterns of Race in the Americas* (Westport CT, 1964)] meaning that Americans of visible African admixture are considered Black, even if that admixture is less than 50 percent. In much of the Caribbean, in contrast, you are White if you look mostly European. This book instead focuses on the most extreme form of one-drop. It examines the history of the idea that Americans who look completely, utterly European, without even a hint of Africa, are still classified as

blackness) became written law in many states starting in 1910 in order to enforce and maintain the oppression of Blacks by Whites during the Jim Crow era. But the very definition of the two groups, "Blacks" and "Whites," depends on the existence of an endogamous color line.

Americans have many overlapping names for demographic groups, names like: "Jews," "liberals," "Hispanics," "Blacks," and the like. Many of the groups (conservatives, liberals, pro-choice, pro-life) are seen as ideological voting blocs, whose members share no cultural or biological traits in common. Other groups (Irish-Americans, German-Americans, Italian-Americans) are perceived as sharing national origin. Still other groups are supposedly delineated by ethnic traditions of language or religion, rather than by nationality. Among these are Jews, Slavs, and Hispanics.[4] Finally, a few groups (Blacks, Asian-Americans, Native Americans, Whites) are visualized as comprising people who share unique biological traits. These last groups are called "races" on U.S. government forms.

The U.S. distinction between "race" and "ethnicity" is not always clear. Until about 1945, most Americans considered Jews to be a separate "race," and some Americans still see them as such (many Orthodox or Hassidic Jews, for example, see themselves thus).[5] Similarly, many matriculation or employment ap-

---

members of the Black endogamous group. That is, they are seen as unsuitable marriage partners by Whites but suitable by Blacks because of an invisible touch (one drop) of Black ancestry.

[4] Neither Ireland, Germany, nor Italy existed as nations when such national-origin labels were coined. Bavarian immigrants did not see themselves as having much in common with Prussians, nor did Corkers identify with immigrants from County Kaman, nor Neapolitans with Milanese. America's "umbrella" ethnicities (each label covering diverse people seen as similar only in America) were invented in the nineteenth century to enhance immigrants' political clout. The process is visible today in the Anglo-American-invented label "Hispanic," which covers both Puerto Ricans and Chicanos, despite their having little in common. A useful introduction to the concept of "ethnicity" is Werner Sollors, *The Invention of Ethnicity* (New York, 1989), especially the introduction and the chapter by Kathleen Conzen.

[5] For a detailed account of the transformation of Jews from "race" to "ethnicity," see Karen Brodkin, *How Jews Became White Folks and What That Says About Race in America* (New Brunswick NJ, 1998) or the earlier

plication forms that today collect data for federal agencies tell
the applicant to check off only one of the following labels:
Black, Asian, Native American, Hispanic, or White, thus assuming that no "Hispanic" can see himself or herself as "White."
The distinction between ethnicity and national origin is also unclear, especially when the "nation" in question did not exist
when the label was coined (German-American, Italian-
American). Nevertheless, although the definitions are sometimes
blurred or confusing, most Americans would agree that they recognize such terms as "Irish-Americans" or "Blacks."

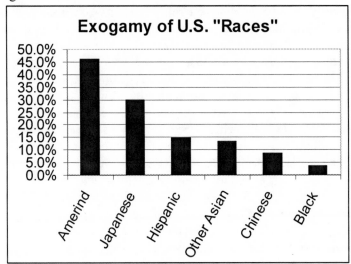

Figure 1. Exogamy of U.S. "Races" [6]

Karen Brodkin Sacks, "How Did Jews Become White Folks?," in *Race*, ed.
Steven Gregory and Roger Sanjek (New Brunswick NJ, 1994), 78-102.

[6] "Exogamy" in Figure 1 is defined as the fraction of married group members who have a White spouse. For the methodology used in arriving at this
figure, see Appendix A, "Census Data Processing Methodology," specifically, the section titled "Exogamy of U.S. 'Races.'" For comparable numbers regarding other ethnic groups, see M. Belinda Tucker and Claudia
Mitchell-Kernan, "New Trends in Black American Interracial Marriage:
The Social Structural Context," *Journal of Marriage and the Family*, 52
(no. 1, 1990), 209-18; Thomas Sowell, *Ethnic America: A History* (New
York, 1981), 9, 94; and Roger Sanjek, "Intermarriage and the Future of
Races in the United States," in Gregory (1994), 103-30.

This book examines one particular American group, African-Americans, because the group is unique in two ways. First, as depicted in Figure 1, "Exogamy of U.S. 'Races,'" it is the most strictly segregated from mainstream society of all U.S. groups (whether the groups are defined by politics, national origin, ethnicity or "race"). No other U.S. group routinely considers Blacks to be suitable marriage partners. And Blacks do not routinely consider any other group to be suitable marriage partners for themselves. Anti-miscegenation laws enforced Black endogamy for about 270 years, and it has been enforced by custom since 1967.[7] The out-marriage rate of the Black community has been negligible for three centuries and remains, as of the 2000 census, much smaller than that of any other U.S. social segment. In other words, no other U.S. group (whether defined by political ideology, national origin, ethnicity, or physical traits) is as harshly endogamous as is the community of Black Americans. In a strict sense, the United States has never had more than two endogamous groups. One U.S. endogamous group comprises everyone who is considered African-American. This group is usually called "Black." The other U.S. endogamous group comprises everyone else. This group is usually called "White."[8]

Second, the Black endogamous group is the only U.S. social category with a one-drop rule of membership. Having even one distant Black ancestor supposedly makes you Black, despite your personal preference or appearance. The latter aspect is the subject of this book. Of course, in reality the one-drop rule is factually untenable. As will be explained in Section I, there are over twice as many White Americans (74 million) with measur-

---

[7] Although mainstream (White)American society enforced the endogamous color line by judicial means throughout most of its history, non-judicial enforcement by peers and family today springs mainly from members of the Black community. For a study of this topic, see Randall Kennedy, *Interracial Intimacies: Sex, Marriage, Identity, and Adoption* (New York, 2003) or the earlier Randall Kennedy, "Interracial Intimacy," *Atlantic Monthly*, December 2002, 103-10.

[8] Later chapters discuss the African-American community as a voluntary, learned ethnicity based on traditions, rather than as a forcibly endogamous group.

able recent African genetic admixture than there are Black ones (36 million).

There are two ways of looking at U.S. racialism. One view sees the color line as delineating an "ethnicity," no different in principle from, say, Hispanics or Jews. The second sees socially coerced endogamy as a unique U.S. phenomenon. The "ethnicity" paradigm treats Blackness as a step in an acculturation process, as a self-identity that is basically voluntary and culturally learned.[9] The "endogamous group" paradigm views which side of the color line you are on as involuntary rather than as self-applied, and based upon presumed biological heredity rather than on learned traditions. For example, on the one hand arriving immigrants from Nigeria or Barbados are not members of the African-American ethnic group; they share few of Black America's history or traditions. On the other hand, U.S. society assigns such newly arrived immigrants to the Black side of the U.S. endogamous color line, in that they are perceived as suitable marriage partners for U.S. Blacks but not for U.S. Whites.

The two paradigms, Blackness as ethnicity and Blackness as assigned endogamous group, are not contradictory. Which of the two views is most appropriate to any particular study depends upon the topic of interest. Most of this book examines the endogamous color line via the second paradigm—involuntary assignment based mainly upon biological heredity. Nevertheless, this book also discusses voluntary African-American ethnic self-identity, with its associated traditions, in several places.[10]

This book does not address the morality of the U.S. system of two endogamous groups—whether any particular feature

---

[9] Robert F. McNergney and Joanne M. Herbert, *Foundations of Education: The Challenge of Professional Practice*, 3rd ed. (Boston, 2001), 549, define the concept of ethnicity as, "a group of people with a common tradition and a sense of identity that functions as a subgroup within the larger society; membership is largely a matter of self-identification."

[10] The historical origins of African-American ethnicity are discussed in *Chapter 13. The Color Line Created African-American Ethnicity in the North.* Today's paradigm clash between Blackness as voluntary, culturally learned ethnicity versus involuntary, biologically inherited membership in an endogamous group is discussed in *Chapter 14. Features of Today's One-Drop Rule.*

is "good" or "bad" in either an abstract moral sense or in a socially utilitarian sense. It takes no position as to what sort of society Americans should seek. Although some political scientists
suggest that injustice is the inevitable consequence of endogamous segregation, others suggest that a society can maintain a
segregated enclave group without its leading to distrust or big-
otry, and still others suggest that America's system of two endogamous groups has benefited U.S. society.[11]

Also, this study also takes no moral stance regarding the
propriety of people of slight African genetic admixture quitting
the Black endogamous group (or African-American ethnicity)
and joining the White group (or one of the European or Native
American ethnicities). Different folks have different goals. Many
people with a knack for language or mimicry exploit society by
cheerfully transforming themselves into whichever ethnicity
pays best. In 1830, for example, about one South Carolina slave
in a hundred was owned by a member of the biracial "Mulatto
elite" and about one Louisiana slave in twenty-five was owned
by a member of the biracial "Creole elite."[12] Few historians tell

---

[11] J.W. Warren and F.W. Twine, for example, suggest that the maintenance
of a permanent endogamous group may benefit the United States as a
whole, even as it sacrifices the enclave group. They suggest that America's
ethnic diversity is precisely what makes the nation uniquely resilient and
creative. They suggest that American diversity has resulted from the acceptance of each new group's transformation from colored "race" to White
ethnicity. They suggest that America's unique hospitality arose because
each new ethnic group was embraced by America's expanding blanket of
Whiteness as soon as they learned to display contempt towards African-
Americans. In other words, in an America without a permanent Black endogamous group from which immigrants could distinguish themselves,
ethno-cultural acceptance into mainstream society might be negligible. Such
an alternate-universe United States would comprise permanently polarized,
mutually hostile groups like Yugoslavia, say, or Rwanda. See Jonathan W.
Warren and France Winddance Twine, "White Americans, the New Minority?," *Journal of Black Studies*, 28 (no. 2, 1997), 203.

[12] James Hugo Johnston, *Race Relations in Virginia & Miscegenation in the
South, 1776-1860* (Amherst, 1970), 47; Peter Kolchin, *American Slavery
1619-1877* (New York, 1993), 242.

of these slaveowners.[13] The ability to switch sides is precisely what defines color-line permeability. Hence, this book's interest in studying those who crossed the barrier should not be misunderstood as either advocacy or opposition.

America's Admixed Population

This book's first section uses recent findings in molecular anthropology to explain that one-third of White Americans carry measurable recent African genetic admixture in their DNA, the equivalent of having a single ancestor of one hundred percent African admixture from around the year 1880. Afro-European admixture is typical of New World populations, but the United States is unique in having a bimodal admixture distribution. Two genetically different populations live in the United States. One population, self-identified as "White," is of overwhelmingly European descent with only zero to twenty percent African genetic admixture. The other group, called "Black," is of mainly African descent with only zero to fifty percent European genetic admixture. No other New World nation has a bimodal scatter diagram, the result of an endogamous color line that has been in place for three centuries.

The physical features associated with African versus European ancestry in the U.S. culture are due to about a dozen genes. Such "racial" traits are so ephemeral that three generations of intermarriage suffice to erase all traces of them. The association of certain features with "race" is culturally dependent and learned in early childhood. Finally, the 0.7 percent average African admixture found in today's White Americans is the result of genes slowly leaking through the color line from Black to White. In every year that has passed since the 1691 invention of the endogamous color line, between 0.10 and 0.14 percent of the

---

[13] But, for exceptions, see Michael P. Johnson and James L. Roark, *Black Masters: A Free Family of Color in the Old South*, 1st ed. (New York, 1984); Larry Koger, *Black Slaveowners: Free Black Slave Masters in South Carolina, 1790-1860* (Jefferson NC, 1985); Daniel L. Schafer, *Anna Kingsley* (St. Augustine, 1994).

Black population on average switched self-identity from the Black side of the endogamous color line to the White side.

The Endogamous Color Line

This book's second section is based upon historical research. It tells the history of America's intermarriage barrier. The endogamous color line is what defines the terms "Black" and "White." Whether you are seen as a suitable marriage partner by Blacks or by Whites is what defines which side of the color line you are on, which of the two endogamous groups you are a member of. For example, Puerto Ricans average 50-50 Afro-European genetic admixture and most have visible African features (skin tone, hair, etc.). Nevertheless, in recent decades Puerto Ricans have been considered suitable marriage partners for Whites (fifteen percent exogamy rate, according to the 2000 census). But it is inaccurate to say that dark-complexioned Puerto Ricans are suitable marriage partners for Whites because they are not "really Black." This reverses cause and effect. Puerto Ricans are not seen as members of the U.S. Black community precisely because they are considered suitable marriage partners for Whites, despite their partial African ancestry.

Although the U.S. endogamous color line was invented in the late seventeenth-century Chesapeake to deter servile insurrection, it gradually spread throughout the North and upper South. It reinforced the aggressive ethnic voting blocs of the Jacksonian urban North. It may have stifled a socialist revolution in the 1840s and 1850s.

In the period between the invention of the color line and the Civil War, Americans in the North and the upper South gradually changed how they identified which side of the color line you were on. Throughout the eighteenth century, the primary criterion was your physical appearance. Although some colonies had blood-fraction laws, courts tended to rule that, if you looked European, then you belonged on the White side of the color line. During the nineteenth century, blood fraction as adjusted by association gradually became important additional criteria. By 1890 in the North and the upper South, if you had a

Black grandparent and associated with Blacks, you were Black even if you looked European. The lower South was different.

Until Reconstruction, the lower South had very different color-line traditions. Louisiana and Alabama had two color lines separating three mildly endogamous groups: Black, White, and Colored. South Carolina had an extraordinarily permeable color line determined as much by socio-economic class as by physical appearance. And Spanish Florida had no endogamous barrier at all. After Reconstruction, the nation as a whole adopted the impermeable single color line and the concept of African-American ethnicity that had been born in Boston, New York, Cincinnati, and Philadelphia.

The One-Drop Rule

This book's third section traces the origin and unfolding of the notion of invisible Blackness by examining travelers' accounts, diaries, fiction literature, advertisements for runaway slaves, and a database of 300 court cases held from 1770 to 1990 to resolve on which side of the color line you belonged. It reveals that the concept, a "White-looking Black person," arose in the 1830s North after the Nat Turner incident. This idea of invisible Blackness or "one-drop rule" then spread slowly through the South, reaching Louisiana shortly after 1900. The one-drop rule then triumphed and became nationwide consensus in a series of court decisions that ostracized many White families to the Black side of the color line, apparently as punishment either for associating with or for defending Blacks during the Jim Crow wave of terror.

* * * * *

This book informs the reader of several under-publicized facts:

• One-third of White Americans have recent African ancestry.

- 35,000-50,000 Black youngsters switch to defining themselves White each year.
- The color line was invented to prevent servile insurrection in 1691.
- The origin and unfolding of the one-drop rule was unrelated to slavery.
- The one-drop rule was invented in the free North during the Nat Turner panic.
- The one-drop rule was embraced by nineteenth-century Black leaders as a means of delineating ethnicity.
- The one-drop rule did not become nationwide consensus until the Jim Crow era.
- The one-drop rule triumphed during Jim Crow as a means of keeping Whites in line, by banishing to Blackness those White families who dared to established friendly relations with Black families.
- The one-drop rule was actively resisted in the nineteenth century by Louisiana Creoles, Florida Hispanics, South Carolina elite, and the maroon (triracial) communities of the Southeast (Melungeons, Lumbees, Redbones, etc.).
- The one-drop rule continues to be resisted today by Louisiana Creoles, Hispanics, the maroon (triracial) communities, and by recent West Indian immigrants.

But resolving controversial or little-known facts of history is not this book's only goal. It can also be used as a reference. Its examination and database listing of the 300 cases that determined Americans' "racial" identity may be the most thorough analysis of the legal history of U.S. endogamous-group membership determination yet published.

Section I.
America's Admixed
Population

Chapter 2.
Afro-European Genetic
Admixture
in the United States

In 1976, California's Los Angeles Unified School District implemented a program where hundreds of schoolteachers were compulsorily transferred to distant schools in order to achieve "racial" balance throughout the county. Unsurprisingly, the teachers resisted having to commute for hours after having made their homes near the schools where they taught. To avoid being transferred, some formerly White teachers declared themselves Black, some formerly Black teachers insisted that they were White, and others (on both sides of the U.S. endogamous color line) asserted that they were of American Indian origin. The predictable bureaucratic response was to create an Ethnic Designation Committee, which justified its existence by launching a costly investigation to sniff out each teacher's "true race." Teachers were ordered to produce their birth certificates, as well as those of their parents and grandparents, and to bring in notarized sworn affidavits by school administrators and clergymen proving each teacher's "real racial identity."[1]

* * * * *

This chapter explains, in three topics, how we know that one-third of White Americans carry two to twenty percent recent African genetic admixture in their DNA. The first topic, *Ancestry-Informative Markers*, introduces the genetic variations that identify ancestral continent of origin. The second, *Admixture Scatter Diagrams*, shows how we can make observations and draw conclusions from charts that plot individuals by their Afro-European admixture ratios. It explains that a broad range of Afro-European admixture is typical of New World populations. This is because most inhabitants of the western hemisphere descend from a blend of European, Amerind, and African ancestors within the past five centuries. Old world peoples, in contrast, are individually much less diverse. The third topic, *Genetic Admixture is not the Same as Appearance*, shows how admixture scatter diagrams reveal that the United States comprises two genetically distinct populations separated by a 300-year-old barrier to intermarriage. It explains that White Americans look European, despite their measurable recent African admixture, due to selection across the endogamous color line.

Ancestry-Informative Markers

The decoding of the human genome has enabled molecular anthropologists to track recent as well as prehistoric human migrations. You carry traces of the past in your DNA—markers that identify the populations and sub-populations to which your ancestors belonged. They reveal facts about your forebears: how they lived, where they came from.

---

[1] *Luther Wright, Jr.*, "Who's Black, Who's White, and Who Cares: Reconceptualizing the United States's Definition of Race and Racial Classifications," *Vanderbilt Law Review*, 48 (no. 2, 1995), 513-70, 539n176.

This has nothing to with "race." Some people, for example, are lactose-tolerant and can digest milk in adulthood without difficulty. Others cannot. Among the former are most Danes, Dutch, Watutsi, and Maasai. Among populations who suffer digestive discomfort if they drink milk as adults are most Sicilians, Greeks, Bantus and the Khoisan (Kalahari Bushmen). It turns out that you are more likely to be lactose-tolerant if your ancestors after the Neolithic agrarian revolution were primarily herders. If your ancestors were mainly cultivators of grains, then you are more likely to be lactose-intolerant. Similar traits reveal whether your ancestors lived at low latitudes, subjected to excess solar ultraviolet radiation, or at high latitudes, with less-than-ideal levels of ultraviolet. Other DNA markers suggest whether your ancestors lived in the thin air of mountain elevations or along the seashore, and still others tell of the diseases to which they were subjected.

The New World was first populated by hunters who migrated across Beringia about 20 millennia ago. Rising sea levels when the last ice age ended cut them off from everyone else. Isolated, their immune systems lagged behind the rest of the human species in the ongoing genetic arms race against germs. Columbus and those who followed him introduced Euro-Afro-Asian germs into the New World. Within a generation, over 90 percent of Native Americans had died of diseases that their immune systems could not recognize.[2] Then, over the next three centuries, eleven million Africans and about one-fifth as many Europeans were carried across the Atlantic in sailing ships to repopulate the devastated New World.[3] Most Africans came involuntarily (although some were indentured servants) and most Europeans volunteered (although some were sold into slavery). But, whether volunteers or slaves, Africans or Europeans, the immigrants came in their tens of millions and blended with the handful of surviving natives into a mixed population. The blend-

---

[2] Woodrow Wilson Borah and Sherburne Friend Cook, *The Aboriginal Population of Central Mexico on the Eve of the Spanish Conquest* (Berkeley, 1963).

[3] Hugh Thomas, *The Slave Trade: The Story of the Atlantic Slave Trade: 1440-1870* (New York, 1997), 793, 804-5.

ing was nearly total in Central and South America—most Ibero-Americans enjoy demographically proportional genetic admixture from both transatlantic sources. The blending was a bit less thorough in the British West Indies, and even less so in North America.[4] Of interest to this work is the extent of genetic admixing among people from different continents to produce the current inhabitants of North America: how, when, where, and to what extent the admixing happened.

Ancestry-informative markers help to answer such questions by enabling estimates of what fraction of an individual's genome was inherited from Africa, what fraction came from Europe, and what fraction descended from the pre-Columbian aboriginal population. Figure 2, titled "Thirty-Nine Ancestry-Informative Markers" shows a typical array of DNA markers used to identify the ancestral continent of origin of New-World peoples.

---

[4] Esteban J. Parra and others, "Estimating African American Admixture Proportions by Use of Population-Specific Alleles," *American Journal of Human Genetics*, 63 (1998), 1839-51; E.J. Parra and others, "Ancestral Proportions and Admixture Dynamics in Geographically Defined African Americans Living in South Carolina," *American Journal of Physical Anthropology*, 114 (2001), 18-29; C.L. Pfaff and others, "Population Structure in Admixed Populations: Effect of Admixture Dynamics on the Pattern of Linkage Disequilibrium," *American Journal of Human Genetics*, 68 (2001a), 198-207.

Marker	dbSNP ss no.	Location	Mb (UCSB)	African	European	Native American	AF/EU	AF/NA	EU/NA
MID-575*1	4387042	1p34.3	36.1	0.124	0.004	0.584	0.121	0.460	0.584
MID-187*1	4387043	1p34.1	45.0	0.759	0.388	0.301	0.370	0.458	0.087
FY-NULL*1	4387025	1q23.2	160.0	0.001	0.998	1.000	0.997	0.999	0.001
AT3*1	4387045	1q25.1	174.8	0.858	0.282	0.061	0.575	0.797	0.222
F13B*1	4387024	1q31.3	201.1	0.704	0.063	0.018	0.641	0.687	0.045
TSC1102055*1	4387029	1q32.1	207.6	0.487	0.917	0.137	0.430	0.351	0.780
WI-11392*1	4390531	1q42.2	242.2	0.878	0.433	0.626	0.444	0.252	0.193
WI-16857*1	4387031	2p16.1	57.0	0.751	0.215	0.181	0.536	0.570	0.034
WI-11153*1	4387032	3p12.3	78.2	0.785	0.133	0.819	0.652	0.033	0.819
GC*1F	NA	4q13.3	72.9	0.853	0.156	0.339	0.697	0.514	0.183
GC*1S	NA	4q13.3	72.9	0.069	0.607	0.542	0.538	0.473	0.065
MID-52*1	4390532	4q24	101.7	0.363	0.077	0.763	0.186	0.500	0.687
SGC30610*1	4387040	5q11.2	51.3	0.401	0.255	0.699	0.146	0.281	0.427
SGC30055*1	4387041	5q23.1	115.9	0.054	0.511	0.753	0.457	0.699	0.241
WI-17163*1	4387033	5q33.2	155.8	0.054	0.175	0.690	0.120	0.636	0.515
WI-9231*1	4387034	7	NA	0.129	0.147	0.548	0.017	0.419	0.401
CYP3A4*1	4390533	7q22.1	101.2	0.198	0.958	0.959	0.761	0.762	0.001
WI-4019*1	4387035	7q22.1	104.5	0.430	0.306	0.618	0.124	0.168	0.311
LPL*1	4387026	8p21.3	22.4	0.971	0.492	0.442	0.479	0.529	0.050
CRH*1	4390534	8q13.1	64.3	0.318	0.927	0.983	0.609	0.624	0.056
WI-11909*1	4387036	9q21.31	72.4	0.805	0.881	0.181	0.075	0.587	0.663
D11S429*1	4387023	11q11	57.9	0.087	0.516	0.119	0.429	0.032	0.397
TYR-192*1	4387030	11q21	98.7	0.005	0.449	0.034	0.444	0.029	0.415
DRD2-Bcl I*1	4387021	11q23.1	118.4	0.063	0.144	0.665	0.080	0.409	0.446
DRD2-Taq I "D"*1	4387022	11q23.1	118.4	0.135	0.670	0.045	0.535	0.090	0.626
APOA1*1	4387046	11q23.3	123.6	0.420	0.925	0.977	0.505	0.557	0.052
GNB3*1	4387018	12p13.31	6.8	0.795	0.332	0.364	0.463	0.431	0.032
RB1*1	4387047	13q14.2	48.3	0.926	0.315	0.175	0.611	0.733	0.122
OCA2*1	4387028	15q13.1	24.9	0.115	0.746	0.488	0.631	0.373	0.258
WI-14319*1	4387037	15q14	30.6	0.386	0.201	0.716	0.185	0.330	0.514
CYP19*1	4387020	15q21.2	47.9	0.332	0.296	0.741	0.037	0.409	0.446
PV92*1	4387048	16q24.1	87.7	0.225	0.152	0.792	0.073	0.568	0.640
MC1R-314*1	4387027	16q24.3	93.6	0.513	0.163	0.035	0.350	0.478	0.127
WI-14867*1	4387038	17p13.2	3.9	0.024	0.472	0.418	0.448	0.394	0.054
WI-7423*1	4387039	17p12	8.7	0.000	0.476	0.058	0.476	0.058	0.418
Sb19.3*1	4387049	19p13.11	27.2	0.415	0.903	0.645	0.488	0.230	0.258
CKM*1	4387019	19q13.32	61.2	0.164	0.313	0.904	0.150	0.740	0.590
MID-154*1	4387044	20q11.22	32.5	0.806	0.362	0.420	0.444	0.368	0.057
MID-93*1	4390535	22q13.2	38.8	0.261	0.815	0.081	0.554	0.179	0.733

Figure 2. Thirty-Nine Ancestry-Informative Markers[5]

Eight columns are of interest, exemplified by the table's third row. The first column gives the common-use name of the marker. "FY-NULL*1" denotes a particular variant of a gene that encodes a protein associated with the Duffy blood group. Column three shows where the marker is located in the genome. The entry "1q23.2" means that this marker is located on the first chromosome (1), on the long arm of the chromosome (q), and 23.2 centimorgans[6] from the chromosome's centromere. Columns five, six, and seven show the marker's rate of incidence in the native populations of sub-Saharan Africa, Europe, and America. Only one African in a thousand carries the FY-Null marker, while every Native American tested does so, as do 998 out of

---

[5] From Mark D. Shriver and others, "Skin Pigmentation, Biogeographical Ancestry, and Admixture Mapping," *Human Genetics*, 112 (2003), 387-99.

[6] A "centimorgan" is a measure of chromosomal distance tied to the likelihood of meiosis recombination.

every thousand Europeans. Columns eight, nine, and ten show the marker's effectiveness in distinguishing between any two of the three populations. FY-Null is very effective at distinguishing between Africans and either Europeans or Native Americans (0.997 and 0.999, respectively), but useless at distinguishing Europeans from Native Americans (0.001).

Figure 3, titled "Twenty-Two Ancestry-Informative Markers" shows a smaller array of DNA markers, used by a different research team than the source of Figure 2, but also to identify the ancestral continent of origin of New-World peoples. That some researchers use more markers than others is a source of discussion in the field. Should you stick to the small handful of extremely reliable and informative markers? Or should you also examine (for any given individual) the greater number of marginally reliable markers because they are cumulatively informative? Say, for instance, that each marker of a set of twenty is only 67 percent reliable in distinguishing European from African admixture. If a person has the European version, he or she may be among the two-thirds of Europeans who have the marker or among the one-third of Africans who also have it. But if all twenty of the individual's 67-percent-reliable markers point to European admixture, their unanimity becomes much more persuasive.[7]

---

[7] For mathematical discussions of this point, see Michael J. Bamshad and others, "Human Population Genetic Structure and Inference of Group Membership," *American Journal of Human Genetics*, 72 (2003), 578-89 or Jinliang Wang, "Maximum-Likelihood Estimation of Admixture Proportions From Genetic Data," *Genetics*, 164 (June 2003), 747-65.

Marker	Location	cM	AF/EU
MID 575	1p34.3	~64	0.130
MID 187	1p34.1	~75	0.370
FY-NULL	1q23.2	~165	0.999
AT3	1q25.1	~191	0.575
WI-11392	1q42.2	~252	0.444
WI-16857	2p16.1	~79	0.536
WI-11153	3p12.3	~106	0.652
GC*1F	4q13.3	79	0.697
GC*1S	4q13.3	79	0.538
SGC30055	5q23.1	~120	0.457
CYP3A4	7q22.1	~111	0.761
LPL	8p21.3	~39	0.479
D11S429	11q11	~70.9	0.429
DRD2-Taq I "D"	11q23.1	~105	0.535
APOA1	11q23.3	~113	0.505
GNB3	12p13.31	~15	0.463
OCA2	15q13.1	~16	0.631
MC1R314	16q24.3	~133	0.350
WI-14867	17p13.2	~10	0.448
WI-7423	17p12	~16	0.476
Sb19.3	19p13.11	~49	0.488
MID 154	20q11.22	~50	0.444

Figure 3. Twenty-Two Ancestry-Informative Markers[8]

Again, it is important to recognize that such markers in the DNA of today's inhabitants of the New World cannot identify one's "race," not even implicitly. They are chosen only to show the continent of origin of their ancestors (Africa, Europe, or Native America). Consider, for instance, row 18 of Figure 3,

---

[8] From Jose R. Fernandez and others, "Association of African Genetic Admixture with Resting Metabolic Rate and Obesity Among Women," *Obesity Research*, 11 (no. 7, July 2003), 904-11.

labeled *MC1R314*. This is the same marker that is depicted as *MC1R-314*1* in row 33 of Figure 2. About 51 percent of Africans, but only 16 percent of Europeans carry this particular marker in their DNA. In other words, if you have this marker at position 16q24.3 of your sixteenth chromosome, then it is two-out-of-three likely that you inherited it from a sub-Saharan ancestor. As it turns out, MC1R314 is one of the few markers associated with a gene whose function is known. It is one of the half-dozen genes associated with dark skin tone.[9] In other words, row 33 of Figure 2 merely says, in essence, that if you are a New-World inhabitant with a dark brown skin tone, you probably inherited it from a sub-Saharan ancestor. The point is that the above markers were chosen because they work, nothing more—even those whose function is unknown. The markers were chosen only because they correlate strongly with continent of origin.

Another important point is that the above-listed genetic markers are not the ones that you would use in order to track prehistoric migrations. For such a purpose you would choose different of sets markers, non-recombinant markers in mitochondrial DNA or those in the Y chromosome, and depending upon the time frame of interest. For example, the markers that you would use to track the African Diaspora that colonized the planet starting 60 millennia ago are different from those used to follow the tribes who re-colonized uninhabited central Europe after the glaciers retreated 16 millennia ago.[10]

The main use of ancestry-informative markers today is in medical research. They help determine whether any given disease (HIV, diabetes, obesity, cystic fibrosis, etc.) is more or less prevalent, or has a consistently different outcome, depending upon a person's continent of ancestry. One way of doing this is with a scatter diagram. Say, for example, that you test a few

---

[9] For a list of all of the genes known to be involved in dermal melanization, see under the topic "Three-to-Six Co-Dominant Skin Tone Genes" in *Chapter 3. The Heredity of "Racial" Traits.*

[10] For introductions to markers tracing prehistoric migrations, see: Bryan Sykes, *The Seven Daughters of Eve*, 1st American ed. (New York, 2001) or Steve Olson, *Mapping Human History: Discovering the Past Through Our Genes* (Boston, 2002).

thousand individuals. You measure each person's Afro-European admixture percentage using ancestry-informative DNA markers. You also measure each person's susceptibility to some disease of interest. You then plot each individual on a graph from left-to-right based upon genetic admixture. People of 100 percent European (0 percent African) admixture are plotted on the left-hand axis. People of 100 percent African (0 percent European) admixture are plotted on the right-hand axis. Everyone else goes somewhere in between, left-to-right depending on admixture ratio. Each dot is also plotted vertically depending on susceptibility to the disease of interest. Those with no vulnerability to the disease are plotted along the bottom axis. Those who have the strongest susceptibility are plotted along the top axis. Everyone else is plotted in between, bottom-to-top depending on disease susceptibility.

Admixture Scatter Diagrams

This process yields a scatter diagram, a cloud of dots spread across the chart. If the cloud trends upwards and to the right, it shows that the disease in question tends to be more prevalent among those with a strong African admixture component. If it trends downwards to the right, it shows that the disease tends to be more prevalent among those of predominantly European admixture component. If it trends in neither direction, then it shows that there is no connection between Afro-European genetic admixture and that particular disease. Such studies have revealed that diabetes, prostate cancer, and hypertension, for example, are more prevalent among Americans of predominantly African genetic admixture, while dementia and osteoporosis are more frequent among those of mostly European genetic admixture.

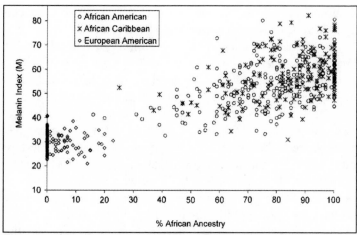

Figure 4. Skin Tone as a Function of Afro-European Admixture Ratio[11]

Figure 4, "Skin Tone as Function of Afro-European Admixture Ratio," shows a typical Afro-European genetic admix-

ture scatter diagram. It was taken from an article produced out of a project headed by Penn State University molecular anthropologist Mark D. Shriver (see Figure 5).

Figure 5. Dr. Mark D. Shriver[12]

Among the other sixteen team-members and collaborators of this study, who work for colleges and private research laboratories throughout the United States, Canada, and England, is Dr. Rick Kittles, a geneticist then at Howard University in Washington DC (see Figure 6). The study analyzed DNA samples from 3,000 indi-

---

[11] Shriver (2003), 387-99.

[12] Photo by Greg Grieco.

viduals in 25 locations. In Figure 4, the vertical scale does not represent susceptibility to any specific disease. Instead, individuals were plotted bottom-to-top based upon how dark was the person's skin tone (as measured by the reflectance of the inner upper arm). Darker individuals are plotted higher than paler ones. The team's intent was to see if dermal melanin correlated with percentage of African genetic admixture, and so might be a predictor of, say, skin cancer. The cloud of points displays a visibly distinct slope rising from lower-left to upper-right. This demonstrates that, in general, the more African genetic admixture you have, the darker your skin.[13]

Figure 6. Dr. Rick A. Kittles

The graph also depicts another variable, one that is of interest to the historian—endogamous group membership or ethnic self-identity. Each dot in Figure 4 is encoded to show whether the person sampled claimed to be a member of the U.S. White endogamous group (diamond shape, 187 individuals) or of the U.S. Black endogamous group (open circle, 232 individuals). (The x-shaped plots represent a population of British West Indian ethnicity living in London.[14]) The graph refers to these

---

[13] Dozens of peer-reviewed journal articles on Afro-European genetic admixture mapping using ancestry-informative DNA markers have sprung from the decoding of the human genome. About 50 such articles from medical, genetic, and molecular anthropological journals are available for download from URL <http:// backintyme.com/admixture>.

[14] The 173 individuals of West Indian ethnicity were all British subjects living in London. Some genetic admixture mapping studies lump British West Indians and African-Americans into a single group. This study tallies them separately because doing so reveals the interesting point that there are virtually no "Black" British West Indians with very slight African genetic admixture. British West Indians of known partial African ancestry who look

three groups as European American, African American, and African Caribbean, respectively, and the text explains that this trait was self-assessed and independent of actual genetics.

With this added information, three aspects of the scatter diagram suddenly jump out at you. First, there is significant overlap between White and Black Americans regarding Afro-European genetic admixture. Some so-called "Black" Americans have less DNA admixture of African ancestral origin than do some so-called "White" Americans. Second, the admixture range of Black Americans spans the entire chart. While most of the subjects who self-identify as Black (marked as circles) have strong African admixture (are found towards the right), some have little or no African admixture (are found at the left edge). Finally, although the range of genetic admixture in those who self-identify as "White" is narrower than the admixture range of Blacks, it is still significant. Many so-called "White" Americans have as much as 20 percent or more of African genetic admixture.

Figure 7, "Afro-European Genetic Admixture as a Function of Ethnicity," was taken from a different study. It also matches ancestral continent-of-origin genetic admixture for several hundred individuals with their ethnic self-identity or endogamous group membership.

European are considered "White" by British society, which lacks an endogamous color line.

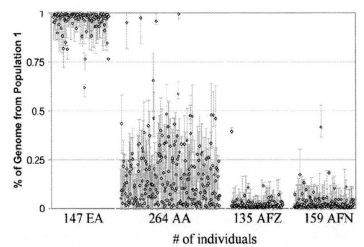

Figure 7. Afro-European Genetic Admixture as a Function of Ethnicity[15]

In the scatter diagram of Figure 7, each point (representing one individual) is plotted vertically to depict Afro-European genetic admixture (100 percent European at the top) and horizontally into four groups representing endogamous group membership or ethnicity. The groups, from left to right, are: 147 Americans of the White endogamous group, 264 Americans of the Black endogamous group, 135 subjects from Zaire (formerly Congo), and 159 subjects from Nigeria.[16]

Three points of interest present themselves upon your examining this graph. First, as in the prior chart, if you look at the range of from zero to thirty percent African genetic admixture, you see a wide overlap between Americans of the Black and

---

[15] Heather E. Collins-Schramm and others, "Markers that Discriminate Between European and African Ancestry Show Limited Variation Within Africa," *Human Genetics*, 111 (September 2002), 566-99.

[16] Again, some would argue that Nigerians and Zaireans are also "Black" and so should be lumped in with the African-Americans. But this confuses genetic admixture and nationality with membership in one of the two U.S. endogamous groups. Nigerians and Zaireans are of preponderantly African genetic admixture with little European admixture, but they do not become members of either of the two U.S. endogamous socio-political groups unless and until they immigrate to the United States.

White endogamous groups. As in the Shriver study of Figure 4, some so-called "White" Americans have over twenty percent African genetic admixture and some so-called "Black" Americans have little or none. Indeed, other studies have found that approximately 5.5 percent of members of the U.S. Black community have no detectable African genetic admixture.[17]

Second, the Black and White groups are not symmetrical. The mean African admixture among White Americans is low—roughly 0.7 percent African and 99.3 percent European admixture.[18] To put this in perspective, this would have been the result if every member of the U.S. White endogamous group alive today had a single ancestor of one hundred percent African genetic admixture seven generations ago (around the year 1850). Of course, African alleles are not distributed evenly. Seventy percent of White Americans (like 5.5 percent of Blacks) have no detectable African genetic admixture at all. Among the thirty percent of Whites with African genetic admixture, the admixture ratio averages to about 2.3 percent, the equivalent of having a single ancestor of one hundred percent African genetic admixture from around the year 1880.[19] Black Americans, on the other hand, have significant European admixture (averaging about 75 percent African and 25 percent European).

Third, the wide admixture spread of the two groups of New-World inhabitants contrasts with the narrow range of admixtures among Old-World inhabitants. A wide spread of genetic admixtures is characteristic of the Western Hemisphere. As evident in Figure 7, on the one hand, the U.S. White population

---

[17] Parra (2001), 18-29, Figure 1.

[18] Shriver (2003), 387-99, Table 2.

[19] UPI, *Analysis: Race Now Not Black and White* (May 8, 2002). Astonishingly, these DNA-based findings confirm an obscure 1958 study that predicted, on the basis of statistical demographics alone, that about 21 percent of White Americans had Black ancestry within the past four generations. See Robert S. Stuckert, "The African Ancestry of the White American Population," *Ohio Journal of Science*, 55 (May, 1958), 155-60. For an accessible survey, see Monica L. Haynes, "Passing: How Posing as White Became a Choice for Many Black Americans," *Post-Gazette*, Oct. 26 2003, Lifstyle, 1.

spans a range of 15-20 percent and the U.S. Black population covers a 30-40-percent range. On the other hand, the Nigerian population covers only a 10-precent spread and the Congolese population spans only a 5-percent range.

The Black and White ranges are typical of the New World. Admixture variation among Latin American populations tends to span ranges as broad as that of the U.S. Black endogamous group, but shifted up or down on the chart depending on the particular nation's colonial ratio of African slaves to European colonists. A plot from Argentina, for example, would resemble a mirror image of the Black scatter diagram, flipped over to start at the top, thereby resembling a slightly stretched version of the White U.S. plot. Scatter diagrams of Puerto Ricans or Dominicans center on the 50-percent line, with decreasing dot densities stretching all the way to both of the 100-percent axes. Haitians produce scatter diagrams resembling those of Black Americans.

Old-World populations, in contrast, display much narrower ranges of variation of genetic admixture. A scatter diagram of Danes or Dutch would resemble a flipped mirror-image of the Zairean population, with a mere 5-percent spread from the 100-percent European axis. A diagram of Spain or Portugal would resemble a flipped, slightly stretched version of the Nigerian diagram.[20]

What is remarkable about the two U.S. endogamous groups is not that each spans a wide range of Afro-European admixture. That many White Americans carry up to 20 percent African genetic admixture may startle the uninformed, but this is typical of New World populations descended from demographically European colonies with few African slaves. And the admixture plot of Black Americans resembles those of the West Indies, where African slaves were a demographic majority. What is re-

---

[20] Interestingly, the slighter broader-than-usual (for the Old World) admixture range of Nigerians and Iberians probably has the same cause. Both of these broader-than-expected scatter diagrams may reflect the faint remaining traces of the population mixing that took place consequent to the Almoravid Empire and its aftermath. The Almoravid Empire (1043-1133) stretched from Senegambia to Barcelona.

markable about the two U.S. groups is that they both live within the same society. Such a bimodal distribution of Afro-European admixture is characteristic of no other nation on earth. The separation, of course, is the result of the endogamous U.S. color line.

Genetic Admixture is not the Same Thing as Appearance

About one-third of White Americans are of between two and twenty percent recent African genetic admixture, as measured by the ancestry-informative markers in their DNA.[21] This comes to about 74 million Americans. And yet, day-to-day experience teaches that virtually all White Americans look, well, White. Some may look more Mediterranean and others may look more Nordic, but very few White Americans have a distinctively African appearance. How can one reconcile DNA measurements with common experience?

An anecdote may help illustrate the problem. Look again at the chart of Figure 4. Consider one of the graph's outlier points—a "European American" individual plotted as having 11 percent[22] African genetic admixture. Dr. Shriver, the project team leader, became curious about this individual for two reasons. First, the person's African genetic admixture was unusually high for someone who self-identified as a member of the U.S. White endogamous group. Second, the sample had been taken from State College, Pennsylvania, the site of Dr. Shriver's own campus.[23] According to Dr. Shriver:

---

[21] Sailer (2002)

[22] The Sailer (2002) article, from which the above anecdote was taken, said "23 percent" African admixture, and so this was the number given in an earlier essay version of this chapter. But the number may have been mistaken. The 11 percent figure, above, is from a conversation between Dr. Shriver and the present author after a lecture in Gainesville, Florida, in November 2003, and matches the number mentioned in Christen Brownlee, "Code of Many Colors," *Science News Online* April 9, 2005.

[23] Sailer (2002).

I had the result for two or three years before I even looked up
the ID number of the person whom we tested. I looked at
who it was and it was me! I checked myself and the rest of
my relatives and tracked it through my family. I never considered that there were any African people in my family.
There's no real variation in my family. The admixture must
have been pretty far back. It just so happens that we can detect it with the markers we have. My mom especially stood
out as being surprised, maybe because I told her it was coming through her father. She still doesn't believe it about her
family! The part of Pennsylvania where my mother's father
came from is where the Underground Railroad ended. There
are several towns right here in Southern Pennsylvania where
there are very light-skinned African-American communities
that are the remnants of the Underground Railroad.[24]

It seems that Dr. Shriver's maternal grandfather moved from
Pennsylvania to Iowa, then to California, leaving behind in the
process most of his ties with his relatives.[25] Dr. Shriver, it turns
out, (see Figure 5) is one of the 74 million White Americans
with significant recent African genetic admixture.

In a coincidentally similar fashion, Dr. Rick Kittles,
Shriver's collaborator then at Howard University in Washington,
discovered that he carries the FY-null genetic marker at genome
position 16q24.3. This marker is found in 998 out of every thousand Europeans but found in only one out of thousand Africans.
Many of Dr. Kittles's other ancestry-informative markers tell the
same unexpected story. Dr. Kittles (see Figure 6) is one of the
many Black Americans with strong European genetic admixture.
And yet, and there is no other way to say this, Dr. Shriver "looks
White" and Dr. Kittles definitely "looks Black." Why is there
such a discrepancy between measured genetic admixture and
physical appearance?

There is an immediate answer to this question, and a
deeper answer. The immediate answer is that many different invisible genes identify continent of ancestry. As of the summer of
2004, the private DNA lab **DNAPrint Genomics, Inc.** uses up

---

[24] Dr. Shriver's comments are from an interview in Sailer (2002).

[25] Idem.

to 175 single nucleotide polymorphisms (markers) in order to analyze a client's ancestral continents of origin.[26] On the other hand only a handful of genes encode for the few superficial, externally visible features (skin tone, hair curliness, etc.) that Americans see as significant to the endogamous color line. Parental genes are randomly recombined with each passing generation. It can happen, through sheer chance, that an individual (like Dr. Shriver) can inherit many invisible African DNA markers, but few or none of the handful of alleles that encode for color-line-related traits. Alternatively, a person (like Dr. Kittles) can inherit those few alleles that encode for visible color-line-related traits but otherwise inherit the invisible but ancestrally informative European admixture markers.

The deeper answer becomes evident if you plot each of the two U.S. endogamous groups from Figure 4 separately. Figure 8, "Blacks' Skin Tone as Function of Admixture," shows just one portion of the population of the Figure 4 chart—those who self-identified as members of the U.S. Black endogamous group. In this diagram you can see a definite positive correlation (R^2=0.211) between skin tone and African admixture. Clearly, if you are considered a Black American, the more African admixture you have, the higher your melanin index. More importantly, the range of skin reflectance as measured by the melanin index of Black Americans is very large, spanning a vertical distance of fifty points from 30 to 80.

---

[26] As of June 7, 2004, see the firm's URL
<http://www.ancestrybydna.com/ancestry25.asp>.

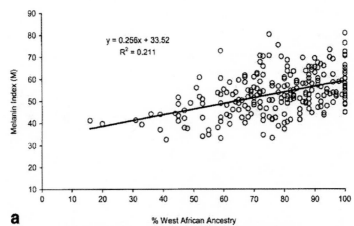

a   % West African Ancestry

Figure 8. Blacks' Skin Tone as Function of Admixture

Figure 9, "Whites' Skin Tone as Function of Admixture," shows the other U.S. endogamous group from Figure 4—those who self-identified as White. In this diagram, you can see that there is no correlation, either way (R^2=0.001), between skin tone and African admixture. Clearly, if you are considered a White American, your melanin index is unrelated to your degree of African admixture. More importantly, the range of skin reflectance as measured by the melanin index of White Americans is very narrow, spanning a vertical distance of only twenty points from 20 to 40. This is less than half of the range of skin-tone variation found among Black Americans.

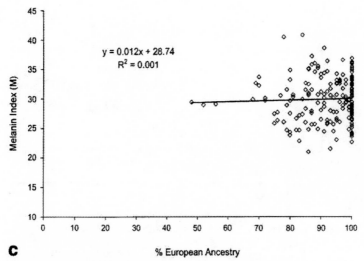

C   % European Ancestry

Figure 9. Whites' Skin Tone as Function of Admixture

The combination of narrow phenotype variation (skin tone) along with a wide range of inter-population (Afro-European) admixture variation among White Americans shows that recent selection has taken place. Narrow phenotype variation alone does not necessarily indicate recent selection. Northern Europeans display little skin tone variation, but they lack a wide range of African admixture. Broad genotype variation alone does not necessarily indicate recent selection. Puerto Ricans average 50-50 Afro-European admixture, but they also display a wide range of skin tones. The late Stephen J. Gould, Harvard biology professor and columnist for *Natural History* magazine, used to explain this principle with a baseball analogy. Plot a scatter diagram of the batting averages of a thousand amateur or minor-league players and you will find a very large range of variation. A few such players are very bad, a few are very good, and most spread across the entire range of batting averages in-between. Now plot the batting averages of professional athletes in the major leagues. All are very good indeed. More importantly, the range of batting averages among them is tiny. The difference between an outstanding star of the game and a rookie is a matter of mere hundredths of a percentage point. The reason, of course, is because you cannot get into the majors unless you are very good at it. Similarly, wild cows vary greatly in the amount of milk that they produce. The cows in a dairy farm produce more milk on average but, more importantly, their milk production varies very little among themselves (compared to wild cows). The reason? Those cows who do not make the cut become hamburger.

And so, why do few if any White Americans display a strongly African appearance (have a high melanin index) despite having detectable African admixture? Because those Americans who "look Black" are assigned involuntarily to the Black endogamous group, whatever their genetic admixture. The scatter diagrams of the two endogamous U.S. groups are not symmetrical because the selection process acts only upon the White group. As revealed in court records, discussed elsewhere, a person of mixed ancestry who "looks European" (like Dr. Shriver or his maternal grandfather) in practice has the option of either adopting a White self-identity, thus joining the White endogamous group or a Black self-identity, thus joining the other group. But a person of mixed ancestry who "looks African" lacks such a choice. U.S. society assigns such a person to membership in the Black endogamous group, like it or not.[27]

In short, U.S. society has unwittingly applied selection pressure to the color line. The only American families accepted into the White endogamous group have been those whose African admixture just happened not to include the half-dozen alleles for dark skin (or the other physical traits associated with membership in the Black endogamous group). Since those particular alleles were sifted out of the portion of the White population that originated in families of mixed heritage, the relative percentage of the remaining, invisible, African alleles in this population cannot affect skin color. That skin-color does not vary with African genetic admixture among Whites demonstrates and confirms that physical appearance has been an important group membership criterion throughout U.S. history. It has resulted in genetic selection of the White U.S. population for a European appear-

---

[27] As discussed elsewhere, exceptions to this rule are made in today's U.S. society for some Hispanics and North African Muslims of slight African appearance.

ance, regardless of their underlying continent-of-ancestry admixture ratio.

* * * * *

This chapter introduced the U.S. endogamous color line. It showed that New World populations have a wide range of Afro-European genetic admixture and that the United States is no exception. One-third of White Americans carry two to twenty percent recent African genetic admixture in their DNA (the mean is 2.3 percent). On the other hand, the United States is exceptional in comprising two genetically distinct populations, called "Black" and "White" and that virtually all U.S. Whites look European despite some having measurable African genetic admixture. Although genetic admixture studies cannot identify one's "race," they do reveal that the distinctive bimodal Afro-European admixture pattern found in the United States is due to a three-centuries-old endogamous barrier called "the color line."

What does this have to do with the history of the one-drop rule? One cannot fully understand historical events except in the light of anthropological reality. The preceding chapter established that millions of Americans born into Black families have redefined themselves as White, despite the color line. The next few chapters will show that "racial" features can change dramatically from one generation to the next through intermarriage, that much of what Americans see as "racial" traits is an illusion, and that the rise and fall of color-line permeability is easily computed. They set the stage for the later historical narrative by letting us see that laws and customs meant to support the endogamous color line were never completely successful.

Chapter 3.
The Heredity of "Racial" Traits

"Because they look different," explained the State Park Service historian in charge of living history at Olustee, Florida. She was answering an ethnic acculturation question. Why has almost every non-White immigrant group in U.S. history—Irish, Jews, even Chinese in Jim Crow Mississippi—been embraced by America's ever-expanding blanket of Whiteness and joined the mainstream via intermarriage within a few generations, while African-Americans remain non-White?[1] The irony in the historian's answer could be seen in the four children playing in the grass nearby—two apparently members of the Black endogamous group and two apparently White.

Every February, the Florida Park Service hosts a Civil War reenactment at Olustee. The real battle, fought in February 1864, comprised about five thousand Union attackers and the same number of Confederate defenders. The reenacted battle is choreographed to replicate actual events. Over a hundred Black re-enactors from Charleston play the role of the famed 54th

---

[1] Noel Ignatiev, *How the Irish Became White* (New York, 1995); Karen Brodkin, *How Jews Became White Folks and What That Says About Race in America* (New Brunswick NJ, 1998); James W. Loewen, *The Mississippi Chinese: Between Black and White* (Cambridge MA, 1971).

Massachusetts. Thousands of other Civil War re-enactors from throughout the Southeast come to portray the other Union and Confederate regiments involved. The event attracts thousands of spectators. Some come for the day to cheer one side or the other, but most are families who bring their children to learn about a dramatic event in the state's past.

In recent years, the local NAACP chapter has picketed the event as a painful reminder of slavery. In response, volunteers involved in the production have increased the number of living history presentations and dioramas by Black History groups, who lecture on the African-American heroes and heroines of abolition and the war. It is a family event for the living history interpreters as well, and the volunteers bring their own children, dressed out in the Alice-in-Wonderland childhood fashions of the 1860s.

One pair of living history presenters are of first-generation mixed heritage. He has one Black parent and one White parent, and so does she. Both display the in-between appearance of, say, Jennifer Beals or Gary Dourdan of the CSI TV show. Technically speaking, both are heterozygotic at each of the three-to-six genes for dermal melanization. But their four children could be used to exemplify Mendel's wrinkled peas and smooth peas without the in-between peas. The two oldest kids are quite dark, taking after their Black grandparents (homozygotic for African skin tone). The two youngest are European-looking, taking after their White grandparents (homozygotic for European skin tone). The standing family joke (which outsiders endure stoically despite having heard it many times) is that the two older children used up all of the family melanin, leaving none for their younger siblings. The parents identify the family as part of the Black community. Nevertheless, the two European-looking children will probably switch to self-identifying as Hispanic or even White after high school. There is little to be gained in today's America, for a young person who looks European, by voluntarily remaining a member of the Black endogamous group.

* * * * *

This chapter explains, in four topics, that much is known about the heredity of those physical features important to U.S. society in assigning someone to one side or the other of the endogamous color line. *Three-to-Six Co-Dominant Skin Tone Genes* discusses the genes that determine skin tone. *Mendelian Inheritance* explains that, on average, half of the children of admixed parents inherit a skin tone between those of their parents, one fourth come out darker than both parents, and one-fourth come out lighter than both. This means that any Afro-European admixed population will not blend homogeneously after many generations, but will continue to produce a few African-looking and European-looking individuals indefinitely. *Appearance is not the Same Thing as Ancestry* explains that, in admixed populations, even people who share identical ancestry may wind up with different Afro-European admixtures due to the random recombination of parental genes at each generation. This is why about five percent of the African-American population has no detectable African genetic admixture. Finally, *Hardy-Weinberg Distribution* shows how to compute the rate at which European-looking children are born into various Black communities in the United States, and the rate at which African-looking children are born into European-looking populations in other countries.

Three-to-Six Co-Dominant Skin Tone Genes

Some people erroneously assume that physical traits associated with the U.S. endogamous color line "blend" in some non-Mendelian way. They assume that children cannot come out looking more European than both parents nor more African than both. They assume that endogamous populations become ever more homogeneously blended with the passage of generations. And they assume that any given New World resident of mixed Afro-European appearance must descend from colonists who were themselves of one hundred percent European or one hundred percent African genetic admixture.[2] All of these assumptions are mistaken.[3]

Parents of mixed intermediate Afro-European genetic admixture can, and often do, produce strongly European-looking or African-looking children. To be precise, there is a 1/2 probability that any given child of two genetically admixed parents will display color-line-related features midway between those of the parents, 1/4 probability that it will look more European than either parent, and 1/4 probability that it will look more African than either parent. Furthermore, most Americans of intermediate Afro-European admixture are not first-generation dual-heritage individuals. Instead, most spring from parents who are also of Afro-European genetic admixture. In fact, many of the New World's alleles for European features came to this hemisphere within the bodies of African slaves, whose ancestors had mingled with Arabs, Berbers, and Mediterranean Europeans for centuries. And many of the alleles for African features came to the Americas within the bodies of European Mediterranean colonists, whose ancestors had mingled with Arabs, Berbers, and Africans for centuries. The Mediterranean has been a genetic mixing bowl for tens of thousands of years.

None of this has anything to do with "race," as many use the term, since what non-scientists mean by "race" is hard to pin down. Americans tend to think of Africans, Europeans, and

---

[2] See, for example, Ira Berlin, *Slaves Without Masters: The Free Negro in the Antebellum South* (New York, 1974), 108-9; Gwendolyn Midlo Hall, *Africans in Colonial Louisiana: The Development of Afro-Creole Culture in the Eighteenth Century* (Baton Rouge, 1992) as quoted in Virginia Meacham Gould, "The Free Creoles of Color of the Antebellum Gulf Ports of Mobile and Pensacola: A Struggle for the Middle Ground," in *Creoles of Color of the Gulf South*, ed. James H. Dormon (Knoxville, 1996), 28-50, 32; Jane G. Landers, ed. *Against the Odds: Free Blacks in the Slave Societies of the Americas* (London, 1996), 86; Frederick P. Bowser, "The Free Person of Color in Mexico City and Lima: Manumission and Opportunity, 1580-1650," in *Race and Slavery in the Western Hemisphere: Quantitative Studies*, ed. Stanley L. Engerman, et al. (Princeton, 1975), 331-61, 333.

[3] See, for example, the extended critique of Berlin (1974) in Gary B. Mills, *The Forgotten People: Cane River's Creoles of Color* (Baton Rouge, 1977), xv-xvi.

Asians as different "races." But nobody else sees it this way. Japanese, Australian Aborigines, Tahitians, Malaysians, Pakistanis, Turks, and Israelis are all Asians, for example, but no one of them would consider themselves to be of the same "race" as any of the others. Even the obsolescent craniofacial anthropometry of the past does not match preconceptions of "race." Carleton S. Coon, the greatest race-defining craniofacial anthropometrist of the twentieth century, whose definitions filled the U.S. textbooks of fifty years ago, considered neither Ethiopians nor Khoisan to be of the "negroid race."[4] Rather than "race," this discussion is interested only in those physical traits that lead U.S. society to assign a person to one side or the other of the endogamous color line—to consider a person a suitable marriage partner for Whites or Blacks.

Understanding the heredity of physical traits associated with the endogamous color line can help us better to grasp how genes leaked through the barrier as much as they have (one third of White Americans having 2-20 percent African genetic admixture). But a difficulty in discussing heredity is the indeterminacy of just which features are associated with the color line. We know that people who "look African" are usually assigned to the Black endogamous group by U.S. society. But precisely what does it mean to say that someone "looks African"? As will be explained in the next chapter, *The Perception of "Racial" Traits*, the features associated with African ancestry depend upon which society is making the determination. As Harry Hoetink pointed out, the very same individual may be considered White in Puerto Rico, Coloured in Jamaica, and Negro in Georgia.[5] Modern craniofacial anthropometrists (forensic anthropologists) give more importance to prognathism than to skin tone,[6] and nineteenth-century Americans once emphasized foot shape.[7] Consequently,

---

[4] See Carleton Stevens Coon, *The Origin of Races* (New York, 1962).

[5] Harry Hoetink, *Caribbean Race Relations: A Study of Two Variants* (London, 1971), xii.

[6] Nova: George W. Gill, *Does Race Exist?: An Proponent's Perspective* <http://www.pbs.org/wgbh/nova/first/gill.html> (2000).

[7] 23 Ark. 50.

the following discussion of heritability simplifies such traits to a single feature—skin tone.

Throughout the following discussion, three things should be kept in mind. First, many societies (Hindu India, for example) do not consider skin tone to be associated with any endogamous barrier. This discussion focuses on skin tone because most Americans consider it significant, hence the term "color line" and the group labels "Black" and "White" corresponding to brown versus pinkish beige skin tone. Second, melanization is mechanically complex. Some people are darker than others before tanning, some tan more easily, some tan more deeply, and some tans last longer than others. Despite its complexity, dermal melanization depends on just a few genes. Finally, the following discussion could be repeated for any feature that depends on a handful of additive genes, each with co-dominant alleles, such as hair curliness, nose width, lip thickness, prognathism, steatopygia, and the like. Hence, it applies to any of the physical traits that U.S. society associates with membership in the Black or White endogamous groups.

Alleles do not blend. They are not analog recordings. They are digitally encoded (the human genome contains about 750 megabytes of data).[8] Because they are digitally encoded, alleles combine in simple, mathematically predictable ways. Since 1910, researchers have known that human skin pigmentation is polygenic, depending on just a few codominant additive genes of essentially two alleles each. We have known that skin tone is polygenic, rather than the result of one gene with many alleles, because breeding of palest with darkest yields a spectrum of offspring genotypes from the same parents, not just the four Mendelian ones. We have known that human pigmentation genes are additive and codominant because half the offspring of differently colored parents have a skin tone between that of their parents, no matter how similar the parents (one-fourth are outside each extreme of the parental span). We have known that at least

---

[8] Three billion nucleotides, each carrying two bits of information, at eight bits per byte.

three genes are involved because histograms of population skin reflectance yield continuous, not discrete, values.[9]

Where knowledge has improved over the past century has been in precisely how many genes are involved and their specific loci. As of 1998, five human pigmentation genes had been identified. Their symbols and genome loci are: "TYR" at 11q14-21 (chromosome eleven long arm, 14 to 21 centimorgans out), "TYRP1" at 9p23, "TYRP2" at 13q31-32, "P" at 15q11.2-12, and "MC1R" at 16q24.3.[10] Subsequent work has identified five non-synonymous polymorphisms at the MC1R site.[11] Some polymorphisms have been related to phenotype.[12] And gene-enzyme-protein reaction chains have been identified.[13]

Much of the genetic mechanism remains to be unraveled but one finding is pertinent here. Skin tone is determined by a (definite) minimum of three and a (probable) maximum of six additive genes, each with two co-dominant alleles. This means that skin-tone inheritance is predictable. Imagine a population composed of two same-sized groups. The first group comprises individuals who (like many sub-Saharan Africans) are homozygotic for dark alleles at all of the (three to six) dermal melanization loci. The other group comprises individuals who (like Nordic Europeans) are homozygotic for fair alleles at the same loci. Given random mating within the population composed of the

---

[9] The two most accessible sources of historical surveys and synopses of current understanding are Curt Stern, *Principles of Human Genetics*, 3d ed. (San Francisco, 1973), 443-65 and L. L. Cavalli-Sforza and W. F. Bodmer, *The Genetics of Human Populations* (Mineola NY, 1999), 527-31.

[10] Richard A. Sturm, Neil F. Box, and Michele Ramsay, "Human Pigmentation Genetics: The Difference is Only Skin Deep," *BioEssays*, 20 (1998), 712-21.

[11] B.K. Rana and others, "High Polymorphism at the Human Melanocortin 1 Receptor Locus," *Genetics*, 151 (no. 4, 1999), 1547-48.

[12] R.M. Harding and others, "Evidence for Variable Selective Pressures at MC1R," *Journal of Human Genetics*, 66 (no. 4, 2000), 1351.

[13] P.A. Kanetsky and others, "A Polymorphism in the Agouti Signaling Protein Gene is Associated with Human Pigmentation," *American Journal of Human Genetics*, 70 (2002), 770-75.

two equal-sized groups, within a few generations the resultant population would fall into a Poisson skin-tone distribution.[14]

Mendelian Inheritance

In other words, if a large population (more than a few thousand individuals) were assembled out of equal numbers of the darkest and the fairest humans on earth, within a few generations, their descendants' skin tone would fall into a normal (Gaussian bell-curve) distribution. The number of genes involved would not affect the form of the distribution. If skin tone were determined by only three genes, then the resultant population would fall into the seventh line of Pascal's triangle with, on average, 1, 6, 15, 20, 15, 6, and 1 out of every 64 individuals having each skin-tone gradation, from the fairest to the darkest possible. If skin tone were set by six genes, then the descendants would fall into the thirteenth line of Pascal's triangle with, on average, 1, 12, 66, 220, 495, 792, 924, 792, 495, 220, 66, 12, and 1 out of every 4096 individuals having every skin-tone gradation from the fairest to the darkest. Neither the shape, the height, nor the width of the consequent distribution would vary with number of genes. The number of genes involved would affect only the fineness of the skin-tone gradations.

The above explanation may seem trivial, but it is important to understanding U.S. color line permeability. It is important because exactly the same results would unfold if one were to start with a homogeneous population where every individual were heterozygotic at each locus. In other words, if you started with a population of first-generation admixture (each with a fair-skin allele from one parent, and a dark-skin allele from the other parent, at each of the three-to-six genes), then their descendants would fall into precisely the same pattern as above, with pre-

---

[14] C. Stern, "Model Estimates of the Frequency of White and Near-White Segregants in the American Negro," *Acta Genetica*, 4 (1953), 281-98, 445-52.

cisely the same numbers of individuals having every skin-tone gradation from the very fairest to the darkest possible.[15]

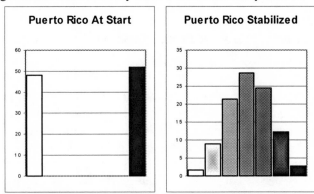

Figure 10. Puerto Rico Skin tone Histogram

As a practical example, consider Puerto Rico. From the late eighteenth century until the U.S. conquest at the turn of the twentieth century, Spanish censuses of the island consistently reported that 45 percent of the population was White (predominantly European-looking) and 55 percent was Black (predominantly African-looking). Census after census, these numbers did not change more than three percentage points until the United States took possession of the island.[16] Today, the native-born island population physically matches the theoretical Poisson distribution almost precisely. About one Puerto Rican in ten looks White to the typical American, about one in ten looks Black, and

---

[15] See, for example, A.K. Kalla, "Inheritance of Skin Colour in Man," *Anthropologist*, Special Volume (1968), 158-68; G.A. Harrison and J.J.T. Owen, "Studies on the Inheritance of Human Skin Colour," *Ann. Human Genetics*, 28 (1964), 27-37; Stern (1953), 281-98.

[16] For 1792, see Francisco Morales Padron, "La Vida Cotidiana en una Hacienda de Esclavos," *Revista del Instituto de Cultura Puertorriquena*, 4 (no. 10, 1961), 23-33, 25. For a census-by-census table of subsequent years, see Frederick P. Bowser, "Colonial Spanish America," in *Neither Slave Nor Free: The Freedmen of African Descent in the Slave Societies of the New World*, ed. David W. Cohen and Jack P. Greene (Baltimore, 1972), 19-58, 38.

the rest look "Hispanic," which in this context means "in between."[17]

Appearance is not the Same Thing as Ancestry

To be precise, Figure 10 shows that a skin-tone histogram
of Puerto Ricans has a single peak at the 50-50 mark with population fractions diminishing in both directions—dark and light.[18]
Nevertheless, judging by the Spanish census data and considering that the Johnson-Reed Act of 1924 cut off immigration, virtually every native-born Puerto Rican on the island today has
equal numbers of African and European ancestors.[19] This means
that those few Puerto Ricans who are of predominantly European appearance as well as those who are of predominantly African appearance descend from the same population of ancestors.
Figure 10 depicts a computer simulation of this result.[20]

This point bears repeating. Those few Puerto Ricans of
European appearance whose families have been on the island
since colonial tines have equal numbers of African and European
ancestors, as do those Puerto Ricans of strongly African appearance. In short, skin tone is so ephemeral and so sensitive to a

---

[17] Since the American occupation, the federal census in Puerto Rico has
conformed to the U.S. viewpoint. Through 1950, all Puerto Ricans were
census-defined as "colored" as per the enumerators' instructions. Since
1960, the census has been self-administered, and about forty percent of
Puerto Ricans have checked off "White," while another fifty percent have
checked off "other" and written in various terms (Hispanic, human, none,
Puerto Rican, Latino, and the like), which the census bureau encodes as
"White." Only one Puerto Rican in ten checks off "Black."

[18] For a similar discussion of Puerto Rican admixture, rather than skin tone,
see under the topic "Admixture Scatter Diagrams" in *Chapter 2. Afro-
European Genetic Admixture in the United States*.

[19] Clara E. Rodriguez, "Challenging Racial Hegemony: Puerto Ricans in the
United States," in *Race*, ed. Steven Gregory and Roger Sanjek (New
Brunswick NJ, 1994), 131-45, 137.

[20] The program (a MS-Excel macro) can be downloaded from URL
<http://backintyme.com/admixture/genetics.xls.>

few genes, that it is nearly useless as an indicator of either Afro-European ancestry or Afro-European genetic admixture (which are themselves different things). As another example of this point, a recent admixture study conducted in Columbia, South Carolina, found that about five percent of Black Americans have no detectable African genetic admixture at all.[21] Their family oral histories accurately trace their descent partly from African slaves. But over the course of many generations, even the negligible intermarriage rate between Whites and Blacks gradually eliminated the genetic markers of African origin from those few families by random chance.

Hardy-Weinberg Distribution

Once a population's genotype stabilizes into a Poisson bell curve, it will remain in that configuration as long as the conditions of Hardy-Weinberg equilibrium hold and mating is random. Hardy-Weinberg equilibrium is not discussed at depth in this work. It suffices to point out that where a closed population is large enough to avoid loss or fixing of alleles by mere chance (termed *drift*), and where no selection mechanism operates on the genes of interest (affecting either survival, reproduction, or mate selection), then the percentages of alleles (fifty-fifty in the above example) within a population will remain unchanged indefinitely.[22]

In the context of this discussion, absence of mate selection implies random mating with regards to skin tone, which may seem inapplicable to this study. After all, in contrast to Puerto Rico, the defining feature of the U.S. color line is that it marks

---

[21] E.J. Parra and others, "Ancestral Proportions and Admixture Dynamics in Geographically Defined African Americans Living in South Carolina," *American Journal of Physical Anthropology*, 114 (2001), 18-29. This study was also mentioned in *Chapter 2. Afro-European Genetic Admixture in the United States.*

[22] An accessible introduction to Hardy-Weinberg equilibrium can be found in Steve Jones, Robert Martin, and David Pilbeam, eds. *The Cambridge Encyclopedia of Human Evolution* (Cambridge UK, 1992), 290.

an endogamous barrier. But the point here is that the U.S. Black community can itself be defined as a closed population precisely because it is endogamous. Whether mate-selection within this group depends on skin tone is an interesting question. Many anthropologists of the 1920s and 1930s reported detecting a Black male mate-selection preference for fair women. Melville J. Herskovitz, Gunnar Myrdal, Edward Reuter, Ralph Linton, Gustavas Steward, and Robert E. Park referred to it.[23] But these finding were eventually overturned because they were based on skin-tone differences between husbands and wives. As it turns out, studies of siblings show that females typically display less melanization than males,[24] just as children display less melanization than adults.[25] It is simply one of the neotenous features associated with human sexual dimorphism.[26] In any event, it is now accepted that, within the U.S. Black community, mating has been essentially random for skin tone.

---

[23] A useful survey of this topic can be found in Joel Williamson, *New People: Miscegenation and Mulattoes in the United States* (New York, 1980), 118-21.

[24] E. Rebato and others, "Sibling Correlations of Skin Pigmentation During Growth," *Human Biology,* 71 (no. 2, 1999), 277-93.

[25] J.H. Relethford, F.C. Lees, and P.J. Bayard, "Sex and Age Variation in the Skin Color of Irish Children," *Current Anthropology,* 26 (no. 3, 1985), 386-97.

[26] Otherwise important distinctions among neoteny, paedomorphosis, and postdisplacement are irrelevant to the point being made.

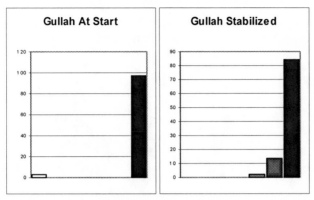

Figure 11. Gullah Skin tone Histogram

How Many White Children are Born Into Black Families?

The occurrence frequency of European admixture (implying alleles for fair skin tone) among members of the U.S. Black community varies by region, from around 3 percent among the Geechee/Gullah people of the Sea Islands of South Carolina, Georgia, and Florida, to about 20 percent among the African-Americans of Philadelphia and Boston.[27] Given these numbers, it is a straightforward task to compute the rate at which any given African-American population will produce members who are as fair as Europeans.[28]

---

[27] C.L. Pfaff and others, "Using Estimates of Individual Admixture to Study the Genetics of Phenotypic Traits: Skin Pigmentation in African Americans," *American Journal of Human Genetics*, 69 (no. 4, 2001b), 410; E.J. Parra and others, "Ancestral Proportions and Admixture Dynamics in Geographically Defined African Americans Living in South Carolina," *American Journal of Physical Anthropology*, 114 (2001), 18-29; Esteban J. Parra and others, "Estimating African American Admixture Proportions by Use of Population-Specific Alleles," *American Journal of Human Genetics*, 63 (1998), 1839-51.

[28] Again, this is easiest done by simulation rather than analytically, using something like the program at URL <http://backintyme.com/admixture/genetics.xls>.

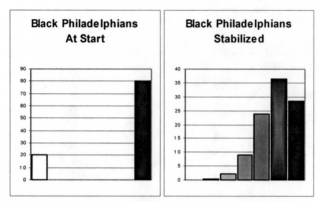

Figure 12. Black Philadelphia Skin tone Histogram

Various sources agree that, on average, people with 12 percent or less African admixture appear White to the average American and those with up to 25 percent look ambiguous (with a Mediterranean skin tone).[29] Given this finding, random chance will produce one such Philadelphian out of every five hundred born to parents who are members of the Black community (rare, but measurable), and one such Gullah out of every 1.4 billion (virtually impossible).[30] (In the accompanying graphs, only the two leftmost bars depict the numbers of people with European skin tone.)

---

[29] Caroline Bond Day and Earnest Albert Hooton, *A Study of Some Negro-White Families in the United States* (Cambridge MA, 1932), 10; Melville J. Herskovits, *The Anthropometry of the American Negro* (New York, 1930); G.A. Harrison and J.J.T. Owen, "Studies on the Inheritance of Human Skin Colour," *Ann. Human Genetics*, 28 (1964), 27-37; A.K. Kalla, "Inheritance of Skin Colour in Man," *Anthropologist*, Special Volume (1968), 158-68; C. Stern, "Model Estimates of the Frequency of White and Near-White Segregants in the American Negro," *Acta Genetica*, 4 (1953), 281-98.

[30] Assuming four genes (eight haplotypes): For Philadelphia, if the probability of any haplotype's being European is 0.20, then the probability of six out of the eight haplotypes being European (giving a European appearance to the individual) would be $0.20^6 \times 28 = 1.8 \times 10^{-3}$. For the Sea Islands, if the probability of any haplotype's being European is 0.03, then the probability of six aligning to yield a European phenotype would be $0.03^6 \times 28 = 2.04 \times 10^{-8}$. Where 28 is the number of two-in-eight combinations n!/j!(n-j)!.

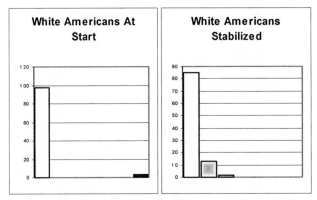

Figure 13. White America Skin tone Histogram

How Many Black Children are Born into White Families?

The mirror-image situation is also easily computed. African admixture averages about 0.7 percent among White Americans, about 8 percent in Portugal, and about 5 percent in Spain, based upon recent genetic admixture studies as well as upon accepted estimates of sixteenth-century sub-Saharan immigration to Iberia.[31] Hence, typical White Americans cannot produce

---

[31] For the U.S. rate, see Mark D. Shriver and others, "Skin Pigmentation, Biogeographical Ancestry, and Admixture Mapping," *Human Genetics*, 112 (2003), 387-99, Table 2. For immigration history, see: University of Chicago, ed. *The New Encyclopaedia Britannica*, 15 ed. (Chicago, 1974), 15:859; Hugh Thomas, *The Slave Trade: The Story of the Atlantic Slave Trade: 1440-1870* (New York, 1997), 22-24, 48-86, 804; Lerone Bennett Jr., *Before the Mayflower: A History of Black America*, 6th rev. ed. (New York, 1993), 32; Frank Tannenbaum, *Slave and Citizen, the Negro in the Americas* (Boston, 1946), 14-15, 44; Leslie B. Rout, *The African Experience in Spanish America, 1502 to the Present Day* (Cambridge UK, 1976), 9, 18-20. For DNA admixture studies, see: Martin Richards and others, "Extensive Female-Mediated Gene Flow from Sub-Saharan Africa into Near Eastern Arab Populations," *American Journal of Human Genetics*, 72 (2003), 1058-64; H.B. Corte-Real and others, "Genetic Diversity in the Iberian Peninsula Determined from Mitochondrial Sequence Analysis," *Annals of Human Genetics*, 60 (no. 4, July 1996), 331-50.

children with unambiguously dark skin but it occurs among Spaniards at the rate of about one in two hundred.[32]

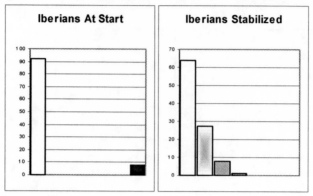

Figure 14. Iberia Skin tone Histogram

This explains why modern-day Chileans and Argentine-ans, as well as Spaniards, look White to Americans, despite hav-ing recently absorbed large African populations.[33] Alleles for African appearance are so thinly distributed throughout these predominantly European populations that the genes seldom hap-pen to match up in any one individual.

As explained above, the same can be said for any trait as-sociated with the U.S. endogamous color line. In short, even without taking into account a steady inflow of genes for Euro-pean appearance, the Black community has always produced a steady and predictable stream of European-looking individuals whose immediate parentage is socially Black. They owe their European phenotype to the random matching up of genes from distant European ancestors. Of course, counting how many peo-

---

[32] Assuming four genes (eight haplotypes): For Spain, if the probability of any haplotype's being African is 0.05, then the probability of three out of the eight haplotypes being African (giving an African appearance to the individual) would be $0.05^3 \times 56 = .007$. For White Americans, if the prob-ability of any haplotype's being African is 0.007, then the probability of three aligning to yield an African phenotype would be $0.007^3 \times 56 = 1.92 \times 10^{-5}$. Where 56 is the number of three-in-eight combinations n!/j!(n-j)!.

[33] George Reid Andrews, *The Afro-Argentines of Buenos Aires, 1800-1900* (Madison, 1980).

ple are born with European appearance measures opportunity, not action. There is no reason to think that all or even most such Americans actually cross the color line and designate themselves White.[34]

*   *   *   *   *

This chapter described the heredity of skin tone, the most important of the physical features used by U.S. society in assigning someone to one side or the other of the endogamous color line. It listed the genes that determine skin tone. It explained that any Afro-European admixed population (such as the African-American community) will never blend homogeneously, but will continue to produce a few European-looking individuals indefinitely. It showed that even people who share identical ancestry may wind up with different Afro-European admixtures due to the random recombination of parental genes at each generation. Finally, it demonstrated how to compute the rate at which European-looking children are born into the African-American community.

This was the second of four chapters meant to illuminate the historical events narrated later. It built upon the previous chapter to show that, not only have millions of Americans born into Black families redefined themselves as White over the decades, but that the process is a natural consequence of Mendelian heredity. One out of every several thousand births within the Black community produces a person who looks completely European and has no more African admixture than 74 million other White Americans.

---

[34] See *Chapter 5. The Rate of Black-to-White "Passing"* for an estimate of Black-to-White gene flow across the U.S. color line in order compute just how many individuals have made this choice over the years.

Chapter 4.
The Perception of "Racial" Traits

A few years ago, Eugene Robinson, a Black writer for the *Washington Post*, visited Brazil. An outgoing, likeable young man, he soon made friends with English-speaking Brazilians his own age. A particularly attractive young woman invited him to join her and her friends in a relaxing day on the incomparable beaches of Rio de Janeiro. Despite minor, often humorous language confusion, the day started well. Eugene was fascinated with Brazilian culture and customs and, while satisfying his curiosity about their world, his Brazilian friends asked him about life in the United States.[1]

The problem started when he asked them what is was like to be Black in Brazil. They tried to answer, but it soon became clear that they had no idea—their answers were based on their impressions of U.S. popular culture. Eugene explained that he already knew what it was like to be Black in the United States. He was American and Black, after all. He wanted to know about Black life in Brazil. Startled, his new friends explained that they did not personally know any Black people. Shocked, he bluntly told them that they were Black and should not deny the fact. Concerned bystanders glanced at the little group as voices were

---

[1] Eugene Robinson, *Coal to Cream* (New York, 1999), 9-13.

raised in mutual frustration. Finally, in desperation, Eugene extended his forearm, placed it alongside that of the gorgeous young woman who had invited him to the beach, and scolded, "Stop denying that you are Black! I am Black and you are darker than me!" As one, the Brazilians rose to their feet, collected their belongings, and left Eugene sitting all alone on one of the most beautiful beaches on earth.

The problem was more than mere language. Brazilians think of "Blacks" as the urban underclass, responsible for more crime than their numbers would predict and who have suffered White domination for so long that many are suspicious of well-meaning Whites. To some extent, this is also true in the United States. But Robinson used "Black" to mean membership in an endogamous group—a phenomenon that does not exist in Brazil. Each saw the other through a cultural filter. In Eugene's eyes, his Brazilian friends displayed some African ancestry, just like him. Since Robinson is a member of the U.S. Black endogamous group, he incorrectly thought that his friends were also members of a Black endogamous group. From the other side, Robinson showed unmistakable middle-class education and status, just like them. Since this made them White by the Brazilian definition, they insisted that Robinson was also White.

To a historian, the interesting point is that neither side was willing to budge from its culturally learned preconceptions. To this day, the intelligent, educated journalist insists in his writings that Brazilians are in denial. We shall never know how Brazilians feel about the crazy White American who, to their minds, claimed that he was a slum-dweller, since only Robinson wrote about the event. But we can guess. As one scientist points out, "Most people believe they know ['racial' appearance] when they see it, but arrive at nothing short of confusion when pressed to define it."[2]

*   *   *   *   *

---

[2] National Human Genome Research Institute (NIH), *The Human Genome Project And Beyond* [Lecture Transcript Web Site] (July 7, 2001).

This chapter reviews what is known about the culturally dependent perception of "racial" traits in four topics. *Harry Hoetink's Somatic Norm Image* considers whether predictable differences in colonial histories determine how people see "racial" group membership. *How U.S. Children Learn to See Two Endogamous Groups* examines the stages through which children learn to identify and to articulate what their culture sees as "racial" traits. *The Instinctive Need to See "Otherness"* identifies the cognitive system, selected by adaptation to hunter-gatherer life over 200 millennia ago, that has been co-opted to identify someone as having "racially" different looks—an encounter that no Paleolithic hominid could ever have experienced. Finally, *The Decline of the Bio-Race Concept* offers a brief explanation of why the biological concept of "race" as applied to humans has been abandoned by the hard sciences.

Harry Hoetink's Somatic Norm Image

That different cultures can assign the same individual to opposite "races" may be hard to grasp. And yet Barbadian South Carolina, Hispano-Florida, Anglo-Alabama, and Franco-Louisiana all had cultural beliefs and attitudes about "race" that differed from today's U.S. customs. Colonial Floridians held public celebrations when the Spanish governor ruled that children of well-liked biracial families had become legally White. English-speaking Alabamians routinely allowed men of the Colored designation to marry women of the White group and accepted their mixed offspring as Whites. And Creole Louisianans fought to retain a three-layer system resembling that of apartheid South Africa a century later.

David Hackett Fischer may have stretched things when he wrote, "People, in various places and times, have not merely thought different things. They have thought them differently. It is probable that their most fundamental cerebral processes have changed through time."[3] But if Fischer stretched things, it was

---

[3] David H. Fischer, *Historians' Fallacies* (New York, 1970), 203-4.

only a bit. North Americans, Haitians, Dominicans, Puerto Ricans, Barbadians, Jamaicans, and Trinidadians all have different subconscious and automatic perceptions of just what features define who belongs to which endogamous group or appearance designation. Americans in the past were sincere that Germans, Irish, Jews, Slavs, Italians, Chinese, and Puerto Ricans could never pass for White because of their distinctive non-White appearance.[4] The Chief Justice of Arkansas wrote in 1861 that, "No one, who is familiar with the peculiar formation of the *negro foot* [emphasis in the original], can doubt, but that an inspection of that member would ordinarily afford some indication of the race."[5] Nowadays, of course, few Americans consider Germans, Irish, Italians, or Slavs to be nonwhite, or think that being Black depends upon your foot shape. Nevertheless, it is a deep cognitive truth that cultures do not ostracize out-groups because they look different; they look different because they are out-groups. More accurately, the two effects operate in mutual feedback. Each phenomenon reinforces the other. Cognition research has demonstrated why people in different cultures, past or present, have not merely seen different "racial" features, but really have seen them differently. Perception is warped by cognition. We see what we want to see.

To Brazilians (and other Latin American continuum societies), skin-tone designations are descriptors of appearance. The terms are analogous to the designations that cosmetologists use to select the best foundation for a client. Some Americans think that the range of terms means that Brazilians (and other Latin American continuum societies) believe in dozens of "races." But this is no more the case than that Americans believe in dozens of "races" based on cosmetic skin tone. Latin American continuum societies lack an endogamous color line. Nevertheless, as the anecdote shows, Brazilians agree that Blacks (a class, not an endogamous group) are a crime-ridden impoverished minority.

---

[4] See "Impermeability" in *Chapter 6. Features of the Endogamous Color Line*.

[5] 23 Ark. 50.

Why does social status correlate with appearance even in continuum societies, which lack endogamous color lines?

Because most Africans came as slaves, the relative preponderance of African versus European features (skin tone, hair texture, etc.) in individuals, still correlates with socioeconomic class throughout the hemisphere. Consequently, almost everyone in the New World today is confident of being able to observe whether someone is Black or White. In reality, as Robinson learned, different cultures disagree dramatically on just who is what. This is because Latin Americans use the terms to denote appearance or class, whereas English-speaking Americans (of both endogamous groups) use them to denote endogamous group membership.[6]

Except for subjects at the extremes of Nordic or Bantu appearance, New World cultures differ in who gets sorted into which category. This makes one wonder if different peoples have systematically different criteria. Can one predict how Jamaicans, say, differ from Puerto Ricans in how they identify "racial" membership, or how both differ from South Carolinians based on their colonial histories? Harry Hoetink believes that the answer is "yes."[7] Although originally from Holland, Hoetink spent most of his career as historian and teacher throughout the Caribbean. He had the opportunity to live and work on West Indian islands of British, French, Dutch, and Spanish traditions. He devised the hypothesis of the *somatic norm image*.

Hoetink suggests that three similar socioeconomic classes formed in most settlements during the New World colonial period. Once the importation of African labor became widespread, Western Hemisphere colonies that lacked significant numbers of Native Americans tended to fall into a three-tiered social structure. The top layer comprised a small number of European landowning planters who produced agricultural products for export using large numbers of African slaves. The slaves themselves

---

[6] This is not to say that some Latin Americans societies are not ruled by light-complexioned people who oppress dark ones. It says only that no endogamous color lines exist in Latin America.

[7] Harry Hoetink, *Caribbean Race Relations: A Study of Two Variants* (London, 1971), xii.

made up the bottom layer. Finally, in most European colonies (Barbados being the exception), an intermediate group arose, composed of free subsistence farmers, who were allowed to opt out of the plantation economy in return for serving as militia in the event of slave insurrection. In each colony, the color line came to be defined by the appearance of typical members of the intermediate class. Anyone more European-looking was seen as White; anyone darker was considered Black. Historical contingency decreed that this intermediate group would have a large admixture of African appearance in Santo Domingo, less so in Puerto Rico and Brazil, even less in Jamaica and Trinidad, and be completely European-looking in Virginia and South Carolina. According to Hoetink, where different New World peoples locate the color line (along the Norway-to-Nigeria continuum) is the legacy of a somatic norm image formed in colonial times. Hoetink's central thesis is that:

> One and the same person may be considered white in the Dominican Republic or Puerto Rico, and 'coloured' in Jamaica, Martinique, or Curaçao; this difference must be explained in terms of socially determined somatic norms. The same person may be called a 'Negro' in Georgia; this must be explained by the historical evolution of social structure in the Southern United States.[8]

Hoetink's somatic norm image hypothesis stumbles a bit in conflating endogamous group membership designations (prevalent in former British, and French colonies) with skin-tone designations (prevalent in former Spanish and Portuguese colonies). But his central thesis seems valid. It is easily demonstrated that people see only what they want to see, and what they want to see is learned from their culture in early childhood.

---

[8] Idem.

How U.S. Children Learn to See Two Endogamous Groups

Eugene Robinson's experience in Rio de Janeiro illustrates that, although members of different cultures differ in how they perceive the meanings of "White" and "Black," everyone is convinced that his or her perception is the only valid one. Furthermore, people find great difficulty in articulating the criteria on which their own perception is based. Skin tone is often cited as the most important "racial" trait, but it is easy to demonstrate that in the middle range of skin tones, darkness is less important to "racial" definition than hair kinkiness and facial features. This suggests that the ability to distinguish "racial" traits is learned early and deeply. It is learned early in that the process seems to start shortly after an infant learns to talk—long before formal schooling. It is learned deeply in that it employs cognitive skills that are only dimly accessible to the conscious mind.

What are the stages through which children learn to perceive and later to articulate what their culture sees as "racial" traits?[9] "Racial" perception develops similarly to most of the cognitive abilities identified by Piaget and others in five major respects. First, like the ability to recognize that one jar can hold more liquid than another, some form of "racial" feature recognition appears in every culture. Second, contrary to folk belief, the ability begins to emerge in very early childhood. Third, it forms gradually in stages. Fourth, with maturity it becomes so entrenched and cognitively automatic that the individual can no

---

[9] The scientific literature on the formation of "racial" perception in childhood is vast. For anthropological surveys of the field, see: Mary Ellen Goodman, *The Culture of Childhood: Child's-Eye Views of Society and Culture* (New York, 1970) and Robyn M. Holmes, *How Young Children Perceive Race* (Thousand Oaks CA, 1995). For psychological surveys, see Judith D. R. Porter, *Black Child, White Child: The Development of Racial Attitudes* (Cambridge MA, 1971); Phyllis A. Katz, *Development of Children's Racial Awareness and Intergroup Attitudes* (Washington, 1981); Jean S. Phinney and Mary Jane Rotheram, *Children's Ethnic Socialization: Pluralism and Development* (Beverly Hills, 1987); Frances E. Aboud, *Children and Prejudice* (New York, 1988); or William E. Cross, *Shades of Black: Diversity in African-American Identity* (Philadelphia, 1991).

longer introspect how it is done. Fifth, it eventually becomes rationalized into a theory-like knowledge structure that sustains inferences about category members that go beyond direct experience. On the other hand, the perception of "racial" traits differs in two important ways from other cognitive abilities that emerge in early childhood. First, although the pattern of development is stable across diverse cultures, the content of "racial" perception varies dramatically (as Eugene Robinson learned). Second, although "racial" perception first appears in infancy, it becomes theory-like relatively late in childhood. Naive theories of biology (dogs beget puppies, cats beget kittens, etc.), of physics (big jars hold more than small jars), and of mind (mothers cannot really read thoughts), in contrast, develop years earlier than those of "racial" group membership.[10]

Experiments with 3-, 4- and 7-year-olds from the U.S. Midwest show that even toddlers believe that "racial" traits are more firmly fixed for life than are occupation or body type. This is important because it shows that counterfactual belief starts early in life. In the children's own experiences (attending an integrated school) skin color and hair texture do in fact change over a person's life (most kids darken at puberty) whereas body type (which correlates with the global latitude of ancestry) does not change. Nevertheless, belief in the permanence of "racial" traits starts by age 3 and grows stronger with age. This demonstrates that, although cognition of "racial" traits may use some of the mechanisms of naive biology, the former does not depend on the latter, nor does it spring merely from observation of the world.[11]

Other experiments show a strong social membership component (as opposed to a presumed biological component) of "racial" perception. Thirty-six 3-, 4-, and 6-year-olds were presented only with speaking voices. They were then asked to tell whether each unseen speaker resembled previously depicted in-

---

[10] Lawrence A. Hirschfeld, *Race in the Making: Cognition, Culture, and the Child's Construction of Human Kinds* (London, 1996), 83.

[11] Lawrence A. Hirschfeld, "Do children have a theory of race?," *Cognition*, 54 (no. 2, February 1995a), 209-52.

dividuals with preponderantly European traits or those with preponderantly African features. Although all of the voices were
unintelligible, some used muffled English syllables and others
used Portuguese sounds. Midwestern U.S. children (members of
both the Black and the White endogamous groups) associated
Portuguese-sounding speech with African appearance.[12]

The most revealing experiments focus on hypodescent
(that if you are partly Black, you are all Black).[13] Seventeen second-graders, fifteen sixth-graders, and forty-three undergraduate
adults were presented with pictures of interracial parents (one
African-looking, one European-looking) pushing a stroller containing a baby that was so bundled up as to be utterly concealed.
After their memories had faded, the subjects were asked which
parent the (actually unseen) infant had most closely resembled.
Second-graders chose randomly. Half recalled that the (unseen)
baby had resembled the European-looking parent and half said
that it had resembled the African-looking parent. Sixth graders
overwhelmingly said that the infant had resembled the African-
looking parent. But when asked why the hidden baby had come
out looking Black, the sixth-graders simply shrugged. Adult subjects also overwhelmingly said that the concealed baby had
looked Black. But, when asked why this was so, American
adults confabulated tales of genetic dominance in order to ra-
tionalize their culture's counterfactual folklore of hypodescent.[14]
Again, in no experiment was there any correlation with the subject's own endogamous group membership.[15]

---

[12] Hirschfeld (1996), 121-57.

[13] Coined in Marvin Harris, *Patterns of Race in the Americas* (Westport CT,
1964), 37, "hypodescent" means that, to the extent that blood fraction influences endogamous group membership, the dividing line is not 50-50. Even a
slight fraction of known Black ancestry usually consigns an English-
speaking American to the Black group. This contrasts with other New
World countries where one is categorized by preponderance of appearance.
If you look mostly White, you are White.

[14] Lawrence A. Hirschfeld, "The Inheritability of Identity: Children's Understanding of the Cultural Biology of Race," *Child Development*, 66 (no. 5,
October 1995b), 1418-37.

[15] The specific numbers cited in the text refer only to the original breakthrough experiments. Their findings have since been replicated many times.

The Instinctive Need to See "Otherness"

It is evident that children of every culture can "correctly" (for their own society) categorize strangers by age three. They can reliably match each "racial" category with its social term or word by about age five.[16] American children internalize the counterfactual hypodescent rule by about age ten. And they can confabulate an intellectual rationalization for hypodescent by early adulthood. The most astonishing finding is the first. As Hoetink demonstrated and Robinson experienced, the number and meaning of "racial" categories and of the traits that delineate them vary dramatically among cultures. Nevertheless, children learn their own culture's rules and categories shortly after learning to walk. Clearly, the cognitive system employed is as adaptable to culture, and yet is as hard-wired in the brain, as is language itself. Logically, it must have been as powerfully selected for as was language itself. And yet, "racial" traits vary geographically so imperceptibly on the scale of a few hundred miles, that until just a few millennia ago, when most humans stopped making a living as hunter-gatherers, no one could ever have seen someone of a different "race." How can the cognitive ability to perceive "racial" categories be so strongly adaptive if the occasion to use it never actually arose?

The answer is revealed in a series of experiments conducted by Robert Kurzban, subsequently confirmed by John Tooby and Leda Cosmides. Sex, age, and "otherness" are the three fundamental attributes that the mind encodes in an automatic and mandatory manner. For example, long after all memory has been lost of the occupation, name, clothing, or hair of a

---

The baby-stroller experiment, for instance, has been adopted into many college-level introductory psychology laboratory assignments. The findings have become part of the cognitive-science consensus. The reader should not be misled by the fact that the seminal breakthrough experiments, discussed in the text, employed only a few subjects in a few locations. The sum of subsequent confirming replications has yielded far greater numbers and no corroborative failures.

[16] Debra Van Ausdale and Joe R. Feagin, *The First R: How Children Learn Race and Racism* (Lanham MD, 2001).

stranger to which one was briefly exposed, one can recall that the individual was "a White woman" or a "Black male child." But age and sex are independent of culture. "Otherness" is not. Kurzban and later investigators demonstrated that the ability to recall a stranger's "otherness" actually detects a culture's social coalitions or alliances. Over the past hundred millennia or so, humans have become adept at detecting competing social groups. The discrimination of facial features enables a child to identify whether a stranger is genetically related (a member of the child's extended family). This ability is strongly selected because one is less likely to be killed and devoured by a relative than by a member of an opposing group.[17] Recall that we (genus *Homo*) evolved as hunting apes for two million years before our brains expanded five-fold in the past 120 millennia (species *sapiens*). You must take the long view when studying adaptive cognition.

Skin tone, hair kinkiness, and the like are the clues used to identify a stranger's "otherness" in the culture of the United States. Other cultures use clues that are unrelated to the U.S. endogamous color line: height, hair-length, clothing, facial features (such as hooked nose versus straight nose or the shape of the eye), even a person's smell (which relates to diet). Interestingly, although the need to remember a stranger's "otherness" is apparently inborn, each culture's particular recognition template is easily changed. In about half an hour, a researcher can alter your template, from whatever it was that your culture imprinted upon you at your mother's knee, to something as silly as the color of a basketball player's jersey. The need is hard-wired but your particular recognition template is easily changed.

---

[17] The most accessible explanation of methodology and results is to be found in Robert Kurzban, John Tooby, and Leda Cosmides, "Can Race be Erased? Coalitional Computation and Social Categorization," *Proceedings of the National Academy of Sciences*, 98 (no. 26, December 18 2001), 15387-15392. For completeness, see also Robert Owen Kurzban, "The Social Psychophysics of Cooperation in Groups" (Ph.D., University of California, 1998) and Lola Cosmides, John Tooby, and Robert Kurzban, "Perceptions of Race," *Trends in Cognitive Sciences*, 7 (no. 4, April 2003), 173-79.

This point is easily misunderstood and has even been reported as suggesting that humans are hard-wired to recognize
"race."[18] The fact is that in no culture does the need/ability to
recall a stranger's "otherness" correlate with Americans' unique
perception of "race," unless you stretch the meaning of "race" to
denote simply "otherness." In the United States, for example,
where the term "race" is applied to differentiate those of Asian
ancestry, subjects quickly forget whether the stranger was Japanese, Native American, Hindu, Irish, Italian, or Pakistani. But
Americans (only) do not forget on which side of the U.S. endogamous color line he seemed to be. In short, it is easily demonstrated within minutes that human subjects notice and subconsciously remember even the most apparently insignificant differences in facial features *if they happen to correlate with "otherness."* On the other hand, even glaring facial differences, such as
skin-tone darkness, are quickly forgotten *if they are irrelevant to
"otherness."* And only in the United States does "otherness"
correlate with the endogamous color line.[19]

The Decline of the Bio-Race Concept

Pull up a live ocean sponge (phylum *Porifera*), grind it in
a blender, and pour the purée back onto the reef. The creature
will reconstitute itself none the worse for the experience.[20] A

---

[18] See for example, Sharon Begley, "The Roots of Hatred: Our brains are
Programmed to Distrust Outsiders But are We Hard-Wired to Hate?,"
AARP, May-June 2004.

[19] For studies suggesting that the development of the ability among social
primates to identify kin via facial features actually caused brain development through natural selection, see Robert A. Barton, "Neocortex Size and
Behavioural Ecology in Primates," *Proceedings of the Royal Society: Biological Sciences*, 263 (no. 1367, Feb. 22 1996), 173-77. For a study measuring the neurological cost of trying to overcome such perceptions learned in
infancy, see BBC News: BBC, *Hidden Race Bias 'Drains Brain'* (Nov. 17,
2003).

[20] The experiment was first reported nearly a century ago by E.V. Wilson of
the University of North Carolina in the article "On Some Phenomena of
Coalescence and Regeneration in Sponges," *Journal of Experimental Zool-
ogy* (1907) 5: 245-58. It has become a traditional demonstration in marine

sponge is merely a loose association—a colony of independent one-celled organisms. To a biologist, the division between single- and multi-celled organisms is just a convenient pedagogical fiction. As the sponge shows, nature herself has few sharp boundaries. The issue is not whether single-celled or multicelled organisms exist. It is whether such a classification scheme is intellectually useful. After all, classification schemes exist only inside our heads. Regarding the example, it turns out that virtually all biologists agree that, except for the sponges, the paradigm dividing single- from multi-celled organisms is very useful indeed.[21]

Bio-race, on the other hand, has lost support among physical anthropologists as a useful paradigm for classifying human variation. In fact, most physical anthropologists today reject bio-race (the biological "race" concept) as useless.[22] According to Matt Cartmill:

> [If "races" are defined as] geographically delimited populations characterized by regionally distinctive phenotypes that do not occur elsewhere in significant numbers, then races no longer exist and have probably not existed for centuries, if ever. And if races are not geographically delimited, then "racial" classificatory categories are merely labels for polymorphisms that vary in frequency from one part of the world to another, like redheadedness or Type A blood. If "Negroid" and "Caucasoid" people occur on every continent, it makes no more sense to describe these groupings as geographical

---

biology labs. Oddly enough, Wilson considered his experiment a failure because he had blended together two sponges of different species in a effort to create a hybrid sponge. The cells simply sorted themselves out before reconstituting their respective sponges. An entertaining account of Wilson's experiment can be found in Richard Dawkins, *The Ancestor's Tale: A Pilgrimage to the Dawn of Evolution* (Boston, 2004), 486-87.

[21] The term "paradigm," here, is used in the strict sense defined by Thomas S. Kuhn, *The Structure of Scientific Revolutions* (Chicago, 1962) as a conceptual framework for experimental observations.

[22] See the results of a survey of 365 physical anthropologists reported in Matt Cartmill, "The Status of the Race Concept in Physical Anthropology," *American Anthropologist*, 100 (no. 3, September 1998), 651-60.

subspecies than it would to describe redheads or people with Type A blood as human subspecies.[23]

The abandonment of bio-race is not unanimous. Some forensic anthropologists make a living providing "racially" framed answers to the peculiar demands of the U.S. justice system. As craniofacial anthropometrist George W. Gill puts it, "I have been able to prove to myself over the years, in actual legal cases, that I am more accurate at assessing race from [bone measurements] than from looking at living people standing before me."[24] Nevertheless, even these professionals admit when pressed that, "If the police want race, I give them race. Maybe afterward, when we're having a beer, we can have a discussion about what race really means."[25] The point is that although the bio-race paradigm has been found useless or worse by biologists, geneticists, and physical anthropologists as a classification scheme for human variation, a few continue to rely on it.

Loss of support for bio-race among physical anthropologists is not new. Its gradual abandonment by science began around the turn of the twentieth century, and may have had an unexpected side effect. It may have been one of the triggers of the 1890s' shift in Americans' conceptualization of "race" (especially in the lower South), from a basis in looks or blood-fraction to one of invisible ancestry. In any event, scientific support for bio-race has fallen steadily over the past century. Where 78 per-

---

[23] idem. For similar rejections of the bio-race paradigm as useless, see: Michael L. Blakey, "Scientific Racism and the Biological Concept of Race," *Literature and Psychology*, 1999 (no. 1/2, Spring-Summer 1999), 29; Nova: C. Loring Brace, *Does Race Exist?: An Antagonist's Perspective* <http://www.pbs.org/wgbh/nova/first/brace.html> (2000); Steve Olson, *Mapping Human History: Discovering the Past Through Our Genes* (Boston, 2002); and Stephen Molnar, *Human Variation: Races, Types, and Ethnic Groups*, 5th ed. (Upper Saddle River NJ, 2002). Also, see the American Anthropological Association's rejection of "race" as useful paradigm at URL <http://www.aaanet.org/stmts/racepp.htm> and their dissociation of "race" from "intelligence" at URL <http://www.aaanet.org/stmts/race.htm>.

[24] Nova: George W. Gill, *Does Race Exist?: A Proponent's Perspective* <http://www.pbs.org/wgbh/nova/first/gill.html> (2000).

[25] James Shreeve, "Terms of Estrangement," *Discover*, November 1994, 56, 61.

cent of the articles in the 1931 *Journal of Physical Anthropology* employed the bio-race paradigm, only 36 percent did so in 1965, and just 28 percent did in 1996.[26] In February, 2001, the editors of the medical journal *Archives of Pediatrics & Adolescent Medicine* asked authors to no longer use "race" as explanatory variable. Other prestigious peer-reviewed journals have done the same.[27] Furthermore, the National Institutes of Health recently issued a program announcement for grant applications through February 1, 2006, specifically seeking researchers who can investigate and publicize among primary care physicians the detrimental effects on the nation's health of the practice of medical "racial" profiling. The program announcement quoted the editors of one journal as saying that, "analysis by race and ethnicity has become an analytical knee-jerk reflex."[28]

* * * * *

---

[26] Leonard Lieberman, Rodney C. Kirk, and Alice Littlefield, "Perishing Paradigm: Race--1931-99," *American Anthropologist*, 105 (no. 1, March 2003), 110-13. A following article in the same issue, by Mat Cartmill and Kaye Brown, questions the precise rate of decline, but agrees that the bio-race paradigm has fallen into near-total disfavor. A third article in the same issue shows that the decline in the paradigm's usefulness has been slower in Poland than in the United States but admits that in Europe the semantic usage of "race" includes the French race, the German race, the Italian race, and so forth.

[27] Frederick P. Rivara and Laurence Finberg, "Use of the Terms Race and Ethnicity," *Archives of Pediatrics & Adolescent Medicine*, 155 (no. 2, February 2001), 119. For similar author's guidelines, see Robert S. Schwartz, "Racial Profiling in Medical Research," *The New England Journal of Medicine*, 344 (no, 18, May 3, 2001); M.T. Fullilove, "Abandoning 'Race' as a Variable in Public Health Research: An Idea Whose Time has Come," *American Journal of Public Health*, 88 (1998), 1297-98; and R. Bhopal and L. Donaldson, "White, European, Western, Caucasian, or What? Inappropriate Labeling in Research on Race, Ethnicity, and Health." *American Journal of Public Health,* 88 (1998), 1303-7.

[28] See program announcement and requests for grant applications at the NIH website, at URL <http://grants1.nih.gov/grants/guide/pa-files/PA-03-057.html>.

This chapter described the culturally dependent perception of "racial" traits. It showed that different cultures, nations, and even different regions of the United States can perceive "racial" traits differently, assigning the same person to different "races." It showed the stages through which U.S. children learn to see "race." It explained that the "race" notion co-opts an ancient adaptive cognitive function—that of recognizing "otherness." It explained why bio-race is no longer a useful way of biologically categorizing humans.

This was the third of four chapters meant to shed light on historical events. The first showed that millions of Americans born to Black families have redefined themselves as White over the decades as a consequence of Mendelian heredity. Their descendants are the 74 million White Americans today who have recent African admixture. The challenge to understanding history is that Americans in the past were just as unalterably convinced that they could see "race" as modern Americans are. They were just as mistaken.

Chapter 5.
The Rate of Black-to-White "Passing"

In early twentieth-century South Carolina, at the height of the Jim Crow era when the one-drop rule was supposedly the law of the land, Louetta Chassereau, an orphaned infant of known, documented, but invisible African ancestry was placed in a White orphanage and adopted by a White family. As the little girl matured, her White adoptive family became influential in the White community. She married very well indeed, to a wealthy White man (F. Capers Bennett), in an upscale White church (Spring Street Methodist Church in Charleston). Throughout her marriage to Bennett, she voted in White primaries (Democrat), her children attended White schools and when they grew up, joined White churches (two became Episcopalians and two were Methodists). The godparents of her children were White (Mr. and Mrs. I. M. Fishburne), he being the president of the local Farmers & Merchants Bank. Upon Mr. Bennett's death, his relatives contested his will leaving all to Louetta, on the grounds that their long and fruitful marriage had been illegal because Louetta had started life as a Black baby. In a terse opinion, *Bennett v. Bennett*, 1940 South Carolina, (most of which is the above summary), South Carolina Supreme Court Justices Milledge L. Bonham, D. Gordon Baker, E. L. Fishburne, Taylor H. Stukes, and L. D. Lide ruled that over her lifetime, Louetta had become irrevocably White, and they dismissed the will contestation unanimously.[1]

* * * * *

     This chapter discusses the annual rate of Black-to-White endogamous-group switching by Americans in four topics. The first topic, *The Average Yearly Rate is Between 0.10 and 0.14 Percent,* uses several independent methods to compute the rate of switching. It shows that all methods converge to the same narrow range of numbers. *The Percentage Rate Has Remained Relatively Steady over the Years,* demonstrates why we know that Black-to-White group switching has been steady and continuous over the centuries. Our DNA reveals that the current African admixture in White Americans was neither the result of a one-time event before intermarriage was outlawed in 1691, nor the result of intermarriage after Loving v. Virginia 1967 ruled anti-intermarriage laws unconstitutional. *How Can so Many People Falsify Their Paper Trail and Cut all Family Ties?,* explains that, except for a brief period in U.S. history—the Jim Crow era—there has never been a need to deceive nor to cut family ties. For most of the past 300 years, endogamous-group switching was done openly, just as it is today. Finally, *The Maroon Escape Hatch,* suggests how, even during Jim Crow, families could pass from Black to White through a two-step process that included an in-between stage.

The Average Yearly Rate is Between 0.10 and 0.14 Percent

     Nowadays (as of the 2000 census), between 35,000 and 50,000 young adults every year, who previously were identified by their parents as Black, switch to identifying themselves publicly as White or Hispanic. The number has fallen and risen more or less in step with the intermarriage rate over the decades and it

---

[1] 195 S.C. 1.

is higher today than during Jim Crow, when switching your endogamous group membership was considered criminal fraud.

There are several ways of measuring the annual rate of Black-to-White self-identity switching, but the most straightforward is simply to ask large numbers of people how they self-identify, repeat the question every few years, and then count how many changed their answer from Black to something else. The Departments of Labor and of Health and Human Services do precisely this (along with many other questions) in longitudinal studies meant to track life-long earnings and health, respectively, of large numbers of Americans. For example, the Department of Labor's NLS79 National Longitudinal Survey has interviewed 12,686 young men and women yearly since 1979 to measure their career progress. Each year they are asked the same hundred or so questions. Between 1979 (when they were 14 to 22 years old) and 1998, 1.87 percent of those who had originally answered "Black," switched to answering the interviewer's "race" question with either "White," "I don't know," or "other."[2] This comes to 0.098 percent per year. Extrapolated to the Black census 2000 population of 36 million, this comes to about 35,000 individuals per year.[3]

Another approach is to start with the 0.7 percent African admixture found in the White U.S. population today.[4] Assuming that the mixing has happened at an unvarying rate for three centuries (since 1704), to reach this number would have required the average yearly injection into the White community of the alleles from one person of one hundred percent African genetic admixture for every 43,000 living White Americans (.0023 percent).[5] Of course, such a flow is unlikely to have happened at a steady rate. Switching between endogamous groups was easier

---

[2] The data can be downloaded from URL <http://www.bls.gov/nls/nlsy79.htm>.

[3] 36,023,000 x .0187 / 19.

[4] See footnote 18, *Chapter 2. Afro-European Genetic Admixture in the United States*, page 28.

[5] 300 / 0.007 = 42,900.

at some times than at others. But you can adjust for historical variation after establishing the baseline.

In practice, real people of one hundred percent African genetic admixture could not possibly have been accepted as members of the White endogamous group and so an adjustment is needed for the fraction of African admixture in those Blacks who did re-identify as White. Most sources agree that families with more than 25 percent African admixture are seldom accepted as White in the United States (although they may be in the Caribbean).[6] On the other hand, many Blacks have no detectable African ancestry at all.[7] Hence, a reasonable estimate is that typical families who successfully switched from the Black endogamous group to the White group had about 12.5 percent of African admixture. This would put them in the median of the White portion of the scatter diagrams of Chapter 2. It would have taken eight such carriers to transport across the color line the allele equivalent of one person of 100 percent sub-Saharan ancestry. And so, to reach the current measured African admixture in White Americans would have required one such person per year switching self-identity for every 5,400 living White Americans.[8]

The next step is to convert this number of group-switching individuals into a fraction of the Black population. As of the 2000 census, the Black population was about 12.8 percent of the total U.S. population, but this has varied from a high of 19.27 percent in 1790 to a low of 9.65 percent in 1930. The weighted average since 1790 has been 13.51 percent. And so, the number of individuals we must account for represents a movement from the Black community to the White of some 0.1382 percent of the Black population (0.007 x 8) / (300 x .1351) per

---

[6] See *Chapter 3. The Heredity of "Racial" Traits*, page 50.

[7] E.J. Parra and others, "Ancestral Proportions and Admixture Dynamics in Geographically Defined African Americans Living in South Carolina," *American Journal of Physical Anthropology*, 114 (2001), 18-29, Figure 1; Mark D. Shriver and others, "Skin Pigmentation, Biogeographical Ancestry, and Admixture Mapping," *Human Genetics*, 112 (2003), 387-99, Figure 3.

[8] 300 / (8 x .007) = 5,400.

year. As of census 2000, this comes to about 50,000 individuals per year.[9]

Another approach would be to use the Philadelphia rate at which European-looking children are born into the Black community (one out of every 500) and extrapolate this to the national Black yearly cohort. This yields about 72,000 individuals per year as of census 2000. Most of these, of course, might choose not to switch.

Finally, Joel Williamson suggests yet another approach. It is based on the assumption that women are less likely than men to cross the color line permanently.[10] Approximately equal numbers of male and female infants are born. But from age 16, millions of African-American men disappear from the census but women do not. In 2000, this came to 2.77 million individuals. Where did they go? The assumption of this method is that they redefined themselves as White. This approach yields 0.1019 percent per year or about 37,000 individuals per year as of census 2000.

The Percentage Rate Has Remained Relatively Steady over the Years

The preceding section used several methods to compute the average yearly rate at which Black Americans became White by switching their "racial" identity. One method was to divide the African admixture presently observed in White Americans equally among the 300 years since the endogamous color line was invented. However, the Chesapeake Bay colonies had been in operation for nearly a century when intermarriage was first outlawed in 1691. There was much Afro-European intermarriage in British North America before the endogamous color line was invented. Perhaps there has been no Black-to-White gene flow ever since. Could the African admixture found in White Ameri-

---

[9] 36,023,000 x .001382 = 49,784.

[10] Joel Williamson, *New People: Miscegenation and Mulattoes in the United States* (New York, 1980) 100-6, 119-20.

cans today merely be an echo of the intermarrying 17th century, rather than evidence of the continual, steady passing of biracials into White society in the 18th, 19th, and 20th centuries?

There are three reasons to think that the African admixture found in today's White Americans is the result of an ongoing process and not the remnant of a one-time event. First, as mentioned in the preceding section, longitudinal studies show that the current rate of openly avowed Black-to-White identity-switching would suffice to yield the observed admixture had it always been going on. Second, if the White-to-Black gene flow that we know has been going on for 400 years (in the form of the children of interracial unions) had not been balanced by an equal Black-to-White flow, Afro-Americans would have vanished by genetic assimilation, as did the Afro-Spanish and Afro-Portuguese by 1700, the Afro-Mexicans by 1800, and the Afro-Argentines by 1900. The third argument comes from molecular anthropology itself. It comes from observing *linkage disequilibrium* (defined below).

Chromosomes come in pairs. You have two copies of chromosome #1, two copies of chromosome #2, two copies of #3, and so forth. One copy of each chromosome came from your mother's egg cell; the other came from your father's sperm cell. Focus on a single chromosome pair; say the pair of chromosomes #5. When your body wants to produce a gamete (a spermatozoon if you are male, an ovum if you are female) it must place a single copy of chromosome #5 into the gamete. Which copy does it choose?

Think about it. You have two copies of #5, but you must place only a single copy of #5 into the new gamete. Does your body pick one or the other at random (either the #5 copy from you father or the one from your mother)? Does your body simply make up a brand new #5 never seen before? Does it blend together the material from your two copies—both the #5 copy from your father plus the one from your mother—and mold a new #5 using only half of the resultant mixture (otherwise the new #5 would be way too big)?

In fact, the process lays your two #5 chromosomes side-by-side, like two strands of yarn. It then cuts them crosswise into matching pieces and swaps the pieces between strands. Imagine that the DNA strand from your father was red, say, and your mother's strand was blue. The cut-and-swap process (called meiosis) with just two cuts would yield one strand that was blue-red-blue and another that was red-blue-red. Many cut-and-swaps later, each new patchwork #5 then goes into a different gamete. And so, the single #5 chromosome in each gamete winds up being a mix of material from your mother's #5 and your father's #5. Only thus can your child inherit your mother's eyes and your father's chin. The single #5 in the gamete is not a "blend" in the sense of being purple (the combination of blue and red). Instead, it resembles a barber pole with broad blue and red stripes. The width of the stripes is called "linkage disequilibrium."

As explained in Chapter 2, markers throughout the genome can be used to distinguish African from European ancestry. A first-generation Afro-European biracial individual will have one purely African chromosome #5 (from one parent) and one purely European chromosome #5 (from the other). But the strands are cut and their pieces swapped in meiosis at each subsequent generation. So if you observe that an individual has barber-pole stripes of African and European DNA within the same strand, then he must be at least a second-generation biracial. Now the chance that, in the next generation, any given cut will just happen to hit the seam between two existing stripes is negligible. Consequently, the stripes of African and European DNA get narrower and narrower (linkage disequilibrium diminishes) with each passing generation. One can estimate how many generations have elapsed since any individual's original Afro-European admixture took place, by the width of the stripes (by the degree of linkage disequilibrium).

A recent one-time wave of intermarriage (since the 1955-65 civil rights movement, say) would result in uniformly high linkage disequilibrium in admixed Americans. This is not observed. An ancient one-time wave of intermarriage (in the seventeenth century, say) would result in uniformly low linkage disequilibrium in admixed Americans. This is not observed either. An ongoing slow but steady Black-to-White genetic leakage across the color line for 400 years would result in a distinctive pattern of linkage disequilibrium distribution (stripes of every width occurring with equal frequency). This, in fact, is what is observed.[11]

How Can so Many People Falsify Their Paper Trail and Cut all Family Ties?

Some people are startled by what, to them, seems an extraordinarily high rate of White-to-Black endogamous-group switching over the past three centuries, a rate that is still going on. They ask:

> You mentioned the phenomenon of "passing," which you define as those who were identified as one race as children but another as adults, generally 'black' as a child and 'white' as an adult. One sees that this was relatively common in the past - but how common is this today, when we are more careful about civil records, tracking, driver's licenses, etc.? Is this in fact a common, modern-day phenomenon? How difficult it must be for someone to cut all ties to family and literally walk away![12]

First, a paper trail indicating "racial" identity was a transitory phenomenon in U.S. history, lasting only from about 1880 to about 1965.[13] Most nineteenth-century births were not recorded on civil birth certificates, just with local churches. And since Alabama ended the practice in 1991, only five states (Connecticut, Hawaii, Mississippi, North Carolina, and Texas) put infant "race" on birth certificates today. Some states never did

---

[11] For details, see C.L. Pfaff and others, "Population Structure in Admixed Populations: Effect of Admixture Dynamics on the Pattern of Linkage Disequilibrium," *American Journal of Human Genetics*, 68 (2001a), 198-207 or Heather E. Collins-Schramm and others, "Markers Informative for Ancestry Demonstrate Consistent Megabase-Length Linkage Disequilibrium in the African American Population," *Human Genetics*, 113 (June 2003), 211-19.

[12] Barbara Yanez, "Taking a Closer Look at the 'One Drop Rule': An Interview with Frank Sweet," *Mulatto Nation Times*, July 2004.

[13] Antebellum American society attempted meticulously to keep track of who was slave and who was free, but this is quite something else again.

so, and most stopped doing so in the late 1960s.[14] Similarly, neither driver's licenses nor voter registration cards record "racial" identity in most jurisdictions today. This is precisely why "racial" profiling is so controversial. In Florida, for example, neither the state voter registration web site nor the Flagler County voter registration card has any entry for "race," while the Alachua County card does. The few civil records today that capture one's "race" (jobs, school matriculation, etc) are voluntary. You can check off or write in whatever you want and, with one exception, nobody questions it.[15] If you look European and claim to be White, nobody cares.

The word "passing" is a misnomer to the extent that it is associated with deceit or pretense. As far as anyone can tell, most of the individuals who redefine themselves from Black to White or Hispanic make no secret of their partial African ancestry. They just do not feel that this trivial fact should stop them from adopting a "racial" self-identity that matches their appearance. There is no need to "cut all family ties and walk away."

White Americans with openly acknowledged partial African ancestry abound in the entertainment industry. The official web sites of many entertainers claim mixed ancestry. As of July 1, 2003, URL addresses

http://www.mixedfolks.com/africans.htm and

http://www.multiracial.com/links/links-celebrities.html

provide links to hundreds of such sites. Among these are blue-eyed blondes like Broadway star Carol Channing and Heather

---

[14] Major W. Cox, "Alabama Quietly Ends Race Certification Policy," *Montgomery Advertiser*, May 1993. Interestingly, in the 1930s, Puerto Rico's birth certificates, like those of most Latin American cultures, recorded the skin tones of both parents (choosing from among the plethora of available designations). This was presumably for identification purposes. But it did not record the infant's skin tone.

[15] The exception, where you can still be prosecuted in America today for claiming to be of a "race" to which you do not "really" belong, is if you claim Blackness in order to reap affirmative action benefits. In such cases, your "true race" is determined by the testimony of local Black community leaders. Your appearance is irrelevant. If local Black community leaders disown you, you may be found guilty of criminal fraud.

Locklear, star of the TV show *Melrose Place*.[16] At the other extreme are brunettes like Jennifer Beals, star of the movie *Flashdance* (who has a Black father). Of in-between skin tone are Oscar-winning film and TV star Martin Sheen (an Afro-Cuban grandmother) and Emmy-winning vocalist Linda Ronstadt (an Afro-Mexican grandfather). Additionally, there are thousands of Hispanic entertainers, such as Geraldo Rivera, Jimmy Smits, Jennifer Lopez, or Mariah Carey, who proudly claim African as well as Spanish roots through their Latin American heritage.

That switching sides has risen in the past few decades makes it likely that many switchers are following the example of the millions of Puerto Ricans who have come to the mainland since 1950. Most Puerto Ricans have obvious African ancestry, but 90 percent check off "White" on the census form anyway.[17] In fact, given that all methods of estimating the rate of Black-to-White identity-switching converge on the 0.10-to-0.14 percent per year figure derived from the observed African admixture in White Americans, legendary tales of "cutting all family ties" and deception more likely belong to the realm of fictional "passing" novels than to the reality of America's notoriously mobile society. (Except perhaps during the Jim Crow period and, even then, apparently only Whites were deceived regarding ongoing family contact.) As Maria P.P. Root put it, "It is not uncommon that many individuals emerge out of college years with a different resolution to their racial identity than when they graduated high school."[18]

---

[16] For Channing, see her autobiography Carol Channing, *Just Lucky I Guess: A Memoir of Sorts* (New York, 2002). For Locklear, see Gerald M. Sider, *Lumbee Indian Histories: Race, Ethnicity, and Indian Identity in the Southern United States* (Cambridge UK, 1993).

[17] See the discussion in *Chapter 3. The Heredity of "Racial" Traits*, page 46

[18] Maria P.P. Root, "Resolving 'Other' Status: Identity Development of Biracial Individuals," *Women and Therapy*, 9 (1990), 185-205, 202.

The Maroon Escape Hatch

On the evening of January 18, 1958, a hundred members of the Ku Klux Klan gathered in Maxton, North Carolina for a rally. They had advertised that their planned marching, speechifying, and cross burning would terrorize and teach respect to the Lumbee Indians of Robeson County. Apparently, the locals were "forgetting their place." One Lumbee woman had been dating a White man and a Lumbee family had moved into a White neighborhood. The Klan had already burned crosses at each of those two homes, and so the large rally was meant to drive the lesson home countywide.

The Klansmen began assembling at 8:00 P.M., shotguns in hand. The Grand Vizier strutted about in full regalia. A huge "KKK" banner was unfurled. A public address system with a microphone was set up. Newspaper reporters and photographers scurried for photo-ops. The Klansmen ignored the 500 Lumbee men who had gathered across the road, also carrying rifles and shotguns.

At a signal, the Lumbees fanned out across the highway, shouting war cries and shooting into the air. The Klansmen dropped their weapons, flags, robes and hoods, jumped into their cars, and raced away, leaving their paraphernalia strewn all about. They had not yet set fire to their cross. The state police arrived within minutes, escorted the fleeing Klansmen to safety and disarmed the Lumbees. Despite thousands of shots fired, no one had been hurt (except one news photographer who was nicked by a bullet). Only one person was arrested—a Klansman who was too drunk to stand.

The Lumbees then put on a show for the newspapers. They marched triumphantly around the field of battle, wrapped themselves in the KKK flag, hollered into the microphone, burned the cross, hanged the Grand Wizard in effigy, and a rousing good time was had by all. The next day, newspapers across the nation ran wild with the story. "The Klan had taken on too many Indians," said *Life* magazine. "Look Who's Biting the Dust! Palefaces," wrote columnist Inez Robb. That the Indians had finally defeated the palefaces in Robeson County, North

Carolina in January of 1958 was the most hilarious story of the week, nationwide.[19]

But wait. Are the Lumbees really American Indians? Although no one has published an admixture study of the Lumbees since the decoding of the human genome made admixture mapping reliable and consistent, an older study used blood proteins and craniofacial anthropometry methods (the latter is the method used today by forensic anthropologists when asked by the police to tell the "race" of a skeleton). That study found that the Lumbees were "about forty percent White, forty-seven percent Negro, and thirteen percent Indian."[20]

The Lumbees have the right to call themselves whatever they wish, of course. They have worked hard to be seen as Native Americans, and some deny having African ancestry. The North Carolina legislature formally designated them "Lumbee Indians" in 1953 (the name is from a Robeson County river). The U.S. Congress officially designated them "Lumbee Indians of North Carolina" on June 7, 1956. And yet, according to the census, there were zero Amerinds in Robeson County in 1950 (although there were 30,000 "mulattos"). In the 1960 census, after the legislative fiats, Robeson county's 30,000 "mulattos" vanished and 30,000 "Lumbee Indians" suddenly appeared. The mulatto "Croatans" had become the "Lumbee Indians." The Lumbees' self-reinvention has not yet been a complete success. The Federal Bureau of Indian Affairs refuses to recognize them as legitimate, in part, because of their very strong African admixture. Genetically, they are a typical U.S. maroon community.

Numerous communities, like the Lumbees, are scattered throughout the eastern United States. They are called *triracial isolate* groups (the anthropological term), *maroon* communities (the historical term), or *Mestizos* (the sociological term).[21] All

---

[19] Brewton Berry, *Almost White* (New York, 1963), 9-11.

[20] William Pollitzer, "The Physical Anthropology and Genetics of Marginal People of the Southeastern United States," *American Anthropologist*, 74 (no. 3, 1972), 723-30.

[21] The term "triracial isolate" was coined in Calvin Beale, "American Triracial Isolates," *Eugenics Quarterly*, 4 (no. 4, 1957), 187-96.

such groups descend from Europeans, Africans, and Native
Americans who escaped involuntary labor in colonial plantations
and formed their own communities on the fringes of civilization.
In 1946, William Gilbert published the first comprehensive survey of these groups in the Southeastern United States. According
to him, these groups comprised, "at least 50,000 persons who
were complex mixtures in varying degrees of white, Amerind,
and Negro blood."[22] The major maroon communities that Gilbert
studied were:

- The Brass Ankles, Red Bones, Red Legs, Turks, and
  Marlboro Blues of South Carolina;

- The Cajans (not the Acadians of Louisiana) and Creoles
  of Alabama and Mississippi;

- The Croatans (called the "Lumbees" since 1953) of
  Robeson County North Carolina, South Carolina, and
  Virginia;

- The Guineas, West Hill Indians, Cecil Indians, and
  Guinea Niggers of West Virginia and Maryland;

- The Issues of Amherst and Rockingham Counties, Virginia;

- The Jackson Whites of New York and New Jersey;

- The Melungeons of the Southern Appalachians, centered on Hancock County Tennessee;

- The Red Bones of Louisiana and Arkansas;

- The Wesorts of southern Maryland.[23]

Today, the two largest maroon groups are the *Seminoles*
of Florida (a corruption of the Spanish word *cimarrones* or "runaways"), who were not studied by Gilbert, and the *Melungeons*
(the largest group to have self-identified as White over the centuries, rather than as Amerind).

---

[22] William Harlan Gilbert, Jr., "Memorandum Concerning the Characteristics of the Larger Mixed-Blood Racial Islands of the Eastern United States,"
Social Forces, 24 (no. 4, 1946), 438-47, 438.

[23] The tabulation is from Wayne Winkler, *Walking Toward the Sunset: The
Melungeons of Appalachia*, 1st ed. (Macon GA, 2004), 19.

Most of the above names were derogatory epithets given by Whites, not self-labels adopted by the maroon communities themselves. In 1960, a friend warned Brewton Berry that he was likely to be murdered on the spot if he called someone a "Melungeon" to their face.[24] During the Jim Crow era, many members of these groups vehemently denied having even the slightest drop of "Black blood." In fact, some were able to receive "White" civil documents and avoid their children's assignment to Negro schools by their willingness to commit mayhem against any official who mistook them for Blacks.[25] The maroon communities are potentially important to the study of people switching from Black to White across the color line because they may form an escape hatch similar to what Carl Degler observed in Brazil.

In 1971, Carl Degler coined the term "mulatto escape hatch" to describe how Brazil differed from U.S. customs. According to Degler, White Brazilians enjoy the privileges of Whiteness, including that of looking down with disdain upon Black Brazilians. According to Degler, this "colorism" resembles White American customs during the Jim Crow era. On the other hand, most White Brazilians have Black parents or grandparents and are proud to acknowledge their fractional African ancestry. This is different from White American customs during the Jim Crow era. The U.S. tradition of hypodescent made it unlikely for any non-Hispanic of known African ancestry to be socially welcomed as White during the Jim Crow era. In Latin America, in contrast, generational acculturation and assimilation took place via intermarriage. Medium-brown offspring of even dark parents were no longer "Black," but were labeled with any of a half-dozen terms denoting class as much as skin tone. Their European-looking descendants, in turn, were accepted as White.[26]

---

[24] Brewton Berry, *Almost White* (New York, 1963), 38.

[25] Ibid., 30-49.

[26] Carl N. Degler, *Neither Black nor White: Slavery and Race Relations in Brazil and the United States* (New York, 1971). Incidentally, Degler's concept of a "mulatto escape hatch" enabling gradual ethnic acculturation or assimilation over the course of generations is sometimes misunderstood. In

A similar mechanism may have operated in the United States during the Jim Crow era through the maroon communities. Three points suggest this. First, these groups have unusually high fractions of African genetic admixture for White Americans. Second, inflow into the groups from those designated "free people of color" has been steady. Third, outflow to the White mainstream has also been steady.

That America's maroon communities have unusually high fractions of African genetic admixture are evident in studies by Pollitzer, Jones and others. The Lumbees have about 47 percent African admixture.[27] The Melungeons (who in the past self-identified as White) have about five percent African admixture.[28] Inflow into these groups by free persons of color has been going on steadily since the mid-1700s.[29] Outflow has also been steady. From 50,000 in 1946 as counted by Gilbert they had grown to at least 77,000 according Beale in 1957.[30] Between 1943 and 1953 hundreds of thousands of these hill people from the Southern Appalachians fled poverty and isolation and migrated to north-

---

1988, reviewer Judy Beiber wrote that recent studies "lay bare the limitations of Degler's 'mulatto escape hatch' [in that Brazilian] mulattos never truly gained white status regardless of social class." See Judy Bieber, "Race, Resistance, and Regionalism: Perspectives from Brazil and Spanish America," *Latin American Research Review*, 32 (no. 3, 1997), 152-68, 160. Of course Degler claimed no such thing. Degler's point was that White Brazilians enjoy the privileges of whiteness, even those White Brazilians who happened to have Black or mixed parents or grandparents.

[27] Winkler (2004), 232-41.

[28] Kevin Jones, "DNA Study Results," in *Fourth Union: A Melungeon Gathering*, ed. N. Brent Kennedy (Kingsport TN, 2000a).

[29] See, for instance Winthrop D. Jordan, "American Chiaroscuro: The Status and Definition of Mulattoes in the British Colonies," in *Slavery in the New World: A Reader in Comparative History*, ed. Laura Foner and Eugene D. Genovese (Englewood Cliffs NJ, 1969), 189-201, 193-36; Larry Koger, *Black Slaveowners: Free Black Slave Masters in South Carolina, 1790-1860* (Jefferson NC, 1985), 12-13; or James Hugo Johnston, *Race Relations in Virginia & Miscegenation in the South, 1776-1860* (Amherst, 1970), 206-10.

[30] Calvin Beale, "American Triracial Isolates," *Eugenics Quarterly*, 4 (no. 4, 1957), 187-96, 187.

ern industrial cities.[31] The major economic change they have undergone is that they have been integrated into the mainstream economy. The major social change is that they have become White (accepted as suitable marriage partners by Whites, but no longer by Blacks).[32]

* * * * *

This chapter computed the annual rate of Black-to-White endogamous-group switching by Americans. It showed that the rate has been continuous over the past three centuries and not a one-time event. It explained that only during the Jim Crow was there ever a need to deceive or to cut family ties. Except during Jim Crow, and for most of America's past, endogamous-group switching was done as openly as it is today. It suggested how, even during Jim Crow, families could pass from Black to White through a two-step process that included an in-between stage.

This was the last of four chapters meant to shed light on historical events. They showed that some 74 million of today's White Americans have detectable recent African admixture, the result of about 0.10 and 0.14 percent of Black Americans per year switching self-identity from Black to White. This happened despite the general conviction that "race" is visible.

This information is important because knowing the actual rate of switching between endogamous groups puts a wider perspective on the court cases, presented in subsequent chapters, that ruled on someone's group membership. Although such cases reveal the reasoning of judges (thus indirectly legislators' and voters' attitudes), they had little impact on the actual rate of group switching. And so, as the case histories emerge, it will be useful to recall the following: For every court case that ruled on

---

[31] Winkler (2004), 153.

[32] Additional accounts of the maroon communities are: Jim Callahan, *Lest We Forget: The Melungeon Colony of Newman's Ridge* (Johnson City TN, 2000); N. Brent Kennedy, *The Melungeons, The Resurrection of a Proud People: An Untold Story of Ethnic Cleansing in America* (Macon, 1997); Bonnie Ball, *The Melungeons: Notes on the Origin of a Race* (Johnson City TN, 1992).

someone's endogamous group membership, between three thousand and fifteen thousand former Black Americans slipped silently through the endogamous color line and they and their progeny thenceforth became irrevocably White.

Section II.
The Endogamous
Color Line

Chapter 6.
Features of Today's
Endogamous Color Line

On May 8, 2003, Halle Berry won an Academy Award for her performance as an executed murderer's widow in the Lion's Gate film *Monster's Ball*. In her acceptance speech, Ms. Berry said that her nomination and triumph as a female member of the Black endogamous group showed how far all members of that group had advanced towards acceptance in the entertainment industry. She said that she accepted the award on behalf of all of the members of her "race" who had struggled before her and prepared the way. In return, she looked forward to paving the way for future Black actresses. Her award, she said, was "for every nameless, faceless woman of color who now has a chance because this door tonight has been opened."[1] As she spoke, the television cameras focused on the beaming face of Ms. Berry's mother, tearfully joyous that her daughter had reached the pinnacle of her chosen career. Probably not one U.S. viewer in a hundred saw anything incongruous about the heart-tugging moment. Probably not one viewer in a hundred who was watching from another country realized that the smiling blonde, fair-skinned woman in the audience was Halle Berry's biological mother. The few people in other countries who were in the know undoubtedly

---

[1] UPI, *Analysis: Race Now Not Black and White* (May 8, 2002).

shook their heads at one more example of Americans' idiosyncratic denial of mixed Afro-European ancestry. The oddity is not that a European-looking woman gives birth to a woman of mixed heritage. The oddity is that mother and daughter are seen as members of different endogamous groups.

*   *   *   *   *

In order to grasp just how unusual is America's endogamous color line, consider it abstractly. Many newcomers to the United States, especially Hispanics, find it astonishing that an endogamous community of apparently African appearance has somehow perpetuated itself (or has been perpetuated) in North America for over three centuries, despite Africans having been a demographic minority. Such a thing happened nowhere else on the planet. America's color line (and its consequent one-drop rule) is a puzzle. It is self-contradictory and counterfactual, and yet many Americans believe it with intensity. It was invented just four centuries ago and has shifted over the years, and yet many think of it as eternal and unchanging. It is based on the assumption that White Americans have no recent African ancestry, and yet, as explained in *Chapter 2. Afro-European Genetic Admixture in the United States*, DNA studies show without doubt that White Americans, like all other New World populations, are a mix of European, Native American, and, yes, African ancestry. The phenomenon cries out for historical explanation.

The U.S. color line is self-contradictory because it is asymmetrical. Most Americans (Black and White) consider it unremarkable when a White mother gives birth to a Black child (if her husband is Black, say). And yet some sincerely think it impossible ("genetically impossible," some insist) for a Black woman to bear a White child, regardless of the father. The color line is counterfactual because the same degree of mixed Afro-European heritage that makes Americans (Black and White) see someone named John Smith as being of the Black "race" causes them to see the same person as being of the Hispanic "race" if named Juan Pérez. Scholars agree that the color line was invented in the late seventeenth century, and yet many Americans

(Black and White) debate whether Hannibal or Nefertiti were Black or White. That the color line is believed intensely is exemplified by college application forms with five "race" check-off boxes (White, Black, Asian, Native American, Hispanic), next to the printed warning that, "if the applicant fails to check a box, or checks more than one box, this application will be discarded unread."[2]

Draw a path on the globe from Norway to Nigeria. Walk along that path and you will notice that most folks at the northern end have fair (pinkish-beige) skin tone, blonde hair, and blue eyes. As you travel south through the Netherlands, Belgium, and France, peoples' skin, hair and eyes get darker. Continue south through Spain, and skin tone gets darker yet—almost light brown. By the time you reach the Mediterranean, hair is mostly black with reddish highlights and blue eyes are rare. Take the ferry to Tangier and hike into the Sahara. Complexions gradually shade from medium to dark brown and hair becomes nearly black. Continue south though Mali, Upper Volta, and Dahomey. When you reach Lagos, you will find that most people's skin and eyes are very dark brown indeed and their hair is black. Other features also changed slowly along your journey, hair became curlier, noses became wider.

The U.S. endogamous color line is rhetorically based on the notion that somewhere along the path of gradually darkening skin tone from Norway to Nigeria lies a border separating White people from Black. In other words, the U.S. system of two endogamous groups assumes that some people are predestined by God or nature to become members of one or the other of America's two groups. There is no real boundary, of course; change is imperceptible at every step. Nevertheless, U.S. folklore upholds four beliefs:

- *Discontinuity* – A single color line exists.

- *Endogamy* – People should not marry across it.

---

[2] See the graduate student application form issued by Nova Southeastern University in Fort Lauderdale FL.

- *Impermeability* – You cannot switch sides from Black to White.

- *Hypodescent* – If you have a parent who is a member of the Black endogamous group then you are Black also, no matter your preference or even your appearance.

Other nations have caste systems and "racial" beliefs but, regarding Africans and Europeans, all differ from the United States in at least one of those four ways. Consider each of the four features in detail.

Discontinuity

The human species diversified after colonizing the planet from an origin in Africa about 60 millennia ago. East Asians developed an epicanthic eyelid fold, Europeans lost dermal melanin, Amerinds lost genetic variation.[3] Explorers and merchants have noted such differences throughout recorded history. Geneticists have observed that wherever different people come into contact and both survive the impact, mixed children are born spanning a continuum of genetic admixture.[4]

---

[3] This is not meant to debate the most recent variant of Milford Wolpoff's theory of multiregional evolution (MRE), which claims (without molecular evidence as yet) that modern humans interbred with prior Eurasian hominins during the African diaspora. It merely acknowledges the fact of the diaspora and the timing of "racially" distinctive features—points supported by most paleoanthropologists today, including MRE supporters.

[4] Although few overall surveys of molecular admixture mapping have yet emerged, Stephen Molnar, *Human Variation: Races, Types, and Ethnic Groups*, 5th ed. (Upper Saddle River NJ, 2002) and John Relethford, *Genetics and the Search for Modern Human Origins* (New York, 2001) discuss it in passing, and Steve Olson, *Mapping Human History: Discovering the Past Through Our Genes* (Boston, 2002) provides a very elementary introduction. Fascinating individual studies abound, however. For example, Elena Bosch and others, "High Level of Male-Biased Scandinavian Admixture in Greenlandic Inuit Shown by Y-Chromosomal Analysis," *Human Genetics*, 112 (April 2003), 353-63 reveals extensive European patrilineal infiltration into the Inuit, presumably because of the natives' well-known hospitality.

"Discontinuity" denotes the practice of socially categorizing the actual human genetic continuum into discrete groups.
The United States is unique in that its color line divides Americans into only two groups separated by a single endogamous
barrier. Most stratified societies imagine three groups: the two
original parent groups, plus a third (hybrid) group comprising
the mixed descendants of both parent groups. Furthermore, most
stratified societies perceive the hybrid group as distinct from
both parent groups. And so, stratified societies are typically
made up of three endogamous groups. These are: high-status
original parent group "A," low-status original parent group "B,"
and hybrid group "AB" (the mixed descendants of both parent
groups).

Where societies differ is in the social rank or status that
they attribute to the hybrid group "AB." In some stratified societies, the hybrid group occupies the lowest social rank or status,
inferior to both of the parent groups. In other stratified societies,
the hybrid group occupies an intermediate rank, lower than
group A, say, but higher or more prestigious than group B. Finally, in some stratified societies, the hybrid group (the mixed
descendants of both parent groups) becomes the uppermost
group, superior to both of the original parent groups. Consider
examples of each.

In Haiti and Mexico today, hybrids are seen as higher
status than both parent groups. Haitians of unmixed European
ancestry (a few Lebanese and Syrian shopkeepers) are not allowed to own Haitian real estate and so cannot legally vote.[5] In
Mexico, the population is mainly a genetic blend of European
(presumably Spanish) and Native American. Spanish rule was
overthrown in 1821. The Spanish-Amerind hybrid group (Mestizos) took power and disenfranchised the remaining Spanish
colonists. Europeans regained power briefly during Austrian
Archduke Maximilian's French-backed regime of 1864-67, but
lost it again thereafter.[6] (Incidentally, Afro-Mexicans vanished

---

[5] F. James Davis, *Who is Black?: One Nation's Definition* (University Park
PA, 1991), 87-88.

[6] Ibid., 88-90.

through genetic assimilation before the nineteenth century; alleles for African appearance are now dispersed throughout Mexico's population.[7])

In Uganda, Canada, India, and Southeast Asia, the hybrid groups occupy a lower rank than either parent group. In Uganda, people of mixed Afro-European ancestry are regarded with condescension and contempt by the Ganda tribes, and are not accepted by European society either. The government once considered a plan to solve the problem by removing all biracials to an island in Lake Victoria where they could be completely isolated.[8] The Métis of Canada, the Anglo-Indians of India, Korean-Americans in Korea, and Vietnamese-Americans in Vietnam are also relegated to the bottom rung. The Métis sprang from seventeenth century unions between Amerind women and French or Scottish trappers in the Canadian wilderness. They developed a strong cultural identity, wore a distinctive sash, and danced their unique Red River jig. They were once considered superior to Amerinds, and worked as buffalo hunters, interpreters, guides, or in transporting supplies for the Hudson's Bay Company by canoe or in distinctive carts. Their downfall came when Canada acquired and settled the Hudson Bay territory and railroads ended their livelihood. After failed rebellions in 1870 and 1884, they became outcasts from both European and Amerind cultures. Today, they number about 750,000 and remain desperately poor with high unemployment, welfare dependency, crime, school dropout, and alcoholism.[9]

---

[7] UPI, *Analysis: Race Now Not Black and White* (May 8, 2002). "Vanished" is a relative term, of course. There are villages along Mexico's Gulf Coast near Vera Cruz where alleles for African appearance are frequent enough to align now and then, producing Mexicans with dark skin-tone. Such individuals consider themselves dark Mexicans and have no "Black" self-identity or ethnicity. See also Rachel Graves, "Forgotten Culture: Ignored by Society, Black Mexicans Deny Their History," *Houston Chronicle*, July 3 2004.

[8] F. James Davis, *Who is Black?: One Nation's Definition* (University Park PA, 1991), 83.

[9] Ibid., 83-84. Amerinds also suffer from some of the same social problems, but look down on the Métis nonetheless.

In the late seventeenth century, Britain's colonial administration in India encouraged intermarriage. Anglo-Indians received hiring preference and many became officials in the bureaucracy. Some even married British nobility. Two centuries later, when intermarriage came into disfavor, they became outcasts, avoided by Indians and Europeans alike. They saw themselves as English and wore English clothes, but the British ignored them. Furthermore, their desperate efforts to become accepted into mainstream British society made natives within the Hindu caste system even more contemptuous of them. Many fled to Australia, Africa, or England when the British pulled out of India. The 250,000 who remained are now a despised out-group. In the traditional Hindu caste system, there is no place for those of mixed blood. [10] And, although the Hindu caste system has been legally abolished in India, it still has enormous social effect. [11]

In Vietnam and Korea, citizenship is based on the father, not the mother. Unknown thousands of Korean-American children and about 80,000 Vietnamese-American children were abandoned in Asia after American soldiers left. Adults now, neither they nor their patrilineal offspring can aspire to civil rights in their own land. Exceptions occur only when the American father claims his child, and jumps through Southeast Asian and U.S. State Department bureaucratic hoops to obtain U.S. visas. [12]

In South Africa and the British West Indies, biracials form an intermediate group whose status within the middle group, as well as their promotion or demotion between groups, depends on their "racial" appearance. [13] Apartheid South Africa enforced segregation and endogamy between each of its three groups: Black,

---

[10] Ibid., 84-85. Incidentally, most pre-DNA scientists of bio-race classified East Indians as "Caucasoids," despite their dark complexion. U.S. courts have continued to waffle on this point.

[11] Tom O'Neill, "Untouchables," *National Geographic*, June 2003, 2-31.

[12] F. James Davis, *Who is Black?: One Nation's Definition* (University Park PA, 1991), 85-86. For what it's worth, the French took their 25,000 biracial children with them when they pulled out of Vietnam after Dienbienphu.

[13] F. James Davis, *Who is Black?: One Nation's Definition* (University Park PA, 1991), 90-98, 105-9.

White, and Coloured. This often confused American visitors, members of the U.S. Black endogamous group, who tried to associate with locals who were members of South Africa's Black group. The problem was that the Black group in the United States includes what South Africans consider two distinct groups, Black plus Coloured. In apartheid South Africa, association between members of the Black and Coloured endogamous groups was forbidden. Even today, after the ending of apartheid, South Africa's three endogamous groups, whose segregation was formerly enforced by criminal law, have become three separate appearance-based political blocs whose segregation is enforced by social custom.

Coloured people in the British West Indies also form an intermediate group between Europeans and those of strong African appearance. Neither status within the group nor movement between groups was ever as institutionalized as in South Africa. Nevertheless, their membership criteria differ both from the United States and from South Africa. Europeans in the British West Indies often marry locals who physically appear to be European but have known partial African ancestry. Similarly, White clubs were closed to members of the Coloured group in the early colonial period, and members of this middle group were not allowed to vote, hold public office, hold military commissions, marry members of the White group, or inherit significant property from a member of the White group. But by the year 1733, these restrictions had been lifted for the intermediate group in Jamaica, Barbados, and Trinidad. The restrictions continued in effect for Blacks until the twentieth century.[14]

Legislation, court decisions, and social custom in Jamaica, Trinidad, and Barbados treated members of the Coloured group as distinct from members of the Black group.[15] According to one scholar, "The English... encountered the problem of race mix-

---

[14] Winthrop D. Jordan, "American Chiaroscuro: The Status and Definition of Mulattoes in the British Colonies," in *Slavery in the New World: A Reader in Comparative History*, ed. Laura Foner and Eugene D. Genovese (Englewood Cliffs NJ, 1969), 189-201.

[15] Davis (1991), 107; Hilary Beckles, *A History of Barbados: From Amerindian Settlement to Nation-State* (Cambridge UK, 1990) 48, 50, 68-69.

ture in very different contexts in their several colonies; they answered it in one fashion in their West Indian islands, and in quite another in their colonies on the continent," and, "The contrast offered by the West Indies is striking."[16] In post-emancipation Jamaica, the beleaguered White population allied with the Coloured elite (the descendants of the famous Maroons) to keep down the free Blacks.[17] A Barbadian historian wrote, "In August 1838, some 83,000 blacks, 12,000 coloureds, and 15,000 whites, embarked on a social course which the ruling elite hoped to charter."[18] A historian of Trinidad wrote, "The people of colour were marginal to Caribbean society: neither black nor white, neither African nor European...."[19] Today, West Indian immigrants to England assimilate into mainstream society within a generation or two. There is no endogamous color line in Great Britain today.[20]

Finally, Latin American societies, including those of the Spanish Caribbean, have always lacked endogamous color lines. Every Hispanic resides on an Afro-Amerind-European continuum where status depends on wealth, breeding, education, and political power as well as phenotype. Latin American countries typically have three economic classes: A lower class of agricultural peasants and urban poor; a middle class of landowning farmers and urban craftsmen; and an upper class of wealthy professionals, educators, or the politically powerful. The structure

---

[16] Winthrop D. Jordan, "American Chiaroscuro: The Status and Definition of Mulattoes in the British Colonies," in *Slavery in the New World: A Reader in Comparative History*, ed. Laura Foner and Eugene D. Genovese (Englewood Cliffs NJ, 1969), 189-201, 190, 197.

[17] Eric Foner, *Reconstruction: America's Unfinished Revolution* (New York, 1988), 547.

[18] Beckles (1990), 90, 104.

[19] Arnold A. Sio, "Marginality and Free Coloured Identity in Caribbean Slave Society," in *Caribbean Slave Society and Economy: A Student Reader*, ed. Hilary Beckles and Verene Shepherd (New York, 1991), 150-59, 151.

[20] Suzanne Model and Gene Fisher, "Unions Between Blacks and Whites: England and the U.S. Compared," *Ethnic and Racial Studies*, 25 (no. 5, September 2002), 728-54.

has a strong hereditary component. It is rigid, offers little social mobility, and is often harsh or unjust. Nevertheless, despite significant class/skin-tone correlation, it has no color line in the sense of endogamy.[21] Enforced endogamy is impossible in Latin America because nearly every Hispanic has immediate blood relatives who are more African-looking and others who are more European-looking than himself. Puerto Rico's dialect of Spanish contains about a dozen words to denote various blends of Afro-European appearance: *prieto, criollo, blanquito, mulato, moreno, trigueño, mestizo, jabao, marrano*, etc. Yet, neither private sector documents (social club applications, job applications) nor government documents (public school registration, birth certificates, census forms) on the island have any category for "race."[22]

The above is not meant to be an exhaustive survey of endogamous systems around the world. Other societies, such as Japan, India, and New Zealand, have endogamous groups. The intent was merely to offer a few examples of variations in discontinuity so as to compare and contrast the U.S. system of two endogamous groups with three-group systems and with societies of mixed ancestry that lack endogamous groups altogether.

---

[21] George Reid Andrews, "Racial Inequality in Brazil and the United States: A Statistical Comparison," *Journal of Social History*, 26 (no. 2, Winter 1992), 229-63. For a survey of the historiography of the remarkably permeable color lines of the British West Indies (if you looked European, you were White by definition), see David Lowenthal, "Post-Emancipation Race Relations: Some Caribbean and American Perpectives," *Journal of Interamerican Studies and World Affairs*, 13 (no. 3/4, Jul-Oct 1971), 367-77.

[22] Some Latin American countries do ask for "color" or skin tone on the census, but the answer has been shown to correlate with wealth. See George Reid Andrews, "Racial Inequality in Brazil and the United States: A Statistical Comparison," *Journal of Social History*, 26 (no. 2, Winter 1992), 229-63. Oddly, the word *negro* in Puerto Rican Spanish today is seldom used to denote appearance. It is simply the most common Puerto Rican term of endearment, like the English *honey*. It is used by affectionate couples, even those who look entirely European.

Endogamy

Endogamy is what defines "Black" and "White" in the United States. This is not the same thing as determining to which group you are assigned by society. As will be explained shortly, Americans at different times and places have used several methods of assigning endogamous group membership: appearance, blood-fraction, association, class. But endogamy is what defines the very groups themselves. In other words, if U.S. society considers you a suitable marriage partner for people on the White side of the color line, then you are White by definition. You may have a dark brown skin tone (like many East Indians, for example) or have recent African genetic admixture (like 74 million White Americans), or have openly acknowledged African ancestry (like many Hispanic celebrities), but if you are seen as marriageable by Whites but not by Blacks then you are termed "White" nonetheless. Similarly, you may have a pink skin-tone (like famed NAACP Secretary Walter White), have no measurable African genetic admixture (like five percent of America's Blacks), and deny having any Black ancestry (as Anatole Broyard did, according to Henry Louis Gates[23]), but if you are seen as marriageable by Blacks but not by Whites then you are labeled as "Black" nonetheless. As mentioned, just which rules U.S. society uses to assign someone to one group or the other will be discussed momentarily. For now, consider the endogamous color line itself.

Endogamy is important because intermarriage measures acceptance. Lack of intermarriage reveals (*reveals*, not *causes*) social ostracism. Social ostracism leads to alienation, then to disdain, then, to contempt, then to oppression and fear. A half-century ago, Gunnar Myrdal wrote:

> The ban on intermarriage has the highest place in the white man's rank order of social segregation and discrimination. Sexual segregation is the most pervasive form of segregation, and the concern about "race purity" is, in a sense, basic. No

---

[23] Henry Louis Gates, "The Passing of Anatole Broyard," in *Thirteen Ways of Looking at a Black man* (New York, 1997), xxvi, 226.

other way of crossing the color line is so attended by the emotion commonly associated with violating a social taboo as intermarriage and extra-marital relations between a Negro man and a white woman. No excuse for other forms of social segregation and discrimination is so potent as the one that sociable relations on an equal basis between members of the two races may possibly lead to intermarriage.[24]

The right to attend birthday parties, weddings, funerals, picnics, and the like cannot be legislated. Folks invite other folks over based on neighborliness. Parents welcome daughters' suitors and sons' girlfriends into their parlors based on friendship and social equality. Such social intercourse is routinely taken for granted today between Irish-Americans and English-Americans though it would have been inconceivable in 1860. As measured by intermarriage, such social intercourse has been virtually nil between white and black America. Anthropologists agree that intermarriage is the ultimate expression of mutual acceptance between societies.

The importance of [intermarriage] cannot be overstated. The family is the primary social unit in society, and as families mix, so do other institutions. In other words, intermarriage is the ultimate form of ethnic assimilation.[25]

Or, as Milton M. Gordon puts it:

Recent studies have pointed to the role of intimate equal-status contact between members of majority and minority groups in reducing prejudice. Structural separation, by definition, denotes a situation in which primary group contacts between members of various ethnic groups are held to a minimum, even though secon-

---

[24] Gunnar Myrdal, Richard Mauritz Edvard Sterner, and Arnold Marshall Rose, *An American Dilemma: The Negro Problem and Modern Democracy* (New York, 1972), 606. Some suggest that Myrdal's statement on the importance of the ban on intermarriage to ostracism of the Black endogamous group reifies "race" in some way. I disagree, but even if this were so, it would be irrelevant. The existence of the U.S. endogamous color line is a measurable phenomenon. Whether it is undesireable in the sense of moral philosophy is not at issue here.

[25] Leonard Dinnerstein and David M. Reimers, *Ethnic Americans: A History of Immigration*, 4th ed. (New York, 1999), 179.

dary contacts on the job, on the civic scene, and in other areas of impersonal contact may abound. In view of the tendency of human beings to categorize in their psychic perceptions and reactions and to form in-groups and, frequently, out-groups on the basis of familiar experiences and contacts, it may plausibly be argued that just as intimate primary group relations tend to reduce prejudice, a lack of such contacts tends to produce hostile ethnic attitudes.[26]

As shown in Figure 15, the out-marriage rate of U.S. Blacks is 3.9 percent as of the 2000 census, and today's rate is the historical maximum. From 1870 through 1970, it languished below one percent. In most other former slave-owning countries, there is no endogamous color line. Marriages between those of different degrees of African genetic admixture are as common as those between people of similar degrees African genetic admixture. Marriages between people of preponderantly European genetic admixture and those of mainly African genetic admixture in Morocco, Puerto Rico, Dominican Republic, Brazil, or the Mascarene Islands occur at the 24-40 percent rate typical of ethnic or cultural groups undergoing acculturation (e.g.: Jamaica, Barbados, Trinidad).[27]

---

[26] Milton M. Gordon, *Assimilation in American Life: The Role of Race, Religion, and National Origins* (New York, 1964), 235-36.

[27] Theodore Allen, *The Invention of the White Race*, 2 vols. (London, 1994), 1:11; Lila E. Salazar, *Love Child: A Genealogist's Guide to the Social History of Barbados* (St. Michael, Barbados, 2000) 151-12.

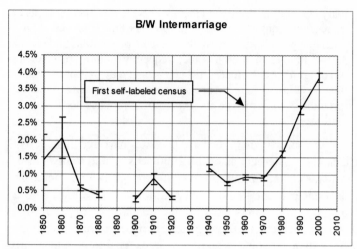

Figure 15. Black/White Intermarriage[28]

The contrast with other U.S. ethnic groups is also striking. Today, about 60 percent of U.S. Hispanics marry non-Hispanics. The exogamy (out-marriage) rate of Amerinds is 54 percent. Irish-, German-, and Polish-American exogamy is at 50 percent. About 45 percent of Italian- and Japanese-Americans marry others, and 40 per cent of Jews marry Christians.[29] The intense endogamy of U.S. Blacks is as unique among ethnic groups within the United States as it is among other nations.

One might ask whether the fact (discussed in *Chapter 2. Afro-European Genetic Admixture in the United States*) that thirty percent of members of the U.S. White endogamous group have significant African genetic admixture, and that over five percent of members of the U.S. Black endogamous group have no African genetic admixture does not suggest that U.S. exogamy is actually higher than the 3.9 percent reported to the census. But this confuses endogamous group membership with genetic admixture. Endogamous group membership is assigned by

[28] For the methodology used in arriving at this figure, see *Appendix A. Census Data Processing Methodology*, specifically, the section titled "Black/White Intermarriage."

[29] See note 4 in *Chapter 2. Afro-European Genetic Admixture in the United States*.

society, once enforced by criminal legislation, and nowadays enforced via peer pressure from both groups.[30] It is measured today by voluntary census data recorded by the head of household. It was measured before 1950 by involuntary census data recorded by a census taker. Measured thus, the exogamy rate is extraordinarily low, much lower than in other countries, much lower than among other U.S. ethnic groups.

Genetic admixture, on the other hand, is the result of African alleles slowly leaking through the endogamous color line over centuries. Most members of the U.S. Black endogamous group are of mostly African genetic admixture. And most members of the U.S. White endogamous group are of mainly European admixture. Indeed, seventy percent of Whites have no African admixture at all. But the tiny rate of interbreeding has had a slow long-term effect. In fact, it is precisely because exogamy is so low that we can measure the impact that each of these two phenomena (group membership and genetic admixture) has on the other. In societies with a Gaussian (normal or bell curve) distribution of genetic admixture (without an endogamous color line), such a study would be impossible.[31] It would be hopeless for example, to try to compare the ethnic self-identity of Irish-Americans with their degree of Celtic versus Anglo-Saxon genetic admixture. This is because Celtic alleles are widely dispersed, Irish-American self-identity is voluntary, and there is no peer pressure preventing Irish-American out-marriage (except, of course, for marriage with Blacks).

Impermeability

This term refers to a person's ability to switch from one endogamous group to another. This feature of the U.S. endogamous color line also differs from other countries' traditions. Dur-

---

[30] See note 5 in *Chapter 2. Afro-European Genetic Admixture in the United States.*

[31] For details, see the final paragraph of the topic "Admixture Scatter Diagrams" in *Chapter 2. Afro-European Genetic Admixture in the United States.*

ing apartheid, South Africans routinely switched group membership by requesting it from their local Race Classification Boards.
Although the bureaucracy was cumbersome and inconsistent, it
enabled change. Individuals were often classified differently
from their siblings and parents, and some people changed more
than once. South Africans could appeal local reclassification decisions to the national Population Registration Board, thence to
the Supreme Court.[32] Like U.S. draft boards of the 1970s, South
Africa's local Race Classification Boards reflected local public
opinion and often found it helpful to cooperate with those wanting to upgrade from Black to Coloured or from Coloured to
White. School principals of schools for children of the White
endogamous group could keep up enrollments (and funding) by
getting some Coloured children reclassified as White members.
But if they pushed too hard, they risked having the whole school
reclassified as a school for members of the Coloured endogamous group.[33]

In contrast, the permeability of the U.S. color line—
peoples' ability to switch between groups—is negligible. In today's United States, openly proclaimed Black-to-White switching by individuals is exceedingly rare, amounting to just 0.10-to-

---

[32] F. James Davis, *Who is Black?: One Nation's Definition* (University Park
PA, 1991), 67, 97.

[33] Graham Watson, *Passing for White: A Study of Racial Assimilation in a
South African School* (London, 1970), 10-24, chap. 4. Incidentally, none of
the above is meant to suggest that South Africans' three-group system is in
any way more logical or beneficial than America's two-group system. All
appearance-based systems tend to crumble around the edges. U.S. courts
have still not resolved whether East Indians are members of the U.S. White
endogamous group. Similarly, in South Africa, Japanese were ruled to be
White whereas Chinese were officially Coloured. One final remark about
South Africa: Due to recent Black political supremacy, their society may be
changing. It may now be in transition, from seeing hybrids as intermediate
in social rank, to relegating them to inferior status, as in Uganda. A Coloured South African recently complained to a newspaper reporter, "In the
old system, we weren't White enough; now we aren't Black enough." See
Lydia Polgreen, "For Mixed-Race South Africans, Equity is Elusive," *The
New York Times International*, July 27 2003, 3.

0.14 percent of the Black population per year.[34] Furthermore, it is often done privately and without fanfare. This is undoubtedly because of the eagerness with which academia and the press "out" those who switched, exposing them to public vilification for betraying their "race."[35]

Of course, that individuals seldom switch does not mean that ethnic groups seldom switch. U.S. immigrant groups have traditionally undergone an acceptance process that moved them from a probationary non-White status to fully White in two or three generations. According to Benjamin Franklin, German-Americans in 1751 Pennsylvania were too dark to pass for White. In his *Observations Concerning the Increase of Mankind* he wrote, "Why should Pennsylvania, founded by the English, become a Colony of *Aliens,* who will shortly be so numerous as to Germanize us instead of our Anglifying them, and will never adopt our Language or Customs, any more than they can acquire our Complexion. … The Germans are generally of what we call a swarthy Complexion. … The English make the principle Body of White People on the Face of the Earth."[36]

The Irish took nearly a century to become accepted as members of the White endogamous group. According to the 1860 *American Encyclopedia: A Popular Dictionary of General Knowledge,* "[The Irish race shares] inherited features such as "low-browed and savage, groveling and bestial, lazy and wild,

---

[34] For details, see the topic "The Average Yearly Rate is Between 0.10 and 0.14 Percent" in *Chapter 5. The Rate of Black-to-White "Passing."*

[35] In addition to Henry Louis Gates, "The Passing of Anatole Broyard," in *Thirteen Ways of Looking at a Black man* (New York, 1997), xxvi, 226, mentioned earlier, see Interracial Voice: A.D. Powell, *When Are Irish-Americans Not Good Enough to Be Irish-American?: 'Racial Kidnaping' and the Case of the Healy Family* <http://interracialvoice.com/powell8.html> (1998); James M. O'Toole, "Racial Identity and the Case of Captain Michael Healy, USRCS," *Prologue: Quarterly of the National Archives & Records Administration,* 29 (no. 3, Fall 1997); Interracial Voice, *Pissing on the Graves of Heroes,* May [Electronic Magazine] (2003); The Multiracial Activist, *The Misidentification of Mother Henriette Delille,* August [Electronic Magazine] (2002).

[36] As quoted in Winthrop D. Jordan, *White Over Black: American Attitudes Toward the Negro, 1550-1812* (Chapel Hill, 1968), 102, 143.

simian [ape-like] and sensual...." Scholars of the time described such uniquely Irish race-distinguishing features as eye and skin color, facial configuration, and physique.[37] As late as 1881, English historian Edward A. Freeman (1823-1892) opined that the United States "would be a grand land if only every Irishman would kill a negro, and be hanged for it."[38] As recently as thirty years ago, some people sincerely believed that they could spot an Irishman trying to pass for White.[39]

Italians, Greeks, and eastern Europeans were considered ineligible for membership in the White endogamous group until well into the twentieth century. Before World War II, some Italian-American children in the South were forced to attend segregated schools for children of the Black endogamous group. Eleven Italian-Americans who tried to pass as members of the White group were lynched in 1891 New Orleans and five more were lynched for the same reason outside the Madison Parish, Louisiana, courthouse in 1899.[40] A nineteenth-century physician wrote, "The Slavs are immune to certain kinds of dirt. They can stand what would kill a White man."[41] American Jews did not become accepted as White until the 1940s. Again, as with the Germans, Irish, and Italians, Americans rationalized rejection as based on hereditary appearance. In 1911, Franz Boas (1858-1952) concluded in his groundbreaking *The Mind of Primitive Man,* "No real biological chasm separated recent immigrants

---

[37] Dale T. Knobel, *Paddy and the Republic: Ethnicity and Nationality in Antebellum America,* 1st ed. (Middletown CT, 1986), 88. As quoted in Jonathan W. Warren and France Winddance Twine, "White Americans, the New Minority?," *Journal of Black Studies,* 28 (no. 2, 1997), 200-18, 203; David R. Roediger, *The Wages of Whiteness: Race and the Making of the American Working Class* (London, 1991), 133.

[38] As quoted in Theodore Allen, *The Invention of the White Race,* 2 vols. (London, 1994), 1:29.

[39] H.L Gates, *Loose Canons: Notes on the Culture Wars* (New York, 1992), 49.

[40] Adam Fairclough, *Race & Democracy: The Civil Rights Struggle in Louisiana, 1915-1972* (Athens, 1995), 6.

[41] As quoted in Mary C. Waters, *Ethnic Options: Choosing Identities in America* (Berkeley, 1990).

from Mayflower descendants."[42] In reply, the *New York Times* book review told readers that this book was "the desperate attempt of a Jew to pass himself off as white."[43]

Nineteenth-century Asian-American men were not considered members of the White endogamous group. Those who dated women of the White group provoked mass lynchings. Twenty were hanged in 1871 Los Angeles, twenty-eight killed in 1885 Rock Springs, and thirty-one in 1887 Hell's Canyon.[44] Their voting rights were similarly restricted. The 1875 and 1880 modifications of the federal Naturalization Act of 1790 were meant to bar citizenship even from Asian Americans born in the U.S.—ironic, considering that the fourteenth and fifteenth amendments to the U.S. Constitution granted citizenship-by-birth to former slaves. After World War II, Chinese-Americans in Mississippi achieved membership in the White endogamous group by deliberately disdaining members of the Black group. Community leaders influenced Chinese males to end relationships with Black females, to expel Afro-Chinese kin, and to force such biracial families to leave the Chinese community. They ended friendships with members of the Black group and ceased interacting courteously with Black customers. In the presence of members of the White group, they joked stereotypically about members of the Black group. They excluded Blacks members from birthday parties, weddings, and funerals. The carefully planned strategy paid off. By the late 1960s, Chinese-American children attended White schools and universities. They joined Mississippi's infamous White citizen's councils, became members of White churches, were recorded as *White* on driver's licenses, and could marry members of the White endogamous group.[45] Asian Americans have been accepted into the

---

[42] Franz Boas, *The Mind of Primitive Man* (New York, 1911).

[43] Lothrop Stoddard, as quoted in Matthew Frye Jacobson, *Whiteness of a Different Color: European Immigrants and the Alchemy of Race* (Cambridge, 1998), 184.

[44] Harry H. L. Kitano and Roger Daniels, *Asian Americans: Emerging Minorities*, 2nd ed. (Englewood Cliffs, 1995), 24.

[45] James W. Loewen, *The Mississippi Chinese: Between Black and White* (Cambridge MA, 1971); Warren (1997), 200-18, 209-11.

White endogamous group so recently that the process has not yet finished. Although many Chinese-Americans in the South can now join exclusive White-only private country clubs, pockets remain on the West Coast where they are still considered Colored.

Judging by census data (see Figure 1 in *Chapter 2. Afro-European Genetic Admixture*) U.S. Hispanics are also becoming accepted into the White endogamous group. In 1950, Florida and Georgia demographers defined all Puerto Ricans as Colored, no matter how pale. It said, "The term 'white person' shall include only persons... who have no trace of... West Indian.... 'West Indian' shall include anyone with a West Indies background, regardless of whether his antecedents were... Spanish or French Caucasians...."[46] And yet, ever since the 1960 census instructions allowed self-labeling, ninety percent of Puerto Ricans have chosen to be census-White.[47]

Finally, growing numbers of British West Indians living in the United States apparently seek mainstream acceptance by deliberately distancing themselves from the Black endogamous group. Actress Gloria Reuben (*The Agency, Salem Witch Trials, Little John, ER*), once said to a dimwitted interviewer who failed to notice several hints, "Stop calling me African-American! I am not African-American; I am Jamaican-Canadian!"[48] West Indi-

---

[46] Stetson Kennedy, *Jim Crow Guide: The Way it Was* (Boca Raton FL, 1990), 47-49.

[47] Clara E. Rodriguez, "Challenging Racial Hegemony: Puerto Ricans in the United States," in *Race*, ed. Steven Gregory and Roger Sanjek (New Brunswick NJ, 1994), 131-45.

[48] One might ask whether Ms. Reuben's scolding does not reflect a desire to deconstruct the U.S. color line, rather than to distance herself from the Black community. It is, of course, impossible to know Ms. Reuben's innermost motives. But the literature of West Indian resistance to being involuntarily assigned to the Black endogamous group by American society (especially by members of the U.S. Black endogamous group) is vast. See, for example, Stephen A. Woodbury, "Culture, Human Capital, and the Earnings of West Indian Blacks," (1993); Mary C. Waters, *Black Identities: West Indian Immigrant Dreams and American Realities* (New York, 1999); Thomas Sowell, *Ethnic America: A History* (New York, 1981), 219; or Malcolm Gladwell, "Black Like Them," *The New Yorker*, April 29 1996. The interpretation presented here makes Ms. Reuben's statement unexcep-

ans' ongoing acculturation is eerily reminiscent of Puerto Ricans' bleaching a generation ago.[49] Like Puerto Ricans then, many British West Indians now are comfortable with their African heritage and enjoy tracing names, music, or folklore back to Wolof, Fulani, or Yoruba customs, while they simultaneously resent being mistaken for members of the U.S. Black endogamous group. They avoid intermarriage with members of the U.S. Black community, but have no objection to marrying other West Indians of partial African ancestry.[50]

Many authors have explained how each immigrant group became accepted into mainstream American society and thereby redefined as "White."[51] To become accepted as White, immigrants had to learn a few vital American attitudes: tolerance of the religion and customs of others who have already been accepted as White, respect for education (for generations, Irish-Americans forbade their children to learn to read because they

---

tional. The alternative (that she wants to defy the U.S. social system, rather than position herself advantageously within it) would be anomalous.

[49] One might also wonder whether this suggests or implies that West Indians are currently following the same trajectory as the earlier Puerto Ricans, Chinese, Jews, and so forth, who achieved acceptance into the White endogamous group. That is precisely what this study suggests. Finally, one might ask: "Why have other ethnic groups (Germans, Irish, Italians, Slavs, Jews, Chinese, Japanese, and Puerto Ricans) achieved acceptance into the White endogamous group, but native-born members of the Black endogamous group have not achieved acceptance into the White endogamous group?" This study does not attempt to answer that question. There is, of course, no physical trait that would prevent it. After all, it is a cliché among forensic anthropologists that the only way to tell if an unidentified corpse is Hispanic, rather than Black with lots of European genetic admixture, is to search the pockets for a shopping list written in Spanish.

[50] See Thomas Sowell, *Ethnic America: A History* (New York, 1981), 219. Incidentally, not all those of B.W.I. lineage reject the Black label. Jamaican-descended General Colin Powell, for example, identifies himself as Black.

[51] See, for example: Karen Brodkin, *How Jews Became White Folks and What That Says About Race in America* (New Brunswick NJ, 1998); Noel Ignatiev, *How the Irish Became White* (New York, 1995); Matthew Frye Jacobson, *Whiteness of a Different Color: European Immigrants and the Alchemy of Race* (Cambridge, 1998); Ian F. Haney-Lopez, *White by Law: The Legal Construction of Race* (New York, 1996).

feared that it was a Protestant plot[52]), acceptance of class mobility (the idea of the self-made man), and finally, they had to learn to display open contempt towards members of the U.S. Black endogamous group. The third item is unfortunate, but the evidence is incontrovertible.[53] In short, the U.S. endogamous color line is the lever by which immigrant groups continue to wrench themselves into the White mainstream using Black Americans as the fulcrum.

The point is that the permeability of the U.S. color line—peoples' ability to switch between groups—is negligible compared to how groups interact in most other countries, as well as compared to other U.S. ethnic groups. In today's United States, openly proclaimed Black-to-White group switching by individuals, as opposed to the Whitening of entire ethnic groups, is exceedingly rare. As shown in *Chapter 5. The Rate of Black-to-White "Passing,"* it has averaged between 0.10 and 0.14 percent of the Black population per year.

Hypodescent

This term "hypodescent" was coined in 1963 by the late University of Florida anthropologist, Marvin Harris.[54] It means that U.S. society assigns individuals with known mixed Afro-European heritage to the Black endogamous group, even though they might be of mostly European descent. This study considers the one-drop rule of invisible blackness as hypodescent taken to its absurd conclusion. In lands where other forms of Afro-European racialism exist, the preponderance of appearance determines a person's "racial" label.

---

[52] Oscar Handlin, *Boston's Immigrants, 1790-1880*, Rev. and enl. ed. (Cambridge MA, 1959), Chapter 5.

[53] The best overall survey of such evidence is Warren (1997), 200-18.

[54] Marvin Harris, *Patterns of Race in the Americas* (Westport CT, 1964), 37.

The Future

Figure 15, "Black/White Intermarriage" shows that the U.S. endogamous color line has weakened since the civil rights movement of 1955-1965 and the Supreme Court ruling in *Loving v. Virginia*, 1967. It shows that the Black-White intermarriage rate has tripled since 1970. Despite appearances, this rate of change is numerically insignificant. Even if this rate of intermarriage increase were to continue unabated, Black exogamy would not approach the 50 percent rate typical of ethnic groups (Jews, Japanese-Americans, Hispanics) for another six centuries. In other words, 2.5 percent in three decades equals 50 percent in sixty decades. Other social trends also suggest the permanence of the color line.

Between 1980 and 1995, Black male earnings fell from 75.1 percent of White male earnings to 71.2 percent. In the same period, the net worth of the median Black family fell from $8,400 to $7,500, while median White family net worth rose from $54,600 to $59,500.[55] Public schools are increasingly becoming racially segregated in a national retreat from integration.[56] Such color line hardening is national, not global. Blacks in the United Kingdom out-marry with Whites at a 20-to-40 percent rate.[57] This is comparable to the exogamy rate of Japanese Americans or Hispanic Americans. In other words, the endogamous color line continues to be a U.S. phenomenon, not one of Western or even of Anglo-Saxon culture.

Some have seen an adjustment in the mechanics of the 2000 census form as indicative of change, but this is also illusory. Although censuses since 1960 have enabled Americans to choose their own "race," only in 2000 were they allowed to

---

[55] Andrew Hacker, *Two Nations: Black and White, Separate, Hostile, Unequal* (New York, 1995), 108.

[56] Gary Orfield and Susan E. Eaton, *Dismantling Desegregation: The Quiet Reversal of Brown v. Board of Education* (New York, 1996).

[57] Suzanne Model and Gene Fisher, "Unions Between Blacks and Whites: England and the U.S. Compared," *Ethnic and Racial Studies*, 25 (no. 5, September 2002), 728-54.

check off more than one box. The decision was made by Congress responding to a campaign launched by more than thirty multiracial organizations across the country, which coalesced into a nationwide political advocacy group: the Association of Multiethnic Americans (AMEA). The "multiracial movement," as it was then called, lobbied to add a "multiracial" box to the census "race" question. The movement failed due to intense pressure by the Congressional Black caucus, who feared that it would dilute Black political influence. Nevertheless, Congress compromised by ordering the Census Bureau to allow Americans to check off "all boxes that apply." This partly satisfied those like the multiracial movement who wanted to undermine the census "race" question, those like the American Anthropological Association who wanted to do away with census "race" entirely, and those like Hispanic and Black advocacy groups who wanted to maximize their constituencies' visibility.[58]

The decision to allow Americans to "check all race boxes that apply" was met with overheated enthusiasm by some social scientists. According to two sociologists,

> [The new federal regulation] illustrates a seismic shift in our understanding of... racial group membership. In fact, the very *idea* [emphasis in original] of races... will never be the same. ... The Census Bureau has dealt a deadly blow to the idea that 'pure' races exist, shattering the... notion of races as genetically distinct groupings of human beings.[59]

The census did nothing of the sort. No seismic shifts shattered anything with deadly blows. The change had no effect on

---

[58] For an excellent overall survey of the multiracial movement, see G. Reginald Daniel, *More than Black?: Multiracial Identity and the New Racial Order* (Philadelphia, 2002). For the American Anthopological Association's plea to the Federal Government to discontinue the census "race" question once and for all, see URL <http://www.aaanet.org/gvt/ombdraft.htm>. For a brief overview of these issues, see Bijan Gilanshah, "Multiracial Minorities: Erasing the Color Line," *Law and Inequality*, 12 (December 1993), 183.

[59] David L. Brunsma and Kerry Ann Rockquemore, "What Does 'Black' Mean? Exploring the Epistemological Stranglehold of Racial Categorization," *Critical Sociology*, 28 (no. 1/2, 2002), 101-21, 112.

how the average American sees "race." Despite pre-census fears (by Black politicians) and hopes (by Hispanic ones) that many Blacks would finally admit their European ancestry, it turned out that 95.2 percent of African-Americans checked only one box: "Black." And despite pre-census fears (by Hispanic politicians) and hopes (by Black ones) that many Hispanics would finally admit their African ancestry, it turned out that 93.7 percent of Hispanic Americans checked only one box: "White."[60]

* * * * *

This chapter offered a comparative inspection of the U.S. endogamous color line. It explained that the intermarriage barrier is the basis upon which all other aspects of the U.S. "race" notion are constructed. It dissected the color line into four folk-loric beliefs: discontinuity, that a single color-line exists; endogamy, that people should not marry across it; impermeability, that you cannot switch sides from Black to White; and hypodescent, that if you have a parent who is a member of the Black endogamous group then you are Black also, no matter your preference or even your appearance. It predicted that the U.S. endogamous color line is not likely to vanish within the next few centuries.

---

[60] Nicholas A. Jones and Amy Symens Smith, "The Two or More Races Population: 2000," (Washington, 2001), 12, page 7 tables 4 and 5. Black political leaders want Hispanics to check off "Black" as well as "White" in order to swell their constituencies, thereby increasing Black affirmative action quotas. Hispanic political leaders want African-Americans to check off "White" as well as "Black" in order to swell the ranks of those seen as multiracial, thereby increasing Hispanic affirmative action quotas.

Chapter 7.
The Invention of the Color
Line: 1691

In 1653 Virginia, one of Anthony Johnson's involuntary
African laborers, a man named John Casor, claimed his freedom
because his term of indenture had allegedly expired seven years
before. He fled his master's plantation and took refuge with a
nearby farmer, Captain Gouldsmith. Johnson insisted that his
runaway laborer was not indentured, but was a lifelong slave and
demanded the African's return. Not wanting to become em-
broiled in a legal fight with a powerful plantation owner, Gouldsmith turned the worker over to planter Robert Parker. Parker
took the worker's side in the dispute, kept him on his own plantation's workforce, and argued on his behalf in court. The case
dragged on for two years, with Johnson at one point agreeing to
manumit Casor, but then reneging on the settlement. On March
8, 1655, the Northampton County Court ruled that Casor had
been a slave all along, ordered that the worker be returned immediately to Anthony Johnson, and ordered Robert Parker to pay
damages for sheltering the runaway for two years, as well as
court costs. A few years later, Parker abandoned his career as a
Virginia planter and returned to England. Twenty years later,
Casor was still owned by Mary Johnson—Anthony Johnson's

widow.[1] What is important about this tale is that Anthony Johnson was also African. His plantation, from whence Casor fled, was named "Angola," and it exploited European forced laborers as well as Africans.

* * * * *

This chapter explains, in three topics, when, where, and how America's endogamous color line was invented. *The Years Before the Color Line was Invented* describes colonial life before the turn of the eighteenth century. It shows that colonists of African and European ancestries mingled and married within all three social classes: forced laborers, shopkeepers, and planters. *The Transition Period* narrates events in and around the Chesapeake leading up to the 1691 law, the first in history to outlaw Afro-European intermarriage. *The Spread of the New Color Line* describes the aftermath as punishments for violating the 1691 law became increasingly harsher, and similar laws were passed in subsequent generations throughout British North America.

The Years Before the Color Line was Invented

African-American colonists arrived in Virginia in August of 1619. Most came as indentured servants (or slaves; the two labor systems had not yet diverged). They were under no initial implication of "racial" inferiority. The endogamous color line had not yet been invented. They soon permeated all three socio-economic classes. "They accumulated land, voted, testified in court, and mingled with whites on a basis of equality."[2] Some remained slaves (or indentured servants). Forced laborers both Afro- and Euro-American, ran away together, attempted servile

---

[1] T. H. Breen and Stephen Innes, *"Myne Owne Ground": Race and Freedom on Virginia's Eastern Shore, 1640-1676* (New York, 1980), 13-17, 19. Incidentally, there is evidence that Casor may have been manumitted after the Johnson's moved from Virginia to Maryland.

[2] Lerone Bennett Jr., *The Shaping of Black America* (Chicago, 1975) 17-19.

insurrections together, and jointly complained about both the greed of the bourgeois and the cruelty of the aristocracy.[3]

Others became artisans and shopkeepers as well as professional lawyers, physicians, or skilled farmers who contributed to colonial life. According to the governor, in 1648, African-American colonists recommended rice planting because conditions in the Chesapeake were favorable to that crop. This middle class, both Afro- and Euro-American, complained about the laziness and dishonesty of their slaves and of taxes imposed by rapacious aristocrats.[4]

Still others became aristocrats. Slave importing was the route to social status. In 1651, Anthony Johnson earned 250 acres for importing five slaves (we do not know their land of origin). Richard Johnson, Anthony's father, received 100 acres for importing two slaves (of unknown complexion). John Johnson, Richard's brother, did better, winning 550 acres for bringing in eleven slaves (again, we do not know how many were African or European). Benjamin Dole received 300 acres for importing six slaves into Surry County. All of these men owned tidewater plantations and left large estates. They were established members of the ruling class.

Northampton County, Virginia, was typical of the early colonial economy. In 1666, about 300 of Virginia's colonists were of African ancestry, like the Johnsons. At that time, 11 percent of African colonists and 18 percent of European colonists owned either land or slaves.[5] This is analogous to a 61 percent ratio of Black-to-White net worth—higher than the United States would ever see again in its history. For comparison, two centuries later in 1860, the county's Black-to-White property ownership ratio was zero percent.[6] By 1980, the overall U.S. Black-to-

---

[3] Bennett (1975) 61-80; Edmund Sears Morgan, *American Slavery, American Freedom: The Ordeal of Colonial Virginia* (New York, 1975) 155.

[4] Lerone Bennett Jr., *Before the Mayflower: A History of Black America*, 6th rev. ed. (New York, 1993) 35-36.

[5] Theodore Allen, *The Invention of the White Race*, 2 vols. (London, 1994) 2:182-85.

[6] Ibid., 2:185.

White net-worth ratio had risen to 15.4 percent, but by 1995 it had fallen again to 12.6 percent.[7]

Intermarriage was common. Visitors reported that the colony "swarms with mulatto children, and these mulattoes, if but three generations removed from the black father or mother [are accepted as White]."[8] Among prominent interracial marriages were those of European attorney William Greensted and his biracial wife Elizabeth Kay, African slaveowner Francis Payne and his European wife Amy, European Francis Skipper and his African wife Ann Cocore, African James Tate and his European wife Hester, and African Phillip Mognum and his European wife Mary Morris.[9] Then attitudes began to change.

The Transition Period

At first, the changes seemed to have little to do with establishing an endogamous color line. In 1630 Jamestown, Hugh Davis was ordered to be "soundly whipt before an assembly of negroes for abusing himself to the dishonor of God and the shame of Christianity by defiling his body in lying with a negro." As many scholars have pointed out, the unfortunate Mr. Davis was caught "lying with a *negro*," not "lying with a *negress*," and so his offense was more likely to have been homosexuality rather than crossing the color line.[10] Still, it is possible that this may have been the first legal document in British North

---

[7] Andrew Hacker, *Two Nations: Black and White, Separate, Hostile, Unequal* (New York, 1995), 108.

[8] Ann Maury, *Memoirs of a Huguenot Family* (New York, 1872) as quoted in James Hugo Johnston, *Race Relations in Virginia & Miscegenation in the South, 1776-1860* (Amherst, 1970), 170.

[9] Edmund Sears Morgan, *American Slavery, American Freedom: The Ordeal of Colonial Virginia* (New York, 1975), 334; Allen (1994), 2:181-82.

[10] 1 *Laws of Virginia* 146; Werner Sollors, *Neither Black Nor White Yet Both* (Cambridge, 1997), 395; Leon A. Higginbotham, Jr. and Barbara K. Kopytoff, "Racial Purity and Interracial Sex in the Law of Colonial and Antebellum Virginia," *Georgetown Law Journal*, 77 (no. 6, August 1989), 1967-2029; Winthrop D. Jordan, *White Over Black: American Attitudes Toward the Negro, 1550-1812* (Chapel Hill, 1968), 78; Morgan (1975), 333.

America to disapprove of intimate contact between people of African and European ancestry.

Ten years later, in 1640 Jamestown, European Robert Sweat was ordered to "do penance in church according to the laws of England," for impregnating an African female. The woman was ordered whipped.[11] Apparently, the couple would not have been punished had they been married. But the point is that she was whipped, while he merely "did penance." At first glance, this seems to reflect "racial" inequality—the African was punished, not the European. If so, this would make it the first documented instance of "racial" inequality in British North America. But it more likely reflected gender inequality instead. The Puritans were coming to power under Oliver Cromwell at the time, and Puritan theology held that women were morally weak and tools of Satan. The colonial leaders may have felt that the pregnant woman had seduced the man. A case nine years later, in 1649 Jamestown, supports the latter interpretation. William Watts (European) and Mary (African) were both ordered to do penance for fornication.[12] Their punishment was equal and nothing suggests that they would have been punished had they been married. If a sense of inequality across an embryonic color line was emerging, it was emerging slowly and haltingly.

In 1662, Virginia passed two laws of interest. The first increased the penalty for interracial fornication:

> if any Christian shall committ ffornication with a negro man or woman, hee or shee soe offending shall pay double the ffines imposed by the former act [500 pounds of tobacco].[13]

This act did not legalize fornication between two Europeans or between two Africans; it merely made the penalty more severe if the parties were of different continental ancestry. Although it did not address intermarriage, it is historically important because it is the first law in British North America that made interracial sex more reprehensible than sex between those of the same ancestry.

---

[11] 1 *Laws of Virginia* 552.

[12] Sollors (1997), 395.

[13] Ibid., 396.

The second Virginia law of 1662 established the doctrine
of *partus sequitur ventrem*, that the free/slave status of a child
was solely determined by the free/slave status of the mother:[14]

> Whereas some doubts have arisen whether children got by
> any Englishman upon a negro woman should be slave or free,
> be it therefore enacted and declared by the present grand as-
> sembly, that all children borne in this country shall be held
> bond or free only according to the condition of the
> mother....[15]

The new law held that neither your continent of ancestry, skin-
tone, nor patrilineal descent had any effect on whether you were
a slave. The law brought Virginia into line with Iberian laws that
had been in effect since 1265.[16] Over the next few decades, identical laws would be adopted throughout the British colonies.
They would remain in effect until U.S. slavery ended over two
centuries later. The new *partus sequitur ventrem* law had four
long-term consequences. First, it set a psychological basis for
popular culture's seeing slaves as less than fully human. Prior
British common law had held that social status passed through
the father; only livestock ownership had been matrilineal. Second, it enabled the emergence of a large population of legitimately freeborn Americans of mixed Afro-European ancestry
who had no connection to slavery within living memory. Third,
it meant that tens of thousands of future slaves would be geneti-

---

[14] "The offspring follows the mother; the brood of an animal belongs to the
owner of the dam; the offspring of a slave belongs to the owner of the
mother, or follows the condition of the mother. A maxim of the civil law,
which has been adopted in the law of England in regard to animals, though
never allowed in the case of human beings, 2 Bl. Comm. 390, 94; Fortes.
42." Black's Law Dictionary, 3d ed, (West Publishing, 1933). See also
background and explanation in Paul Finkelman, "The Crime of Color,"
Tulane Law Review, 67 (no. 6, 1992), 2063-112, 2085.

[15] William Waller Hening, *The Statutes at Large: Being a Collection of all
the Laws of Virginia, from the First Session of the Legislature in the Year
1619* (Richmond [Va.], 1809), 2:170; Kathleen M. Brown, *Good Wives,
Nasty Wenches, and Anxious Patriarchs: Gender, Race, and Power in Colonial Virginia* (Chapel Hill, 1996), 132; Paul Finkelman, "The Crime of
Color," *Tulane Law Review*, 67 (no. 6, 1992), 2063-112, 2082-83

[16] *Las Siete Partidas del Rey Alfonso X* (1265).

cally European, due to European alleles from fathers gradually replacing African alleles from mothers, through random DNA mixing (meiosis) at each generation.[17] Within two centuries, this would lead to such runaway slave advertisements as, "A beautiful girl, about twenty years of age, perfectly white, with straight light hair and blue eyes." — 1847 Hannibal MO.[18] Finally, the new law launched a 143-year period in U.S. history when slavery had no legal connection to continent of ancestry. If your mother was a slave, you were a slave, even if you were European. If your mother was free, then you were free, even if you were African. As will be explained in Chapter 9, this period ended with *Hudgins v. Wrights*, 1806 Virginia.

Three years later, Maryland passed a 1664 law punishing free women who married slaves. Offenders would themselves be enslaved for their husband's lifetime, and their children would be hereditary slaves from birth:[19]

> For deterring such free borne women from such shamefull Matches... whatsoever free borne woman shall inter marry with any slave... shall Serve the master of such slave dureing the life of her husband And that all the issue of such free-borne woemen soe marryed shall be Slaves as their fathers were.[20]

Although this law is often cited as the first prohibition of Black/White intermarriage in British North America,[21] it makes no mention of "race" or continent of ancestry. A careful reading shows something quite different. It punished inter-class mar-

---

[17] See the detailed explanation under topic "The Percentage Rate Has Remained Relatively Steady over the Years" in *Chapter 5. The Rate of Black-to-White "Passing."*

[18] For this and many similar advertisements for runaways, see Lawrence Raymond Tenzer, *The Forgotten Cause of the Civil War: A New Look at the Slavery Issue* (Manahawkin NJ, 1997), 32.

[19] Ibid., 395-96.

[20] Helen Tunnicliff Catterall and James J. Hayden, *Judicial Cases Concerning American Slavery and The Negro* (New York, 1968), 4:2.

[21] See, for example, Ruth Frankenberg, *White Women, Race Matters: The Social Construction of Whiteness* (Minneapolis, 1993), 72.

riages. It did not prohibit free Europeans from marrying free Africans, nor did it forbid forced-laborer Europeans from marrying forced-laborer Africans. It forbade only marriages between free women (of any ancestry) and slaves (of any ancestry).

Early in 1681, Lord Baltimore returned to Maryland from a four-year sojourn in England. He was displeased to learn of the evils resulting from the 1664 law that had enslaved the offspring of free women and slave men. They were brought to Lord Baltimore's attention by his house servant, Eleanor Butler, better known as "Irish Nell."[22] The law had created three problems:

First, it conflicted with the 1662 Virginia *partus sequitur ventrem* law that assigned the status of the mother to children of mixed marriages. The legal incompatibility had inspired mass flight between the two colonies. Interracial families headed by African men and European women fled from Maryland to Virginia, while those headed by African women and European men ran away from Virginia to Maryland. The second problem was that some Maryland planters, with a view towards breeding additional human assets, were exploiting the law by deliberately "purchasing white women" and forcing them to wed African men.[23] But worst of all, according to Irish Nell, was that she herself had married Charles, one of Lord Baltimore's slaves, and so her own future children were now doomed to slavery.

In December of 1681, Lord Baltimore, with Irish Nell's help, induced the Maryland legislature to revoke their peculiar 1664 law and adopt Virginia's system instead. In the same session, Maryland also made it illegal for masters to order European female servants to marry African male slaves against their will.[24] Nevertheless, for seventeen years Maryland and Virginia had enforced contradictory laws regarding the heredity of slave

---

[22] Joel Williamson, *New People: Miscegenation and Mulattoes in the United States* (New York, 1980), 10.

[23] The quote is from Catterall (1968), 4:2. For a specific case, see *Butler v. Boarman*, 1770 Maryland (1 H. & McH. 371). For the complete story of Irish Nell, Charles, and their descendants see Martha Elizabeth Hodes, *White Women, Black Men: Illicit Sex in the Nineteenth-Century South* (New Haven, 1997), 19-38.

[24] Sollors (1997), 396; Catterall (1968), 4:2.

status. The ensuing confusion spawned a series of lawsuits that continued even after independence a century later, as individuals tried to prove that they were not hereditary slaves, and masters tried to prove that they were, based on matrilineal or patrilineal ancestry.

Finally in 1691, the Virginia colony passed and enforced the first law on earth against voluntary marriage between free individuals of predominantly European ancestry and free individuals of predominantly African ancestry.[25] At first, the law was weak. It punished interracial couples by banishing them from the colony. It did not punish the ministers who married them, nor did it punish their children. Within years, however, punishments became increasingly harsh for anyone complicit in a crime of intermarriage, up to and including death by torture.[26] Dozens of interracial families (including the descendants of Anthony Johnson) fled from Virginia to Maryland. Such innovative legislation had never happened before in world history. It would never happen independently again. But it happened this once, and once was enough.

The Spread of the New Color Line

The following year, in 1692, Maryland also outlawed intermarriage, virtually copying the 1691 Virginia law.[27] Dozens of interracial families, among them those who had fled from Virginia, now fled from Maryland to Pennsylvania.

Four years later, in 1696, Virginia's rulers made their anti-intermarriage law harsher. Apparently, the colonists were not taking the law seriously enough. The 1696 change added the offending minister as complicit in the crime of intermarriage. After this change, interracial married couples would be banished, as before, but now the minister who married them would

---

[25] 3 *Laws of Virginia* 86, 87.

[26] Lerone Bennett Jr., *The Shaping of Black America* (Chicago, 1975), 74-75.

[27] *Acts of Maryland* 76.

be fined 10,000 pounds of tobacco.[28] Since this amount was far
beyond the reach of even some landed gentry, it meant the minister's defrocking. In addition, the new law explicitly ordered
ministers to preach against intermarriage. Priests who refused to
comply were also defrocked and replaced. How the landed gentry acquired the church authority to appoint and fire priests and
bishops will be explained momentarily.

Over the next few decades, penalties became increasingly
cruel. According to one historian, a horror of intermarriage was
planted in the minds of the colonists:

> by the creation of a total system of domination, a system that
> penetrated every corner of Colonial life and made use of
> every Colonial institution. Nothing was left to chance. The
> assemblies, the courts, the churches, and the press were
> thrown into the breach. A massive propaganda campaign con-
> fused and demoralized the public, and private vigilante
> groups supplemented the official campaign of hate and ter-
> ror.[29]

Ministers were ordered to read decrees that not only forbade intermarriage, but that also referred to Africans in dehumanizing
terms. Even Winthrop Jordan, a highly respected historian who
believes that hatred of the "negro race" is an inborn instinct of
the "white race" that goes back thousands of years, admits that
the Virginia laws outlawing intermarriage were aimed at freeborn colonists, not at Black slaves:

> While the colonial slave codes seem at first sight to have
> been intended to discipline Negroes, to deny them freedoms
> available to other Americans, a very slight shift in perspec-
> tive shows the codes in a different light; they were aimed,
> paradoxically, at disciplining white men. Principally, the law
> told the white man, not the Negro, what he must do; the
> codes were for the eyes and ears of slaveowners.... Members
> of the assemblies, most of whom owned slaves, were at-
> tempting to enforce slave-discipline by the only means avail-

---

[28] 3 *Laws of Virginia* 252, 453.

[29] Bennett (1975), 71. For corroboration, see Theodore Allen, *The Invention
of the White Race*, 2 vols. (London, 1994), 1:21.

able, by forcing owners, individually and collectively, to exercise it.[30]

No endogamous barrier is perfect, however, and America's new color line leaked. Despite the threat of law, the preaching of religious leaders, and the pressure of social peers, people of mixed heritage continued to be born. Conventional wisdom holds that such mixing was the result of European male slave-owners raping or at least economically coercing female slaves. In fact, although colonial interracial mating was somewhat asymmetrical, it was not all that one-sided. Many Americans today carry mitochondrial DNA of matrilineal European descent and Y chromosomes of patrilineal African ancestry.[31] Nevertheless, whether the continued production of biracial children was the result of African males joining with European females or vice-versa, colonists of every intermediate gradation continued to be born during the eighteenth century. Multiracial colonists had no legal existence then, just as multiracial Americans have no legal existence today. Mixed-ancestry individuals, then as now, were legislated out of existence. And so, for the first time, Americans faced a problem that remains unsolved and plagues the nation to this day: how to decide to which side of the color line to assign someone?

In 1705, Virginia passed the first law in history defining who was considered a member of the Black endogamous group. The law used a one-eighth blood-fraction rule; You belonged on the Black side of the color line if you had one or more great-grandparents who had belonged on the Black side of the color line. In addition, the fine for ministers performing interracial

---

[30] Winthrop D. Jordan, *The White Man's Burden: Historical Origins of Racism in the United States* (New York, 1974), 61.

[31] Esteban J. Parra and others, "Estimating African American Admixture Proportions by Use of Population-Specific Alleles," *American Journal of Human Genetics*, 63 (1998), 1839-51. Also, for an outstanding historical account of sex-symmetrical miscegenation common in colonial and early antebellum America, in contrast to the conventional tale of White male exploitation of Black females, see Martha Elizabeth Hodes, *White Women, Black Men: Illicit Sex in the Nineteenth-Century South* (New Haven, 1997).

marriages was increased even farther beyond reach.[32] This law was the first instance in history of legalized hypodescent.[33]

Punishment of intermarriage became ever harsher. In 1715, Maryland and Virginia condemned women who married across the color line to seven years of bondage, and their mixed children to thirty-one years of bondage.[34] One historian counted 367 court cases in this period punishing women alone. Of these, 140 identified the male partner: 89 cases punished White females for consorting with African-American males; 9 cases punished African-American females for consorting with White males.[35]

In 1705, Massachusetts outlawed interracial marriage. Other British colonies followed: North Carolina outlawed interracial marriage in 1715. Delaware outlawed interracial marriage in 1721. Pennsylvania outlawed interracial marriage in 1725.[36] Dozens of interracial families, among them those who had fled from Maryland, now fled from Pennsylvania to New York, apparently seeding the maroon community knows as the Jackson Whites.[37] Fear/hatred of intermarriage spread throughout British North America until, by 1776, 12 of the 13 colonies that declared their independence legally enforced endogamous color lines.

Oddly, the idea of a forcibly endogamous color line did not jump the Atlantic to Europe. Throughout the 1600s, the New World was all the rage in Europe. Women's fashions aped the feathers and fringes of Native American dress. Tobacco became

---

[32] Paul Finkelman, "The Crime of Color," *Tulane Law Review*, 67 (no. 6, 1992), 2063-112, 2085-86, 2106.

[33] See the topic "Hypodescent" in *Chapter 6. Features of the Endogamous Color Line* for an explanation of this term coined by Marvin Harris.

[34] 3 H. & McH. 504.

[35] Theodore Allen, *The Invention of the White Race*, 2 vols. (London, 1994) 2:158-59, 328.

[36] Werner Sollors, *Neither Black Nor White Yet Both* (Cambridge, 1997), 396-97.

[37] David Steven Cohen, *The Ramapo Mountain People* (New Brunswick NJ, 1974).

the most lucrative crop ever known, as smoking swept the Old World. New foods like tomatoes, potatoes, corn, lima beans, were served in the best homes in Europe. The old languages absorbed new words like *hurricane* and *tomahawk*. Previously unknown creatures, like opossums, raccoons, and turkeys filled the zoos. Shakespeare's plays abound with references to the mysterious and fascinating New World. Novels and stage musicals were set in the exotic "Indies." And yet, Europeans never seemed to grasp the colonial notion that Afro-European intermarriage was to be prevented.

England's highest social level welcomed Afro-European intermarriage as late as 1761. According to PBS Frontline historian Mario Valdes y Cocom, King George III's wife of more than 50 years, Charlotte Sophia of Mecklenburg-Strelitz, whom he wed in that year, was openly biracial, a dark noblewoman descended from Margarita de Castro y Sousa, of the Afro-European branch of the Portuguese Royal House. Her biracial features are clear in contemporary portraits, the most famous being the one by Sir Allan Ramsay.

Figure 16. Queen Charlotte

Two centuries later, according to Valdes y Cocom, during Queen Elizabeth II's coronation, the Royal Household referred to the present queen's African bloodline (through her ancestor, Queen Charlotte) in a white paper it published defending her

position as head of the Commonwealth.[38] The point, of course, is
not whether Queen Charlotte actually had recent African ances-

Dido Elizabeth Lindsey and her Cousin Lady Murray

Figure 17. Dido Lindsey

try. (As explained in "Chapter 2. Afro-
European Genetic Admixture in the
United States," millions of people un-
knowingly do.) It is that such a possibility was once welcomed and not
seen as disgraceful.

Similarly, Dido Lindsey was a family member in the
household of William Murray, first Earl of Mansfield and
Speaker of the House of Lords. She was the biracial daughter of
Mansfield's nephew, Rear Admiral Sir John Lindsey, and an Af-
rican-born woman that the naval officer met in Cuba. Dido appears in several contemporary paintings, the most famous being
one by Zoffany, the court painter to the royal family, for whom
Queen Charlotte sat on a number of occasions.[39]

Incidentally, Lord Mansfield was the man who ended
slavery in England when, as Chief Justice of the King's Supreme
Court in 1773, he ruled it unconstitutional. His ruling that, "the
air of England is too pure for a slave to breathe, and so everyone
who breathes it becomes free. Everyone who comes to this island is entitled to the protection of English law, whatever oppression he may have suffered and whatever may be the colour
of his skin," meant that thenceforth, any slave would become
free the instant he or she set foot on English soil. Lord Mansfield's words are still memorized by British schoolchildren today. William Cowper (1731-1800) made a poem out of this ruling:

---

[38] University of Chicago, ed. *The New Encyclopaedia Britannica*, 15 ed.
(Chicago, 1974) 7:1125; see also web page
www.pbs.org/wgbh/pages/frontline/shows/secret/famous/royalfamily.html.
Incidentally, despite the PBS Frontline documentary, the present author has
been unable to confirm that such a white paper was actually published. As
of September 2, 2004, the Royal Archivist at Windsor Castle was unable to
find any record of it.

[39] Hugh Thomas, *The Slave Trade: The Story of the Atlantic Slave Trade:
1440-1870* (New York, 1997) 471.

Slaves cannot breathe in England; if their lungs
Receive our air, that moment, they are free!
They touch our country and their shackles fall.

Figure 18. Lord Mansfield

To be sure, this was the same period when the idea of "racial" African inferiority spread among Enlightenment thinkers.
We can trace its spread during these years. Hobbes (1650, 1651)
never used the word "race" in the modern sense. To Locke
(1690), our species has different "stocks" of equal merit. The
first scholarly work identifying Africans as somehow unworthy
is the first volume of *Natural History* by George Louis Leclerc
de Buffon (1749).[40] Immanuel Kant (1775) solidified what became the nineteenth century concept of "degenerate" sub-human

---

[40] Thomas F. Gossett, *Race: The History of an Idea in America*, New ed.
(New York, 1997) 35.

Africans.[41] Finally, Blumenbach (1791) (who invented the term later used to denote white folks, based on the most beautiful skull in his collection—one from the Caucasus mountains) was the first European to speak of different "races" in the modern sense.[42] But none of this relates directly to the social enforcement of a compulsorily endogamous color line. That particular innovation was unique to British North America three centuries ago, and remains so to this day.

* * * * *

This chapter explained when, where, and how America's endogamous color line was invented. It showed that through most of the seventeenth century, colonists of African and European ancestries intermingled and intermarried within all three social classes. It showed that, although there may have been early hints that Americans were becoming conscious of "racial" differences in the 1670s, the law of 1691 outlawing intermarriage struck like a thunderclap and drove refugees fleeing from colony to colony. The outlawing of intermarriage never spread to Europe, and so the U.S. endogamous color line remained unique.

---

[41] See Kant's *On the Different Races of Men* pp. 160-64 as quoted in Ivan Hannaford, *Race: The History of an Idea in the West* (Baltimore, 1996) 218-22.

[42] Hannaford (1996); Gossett (1997); Audrey Smedley, *Race in North America: Origin and Evolution of a Worldview*, 2nd ed. (Boulder, 1999), 27.

Chapter 8.
Why Did Virginia's Rulers Invent a Color Line?

About 3,750 years ago, speakers of Indo-European languages who called themselves *Aryans* migrated into India from the northwest, displacing the speakers of Dravidian languages who had inhabited the subcontinent since the Neolithic revolution.[1] The written history of the Aryan newcomers, the *Rig-Veda*, describes this replacement as the military conquest of savage tribes by civilized people. But this image is not supported by archaeology. Instead, the Dravidian Indus Valley civilization was a highly developed urban culture with labor specialization and literature. Mohenjo-daro and Harappa were the society's most advanced and well-excavated cities. Nevertheless, the Indo-Aryans were more advanced militarily. Despite the high level of Dravidian civilization, their culture collapsed and they were conquered by the Aryans, who occupied and ruled India thenceforth.[2] Only the Aryan records of this conquest survive, since

---

[1] Originally meaning "plowman," the term *Aryan* later came to denote "noble" in Sanskrit. Unfortunately for the historian, the Nazis' co-opting of a pseudo-history of India by Houston Stewart Chamberlain (1855-1927) to devise a mythology of an Aryan super-race, gave the term *Aryan* a bad smell and has thereby tainted subsequent discussions of these events.

[2] "History of the Indian Subcontinent" in University of Chicago, ed. *The New Encyclopaedia Britannica*, 15 ed. (Chicago, 1974), 9:334-46; "Dravid-

Dravidian script is still undecipherable whereas Aryan writing (Sanskrit) is easily read, being the ancestor of English (and German, Latin, Greek, Russian, etc.).

The Dravidians were not exterminated. They were enslaved. They were forced to labor for their conquerors, and their mixed descendants were allowed only limited opportunities to rise in Aryan society. In order to keep their forced laborers under control, elite Aryans introduced Hinduism and its caste system.

The Hindu caste system delineates four endogamous groups (*varna*). These are: priests (*Brahmana*), warriors (*Ksatriya*), farmers and merchants (*Vaisya*), and menial laborers (*Sudra*). Priests as well as rulers enforced the three endogamous barriers separating the four groups. The top three castes were reserved for Aryans and for the children of those few male Aryans who were socially powerful enough to defy the system and sire children upon Dravidian females. Unmixed Dravidians were consigned to the lowest caste, along with the despised children of lower-caste fathers and higher-caste mothers. Centuries later, Hindu society added a fifth group, the outcasts or untouchables (*Achuta* or *Harijana*), relegated to the most unclean tasks (burying the dead, unclogging latrines, slaughtering animals).[3]

Thousands of years ago, the Hindu endogamous barriers were erected to stabilize a stratified society and to prevent alliances that might overthrow rulers. The system has endured for nearly four millennia without being toppled. On paper, the modern nation of India repealed the caste system decades ago. Nevertheless, the four castes remain as endogamous as ever, and their associated civil liabilities remain as strong as ever.[4]

*   *   *   *   *

As explained in the previous chapter, a successful endogamous barrier between those of African descent and those of

---

ian Local Race" in *Britannica*, 15 ed. (1974), iii:658; "Human Populations" in *Britannica*, 15 ed. (1974), 14:846; *Britannica*, 15 ed. (1974), 15:361.

[3] "Hinduism" in *Britannica*, 15 ed. (1974), 8:903.

[4] Tom O'Neill, "Untouchables," *National Geographic*, June 2003, 2-31.

European descent appeared only once in history—in the Chesapeake around the turn of the eighteenth century. It had never arisen before, anywhere else on earth. And, although it gradually spread through British North America over the next half-century, an endogamous color line has never arisen since.

Two questions are irresistible. Why was the endogamous color line invented in the Chesapeake and nowhere else? Why was it invented at the turn of the eighteenth century and not before nor after? This chapter presents several theories. *It Was a "Divide and Conquer" Tactic* suggests that it was a deliberately calculated solution to a unique problem of: too few yeomen, too many European laborers, and too little time. *Other Voices* presents a collection of alternative theories including: fair-skinned people have an instinctive loathing for those with dark skin tone, people of certain religions or cultures were taught to reject Africans, and it was related to the numbers of European women.

It was a "Divide and Conquer" Tactic

For decades, forced laborers had fled the Chesapeake. The first person known to have his servitude extended for trying to escape was English bound laborer John Joyce, in August 1623. He was also whipped with thirty strokes of the lash.[5] Thousands fled into the forests, some singly, some in small multiracial bands of two to ten. During 1676, the watershed year of Bacon's rebellion, between 880 and 890 laborers of every ancestry fled Virginia in large groups.[6] Most were soon recaptured by Native Americans and returned in chains. But others succeeded in getting away. They created the maroon communities of the Cumberland Plateau which have survived to this day.[7]

Others committed suicide rather than endure the unendurable. In October 1656, Thomas, an Irishman owned by John

---

[5] Theodore Allen, *The Invention of the White Race*, 2 vols. (London, 1994), 2:108.

[6] Ibid., 2:153.

[7] For an overview, see "The Maroon Escape Hatch" in *Chapter 5. The Rate of Black-to-White "Passing."*

Custis slashed his own throat and threw himself down a well. Another coerced worker "willfully Cast himself away" in a creek near his owner's Westmoreland County plantation during a period when tobacco prices were low and laborers were being left to die of famine (the seventeenth-century version of downsizing). That same year, Cork County servant Walter Catford "for want of Grace tooke a Grind stone and a Roape and tyed it around his Middle and Crosse his thighs and most barbarously went and drowned himselfe contrary to the Laws of the King and this Country."[8]

Others turned their despair into attacks on their owners. In 1658, English servant Huntington Ayres killed his owner and the owner's wife with a "lathing hammer" as they slept. In 1671, three Elke River workers (two English and one African) axed their owner, John Hawkins, to death. They were hanged, as were those whose attacks had less success. Englishman Charles Rogers took a hoe to his Norfolk County owner in August 1666, as did Lancaster County African William Page in 1671. The latter had previously warned, "God damn him. If [the owner] strock him again he would beat out his braynes." In 1672, Northampton County Portuguese laborer Nicolas Silvio attacked his owner John Savage. In 1687, African John Parris set fire to the plantation before running away.[9]

To the landlords, the most threatening form of defiance was armed revolt. Virginia planters knew that in 1634 Barbados, 800 forced laborers revolted and were quelled only after pitched battles against English troops. In 1648, it was reported that, "many hundreds of Rebell negro slaves were in the woods." Among four major revolt plots that shook the island between 1675 and 1701, African and European workers launched a failed 1686 rebellion, and a biracial conspiracy tried to seize the fortress at Bridgetown in 1692. Rebellion was also a permanent

---

[8] Allen (1994), 2:149-51.

[9] The quotes are taken from the summary of coerced labor resistance in Allen (1994), 2:149-51. For additional accounts, see Lerone Bennett Jr., *The Shaping of Black America* (Chicago, 1975), 39-57 and Edmund Sears Morgan, *American Slavery, American Freedom: The Ordeal of Colonial Virginia* (New York, 1975), 235-49.

feature of Jamaica. When the Spanish left in 1655, about 1,500 forced laborers escaped to the mountains. They became the Jamaica maroons, who fought the British, on and off, until 1796.[10] According to Richard Price, "for more than four centuries, the communities formed by... [self-liberated laborers] dotted the fringes of plantation America, from Brazil to the southeastern United States, from Peru to the American Southwest." They "struck directly at the foundation of the plantation system, presenting military and economic threats that often taxed the colonists to their very limits."[11] A maroon community led by Yanga, an African of reputed royal rank, was founded in the mountains near Vera Cruz and successfully negotiated its right to exist in 1580 after defeating the Spanish military force sent to destroy it. Another supposedly African king, Domingo Biolto, similarly founded San Basilio, Colombia, and won its freedom in 1619. The maroon settlement of Palmares in Bahia fought off Brazilian troops for 122 years (1575-1694) before succumbing to overwhelming military force after a six-week siege.[12] Meanwhile, back in Virginia, the Lawnes Creek Mutiny was put down in 1673. It served notice that full-scale revolt was imminent.[13]

Three years later, the Virginia planters' nightmare came to life. Bacon's Rebellion of 1676 began as a war of Amerind extermination, but soon became a massive uprising of coerced laborers. In its last nine months, thousands of African, European, and mixed forced laborers captured weapons and crushed the gentry's small militia. A half-century earlier, in 1624, Captain John Smith had predicted that basing his colony on forced labor was bound to "bring... [Virginia] to misery."[14] His prophesy seemed to be coming true. The siege of Jamestown lasted until British regulars arrived from Europe and rescued Governor Berkeley. The landowners promised amnesty if no more blood

---

[10] Allen (1994) 2:224-26.

[11] Richard Price, *Maroon Societies: Rebel Slave Communities in the Americas*, [1st] ed. (Garden City NY, 1973), 2, 3.

[12] Allen (1994), 2:149, 261-62.

[13] Ibid., 2:160.

[14] As quoted in Allen (1994), 2:203.

was shed, then (to the king's disgust) promptly hanged 23 rebel leaders when they surrendered.[15]

Virginia was not unique in being under the threat of rebellion by forced laborers. All New World colonies ran the risk of servile insurrection. All needed to have sufficient yeomen (landowning subsistence farmers available to take up arms) to deter or quickly crush a slave uprising. Many home governments had promised to send regular army troops if an insurrection ever got out of hand. But this still meant that the landlords and their loyal yeomen would have to hold out under siege for the weeks that it would take military rescuers to cross the Atlantic.[16] Furthermore, every early New World colony seemed to be run by profit-hungry landlords who regularly drove their forced laborers to starvation. In short, they were tinderboxes of servile revolt. By the middle of the seventeenth century, it was clear to all colonial masters that risk of insurrection had to be taken seriously. Not only was it necessary to deter runaways by making examples of those caught, but it was also vital to deter revolts by keeping on hand a traditionally large buffer class of armed yeomen.

The challenge faced by colonial rulers was that the buffer class had to be roughly as numerous as the colony's forced labor population, and the forced laborers themselves were its only possible source. Like it or not, every New World colony lacking sufficient yeomen had to transform at least half of its forced laborers into landed yeomen if it was to survive. Each colony adopted a solution that suited its own particular situation. How they went about it reveals something important. Each strategy was carefully crafted by men who found a way to maximize profit, given their colony's peculiar circumstance.

For several reasons, few of the forced laborers in Iberian New World colonies were of European ancestry. Portuguese colonies used Africans. Spanish colonies used Africans plus

---

[15] R. Ernest Dupuy and Trevor N. Dupuy, *The Harper Encyclopedia of Military History*, 4 ed. (New York, 1993), 660; Allen (1994), 203-22; Edmund Sears Morgan, *American Slavery, American Freedom: The Ordeal of Colonial Virginia* (New York, 1975), 268.

[16] Allen (1994), 2:97-116; Audrey Smedley, *Race in North America: Origin and Evolution of a Worldview*, 2nd ed. (Boulder, 1999), 104.

comparable numbers of Amerinds (where they did not simply exterminate the latter, as in the Caribbean). But Iberians had a centuries-long tradition of accepting Africans into mainstream society (the Almoravid Empire had stretched from Senegambia to Barcelona). They thus created the continuum societies of Latin America, three-class societies that, to this day, are of Afro-European genetic admixture from top to bottom, small copies of sixteenth-century Spain and Portugal.

Planters in the British and French West Indies also had been unable to periodically repopulate their European workers as often as they could acquire new Africans. Their proportion of European forced laborers was larger than that of the Iberian colonies. Nevertheless, most of their laborers were also Africans. But neither Holland, France, nor England had any tradition of accepting Africans into mainstream society. Rulers were unsure of the future loyalty of African yeomen. So planters and the few yeomen were ordered or encouraged to beget children upon servant or slave women, expand the already growing biracial population, and select their own children as new yeomen. They thus created the three-caste societies common to most colonial empires—White rulers, Coloured yeomen, and Black laborers.

Virginia was unique in its demographic mix. Virginia alone had too many European forced laborers to adopt such solutions. Jamestown had been a dumping ground for British (including Scots and Irish) poor, landless, homeless, and criminals. Unlike Massachusetts, Chesapeake plantations were too lucrative to be abandoned to subsistence farmers, and yet over half of their forced laborers were of European descent. They had waited too long to adopt the British West Indies solution of creating a biracial yeoman class in the next generation. With too many European workers to take the Spanish approach, Virginia alone found it useful to adopt a divide-and-rule strategy.

At the turn of the eighteenth century, Virginia's rulers faced a problem that no other New World colony had ever faced before, nor ever would again. They had about 15,000 adult colonists. Of these, roughly 9,000 were involuntary laborers. About 7,000 of the 9,000 Virginians held in bondage were of European descent and 2,000 were of Native American and/or African ancestry.[17] In order to suppress rebellion, Virginia had to create a free yeoman class virtually overnight. They did not have enough time to grow one. They did not even have time to train one. Somehow, they had to split about 5,000 instantly recognizable yeomen from the total forced-labor population, so as to wind up with just as many Virginians with a stake in suppressing servile insurrection as there were in fomenting it. Again, what was unique was that 7,000 of the 9,000 Virginians held in bondage were Europeans.[18]

The Virginia Assembly's solution was to drive a wedge vertically through the three existing social ranks: planters, yeomen, and forced laborers. Once separated, the Whites (a newly coined term for people of mainly European ancestry) would become the new upper endogamous group, keeping Blacks (the newly invented lower endogamous group) permanently in check. The gentry foresaw that all members of the White group would eventually rise socially to become free Englishmen. All members of the Black group would eventually descend to become slaves.[19]

At first, human nature threatened to make a mockery of the plan. Ordinary Virginians did not yet perceive those few physical features that differ between Europeans and Africans as indicating "otherness."[20] How could the rulers successfully split African from European when the population was quickly becom-

---

[17] Allen (1994) 2:218; Edmund Sears Morgan, *American Slavery, American Freedom: The Ordeal of Colonial Virginia* (New York, 1975) 395-432; Joel Williamson, *New People: Miscegenation and Mulattoes in the United States* (New York, 1980), 7.

[18] Idem.

[19] Morgan (1975), 328; Allen (1994), 2:240; T. H. Breen and Stephen Innes, *"Myne Owne Ground": Race and Freedom on Virginia's Eastern Shore, 1640-1676* (New York, 1980).

[20] Kathleen M. Brown, *Good Wives, Nasty Wenches, and Anxious Patriarchs: Gender, Race, and Power in Colonial Virginia* (Chapel Hill, 1996), 215.

ing mixed Afro-European through intermarriage?[21] The legislative solution passed in 1691 was to criminalize intermarriage.[22]

Not everyone in government thought an endogamous color line a good idea. Virginia's Attorney General Richard West wrote to his superiors in London, the Lords of Trade and Plantations. He expressed misgivings about interfering with the Christian tradition that marriage was a sacrament between a pledged couple and their God. For his part, Governor General William Gooch advocated criminalizing marriage between servants of European and African ancestry.[23] Gooch feared the eruption of another bloody servile insurrection, a replay of Bacon's Rebellion in 1676.

As Gooch explained in his own 1723 letter to the Lords of Trade and Plantation, the new endogamous color line depended on colonists' being "sensible that a distinction ought to be made between [Black] offspring and the descendants of an Englishman." Gooch spelled out that Virginia's necessary, but still weak color line was in jeopardy from biracial colonists, who were "descended from a white Father or Mother." And so, he wrote, making intermarriage illegal was contrived "as a way of discouraging that kind of copulation."[24]

In short, this theory says that the endogamous color line was designed to avert servile insurrection at a unique time and place. It was the only time and place with more forced laborers of European descent than of African descent. Virginia was the only New World colony where such a method of permanently splitting potential insurrectionist allies could have worked. No other colony would have benefited from splitting Europeans from Africans by an endogamous barrier. This is because no other colony, whether British, French, Dutch, Spanish, or Portu-

---

[21] Ibid., 206.

[22] Paul Finkelman, "The Crime of Color," *Tulane Law Review*, 67 (no. 6, 1992), 2063-112, 2086.

[23] Allen (1994), 2:248.

[24] As quoted in Allen (1994), 2:241-42; also see Audrey Smedley, *Race in North America: Origin and Evolution of a Worldview*, 2nd ed. (Boulder, 1999), 145.

guese, had such a high fraction (more than half) of European forced laborers. None could benefit by preventing mixing between Europeans and Africans, and so none had to criminalize intermarriage.Consequently, none ever needed to invent or enforce an endogamous color line.[25]

The strength of this theory is that it starts from the two pivotal facts that we know unambiguously. First, the endogamous color line was (and remains) unique to British North America. Second, Virginia's rulers implemented it deliberately via 1691 legislation, followed by ruthless enforcement lasting generations. To explain why they did it, this theory accepts the words of the decision-makers themselves. They claimed that they did it in order to prevent a servile insurrection by an alliance of European and African forced laborers. Among scholars who support this explanation are: Allen, Bennett, Breen, Harris, Morgan, Morner, and Smedley.[26]

Other Voices

The "divide and conquer" theory is said to have six weaknesses. It skips the fact that Virginia's military governors used a well-known tactic. It skips the role of the church. It fails to explain why Spaniards did not need a yeoman class. It does not connect attitudes to numbers of European women. It does not explain why the endogamous color line was so easily accepted by North American colonies (like Massachusetts, for example) that had no risk of servile insurrection. Finally, it traces horrific results to a trivial cause.

It skips the fact that Virginia's military governors used a well-known tactic. This somehow suggests that they invented "divide and conquer" on their own. In fact, neither Attoney-

---

[25] George M. Fredrickson, *White Supremacy: A Comparative Study in American and South African History* (New York, 1981b), Chapter 11.

[26] Allen (1994); Bennett (1975); Breen (1980); Marvin Harris, *Patterns of Race in the Americas* (Westport CT, 1964); Morgan (1975); Magnus Morner, *Race Mixture in the History of Latin America* (Boston, 1967); Smedley (1999).

General Richard West, Governor-General William Gooch, nor Governor-General William Berkeley—the governor who had come close to being hanged when Bacon's Rebellion almost transformed Virginia into a maroon colony—originated the idea of an enforced endogamous barrier as a way of preventing an insurrection alliance of subjugated groups. The tactic was well-known and of ancient usage among military governors. The British later used the technique in their treaty with the Jamaica Maroons whose 1,500 ancestors had fled slavery nearly a century before. The treaty guaranteed the Maroons their lands and freedom in return for their promise to crush any future slave uprisings without British army help. Indeed, a militarily enforced endogamous barrier between Protestants and Catholics had been applied earlier in mid 17-century Ireland by some of the very same men who applied it later in the Chesapeake. They merely adopted it from their predecessors as a way of discouraging rebellious alliances.

Their immediate predecessors were the Roundheads in Ireland. They copied the idea from Oliver Cromwell's successful crushing of Irish resistance. The English in Ireland had to quell a new rebellion every few generations. Conquering landlords married conquered women, who then raised their sons in the Irish culture. The Irish descendants of English invaders—Catholics and Protestants alike—would ultimately rebel against English rule in their turn. Ireland suffered under ever-repeating cycles of conquest, intermarriage, and revolt. Cromwell's men found a permanent solution. They made intermarriage between Protestant English landlords and Catholic Irish serfs a crime.[27]

And yet when you come down to it, Cromwell's officers did not invent enforced endogamy to suppress insurrection alliance either. Just thirty years before Cromwell's 1649 invasion of Ireland, the first East India Company ships returned from Surat, Gujarat—from the court of the Mughal Emperor, Jahangir.[28] They docked in London bringing wondrous tales of a Hindu

---

[27] Allen (1994), volume 1.

[28] University of Chicago, ed. *The New Encyclopaedia Britannica*, 15 ed. (Chicago, 1974), iii:762, ix: 687.

caste system, invented 3,400 years before to accomplish that very same goal—avoiding joint insurrection by averting the birth of people with dual heritage (Aryans and Dravidians in the Hindu case).[29] In fact, one could probably find cases of "divide and conquer" stretching back into the mists of time. It is why the phrase rings a bell, after all.

It skips the role of the church. An alliance between the Catholic Church and the Spanish Crown fought and won a centuries-long struggle against local elites to defend and maintain the humanity of both Amerinds and Africans against inhumane treatment. They were inspired by Las Casas's writings in favor of Indian rights. In the same manner, independent, London-appointed clergymen in Barbados undermined planter goals by surreptitiously flouting laws forbidding them to baptize African slaves.[30] Other colonies had similar experiences. Churches throughout the New World resisted the ostracism of any group of God's children. Church resistance thereby defeated or softened planter-imposed systems of segregation in Jamaica, Trinidad, Montserrat, St. Kitts, and Nevis. Ethical religious leaders of many denominations foresaw the destructive legacy that such a society-sundering tactic would leave behind.

Virginia's church, in contrast, supported the color line. This was the result of a chain of events that involved the dissolution of the Virginia Company in 1624, the deaths of local bishops, and the financial poverty of the Anglican Church consequent to the English Civil War. The church in England lacked the funds to appoint new bishops and ship them to the colonies. Consequently, Virginia gentry seized the authority to appoint or fire ministers and no independent religious organization was ever allowed to form in the seventeenth-century Chesapeake.[31]

---

[29] Ibid., 9:334-46,

[30] Lila E. Salazar, *Love Child: A Genealogist's Guide to the Social History of Barbados* (St. Michael, Barbados, 2000), 38-40.

[31] An excellent account of the overwhelming power of the Catholic Church in Iberian colonies as well as of the chain of events that handed clerical power to the landed gentry in Virginia can be found in Herbert S. Klein, "Anglicanism, Catholicism, and the Negro Slave," in *Slavery in the New*

In the end, Virginia was the only British colony where planters controlled who was allowed to preach. And Virginia was also the only British colony where the clergy, whose jobs were at stake, followed planter orders and preached against intermarriage and in support of a forcibly endogamous color line.[32]

Some have taken a different approach to analyzing the impact of religion on the color line. They suggest that, since the endogamous color line was devised by Protestant Englishmen rather than by Catholic Spaniards, it must have had something to do with the Reformation. The problem here is that Catholic Marylanders joined with Protestant Virginians in enforcing the endogamous barrier, while Protestant colonists in the British West Indies intermarried as consistently as Catholic colonists in the Spanish and French West Indies. Indeed, the flaw in all theories that seek explanations by contrasting Englishmen with Spaniards is that the world is much vaster than either. Neither pre-reformation Europeans, Muslims, the people of the Indian Ocean, nor Englishmen outside North America ever felt the need for an endogamous barrier between Europeans and Africans.

It fails to explain why Spaniards did not need a yeoman class. Where Virginia's governors decreed a forcibly endogamous color line, the Spanish crown explicitly allowed colonists to intermarry. On October 9, 1514, Habsburg Holy Roman Emperor Charles V decreed a Spanish law that explicitly permitted intermarriage between Spaniards and Indians. The law was reenacted in 1515 and 1556. No mention was made regarding intermarriage with Africans, since intermarriage between free Christian Iberians and free Muslim Africans had been common for many centuries.[33] On May 11, 1527, a Spanish royal decree ruled that marriages between African slaves were of equal valid-

---

World: A Reader in Comparative History, ed. Laura Foner and Eugene D. Genovese (Englewood Cliffs NJ, 1969b), 138-66.

[32] Bennett (1975), 71; Allen (1994), 1:21.

[33] Werner Sollors, *Neither Black Nor White Yet Both* (Cambridge, 1997), 395. It should be noted that, two centuries later, during the Bourbon period, Spanish imperial law changed to require permission for intermarriage. Also, the extent to which Spanish imperial laws were obeyed varied dramatically over time and place.

ity as between free Africans and Spaniards, and encouraged them.[34]

Spanish colonists did not need to create a yeoman class because they took over existing stratified imperial civilizations. British colonists in Virginia brought civilization to a land populated by pre-literate hunter-gatherers and early agriculturalists. They had to create a three-tier society (planter, yeoman, forced laborer) from scratch, and so they had to establish the social controls necessary to stabilizing and preserving such a structure. The Spanish hidalgos, in contrast, insinuated themselves into two geographically huge, militarily powerful, and organizationally advanced (though technologically retarded) empires. The hidalgos exterminated the indigenous aristocracies of the Aztecs and Incas, and took their places, leaving their social structures untouched. They married females of the indigenous nobility in order to legitimize their rule.

The crown explicitly authorized intermixing in the New World in order to merge the nobilities of Spain with those of the native civilizations. That they succeeded in merging these nobilities through intermarriage is clear in the following statement by one of Cortez's soldiers:

> Before I go any further, I wish to say about the Cacica the daughter of Xicotenga, who was named Doña Luisa and was given to Pedro de Alvarado, that when they gave her to him all the greater part of Tlaxcala paid reverence to her, and gave her presents, and looked on her as their mistress, and Pedro de Alvarado, who was then a bachelor, had a son by her named Don Pedro and a daughter named Doña Leonor, who is now the wife of Don Francisco de la Cueva, a nobleman, and a cousin of the Duke of Albuquerque, who had by her four or five sons, very good gentlemen.[35]

It does not connect attitudes to numbers of European women. That America's uniqueness had something to do with

---

[34] Idem. Again, Spanish laws changed two centuries later and were often ignored.

[35] Bernal Diaz del Castillo and J. M. Cohen, *The Conquest of New Spain* (Baltimore,, 1963), 156.

the presence or absence of women is a misunderstanding. Some suggest that Virginia's rulers forbade Afro-European intermarriage because they had so many English women that they did not need to marry Africans.[36] Others say that Virginia's rulers forbade intermarriage because they had so few English women, that they wanted to keep those few to themselves.[37] Some writers claim both, writing on one page that Virginia had fewer White women than did other New World colonies, and on another page that it had more. In fact, detailed studies show that Virginia had about the same proportion of English women as the other British colonies in the West Indies, who intermarried freely. Until 1620, White women were generally unavailable either in Virginia or in the British West Indies, and English males often "took recourse" to Indian or African women.[38] Furthermore, even the earliest Spanish conquerors brought their wives on their military campaigns, and subsequent shiploads of immigrants from Spain to the New World (amounting to 200,000-300,000 souls during the sixteenth century alone) carried roughly equal numbers of males and females.[39] The explanation for Virginia's uniqueness must rest on something other than too many or too few European women.

It does not explain why the endogamous color line was so easily accepted by North American British colonies that had no risk of servile insurrection. As mentioned earlier, within a few decades after 1691 Virginia, other colonies also

---

[36] Smedley (1999) 140.

[37] Morgan (1975) 336.

[38] Gary B. Nash, *Red, White, and Black: The Peoples of Early America*, 2nd ed. (Englewood Cliffs NJ, 1982) 276.

[39] For accounts of the wives of Cortez's officers, see Bernal Diaz del Castillo and J. M. Cohen, *The Conquest of New Spain* (Baltimore,, 1963), 320. For numbers of Spanish colonists, see Murdo J. MacLeod, "Spain and America: The Atlantic Trade 1492-1720," in *The Cambridge History of Latin America: Colonial Latin America*, ed. Leslie Bethell (Cambridge UK, 1984), 341-88, 356. For ratio of female to male Spanish colonists, see Analola Borges "La mujer pobladora en los origenes americanos," *Anuario de Estudios Americanos*, 29 (1972) 389-444 or Peter Boyd-Bowman, "Patterns of Spanish Emigration to the Indies until 1600," *Hispanic American Historical Review*, 56 (no. 4/November, 1976), 580-604.

decreed forcibly endogamous color lines: Massachusetts in 1705, North Carolina in 1715, Delaware in 1721, Pennsylvania in 1725.[40] With this in mind, some scholars suggest that British North American colonists were "primed" somehow by instinct to de-humanize Africans and see them as the "other."[41]

Winthrop Jordan, one of the most influential historians of U.S. racialism, says that Negroes are an "incipient sub-species,"[42] and claims that horror of intermarriage and passing arises from within the White psyche as an instinctive dislike of people with dark skin tone.[43] Social intolerance, he suggests, is like word usage. Englishmen, according to Jordan, could not help harboring an instinctive loathing of Blacks because:

> No other color except white conveyed so much emotional impact. As described in the *Oxford English Dictionary*, the meaning of *black* before the sixteenth century included, "Deeply stained with dirt; soiled, dirty, foul.... Having dark or deadly purposes, malignant; pertaining to or involving death; baneful, disastrous, sinister.... Foul, iniquitous, atrocious, horrible, wicked.... Indicating disgrace, censure, liability to punishment, etc." Black was an emotionally partisan color, the handmaid and symbol of baseness and evil, a sign of danger and repulsion.[44]

Jordan further explains "inchoate" British disgust at dark skin tone by comparing it to Englishmen's reaction to apes, nudity, lust, debauchery, and Shakespeare's *Othello*. Jordan presents the past as a conflict between Evil (enslavement and degradation of poor benighted beasts) and Good (compassion for helpless, less advanced creatures). These two elemental forces wrestle for control of the Anglo-Saxon psyche. In the end, Jordan assures us that hope still arises that the White man can "turn

---

[40] Sollors (1997), 396-97.

[41] See "The Instinctive Need to See 'Otherness'" in *Chapter 4. The Perception of "Racial" Traits.*

[42] Winthrop D. Jordan, *White Over Black: American Attitudes Toward the Negro, 1550-1812* (Chapel Hill, 1968) 584.

[43] Jordan (1968) 582-84.

[44] Ibid., 7.

to stare at the animal within him" and "recognize that what had happened and was still happening with himself and the Negro in America,... [and so] he might set foot on a better road."[45] Many other scholars, like Jordan, have found evidence of "race" consciousness among Europeans earlier than 1691. Among them are: Kathleen Brown, David Eltis, Oscar and Mary Handlin, and Richard Williams.[46]

The two drawbacks of these explanations are complementary. First, no evidence exists of a pre-1691 endogamous color line. Second, in order to collect evidence, one must broaden the meaning of "racism" to include virtually any inter-ethnic disdain. The notion that the endogamous color line came about because the terms "white" and "black" had previous connotations misses the fact that those terms were not applied to Europeans and Africans (*Christians* and *heathens*, in seventeenth-century phrasing) until after the color line was invented. The suggestion that when Europeans first saw Black people during Elizabethan times, they were doomed to instinctive revulsion, founders on the ubiquity of prior Afro-European contact. Africans had been steadily imported across the Mediterranean since ancient times. At least one Roman emperor—Pescennius Niger—was very dark indeed.[47] Fifteenth-century Flemish paintings of busy street scenes depict as many Blacks as in today's Brussels.[48] And upper-class ancient Egyptian portraits reveal a skin-tone range as great as in downtown Cairo today.[49]

---

[45] Ibid., 582.

[46] Kathleen M. Brown, *Good Wives, Nasty Wenches, and Anxious Patriarchs: Gender, Race, and Power in Colonial Virginia* (Chapel Hill, 1996); David Eltis, *The Rise of African Slavery in the Americas* (Cambridge UK, 2000); Oscar Handlin and Mary F. Handlin, "Origins of the Southern Labor System," *William and Mary Quarterly*, 7 (no. 2, April 1950), 199-222; Richard Williams, *Hierarchical Structures and Social Value: The Creation of Black and Irish Identities in the United States* (Cambridge UK, 1990).

[47] J.A. Rogers, *Sex and Race*, 3 vols. (St. Petersburg, Fla., 1944), 1:86.

[48] See the 1504 Hieronymus Bosch triptych "The Garden of Earthly Delight"

[49] See, for instance, the Old Kingdom, early Fourth Dynasty statues depicting Prince Rahotep and his Consort Nefret. He is dark brown. She is light

Regarding pre-1691 evidence of "race" consciousness, opposing groups have dehumanized each other since the dawn of history. According to the Aryan Rig-veda, their god Indra blew "away with supernatural might from earth and from the heavens the black skin which Indra hates." They wrote how Indra "slew the flat-nosed barbarians" and decreed that the foe was to be "flayed of his black skin."[50] Han Dynasty Chinese historians in the third century B.C. told of a yellow-haired, green-eyed people in a distant province "who greatly resemble the monkeys from whom they descend." From 1350 B.C., Egyptian paintings depict lower Nile peoples with red bodies, those from the east (Semites, Hittites) as being yellow, those from upper Egypt as white, and Nubians as black. When lighter Egyptians were in power, they referred to the subordinate group as "the evil dark-skinned race of Ish." When darker Egyptians dominated, they called the conquered "the pale, degraded race of Arvad."[51] Even the biblical prophet Jeremiah asked, "Can the Ethiopian change his skin or the Leopard his spots?"[52] Medieval Europeans invented the idea that the biblical Ham was African. Elizabethans fretted over interracial marriage. Some Virginians taxed some Africans by 1645. Slaveowners morally justified lifelong hereditary forced labor by the inferiority of their victims as early as in 1662. Ronald Takaki, traces "racism" to the age of European conquest, colonization, and exploitation and asserts that European colonization itself was a manifestation of capitalism, and so a "racist" project by its very nature.[53]

Nevertheless, this book section is neither about "racism" nor "racial consciousness." It is about people deprived of their lives, their liberty, or their property as society's punishment for

---

pink P.P. Kahane, *Ancient and Classical Art*, ed. Hans L. C. Jaffe, 6 vols., vol. 1 (New York, 1967), 1:47.

[50] Thomas F. Gossett, *Race: The History of an Idea in America*, New ed. (New York, 1997) 3-4.

[51] Ibid., 4-16.

[52] Jeremiah, 13:23.

[53] Ronald T. Takaki, *Iron Cages: Race and Culture in Nineteenth-Century America*, Revised ed. (New York, 2000), 11-12.

their marrying someone of the same nationality, class, religion, and language, but across an endogamous barrier separating those of African ancestry from those of European ancestry. This phenomenon was and is unique to British North America, and it emerged in 1691.[54] This study excludes as explanatory, those factors (ethnocentrism, slavery, exploitation, capitalism) that are ubiquitous. This study seeks to explain a phenomenon found only in the land that became the United States, and so it focuses upon precursor phenomena found only in the land that became the United States.

Finally, it traces horrific results to a trivial cause. The origin of the U.S. endogamous color line seems strange because we expect great results to emerge from great acts and trivial results from trivial acts. And yet here was an act that was done in an apparently off-hand manner, without serious forethought, just to keep some forced laborers under control. A few people, like Attorney-General West, worried about the long-term consequences. But the consensus was that an endogamous barrier was necessary to the colony's survival. The long-term consequences have been dreadful for the United States, of course. Worse yet, after three centuries of this bizarre social pathology, Americans are still coming up with fresh new rationalizations as to why it must be preserved for their grandchildren. Many scholars who research this tale feel the same way about it. It was a terrible decision by a few shortsighted men. It would somehow seem more satisfying if the U.S. endogamous color line had begun in some cataclysmic occurrence, a plague, or a war that slew millions, but there you have it. Trivial events sometimes have horrific consequences.

*   *   *   *   *

This chapter suggested: (1) That the endogamous color line was a consequence of planter-controlled governments outlawing intermarriage and brutally punishing offenders in the circa-1700 Chesapeake. (2) That the laws were passed in order

---

[54] Gossett (1997), 3.

to split potential servile insurrectionists. (3) That "race" consciousness, colonialism, capitalism, sexism, racism, and even slavery were incidental or peripheral to the main point because they appeared everywhere that Africans were carried, whereas the U.S. endogamous color line remains unique to this day. This means that the color-line-forming laws were not passed in order to consolidate power or dominance by one group over another beyond the obvious desire of the landed gentry to control their involuntary labor force. It means that Virginia ministers preached obedience to the law and revulsion towards Africans in demeaning terms, not because Virginia's ministers were wickeder than those in Cuba, Jamaica, Brazil, or Barbados, but because (in contrast to the latter groups) Virginia's preachers could be replaced by the local gentry. It means that U.S. popular culture originally adopted color-line endogamy (and its "black" and "white" terminology) in response to enforced laws, not as their cause.

Chapter 9.
How the Law Decided if You Were Black or White: The Early 1800s

In February of 1815, two young friends of John Adams traveled to Virginia, visited Monticello, and met Thomas Jefferson. Their names were George Ticknor and Francis Gray. Gray had never known slavery as an adult (which had ended 32 years earlier in his state of Massachusetts). He was fascinated that many of Jefferson's slaves looked European. He asked the former president how Virginians went about determining whether someone was Black or White (in the color-line sense), and how this determination related to slavery.[1] On March 4, 1815, Jefferson wrote a chatty 4-page letter in reply.[2] He explained that slavery and endogamous group membership were unrelated in Virginia law. On the one hand, mulattos were legally Black and the law defined "mulatto" as anyone with one or more "negro" grandparents. Jefferson thereupon filled two pages with mathematical equations to show that anyone with less that 1/4 African

---

[1] Joshua D. Rothman, *Notorious in the Neighborhood: Sex and Families Across the Color Line in Virginia, 1787-1861* (Chapel Hill, 2003), 47.

[2] Thomas Jefferson and others, *The Writings of Thomas Jefferson* (Washington DC, 1905). XIII: 268-71.

admixture was legally White.[3] On the other hand, slavery passed through the mother with no diminution regardless of ancestry, and had nothing to do with the color line. Only upon emancipation would a former slave's membership in either of America's endogamous groups become an issue. And so, Jefferson explained, specifically referring to one of his European-looking slaves, "if emancipated, he becomes a free *white* man [emphasis Jefferson's], and a citizen of the United States to all intents and purposes."[4]

Who was Jefferson talking about? The most European-looking slave in his household at the time was his own son: fair-complexioned, freckled, red-haired Eston Hemings.[5] Eston had, at most, 1/8 African genetic admixture. Eston's mother, Sally Hemings, was Jefferson's sister-in-law. She was his deceased wife's half-sister. She was the daughter of Jefferson's father-in-law, John Wayles, whose antecedents were all of one hundred percent European admixture, as far as anyone knows. Sally's mother, Betty Hemings, was the daughter of a Welsh sea captain named Hemings and an African woman.[6] Since Sally had one "negro" grandparent, she would have been legally Black even if

---

[3] For an explanation that Jefferson in fact interpreted the law correctly, see Paul Finkelman, "The Crime of Color," *Tulane Law Review*, 67 (no. 6, 1992), 2063-112, 2088, 2090.

[4] Idem. The quotation is from page 3 of the letter. A scanned-in picture of all four pages of the original letter can be viewed at URL <http://www.artsci.wustl.edu/~landc/html/tj_to_gray1.html>.

[5] That the Eston brothers were Jefferson's offspring is not essential to the point being made. But for the DNA evidence that persuaded the Thomas Jefferson Memorial Foundation, Inc. to acknowledge this paternity, see Daniel P. Jordan, "Statement on the TJMF Research Committee Report on Thomas Jefferson and Sally Hemings," (2000), 54.

[6] Although no portraits of Sally are known to have survived, judging by her twenty-five percent African genetic admixture she probably looked somewhat like Gloria Estefan or Rosie Perez. This point is important because one must have a rough idea of what people with different percentages of Afro-Euro genetic admixture look like in order to grasp the impact of the one-drop rule. Simply put, people with less than 20 percent African admixture look White to most Americans. See note 30 of *Chapter 3. The Heredity of "Racial" Traits* for details.

manumitted. But since her son Eston had only 1/8 African ancestry, Jefferson's prediction most likely applied to him.

When Jefferson died eleven years after writing the letter
to Francis Gray, his prediction was fulfilled. Eston Hemings was
freed by his father's will. He set up house in Charlottesville as a
White man. As Jefferson had foreseen, Hemings was accepted as
a member of the White endogamous group "and a citizen of the
United States." He was recorded as White in the Charlottesville
census of 1830.[7] He did not "pass for White" in the sense of deceiving anyone. There was no deception. Charlottesville had
only a few hundred residents at the time. Sally had moved in
with her son and she was listed as "colored" in the same census.
For reasons to be explained later, Eston, his mother, Sally, and
his wife, Julia Ann Isaacs (also a White person with an insignificant touch of known African ancestry), moved to Chillicothe
Ohio after 1830. After his mother's death, Eston and his family
moved to Wisconsin as members of the White endogamous
group and changed their surname to "Jefferson." Their children
were accepted as White.[8] Their descendants still live on the
White side of America's endogamous color line today.[9]

Sally and Jefferson's other son, however, was not so fortunate in the random mixing of his DNA strands. Eston's brother
was named James Madison Hemings after the husband of Dolly
Payne Madison, who had been Sally's close friend and mentor
during her days in Paris. He was known as "Jim-Mad" to his
friends and relatives, and he was of "bronze" skin tone. Although the letter of Virginia law held Jim-Mad to be legally
White, like his brother, his features were apparently not quite
European enough for acceptance by White society. Despite the
law, he was listed as "colored" in the 1830 census, like his

---

[7] Charlottesville census, 1830, as quoted in Jordan (2000), 47.

[8] "A Sprig of Jefferson was Eston Hemings," *Scioto Gazette*, Aug. 1 1902.

[9] Joshua D. Rothman, *Notorious in the Neighborhood: Sex and Families
Across the Color Line in Virginia, 1787-1861* (Chapel Hill, 2003), 86-87.

mother. He also moved to Ohio after 1830 but lived out his life
on the Black side of America's endogamous color line.[10]

* * * * *

The above tale exemplifies three of America's traditional
methods of determining on which side of the color line someone
belongs: blood fraction, appearance, and invisible blackness.
The letter of Virginia's law was clear. It defined group membership in terms of blood fraction. The blood-fraction rule was accepted and applied to Eston Hemings, to his wife Julia Ann, and
to many others of the time. On the other hand, the letter of the
law did not apply to Jim-Mad. Instead, he apparently came under
a second, unwritten law that said that, in addition to having the
correct blood fraction, you also had to look reasonably European. The third rule that determines group membership is illus-
trated by the way that this tale is told today in the popular press.
Dozens of accounts write that Eston Hemings and his wife
"passed for White" or "pretended to be White," and that their
children "thought that they were White."[11] Any explanation that
Eston and his family really were White, and that they well knew
that they were legitimately White despite their trace of African
ancestry, simply confuses many modern Americans. Ironically,
the White endogamous group membership that was assigned to
Eston Hemings's children by their contemporaries in the 1820s,

---

[10] Annette Gordon-Reed, *Thomas Jefferson and Sally Hemings: An American Controversy* (Charlottesville, 1997) 7-58.

[11] See, for instance, the accounts at: URLs:
<http://www.monticello.org/plantation/lives/sallyhemings.html>,
<http://www.cincypost.com/2001/feb/19/jeffer021901.html>,
<http://www.enquirer.com/columns/kiese/2000/02/13/loc_jefferson-
hemings_is.html>, and <http://www.nature.com/nsu/981112/981112-
1.html>. Another example of the inability of today's popular culture to
break free of the idea of invisible blackness was a PBS documentary about
Eston Hemings. The producers chose not to air filmed interviews with Eston's current descendants because they resemble every other Nordic-looking
Wisconsinite and the TV viewers might miss the point. Instead, a voice-over
carried the interview with Eston's descendants while the camera focused on
an unrelated family of Black children playing on a swing set.

following the letter of a blood-fraction rule and the spirit of an unwritten appearance-based rule, was revoked nearly two centuries later by a society wedded to the notion of invisible blackness.

This chapter introduces the three legal rules that emerged in the early 1800s for deciding if you were a member of the Black endogamous group or a member of the White endogamous group: physical appearance, blood fraction, and association. It comprises three topics: *Slavery Depended on Matrilineal Descent, Not on the Color Line* shows that endogamous group membership neither affected nor was affected by slave status. Slave status was decided by a different rule entirely: the rule of matrilineal descent. *The Color Line Became Legally Important Around 1800* explains why it became increasingly necessary for courts to decide whether someone was White or Black. At first, it was only to decide where the burden of proof fell in slavery cases, but state legislatures soon passed dozens of laws requiring distinctions across the color line. *Physical Appearance, Blood Fraction, Association* presents with examples, the strengths and weaknesses of each of the three rules that were applied in court.

The primary historical data source that this book examines and relies upon in order to interpret the unfolding of the U.S. one-drop rule is the record of court cases. As explained in *Appendix B. Court Case Data Processing Methodology* court reports were assembled into an Excel database. Hundreds of thousands of cases that were held in the United States and its ancestral British colonies were examined and considered for inclusion in this book's database. The database includes every single court case on record from the colonial period through 1980 where: (1) a person's endogamous group membership—Black or White— was an issue to be judicially resolved and (2) the rationale for the decision was written down. This yielded about 300 cases.[12]

---

[12] Several issues are raised regarding the usefulness of the U.S. court record in interpreting American history. Among these are: (1) Court cases do not reflect all of society; they reflect only the opinions of elite powerful males. (2) Written decision rationales may deceive, either deliberately or subconsciously. (3) As many as ten cases may have been decided for every one case that was appealed. (4) The ratio of cases where people were found to be White does not reflect the severity of the color line. (5) The number of

Slavery Depended on Matrilineal Descent, Not on the Color Line

Jefferson's explanation, that which side of the color line a person was on had no impact on their slave status, was incomplete. The very fact that Francis Gray asked the question shows that the color line and slavery were linked somehow in popular understanding. As explained elsewhere, the uniquely American connection between slavery and the color line came about because the intermarriage barrier was designed to prevent rebellious alliances among forced laborers in the only colony where such a tactic could have worked—the only colony with more European forced laborers than Africans. The result of the barrier's enforcement was that European laborers in British North America were eventually freed and that slavery (lifelong hereditary forced labor) became associated with those of mostly African ancestry.[13] And so, when Gray asked his question, the link between the color line and the American version of slavery had echoed for more than a century.

On the other hand, Jefferson's answer was perfectly accurate. Although slavery was linked to endogamous group membership in the popular mind, there was no legal connection between the two until 1802, as discussed below. In the century since the 1691 invention of the color line, many Americans had been members of the White endogamous group but had been slaves nonetheless, like Eston Hemings before his 1826 manumission. Conversely, many Americans had been members of the Black endogamous group but were free nonetheless, like Sally Hemings after Jefferson's death. As Jefferson wrote, whether you were legally a slave had nothing to do with which side of

---

cases per decade also does not reflect the severity of the color line. Each of these questions is addressed, and data collection, selection, and tabulation methodologies are described in *Appendix B. Court Case Data Processing Methodology.*

[13] The Latin American lifelong hereditary compulsory labor system named *encomienda* applied to Amerinds, and the Islamic Middle East and North Africa (especially the Barbary Coast) enjoyed colorblind equal opportunity slavery.

the color line you were on. From the 1662 *partus sequitur ventrem* law until slavery's end over two centuries later, the only factor that determined whether someone was legally born a slave was whether the mother was legally a slave at the time. No other factor entered the equation: not skin tone, not endogamous group membership, not ancestry, not anything but matrilineal descent *ad infinitum* and nothing more.[14]

The question was not trivial. Whether someone was slave or free had to be decided many times in the years between 1691 and 1800. Virginia alone imported about 45,000 African slaves between 1700 and 1750.[15] This comes to about ten percent of all the slaves ever imported into British North America.[16] Consequently, the number of Americans of African heritage exploded during this period. Members of the Black endogamous group went from 7 percent of Virginia's population to 44 percent.[17] Some of these individuals were recently imported slaves, and some were the children of slave mothers—also slaves under the law. But others had European mothers, and still others descended from African planters, shopkeepers, or indentured servants of the

---

[14] This may seem to belabor an obvious point, but the number of historians who claim without evidence that slave status was determined by fraction of African ancestry is truly distressing. Among these, for example, are Steve Olson, *Mapping Human History: Discovering the Past Through Our Genes* (Boston, 2002), 60; G. Reginald Daniel, *More than Black?: Multiracial Identity and the New Racial Order* (Philadelphia, 2002), x; David L. Brunsma and Kerry Ann Rockquemore, "What Does 'Black' Mean? Exploring the Epistemological Stranglehold of Racial Categorization," *Critical Sociology*, 28 (no. 1/2, 2002), 101-21, 106-7; and David A. Hollinger, "Amalgamation and Hypodescent: The Question of Ethnoracial Mixture in the History of the United States," *American Historical Review*, 108 (no. 5, December 2003), 1363-90, 1369. These also claim that the 1662 *partus sequitur ventrem* law was motivated by the desire to maximize human assets. In fact, the law as written reduced by one-half the annual crop of newborn slaves that would have resulted from a biologically based law of slave status (a law decreeing that having either parent a slave made one a slave).

[15] Edmund Sears Morgan, *American Slavery, American Freedom: The Ordeal of Colonial Virginia* (New York, 1975), 301.

[16] Hugh Thomas, *The Slave Trade: The Story of the Atlantic Slave Trade: 1440-1870* (New York, 1997), 804.

[17] Peter Kolchin, *American Slavery 1619-1877* (New York, 1993), 11.

seventeenth century, from before the color line was invented. How did the courts decide who was legally a slave and who was free? They did it precisely as Jefferson had explained.

Eleven appealed court cases were held in British North America between 1770 and 1800 to determine whether someone was legally a slave. All followed *partus sequitur ventrem.* In every case, plaintiff and defendant alike tried to prove the individual's status by tracing his or her matrilineal ancestry. In six of the eleven cases, the party arguing for freedom traced matrilineal ancestry to free British women.[18] In three cases, ancestry was traced to Amerind women.[19] The remaining two cases traced matrilineal ancestry to Spain and to China.[20] In every case, the court's ruling was based on whether the matrilineal ancestor had been legally free or slave. In no case was appearance or African ancestral blood fraction an issue. Indeed, in *Higgins v. Allen,* 1796 Maryland, a man's ancestry was traced from his great-grandmother, a Scotswoman, who had married an African slave, and whose mulatto daughter also married an African slave, and whose granddaughter also married an African slave, giving birth to the individual in question—a man of overwhelmingly African ancestry and of utterly African appearance. And yet, despite his appearance, the court set him free due to his matrilineal descent from a free woman, however distant.[21] The ancient principle of

---

[18] *Butler v. Boarman 1770 Maryland* (1 H. & McH. 371), *Howell v. Nether-land 1770 Virginia* (Jeff. 90), *Butler v. Craig 1787 Maryland* (2 H. & McH. 214), *Shorter v. Rozier 1794 Maryland* (3 H. & McH. 238), *Thomas v. Pile 1794 Maryland* (3 H. & McH. 241), and *Higgins v. Allen 1796 Maryland* (3 H. & McH. 504).

[19] *Jenkins v. Tom 1792 Virginia* (1 Va. 123), *Rawlings v. Boston 1793 Maryland* (3 H. & McH. 139), and *Coleman v. Dick and Pat 1793 Virginia* (1 Va. 233).

[20] *Phillis v. Lewis 1796 Delaware* (1 Del. Cas. 417) and *State v. Van Waggoner 1797 New Jersey* (6 N.J.L. 374).

[21] 3 H. & McH. 504. This case parallels, in mirror image, that of Eston Hemings, who sprang from the union of a free Englishman and a slave woman, whose mother also was born of a free Englishman and a slave woman, whose parents were a free Welshman man and an African slave woman. Eston Hemings was of overwhelmingly British ancestry and looked

partus sequitur ventrem was thereafter applied without exception by every U.S. court until slavery was ended by the Civil War.

Nevertheless, although the ancient principle of *partus sequitur ventrem* was universally applied, it was sometimes inadequate in practice due to lack of evidence. One could be a slave by birth, without personally having been purchased or captured. Hence, a legitimate slaveowner might be unable to present a bill of sale. On the other side, government-recorded birth certificates would not be invented for another half-century, and so a person might be unable to document having been born free. According to Kenneth Stampp, freedom papers or travel passes were in use (and being forged by literate slaves) at least as early as 1833.[22] But a runaway might discard a pass or forge freedom papers, and an avaricious slave-trader might claim that the freedom papers in a person's possession were forged. Credible documents were scarce in the messy real world of the early republic. And so the question was, how could a court decide between someone claiming, without documents, to be held illegally and someone else claiming, also without documents, to be the other's rightful owner? Which party had the burden of proof?

Looking backwards in time, American courts' problem— how to resolve property in a person—had already been faced and solved previously by every slave-owning nation ruled by laws. According to British common law, in civil suits the burden of proof falls upon the plaintiff. But lawsuits over slave status were as likely to be brought by the slave as by the owner. A sense of fairness would seem to demand a more objective rule. In fact, colonial courts regarding slavery in British North America followed Spanish, not British precedent. Since 1265, Spanish law had upheld the doctrine that the burden of proof always lay upon the party arguing that someone was a slave. Spanish King Alfonso X had decreed that, since slavery was odious and contrary to Church teachings, it had to be supported by positive evidence. If an alleged slaveowner was unable to provide positive evi-

---

European, but he was legally a slave nonetheless (until freed by the deceased Jefferson's will).

[22] Kenneth M. Stampp, *The Peculiar Institution* (New York, 1953), 115.

dence, the person was to be freed. The alleged slave did not need to provide any evidence, except to contest evidence by the alleged owner. Spanish courts throughout the Americas followed this principle in theory.[23] It was also followed throughout British North America until 1802.

The Color Line Became Legally Important Around 1800

The first appealed court case on record where a person's endogamous group membership was an issue was decided in 1802. This seems strange. The endogamous color line had been in force since 1691, and penalties for intermarriage became increasingly severe in the decades immediately thereafter. Nevertheless, for over a century no appealed case was recorded where a court had to decide on which side of the color line someone belonged. Some have suggested that this is because virtually all Americans in this period were visibly of either northern European or African descent; that few ambiguous-looking people of dual heritage had yet emerged. But this explanation seems unlikely. As explained elsewhere, it takes only three generations of intermarriage—under 75 years—to produce European-looking adults with as much as 25 percent African admixture.[24] A more likely explanation is that endogamous group membership *per se* (as opposed to slavery) had few legal ramifications under British colonial law. Laws restricting the rights of free Black citizens (other than laws forbidding their marrying Whites) seem to be a post-Revolutionary invention. Whatever the reason for the hiatus, the first court case where endogamous group membership was an issue was also the first case that overturned the burden-of-proof precedent.

---

[23] *Las Siete Partidas del Rey Alfonso X* (1265), Partida 3, tit. 14, l. 5. Of course, New World colonists did not always follow the king's law in practice.

[24] See *Chapter 3. The Heredity of "Racial" Traits.*

The change in burden of proof for slavery arose in 1802 North Carolina. A twelve-year-old girl surnamed Gobu claimed to have found an abandoned eight-day-old male infant lying in a barn. The baby had straight hair and an "olive color" (yellowish) skin tone. The girl took the baby home and raised him as her slave. Upon reaching maturity, the young man sued for his freedom. He argued, in *Gobu v. Gobu*, 1802 North Carolina, that Ms. Gobu lacked evidence proving his legal slave status.[25] Her lawyer argued that, because it was clear that the plaintiff was not of pure European ancestry, the burden of proof should rest upon him, not upon his alleged owner. The judge agreed with this altered burden of proof.

> I acquiesce in the rule laid down by the defendant's counsel, with respect to the presumption of every black person being a slave. It is so, because the negroes originally brought to this country were slaves, and their descendants must continue slaves until manumitted by proper authority. If therefore a person of that description claims his freedom, he must establish his right to it by such evidence as will destroy the force of the presumption arising from his color.[26]

The judge thus overturned six centuries of Spanish law and established two new precedents that reverberated in U.S. courts from then on. First, he ruled that the burden of proof was not always upon the alleged slaveowner. Second, he ruled that the burden of proof depended on the alleged slave's endogamous group membership ("the presumption of every black person being a slave"). Thenceforth, a Black person would be presumed a slave unless proven otherwise. A White person would be presumed free.

Interestingly, the *Gobu v. Gobu* judge then went on to free the young man, denying that the new burden of proof standard applied to him, thereby establishing a third precedent: a person of dual heritage did not necessarily fall on the Black side of the color line.

---

[25] 1 N.C. 188.

[26] Idem.

> I am not aware that the doctrine of presuming against liberty has been urged in relation to persons of mixed blood, or to those of any color between the two extremes of black and white; and I do not think it reasonable that such a doctrine should receive the least countenance. Such persons may have descended from... a white parent in the maternal line or from mulatto parents originally free, in all which cases the offspring, following the condition of the mother, is entitled to freedom. Considering how many probabilities there are in favor of the liberty of these persons, they ought not to be deprived of it upon mere presumption, more especially as the right to hold them in slavery, if it exists, is in most instances, capable of being satisfactorily proved.[27]

And so, the *Gobu v. Gobu* ruling thus established that a person of mixed ancestry was not necessarily a member of the Black endogamous group for the purpose of determining *onus probandi* in slavery case.

Four years then passed before the issue arose again. The court in the second case then confirmed the *Gobu v. Gobu* ruling and accepted case law was changed once and for all. That case was *Hudgins v. Wrights*, 1806 Virginia.[28] Hanna Hudgins and her daughter sued for their freedom. They won in the lower court, on the ground that the alleged owner had not made a case. The lower court explicitly followed the old Spanish law of 1265, ruling that:

> freedom is the birthright of every human being, which sentiment is strongly inculcated by the first article of our 'political catechism,' the bill of rights... [and] that whenever one person claims to hold another in slavery, the *onus probandi* lies on the claimant.[29]

The five appeals judges in *Hudgins v. Wrights* unanimously voided the principle upon which this decision was based. They held, following *Gobu v. Gobu*, that the burden of proof did not always lie on the alleged slave owner:

---

[27] Idem.

[28] 11 Va. 134.

[29] Idem.

where white persons, or native American Indians, or their descendants in the maternal line, are claimed as slaves, the *onus probandi* lies on the claimant; but it is otherwise with respect to native Africans and their descendants, who have been and are now held as slaves.[30]

Also, as in *Gobu v. Gobu*, the appeals court freed the plaintiffs because, "the youngest of the appellees was perfectly white, and that there were gradual shades of difference in colour between the grand-mother, mother, and grand-daughter, (all of whom were before the court)." Three of the judges wrote a separate opinion stressing even more firmly that the burden of proof depended on an alleged slave's endogamous group membership.[31]

Hudgins v. Wrights decisively confirmed the case law that slavery's burden of proof depended on the color line. This principle was then followed regularly in U.S. courts thereafter. Subsequent courts, even outside Virginia, cited *Hudgins v. Wrights* as precedent.[32] *Hook v. Nanny Pagee and her Children*, 1811 Virginia, ruled that a single mother and her children were presumed free because "clear and distinct perception" revealed

---

[30] Idem.

[31] For a detailed analysis of *Hudgins v. Wrights*, 1806 Virginia, as the first case where two nineteenth-century criteria for endogamous group membership (blood fraction and appearance) were at odds, see Adrienne D. Davis, "Identity Notes Part One: Playing in the Light," *American University Law Review*, 45 (1996), 695-720.

[32] For an account that sees *Hudgins v. Wrights 1806 Virginia* as the most important precedent-setting case that endogamous group membership determined *onus probandi* regarding slave status, see Paul Finkelman, "The Color of Law," *Northwestern University Law Review*, 87 (no. 3, 1993), 937-91, 952-54. Other studies that discuss the importance of this case are: Daniel J. Sharfstein, "The Secret History of Race in the United States," *Yale Law Journal*, 112 (no. 6, 2003), 1473-509, 1478; Adrienne D. Davis, "Identity Notes Part One: Playing in the Light," *American University Law Review*, 45 (1996), 695-720, 702-17 (as mentioned above); Ariela J. Gross, "Litigating Whiteness: Trials of Racial Determination in the Nineteenth-Century South," *Yale Law Journal*, 108 (no. 1, 1998), 109-88, 129-30; Ian F. Haney-Lopez, *White by Law: The Legal Construction of Race* (New York, 1996), 1-5; and Leon A. Higginbotham, Jr. and Barbara K. Kopytoff, "Racial Purity and Interracial Sex in the Law of Colonial and Antebellum Virginia," *Georgetown Law Journal*, 77 (no. 6, August 1989), 1967-2029, 1985-87.

them to be White.[33] In *Edwards v. M'Connel,* 1813 Tennessee, a "deep yellow" family was ruled to be Black (hence, presumed slaves) despite being from Guadalupe.[34] In *Welborn v. Little,* 1818 South Carolina, an indigent young apprentice was freed from an attempt to enslave him by the presumption of his freedom, based on his being a member of the White endogamous group by virtue of his appearance.[35]

Endogamous group membership soon became important in courts well beyond just those cases held to resolve slave status. Many states forbade Black witnesses from testifying in trials involving White litigants. Between 1794 and 1811, five cases hinged on whether a witness would thus be allowed to testify.[36] And, of course, people continued to intermarry despite the law. One case in this period resolved on which side of the color line someone belonged in order to decide the validity of a marriage.[37] Before long, dozens of laws were passed and precedents established that hinged upon upon whether you were Black or White. Which side of the color line you were on affected more than just your slave status, testimony, and marriage. It also determined: what school you could attend, whether you could inherit, whether you could vote, the taxes you paid, public transportation carrier liability for your escape, whether a "racial" epithet was slanderous, how you would be sentenced as a criminal,

---

[33] 16 Va. 379.

[34] Helen Tunnicliff Catterall and James J. Hayden, *Judicial Cases Concerning American Slavery and The Negro* (New York, 1968), 2:484-85; Cooke 305.

[35] Catterall (1968), 2:310; 1 N. and McC 263.

[36] *Thomas v. Pile   1794 Maryland* (3 H. & McH. 241), *U.S. v. Fisher 1805 District of Columbia* (25 F. Cas. 1086), *State v. Fisher, 1805 Maryland* (1 H. & J. 750), *U.S. v. Mullany 1808 District of Columbia* (27 F. Cas. 20), and *Chaney v. Saunders 1811 Virginia* (17 Va. 51).

[37] *Inhabitants of Medway v. Inhabitants of Natick 1810 Massachusetts* (7 Mass. 88).

whether you could carry a gun, and dozens of other aspects of daily life.[38]

A century before Jefferson wrote his explanation, Governor Gooch had realized that preserving an endogamous color line, based on the notion that colonists of African descent were slaves and those of European descent were free, would depend upon preventing the birth of hybrids. He probably did not foresee just how hopeless this goal would turn out to be. As explained in *Chapter 5. The Rate of Black-to-White "Passing,"* the steady rate of Black-to-White genetic leakage across the color line had produced, by the turn of the nineteenth century, many thousands of Americans who were of mixed Afro-European ancestry. As explained in *Chapter 3. The Heredity of "Racial" Traits*, less than a dozen superficial genes determine the physical features that Americas see as "racially" significant, and the non-European versions of those few genes are often replaced by the genetic recombination (meiosis) that takes place with each generation, thus erasing "racialized" features in mixed descendants. Finally, as explained in *Chapter 2. Afro-European Genetic Admixture in the United States*, Americans of about 15 percent African admixture or less are usually accepted as members of the White endogamous group. And those of roughly 35 percent African admixture or more are usually relegated to the Black side of the U.S. color line.[39] This means that, while some Americans of mixed ancestry looked European and some looked African, many others looked ambiguously Mediterranean. How could law courts be expected to resolve to which side of the color line such people belonged?

---

[38] For a complete list of the reasons why U.S. courts had to rule on someone's endogamous group membership, see "Court Case Data Dictionary" in *Appendix B. Court Case Data Processing Methodology.*

[39] Other lands differ, of course. As explained in *Chapter 4. The Perception of "Racial" Traits*, you must have over 80 percent African admixture to be termed "Black" in the skin-tone sense in some Caribbean nations.

Physical Appearance, Blood Fraction, Association

Even in affirmative action litigation today, courts do not have complete freedom to set the criteria themselves. Two important restrictions limit courts' scope of reasoning. First, courts cannot in practice base their decisions solely upon endogamy itself—whether the person has married across the color line. Acceptance as suitable marriage partner by one endogamous group or the other is important, but this must be shown by the testimony of community leaders. Cases where all parties already agree which side of the color line someone is on would not require intervention by the judicial system. In cases held specifically to determine someone's endogamous group membership, the endogamous group membership in question must be proven and cannot be stipulated. Second, traditionally, U.S. courts have viewed endogamous group membership as something biologically inherent in the individual, something called "race." Although some U.S. judges may have secretly considered "race" to be a social construct and realized that they were actually assigning an individual to one side or the other of an imaginary social barrier, this is seldom if ever what they wrote. An inspection of the rhetoric of the nearly 300 written decisions regarding "racial identity" reveals that, after the one-drop rule emerged in the 1830s, judges usually expressed their task as that of exposing hidden reality.[40] Even today, the rhetoric of America's judicial credo is that everyone biologically falls on one side of the color line or the other. Presumably, everyone in the United States has a single true "race" in the eyes of the law, and the law's task is to sniff out what that persons "true racial identity" is. On what criteria did appellate judges base their decisions? Fortunately, they usually wrote their reasoning down.

---

[40] On the other hand, Daniel J. Sharfstein, "The Secret History of Race in the United States," *Yale Law Journal*, 112 (no. 6, 2003), 1473-509 finds evidence "that many of the historical actors [in Jim Crow period courtroom dramas] *understood* that race is a social construction." This may be so, but the written opinions of appellate judges' usually see "race" as real. See *Appendix B. Court Case Data Processing Methodology*.

Until the advent of the one-drop rule of invisible Black-ness in the 1830s, courts relied on a combination of three rules to determine whether someone was Black or White. The first was the rule of physical appearance. The second was the rule of blood fraction. The third was the rule of association.

Nineteen appellate cases were held from colonial times through 1829 to determine an American's "racial identity" or endogamous group membership. Of these, fifteen were decided on the basis of the person's physical appearance. You were Black if you looked African; you were White if you looked European. Ten were slavery cases where the person's endogamous group membership established the burden of proof.[41] Three decided whether a person could testify in a case involving Whites.[42] One resolved whether a defenefdant could demand a jury trial (Blacks lacked the right to a trial by jury).[43] And one determined the validity of a marriage.[44] In only one of these ten cases was the person found to be Black for the purposes of the case.[45] One might think that today's appearance-based clues to a person's endogamous group membership (skin tone, hair curliness, nose width, lip thickness, and the like) would always have been im-portant.[46] But in fact, some nineteenth-century cases depended upon the shape of the jaw or of the foot, or on purple- or blue-

---

[41] *Jenkins v. Tom 1792 Virginia* (1 Va. 123), *Coleman v. Dick and Pat 1793 Virginia* (1 Va. 233), *Gobu v. Gobu 1802 North Carolina* (1 N.C. 188), *Hudgins v. Wrights 1806 Virginia* (11 Va. 134), *Adelle v. Beauregard 1810 Louisiana* (1 Mart o.s. 183), *Hook v. Pagee 1811 Virginia* (16 Va. 379), *Edwards v. M'Connel 1813 Tennessee* (Catterall 2:484), *State v. Wilson 1818 South Carolina* (Catterall 2:308), *Welborn v. Little 1818 South Caro-lina* (Catterall 2:310), and *Scott v. Williams 1828 North Carolina* (12 N.C. 376).

[42] *State v. Cecil 1812 Louisiana* (2 Mart. o.s. 208). *Pilie v. Lalande 1829 Louisiana* (7 Mart. n.s. 648), and *State v. Scott 1829 South Carolina* (Cat-terall 2:339).

[43] *Bore v. Bush 1827 Louisiana* (6 Mart. n.s. 1).

[44] *Weaver v. Cryer 1827 North Carolina* (12 N.C. 337).

[45] This was *Edwards v. M'Connel 1813 Tennessee* (Catterall 2:484), where the individual, who was from Guadaloupe, was seen to be of a "deep yel-low" skin tone.

[46] See *Chapter 4. The Perception of "Racial" Traits.*

colored marks on certain parts of the body. Nevertheless, despite its popularity (cases were decided on the basis of appearance until the 1950s), appearance-based endogamous group member-ship had its drawbacks.

There were two problems with using only appearance as color line determinant. The first was that it ignored ethnic self-identity. After the endogamous color line was artificially im-posed around 1700, it soon gave rise to a unique ethnic self-identity among Americans of the Black endogamous group. Socio-cultural traits associated with ethnic self-identity are passed down from parent to child. Hence, then as now, many European-looking Americans with parents who were members of the Black endogamous group considered themselves to be Black, despite their own fair-skinned physical appearance. In-deed, as mentioned earlier, about five percent of modern Black Americans have no detectable African genetic admixture at all.[47] What's more, since language, religion, folklore, and other traits are culturally learned, subtle differences in accent or even movement patterns can enable Americans to perceive which side of the color line someone self-identifies with, regardless of their appearance. A strictly appearance-based legal rule would thus result in many legally White Americans insisting that they were socially and culturally Black. In a taped interview conducted by a blind, black anthropologist, a black man nearly ninety years old said:

> Now you must understand that this is just a name we have. I am not black and you are not black either, if you go by the evidence of your eyes.... Anyway, black people are all colors. White people don't all look the same way but there are more different kinds of us than there are of them. Then too, there is a certain stage [at] which you cannot tell who is white and who is black. Many of the people I see who are thought of as black could just as well be white in their appearance. Many of the white people I see are black as far as I can tell by the way they look. Now, that's it for looks. Looks don't mean

---

[47] See "Appearance is not the Same Thing as Ancestry" in *Chapter 3. The Heredity of "Racial" Traits.*

much. The thing that makes us different is how we think. What we believe is important, the ways we look at life.[48]

The second problem with appearance-based group membership determination was that it was too subjective to give the appearance of justice. The public well knew that appearance is elusive and subject to illusion and rationalization.[49] Actual court cases showed a tendency to rule that community leaders were perceived to be on the White side of the color line while vagabonds of the same skin tone were seen as Black.[50] Nevertheless, as will be explained shortly, the rule of physical appearance—in a one-sided sense—remained in effect as an adjunct to the other rules. To this day, although having a European appearance will not guarantee your acceptance into the White endogamous group, a strongly African appearance will definitely relegate you to the Black endogamous group.

In an effort to make endogamous group determination more consistent and objective, colonial and then state legislatures adopted blood-fraction laws. These laws spelled out just what fraction of your ancestors had to be on which side of the color line in order to determine your own group membership. And so, the rule of blood fraction became an alternative criterion used by courts to determine which side of the color line someone was on.

The earliest blood-fraction law in British North America was that of 1705 Virginia, which defined "Black" as anyone with one or more "Negro" great-grandparents (1/8 or more Negro blood made you Black). This was amended in 1785 Virginia to be anyone with one or more "Negro" grandparents (1/4 or more Negro blood made you Black).[51] Over the next century, almost

---

[48] John Langston Gwaltney, *Drylongso: A Self Portrait of Black America* (New York, 1980) as quoted in F. James Davis, *Who is Black?: One Nation's Definition* (University Park PA, 1991), 1.

[49] See *Chapter 4. The Perception of "Racial" Traits.*

[50] As Justice Harper aptly articulated in *State v. Cantey 1835 South Carolina* (Catterall 2:358).

[51] Werner Sollors, *Neither Black Nor White Yet Both* (Cambridge, 1997), 396.; Paul Finkelman, "The Crime of Color," *Tulane Law Review*, 67 (no. 6, 1992), 2063-112, 2085-86, 2106.

every state legislated a statutory definition of endogamous group membership based on blood fraction. By 1910, Florida, Georgia, Indiana, Missouri, South Carolina, Kentucky, Maryland, Mississippi, North Carolina, Tennessee, and Texas defined anyone with 1/8 or more Negro blood to be Black, as in 1705 Virginia. Nebraska, Oregon, Virginia, and Michigan used a 1/4 rule. Alabama used a 1/32 rule. At the other extreme, Massachusetts's statutes and Ohio case law (not statutes) ruled that someone was legally of the White endogamous group if they were mostly of European blood (a 1/2 rule).[52] As indicated, the most popular blood-fraction rule before Jim Crow was the 1/8 rule. This was probably because 12.5 percent African admixture really does reflect physical appearance better than other fractions.[53] As Caroline Bond Day put it, "I have been able so far to see no traces whatever of Negro admixture [in octoroons]."[54]

Since blood-fraction laws were devised in an effort to make the law impartial and objective, court cases that were decided on the basis of blood fraction reflected attempts to rule that a person was White or Black regardless of appearance. Of the nineteen appellate cases held from colonial times through 1829 to determine an American's "racial identity" or endogamous group membership, just four were decided on the basis of blood fraction. One was a slavery case, where the person's endogamous group membership established the burden of proof.[55] Two decided whether a person could testify in a case involving Whites.[56] And one determined the validity of a marriage.[57] In only one of these four cases was the person found to be White

---

[52] Gilbert Thomas Stephenson, *Race Distinctions in American Law* (New York, 1910), 15.

[53] See "How Many White Children are Born Into Black Families?" in *Chapter 3. The Heredity of "Racial" Traits.*

[54] Caroline Bond Day and Earnest Albert Hooton, *A Study of Some Negro-White Families in the United States* (Cambridge MA, 1932), 10.

[55] *Bob v. State 1827 Tennessee* (8 Tenn. 5).

[56] *Chaney v. Saunders 1811 Virginia* (17 Va. 51) and *State v. Barrow 1819 North Carolina* (7 N.C. 121).

[57] *Inhabitants of Medway v. Inhabitants of Natick 1810 Massachusetts* (7 Mass. 88).

for the purposes of the case.[58] Because of its presumed objectivity, blood fraction became a widely used criterion, along with physical appearance, and court cases were decided on this basis until the 1940s.[59]

There were two problems with using the rule of blood fraction to determine someone's endogamous group membership. The first was that the rule of blood fraction could not be used independently of the rule of physical appearance, but it had to be buttressed by that earlier rule. Due to randomness in the way that features are inherited, many people with significant African ancestry look European to most Americans and an equally large fraction with preponderantly European ancestry look African.[60] This created a problem as evidenced by the selection apparent in phenotype versus genotype variation. Since about 1700, Anglo-Americans of what eventually became the hegemonic U.S. mainstream culture have relegated African-looking families to the Black side of the endogamous color line.[61] A strictly interpreted blood-fraction rule would have in-

---

[58] This was *Inhabitants of Medway v. Inhabitants of Natick 1810 Massachusetts* (7 Mass. 88), where the individual, of significant African ancestry, was ruled White due to the state's 1/2 blood fraction law.

[59] See Adrienne D. Davis, "Identity Notes Part One: Playing in the Light," *American University Law Review*, 45 (1996), 695-720, especially page 706 for a contrasting analysis of blood fraction versus appearance as endogamous group membership criteria. Davis sees the two criteria as fundamentally opposed. Daniel J. Sharfstein, "The Secret History of Race in the United States," *Yale Law Journal*, 112 (no. 6, 2003), 1473-509, 1479 also sees these two criteria as being in conflict. This study, in contrast, depicts them as orthogonal, or better yet, serial. During most of the nineteenth century, one had to leap both hurdles (a low documented ancestral blood fraction and European appearance). Both qualifications for White endogamous group membership were necessary. Neither was sufficient by itself.

[60] See "Genetic Admixture is not the Same Thing as Appearance" in *Chapter 2. Afro-European Genetic Admixture in the United States.*

[61] This is not to say that every resident of North America since 1607 has always insisted that any visible trace of African ancestry makes one Black. As discussed in *Chapter 7. The Invention of the Color Line*, the color line itself was invented in 1691. And, as discussed in *Chapter 4.The Perception of "Racial" Traits*, the principle is resisted today within the United States by non-Anglo-Americans (Hispanics, Muslims). That this principle was only slowly accepted over resistance by now-vanished non-mainstream

evitably resulted in some African-looking people being ruled to be of the White group and some European-looking people being ruled to be of the Black group. Judging by the genetic evidence, the latter situation has seldom been a problem. But the former (accepting an African-looking person as White) was usually intolerable. As Justice Battle of the North Carolina Supreme Court wrote in *State v. William Chavers*, 1857 North Carolina, "Can it be then, that a remove by one [last] generation [in a series] has the effect, in law, of turning a half negro into a free white man in spite of the color of his skin or the kinking of his hair? It seems to me both unreasonable and absurd..."[62]

The second problem with the rule of blood fraction was that such a rule is recursive. The concept of recursion or infinite regress is best explained with an example.

Whitmell Dempsey, Jr. of 1849 North Carolina was of European appearance, although some said that he had Black ancestry. Like many men of that place and time, he supplemented his family's diet by shooting squirrels, rabbits, woodchucks, and such. In *State v. Whitmell Dempsey*, 1849 North Carolina, he was charged with violating Chapter 30 of the North Carolina act of 1840, which made it a misdemeanor for, "any free negro, mulatto, or free person of color, to carry about his person or keep in his house any shotgun or other arms, specified, unless he obtain a license from the county court."[63]

At trial, the prosecution argued that Dempsey was a White-looking Black man. Dempsey argued that he was legally White despite having a trace of African ancestry. The North

---

cultures (Barbadian South Carolina, Spanish Florida, French Louisiana) is a point that subsequent chapters discuss in detail. For the importance of slight African appearance today, see Employer Information Report EEO-1 and Standard Form 100, Appendix § 4, Race/Ethnic Identification, 1 Empl. Prac. Guide (CCH) § 1881, (1981), 1625. The Equal Employment Opportunity Commission (EEOC) is a federal executive agency that investigates discrimination and negotiates settlements under 42 U.S.C. §§ 2000e-4 to 2000e-5b. It has the responsibility of defining racial classifications for federal litigation.

[62] 50 N.C. 11. For details, see under the topic "Transitional Cases" in *Chapter 17. The Antebellum South Rejects the One-Drop Rule*.

[63] 31 N.C. 384.

Carolina act of 1777 defined as White anyone of less than 1/8 Negro blood.

According to trial testimony, only one of Dempsey's sixteen great-great-grandparents had any Black ancestry at all. This individual married a White woman and had a red-haired blue-eyed son named Joseph (at most 1/2 Black, although probably much less). Joseph married a White woman and had a European-looking son named William (1/4, at most). William married a White woman and had a son named Whitemell (1/8, at most), who was the defendant's father. And so, Whitmell Jr. the defendant had at most, 1/16 Black ancestry. Therefore the defense argued that the defendant fell within North Carolina's legal definition of a White man. The jury convicted Dempsey anyway and he appealed.[64]

The Supreme Court of North Carolina, Justice C. J. Ruffin presiding, upheld Dempsey's conviction. Ruffin used recursive logic to rule that the defendant's own testimony had convicted the man. Dempsey had admitted that his great-grandfather had been more than one-sixteenth Negro and, by law, this made the ancestor legally Black. Dempsey's grandfather thus had a Black father, and so, being half Black, he was also legally Black as well. Following the same rationale, Dempsey's father was also half-Black, hence Black, and so was Dempsey. It is inconceivable that Justice Ruffin was unaware that such reasoning made the statute meaningless. If pursued to its logical absurdity, as in this case, any recursive definition is nonsense. Mathematically, every purely recursive definition is irresolvable. As Alabama Supreme Court Judge J. Parsons wrote the very next year, in an 1850 *reductio ad absurdum* decision overturning a lower court finding that a light-brown defendant was Black, "If the statute against mulattoes is by construction to include quadroons, then where are we to stop? If we take the first step by construction,

---

[64] Interestingly, James Hugo Johnston, *Race Relations in Virginia & Miscegenation in the South, 1776-1860* (Amherst, 1970), 196 reports that the trial judge acquitted Dempsey and "declared that the man was not a mulatto and that he therefore had the right to possess firearms and to exercise all the rights of other white citizens." Nevertheless, the court records are as narrated above.

are we not bound to pursue the line of descendants, so long as there is a drop of negro blood remaining?"[65]

Beyond blood fraction and physical appearance was a third rule for deciding endogamous group membership. It was the rule of association—did the person spend most of his or her time associating with White folks or Black? The rule of association was seldom applied independently before the twentieth century, but it was sometimes used in conjunction with the other two. Courts sometimes gave weight to a person's associating only with White people. It may seem odd that, in order to be allowed legally to exercise the privileges of White endogamous group membership, one had to demonstrate that one had already violated law and custom by exercising those very privileges, but such was often the case.[66] In some cases, especially in the Jim Crow era, the actual evidence contradicted the judge's rhetoric in the written decision. A judge might write that his ruling was based on blood fraction, but the trial details on record might show that little or no evidence was ever presented as to ancestral birth records. Instead, although the decision rhetoric might have been about blood fraction, the actual evidence cited might have been about the performance of social roles.

The first case when association was cited as significant was *Thomas v. Pile*, 1794 Maryland.[67] Robert Thomas, an alleged slave of biracial appearance won his freedom from slaveowner The Reverend Henry Pile through the testimony of a female witness that Thomas's mother had been White and not a

---

[65] *Thurman v. State 1850 Alabama* (18 Ala. 276). Incidentally, Judge Parsons's decision was the first time that the words "a drop of negro blood" were used in this sense in a U.S. appellate decision. The irony, of course, is that they were used as an example of an obviously irrational and invalid criterion of group membership.

[66] An excellent and informative study of the gradually increasing importance of association as legal criterion for determining whether someone belong on the White or Black side of the endogamous color line, leading up to the actuality behind the rhetoric of the one-drop rule during the Jim Crow era is Ariela J. Gross, "Litigating Whiteness: Trials of Racial Determination in the Nineteenth-Century South," *Yale Law Journal*, 108 (no. 1, 1998), 109-88.

[67] 3 H. & McH. 241.

slave. Thomas's own endogamous group membership was not at issue and he was willing to shoulder the burden of proof. The question was raised about Mrs. Smith, the female witness who testified on Thomas's behalf. Although the woman was free and entirely of European descent, the slave-owner objected to her testimony on the basis that she, "associated and kept company with negroes." This was the first case on record where it was argued that mere association could determine one's endogamous group membership. The principle would become increasingly important through the nineteenth century. By the late twentieth century, group membership decided by association would become virtually conclusive in affirmative action cases.

A puzzle regarding how the Law decided if you were Black or White is the mystery of why only the rule of blood fraction was ever written into state laws. The rule of association (you were Black if you associated with Blacks) and the rule of physical appearance (you were Black if you looked African) were never legislated. Throughout U.S. history, they were left to case law or precedent. One might argue that legislators avoided codifying the rule of association because it is too vague a concept and too hard to measure subjectively. But this argument fails when applied to the rule of blood fraction. As explained above, courts were clearly aware that the rule of blood fraction was inherently recursive, and thus nonsensical. Nevertheless, legislators throughout the nation wrote the rule of blood fraction into laws.

An even deeper puzzle is why state legislators failed to codify the rule of physical appearance. No state ever defined a formal set of appearance-based criteria for determining endogamous group membership. It can easily be done, after all, and other Americans have embraced it eagerly. When the service organization Jack and Jill of America, Inc. was founded in 1938 Philadelphia, its membership criteria included having a skin tone lighter than kraft paper and hair smooth enough to pass a comb through.[68] The blue-vein societies of nineteenth-century New

---

[68] Lawrence Graham, *Our Kind of People: Inside America's Black Upper Class* (New York, 1999), 19-44.

Orleans,[69] or Nashville,[70] and the Brown Fellowship Society of antebellum Charleston[71] similarly restricted membership based on physical appearance.

One speculative answer presents itself. Appearance was best decided at the local level. Even though state statutes referred only to blood fraction, Americans actually knew that physical appearance was equally important in deciding someone's endogamous group membership. But they also knew that appearance is subjectively in the eye of the beholder. The point is that, being aware of the slippery nature of appearance-based color line determination, Americans were happy to leave the rule of appearance unwritten precisely in order to give local communities the power to decide.[72]

*   *   *   *   *

This chapter presented the three legal rules that emerged in the early 1800s for deciding if you were Black or White: the rule of physical appearance, the rule of blood fraction, and the rule of association. It showed that slave status was decided by a

---

[69] Joel Williamson, *New People: Miscegenation and Mulattoes in the United States* (New York, 1980), 81-82; James Hugo Johnston, *Race Relations in Virginia & Miscegenation in the South, 1776-1860* (Amherst, 1970), 47; Peter Kolchin, *American Slavery 1619-1877* (New York, 1993), 242.

[70] Kathy Russell, Midge Wilson, and Ronald E. Hall, *The Color Complex: The Politics of Skin Color Among African Americans*, 1st ed. (New York, 1992), 25; Bart Landry, *The New Black middle Class* (Berkeley, 1987), 34.

[71] Marina Wikramanayake, *A World in Shadow: The Free Black in Antebellum South Carolina* (Columbia, 1973), 81-85.

[72] This speculation is buttressed by the U.S. Congress's present unwillingness to legislate endogamous group membership criteria for federal affirmative action programs despite strong pleas for such standards from those who must litigate claims. See, for example, *Luther Wright, Jr.*, "Who's Black, Who's White, and Who Cares: Reconceptualizing the United States's Definition of Race and Racial Classifications," *Vanderbilt Law Review*, 48 (no. 2, 1995), 513-70; Neil Gotanda, "A Critique of 'Our Constitution is Color-Blind'," *Stanford Law Review*, 44 (no. 1, November 1991), 1-68; Trina Jones, "Shades of Brown: The Law of Skin Color," *Duke Law Journal*, 49 (no. 6, April 2000), 1487-558.

different rule entirely: the rule of matrilineal descent. It explained why it became increasingly necessary for courts to decide whether someone was White or Black. And, with examples, it presented the strengths and weaknesses of each of the three rules.

The next three chapters introduce four antebellum societies, within what became the United States, whose color-line customs differed from the mainstream—South Carolina, Alabama, Louisiana, and Florida. South Carolina had a class-based rule of endogamous group membership defining an unusually permeable color line. Alabama and Louisiana had two mildly endogamous color lines separating three groups: White, Colored, and Black. Group membership depended on physical appearance as well as on socioeconomic class. Florida initially lacked an endogamous color line, but American rulers imposed one soon after acquiring the territory from Spain.

The next three chapters mean to show that the antebellum lower South differed significantly from the upper South and the North regarding the endogamous color line. Their differences had all vanished by the mid-twentieth century. These odd enclave traditions were probably doomed even without the Civil War. Transportation technology (railroads, steamships, automobiles) brought national economic integration on a scale previously unimagined, and the nation became more homogenous regarding "racial" perceptions.

Chapter 10.
Barbadian South Carolina:
A Class-Based Color Line

In 1826 South Carolina, Justice Colcock had to decide a probate case on appeal: *Real Estate of Hardcastle*, 1826. The issue was whether the late Mrs. Hardcastle's 2,377 acres of prime South Carolina land should go to her niece, Catharine Cleveland, or escheat to the state instead. Mrs. Hardcastle had died six years earlier. The problem was that no record could be found of her parents' marriage. Cleveland would not be considered a niece if her aunt had been illegitimate. Given the absence of a marriage record, Colcock ruled for the state and that was the end of it. But the case is remarkable because of an argument made by the state and how it was dismissed. It opens a window through which you can glimpse the color line of early antebellum South Carolina.

The state's attorney had argued that Mrs. Hardcastle had been born in Africa, the daughter of a Captain Cleveland of the British Royal Navy and an African princess. This, he said, made her a "colored woman" and so she could not legally own Charleston real estate. True, he admitted, she had achieved wealth and was "well connected" to the powerful Kinloch family of South Carolina, but she was colored nonetheless

Judge Colcock's answer had two parts. "Free persons of color" had only limited rights by South Carolina law and custom. "They have not, like the freed men of Rome, or Athens, become incorporated into the body politic." Colcock knew very well that the United States would never emulate those alien or ancient lands where former slaves were embraced and welcomed into society. But then he said:

> [Free Black subordination] has no doubt been the result of the mark which nature has put upon them. For where this has been obliterated, some have obtained, and now enjoy all the rights of citizens; some who have lost that distinctive mark, hold offices, as well as lands, and even seats in the legislature. My earliest recollections are associated with the knowledge of one of this description, who owned a plantation and negroes.[1]

* * * * *

This chapter introduces the first of four societies, within what became the United States, whose color-line customs differed from the mainstream—Barbadian South Carolina. It presents three topics. *The Rule of Socioeconomic Class* explains that antebellum South Carolina lacked a rule of blood fraction but used a rule of socioeconomic class instead. *A Permeable, Shifted Color Line* shows that it was acceptable for wealthy White adults to have a Black parent, and that some swarthy White South Carolinians might have been seen as Black elsewhere in the United States. *An Echo of Barbados* suggests that South Carolina's unique color line had been adapted from the Barbadian color line.

The Rule of Socioeconomic Class

At first glance, Justice Colcock's decision in *Real Estate of Hardcastle* seems to suggest that he applied the rule of physical appearance, "the mark which nature has put upon them." But

---

[1] Helen Tunnicliff Catterall and James J. Hayden, *Judicial Cases Concerning American Slavery and The Negro* (New York, 1968), 2:334; 2 Harper 495, 1826.

a closer reading reveals that who was deemed White was not just anyone in whom "this [mark] has been obliterated." Colcock specifically cited only people who held offices, lands, seats in the legislature, plantations, negroes. In a one-sided sense, of course, the rule of physical appearance has always applied. The genetic selection apparent in phenotype versus genotype variation shows that the U.S. mainstream has consistently relegated African-looking families to the Black side of the color line.[2] But Colcock was citing another rule, beyond the rule of physical appearance, beyond the rule of blood fraction, beyond the rule of association. It was the rule of socioeconomic class. The following case shows that acceptance into upper class White society was more important than mere appearance.

In *State v. Davis / State v. Hanna*, December 1831, Justice William Harper granted a new trial because the original jury had allowed predominantly European-looking witnesses to testify in a case involving members of the White endogamous group. The jury had found the witnesses also to be White by inspecting them. Judge Harper ruled that:

> It is certainly true, as laid down by the presiding judge, that "every admixture of African blood with the European, or white, is not to be referred to the degraded class." It would be dangerous and cruel to subject to this disqualification, persons bearing all the features of a white, on account of some remote admixture of negro blood; nor has the term mulatto, or person of color, I believe, been popularly attributed to such a person.[3]

Nevertheless, Harper ruled that the jury should also have taken into account whether the witnesses had been "received into society." Membership in South Carolina's White endogamous group, it seems, depended on both appearance and social standing. Each was insufficient by itself. The witnesses in ques-

---

[2] See "Physical Appearance, Blood Fraction, Association" in *Chapter 9. How the Law Decided if You Were Black or White* and "Genetic Admixture is not the Same Thing as Appearance" in *Chapter 2. Afro-European Genetic Admixture in the United States.*

[3] Catterall (1968), 2:346; 2 Bailey 558.

tion had not been so received into society, and so Justice Harper ruled them to be Black, despite their mostly European physical appearance.[4]

In this case and in others like it, Justice Harper was troubled by the lack of clear legislative intent. He would have preferred a statute codifying a blood-fraction rule, as in Louisiana. In another case, he wrote:

> In Louisiana, as I understand, and by the *Code Noir* of France for her colonies, the descendant of a white and a quadroon is accounted a white. Perhaps it would be desirable, that the Legislature should adopt some such uniform rule here. The rule may be of use to juries—not as a rule of law, which we have no authority to declare it, but as being founded on experience and conformable to nature.[5]

Harper's suggested ratio was also Spanish colonial law at the time, under the *Recopilación de leyes de los reinos de las Indias*.[6] In fact, this very same ratio was in effect in Virginia in Justice Harper's time, and eventually became the law in Florida, Georgia, Indiana, Missouri, Kentucky, Maryland, Mississippi, North Carolina, Tennessee, and Texas.[7] Alas, Justice Harper's wish that the legislature establish a fixed blood fraction for endogamous group membership was never granted.

Four years later, it was Harper himself who wrote the legal precedent that continued in effect in South Carolina thereafter. A larceny conviction, *State v. Cantey*, 1835, was appealed on

---

[4] An interesting point raised by Ariela J. Gross, "Litigating Whiteness: Trials of Racial Determination in the Nineteenth-Century South," *Yale Law Journal*, 108 (no. 1, 1998), 109-88 is whether association or social acceptance (what she calls "performance") was more or less determinative of group membership than the other rules (physical appearance, blood fraction, socioeconomic class).

[5] Catterall (1968), 2:347; 2 Bailey 558.

[6] This is not to suggest that the law was enforced or even obeyed throughout Spain's empire.

[7] For an explanation of why 1/8 was so popular, see Physical Appearance, Blood Fraction, Association" in *Chapter 9. How the Law Decided if You Were Black or White.*

the grounds that Black witnesses had been allowed to testify. The original trial judge had accepted the witnesses because:

> The father of the witnesses was a white man. ... The maternal grandfather of the witnesses, although of dark complexion, had been recognized as a white man, received into society and exercised political privileges as such; their mother was uniformly treated as a white woman; their relations of the same admixture have married into respectable families, and one of them has been a candidate for the legislature. The witnesses were ordinarily fair and exhibited none of the distinctive marks of the African race; they are respectable, have always been received into society, and recognized as white men—one of them is a militia officer, and their caste has never been questioned until now.[8]

In deciding the appeal, William Harper resigned himself to the fact that it was going to be up to him, not the legislature, to lay this problem to rest. And so, in May 1835, Harper and two other justices (Johnson and O'Neall) unanimously wrote the decision that would be followed as South Carolina law until 1895:

> It would be an absurdity to say that such a one [as the witness in question] is, in the popular sense a person of color. If we should say that such an [sic] one is to be regarded as a person of color, on account of *any* [emphasis in the original] mixture of negro blood, however remote, we would be making, instead of declaring the law, and making a very cruel and mischievous law. We cannot say what admixture will make a colored person. The condition is not to be determined solely by visible mixture but by reputation and it may be proper, that a man of worth should have the rank of a white man, while a vagabond of the same degree of blood should be confined to the inferior caste. It is hardly necessary to say that a slave cannot be a white man. We wish it to be understood that this matter is regarded as settled. I think it to be regretted that the question was made in the present case, it is doing unnecessary violence to the feelings of persons of much worth and respectability.[9]

---

[8] Catterall (1968), 2:358-59; 2 Hill 614.

[9] Idem.

This above case law was not overturned until the redemptionist South Carolina Constitutional Convention of 1895 legislatively codified a rule of blood fraction.

South Carolina's rule of socioeconomic class to determine whether you were White or Black was unusual for the United States. In most regions and periods of U.S. history, even a very wealthy member of the Black endogamous group was still Black. But basing group membership (and appearance designation) partly upon class was the norm throughout the rest of the Western Hemisphere. "Money whitens" is a cliché elsewhere in the New World and it has been demonstrated statistically in Brazil.[10]

A Permeable, Shifted Color Line

In addition to the absence of a rule of blood fraction, and the presence of a unique rule of socioeconomic class, the color line in antebellum South Carolina had two other distinctive features. First, it was unusually permeable.[11] The children of Black parents were routinely accepted into White society if they passed the two rules of socioeconomic class and appearance. Second, the color line was shifted towards the African end of the Afro-European genetic admixture continuum. The same individual seen as physically Black-looking in Massachusetts, say, could be seen as physically White-looking in South Carolina.

The permeability of South Carolina's color line is apparent in marriage and tax records, as studied by Larry Koger. The historian faced an epistemological (or perhaps semantic) challenge in researching records for his book, *Black Slaveowners: Free Black Slave Masters in South Carolina, 1790-1860*. That is,

---

[10] See George Reid Andrews, "Racial Inequality in Brazil and the United States: A Statistical Comparison," *Journal of Social History*, 26 (no. 2, Winter 1992), 229-63 for a study showing that the skin-tone designations assigned to individual Brazilians in their census lighten or darken from one census to the next depending upon the individuals' income and net worth.

[11] For a definition, see "Impermeability" in *Chapter 6. Features of the Endogamous Color Line.*

"Whom should you count as within the ranks of Black slaveowners, assuming that you want to be understood by modern
Anglo-American readers?" Clearly, you must count it when a
former Negro slave becomes a slaveowner, even if he marries a
woman who is a member of wealthy White society. But what of
their children? Say, for instance, that you count the first generation of mixed offspring as Black group members also, even if
they marry White spouses in their turn. But then, what of their
children? What of the fourth generation, the fifth? Koger discovered that if you adopt modern America's one-drop rule, you
wind up counting many White slaveowners in South Carolina as
"Black," including the state's wealthiest and most influential
White families. And so, in order to keep his results within commonsense reason, Koger arbitrarily cut off hereditary "Blackness" at the second generation, and tallied third-generation and
subsequent descendants of Black slaveowners and White
spouses as members of the White endogamous group.[12]

As mentioned in Chapter 6, color line permeability comprises two components. The first is made up of children with at
least one Black parent who, even as infants or toddlers, are assigned to the White endogamous group by their families and by
mainstream society (usually, in the form of a census taker). The
second component consists of young adults with at least one
Black parent who reject their families' designations and reinvent
themselves as White when starting adult life on their own.

Judging by the many South Carolina court cases accepting
people with known African ancestry into the White endogamous
group, and by Koger's study of Black slaveowners, crossing the
color line in infancy was higher in South Carolina than anywhere else in the English-speaking United States of the time.
Indeed, the practice of European-looking infants of Black parentage being accepted into White society by the rule of socioeconomic class remained a hallmark of South Carolina well into

---

[12] Larry Koger, *Black Slaveowners: Free Black Slave Masters in South
Carolina, 1790-1860* (Jefferson NC, 1985), 17.

the twentieth century.[13] The second component, color-line switching in young adulthood, is harder to measure but the few known cases suggest that it was not particularly socially accept-able when attempted openly.[14]

It is important to understand that the children of Black parents who were seen as members of the White endogamous group in South Carolina really were accepted as White. South Carolinians then, like most Americans now, were convinced that they could distinguish a Black person from a White person on sight.[15] The difference was that the very same person seen as visibly a member of the Black endogamous group in, say, New York or Virginia, might be seen as visibly White in South Caro-lina. There are accounts of swarthy professionals (physicians, lawyers) moving to South Carolina for that very reason. An eld-erly North Carolina judge advised a would-be lawyer:

> As you have all the features of a white man, you would, at least in South Carolina, have simply to assume the place and exercise the privileges of a white man.... [T]he matter has been adjudicated there in several cases, and on the whole I think South Carolina is the place for you.[16]

Alexis de Tocqueville was a French political scientist whose government sent him on a nine-month study of the American penal system in 1831-32. De Tocqueville took advantage of his visit to write *Democracy in America*, a combination travelogue and social commentary on the United States, which he published

---

[13] See, for example, 195 S.C. 1, It is the anecdote that opens *Chapter 5. The Rate of Black-to-White "Passing."* Of course, one case does not prove a point. It is merely an example.

[14] See, for example, the arduous process that the Gibsons had to follow to become White in Larry Koger, *Black Slaveowners: Free Black Slave Mas-ters in South Carolina, 1790-1860* (Jefferson NC, 1985), 12-13. Today in contrast, switching from Black to White in young adulthood is much more common than in infancy. See "The Average Yearly Rate is Between 0.10 and 0.14 Percent" in *Chapter 5. The Rate of Black-to-White "Passing."*

[15] See *Chapter 4. The Perception of "Racial" Traits.*

[16] Charles Waddell Chesnutt, *The House Behind the Cedars* (Boston, 1900), 172. See also Daniel J. Sharfstein, "The Secret History of Race in the United States," *Yale Law Journal,* 112 (no. 6, 2003), 1473-509, 1489-91.

upon returning to Europe. During his visit to the lower South, he wrote:

> There are parts of the United States where the European and Negro blood are so crossed that one cannot find a man who is either completely white or completely black; when that point has been reached, one can really say that the races are mixed, or rather that there is a third race derived from the two, but not precisely one or the other.[17]

Similarly, when General Joshua Lawrence Chamberlain, of Little Round Top, Gettysburg fame, was in the occupied South after Appomattox, he saw:

> wild-looking men in homespun gray, standing sulkily by, or speaking only to insist that they are civilians and not soldiers; sometimes white men, or what seem to be, declaring that they are not white, but colored;--a claim not often set up in that part of the Republic, though there may be some truth in it for all that; for there was in those days a whimsical variance between law and fact,--between being actually white and legally white...[18]

That the South Carolina color line was shifted towards more African admixture does not mean that the state had a "Colored" endogamous group, intermediate between Black and White, as did Louisiana and Alabama, discussed below. It is true that South Carolina had a large and powerful Mulatto elite within the Black endogamous group. Some Mulattos were among the wealthiest men in the state. William Ellison's slaveholdings put him in the top one percent of South Carolina planters.[19] Six Mulattos owned more slaves than Ellison. One owned 152 slaves; another was worth $250,000 (twelve and a half million in today's money).[20] The South Carolina Mulatto elite

---

[17] Alexis de Tocqueville, *Democracy in America* (New York, 1966), 356.

[18] Joshua Lawrence Chamberlain, *The Passing of the Armies* (New York, 1915), 158.

[19] Michael P. Johnson and James L. Roark, *Black Masters: A Free Family of Color in the Old South*, 1st ed. (New York, 1984).

[20] William W. Freehling, *The Road to Disunion: Secessionists at Bay 1776-1854* (New York, 1990), 43.

founded their own exclusive clubs. The Brown Fellowship Society of Charleston is the earliest known instance of the grocery-bag rule of the Colored upper-crust of the 1930s.[21] To be admitted, the skin of your forearm had to be lighter than kraft paper.[22] As of 1830, 474 South Carolina Mulattos owned 2,794 slaves, about one South Carolina slave in a hundred.[23] Nevertheless, despite the efforts and occasional successes of the South Carolina Mulatto elite to create a middle ground for themselves, no officially recognized intermediate endogamous group ever existed in the eyes of mainstream society. The Mulatto elite may have tried to create an intermediate group resembling Louisiana's and Alabama's. But court case records reveal only one color line, not two. To White South Carolinians, the Mulatto elite were all just free members of the Black group.

In short, South Carolina employed a rule of socioeconomic class to determine if you were White or Black, but the state lacked a rule of blood fraction. The color line was permeable in that it was acceptable for a wealthy White person to have a Black parent. For today's English-speaking Americans, in contrast, a person's parentage trumps his or her appearance, even among children.[24] Finally, the color line's endogamous barrier was shifted towards the African end of the Afro-European admixture continuum.

---

[21] Marina Wikramanayake, *A World in Shadow: The Free Black in Antebellum South Carolina* (Columbia, 1973), 81-85.

[22] Eric Foner, *Reconstruction: America's Unfinished Revolution* (New York, 1988), 101; Lawrence Graham, *Our Kind of People: Inside America's Black Upper Class* (New York, 1999), passim.

[23] James Hugo Johnston, *Race Relations in Virginia & Miscegenation in the South, 1776-1860* (Amherst, 1970), 47; Peter Kolchin, *American Slavery 1619-1877* (New York, 1993), 242.

[24] See "How U.S. Children Learn to See Two Endogamous Groups" in *Chapter 4. The Perception of "Racial" Traits.*

An Echo of Barbados

Consider all of the features of South Carolina's endoga-mous color line in combination. It was discontinuous, dichoto-mous, legally enforced, impermeable by adults, permeable by children, dependent upon socioeconomic class, and shifted darkwards. Only one other former colony in the New World had a color line with those very features—Barbados.[25] Barbadians, of course, had colonized South Carolina in 1670, and so similar-ity of customs is not a surprise. What is strange is that Barbados was the only British West Indian colony that, like South Caro-lina, lacked a large intermediate group of Coloured landowning yeomen. There was good reason for this in Barbados, but the reason did not apply to South Carolina.

Geography explains the lack of an intermediate yeoman group in Barbados. Although often considered part of the Lesser Antilles, geographically the 14-by-21-mile island is not vol-canic, but a coral-capped sedimentary seamount, a hundred miles to the east—upwind—of the nearest other island (the way that Bermuda lies off South Carolina, but not as far). It is the first New World landfall for ships following the trade winds, and this made it unique in three ways. First, it was never attacked because there is nowhere to stage an assault. Invasion fleets must refit and resupply shortly before attacking, oceangoing ships could not sail upwind very well, and Europe or Africa are too distant. So, unlike all other Caribbean islands, that bled their wealth into defense, Barbados could single-mindedly develop its economy. Second, Britain used Barbados as military staging area for its near-constant warfare against the downwind Spanish, Por-tuguese, French, and Dutch colonies. Consequently, Barbados was usually crawling with imperial soldiers. And so, unlike

---

[25] See Hilary Beckles, *A History of Barbados: From Amerindian Settlement to Nation-State* (Cambridge UK, 1990) for an overview. A humorous view of Barbados's darkwards-shifted color line comes from Anthony Trollope's 1850 visit to the island, when he reported that only White men could legally run for public office, but then said, "How it is decided whether a man be white or not, I did not hear." Anthony Trollope and Fred D'Aguiar, *The West Indies and the Spanish Main* (New York, 1999), 151-52.

every other slave-based economy in history, Barbados did not need a yeoman class to crush slave revolts. Finally, since Barbados did not need a landowning middle class, the younger sons of Euro-Barbadians and upwardly mobile biracial Barbadians were economically driven off the island. (Some of these exiles founded South Carolina.) Consequently, Barbados quickly evolved into a unique population of wealthy Euro-Barbadian planters who owned nearly every scrap of land, a large number of Afro-Barbadian slaves who did all the work, and a small, landless, biracial group sandwiched uncomfortably between.[26]

But South Carolina did not enjoy the presence of a permanent garrison of imperial troops, and so one would have expected them to adopt the three-layer systems of, say, Jamaica or Trinidad after the Stono Rebellion of 1739.[27] Instead, they apparently copied one feature of the Chesapeake two-layer system—the use of poor Whites for the social control of slaves.[28] This then prevented even the Mulatto elite of the free Black South Carolinians from forming an intermediate group (see the mention of the Brown Fellowship Society, above), and so South Carolina's culture retained the Barbadian style of color line.

* * * * *

This chapter introduced Barbadian South Carolina, the first of four U.S. societies whose color-line customs differed from the mainstream. It explained that antebellum South Carolina lacked a rule of blood fraction but used a rule of socioeconomic class instead. It showed that it was acceptable for wealthy White adults to have a Black parent, and that some swarthy White South Carolinians might have been seen as Black elsewhere in the United States. It suggested that South Carolina's

---

[26] Beckles (1990).

[27] See Peter H. Wood, *Black Majority: Negroes in Colonial South Carolina From 1670 Through the Stono Rebellion*, 1st ed. (New York, 1974) for an account of this decision.

[28] William W. Freehling, *The Road to Disunion: Secessionists at Bay 1776-1854* (New York, 1990), 215-52.

unique color line had been adapted from the Barbadian color line.

Chapter 11.
Antebellum Louisiana and Alabama:
Two Color Lines, Three Endogamous Groups

In November of 1825, dark biracial Alabamian Girard Hansford took Maria George as his bride "in accordance with the laws of Alabama," even though she was some twenty years his junior and much fairer of skin.[1] Her mother was White and her father was a European-looking member of the Colored endogamous group, so Maria could likely have passed through the color line had she chosen to do so. Come to think of it, perhaps she did. The court records refer to her as a White woman. Two decades later, their marriage had collapsed and, in *Hansford v. Hansford*, 1846 Alabama, Girard asked the court of Montgomery Alabama to grant him a divorce on the grounds of his wife's adultery. Adultery was proven to the court's satisfaction, but Girard felt the need to explain why he wanted to cast off his wife. He had repeatedly forgiven young Maria's indiscretions because he knew of the "temptations which were held out to one of her cast [sic] in society." But he had drawn the line when she swore

---

[1] 10 Ala. 561.

that her most recent child (a blonde, blue-eyed toddler) was by a
White man and she vowed, "that all the ballance [sic] of her
children should be white." Even worse, to add gender insult to
marital injury, his wife's lover insisted on supporting and seeking custody of his White child by Maria.[2] The court ruled in Girard's favor and granted him a divorce.

* * * * *

This chapter discusses two out of the four societies, within
what became the United States, whose color-line customs differed from the mainstream—Alabama and Louisiana. Both cultures had two mildly endogamous color lines separating three
groups: White, Colored, and Black. Both could trace their color
line traditions to French colonies in general and to Haiti in particular. They are presented in three topics: *English-Speaking
Alabama* describes an English-speaking version three-caste society. *French-speaking Louisiana* depicts the better known Colored Creole society. *An Echo of Haiti* summarizes the origins of
these cultures.

English-Speaking Alabama

The *Hansford v. Hansford* 1846 divorce case reveals four
aspects of Anglo Alabama in the 1820-1840 period. First, marriage across the White-to-Colored color line was neither illegal
nor uncommon. Second, Alabama had the distinguishing features of a three-caste system with two endogamous color lines.
Third, the wives in most exogamous marriages, then as now,
were members of the White group.[3] Fourth, it was legally (and,

---

[2] Chancery Court Record 1847, 639-57.

[3] One might argue that Maria was not fully accepted as a member of the
White endogamous group. The record is ambiguous. She appears as Colored
in early documents and White in later ones. But her parents were married
and her mother was definitely a member of the White endogamous group,
so this possibility simply pushes the White-Colored intermarriage back one
generation. However you look at it, the Hansford case involves a marriage
between a Colored husband and a White wife.

one presumes, socially, based upon frequency of occurrence) accepted at that place and time for a White child to have a parent or grandparent who was a member of the Colored or Black endogamous groups. Consider each of these aspects in detail.

Marriage across the White-Colored color line was neither illegal nor uncommon. The Alabama codes of both 1805 and 1833 designated officials to "solemnize the rites of matrimony between any free persons" not within the prohibitions of consanguinity and who presented a license, with no mention of "race" or color.[4] Two customary and mildly endogamous color lines existed, but neither of them was legally enforced.[5] Judging from marriage and census records, the fraction of married Colored or Black Alabamians who had a White spouse was 17.8 percent. This is comparable to today's Hispanic-Anglo intermarriage rate. It is over ten times higher than the national Black-White intermarriage rate during Jim Crow. It is five times higher than today's Black-White intermarriage rate.[6]

---

[4] Harry Toulmin *A Digest of the Laws of the State of Alabama, Containing the Statutes and Resolutions in Force at the End of the General Assembly in January, 1823* (Cahawba, Ala. 1823), 576-79; and John G. Aikin *A Digest of the Laws of the State of Alabama, Containing the Statutes of Public and General Nature, in Force at the Close of the Session of the General Assembly, in January, 1833* (Philadelphia, 1833), 305; both as quoted in Gary B. Mills, "Miscegenation and the Free Negro in Antebellum 'Anglo' Alabama: A Reexamination of Southern Race Relations," *Journal of American History*, 68 (no. 1, 1981), 16-34, 18.

[5] Much later, Alabama's 1852 code attempted to discourage people from intermarrying within the state. According to article 1946, "marriage may be solemnized between free white persons, or between free persons of color, by any licensed minister." And article 1956 says, "Any person solemnizing the rites of matrimony... when one of the parties is a negro and the other a white person is guilty of a misdemeanor." But even this restriction was not applied to colored persons (as opposed to "Negroes"), did not apply to marriages performed out of state, and criminalized only the minister's performing the ceremony. It did not declare an interracial marriage void, nor did it impose any penalty on the bride and groom. See John J. Ormand, Arthur P. Bagby, and George Goldthwaite, *The Code of Alabama* (Montgomery, 1852), 376-77 as quoted in Mills (1981), 16-34, 18.

[6] Ibid., 18-19. For the comparisons, see "The Endogamous Color Line" in *Chapter 2. Afro-European Genetic Admixture in the United States.*

It may seem plausible that such acceptance of intermarriage was found only among Alabamians of French or Spanish descent, who were prevalent at the time along Alabama's Gulf Coast. But this was not the case. Intermarriage was accepted among Anglo-Alabamians as well. The above numbers exclude Mobile and Baldwin counties, where 46 percent of Alabama's free Black and Colored resided, and which were of Latin culture. Instead, the interracial marriages counted above were evenly distributed throughout the south-central wiregrass region, the northwest mountain and valley region, the northeastern Appalachian mountain range, and in the city of Montgomery—all English-speaking areas.[7] In addition, the birth records of both males and females of the White group involved in exogamous marriages show that the overwhelming majority were native Alabamians, 24 percent came from South Carolina, and only 1.5 percent were born in other countries.[8]

Antebellum Alabama had the distinguishing features of a three-caste system. Census records reveal that marriage across the customary Black-to-Colored endogamous color line barrier was 6.4 percent, while exogamy across the traditional Colored-to-White color line was 16.6 percent, and between the Black and White groups it was a negligible 0.9 percent.[9] This leads to two conclusions. First, the endogamous color line barrier between free Blacks and free Coloreds was over twice as strong, in practice, as that between the Coloreds and Whites. This may seem startling, but, as shown also in Louisiana, it was not uncommon in three-caste societies. Alabama laws regarding intermarriage, association, civil rights, and public education of children clearly distinguished between the Black and Colored endogamous groups.[10]

---

[7] Mills (1981), 16-34, 19.

[8] Ibid., 24-25.

[9] Ibid., 20-21.

[10] For a brief survey of Alabama laws regarding Colored Creoles, see Virginia Meacham Gould, "The Free Creoles of Color of the Antebellum Gulf Ports of Mobile and Pensacola: A Struggle for the Middle Ground," in *Creoles of Color of the Gulf South*, ed. James H. Dormon (Knoxville, 1996), 44.

The second conclusion is that the Colored endogamous group enjoyed intermediate social status between Whites and Blacks. Specifically, as seen in the above intermarriage statistics, Blacks and Whites alike considered members of the Colored endogamous group to be more suitable marriage partners than members of the opposite unmixed group. This may seem unexceptional at first glance, but as explained earlier, many three-caste societies relegate the hybrid group to a lower status that either unmixed group (Métis, Anglo-Indians, Ugandans) and others raise the hybrid group to a higher status than either unmixed group (Haiti, Mexico).[11] The positioning of the hybrid group to a status rank between those of both unmixed groups is characteristic of French, British, and Dutch New World colonies. Since Alabama was sandwiched between a Barbadian English culture with a uniquely permeable and dark-shifted single color-line (South Carolina) on the one side, and a French culture with two color lines separating three endogamous groups (Louisiana) on the other, the custom probably seeped inland from the French-speaking coast to be partly absorbed by people of Anglo-Saxon customs.

A question arises whether the census and marriage records that distinguished between the Black and Colored groups were accurate or even consistent. The U.S. census is often considered unreliable in this regard, since it is impossible to know exactly what was going through the census-taker's mind when classifying someone. Unfortunately, there is no good answer to this question. The fundamental problem is that there is no objective way to predict the endogamous group to which a person will be assigned by his neighbors. Endogamous group membership is socially determined, after all. Genetic admixture mapping can measure how much of an individual's DNA has African versus European origin. But appearance varies widely within the intermediate admixture ranges, and there is significant U.S. endogamous group overlap in the Afro-European genetic admixture range below 25 percent African (above 75 percent European).[12]

---

[11] See in "Discontinuity" in *Chapter 6. Features of the Endogamous Color Line*.

[12] See *Chapter 2. Afro-European Genetic Admixture in the United States*.

Nevertheless, absolute census accuracy or consistency *per se* is not this study's concern. The central question is whether the census-taker's perception reflected that of the surrounding culture. Census data seems to match court cases in numbers of endogamous groups (there were three), in numbers of endogamous intermarriage barriers (there were two), and in intermarriage patterns (the White-to-Colored barrier was weakest, the Colored–to-Black barrier was stronger, and the White-to-Black barrier was strongest). Hence, this study sees no reason to doubt that census-takers, by and large, were typical members of the middle-class White society in which they lived.

The wives in most exogamous marriages, then as now, were members of the White group. Fifty-one percent of the openly acknowledged, stable exogamous alliances in Anglo Alabama involved women of the White endogamous group and men of the Colored endogamous group. Counting clandestine or short-term alliances resulting in publicly acknowledged children increases the number to about 65 percent involving a White female.[13] This ratio is not unexpected. John Hope Franklin wrote "the practice of white women mixing with Negro men was fairly widespread during the colonial period and had not entirely ceased by 1865."[14] Incidentally, the sexual asymmetry ratio towards a 65-35 preponderance of White females in open relationships with Black or Colored males has remained remarkably stable for the United States as a whole since about 1850.[15] On the other hand, DNA admixture mapping reveals that, where the continent of origin of an American's patrilineal SR-Y markers differs from his matrilineal mtDNA, a slight majority have the opposite asymmetry (European male, African female).[16] Why does genetic admixture mapping tell a different history than

---

[13] Mills (1981), 16-34, 22.

[14] John Hope Franklin, *From Slavery to Freedom*, [1st] ed. (New York, 1947), 215-17.

[15] See "Appendix C – Census Data Processing Methodology" for details.

[16] E.J. Parra and others, "Ancestral Proportions and Admixture Dynamics in Geographically Defined African Americans Living in South Carolina," *American Journal of Physical Anthropology*, 114 (2001), 18-29.

court and census records? The most likely possibility is that interbreeding of male European masters with female African slaves was hidden from both the census and the courts.

It was legally (and, one presumes, socially, based upon frequency of occurrence) accepted at that place and time for a White child to have a parent or grandparent who was a member of the Colored or Black endogamous groups. For example, a Russell County freedom paper filed in 1844 by a man on behalf of his full sister deposed that he was White and their mother was White, but that their father was Colored and his sister was "a brown woman" married to a man of the Colored endogamous group and the mother of several Colored children. To avoid misunderstanding, the man attached affidavits from eleven respectable citizens, including two justices of the peace, a state legislator, and a U.S. senator that he himself was White.[17]

According to Gary Mills, who exhaustively traced the life of literally every free Black in antebellum Anglo-Alabama, "each man, woman and child—5,614 in all—...from birth to death:"[18]

> Numerous free mulattoes were permitted to cross the color line into white society in spite of obvious Negro physical features and a well-remembered ancestry that they made no attempt to shake. As did most southern states, Alabama defined Negroes or mulattoes [with a rule of 1/8 blood fraction].... In actual practice, both the Alabama judiciary and popular custom were far less discriminatory.[19]

As the cotton-growing industry spread westwards towards the Mississippi River, Alabama, like Florida and Louisiana, received an influx of English-speaking immigrants from Virginia and North Carolina. And, as in Florida and Louisiana, the immigrants achieved political power and worked to transform their

---

[17] As quoted in Mills (1981), 28.

[18] Ibid., 17.

[19] Ibid., 29. Like a plurality of states, antebellum Alabama had a statutory 1/8 blood-fraction rule. For an explanation of why 1/8 was so popular, see Physical Appearance, Blood Fraction, Association" in *Chapter 9. How the Law Decided if You Were Black or White.*

new homeland into an image of the old. They passed laws outlawing intermarriage and decreed a single, legally enforced, endogamous color line. The new laws ignored Alabama's traditional Black-to-Colored intermarriage barrier. They attempted to
legislate a joining of the Black and Colored communities into a
single endogamous group, as was common in states to the north.
The Alabama code of 1833 included a section decreeing that,
"All negroes, mulattoes, Indians and all persons of mixed blood,
descended from negro or Indian ancestors, to the third generation inclusive, though one ancestor of each generation may have
been a white person, whether bond or free; shall be taken, and
deemed incapable in law, to be witnesses in any case whatever,
except for and against each other."[20] The law's strict wording
suggests that the legislators were aware of the judicial resistance
of Franco-American Louisiana judges to Anglo-American legislators, discussed momentarily. They did not want judges to defy
lawmakers in Alabama, they way they were defying lawmakers
in Louisiana. The Alabama law was designed to offer no wiggle-
room to a recalcitrant judge. Its wording could not have been
clearer in defining a single non-White endogamous group,
eliminating the ancient distinction between Colored and Black.
And yet, the courts still diverged.

     Early in 1835, Ivey (a member of the White endogamous
group) sued Hardy (a member of Alabama's Colored endogamous group) for $20. Ivey testified under oath that Hardy owed
him the money, then objected when Hardy was called to the
stand to give his side of the story. The local justice of the peace
ruled that Hardy could not testify in his own defense. The law
was clear. Hardy was member of the Colored group, "descended
from Negro... to the third generation inclusive." And so, he was
"incapable in law, to be witness in any case whatever, except for
[cases involving only non-Whites]." Unable to present evidence,
Hardy was found liable and ordered to pay Ivey. He appealed to
the District Court instead. The district court reluctantly upheld
the adverse ruling, and so Hardy appealed to the Alabama Supreme Court.

---

[20] 2 Port. 548.

In *Ivey v. Hardy*, June of 1835, Justice Hitchcock of the Alabama Supreme Court reversed both lower courts and remanded the case back for trial with orders that Hardy be allowed to testify. "We do not think these statutes are to be thus construed," he wrote. "To give the plaintiff the benefit of this statute, and exclude the defendant from it, under the prohibition of the other, would open a door to very great frauds, and would be subversive of every principle of justice."[21] With wiggle-room or without it, judges raised in three-caste societies with two color lines continued to defy legislatures determined to impose a single color line separating two endogamous groups.

Incidentally, not only did the Montgomery court award Girard Hansford a divorce from his young White wife (who, you may recall, had vowed that all her future children would be the White offspring of her lovers), but it also awarded him sole custody of their children. This stunned Maria's latest White lover who had wanted to adopt and support his White child. The White lover and Maria thereupon launched a series of lawsuits to gain custody of the child.

In their final appeal, the ex-wife and her lover adopted a buckshot legal strategy. They argued that: (1) If Maria were White, then her marriage to Colored Girard had been void all along, and the lower court could neither grant divorce nor assign custody. (2) On the other hand, if Maria were not White, then by the rule of *onus probandi* regarding slave status, she must be presumed to have been a slave, and so could not legally contract marriage in any case, and so the original marriage was void, etc. Furthermore, (3) even if the marriage had been valid, then the divorce was still invalid because it had allowed the testimony of a Colored witness (either Maria or Girard) in a case involving a White person (the child). Finally, (4) even if the testimony and the divorce had been valid, then it was still in every child's best interest to stay with its mother. Appellate justice J. Goldthwaite tersely dismissed the first three arguments and ruled against the unfaithful wife on the fourth.[22]

---

[21] Idem.

[22] 10 Ala. 561. See Martha Elizabeth Hodes, *White Women, Black Men: Illicit Sex in the Nineteenth-Century South* (New Haven, 1997) for the most

French-Speaking Louisiana

As discussed earlier, *Gobu v. Gobu*, 1802 North Carolina, overturned six centuries of Spanish law under the 1265 *Siete Partidas* of King Alfonso X by placing the burden of proof upon the slave in a case for freedom, if the slave were Black.[23] Eight years later, a Louisiana case decided a similar situation. In *Adelle v. Beauregard*, 1810 Louisiana, a Colored woman sued her master and claimed her freedom under the ancient Spanish law that put the burden of proof upon the slave owner. Mr. Paillette, the owner's lawyer, cited Anglo-Saxon common law that the burden of proof lay on the plaintiff in a civil suit. The Superior Court of the Territory of New Orleans, First District quoted *Gobu v. Gobu* to rule that:

> Although it is in general correct, to require the plaintiff to produce his proof before the defendant can be called upon for his, it is otherwise, when the question is slavery or freedom. The law [*Siete Partidas*] cited by the plaintiff is certainly applicable to the present case. We do not say that it would be so, if the plaintiff were a negro, who perhaps would be required to establish his right by such evidence, as would destroy the force of the presumption arising from colour....

Nevertheless, the court placed the burden of proof on the alleged owner anyway and Adelle won her freedom. The court ruled that case law only said that Negroes were presumed to be slaves, and

---

useful study of marriages across the color line before Jim Crow. Hodes's study is more valuable than its subtitle suggests because, in fact, it starts in the mid seventeenth century and ends in the twentieth. Interestingly, in describing the Hansford case on page 107, Hodes writes, "Perhaps the judges wished to explain away the marriage of a white woman and a black man— and to erase racial ambiguity—by hastily agreeing that the woman was not really white at all." This is an interesting interpretation because the record shows that: (1) the judges explicitly reaffirmed the validity of the marriage since it was perfectly legal (it was her lawyer who had suggested otherwise), (2) the judges explicitly recorded her as White (it was her lawyer who had suggested otherwise), and (3) Girard was definitely not Black, he was legally and socially Colored, a vital distinction at that time and place.

[23] 1 N.C. 188. See "The Color Line Became Legally Important Around 1800" in *Chapter 9. How the Law Decided if You Were Black or White.*

Adelle was "Colored" not "Negro."[24] *State v. Cecil*, 1812 Louisiana was resolved similarly. A colored woman's testimony was objected to in a criminal case. Recent legislation had forbidden Blacks to testify in cases involving Whites because they were presumed to be slaves. Citing *Adelle v. Beauregard*, the court held that, while Blacks are presumed slaves, "Coloured persons are presumed free."[25]

Such judicial resistance to legislative intent continued until the 1850s, when Louisiana courts finally began to treat all but the wealthiest and most powerful Colored Creoles as free Blacks.[26] For contrast, consider that a North Carolina court in *State v. Barrow*, 1819 ruled that a woman with one Black great-grandparent and seven White ones was Black and so could not testify in a case involving the White father of her own children.[27]

Figure 19. Joseph Pilie

Late in 1828, in the Eastern District of Louisiana, Joseph Pilie went shopping for domestic help. Commercial slave trader, Joseph Lalande Ferrière told Pilie that he had just the thing—a female slave who knew the crafts of washing and ironing. Best of all, Lalande told his customer, the woman was also a skilled cook. Pilie paid cash and took the slave home with him. It did not take long for Joseph and his other domestic servants to discover that the new slave did a wretched job of washing and iron-

---

[24] 1 Mart o.s. 183.

[25] 2 Mart. o.s. 208.

[26] For a summary of this judicio-legislative struggle, see Virginia Meacham Gould, "The Free Creoles of Color of the Antebellum Gulf Ports of Mobile and Pensacola: A Struggle for the Middle Ground," in *Creoles of Color of the Gulf South*, ed. James H. Dormon (Knoxville, 1996), 28-50, 44.

[27] 7 N.C. 121.

ing, and could not cook at all. Her only skill in fact, seemed to be in running away, a talent that she demonstrated several times before the year was out.

Now, one of the innovations introduced to Louisiana's Spanish law by the Napoleonic Code, which was incorporated into the Louisiana Civil Code of 1808, had been the doctrine of redhibition—the original lemon law.[28] In Louisiana, then as now, if a product is so defective that the buyer would not have purchased it had its defects been known, the buyer can demand that the seller make it right or refund an appropriate fraction of the sale price.[29] In *Pilie v. Lalande*, 1829 Louisiana, the buyer filed a redhibitory suit in district court and won a $170 partial refund. In April of 1829, Lalande Ferrière appealed the verdict on the grounds that one of the witnesses to the slave's technical incompetence was a slave herself, and so should not have been allowed to testify in a case involving members of the White endogamous group. Contesting the appeal, Pilie hardened his own stance, demanding that the sale be rescinded and his entire purchase price refunded.[30]

Justice Porter agreed that, "the slave was sold as a washer, ironer and cook. The evidence shews that she possessed these qualities very defectively, if at all." Regarding the witness, the court ruled that, "The bill of exceptions does not state whether

---

[28] For brief accounts of Spanish versus French influences on Louisiana's 1808 Civil Code, see Ferdinand Stone, "The Law with a Difference and How it Came About," in *The Past as Prelude: New Orleans, 1718-1968*, ed. Hodding Carter (New Orleans, 1968), 42-70; William Wirt Howe, "Roman and Civil Law in America," *Harvard Law Review*, 16 (1903 1903), 142-58; Rodolfo Batiza, "The Influence of Spanish Law in Louisiana," *Tulane Law Review*, 23 (1958), 29-34; Rodolfo Batiza, "The Louisiana Civil Code of 1808: Its Actual Sources and Present Relevance," *Tulane Law Review*, 46 (1971), 4-31; and A. N. Yiannopoulos, "The Early Sources of Louisiana Law: Critical Appraisal of a Controversy," in *An Uncommon Experience: Law and Judicial Institutions in Louisiana, 1803-2003*, ed. Judith Kelleher Schafer and Warren M. Billings (Lafayette, 1997), 93-108.

[29] That the law is actively applied today is explained in the Louisiana Department of Justice web site at URL <http://www.ag.state.la.us/publications/redhibiton.htm>.

[30] 7 Mart. n.s. 648.

she was a negro, or mulatto. If the latter, the presumption was in favor of her being free...." For his part, the unhappy Pilie was sent home with his defective slave and only the $170 partial refund.

An Echo of Haiti

France began colonizing Louisiana in 1699, and New Orleans was founded in 1718.[31] As in almost every other slave-based New World colony, a buffer class of yeomen became necessary to prevent servile insurrection. As in Haiti and Jamaica—but in contrast to Virginia—Louisiana landowners bred their own yeoman class. At the very time that Governor Gooch was ripping Afro-European Virginia into two endogamous groups, article IX of France's *Code Noir* explicitly encouraged intermarriage between European colonists and their African slaves for just this purpose.[32]

French "racial" attitudes differed slightly from the Spanish. Like the Spanish, French New World planters lacked large labor-class populations of European descent. But, unlike the Spanish, they also lacked a long-standing tradition of intermarriage. So, instead of blending, as did the Spanish, they evolved a biracial buffer class, a distinctly separate group who considered themselves, and were considered by their society, to be of higher rank than Black slaves, but not fully members of the White endogamous group. The individuals of each biracial cohort who inherited unmistakably European appearance were accepted into White society. The remainder married among themselves.

Most Louisianans were involved with slavery one way or another. Wage labor was rare before the Industrial Revolution. Most unskilled and semiskilled workers, especially in agriculture, were acquired by apprenticeship, indenture, hereditary

---

[31] University of Chicago, ed. *The New Encyclopaedia Britannica*, 15 ed. (Chicago, 1974), 11:125.

[32] Werner Sollors, *Neither Black Nor White Yet Both* (Cambridge, 1997), 396.

peasantry, or slavery.[33] So, like other French colonies, Louisianans soon sorted themselves into a three-layer society: White European rulers, Black slaves, and a large in-between group of Colored yeoman Creoles. By the mid 1700's, the two free layers were solidly in place as endogamous groups. Most marriages were within each group. Few individuals passed between White and Creole groups. Few slaves were of European appearance. Most African-looking people were slaves.

Then, in 1762, the Seven Years' War (called the "French and Indian War," in North America) changed Louisiana unexpectedly. After conquering Canada, the British expelled French-speaking Acadians from Nova Scotia. These homeless refugees sought sanctuary in the French colony at the mouth of the Mississippi. Meanwhile, the treaty ending the Seven Years' War ceded Louisiana to Spain. So, the colony, formerly a satellite of Haiti, suddenly became a satellite of Cuba. This meant that Louisiana received a strong influx of French Acadians (Cajuns) at the very time that Spain was trying to impose its own laws and customs.[34] The long-term result of the culture clash was a land where many still speak French, but whose folk dances, festivals, and food reflect Spain. Mardi Gras is Spain's *Carne Vale* (*Carnaval*) and jambalaya is simply New World *paella*. But the immediate result of the Spanish takeover was the freeing of thousands of slaves and the rapid formation of a large free Black population.

The freeing of large numbers of slaves resulted from Spanish laws, which differed from the French. At this time, Spanish slavery resembled French and British slavery in two ways. Like them (but unlike slavery in medieval Europe or in eighteenth century west equatorial Africa), it was lifelong and hereditary through the mother.[35] But it differed in one important

---

[33] Peter Kolchin, *American Slavery 1619-1877* (New York, 1993), 4-5.

[34] R. Ernest Dupuy and Trevor N. Dupuy, *The Harper Encyclopedia of Military History*, 4 ed. (New York, 1993), 741.

[35] A. Norman Klein, "West African Unfree Labor Before and After the Rise of the Atlantic Slave Trade," in *Slavery in the New World: A Reader in Comparative History*, ed. Laura Foner and Eugene D. Genovese (Englewood Cliffs NJ, 1969a), 87-95.

way. Over the prior three centuries, Spanish law—*Las siete partidas* and the *Recopilación de leyes de los reinos de las Indias*—had been influenced by the powerful Catholic Church to treat slavery as a form of voluntary labor contract.[36] Spain had invented the doctrine of *coartación*.

Coartación meant that any slave who acquired five percent of his own value—typically by loan—had the right to demand his freedom, along with the obligation to gradually pay his former owner the remaining ninety-five percent.[37] The owner's only recourse was to dispute the person's market value by hiring an appraiser to testify against the appraiser hired by the slave. From 1762 to 1801, one Louisiana case is recorded where a court ruled against the slave—insufficient funds. Thousands of cases went the other way. In just one parish, between 1771 and 1803, 477 slaves thus freed themselves. Throughout the colony, these cases add up to more compulsory, court-ordered *coartación* manumissions than all other manumissions combined (voluntary, willed, conditional).[38] Consequently, the freed Black population of Louisiana grew seven-fold from 165 in 1769 to 1,175 by 1785.[39]

The exploding number of people of African ancestry freed by *coartación* created a three-caste system apart from the slaves: a few White Europeans, a large majority of biracial Creoles, and a new population of Black former slaves. It superficially resembled Haiti or Jamaica. But, in contrast to the West Indies, Louisiana's two color lines were relatively permeable. As Black descendants of former slaves ascended the economic ladder they were accepted into the Colored Creole community. Similarly,

---

[36] Frank Tannenbaum, *Slave and Citizen, the Negro in the Americas* (Boston, 1946), 43-58.

[37] Ibid., 54.

[38] Kimberly S. Hanger, "Origins of New Orleans Free Creoles of Color," in *Creoles of Color of the Gulf South*, ed. James H. Dormon (Knoxville, 1996b), 1-27. This is not meant to imply that such a high manumission rate was typical of anywhere other than the Gulf coast and Florida.

[39] Laura Foner, "Free People of Color in Louisiana and St. Domingue: A Comparative Portrait of Two Three-Caste Societies," *Journal of Social History*, 3 (no. 4, 1970), 406-30.

impoverished planters fleeing the bloody chaos of Haiti's revolution (1791-1806) descended into Louisiana's middle group. Within their own group, the Colored Creoles developed a social system resembling that of pre-Reformation Europe: a social hierarchy based on religion, breeding, and wealth, with little significance given to shades of skin color among themselves. Nevertheless, many were powerful slave owners whose customs forbade intermarriage with free Blacks (former slaves). They founded the earliest "blue-vein" societies for Afro-Europeans of preponderantly European appearance.

According to Eric Foner, "The wealth, social standing, education, and unique history of this community set it apart... from most other free persons of color." The Colored Creoles identified more with European than with American customs. Most spoke only French and many enrolled their children in private academies in Brussels or Paris. As aristocrats, they were acutely self-conscious of a military tradition dating back to when they had helped Andrew Jackson win the 1814 Battle of New Orleans.[40] As of 1830, the U.S. census showed that 967 of them owned 4,382 slaves, about one Louisiana slave in twenty-five.[41] Seen another way, of the 1,834 Colored Creole and free Black heads of households who lived in 1839 New Orleans, 752 of them (41 percent) owned at least one slave.[42]

But after the 1803 Louisiana Purchase, English-speaking Americans with English-speaking slaves flooded into Louisiana. Although *coartación* was repealed at once and slaves were forbidden to read, the rights of members of Louisiana's native free Black and Colored Creole endogamous groups were not curtailed overnight. Instead, the next half-century saw a loss of free

---

[40] Eric Foner, *Reconstruction: America's Unfinished Revolution* (New York, 1988), 47.

[41] Joel Williamson, *New People: Miscegenation and Mulattoes in the United States* (New York, 1980), 81-82; James Hugo Johnston, *Race Relations in Virginia & Miscegenation in the South, 1776-1860* (Amherst, 1970), 47; Peter Kolchin, *American Slavery 1619-1877* (New York, 1993), 242.

[42] Virginia R. Dominguez, *White by Definition: Social Classification in Creole Louisiana* (New Brunswick NJ, 1986), 252.

Black' rights and a slower but steady erosion of the Colored Creoles' interracial way of life. At the heart of the change lay the distinction between "free Black" and "Colored Creole." To French-speaking Louisianans, the color line between the Black and Colored groups was obvious. Hence, the Colored Creoles did not initially fear anti-Black laws because they did not consider themselves to be Black. But to English-speaking newcomers, the only color line was between members of the White endogamous group and everyone else. To them, light Colored Creoles were also free Blacks.

Two other appealed court cases in Louisiana between 1820 and 1840 are of interest. In a suit for slander, *Cauchoix v. Dupuy*, 1831, the defendant had publicly stated that Cauchoix had African ancestry. Dupuy's defense was that his statement had been accurate and that Cauchoix did, in fact, descend partially from Negro stock. For his part, the plaintiff presented family records to show that all of his ancestors immigrated from Europe within the past century.[43] The case reveals that living under a three-caste system did not imply "racial" tolerance. To accuse someone of a trace of African ancestry was considered an insult to a member of the White endogamous group. Furthermore, judging by intermarriage rates across the two color lines, to accuse a Colored Creole of being Black would also have been an insult. Also, it is noteworthy that Cauchoix's ancestors' having immigrated from Europe was considered evidence of their suitability for membership in the White endogamous group. This would change a century later during the Jim Crow era. After the triumph of the one-drop rule, merely being of one hundred percent European ancestry would not mandate White group membership—there may have been "racial" mixing in Europe.[44]

One final Louisiana court case of this period is of interest. *Bore v. Bush*, 1827, was an appeal by a Colored Creole of his arrest and conviction for disrespect towards a White person.[45] It

---

[43] Helen Tunnicliff Catterall and James J. Hayden, *Judicial Cases Concerning American Slavery and The Negro* (New York, 1968), 3:493.

[44] See, for example, 18 Ala. App. 354.

[45] 6 Mart. n.s. 1.

seems that one of the laws passed by incoming Anglo-American legislators in the decades after the Louisiana purchase, in an effort to transform Louisiana from a three-caste to a two-caste society, made it a crime for any "free person of color" to be disrespectful towards a member of the White endogamous group.[46] The law used those very words, "free person of color," in order specifically to target the arrogant (in Anglo-American eyes) Creole Coloreds, who called themselves *gens de couleur libre*. The law further stated that any free Black accused of such disrespect could be summarily tried and convicted by a local justice of the peace, and had no right to a jury trial. Bore, a Colored Creole, underwent such an experience. He sued for false imprisonment on the grounds of having been denied a trial by jury. Justice Porter agreed with the prosecution that, "Free persons of colour, are certainly bound to treat the citizens of the state with respect; and if they do not, they are subject to fine and imprisonment." And he also agreed that free Blacks did not have the right to a jury trial in such cases. But, he pointed out, Bore was Colored, not Black, and "Free persons of colour are entitled to a trial by jury, and cannot be tried for offenses by a justice of the peace." Justice Porter went on to explain that, since the defendant was not Black, the justice of the peace had only the right to turn Bore over to district court for trial by jury on the disrespect charge. He did not have the authority to try, convict, and imprison a Colored man on his own. The original conviction was overturned and the local magistrate ordered to pay damages for having acted outside of his jurisdiction.

All of these cases confirmed the trend observed earlier in Louisiana (*Adelle v. Beauregard* 1810 and *State v. Cecil* 1812) and in Alabama (*Ivey v. Hardy* 1835). For the first few decades after Anglo-American legislators created laws designed to impose the U.S. single-color line system, local courts struggled to exercise judicial resistance. Even State Supreme Court justices evaded such legislation in order to preserve the three-caste system associated with French society. The single Mississippi case

---

[46] The Black Code, sec. 40; Paul A. Kunkel, "Modifications in Louisiana Negro Legal Status Under Louisiana Constitutions, 1812-1957," *Journal of Negro History*, 44 (1959), 1-25.

of the period also supported a three-caste system, but through a maroon community. In *Mitchell v. Sherman*, 1835, a person named Locklear, a member of the Lumbee maroon community of Robeson County, North Carolina (called "Croatans" before 1953), was ruled to be of the White group, despite the Lumbees' known African admixture.[47]

*   *   *   *   *

This chapter described the second and third of four U.S. regions whose color-line customs differed from the mainstream—Alabama and Louisiana. Both cultures had two mildly endogamous color lines separating three groups: White, Colored, and Black. Both could trace their color line traditions to French colonies in general and to Haiti in particular.

---

[47] Catterall (1968), 3:288. "Locklear" is one of the most common of Lumbee family names. In a July 22, 2003 discussion thread on the H-South discussion group, the group moderator posted the following informational website: URL
<http://www.pbs.org/wgbh/pages/frontline/shows/secret/famous/locklear.html>. For an overview of U.S. maroons, see "The Maroon Escape Hatch" in *Chapter 5. The Rate of Black-to-White "Passing."* Also, see "It was a 'Divide and Conquer' Tactic" in *Chapter 8. Why Did Virginia's Rulers Invent a Color Line?*

Chapter 12.
Spanish Florida:
No Endogamous Color Line

Job Wiggins died in 1797, leaving several properties in northeast Florida and in Cuba. The court in St. Augustine, finding no will on record, ordered a militia officer to take some men and secure the Wiggins plantation, on the St. Johns River near Tocoi. The soldiers marched to the site and took possession of the deceased planter's livestock and slaves pending the estate sale. Following the court's instructions, they also brought the Wiggins children into town to stay temporarily with a court-appointed guardian. One of the female slaves—a brown-skinned woman with long black hair—protested loudly. She insisted, even after being locked into the slave-holding pen in St. Augustine with the others, that she was not a slave. She said that she just happened to be dressed for labor, supervising slaves in a field, when the soldiers arrived. She said that she was Mrs. Nancy Wiggins, the planter's widow, and that she was now owner and mistress of the Wiggins properties. And so, what started as a routine probate hearing became one of only two cases before 1840 where someone's "racial" status was determined by a Florida court. The court documents in this case offer a glimpse of social attitudes of that place and time, not by what they said, which is straightforward, but by how they said it.

In the case's earliest depositions and transcripts, Nancy was referred to as a "black woman" (*mujer morena*),[1] and only by her first name. When her own lawyers arrived in court (contacted by her determined thirteen-year-old-daughter), the documents began to refer to her by surname and as a "colored woman" (*mujer parda*), no longer "Black."[2] Once her own witnesses arrived in town to testify, the court reporter began to see her as a "colored lady" (*señora parda*), no longer a mere "woman." Finally, by the time that politically powerful Juan Leslie, CEO of the Panton and Leslie trading company, arrived in the colonial capital to testify that the Wiggins family were personal friends, and that Job had left his will with the company for safekeeping, she had become "Milady Nancy" (*Doña Nansi*) in court documents, and subsequent records make no mention of her skin tone.[3]

The Wiggins probate case exemplifies social attitudes in Spanish Florida. It reveals more than merely the bleaching effects of wealth. As it turned out, Panton and Leslie's office staff never did manage to find Job's will. But the reason why the court balked at letting Mrs. Wiggins and her children inherit anyway was that Job and Nancy were Protestants. They had been married in an Anglican church during British rule. Only Catholic marriages were legal under the Spanish regime. Even more illu-

---

[1] It is impossible perfectly to translate Spanish Florida's color designations into English. The usage above equates the darkest designation found in public documents, "*moreno*," with the English term "black," which has the same usage. Neither of the Spanish words for the color black (*prieto* or *negro*) are found in official documents as color designations for people. Similarly, the term "*pardo*" used in official documents of Spanish Florida to designate biracial or mixed-looking people literally means "brown." It is translated above as "Colored," which is the closest equivalent in the three-caste systems of the contemporary lower South.

[2] That the terms "pardo" and "moreno" were not interchangeable in Spanish Florida, is evidenced by Cathedral Parish records of marriages, baptisms, and burials as well as civil marriage licenses being recorded separately for "pardos" and "morenos" with meticulous consistency.

[3] Estate probate of Job Wiggins, *East Florida Papers*, Section #71, Reel #136 (St. Augustine Historical) or #137 (P.K. Yonge). This case is not included in the tabulations of Appendix B because it was never appealed.

minating is that "Nancy" was just her nickname. Her maiden name was Anna Gallum, and she had no African ancestry at all. She was originally from India, a brown-skinned Bengali who had come from London many years before, to be a member of Rollestown, a utopian commune founded by a British nobleman dreamer named Denys Rolle.[4] She had moved west of the St. Johns when the commune collapsed, and became a Seminole—an Indian Indian, as it were. There, she met and married the young Job when he was working as an Indian trading-post supervisor for Panton and Leslie.[5] The point is that her being labeled *morena* (black) due to her dark-brown skin tone had no effect on her legal or social status. As we shall see below, it did not affect the marriage prospects of her children.

* * * * *

This chapter introduces the fourth society, within what became the United States, whose color-line customs differed from the mainstream—Spanish Florida. It is presented in three topics: *Echoes of Spain and Latin America* traces the lack of an endogamous color line to Latin American and, ultimately, to Spanish customs. *Legal Policy Regarding Afro-Hispanic Colonists* shows how the state inadvertently encouraged people to switch "racial" identities by attempting unsuccessfully to impose an endogamous barrier. *Society Changed When Americans Arrived* narrates the transition from Spanish to Anglo-American laws and customs.

---

[4] Carl Bohnenberger, "The Settlement of Charlotia (Rolles Town), 1765," *The Florida Historical Quarterly*, 4 (no. 1, 1925), 43-49.

[5] William Bartram and Mark Van Doren, *The Travels of William Bartram* (New York, 1928), 100. For more biographical details, see also the January 14, 1812, wedding of Benjamin Wiggins (Job and Nancy's son) with Nicolassa Edimburgh (Francis Philip's daughter), St. Augustine Cathedral Parish Records, Reel #248L (P.K. Yonge).

Echoes of Spain and Latin America

To understand why Spanish Florida lacked an endoga-mous color line, look at Iberia in the colonial period. Spanish and Portuguese parents often have children who span a wide skin-tone range.[6] This is why Castilian has so many words for every skin tone from *trigueño* (wheat colored) to *moreno* (moor-ish colored). Most Spaniards attribute their diversity to seven centuries of North African military occupation. In fact, after the reconquest decimated Iberia's labor class, Spain and Portugal repopulated by importing equatorial African slaves.

> [After the reconquest] Black slaves were imported in ever-increasing numbers into Southern Portugal and neighboring regions of Spain, where Seville became an important slave market. These regions had greatly suffered from wars be-tween Christians and Muslims, and their populations had been largely depleted. Imported Africans were employed not only for service in wealthy households but also for work in the fields and for a variety of tasks in the cities, especially as stevedores in the harbours. Because the Portuguese, and to a lesser degree also the Spaniards, as a result of the many con-quests, had little race or colour consciousness, the various elements of the population mixed relatively freely and ulti-mately merged.[7]

By 1500, Iberia was landing over one thousand sub-Saharan Af-ricans a year.[8] By 1550, biracials outnumbered Europeans from the Algarve to as far north as Lisbon.[9] By 1600, according to Mary Wilhelmina Williams, "there was no marked color line, and the blood of the two races mingled freely, resulting eventu-

---

[6] See "How Many Black Children are Born into White Families?" in *Chap-ter 3. The Heredity of "Racial" Traits.*

[7] University of Chicago, ed. *The New Encyclopaedia Britannica*, 15 ed. (Chicago, 1974), 16:859.

[8] Hugh Thomas, *The Slave Trade: The Story of the Atlantic Slave Trade: 1440-1870* (New York, 1997), 22-24.

[9] Lerone Bennett Jr., *Before the Mayflower: A History of Black America*, 6th rev. ed. (New York, 1993), 32.

ally in Negroid physical characteristics in the Portuguese nation."[10] At their peak population, Africans amounted to about eight percent of Portugal's population (less than the United States') and five percent of Spain's.[11] African communities had their own craftsmen's guilds, churches, schools, neighborhoods, and "Black" burial societies.[12] Yet within a few generations, Iberia's Africans vanished without a trace, their genes absorbed and dispersed into the European melting pot as thoroughly as the Danes into England.[13] The Black burial societies of Barcelona and Valencia still exist today. Membership has passed directly from father to son for four centuries, but the members have become White Europeans.[14]

To be sure, each of the sources cited in the preceding paragraph can be contested because some say that Africans imported to Spain were urban workers, not farm laborers; that the reconquest decimated the hidalgo class, not the peasant class; that the genetic absorption and dispersal of alleles from African laborers does not appear in written Portuguese histories; that the characterization of Portuguese as having "Negroid" traits is mistaken; and that the numbers of Africans imported and assimilated were fewer than the above estimates. Nevertheless, more than one study has confirmed 8 percent of recent sub-Saharan DNA genetic admixture in modern Portuguese and 5 percent of recent sub-Saharan genetic admixture in modern Spaniards.[15]

---

[10] As quoted in Bennett (1993), 32.

[11] Thomas (1997), 48-86, 804.

[12] David Brion Davis, *The Problem of Slavery in Western Culture* (Ithaca, 1966), 53.

[13] Frank Tannenbaum, *Slave and Citizen, the Negro in the Americas* (Boston, 1946), 14-15, 44.

[14] Leslie B. Rout, *The African Experience in Spanish America, 1502 to the Present Day* (Cambridge UK, 1976), 9, 18-20.

[15] Martin Richards and others, "Extensive Female-Mediated Gene Flow from Sub-Saharan Africa into Near Eastern Arab Populations," *American Journal of Human Genetics*, 72 (2003), 1058-64; H.B. Corte-Real and others, "Genetic Diversity in the Iberian Peninsula Determined from Mitochondrial Sequence Analysis," *Annals of Human Genetics*, 60 (no. 4, July 1996), 331-50.

The alleles are undeniably there. One might argue that this genetic component did not come from assimilated African slaves. Nevertheless, it is present, it is from sub-Saharan Africa, and it arrived within the past 500 years. As one study put it, "the detection of L sequences at 7.1% in the [Portuguese] mitochondrial pool [seems] to support the above-mentioned pattern of admixture with African slaves."[16] (The comparable recent sub-Saharan genetic admixture fraction for the White U.S. population is one-tenth of that number, about 0.7 percent.[17])

Africans and Iberians merged in the New World also. As noted by Du Bois, Boas, Frazier, Harris, Mörner, Degler and many others, Iberians in the New World, like Muslims in the Old, continued genetic absorption and dispersal.[18] Where Africans were a minority (Mexico, Argentina) people of African appearance were absorbed and eventually vanished. Parish records from Santiago de Guatemala between 1626 and 1769 reveal that on average, 7.9 percent of free people seen as Black or biracial married "pure" Spaniards. In one decade (1750-59), such intermarriages exceeded 12 percent—well over ten times the mean U.S. twentieth century rate. [19] In 1830s Cuba, the rate was 19 percent.[20] In 1646-1746 Mexico City, it was 8.5 percent.[21] These

---

[16] L. Pereira, M.J. Prata, and A. Amorim, "Diversity of mtDNA Lineages in Portugal: Not a Genetic Edge of European Variation," *Annals of Human Genetics*, 64 (2000), 501.

[17] See "Admixture Scatter Diagrams" in *Chapter 2. Afro-European Genetic Admixture in the United States*.

[18] Dubois: The Crisis 7 (April 1914), 286-87 as quoted in David J. Hellwig, ed. *African-American Reflections on Brazil's Racial Paradise* (Philadelphia, 1992), 32; Boas: as quoted in Roger Sanjek, "Intermarriage and the Future of Races in the United States," in *Race*, ed. Steven Gregory and Roger Sanjek (New Brunswick NJ, 1994), 103-30, 104; Frazier: As quoted in Hellwig (1992), 121; Marvin Harris, *Patterns of Race in the Americas* (Westport CT, 1964); Magnus Morner, *Race Mixture in the History of Latin America* (Boston, 1967); Carl N. Degler, *Neither Black nor White: Slavery and Race Relations in Brazil and the United States* (New York, 1971).

[19] Christopher Lutz, *Santiago de Guatemala, 1541-1773: City, Caste, and the Colonial Experience* (Norman, 1994), 179, 180.

[20] Ramón de la Sagra, *Historia Economico-Política y Estadística de la Isla de Cuba* (Havana, 1831), 20-24.

rates were sufficient to thoroughly mix the groups within a few generations, dispersing African alleles throughout the population thus eliminating or absorbing the African phenotype.[22] Where colonial Africans were a majority (the Caribbean, Brazil), the same thorough mixing resulted in today's populations, which display a genetically predictable normal (Gaussian or bell-shaped) skin-tone distribution. Roughly one Puerto Rican, Cuban, or Dominican in ten looks White to modern Americans, about one in ten looks Black, and the rest look "Hispanic" (meaning in-between).[23] The point is not that Hispanic populations enjoy wide diversity. It is that there was and is no endogamous color line in Hispanic societies.[24]

An example may illustrate the point. Spain's army in the New World was a ruthless meritocracy. And so, they sometimes rewarded those with a knack for leading troops to victory, whatever their ancestry. Although other former African slaves reached high military rank, the best-known was Juan Valiente of New Spain, who served under Diego de Almagro in the failed conquest of Chile in 1535-37 and under Pedro de Valdivia in the successful conquest of Chile in 1550-51. He was granted hidalgo status and an *encomienda* (a village of Native Americans to serve as hereditary forced laborers) by Holy Roman Emperor Charles V.[25] He was killed in combat against the Araucanians

---

[21] Edgar F. Love, "Marriage Patterns of Persons of African Descent in a Colonial Mexico City Parish," *Hispanic American Historical Review*, 41 (no. 1, February 1971), 79-91.

[22] Robert S. Stuckert, "The African Ancestry of the White American Population," *Ohio Journal of Science*, 55 (May, 1958), 155-60.

[23] Curt Stern, *Principles of Human Genetics*, 3d ed. (San Francisco, 1973), 443-52; L. L. Cavalli-Sforza and W. F. Bodmer, *The Genetics of Human Populations* (Mineola NY, 1999), 527-31.

[24] L. L. Cavalli-Sforza and W. F. Bodmer, *The Genetics of Human Populations* (Mineola NY, 1999), 788-90.

[25] Leslie B. Rout, *The African Experience in Spanish America, 1502 to the Present Day* (Cambridge UK, 1976), 76; John Kelly Thornton, *Africa and Africans in the Making of the Atlantic World, 1400-1800*, 2nd ed. (New York, 1998), 141; Frederick P. Bowser, "Colonial Spanish America," in *Neither Slave Nor Free: The Freedmen of African Descent in the Slave So-*

(who were not defeated until 1883),[26] but his son also became a military officer, as did his own son and so on. According to Valiente family lore, his descendants flourished in Colombia during the Bourbon dynasty, and a family branch moved to Puerto Rico in the 1880s, where its military tradition continues in the U.S. Army.

That Spanish Florida (like Spain and Latin America) lacked an endogamous color line is often misunderstood. When this point is made by a Hispanic, Anglo-American scholars often insist that Latin Americans were, or are, just as "racist" as North Americans. As David Brion Davis wrote, comparing Latin America with the United States, "It is an open question whether a society that sees every addition of white blood as a step towards purification is more, or less, prejudiced than a society that sees any appreciable trace of Negro blood as a mark of degradation."[27] And V. Martínez-Alier pointed out that Spanish colonial leadership was often "racist" in rhetoric, vilifying colonists of African appearance.[28] But nothing herein suggests that Hispanics were less "racist" than Americans. Davis may be correct that elite colonial Iberians tried to bequeath to their New World posterity a rigidly stratified society with negligible upward mobility. If so, compared to North America, they succeeded. Martínez-Alier may also be correct that they strove to tie these hermetic social layers to degree of African ancestry. If so, compared to North America, they failed. In short, despite near-impenetrable class divisions that are still in place, and although dark Hispanics tend to be poorer on average than fair ones, no endogamous color line ever formed in Latin America (or in the Islamic world, for that matter).

---

cieties of the New World, ed. David W. Cohen and Jack P. Greene (Baltimore, 1972), 20.

[26] Benjamin Keen, *A History of Latin America*, 5th ed. (Boston, 1996), 731.

[27] David Brion Davis, *The Problem of Slavery in Western Culture* (Ithaca, 1966), 275n24.

[28] Verena Martinez Alier, *Marriage, Class and Colour in Nineteenth-Century Cuba: A Study of Racial Attitudes and Sexual Values in a Slave Society* (London, 1974).

Part of the misunderstanding may spring from moral judgment. Raw facts cannot tells us whether Iberian and Latin American acceptance of Afro-European intermarriage is either praiseworthy or reprehensible. Nevertheless, many historians express themselves on this point. G.R. Andrews shows that unimpeded out-marriage caused the African-looking population of Buenos Aries to fall steadily from 15,000 in 1838, to 8,000 in 1887, to nil today. It vanished by genetic absorption and dispersal, as did the African-looking populations of sixteenth-century Spain or of Mexico.[29] Andrews concludes that this shows that Buenos Aires was intensely "racist."[30] Frederick P. Bowser wrote that Latin American intermarriage "was not conducive to racial solidarity among those of African descent."[31] P. Wade wrote that colonial Hispanic intermarriage was deliberately calculated to destroy the Black "race."[32] J.R. Washington, Jr. wrote that colonial Hispanic intermarriage ruled out "cultural acceptance of blackness as a firm and rich experience," and that it was "unconsciously bent on genocide."[33] R.L. Jackson wrote that colonial Hispanic intermarriage was deliberate genocide, "a process that, while loosely defined as ethnic and cultural fusion, is often understood to mean the physical, spiritual, and cultural

---

[29] UPI, *Analysis: Race Now Not Black and White* (May 8, 2002).

[30] George Reid Andrews, "Race Versus Class Association: The Afro-Argentines of Buenos Aires," *Journal of Latin American Studies (UK)*, 11 (no. 1, 1979), 19-39.

[31] Frederick P. Bowser, "Colonial Spanish America," in *Neither Slave Nor Free: The Freedmen of African Descent in the Slave Societies of the New World*, ed. David W. Cohen and Jack P. Greene (Baltimore, 1972), 58; Frederick P. Bowser, "The Free Person of Color in Mexico City and Lima: Manumission and Opportunity, 1580-1650," in *Race and Slavery in the Western Hemisphere: Quantitative Studies*, ed. Stanley L. Engerman, et al. (Princeton, 1975), 360.

[32] Peter Wade, *Blackness and Race mixture: The Dynamics of Racial Identity in Colombia* (Baltimore, 1993), 7-8.

[33] As quoted in Roger Sanjek, "Intermarriage and the Future of Races in the United States," in *Race*, ed. Steven Gregory and Roger Sanjek (New Brunswick NJ, 1994), 105.

rape of black people."[34] He also wrote that colonial Hispanic intermarriage was "tantamount to white lynching."[35] Such moral judgments may be reasonable. Nevertheless, the only point made here is that, genocidal or not, Spanish Florida lacked an endogamous color line.

Legal Policy Regarding Afro-Hispanic Colonists

During Spain's Habsburg dynasty (1516-1700) royal policy had been a mix of idealism and pragmatism. Ideally, no one unable to prove purity of blood (*limpieza de sangre*) could become *hidalgo* (the social rank immediately above slaves, servants, artisans, and peasants), and only *hidalgos* could hold public office.[36] Pragmatically, Spain's was a huge empire, and those who could help run it might be rewarded. Hence, the Holy Inquisition met two goals at once by selling certificates of *limpieza* for a steep price. The certificates gave a legitimate way for the socially powerful to become *hidalgo*, regardless of ancestry. The certificates also made money for the Church.[37]

Spain's Bourbon dynasty (1700-today) was more practical. The reformer king, Charles III (1759-1788), tried to

---

[34] As quoted in David J. Hellwig, ed. *African-American Reflections on Brazil's Racial Paradise* (Philadelphia, 1992), 217.

[35] As quoted in Judy Bieber, "Race, Resistance, and Regionalism: Perspectives from Brazil and Spanish America," *Latin American Research Review*, 32 (no. 3, 1997), 159.

[36] Originally, *limpieza de sangre* meant the absence of Moorish or Jewish ancestry. See Antonio Dominguez Ortiz, *La Sociedad Espanola en el Siglo XVIII* (Madrid, 1955), 233. In the New World, the concept came also to be associated with African ancestry. See Verena Martinez Alier, *Marriage, Class and Colour in Nineteenth-Century Cuba: A Study of Racial Attitudes and Sexual Values in a Slave Society* (London, 1974), 15.

[37] Marcelo Martinez Alcubilla, *Codigos antiguos de Espana: coleccion completa de todos los codigos de Espana, desde el Fuero juzgo hasta la Novisima recopilacion, con un glosario de las principales voces anticuadas, notas, bindices parciales y un repertorio general alfabbetico de materias* (Madrid, 1885), 890-91.

strengthen racialist ideals by decreeing that marriage between *hidalgos* and Afro-Americans was forbidden without case-by-case government permission.[38] For practicality, he delegated permission-granting authority to local governors. Given the demands of a contentious empire, New World Hispanics were soon interpreting "race" as a synonym for "rank."

Although there were exceptions, Bourbon "racial" policies often decreed that military officers in the New World (who, by definition were *hidalgo* elite) could receive permission to marry only if they wed Spanish-born women of "pure" blood. Apparently, too many soldiers had been marrying mixed women in the New World. All officers were required to follow the decree—even the Black officers. Hence, within three generations, the Valiente family and hundreds like it, lost their African looks and became European-looking. This sometimes caused confusion. Now and then, a light-brown youngster of hereditary military, commercial, or scholarly rank (the three routes to becoming *hidalgo*) was refused entry to an exclusive university or medical school in Spain or Latin America. The king's solution was to issue a specific document in each case (a *real cédula de gracias al sacar*) patterned on the old *limpieza de sangre* certificates, decreeing that young Francisco Valiente, say, was legally White by royal edict.[39]

Until 1821, when it was acquired by the United States, historical contingency had made Florida into a multicultural community. When Spain took over the colony from the British in 1784 and Governor Zéspedes took office, the colony had only five Spanish-born families. The rest were from Scotland, England, Ireland, Switzerland, France, Turkey, Italy, Corsica, Greece, the Balearics, the United States, Africa, and (like Anna Gallum) India.[40] It was also a society under Bourbon Spain's

---

[38] Martinez Alier (1974), 11.

[39] Frederick P. Bowser, "Colonial Spanish America," in *Neither Slave Nor Free: The Freedmen of African Descent in the Slave Societies of the New World*, ed. David W. Cohen and Jack P. Greene (Baltimore, 1972), 46.

[40] Abel Poitrineau, "Demography and the Political Destiny of Florida During the Second Spanish Period," *The Florida Historical Quarterly*, 66 (no. 4 April, 1988), 422.

laws and customs, a system that focused more on social rank or class than on skin tone.

Spanish Florida courts seldom had to adjudicate slave status, as they did in the English-Speaking United States. Consequently, no rule of physical appearance, of blood fraction, or of association ever arose under Spanish law. A social tradition that Hidalgo ranks and above enjoyed privileges over those of lower rank may superficially seem to resemble South Carolina's rule of socioeconomic class, but there was no connection between rank and which side of an endogamous color line you were on. There was no endogamous color line.

To grasp how this worked, consider the case of the three Sánchez daughters. On February 6, 1795, 49-year-old Francisco Pérez, a White physician from the royal hospital at El Escorial in Castile received the colonial governor's permission to marry 20-year-old María Beatriz Sánchez of Saint Augustine, Florida. The bride was the daughter of European planter Francisco Xavier Sánchez from Spain and his biracial concubine of the South Carolina Mulatto Elite, Beatrice Stone. The wedding was widely celebrated because Governor Quesada's permission was phrased as a *cédula de gracias al sacar*, thus officially conferring legal Whiteness upon the bride. Father O'Reilly inscribed the nuptial sacrament into the parish book of White weddings and, from that day forth, María was invariably addressed with the *Doña* honorific and referred to as White.[41]

On May 10, 1795, 40-year-old José Manuel Fernández, a European sailor from Galicia married 16-year-old Ana Sánchez, the next younger daughter of Francisco Xavier Sánchez and his concubine. (Apparently, Sánchez's two younger daughters were allowed to wed only after the eldest was married off.) In a replay of her sister's wedding three months earlier, the colonial governor again bestowed both permission on the happy couple and legal Whiteness upon the bride, and again the Church sanctioned the transformation. Ana also became a White Doña, like her older sister María.[42]

---

[41] East Florida Papers, Section #69, Reel #132, Marriage License #82.

[42] Ibid., Marriage License #83.

Finally, on January 4, 1802, Francisco Sánchez, a European soldier from Granada married Catalina Sánchez. This was the wedding of the third and final daughter of European Francisco Xavier Sánchez and Beatrice Stone of the South Carolina Mulatto elite. For the third time, official Whiteness bestowed upon a child of this illustrious and influential family sparked public celebrations.[43]

Slavery in Spanish Florida also differed from slavery in the English-speaking United States. Like Louisiana, Spanish Florida interpreted slavery as a form of lifelong, hereditary but ultimately voluntary labor contract between juridically equal citizens. According to Michael Gannon:

> Slaves enjoyed a legal right to protest (file lawsuit) against harsh treatment. Masters were not allowed to make slaves work on Sundays and Holy Days. Slaveowners convicted of undue severity were fined [and, if recidivists, their slaves were court-confiscated and sold to reputable owners]. Slave marriages were encouraged and protected. Under no circumstances could a slave family be split and, if one member was sold, the others had to go to the same buyer. Slaves had to be properly fed and clothed, and required to be given Christian instruction necessary to fit them for worthy reception of the Church's sacraments [reading, writing, arithmetic].[44]

---

[43] Ibid., Marriage License #142.

[44] Michael V. Gannon, *The Cross in the Sand* (Gainesville FL, 1965), 111. Whether these laws were enforced against slaveowners in practice or were just empty legal promises is a fascinating question with a vast literature. Tannenbaum, Elkins, Genovese, Gannon, and Landers provide a wealth of data and anecdotes supporting the position that slaves in some places and times (notably Spanish Florida, Alabama, and Louisiana in the late eighteenth and early nineteenth century) were in fact protected by vigorous law enforcement of their rights as Spanish citizens. See Frank Tannenbaum, *Slave and Citizen, the Negro in the Americas* (Boston, 1946) 120-26; Stanley M. Elkins, "Slavery in Capitalist and Non-Capitalist Countries," in *Slavery in the New World: A Reader in Comparative History*, ed. Laura Foner and Eugene D. Genovese (Englewood Cliffs NJ, 1969), 8-26; Eugene D. Genovese, "The Treatment of Slaves in Different Countries: Problems in the Application of the Comparative Method," in *Slavery in the New World: A Reader in Comparative History*, ed. Laura Foner and Eugene D. Genovese (Englewood Cliffs NJ, 1969), 202-10; Michael V. Gannon, *The Cross*

As in Louisiana, *coartación* was often invoked in Spanish Florida. In July of 1794, Francis Philip Edinburgh sued for his freedom. His owner was Francisco Xavier Sánchez, the father of the three girls mentioned above, María, Ana, and Catalina. Sánchez was also East Florida's wealthiest rancher and the government's meat and timber contractor (and creditor). Sánchez's plantations were the main source of supplies to the Florida militia. The dispute hinged on Edinburgh's value. The slave was a manager who operated several of Sánchez's plantations with little supervision. So, Sánchez argued, Edinburgh's value on the labor market was that of an executive, far more than the pittance that the slave offered to buy himself. Edinburgh's lawyer argued that a slave's *coartación* value is that of an unskilled laborer, no matter his marketable skills. The court ruled in Edinburgh's favor, citing his greater potential contribution to society as a free man. Having freed him, the authorities promptly commissioned

---

in the Sand (Gainesville FL, 1965), 111; Jane Landers, *Black Society in Spanish Florida* (Chicago, 1999) 95. Harris, Davis, Mintz, and Thomas have found that in other times and places (notably 1830's Cuba and 1840's Puerto Rico), the landed gentry were immune to action by either the state or the Church. See Marvin Harris, "The Myth of the Friendly Master," in *Slavery in the New World*, ed. Laura Foner and Eugene D. Genovese (Englewood Cliffs NJ, 1969), 38-47; David Brion Davis, *The Problem of Slavery in Western Culture* (Ithaca, 1966) 274-76; Sidney W. Mintz, "Labor and Sugar in Puerto Rico and Jamaica, 1800-1850," in *Slavery in the New World: A Reader in Comparative History*, ed. Laura Foner and Eugene D. Genovese (Englewood Cliffs NJ, 1969), 170-77; Hugh Thomas, *The Slave Trade: The Story of the Atlantic Slave Trade: 1440-1870* (New York, 1997) 567-68. But the debate over the comparative harshness of slave systems is irrelevant to the topic at hand—criteria of membership in one of the two U.S. endogamous groups. Spanish laws are mentioned only because the Spanish doctrine of coartación reduced or even eliminated the number of freedom trials on the Gulf coast. This is because, in cases of irresolvable difference, Spanish law—*Las siete partidas* and the *Recopilación de leyes de los reinos de las Indias*—applied the practice of coartación. A Gulf Coast slave who acquired a court-set fraction of his own value (typically about five percent, usually through a loan) was immediately freed on the condition that he pay off the balance in installments. See Kimberly S. Hanger, "Origins of New Orleans Free Creoles of Color," in *Creoles of Color of the Gulf South*, ed. James H. Dormon (Knoxville, 1996b), 6-9. Also, it is stressed that nothing here is meant to suggest that Spanish Florida, Alabama, and Louisiana reflected Spanish society in general.

him an officer in Florida's militia.[45] Local legend has it that his
duty assignment was to negotiate supply contracts with his former owner. A few years later, one of Edinburgh's own slaves, a
man named Holbran sued Edinburgh for his own *coartación*.[46]
He lost. How this tale of slavery and manumission relates to the
unfolding of the endogamous color line will become clear within
a few paragraphs.

Society Changed When the Americans Arrived

The Spanish negotiators of the Adams-Oniz Treaty ceding
Florida from Spain to the United States knew that, one way or
another, the United States was going to take possession of Florida. They tried to prevent a repetition of the mass disfranchisement that had been inflicted upon Louisiana's Colored Creoles a
decade earlier. To safeguard the rights of Hispanic Floridians,
they proposed Article VI of the treaty. It read:

> The inhabitants of the territories which his Catholic Majesty
> cedes to the United States shall be incorporated in the Union
> of the United States, as soon as may be consistent with the
> principles of the Federal Constitution, and admitted to the en-
> joyment of all privileges, rights, and immunities of the citi-
> zens of the United States.[47]

Article VI was vital because two points about U.S. citizenship were foremost in every Spanish Floridian's mind. First,
not everyone born within the United States was automatically a
citizen. The citizenship of free members of the U.S. Black endogamous group was undecided. (Decades later, the U.S. Su-

---

[45] Jane L. Landers, "Traditions of African American Freedom and Community in Spanish Colonial Florida," in *The African American Heritage of
Florida*, ed. David R. Colburn and Jane L. Landers (Gainesville, 1995), 30-
32.

[46] Jane Landers, *Black Society in Spanish Florida* (Chicago, 1999) 95.

[47] John K. Mahon, *History of the Second Seminole War 1835-1842*, revised
ed. (Gainesville, 1985), 29.

preme Court would rule in *Dred Scott v. Sandford*, 1857, that free Blacks could not become citizens and had no more civil rights than livestock.[48]) Second, the Naturalization Act of 1790, which remained in force until the 1950s, allowed only members of the White endogamous group to apply for U.S. citizenship.[49] Without Article VI, U.S. authorities could go through Florida's population after annexation, apply the dreaded *free Black* label to some and strip them of their civil rights, as they had done in Louisiana. Without Article VI, U.S. authorities could require Floridians to apply for naturalization and, obeying federal law, refuse even to consider papers from those not seen as White. On the other hand, once Article VI was signed by both heads of state and their legislatures, Floridians of every ancestry would automatically become U.S. citizens upon annexation. The treaty meant that all non-slave Floridians would be considered equal under the law, no matter which side of the U.S. endogamous color line they were on. The issue of non-Whites applying for citizenship would not even arise.

The Adams-Oniz treaty, with Article VI intact, was approved by both nations. Florida was transferred to the U.S. in 1821. The 20-year flow of immigrants became a tidal wave of English-speaking newcomers. Catholic churches were closed, their property confiscated. Spanish was forbidden in schools, official documents, or in court.[50] St. Augustine's "Minorcans," who had long been a civic-minded, politically active segment of the Hispanic melting pot were promptly renamed "Turnbull's niggers."[51] The first public act by Florida's new governor, Andrew Jackson, was to decree that Article VI was no longer in effect, that Hispanic Floridians had to apply for naturalization,

---

[48] James A. McPherson, *Battle Cry of Freedom: The Civil War Era* (New York, 1988), 170-81.

[49] Matthew Frye Jacobson, *Whiteness of a Different Color: European Immigrants and the Alchemy of Race* (Cambridge, 1998); Ian F. Haney-Lopez, *White by Law: The Legal Construction of Race* (New York, 1996).

[50] Michael V. Gannon, *The Cross in the Sand* (Gainesville FL, 1965), 119-30.

[51] Thomas Graham, *The Awakening of St. Augustine* (St. Augustine, 1978), 18.

and that Floridians thenceforth considered "free Blacks" would be ineligible for citizenship (as would be Seminoles, former slaves, and anyone with a runaway slave in their ancestry).[52] Florida's Hispanic culture was being buried under an avalanche of English-speaking people who saw the world in stark black and white.[53] New laws by the new Floridians fined owners who freed their slaves, jailed those who married them, and barred free members of the Black endogamous group from assembly, carrying firearms, serving on juries, testifying against members of the White endogamous group, or owning property.[54]

And yet, despite the deluge of laws attempting to impose U.S. customs, Florida courts, like those in Louisiana and Alabama, also initially resisted the two-caste system. In the early years of U.S. rule, the courts adopted criteria resembling those of South Carolina—a rule of physical appearance modified by a rule of socioeconomic class. These rules were applied when a tax collector charged the Clarke brothers with refusing to pay the newly imposed capitation tax on free Blacks. The Clarke brothers were the sons of Jorge and Flora Clarke.

Decades earlier, near the end of Florida's British period, Thomas Clarke from Scotland and Honoria Cummings from Ireland had immigrated to Florida. Their son, Jorge J. F. Clarke was raised in Spanish society. When Jorge turned 13, his parents apprenticed the boy to Panton, Leslie, and Co., the sole licensed Indian-trading company in the colony, run by its general manager Juan Leslie. The youngster promptly fell in love with Flora Leslie, his master's teenaged biracial slave girl. As soon as he became self-supporting, as a surveyor in 1797 at age 24, Jorge J. F. Clarke purchased and married Flora. Clarke eventually became the local judge of Fernandina and, after a respected and successful life, provided handsomely for Flora and their two

---

[52] Kathryn Abbey Hanna, *Florida: Land of Change* (Chapel Hill, 1941), 146-47.

[53] Jane Landers, *Black Society in Spanish Florida* (Chicago, 1999), 227-48.

[54] Daniel L. Schafer, *Anna Kingsley* (St. Augustine, 1994), 30-31.

boys in his will.[55] Now grown, the Clarke brothers (roughly one-fourth African admixture) were accused of being Black. The judge ruled that, despite their mother's childhood status as a slave, they had been declared officially White by the Spanish authorities and so, by treaty, they were members of the White endogamous group under U.S. law.[56]

Despite such early judicial resistance, the U.S. endogamous color line system was gradually imposed on Florida throughout the 1830s and early 1840s. Some adapted. Former slave Philip Edinburgh, as it turned out, was so wealthy and European-looking that he was accepted into the White U.S. endogamous group (like Eston Hemings).[57] His daughter Nicolassa married Nancy Wiggins's son Benjamin and they also became White. Other families, who could not adapt, fled. Those who could afford it took ship for Mexico, the Caribbean, or back to Spain. The families of the three slave-owning Sánchez girls (now grandmothers) were too dark for Anglo-American acceptance (like Jim-Mad Hemings), and so they fled to Cuba. Military veterans were rescued at the Spanish Crown's expense and also resettled in Cuba. Families who could not flee adapted. Those who could neither be accepted as White in U.S. society, buy commercial passage, nor evidence past military service moved westwards and joined the Seminoles or made it to the Bahamas in small boats.[58] And yet, color-line permeability for those who looked European remained high in Florida until well after the Civil War.

---

[55] Census records of 1786 and 1793, as tabulated in Donna Rachal Mills, *Florida's First families: Translated Abstracts of pre-1821 Spanish Censuses* (Tuscaloosa, AL, 1992), 4, 39; also see Louise Biles Hill, "George J. F. Clarke, 1774-1836," *The Florida Historical Quarterly*, 21 (no. 3, 1943), 197-253.

[56] Larry Eugene Rivers, *Slavery in Florida: Territorial Days to Emancipation* (Gainesville, 2000), 154, 157; Canter Brown Jr., "Race Relations in Territorial Florida, 1821-1845," *Florida Historical Quarterly*, 73 (no. 3, January 1995), 290.

[57] See the opening anecdote of *Chapter 9. How the Law Decided if You Were Black or White*.

[58] Jane Landers, *Black Society in Spanish Florida* (Chicago, 1999), 238.

Of course, the rule of socioeconomic class, the idea that the "White" label was negotiable by those of rank was not unique to Florida. As Williamson shows, it was common in South Carolina until Reconstruction.[59] As Dominguez shows, it flourished in Louisiana until Jim Crow.[60] Spanish Florida was simply more open about it. In the United States, even in South Carolina, adults crossed the color line in secret and usually moved to a new town.[61] In Florida, as in other Spanish colonies, one became White in a public ritual, an open celebration.

To recap, court cases as well as tax and census records reveal no endogamous color line in Spanish Florida. Documents of the time used three gradations of skin color (*blanco*, *pardo*, and *moreno*) roughly corresponding to the British West Indian labels: White, Coloured, and Black.[62] But the designations did not delineate marriage barriers. They were merely an aspect of Bourbon modernization—a bureaucratic simplification of the dozens of names for skin tones that had become popular two centuries earlier. In fact, newspaper accounts, the vernacular, and literature continued to use the older myriad of skin-tone labels well into the twentieth century.

*   *   *   *   *

This chapter introduced Spanish Florida, the fourth society, within what became the United States, whose color-line cus-

---

[59] Joel Williamson, *New People: Miscegenation and Mulattoes in the United States* (New York, 1980), 93.

[60] Virginia R. Dominguez, *White by Definition: Social Classification in Creole Louisiana* (New Brunswick NJ, 1986).

[61] Michael P. Johnson and James L. Roark, *Black Masters: A Free Family of Color in the Old South*, 1st ed. (New York, 1984), 53-54; Gary B. Mills, "Miscegenation and the Free Negro in Antebellum 'Anglo' Alabama: A Reexamination of Southern Race Relations," *Journal of American History*, 68 (no. 1, 1981), 16-34.

[62] As mentioned in notes 1 and 2 above, neither of the Spanish words for the color "black" (*negro* or *prieto*) appears as a complexion designation in any Spanish Florida document that the present author has yet uncovered. This does not imply that other Spanish colonies were similar.

toms differed from the mainstream. It traced the lack of an endogamous color line to Latin American and, ultimately, to Spanish customs. It showed how the state inadvertently encouraged
people to switch "racial" identities by attempting unsuccessfully
to impose an endogamous barrier. It narrated the transition from
Spanish to Anglo-American laws and customs.

The three preceding chapters showed that the antebellum
lower South differed significantly from the upper South and the
North regarding the endogamous color line. Such enclave differ-
ences had vanished by the mid-twentieth century, as the lower
South's customs were overlaid and replaced by those of the
North and of the upper South.

Chapter 13.
The Color Line Created African-American Ethnicity in the North

When Frederick Augustus Washington Bailey extricated himself from slavery, he hoped to become a member of mainstream society, as had other former slaves before him.[1] He changed his surname to "Douglass," after a hero in Sir Walter Scott's poem *The Lady of the Lake*. He reasoned that, "the basic characteristic of Scott's Douglas is his unflinching fortitude in adversities brought about by the wrongful loss of his patrimony."[2]

Strictly speaking, Douglass's "patrimony" was the legacy of his slave overseer father, Aaron Anthony. Rejection by his father's society is what Douglass meant by "wrongful loss." His criticism of his father in *The Narrative of the Life of Frederick Douglass, an American Slave* (1845) was not directed at the man's "race" nor at his "racism." Instead, Douglass's indictment

---

[1] See, for example, the tale of Eston Hemings in the opening anecdote of *Chapter 9. How the Law Decided if You Were Black or White: The Early 1800s.*

[2] As quoted in Peter Walker, *Moral Choices: Memory, Desire, and Imagination in Nineteenth-Century American Abolition* (Baton Rouge, 1978), 256.

of his father was about Anthony's repudiating his own children by hiding behind a wicked law that, in contrast with the French and Spanish laws once enforced in the lower South, allowed him to disown his slave offspring.[3]

Douglass considered himself to be neither White nor Black, but both. His multiracial self-identity showed in his first autobiography. Introducing his father in *Narrative*, Douglass wrote, "My father was a white man." In this text, his mother was a stranger whom he had never seen in daylight, he could not picture her face, and he was unmoved by news of her death.[4] Not only did Douglass adopt a fictional Scottish hero's name, he emphasized his (perhaps imagined) Scots descent through his father. When visiting Great Britain in 1845-47, Douglass extended his stay in Scotland. He immersed himself in Scottish music and ballads, which he played on the violin for the rest of his life. Having plunged into a Scottish ethnic identity, Douglass wrote to his (then) friend, William Lloyd Garrison, "If I should meet you now, amid the free hills of old Scotland, where the ancient 'black Douglass' [sic] once met his foes... you would see a great change in me!"[5] Upon arriving in Nantucket, Douglass hoped to represent a blending of both endogamous groups, a man who was half White Scot and half Black African:

> Young, ardent, and hopeful, I entered upon this new life in
> the full gush of unsuspecting enthusiasm. The cause was
> good, the men engaged in it were good, the means to attain
> its triumph, good.... For a time, I was made to forget that my
> skin was dark and my hair crisped.[6]

But acceptance by White society was out of reach for Douglass. He discovered that, in the North, there was no such thing as a man who was half-Black. White ships' caulkers in New Bedford denied him a chance to work at his craft because

---

[3] Ibid., 254.

[4] Lewis Hyde, *Trickster Makes This World: Mischief, Myth, and Art* (New York, 1998), 244.

[5] As quoted in Walker (1978), 256.

[6] As quoted in Hyde (1998), 243.

in their eyes he was all Black.[7] When he joined the Garrisonians on a boat to an abolitionist convention in Nantucket, and a squabble broke out because the White abolitionists demanded that the Black abolitionists take lesser accommodations, Douglass found himself classified as Black by his friends. Later in Nantucket, Douglass so impressed the Garrisonians with his public speaking that abolitionist Edmund Quincy exchanged reports with others that Douglass was an articulate public speaker, "for a nigger."[8] Repeatedly, Douglass tried to present himself as an intermediary between America's two endogamous groups. But the Garrisonians made it clear that he was expected to present himself as nothing more than an intelligent "Negro." He was told to talk only about the evils of slavery and ordered to stop talking about the color line. "Give us the facts [about being a slave]. We will take care of the [racial] philosophy." They also ordered him to "leave a little plantation speech" in his accent.[9] In their own words, they wanted to display a smart "nigger," but not too smart.

Douglass's cruelest discovery came after he broke with the Garrisonians and went out on his own. Abolitionist friends of both endogamous groups had warned him that there was nothing personal in how Garrison had used him. The public did not want an intermediary; they wanted an articulate Black. Douglass soon discovered that his friends were right. His newspaper, *The North Star*, failed to sell because it had no market; White Yankees wanted to read White publications and Black Yankees wanted to read Black ones. Indeed, Black political leaders resented Douglass's distancing himself from Black ethno-political society. There was no room in Massachusetts for a man who straddled the color line.

Douglass dutifully reinvented himself. He applied himself to learning Black Yankee culture. "He began to build a closer relationship with... Negro leaders and with the Negro people themselves, to examine the whole range of Negro problems, and

---

[7] Walker (1978), 241.

[8] As quoted in Walker (1978), 245.

[9] Idem.

to pry into every facet of discrimination."[10] Eight months later, *The North Star*'s circulation was soaring and Black leader James McCune Smith wrote to Black activist Gerrit Smith:

> You will be surprised to hear me say that only since his Editorial career has he seen to become a colored man! I have read his paper very carefully and find phrase after phrase develop itself as in one newly born among us.[11]

From that day on, Douglass never looked back. The public wanted him to be hyper-Black and so hyper-Black he became. His later autobiographies reveal the change.[12] *Narrative* (1845) says that his "father was a white man," *My Bondage and My Freedom* (1854) says that his father "was shrouded in mystery" and "nearly white," and *The Life and Times of Frederick Douglass* (1882-1892) says flatly, "of my father I know nothing."[13] *Narrative* says that his mother was a stranger whose death did not affect him, and *Bondage and Freedom* reports that he was "deeply attached to her," *Life and Times* says that "her image is ineffably stamped upon my memory," and describes her death with "great poignancy and sorrow."[14]

And yet, although he donned a public persona of extreme Blackness, he continued to see himself as half White Scottish in his private life. When he eventually married Helen Pitts, a woman of the White endogamous group, even close friends were

---

[10] Philip Sheldon Foner, *Frederick Douglass, a Biography* (New York, 1964), 94.

[11] Idem. Incidentally, Benjamin Quarles also perceives the sea-change in Douglass. He writes that, until this time, Douglass was "immature" or "incomplete" as a Negro. See Benjamin Quarles, "Abolition's Different Drummer," in *The Antislavery Vanguard: New Essays on the Abolitionists*, ed. Martin B. Duberman (Princeton, 1965), 130.

[12] A history of Douglass's often-altered autobiographies can be found in Frederick Douglass, *Narrative of the Life of Frederick Douglass, an American Slave*, ed. Benjamin Quarles (Cambridge MA, 1960), xiii-xvi.

[13] As quoted in Lewis Hyde, *Trickster Makes This World: Mischief, Myth, and Art* (New York, 1998), 244-45.

[14] As quoted in Peter Walker, *Moral Choices: Memory, Desire, and Imagination in Nineteenth-Century American Abolition* (Baton Rouge, 1978), 250-51.

bothered by the mismatch between the public and private Douglasses.[15] In a speech in 1886 Jacksonville, Florida, Douglass justified his intermarriage on the grounds of his own multiracial self-identity. According to James Weldon Johnson:

> Douglass spoke, and moved a large audience of white and colored people by his supreme eloquence. ... Douglass was speaking in the far South, but he spoke without fear or reservation. One statement in particular that he made, I now wonder if any Negro speaker today, under the same circumstances, would dare to make, and, if he did, what the public reaction would be; Douglass, in reply to the current criticisms regarding his second marriage, said, "In my first marriage I paid my compliments to my mother's race; in my second marriage I paid my compliments to the race of my father."[16]

* * * * *

The clash between how Douglass saw himself in 1838 and the public persona that he was forced to portray, was due to the presence of African-American ethnicity in the North.[17] Free citizens of part-African ancestry in the South, especially in the lower South, lacked the sense of common tradition associated with ethnic self-identity. This chapter traces the emergence of African-American ethnicity and the subsequent evolution of the color line in five topics: *Origins of African-American Ethnicity* explains how the imposition of a unique endogamous color line eventually led to the synthesis of a unique ethno-cultural com-

---

[15] See, for example, the exchange of letters between Elizabeth Cady Stanton and Susan B. Anthony on Douglass's 1884 marriage to Helen Pitts, as published in Geoffrey C. Ward, *Not for Ourselves Alone: The Story of Elizabeth Cady Stanton and Susan B. Anthony* (New York, 1999), 178.

[16] James Weldon Johnson, *Along This Way: The Autobiography of James Weldon Johnson* (New York, 1973), 61.

[17] *Ethnicity*: a term for describing a group of people with a common tradition and a sense of identity that functions as a subgroup within the larger society; membership is largely a matter of self-identification. Robert F. McNergney and Joanne M. Herbert, *Foundations of Education: The Challenge of Professional Practice*, 3rd ed. (Boston, 2001), 549.

munity in the Jacksonian Northeast. *African-American Ethnic Traits* outlines the customs of the Black Yankee ethnic group to show that they gave birth to many of today's Black traditions. *The Integration versus Separatism Pendulum* introduces a debate that has occupied Black political leaders since colonial times. *The Color Line in the North* contrasts the harsh enforcement of the intermarriage barrier in the free states with the more permeable systems of the lower South (as presented in the preceding three chapters). *The National Color Line's Rise and Fall* concludes this section on the endogamous color line by presenting two graphs. The first shows that which side of the endogamous color line you were on was most hotly contested in U.S. courts between 1840 and 1869. The second shows that the color line grew abruptly stronger during Reconstruction, was at its harshest during Jim Crow, and began to recover only around 1980.

Origins of African-American Ethnicity

Early in the nineteenth-century, the American North saw the emergence of invented ethnic self-identities that became political power groups: Germans, Irish, Jews, Hispanics (from Louisiana and Florida), and, of course, Black Yankees. Each ethnicity was synthetic in the sense that, while adopting symbols (traditions, language, rituals) associated with some land of origin, it absorbed diversity under a single label. Residents of what would become western Germany (Bavaria or Hesse-Kassel), for example, did not think of themselves as kin to Prussians until after they became a U.S. ethnicity.[18]

An incident in early nineteenth-century Buffalo, New York, exemplifies immigrants' initial perception of separate identity, before the formation of a shared sense of common eth-

---

[18] The process is visible today in the Anglo-American-invented label "Hispanic," which covers both Puerto Ricans and Chicanos, despite their having little in common. A useful introduction to ethnicity formation is Werner Sollors, *The Invention of Ethnicity* (New York, 1989), especially the introduction and the chapter by Kathleen Conzen.

nicity. Some fifty families of German Jews came to Buffalo. They soon felt compelled to build their own synagogue, to avoid attending services with prior American Jews who had already been accepted as Americans. Before long, they had to split again into two congregations because of doctrinal differences between those from western and eastern Germany. Finally, the eastern congregation split in half due to liturgical disagreements between Prussians and Poles.[19] Similarly, residents of county Kaman in Ireland looked down on Corkers as profligates, and those from Cork or County Claire used the term "meanKamanBastard" as a single word (rather like "damnYankee" in the U.S. South).

Despite such initial divisions, immigrants quickly learned that power in America comes to those who command bloc votes. Each ethnic label became an umbrella designation covering all who joined. Voting was not the only manifestation of group power. Parades, public rituals, even riots and gang wars pitted group against group. Ultimately however, the aggressive, in-your-face umbrella ethnicities of the period arose as a consequence of democracy and surged with the widening Jacksonian franchise. Ethnic groups were voting blocs.[20]

One might think that Black Yankees would have been initially more diverse than Europeans because Africa is larger and more populous than Europe. The geographic triangle bounded by Cape Town, Casablanca, and Cairo is a vast kaleidoscope of thousands of cultures, religions, and mutually unintelligible lan-

---

[19] David A. Gerber, *The Making of an American Pluralism: Buffalo, New York, 1825-1860* (Urbana, 1989), 164.

[20] Among important recent works on the formation of ethnicities during this period, in addition to Gerber (cited above) are: Elliott J. Gorn, "'Good-Bye Boys, I Die a True American': Homicide, Nativism, and Working-Class Culture in Antebellum New York City," *The Journal of American History*, 74 (no. 2, September 1987), 388-410; Kerby A. Miller, *Emigrants and Exiles: Ireland and the Irish Exodus to North America* (New York, 1985); Richard Briggs Stott, *Workers in the Metropolis: Class, Ethnicity, and Youth in Antebellum New York City* (Ithaca, N.Y., 1990); David R. Roediger, *The Wages of Whiteness: Race and the Making of the American Working Class* (London, 1991); Noel Ignatiev, *How the Irish Became White* (New York, 1995); and Susan G. Davis, *Parades and Power: Street Theatre in Nineteenth-Century Philadelphia* (Philadelphia, 1986).

guages. Nevertheless, Northerners of the Black endogamous group were not exempt from the need to define themselves as a a single, solid ethnic group. Like other ethnicities, Black Yankees in Boston, New York, Philadelphia, and Cincinnati also conducted parades, processions, and festivals to, "strengthen and solidify the boundaries of class and ethnicity that buttressed and circumscribed American politics of self-interest."[21]

> Amid much pomp and parade, with carriaged processions of Revolutionary War veterans, members of benevolent and literary societies, and the committee on arrangements, entire communities made a public show of their "industry, integrity, [and] temperance." Women and children joined the parades, waving flags from the windows of omnibuses. Along waterways like the Hudson and Susquehanna rivers, chartered steamboats brought 'large delegations from different localities' to common points of celebration like Geneva, New York, and Harrisburg, Pennsylvania. In a resonant declaration of Pan-African unity, African-American communities made clear [their solidarity].[22]

In Cincinnati, a three-way fight for jobs, among Black Yankees, Irish, and Germans, led to an attempt to exile Black Yankees from the state.[23] The struggle among Irish, German, and Black laborers for lucrative work on Cincinnati's docks led to demonstrations, then parades, then riots. Previously, Cincinnati's Black caste had provided the bulk of construction laborers, porters, vendors, shoeblacks, messengers, and domestic workers—steady work in an expanding economy. The growing political power of Irish and German immigrants struggling to distinguish themselves as White men too, manifested itself in the enforcement of the repressive Ohio Black Codes, laws that had long been on the books but ignored.[24] The city expelled Black

---

[21] Elizabeth Rauh Bethel, *The Roots of African-American Identity* (New York, 1997), 3.

[22] Ibid., 6.

[23] Ibid., 119-24.

[24] Enacted in 1804 and 1807, the Ohio Black Codes were meant to stop Blacks from moving to Ohio. The most onerous of these was a law that required Blacks to pay a $500 bond signed by two White men within 20

Yankee children from public schools and forbade the construction of Black private schools.

By the summer of 1829, Black Cincinnatians were avoiding going out in public. They stopped going to hotels, restaurants, theaters, or riding public transportation. They found that they were no longer welcome to attend White church services."[25] Former Virginian John Malvin organized a petition drive calling for a repeal of the Black codes. In angry reaction, the city council gave each Black Cincinnatian thirty days to leave the state or post $500 surety bond (roughly $25,000 apiece, in today's money). Desperate, Malvin negotiated a sixty-day extension from the city in order for the refugees to find new homes in exile. The city's White zealots—led by not-yet-fully-White immigrant German and Irish laborers—responded to the extension on August 19, 1829 with a riot that burned down all of Cincinnati's Black residential areas.[26]

The expulsion order and subsequent arson riot shocked Americans everywhere. It was even reported overseas. Compassion for the victims sparked collection drives for money, food, and clothing even among Southern slave-owners, and brought about the first meeting of the National Convention movement. Zephaniah Kingsley, one of Florida's wealthiest slaveowners, a man who, seven years earlier had been appointed by President Monroe to Florida's Legislative Council wrote that, "[racial tolerance] may be considered as a standard measure by which the comparative state of civilization... may be fairly estimated." He opined that Ohio had stepped outside the limits of civilized society, "in its acts of oppression against its free colored inhabitants, by which their existence seems so far to have been threatened...."[27]

days of arrival in order to remain in the state. See Leon F. Litwack, *North of Slavery: the Negro in the Free States, 1790-1860* (Chicago, 1961), 72.

[25] Bethel (1997), 119-24.

[26] Carter G. Woodson, "The Negroes of Cincinnati Prior to the Civil War," *The Journal of Negro History*, 1 (no. 1, January 1916), 1-22.

[27] Zephaniah Kingsley, *Balancing Evils Judiciously: The Proslavery Writings of Zephaniah Kingsley*, ed. Daniel W. Stowell (Gainesville, 2000), 77-78. Of course, slave-owning planter Kingsley was not impartial regarding

Looked at rationally, immigrant Irish and German resentment of Cincinnati's Black workers made little sense. From the viewpoint of strict self-interest, the most severe competition that each unskilled Irish worker faced in selling his labor was not from already-employed Black workers, but from the dozens of identically unskilled Irish laborers who had just stepped off the same boat.[28] Returning to the experience of Frederick Douglass, the former slave had no more success at portraying himself as biracial in such an environment than an agnostic resident of Belfast would have in adopting a dual Catholic/Protestant persona today. Membership in an ethnicity in many ways resembled membership in a gang.[29]

African-American Ethnic Traits

The newly formed Black Yankee ethnicity of the early 1800s differed from today's African-American ethnicity. Modern African-American ethnic traits come from a post-bellum blending of three cultural streams: the Black Yankee ethnicity of 1830, the slave traditions of the antebellum South, and the free Creole or Mulatto elite traditions of the lower South. Each of the three sources provided elements of the religious, linguistic, and folkloric traditions found in today's African-American ethnicity.[30]

---

either race relations or slavery. His slave-trading wife (she had her own plantations) was from Senegal, and so his children (who were also slave-owning planters) were of 40-50 percent sub-Saharan genetic admixture. By the turn of the twentieth century, most of their descendants had assimilated into upper-crust White Florida society.

[28] David R. Roediger, *The Wages of Whiteness: Race and the Making of the American Working Class* (London, 1991).

[29] Herbert Asbury, *The Gangs of New York: An Informal History of the Underworld*, 1st Paragon House ed. (New York, 1990).

[30] See Joel Williamson, *New People: Miscegenation and Mulattoes in the United States* (New York, 1980) for a summary of this threefold blending. For a more detailed account, see Joel Williamson, *The Crucible of Race: Black/White Relations in the American South Since Emancipation* (New York, 1984).

Black Yankee ethnicity was also not the same thing as membership in America's Black endogamous group. The difference between Black Yankee ethnicity and Black endogamous group membership is that ethnicity is to some extent voluntary whereas which side of the color line you are on is usually involuntary. Mainstream America assigns to the Black side of the endogamous color line people of many different ethnicities whose only common trait is a dark-brown skin tone. These include West Indians, some East Indians (sometimes), recent African immigrants, and (until recently) African-looking Muslims and Hispanics. Finally, the endogamous color line was imposed in 1691 but the earliest evidence of Black Yankee ethnicity dates from the mid 1700s.

Although less wealthy than the Louisiana Creoles, the Black Yankees had developed a strong supportive culture that could withstand the buffeting of social upheaval. They were usually ostracized from mainstream society due to the endogamous color line. According to contemporary accounts, they responded with grace and dignity, making a virtue of their separation. It was not uncommon to see lines of quiet, well-behaved children following their parents to Sunday service with the *gravitas* and *pietas* of Roman elders.[31] Their preachers taught that they were put on earth to be tested. Their lot was to serve as example to the white folks of how civilized Christians behave.

Most Black Yankees distinguished themselves from slaves—indeed many families had no history of slavery but descended from indentured servants. Nevertheless, many were active contributors to and activists in the abolition movement. This is in contrast to the biracial elite of the Gulf coast and Latin America, who owned slaves and defended slavery as a noble institution.[32] The contrast was due to the lack of an independent Black ethnicity among Hispanic planters of part-African ancestry, and this lack was due, in turn, to the absence of an endogamous color line.

---

[31] The chief Roman virtues. Elizabeth Rauh Bethel, *The Roots of African-American Identity* (New York, 1997).

[32] Kingsley (2000).

In some ways, Black Yankee culture (religion, language, music, dance, food, costume) was indistinguishable from that of White Yankees. For example, the boisterous interactive style of many African-American church services today would have been alien to them, since it originated in the slaveholding South. Daniel A. Payne was a Black Yankee, a career AME minister in Philadelphia. He was a sympathizer of the Underground Railroad, so its organizers asked him to preach to a group of newly escaped slaves. His diary reports:

> After the sermon, they formed a ring, and with coats off sung, clapped their hands and stamped their feet in a most ridiculous and heathenish way. I requested that the pastor go and stop their dancing. At his request they stopped their dancing and clapping of hands, but remained singing and rocking their bodies to and fro.[33]

Although the endogamous color line was stricter in the antebellum North than in the antebellum South, it was less strict in 1850 and 1860 than in 1970 and 1980.[34] The children of interracial marriages in the Northeast were usually census-reported as "Negroes" rather than as "Mulattoes." This resembles today's customs and contrasts with the more permeable color lines of the lower South. According to Joel Williamson, "In 1850 in the five states of Ohio, Indiana, Illinois, Michigan, and Wisconsin, [people designated as] mulattoes actually outnumbered blacks by 24,000 to 22,000, while in the older-settled New England and Middle Atlantic states [those labeled as] blacks outnumbered mulattoes by about three to one."[35]

The Black Yankees set many of the patterns of modern African-American life. They developed the supportive church-centered social structure found in African-American communities today. Long before the South was segregated, they faced

---

[33] Eileen Southern, *The Music of Black Americans: A History*, 2nd ed. (New York, 1983), 130.

[34] See Figure 1 under "Endogamy" in *Chapter 6. Features of the Endogamous Color Line*.

[35] Joel Williamson, *New People: Miscegenation and Mulattoes in the United States* (New York, 1980), 58.

isolation and cyclical rejection by mainstream society. They were also the first to articulate the dilemma that continues to occupy Black thinkers to this day: integration versus separatism.

The Integration versus Separatism Pendulum

The ethnicity invented by Black Yankees oscillated between two poles, just as African-American ethnicity does today. It was "a cleavage within the community, similar... to one familiar today between aspects of Negro life started by and based on white insitutions and those that are indigenous or nativistic."[36] At one extreme, they coined the term *African-American*, invented a fantasy image of Africa as a civilized, Eden-like homeland, strove to emigrate to lands where Blacks still ruled, and demanded segregated churches for worship by their adults and segregated schools for the education of their children in order to preserve their cultural integrity. At the other extreme, they considered themselves true Americans, their families having lived in the United States since long before the first Irish and Germans arrived, demanded integrated schools where their children could learn American mainstream values, demanded full membership in the body politic, and rejected colonization overseas as unjust exile. Although at any given instant in time, at least some Black Yankees populated the entire ideological spectrum between these two extremes of separatism on the one hand and integration on the other, fashions changed over the years.[37]

---

[36] The quotation, as well as an analysis of the two poles of ongoing Black Yankee self-image (as Africans who happen to be in America versus as Americans who happen to come from Africa) can be found in Adelaide M. Cromwell, *The Other Brahmins: Boston's Black Upper Class, 1750-1950* (Fayetteville, 1994), 33.

[37] For an account of the formation of the Black Yankee component of African-American ethnicity, see Scott Hancock, "The Elusive Boundaries of Blackness: Identity Formation in Antebellum Boston," *Journal of Negro History*, 84 (no. 2, Spring 1999), 115-29.

From the Revolution to about 1826, Black Yankee ethnic self-image leaned towards separatism. They spoke longingly of returning to Africa. Yet, few emigrated although many had the opportunity. Instead, Africa became a fantasized Eden, spoken of in hushed tones the way European Jews would say "next year in Jerusalem." They made up rituals and customs, which they attributed to the Dark Continent. They founded the traditional African-American churches. The African Society, founded in 1796, was the first known use of the term *African* to denote upper-class Black Yankees. Using his own money, Black Yankee ship's captain Paul Cuffee of Boston personally conveyed 38 emigrants who wanted to return to Africa to Sierra Leone in 1815.[38] Bostonian Prince Hall, who was born on September 12, 1748 in Barbados, organized the first chapter of African-American Masonry on March 6, 1775 and led the 1787 petition drive to open segregated schools in Boston, so that Black children could be taught by members of their own culture.[39] After the Revolution, Peter J. Williams, Jr. and Samuel Cornish founded segregated schools for Black children in New York city.[40] And shortly before the great Philadelphia yellow fever epidemic of 1793, Richard Allen and Absalom Jones both founded Black churches, the former the AME Church, the latter an African branch of the Episcopal Church. Allen and Jones both vowed that their churches, "would admit none to be enrolled members but descendants of the African race."[41]

The Black Yankee ideological pendulum swung the other way around 1826. Black Yankees demanded full citizenship. Many Black Yankee families tried to enroll their children in

---

[38] Elizabeth Rauh Bethel, *The Roots of African-American Identity* (New York, 1997), 66-67.

[39] A brief biography of Prince Hall can be found in Adelaide M. Cromwell, *The Other Brahmins: Boston's Black Upper Class, 1750-1950* (Fayetteville, 1994), 31.

[40] Bethel (1997), 66-67

[41] Ibid., 70.

mainstream schools.[42] And Africa was no longer seen as a desirable homeland. According to one editor:

> Our claims are on America, it is the land that gave us birth; it is the land of our nativity, we know no other country, it is a land in which our fathers have suffered and toiled; they have watered it with their tears, and fanned it with their sighs. Our relation with Africa is the same as the white man's is with Europe. ... We have passed through several generations in this country, and consequently we have become naturalized, our habits, our manners, our passions, our dispositions have become the same.... I might as well tell the white man about England... and call him a European, as for him to call us Africans.[43]

Ship's captain Paul Cuffee had died in 1817, but his dream had been carried forward by the American Colonization Society. In part, AME founder Richard Allen and the other delegates were unhappy that the White-run ACS had taken over governing what would eventually become the Liberia colony, rather than let Blacks control it. But, also in part, migrating back to an imagined African homeland was no longer fashionable. Black emigrants were starting to emigrate to Canada or to Haiti instead.

In September of 1830, Baltimore ice dealer Hezekiah Grice suggested to Philadelphia AME Church founder Richard Allen that he convene a national meeting of Black Yankee leaders. The first goal was to debate colonization. They decided against it. The second was to collect money for the 1200-2000 Black refugees who had been exiled from Cincinnati to Canada on short notice. The convention met annually for six years, debating all aspects of the integration versus separatism pendulum. The sixth and final National Black Convention was held in 1835, its activist civil-rights agenda taken over by self-help (temperance) advocates.[44] Hezekiah Grice, the Baltimore ice dealer who

---

[42] Helen Tunnicliff Catterall and James J. Hayden, *Judicial Cases Concerning American Slavery and The Negro* (New York, 1968), 5:4.

[43] *Freedom's Journal*, April 4, 1828.

[44] Bethel (1997), 83-84, 116, 124, 127-38.

had started it all, moved to Haiti in 1832 and was named director of Public Works for Port-au-Prince in 1834.[45]

Thirteen years later, Frederick Douglass (1818-1895) founded his newspaper, *The North Star*. Douglass handled the editorial end while Martin R. Delany (1812-1885) traveled throughout Ohio, Pennsylvania, and Kentucky lecturing, reporting, and obtaining subscriptions for the newspaper.[46] Although both men were uncompromising and eloquent in their support of America's Blacks, they came to represent both ends of the integration-versus-separatism spectrum. Delany, who epitomized Black nationalism, advocated emigration and cultural integrity. Douglas continued to advocate integration, assimilation, and American patriotism.[47]

A particularly instructive episode in the ideological struggle between separatism and assimilation within the Black Yankee ethnic community appeared in the case *Roberts v. City of Boston*, 1849.[48] Sixty-two years after Prince Hall had persuaded Boston's city fathers to open segregated schools for Black children so that they could be taught their cultural heritage, the parents of Sarah C. Roberts sued the city for not allowing Sarah to attend a White school. The African-American community was split on the topic. Heated intra-group debates erupted over the desirability of segregated schools for Boston's Black children.[49]

---

[45] Ibid., 165.

[46] The best biography of Delany is Victor Ullman, *Martin R. Delany: The Beginnings of Black Nationalism* (Boston,, 1971).

[47] The best example of the hate/love relationship between these two Black activists is a letter from Delany to Douglass published in the North Star of July 10, 1852. For Douglass's July 23, 1852, reply, see Victor Ullman, *Martin R. Delany: The Beginnings of Black Nationalism* (Boston,, 1971), 145.

[48] 59 Mass. 198.

[49] See Douglas J. Ficker, "From Roberts to Plessy: Educational Segregation and the 'Separate but Equal' Doctrine," *Journal of Negro History*, 84 (no. 4, Autumn 1999), 301-14; Adelaide M. Cromwell, *The Other Brahmins: Boston's Black Upper Class, 1750-1950* (Fayetteville, 1994), 36; or Leonard W. Levy and Harlan B. Philips, "The Roberts Case: Source of the "Separate but Equal" Doctrine," *American Historical Review*, 56 (no. 3, April 1951), 510-18.

The Color Line in the North

The endogamous color line was enforced more strictly in the North than in the antebellum lower South (South Carolina, Alabama, Louisiana, Florida). In 1800, Boston deported 240 violators of anti-intermarriage laws. The record says they were deported for intermarriage and for not having been born in Massachusetts. It is not clear if all 240 committed both crimes, or if some were convicted of one thing and some the other. Obviously, the latter charge could not be applied to Black Yankees. So, although it appears that at least some Black Yankees may have been prosecuted for intermarriage at this time, it is likely that the law was enforced only against Black immigrants.[50]

Massachusetts repealed its anti-intermarriage law in 1843 and marriages across the color line became more common, although they never approached the intermarriage rates of the lower South. The rate of Black/White intermarriage exceeded that of Irish/White intermarriage for a time. According to Oscar Handlin, Boston's Irish out-marriage rate in the 1860s "was lower than that of any other group including the Negroes, 12 percent of whose marriages were with whites."[51] To put this in context, between 45 and 55 percent of Irish-Americans out-marry today. Yet as recently as 1920, Irish-American exogamy was at less than half that—20 percent.[52] In other words, Irish-Americans in Boston quadrupled this index of acceptance over the very same period that social acceptance of the Black endogamous group in the same city fell to one-fourth of its prior value. Why was Black/White intermarriage relatively high in mid-nineteenth-century Boston?

---

[50] Leon F. Litwack, *North of Slavery: the Negro in the Free States, 1790-1860* (Chicago, 1961), 16.

[51] Oscar Handlin, *Boston's Immigrants, 1790-1880*, Rev. and enl. ed. (Cambridge MA, 1959), 177.

[52] Patrick J. Blessing, "The Irish," in *Harvard Encyclopedia of American Ethnic Groups*, ed. Stephan Thernstrom and Oscar Handlin (Cambridge MA, 1980), 524-45, 541.

The puzzle is solved by noting that impoverished female Irish servants and housemaids comprised the bulk of the initial wave of Irish famine immigrants. Once employed in America, they sent money home so that their relatives could come over as well.[53] But their lack of acceptance in White society limited their choices of marriage partners. Boston's Black Yankee elite, in contrast to most Whites, preferentially hired Irish servant girls. According to one contemporary, "Negroes were avoided both as servants in the home or as instructors for the children, for it was felt that more gentility and culture would come from exposure to whites."[54] Proximity led to affection, then to love, and many Irish servant girls wound up marrying the sons of established Black craftsmen and shopkeepers.[55] According to Wirth and Goldhammer, Black male/White female marriages were thirty times more common in mid-nineteenth-century Boston than White male/Black female marriages.[56]

Nevertheless, Massachusetts in the 1840-1860 period, with its demographic imbalance of marriageable but poor Irish females was an exception. Most of the North continued to abhor intermarriage. During De Tocqueville's visit to the North, he wrote:

> Race prejudice seems stronger in those states that have abol-
> ished slavery than in those where it still exists, and nowhere
> is it more intolerant than in those states where slavery was
> never known.[57]

Abraham Lincoln represented his constituency in Springfield, Illinois, on June 26, 1857. He repeated the following speech in a dozen later venues, and referred back to it for the rest of his life:

---

[53] Handlin (1959), 61-63

[54] Adelaide M. Cromwell, *The Other Brahmins: Boston's Black Upper Class, 1750-1950* (Fayetteville, 1994), 57.

[55] Ibid., 183.

[56] Ibid., 271n40.

[57] Alexis de Tocqueville, *Democracy in America* (New York, 1966), 343. See also "A Permeable, Shifted Color Line" in *Chapter 10. Barbadian South Carolina.*

Judge Douglas is especially horrified at the thought of the mixing blood by the white and black races: agreed for once— a thousand times agreed. ... On this point we fully agree with the Judge; and when he shall show that his policy is better adapted to prevent amalgamation than ours we shall drop ours, and adopt his. Let us see. In 1850 there were in the United States, 405,751, mulattoes. Very few of these are the offspring of whites and free blacks; nearly all have sprung from black slaves and white masters.[58] A separation of the races is the only perfect preventive of amalgamation but as an immediate separation is impossible the next best thing is to keep them apart where they are not already together. If white and black people never get together in Kansas, they will never mix blood in Kansas. ... I have said that the separa-

---

[58] Although Lincoln apparently believed this, it is factually inaccurate. DNA admixture studies show that genetically speaking, African male with European female mixing has been nearly as common nationwide as the reverse. See "English-Speaking Alabama" in Alabama in *Chapter 11. Antebellum Louisiana and Alabama*. Also see the account of the marriages of Boston's Black males with Irish females in the paragraphs immediately above. In general, Afro-European admixture is sexually asymmetrical towards African males in the Northeast but leans the other way (towards European males) in the lower South. (It is very asymmetrical towards European males in Latin America and in the British West Indies.) See, Bernardo Bertoni and others, "Admixture in Hispanics: Distribution of Ancestral Population Contributions in the Continental United States," *Human Biology*, 75 (no. 1, 2003), 1-11; Maria Catira Bortolini and others, "African-Derived South American Populations: A History of Symmetrical and Asymmetrical Matings According to Sex Revealed by Bi- and Uni-parental Genetic Markers," *American Jornal of Human Biology*, 11 (1999), 561-63; Ricardo M. Cerda-Flores and others, "Genetic Admixture in Three Mexican Mestizo Populations Based D1S80 and HLA-DQA1 Loci," *American Journal of Human Biology*, 14 (2002), 257-63; Manfred Kayser and others, "Y Chromosome STR Haplotypes and the Genetic Structure of U.S. Populations of African, European and Hispanic Ancestry," *Genome Research*, 13 (2003), 624-34; D. Andrew Merriwether and others, "Mitochondrial Versus Nuclear Admixture Estimates Demonstrate a Past History of Directional Mating," *American Journal of Physical Anthropology*, 102 (1997), 153-59; or Clemencia Rodas, Nancy Gelvez, and Genoveva Keyeux, "Mitochondrial DNA Studies Show Asymmetrical Amerindian Admixture in Afro-Colombian and Mestizo Populations," *Human Biology*, 75 (no. 1, 2003), 13-30. Also, see Paul Heinegg, *Free African Americans of Maryland and Delaware from the Colonial Period to 1810* (Baltimore, 2000) for exhaustive genealogical research showing the same finding.

tion of the races is the only perfect preventive of amalgamation. I have no right to say all the members of the Republican
party are in favor of this, nor to say that as a party they are in
favor of it. There is nothing in their platform directly on the
subject. But I can say a very large proportion of its members
are for it, and that the chief plank in their platform—
opposition to the spread of slavery—is most favorable to that
separation.[59]

Like Lincoln, many Midwestern Abolitionists became peculiarly
enraged at the possibility of intermarriage. In 1862 Ohio, abolitionist newspaperman Calvin Kingsley wrote:

Where is this social equality, the fruits of which appear in
amalgamation, to be found but among the slaveholders of the
South? In the North it is a strange and disgusting sight to see
a white man with a colored wife. In the South it can be practically seen everywhere. As to political equality, it has nothing whatever to do with the question of emancipation.[60]

In 1863 Illinois, The *Chicago Tribune* said that Republican doctrine was to:

let the African race alone; neither marry or cohabit with
them;… separate the whites from adulterous communication
with them; and preserve the purity of Caucasian blood from
African admixture.[61]

 In 1863 Chicago and Columbus, editors responding to Lincoln's
Emancipation Proclamation by saying that Republicans were
"actively promoting miscegenation, the most dreaded form of
equality." They said this would destroy "the identity of both

---

[59] *Illinois State Journal* , June 29, 1857. Copies of this speech were advertised by the Journal for sale. It was copied and commented on widely
throughout the state, at least two papers copying it in full (Decatur, Illinois
State Chronicle , July 2; *Clinton Central Transcript* , July 9). Also see Leon
F. Litwack, *North of Slavery: the Negro in the Free States, 1790-1860* (Chicago, 1961), 276-77.

[60] As quoted in V. Jacque Voegeli, *Free But Not Equal: The Midwest and
the Negro During the Civil War* (Chicago, 1967), 59-60.

[61] Ibid., 87.

[races] and substitute in their stead human mongrels."[62] Even the Government-appointed American Freedman's Inquiry Commission reported in 1864 that amalgamation between the races led to degeneration.[63] In 1864, Democrat John McClernand of Illinois said, "We wanted no intermixture of white blood with theirs..."[64] and Republicans answered that it was the Democratic slaveowners... who had long been guilty of trying "to bleach out the black race."[65] Congressman George W. Julian "recoiled in disgust" at the prospect of miscegenation, saying that in the North there were "no such intimate relations as there were in the South where slave mothers and slave masters are brought on to the level of social equality in its most loathsome forms."[66] In short, Midwesterners in general, Democrats, Republicans, Free-Soilers, Know-Nothings, Popular Sovereignty advocates, and Abolitionists alike fully agreed on only one thing—the importance of the endogamous color line.

What interests this study is not how much of the above was political rhetoric, aimed merely at discrediting the opposition. The point is that some scholars interpret the accusation that many slaveowners in the South openly intermarried as hyperbole. In fact, as shown in the prior three chapters, the accusers were correct. More Southern slaveowners married interracially than Northern abolitionists ever did. This was especially true of the thousands of Creole, Hispanic, and West Indian slaveowners in the lower South who were themselves of partial African ancestry.

The National Color Line's Rise and Fall

Each advance in transportation technology: canals, steamboats, railroads, hastened national integration. The venerable

---

[62] Ibid., 77.

[63] Ibid., 181.

[64] Ibid., 127.

[65] Ibid., 179.

[66] Ibid., 182.

Civil War debate about the extent to which cultural difference between North and South exacerbated sectionalism may be answered by noting that it was not difference per se that caused friction, but the clash of cultures brought forcibly into contact by merchants, traders, and families seeking a better life by pulling up roots.[67] Northern attitudes towards the endogamous color line affected and were affected by those of the upper South, and upper South attitudes similarly clashed with the odd "racial" systems of the lower South.

The aftermath of the Civil War dramatically accelerated the process of cultural osmosis. In the same way that Northern entrepreneurs (carpetbaggers) flooded the Reconstruction South seeking business opportunities, tens of thousands of Black Yankees left homes and careers and also migrated to the defeated South. They built the schools, printed the newspapers, and opened the businesses that taught the newly freed to flourish as Americans.[68] Joel Williamson particularly distinguishes between Northern Black Yankees and Southern former slaves, especially among former Union soldiers:

> The channels though which mulatto leadership moved from the North to the lower South are clearly visible. Many of the migrants, women as well as men, came as teachers sponsored by a dozen or so benevolent societies, arriving in the still turbulent wake of Union armies. Others came to organize relief for the refugees.... Still others... came south as religious missionaries... Some came south as business or professional people seeking opportunity on this... special black frontier. Finally, thousands came as soldiers [Black Yankees in regiments that served in the South], and when the war was over, many of [their] young men remained there or returned after a stay of some months in the North to complete their education.[69]

---

[67] See Kenneth M. Stampp, *The Causes of the Civil War* (New York, 1959) for a discussion of this point.

[68] Eric Foner, *Reconstruction: America's Unfinished Revolution* (New York, 1988), 286.

[69] Joel Williamson, *New People: Miscegenation and Mulattoes in the United States* (New York, 1980), 79-80.

Culture clash made for bumpy times for some of the volunteers. Slave religious services were characterized by the ring-shout ceremony. In a ring-shout, as Daniel Payne had noticed,[70] the outdoor congregation shuffles, dances, claps, and sings as they circle the preacher, loudly responding to his or her every utterance. Although the ring-shout is ostensibly Christian, the old Yoruba *orixas* Exu, Ogun, Xango, Oxossi often make an appearance by taking possession of a dancer, especially in the Sea Islands and in Louisiana bayous.[71] Black Yankees, in contrast, were staid Methodist Episcopalians. Slave music had exceedingly simple melodies and harmony was unknown, but the music gloried in dazzling rhythmic syncopation. Black Yankee music was characterized by the subtle and changing harmonies of Anglican hymns and a steady British beat.[72]

Many AME ministers sent south insisted on an educated ministry, undercutting the authority of self-taught slave-born preachers, and demanded more sedate services than new freedmen were used to. "The old people were not anxious to see innovations introduced in religious worship," one wrote home, telling how a Black Yankee preacher was mocked as a "Presbyterian" by his new flock.[73] Nevertheless, the overall attitude of the Black Yankees reflected solidarity with their charges. New England Black Yankee teacher Virginia C. Greene wrote home, "I class myself with the freedmen. Though I have never known

---

[70] See the quotation at note 33 in this chapter.

[71] An *orixa* (pronounced oh-ree-SHAH) is a supernatural being roughly combining the attributes of a god and a patron saint. Orixa worship originated with the Yoruba, but spread widely among the polyglot diverse cultures who were carried across the Atlantic by the slave trade. Similar pantheons of Orixas are worshipped today in Voudum (Haiti), Santeria (the Spanish Caribbean), Cadomblé (Brazil), in the Sea Islands, and in Louisiana. See John Kelly Thornton, *Africa and Africans in the Making of the Atlantic World, 1400-1800*, 2nd ed. (New York, 1998), 242-43, 252-53.

[72] The Fisk Jubilee Singers became world-famous post-bellum precisely by melding European harmonies with African syncopation. See Eileen Southern, *The Music of Black Americans: A History*, 2nd ed. (New York, 1983), 130.

[73] As quoted in Eric Foner, *Reconstruction: America's Unfinished Revolution* (New York, 1988), 92.

servitude they are in fact my people."[74] Some of the southbound migrants even married white southern Republicans during Congressional Reconstruction. Carrie Highgate, a Black Yankee schoolteacher from New York married White Mississippi state senator Albert T. Morgan.[75]

The culture clash led to an unusually large number of court cases held to resolve endogamous group membership. The volume of such cases indicates social uncertainty. At some places and times, color line criteria were clearly understood and stable enough to be passed on from one generation to the next as part of childhood socialization. During such periods and regions, people knew precisely what yardstick was used to measure endogamous group membership. With little element of uncertainty, relatively few occasions would arise when both of two contending parties would think that they could prevail in court. And so, few court cases would be litigated and even fewer appealed.

On the other hand, when society was in transition from one criterion to another, as in the late antebellum period, then rules were uncertain. Generation gaps appeared as those who had learned and internalized one set of rules in their youth were overtaken by a younger generation with a new outlook. Class gaps, gender gaps, and caste gaps might also open. Those of different social rank might apply different rules, men might differ from women, and Blacks might conceivably adopt or advocate a different yardstick than that used by Whites. Where people apply different rules to the same issue, each of two opposing parties can anticipate a favorable outcome. Where each side's risk/benefit assessment justified fighting it out, court cases soared.

---

[74] As quoted ibid., 100.

[75] Dorothy Sterling, ed. *The Trouble They Seen: The Story of Reconstruction in the Words of African Americans* (New York, 1994), 233.

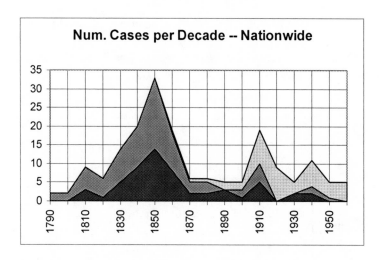

Figure 20. Number of Cases per Decade Nationwide

Figure 20. Number of Cases per Decade Nationwide, shows the number of appeals cases heard to resolve someone's endogamous group membership. The volume of such cases peaked at thirty-six cases in the decade of the 1850s. The number of cases appealed then declined in stages (with two lesser peaks in the 1910s and the 1940s) until, by 1960, they numbered only five per decade. Since this study is limited to cases that were appealed, one might ask whether the measured rise and fall reflects the total number of cases or merely the number that were appealed. For example, does the abrupt drop from over 35 cases per decade in the 1850s to under 10 cases in the 1870s show an overall decline in color-line litigation, or just a drop in the fraction of cases that were appealed? The answer seems to be the former. Ariela Gross sampled both number of cases and number of appeals for the early-to-mid nineteenth century and found that the relative fraction of appealed cases did not change. Furthermore, most states did not add intermediate courts, nor limited the number of appeals to their highest courts until the twentieth century.[76] In short, it seems apparent that the period 1840-1869 represented a peak of uncertainty regarding how the color line was defined. This was also the swiftest period of national integration, due to advances in transportation technology.

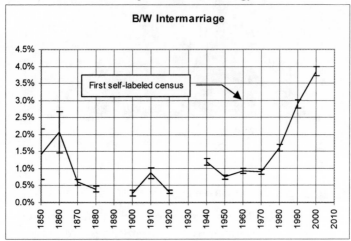

Figure 21. Black/White Intermarriage[77]

Figure 21. Black/White Intermarriage, shows the strength of the endogamous color line from 1850 to 2000.[78] We cannot precisely measure intermarriage before 1850 because prior censuses recorded only households, not individuals. The most eye-catching feature of the graph is the plunge in intermarriage rate between 1860 and 1870, followed by a bottoming-out that lasted throughout the Jim Crow period, and began to recover around 1980. What happened in the 1860s, of course, was the Civil War, the ending of North American slavery, and the abrupt freeing of four million slaves. Others have noted the plunge in intermar-

---

[76] Ariela J. Gross, "Litigating Whiteness: Trials of Racial Determination in the Nineteenth-Century South," *Yale Law Journal*, 108 (no. 1, 1998), 109-88, 178.

[77] For the methodology used in arriving at this figure, see *Appendix A. Census Data Processing Methodology*, specifically, the section titled "Black/White Intermarriage."

[78] This figure is repeated from Figure 1, in the topic "Endogamy" in *Chapter 6. Features of the Endogamous Color Line*.

riage. According to Joel Williamson, "... the drop in unions between Negroes and whites after 1860... remains dramatic and
represents a fundamental change in the history of miscegenation
in America."[79] It is surprising that that the U.S. intermarriage
rate was higher in the years before 1850 to 1860 than ever again
until 1990. To put things in perspective, black-white intermarriage of the time approximated Irish-American intermarriage of
the time. Today, the former is a tiny fraction of the latter.[80]

*   *   *   *   *

This chapter traced the emergence of African-American
ethnicity and the subsequent evolution of the color line in five
topics: It explained how the imposition of a unique endogamous
color line eventually led to the synthesis of a unique ethno-
cultural African-American community in the Jacksonian Northeast. It outlined the features of the Black Yankee ethnic group to
show that its customs became an important source of many of
today's Black traditions. It introduced an integration-versus-
separatism debate that has occupied Black political leaders since
colonial times. It contrasted the harsh enforcement of the intermarriage barrier in the free states with its non-enforcement in the
lower South. It presented graphs showing that endogamous
group membership was most hotly contested in U.S. courts between 1840 and 1869, and that the color line grew abruptly
stronger during Reconstruction, was at its harshest out during
Jim Crow, and began to recover only around 1980.

This was the last of eight chapters that depicted the evolution of the U.S. endogamous color line, from its invention in the
seventeenth-century Chesapeake, to its synthesis of a Black

---

[79] Joel Williamson, *New People: Miscegenation and Mulattoes in the
United States* (New York, 1980), 89; Caroline Bond Day and Earnest Albert
Hooton, *A Study of Some Negro-White Families in the United States* (Cambridge MA, 1932); Herbert George Gutman, *The Black Family in Slavery
and Freedom, 1750-1925* (New York, 1976a).

[80] Thomas Sowell, *Ethnic America: A History* (New York, 1981), 112;
Leonard Dinnerstein and David M. Reimers, *Ethnic Americans: A History
of Immigration*, 4th ed. (New York, 1999) 178-83.

Yankee ethnicity in the Jacksonian Northeast. These chapters showed the ways in which the U.S. endogamous color line is unique. They showed when, where, how, why, and by whom the color line was invented. They showed how the courts in the North and in the upper South strove to devise criteria that could be used to determine which side of the color line someone was on, and that these criteria were: physical appearance, blood fraction, and association.

More importantly, these chapters showed that the lower South (South Carolina, Alabama, Louisiana, and Florida) had very different color lines than did the upper South and the North. South Carolina had an extraordinarily permeable color line. Alabama and Louisiana had two mildly endogamous color lines separating three groups. And Florida lacked any endogamous color line at all. The North, on the other hand, evolved a color line similar to today's: it was strict, it was based on hypodescent, and it supported a shared ethnic self-identity.

Most importantly of all, the preceding eight chapters reveal that the very concept of "invisible blackness" had not even been argued in an appeals court anywhere in the United States as of 1830. The one-drop rule, in the sense of an utterly European-looking person being seen as a member of the Black endogamous group due to an un-measurable trace of distant Black ancestry, was still in the future. This is important because it lets us focus on the late antebellum period and thereafter in determining when, where, how, why, and by whom the one-drop rule was invented.

Section III.
The One-Drop Rule

Chapter 14.
Features of Today's One-Drop Rule

Twin brothers Phillip and Paul Malone applied to become Boston firefighters in 1975 but were rejected due to low civil service test scores. After the city instituted an affirmative action program that added test points for Blacks, the Malone brothers claimed that their mother suddenly revealed that a great-grandmother was Black. They thereupon re-applied as Blacks in 1977 and successfully completed the exam due to the extra points that they received for their newly discovered Blackness. For ten years, they led successful careers and their names were submitted to the Boston Fire Commission for promotion to lieutenants in 1987. Both men passed the qualifying exams with exceptional scores (without affirmative action points).[1]

Then, a fire commissioner who had been reviewing promotion paperwork observed the Malones and accused the brothers of "racial" fraud. The accusation sparked a political firestorm. One minority leader claimed that as many as 60 of Boston's 351 Black and 51 Hispanic firefighters were actually lying

---

[1] The Malones' story can be found in newspaper articles spanning a one-year period: The Boston Globe, *Two Fight Firing over Disputed Claim They are Black*(September 29, 1988); The Boston Globe, *Firemen Who Claimed to be Black Lose Appeal*(July 26, 1989).

Whites. Another complained that the authorities had "looked the other way" for ten years. "If a black person came waltzing into the fire department in the '70s and it was in his interest to claim he was white, I have no doubt the Boston Fire Department would say, 'Wait a minute, you're not white." [But] When a white person said he is black, they look the other way."

Stung by the attacks, Boston's enraged Mayor Flynn ordered investigations into all city departments—fire, police, schools—to root out other Whites who may have fraudulently claimed minority status. As in 1976 Los Angeles, a frenzy of bureaucratic evil-seeking ensued.[2] The fire department's investigation turned up eleven Spanish-surnamed individuals who were accused of not being "racially" Hispanic enough. Seven were exonerated; two resigned under pressure; the other two remained under investigation until the firestorm dwindled away. Two departments—Police and Schools—refused to participate in the widening hunt for "racial" frauds and the mayor complained publicly about their insubordination. The following year, a twenty-three-page ruling by Justice Herbert Wilkins of the state Supreme Judicial Court convicted the Malones of fraud and upheld their expulsion. In his decision, Justice Wilkins referred to the position taken by the Black political leadership. Had the Black community supported the Malone brothers (and presumably the disgraced Hispanic firefighters as well), they would have been allowed to keep their jobs.

*　*　*　*　*

This chapter explains, in six topics, the phenomenon of the one-drop rule in America today. *Definition* explains that the one-drop rule is hypodescent taken to absurd conclusion—that someone with trivial African ancestry is considered Black. *Many Scholars Believe the One-Drop Rule is Stronger Than Ever* surveys the writings of about two-dozen scholars of U.S. race relations publishing today to reveal a clear academic consensus.

---

[2] See the opening anecdote of *Chapter 2. Afro-European Genetic Admixture in the United States.*

Some Evidence Disputes the One-Drop Rule's Universality presents recent cases to show that nowadays the one-drop rule is often rejected by Blacks and Whites alike. *Other Evidence Confirms the One-Drop Rule's Popularity* presents another series of examples to show the opposite—that the one-drop rule is also often enforced by Blacks and Whites alike. *Scholarly Pronouncements are Unpersuasive* explains that moral position-taking and hidden assumptions make unsubstantiated assertions suspect, even those made by scholars. Finally, *The Future* examines census data as to how interracial parents label their children to conclude that the one-drop rule may possibly become less fashionable in the coming decades, although advocating it will continue to be a lucrative practice.

Definition

This book uses "one-drop rule" to mean that some people without even a hint of African features or skin tone, like *New York Times* critic Anatole Broyard or Anthony Hopkins's character in the film *The Human Stain*, are classified as members of the Black endogamous group by press and public despite their European appearance. They are seen as unsuitable marriage partners by Whites but suitable by Blacks because of an unmeasurable, invisible touch (one drop) of Black ancestry. As Naomi Zack puts it, "One-drop rule: American social and legal custom of classifying anyone with one black ancestor, regardless of how far back, as black."[3]

Not everyone uses the term "one-drop rule" thus. To some, "one-drop rule" is synonymous with Marvin Harris's term "hypodescent," meaning that Americans of African physical appearance are considered Black, even if their African admixture is less than 50 percent.[4] This differs from the Caribbean, where you are "White" if you look preponderantly European. To others, "one drop rule" refers to the U.S. folkloric belief that anyone

---

[3] Naomi Zack, *Thinking About Race* (Belmont, CA, 1998), 116.

[4] Marvin Harris, *Patterns of Race in the Americas* (Westport CT, 1964), 37.

who has even one drop of African blood in his veins is marked by some subtle physical trait, a clue that reveals the African ancestry. Some say that it is revealed in the color of the half-moons at the base of the thumbnails, or in the shape of the heel, or in blue or purple marks at specific locations on the body. To them, "one-drop rule" is the belief that no matter how diluted African blood may be, a residue of visible evidence will always remain, generation after generation. For some purposes, these may be useful definitions, but neither is the meaning used here. In this work, "one-drop rule" means "invisible Blackness." It means that someone who looks utterly European is considered Black anyway, presumably due to having some distant intangible Black ancestry.

Incidentally, the folkloric belief in a physical mark or stigma that remains visible despite infinite dilution of Negro blood is important in U.S. history, and turns up in many nineteenth-century court cases. Nevertheless, such a belief in a permanent stigma is not the topic of this study. The difference may seem historically trivial, but it is epistemologically vital. The belief that anyone with one drop of Negro blood, no matter how dilute, will carry some visible mark of ancestry is a statement about observable reality. It is easily refuted precisely because it is thereby subject to experience and demonstration.[5] In contrast, the belief that a person *with no detectable African ancestry* is Black nonetheless and merely "looks White" is not a claim about observable reality. It is a statement about something intangible. Hence, it cannot be tested; it cannot be refuted. This is precisely why such a belief is a fascinating subject of study. Americans live in a world where many educated intellectuals use word processors on computers that exploit the laws of quantum mechanics, to express sincere pre-enlightenment beliefs in an unseen world. This is not to suggest that all social constructs are

---

[5] Whether distinguishing marks really exist is best addressed by considering that about 30 percent of today's White Americans and virtually all Hispanics have measurable recent African genetic admixture. If there were any such marks, they would be visible in one White American out of every three. See *Chapter 2. Afro-European Genetic Admixture in the United States.*

irrational. Gender, class, religion, even criminality are social constructs. But a person's gender, class, religion, or criminal record can be determined by evidence, by observation. Physical observation may be impractical in any given case, and objectivity may be elusive. Nevertheless, tangible observation is theoretically definitive for such constructs. Invisible Blackness, on the other hand is no more tangible in principle than Original Sin. As Scott L. Malcomson explains:

> The one-drop rule held that one drop of black blood made a person black. At first glance, this might seem to fix racial matters in a final shape and settle the problem of determining who's who. Yet it did just the opposite.... Seeking to pin down the essence of race, the one-drop rule actually made that essence unknowable, indeed invisible. It jettisoned the perceptible reality of skin tone for the dream of racial essence; it made the physical metaphysical. It was simply not possible to know whether you had a drop of black blood—to know whether you were really a white person or an imitation. There was no way to find out, no way to be sure. The one-drop rule made whiteness imaginary, pushed one's whiteness back into an indefinitely receding past of unknown ancestors. It took a crucial social fact of your life and made it a legacy bequeathed by ghosts—all in the form of a fine legal distinction meant to clarify a permanent system of racial separatism.[6]

The one-drop rule's notion of invisible Blackness exists only in the United States.[7] To be sure, a few Old World castes are also based on invisible ancestry, rather than on genotype: the Harijans of India, the Burakumin of Japan. But such customs trace membership through one parent or the other, and are unrelated to African-European racialism.

---

[6] Scott L. Malcomson, *One Drop of Blood: The American Misadventure of Race* (New York, 2000), 356.

[7] Gary B. Mills, *The Forgotten People: Cane River's Creoles of Color* (Baton Rouge, 1977), 193; Carl N. Degler, *Neither Black nor White: Slavery and Race Relations in Brazil and the United States* (New York, 1971), 101; Joel Williamson, *New People: Miscegenation and Mulattoes in the United States* (New York, 1980), 2; James Baldwin, *Nobody Knows My Name* (New York, 1962), 19.

The one-drop rule spawns the corollary notion of "passing for White," an Americanism that is not even listed in the first edition of the Oxford English Dictionary.[8] The concept is exceedingly difficult to explain to students and visitors from other countries, whether they hail from former British, French, or Dutch Caribbean colonies or from Muslim or Latino lands.[9] According to F. James Davis, they typically ask, "Shouldn't Americans say that a person who is passing as white *is* white, or nearly all white, and had previously been passing as black?" or "To be consistent, shouldn't you say that someone who is one-eighth white is passing as black?"[10] Indeed, what Alessandro de Medici, Queen Charlotte, Alexander Pushkin, Alexandre Dumas, and John James Audubon had in common was their openly avowed partial African ancestry.[11] Yet, no one in Italy, England, Russia, France, or early America respectively, labeled them "Black."[12] In today's United States, on the other hand, Americans who claim recent African ancestry risk becoming irrevocably Black in the eyes of the press and public.[13]

---

[8] Werner Sollors, *Neither Black Nor White Yet Both* (Cambridge, 1997), 247.

[9] Hilary Beckles, "Black Men in White Skins: The Formation of a White Proletariat in West Indian Society," *The Journal of Imperial and Commonwealth History*, October (no. 15, 1986), 5-21.

[10] F. James Davis, *Who is Black?: One Nation's Definition* (University Park PA, 1991), 13-34; Carl N. Degler, *Neither Black nor White: Slavery and Race Relations in Brazil and the United States* (New York, 1971).

[11] University of Chicago, ed. *The New Encyclopaedia Britannica*, 15 ed. (Chicago, 1974), 11:820; 7:1125; 15:308-9; iii:700. For Queen Charlotte, see also web page www.pbs.org/wgbh/pages/frontline/shows/secret/famous/royalfamily.html by PBS research historian Mario de Valdes y Cocom. For Audubon, see Kathryn Hall Proby, *Audubon in Florida* (Coral Gables FL, 1974), 5. Incidentally, Audubon's work often shows up in modern-day exhibits of Black art. See, for example, the touring exhibit, "Two Centuries of Black American Art," as described in Diana Loercher, "Black Art Exhibit," *The Ann Arbor News*, July 27 1977, B5.

[12] Although Dumas was sometimes referred to as "mulatto."

[13] Zack (1998), 5.

Many Scholars Believe the One-Drop Rule is Stronger Than Ever

Many scholars of contemporary race relations assert that the one-drop rule is stronger than ever among Americans today. In a standard undergraduate text on contemporary U.S. racialism, Naomi Zack explains:

> The formal basis for black and white racial identity amounts to this: ... A person is black if he or she has a black ancestor anywhere in family history. This is known as the "one-drop rule".... Thus, Americans with both white and black ancestry are always officially classified as black and often encouraged to identify as black in personal and social contexts. ... A person is white if he or she has no black ancestry anywhere in family history. This means that in order to be white, a person has to be purely white. This is a condition impossible to prove....[14]

According to legal scholar Neil Gotanda, American racial classifications in court cases today follow two formal rules:

> 1) *Rule of recognition*: Any person whose Black-African ancestry is visible is Black.
> 2) *Rule of descent:* (a) Any person with a known trace of African ancestry is Black, notwithstanding that person's visual appearance; or; stated differently, (b) the offspring of a Black and a white is Black. Historians and social scientists have noted the existence of these rules, often summarized as the "one drop of blood" rule, in their analysis of the American system of racial classification.[15] ... White is unblemished and pure, so one drop of ancestral Black blood renders one Black.[16]

Anthropologist Michael L. Blakey writes, "The 'one drop theory'... [is] still operative today, by which one is defined as

---

[14] Idem.

[15] Neil Gotanda, "A Critique of 'Our Constitution is Color-Blind'," *Stanford Law Review*, 44 (no. 1, November 1991), 1-68, 24.

[16] Ibid., 26.

'Black' when they have any African admixture, or defined as 'White' by the absence of non-European admixture."[17] Legal scholar Julie C. Lythcott-Haims writes, "[The one-drop rule] still exists today; Americans who are part-Black are socially considered Black, and only Black by most Americans. ... The one-drop rule is so ingrained in the American psyche that Blacks and Whites do not think twice about it."[18] Legal scholar Christine Hickman writes, "For generations, the boundaries of the African-American race have been formed by a rule, informally known as the 'one drop rule,' which, in its colloquial definition, provides that one drop of Black blood makes a person Black. In more formal, sociological circles... its meaning remains basically the same: anyone with a known Black ancestor is considered Black."[19]

Historian David A. Hollinger writes, "The stigma carried by blackness is unique, and is affixed and perpetuated resolutely by the American practice of treating blackness as a monolithic identity that an individual either has or does not have on the basis of the principle that any African ancestry at all determines that one is simply black."[20] Historian Thomas E. Skidmore writes, "For me, as a historian of Brazil, North America's "one-drop rule" has always seemed odd. No other society in this hemisphere has defined its racial types in such absolutist terms."[21] Sociologist G. Reginald Daniel writes:

---

[17] Michael L. Blakey, "Scientific Racism and the Biological Concept of Race," *Literature and Psychology*, 1999 (no. 1/2, Spring-Summer 1999), 29, 36.

[18] Julie C. Lythcott-Haims, "Where Do Mixed Babies Belong-Racial Classification in America and Its Implications for Transracial Adoption," *Harvard Civil Rights-Civil Liberties Law Review*, 29 (1994), 531-58, 532, 539.

[19] Christine Hickman, "The Devil and the One Drop Rule," *Michigan Law Review*, 95 (no. 5, March 1997), 1161-265, 1163.

[20] David A. Hollinger, "Amalgamation and Hypodescent: The Question of Ethnoracial Mixture in the History of the United States," *American Historical Review*, 108 (no. 5, December 2003), 1363-90, 1368.

[21] Thomas E. Skidmore, "Racial Mixture and Affirmative Action: The Cases of Brazil and the United States," *American Historical Review*, 108 (no. 5, December 2003), 1391-96, 139.

But... theories have not taken into consideration the fact that no matter how well African Americans are integrated into the primary structural sphere through racial intermarriage, the one-drop rule guarantees that African ancestry is passed on in perpetuity as a means of racially designating all future multi-racial offspring as black. As long as this device remains intact, whether formally or informally, it precludes a multiracial identification. ... The one-drop rule has become such an accepted part of the U.S. fabric that most individuals—except perhaps African Americans—are unaware of its oppressive origins."[22]

Sociologist F. James Davis writes, "This American cultural definition of blacks is taken for granted as readily by judges, affirmative action officers, and black protesters as it is by Ku Klux Klansmen."[23] Sociologist Joe R. Feagin writes, "The infamous one-drop-of-blood rule... has long characterized any American with a little African ancestry as 'black.'"[24] Legal scholar Ian F. Haney-Lopez writes, "Under this [one-drop] rule, historically given form in numerous state statutes, any known ancestry renders one Black. ... Stated differently, Whites are those with no known African... ancestry."[25] Historian Barbara Fields writes, "Throughout U.S. history, racial identity has been legally, and later culturally determined by the one-drop rule."[26]

Of those who believe that the one-drop rule is today's national consensus, some say that it is used by Whites to exploit Blacks, who are powerless to resist it. Barbara Fields writes that it is "used as an ideological weapon to support the continued

---

[22] G. Reginald Daniel, *More than Black?: Multiracial Identity and the New Racial Order* (Philadelphia, 2002), 19.

[23] F. James Davis, *Who is Black?: One Nation's Definition* (University Park PA, 1991), 5.

[24] Joe R. Feagin, *Racist America: Roots, Current Realities, and Future Reparations* (New York, 2000), 200-1.

[25] Ian F. Haney-Lopez, *White by Law: The Legal Construction of Race* (New York, 1996), 27.

[26] As quoted in David L. Brunsma and Kerry Ann Rockquemore, "What Does 'Black' Mean? Exploring the Epistemological Stranglehold of Racial Categorization," *Critical Sociology*, 28 (no. 1/2, 2002), 101-21, 104.

exploitation of African Americans...."[27] She explains that the one-drop rule is imposed against Black resistance and gives "individuals with any known black ancestry no choice other than to identify as black."[28] And she writes, "White Americans... generally regard passing as a particularly insidious form of deceit."[29] Similarly, Christine Hickman writes, "[Whites] fashioned [the one-drop rule] out of racism, malice, greed, lust, and ignorance...."[30]

Others, who are equally convinced that the one-drop rule reflects today's attitudes, say that it survives only because Blacks embrace it and use it to resist White "racism." According to Dinesh D'Souza:

> All the major civil rights organizations, such as the NAACP, the Urban League, and the Leadership Conference on Civil Rights, now strongly support the one-drop rule and would strongly resist getting rid of it. As activist Julian Bond puts it, "I very much oppose diluting the power and strength of numbers as they affect legal decisions about race in this country."[31] ... The one-drop principle continues to define blackness in America and now serves as a unifying force for African Americans.[32]

Historian Joel Williamson writes, "Millions of Americans who are more European than African in their heritage continue to insist, sometimes defiantly, upon their blackness."[33] Sociologist Mary C. Waters writes, "Black Americans are highly socially constrained to identify as blacks, without other options

---

[27] As quoted in Brunsma (2002), 108.

[28] As quoted by Brunsma (2002), 104.

[29] Barbara Fields, "Of Rogues and Geldings," *American Historical Review*, 108 (no. 5, December 2003), 1397-405, 1404.

[30] Christine Hickman, "The Devil and the One Drop Rule," *Michigan Law Review*, 95 (no. 5, March 1997), 1161-265, 1166.

[31] Dinesh D'Souza, *The End of Racism* (New York, 1995), 205.

[32] Ibid., 204.

[33] Joel Williamson, *New People: Miscegenation and Mulattoes in the United States* (New York, 1980), 2.

available to them, even if they believe or know that their fore-bears included many non-blacks."[34] F. James Davis writes:

> Blacks are just as anxious as whites to instruct the young and the deviant about how the rule works and how important it is to follow it. The rule is now strongly enforced within the black community. American blacks now feel that they have an important vested interest in [the one-drop rule]. ... The overwhelming reality is that most blacks in the United States... feel that they have an important stake in maintaining [the one-drop rule], socialize their children to accept it, and rally to its defense when it is challenged.[35]

Julie C. Lythcott-Haims writes, "Part-Black people of all hues joined Blacks in embracing the [one-drop rule] in the late 1960s. ..."[36] Christine Hickman writes, "[The one-drop] rule created the African-American race as we know it today, and while this race has its origins in the peoples of three continents and its members can look very different from one another, over the centuries the [White] one drop rule united this race as a people...."[37] Journalist and author Debra J. Dickerson writes, "No one believes as fervently in the 'one drop' rule as blacks do."[38]

How could a Black minority have the power to force an unwilling White society to pay obeisance to the one-drop rule against its will? Some suggest that the strength of the one-drop rule many be due to the fact that both civil and criminal federal and state courts engaged in affirmative action cases today enforce the one-drop rule as the law of the land. According to Dinesh D'Souza:

---

[34] Mary C. Waters, *Ethnic Options: Choosing Identities in America* (Berkeley, 1990), 18.

[35] F. James Davis, *Who is Black?: One Nation's Definition* (University Park PA, 1991), 137-39.

[36] Julie C. Lythcott-Haims, "Where Do Mixed Babies Belong-Racial Classification in America and Its Implications for Transracial Adoption," *Harvard Civil Rights-Civil Liberties Law Review*, 29 (1994), 531-58, 533.

[37] Hickman (1997), 1166.

[38] Debra J. Dickerson, *The End of Blackness: Returning the Souls of Black Folk to Their Rightful Owners*, 1st ed. (New York, 2004), 15.

[The one-drop rule] serves as the official instrument of enforcement of civil rights laws. Ever since 1965, when the
Equal Employment Opportunity Commission required race-
conscious record-keeping and reporting on the part of companies, racial classification has been an organizing principle
for the American work force.[39]

Some Evidence Disputes the One-Drop Rule's Universality

Despite such scholarly assertions, the fact is that not every
American with an invisible trace of African ancestry is inevitably assigned to the Black endogamous group by U.S. society. In
June 2004, the author presented a historical paper to the 5th bi-
ennial Melungeon Union in Kingsport, Tennessee. Several hundred members of this famous maroon community of the Cumberland Plateau attended the conference, along with members of
the Redbones and other maroon communities. All of the atten-
dees openly embrace all of their ancestries, including African
(about five percent genetic admixture, on average), and yet they
consider themselves White nonetheless (that is, they see themselves as suitable marriage partners for other members of the
U.S. White endogamous group).

The entertainment industry also often rejects the one-drop
rule. Many actors, musicians, and professional athletes have
found that acknowledging a trace of African ancestry can help,
rather than hinder, one's career. And so, the official web sites of
many such entertainers claim mixed ancestry.[40] Like the maroons, such individuals defy the one-drop rule by considering
themselves White while simultaneously acknowledging partial
African heritage. Others reject racialism entirely by refusing to

---

[39] D'Souza (1995), 205.

[40] As of July 1, 2003, URL <http://www.mixedfolks.com/africans.htm> and
URL <http://www.multiracial.com/links/links-celebrities.html> provide
links to hundreds of such sites. See also topic "How Can so Many People
Falsify Their Paper Trail and Cut all Family Ties?" in *Chapter 5. The Rate
of Black-to-White "Passing."*

adopt any "race" at all, thus emulating many Hispanics and Muslims.[41]

Self-identification as White along with public pride in fractional African ancestry is not limited to the entertainment industry, where such a strategy may be lucrative. A survey of 177 Detroit college students, each with one Black and one White parent, offered the subjects seven choices of "racial" self-identification. The choices were: (1) exclusively Black, (2) sometimes Black and sometimes not, (3) biracial but "experience the world as Black", (4) exclusively biracial, (5) exclusively not Black, (6) "race is meaningless," and (7) other.[42] Notice that "White" was not offered as an option. This was because the researcher himself believed that the one-drop rule was the insuperable norm. He wrote, "current research... assumes that individuals with one black and one white parent have only two options for "racial" identity: 'black' or 'biracial.'"[43] Since the survey was limited to first-generation biracials, its very format made a "White" self-image exceedingly unlikely to be reported. And yet, despite the odds stacked against White self-identity, 3.6 percent of the subjects deliberately ignored the given choices and the implicit assumptions built into the form and painstakingly wrote in "White (only)."[44]

On a 1982 TV talk show, a Jamaican singer said in her clipped British accent, "I like to do Black songs sometimes. I am half Black, you know." According to F. James Davis, the statement startled American viewers. One could not be "half Black" in the United States of 1982.[45] Davis wrote:

> Challenges to the [one-drop] rule in court have been rare, especially in the twentieth century. As the Phipps case demonstrates, the rule still seems to be well settled in both state and federal law in the United States. That case has raised wide-

---

[41] See discussion of this point in Brunsma (2002), 100.

[42] Ibid., 108n7.

[43] Ibid., 335.

[44] Ibid., 110.

[45] F. James Davis, *Who is Black?: One Nation's Definition* (University Park PA, 1991), 99.

spread interest, however, and could encourage other legal tests. Cases could come from the Hispanic community, where racial classification has often been a local issue. Before long, Hispanics will become the nation's largest minority group, and they are already increasingly active in politics and in court. Legal challenges to the federal rule might come from Hawaii, where the one-drop rule is contrary to the traditional pattern of race relations. However, the probability of major judicial or legislative challenges to the rule for the nation as a whole seems small. Overall, both individual and patterned deviations from the one-drop rule are likely to continue to symbolize and strengthen it more than pose significant challenges to the rule.[46]

And yet, just twelve years after Davis wrote those words, a magazine article about a professional tennis star headlined, "James Blake may hit the books as hard as the ball, but that doesn't mean this young, gifted, *half-black* [emphasis mine] Harvard-educated heartthrob isn't the future of tennis."[47]

Rejection of the one-drop rule is neither recent nor limited to such peripheral communities as the entertainment industry. The one-drop rule was sometimes rejected by the White elite even before the civil rights movement, as was exemplified by the tale of Louetta Chassereau. She was ruled by her state Supreme Court in *Bennett v. Bennett*, 1940 South Carolina, to have become White despite having been born Black.[48]

As discussed above, much scholarly opinion holds that members of the U.S. Black endogamous group embrace the one-drop rule. Nevertheless, the reality is that African-American disputants routinely reject the one-drop rule whenever it is politically advantageous to do so. Affirmative action litigation provides many examples.

The inconsistency and ambiguity of EEOC regulations provide a rich environment for claims and counter-claims based

---

[46] Ibid., 176.

[47] Melanie D. G. Kaplan, "Different Strokes," *USA Weekend*, June 20-22 2003, 10.

[48] 195 S.C. 1. The story is related in detail as the opening anecdote of *Chapter 5. The Rate of Black-to-White "Passing."*

on acceptance or rejection of the one-drop rule. The Equal Employment Opportunity Commission (the executive agency that investigates discrimination and negotiates settlements under 42 U.S.C. §§ 2000e-4 to 2000e-5b) was given the responsibility of defining "racial" classifications for federal litigation.[49] The EEOC recognizes five "races." Three of those "races" are of interest here:

> **White** (not of Hispanic origin)—All persons having origin in any of the original peoples of Europe, North Africa, or the Middle East.
>
> **Black** (not of Hispanic origin)—All persons having origins in any of the Black racial groups of Africa.
>
> **Hispanic**—All persons of Mexican, Puerto Rican, Cuban, Central or South American, or other Spanish culture or origin regardless of race.[50]

None of the definitions is internally consistent or even makes logical sense. More importantly, the definitions of Black and White assume that all litigants are of pureblooded ancestry; the law cannot contemplate the existence of hybrids.

Similarly, other federal and state regulations refer to minority set-asides, but the term "minority" is not defined in law. Perhaps this is because it seems mathematically to be based on population counts. And yet, when asked to identify their "ethnic heritage" on the census long form, fewer than one percent of Americans claim to be "White." The most popular choices of ethnicity are: German (23.3%), Irish (15.6%), English (13.1%), African-American (10.0%), and Italian (5.9%). In other words speaking mathematically, self-assessed "Blacks" are among the four largest "majorities" in America (pluralities, actually) and the term "White" is insignificantly buried just below Puerto Ricans and Slovaks (0.7%) and just above Danes and Hungarians

---

[49] *Luther Wright, Jr.*, "Who's Black, Who's White, and Who Cares: Reconceptualizing the United States's Definition of Race and Racial Classifications," *Vanderbilt Law Review*, 48 (no. 2, 1995), 513-70, 535.

[50] Employer Information Report EEO-1 and Standard Form 100, Appendix § 4, Race/Ethnic Identification, 1 Empl. Prac. Guide (CCH) § 1881, (1981), 1625.

(0.6%).[51] The point, of course, is not that Blacks rule or that Whites are subordinate, but that, like "race" and "ethnicity," the term "minority" itself is inconsistent and ambiguous.[52]

The Malone brothers, whose tale opened this chapter, claimed one-drop membership in the Black endogamous group. They were convicted of fraud due to the testimony of Black political leaders who rejected their claim to invisible Blackness because they were not ethnically African-American. Similarly, Mostafa Hefny, an African-looking immigrant, actually from Africa, was rejected by local U.S. Black leaders as not being "African-American" in the ethnic sense intended by EEOC regulations.[53]

That Blacks reject one-drop and bar the door to membership in the Black community against people who were not brought up within the African-American ethnic tradition may seem unsurprising. But Black leaders have also been known to bar the door to Blackness against political opponents who were born, raised, and lived their lives as African Americans. Consider the tale of Mark Stebbins and Ralph White.

"If the momma is an elephant and the daddy is an elephant, they durn sure can't have no lion. They got to have a baby elephant," said Ralph White. After a newcomer unseated this twelve-year City Council incumbent in a March, 1984, election in Stockton, California, the millionaire loser demanded a recall. Ralph White claimed that Mark Stebbins had lied to the voters

---

[51] Borgna Brunner, ed. *Time Almanac: The Ultimate Worldwide Fact and Information Source* (Boston, 1999) 364.

[52] For arguments that the term "minority" is deliberately crafted to be ambiguous, see Peter J. Aspinall, "Collective Terminology to Describe the Minority Ethnic Population: The Persistence of Confusion and Ambiguity in Usage," *Sociology*, 36 (no. 4, 2002), 803-16 and Phillip Gleason, "Minorities (Almost) All: The Minority Concept in American Social Thought," *American Quarterly*, 43 (no. 3, September 1991), 392-424.

[53] See URL <http://edition.cnn.com/US/9707/16/racial.suit>. As mentioned above, the letter of EEOC regulations speaks only to a person's continent of origin, not to their ethnic allegiance. Nevertheless, courts often enforced the "spirit" (that affirmative action does not apply to recent African immigrants) and ignore the letter of the law.

about his "race."[54] The defeated councilman said that the victor
falsely claimed to be Black in order win votes in a district
where, according to the Associated Press, "37 percent of the residents are black, 46 percent Hispanic, 8 percent white and 9 percent of other ancestry."[55]

Mark Stebbins, the accused victor, had been a pro-
integration civil rights activist for two decades. He had led the
San Francisco Hunter's Point demonstrations in the early 1960s.
He had moved to Stockton with a church group trying to organize the city's disadvantaged and had become coordinator of several dozen city-sponsored community gardens. He is fair complexioned and—discounting a broad nose and frizzy hair—looks
preponderantly Euro-American. His wife is African-dark. Stebbins claimed to be "culturally, socially, and genetically" black,
tracing his African ancestry through an unspecified grandparent.
He said, "it's terribly significant that you can still ask [a man's
"race"] 20 years or more after the initial Civil Rights Act."

Ralph White, the defeated accuser, had also been a civil
rights activist, but of separatist (Black pride), rather than integra-

---

[54] The detailed story of Stebbins's election and recall can be found in a nine-
month-long series of newswire reports: AP Domestic News, *Defeated
Councilman Says Winner Lied About Being Black*(March 10, 1984e); UPI
Domestic News, *Black or White? Race Becomes Political Issue*(April 19,
1984a); UPI Domestic News, *Race the Major Issue in Recall Election*(May
8, 1984d); AP Domestic News: AP, *City Council Recall Vote Hinges on
Councilman's Race* (May 8, 1984b); UPI Domestic News: UPI, *Candidate's
Race a Major Issue in Recall Election* (May 8, 1984b); AP Domestic News:
AP, *'Black' Councilman Retains Seat* (May 9, 1984a); AP Domestic News:
AP, *'Culturally Black' Councilman Keeps His Seat* (May 9, 1984d); UPI
Domestic News: UPI, *Green-Eyed 'Black' Man Wins Recall Election* (May
9, 1984c); AP Domestic News: AP, *'Culturally Black' Councilman De-
feated* (December 20, 1984c).

[55] This sentence, of course, reveals the AP staffer's own ideas about race.
The 46 percent Hispanic (versus 8 percent white) is questionable because
over ninety percent of those who identify themselves as "Hispanic" in the
U.S. census also report themselves as "White" (or an equivalent) on the
same census form. And, according to Yu Xie and Kimberly Goyette, "The
Racial Identification of Biracial Children with One Asian Parent: Evidence
from the 1990 Census," *Social Forces*, 76 (no. 2, December 1997), 547-70,
most Americans of mixed Euro-Asian parentage (like Keanu Reeves, say)
also consider themselves to be census White.

tionist, persuasion. He had been a butcher when first elected to the Council twelve years earlier, and had become a millionaire since. He looks distinctly Afro-American. White had uncovered a copy of Stebbins's birth certificate, which listed his parents as "white." It was then that White called a press conference to explain the heredity of elephants and lions. He responded to a question about his harping on his victorious opponents "race" by explaining, "It's not a racist issue. He lied to my people and said he was something he wasn't. He deceived and defrauded my people by tricking them and lying to them about being one of them."

On the other hand, some members of Stockton's Black community defended Stebbins. The Rev. Bob Hailey, chairman of the Stockton chapter of the Black American Political Association of California said that Stebbins was, "one of the bright spots here. In my estimation, he thinks black and is black." Hailey said that the voters were tired of White, who had done nothing since his election twelve years before other than build himself a 27-room mansion with a tennis court and swimming pool. He also bought a nightclub, 32 rental properties, and a grocery store. "He's been more detrimental to the black community than anybody I know of."

White replied that, "Any time a black person gets a couple of dollars more than other folks, they accuse him of doing something wrong." For his part, Stebbins pointed out that if he had wanted to lie about his "race" in order to get elected, "I should have said I'm Hispanic. My Spanish isn't that bad." Stebbins survived White's first recall petition and a subsequent court-ordered run-off election in June. But his opponent simply filed another recall petition, and Stebbins's political support slowly dwindled. In the end, Stebbins lost a December recall vote. Nine months after having been voted out in the regular election, White was reinstated as councilman and Stebbins was expelled from office—presumably for having committed "racial" fraud.

At least two scholars believe that America's one-drop rule may be waning. According to David L. Brunsma and Kerry Ann Rockquemore, "The cultural space has emerged where the one-drop rule has been challenged—particularly among young multiracial people. ... Such experiences have allowed a rejection of the one-drop rule and forced a reconsideration of the mutual exclusivity of racial categories."[56]

Other Evidence Confirms the One-Drop Rule's Popularity

On the other hand, much evidence suggests that the one-drop rule is still invoked whenever it seems useful. Court cases as well as scholarly papers and policy pronouncements show this. As recently as 1986, the U.S. Supreme Court upheld the one-drop rule by refusing to hear a case against Louisiana's "racial" classification criteria.

In 1985, fair-complexioned Mrs. Susie Guillory Phipps of Louisiana checked "White" on her passport application. It was denied because, decades before on her birth certificate, a midwife had checked "colored" for one of her parents. Mrs. Phipps sued (see *Jane Doe v. State of Louisiana*, 1985 Louisiana).[57] She testified that, "this classification came as a shock, since she had always thought she was White, had lived as White, and had twice married as White." The state argued that Mrs. Phipps possibly descended from some eighteenth century planter who had married a former slave, long before Louisiana was part of the United States. (In 1970, Louisiana had passed legislation that anyone with 1/32 Negro ancestry or more was legally Black.) Mrs. Phipps was unable to disprove this possibility. So, the court ruled that she was legally Black and could not receive a White passport. She appealed to the three levels of state court and lost each time. In 1986, she appealed to the U.S. Supreme Court. She lost again. The court refused to consider the case, saying that "racial" determination was not a federal issue.[58] The 1986 U.S. Supreme Court thus upheld *Plessy v. Ferguson*, 1896. (Homer Plessy was also genetically White but legally Black.) The courts

---

[56] Brunsma (2002), 108.

[57] 479 So. 2d 369; 485 So. 2d 60.

[58] 479 U.S. 1002.

Figure 22 Patrick Francis Healy

also upheld an earlier Louisiana Supreme Court ruling (*State ex rel. Joseph Jules Schlumbrecht, Jr. v. Louisiana Board of Health*, 1970 Louisiana) that once a Black designation has been officially recorded on a birth certificate, "vital statistics cannot be changed unless the proof and support [of Whiteness] leaves *no doubt at all* [emphasis added]."[59]

In 1815, Irish immigrant Michael Morris Healy founded a slave plantation near Macon, Georgia. He and his biracial wife, Eliza Clark Healy, raised ten children. All were educated in the North and five subsequently achieved success as Irish-Americans.

James Augustine Healy became Bishop of Portland, Maine, Patrick Francis Healy became president of Georgetown University, Michael Morris Healy, Jr. became a captain in the U.S. Coast Guard and the sole U.S. government representative in newly purchased Alaska, Alexander Sherwood Healy became rector of the cathedral in Boston, and their sister became mother superior of a convent.

---

[59] 231 So. 2d 730.

Figure 23 Michael Morris Healy, Jr.

Their photographs show no sign of African features. Their writings show them to have been neither more nor less prejudiced than other prominent Irish-Americans of their time, but one thing is overwhelmingly clear: they saw themselves and were seen by their community as White. They left numerous written documents to this effect, and even the sea-captain's teenaged son once scratched his name on a remote rock above the Arctic Circle during an exploration voyage as "the first white boy" to have visited the region.[60] And yet the Catholic Church today publicizes James as America's first Black bishop,[61] Georgetown University publicizes Patrick as the nation's first Black university president,[62] and the National Archives and Records Administration publicizes Michael as the first Black Coast Guard captain.[63] Each of these sources refers to these men as African-Americans, each portrays them as praiseworthy, and each laments that their only moral flaw was to falsely deny their true "race."

---

[60] Interracial Voice: A.D. Powell, *When Are Irish-Americans Not Good Enough to Be Irish-American?: 'Racial Kidnaping' and the Case of the Healy Family* <http://interracialvoice.com/powell8.html> (1998).

[61] See *Black Catholics in the United States*, a Vatican publicity handout for Pope John Paul II's visit to the United Nations in October, 1995 at URL <http://shamino.quincy.edu/tolton/black.html>, also available from NCCB Secretariat for African American Catholics, 3211 4th Street, N.E., Washington, D.C. 20017, (202) 541-3177.

[62] See Georgetown University, *Rev. Patrick F. Healy, SJ Papers: Collection Description* at URL <http://gulib.lausun.georgetown.edu/dept/speccoll/cl57.htm>.

[63] James M. O'Toole, "Racial Identity and the Case of Captain Michael Healy, USRCS," *Prologue: Quarterly of the National Archives & Records Administration*, 29 (no. 3, Fall 1997).

Calvin Clark Davis of Bear Lake, Michigan, died heroically in 1944 while attacking the oil refineries in Meresburg, Germany with the U.S. Army Air Corps. He was posthumously awarded several medals, including the Distinguished Flying Cross. Davis considered himself to be White, nothing more, and his neighbors agreed. Staffers for a U.S. congressman recently discovered and made public that Davis had undetectable but proven African ancestry. U.S. newspapers portrayed him as: "passed for white" (*Traverse City Record-Eagle*), "lied about who he was" (*Traverse City Record-Eagle*), "claimed to be white" (*Chimes*, student newspaper of Calvin College, Grand Rapids, MI), "pretended to be white" (*Associated Press, Los Angeles Times*), "concealed his race" (Rep. Peter Hoekstra, R-Holland, MI), "faked being white" (*Associated Press, Los Angeles Times*), "black man who pretended to be white" (*The Holland Sentinel*).[64] This unanimity of interpretation defied common knowledge in the region that early twentieth-century Michiganers routinely accepted European-looking people with trace Black ancestry as White.[65] Only the BBC reported his story as a "white airman with black ancestry."[66]

The Catholic Church recently nominated Mother Henriette Delille, the founder of the Order of the Sisters of the Holy Family, for canonization. The honor is due to the aid that she and her order gave selflessly to slaves, freedmen, *gens de couleur libre*,[67] children, elderly and the sick, from 1842 to 1862, when no one else in Louisiana seemed to care. Mother Henriette Delille was the daughter of Jean Baptiste Delille Sarpy (of French and Italian descent) and Marie Diaz, (of French, Hispanic, and African descent). Her canonization had been supported by Lou-

---

[64] Interracial Voice, *Pissing on the Graves of Heroes*, May [Electronic Magazine] (2003).

[65] For a detailed account of this phenomenon, see James E. DeVries, *Race and Kinship in a Midwestern town: The Black Experience in Monroe, Michigan, 1900-1915* (Urbana, 1984), 150.

[66] Powell (2003).

[67] Literally, "free people of color." In practice, the term refers to members of the Louisiana Creole community who, even today, adamantly refuse to self-identify racially. They insist that they are neither Black nor White.

isiana's Creole community, including descendants of Mother Henriette's family. To the family's horror, the Church has publicized the process as the proposed canonization of the first "Black" American saint.[68]

To grasp the controversy, one must understand that many if not most Creoles today reject the U.S. "race" notion (rather like Hispanics, unsurprisingly). In 1976, for instance, a historian interviewed the president of *Jeunes Amis,* a fraternal association for gens de couleur libre, requesting access to its historical documents. The scholar said that he wanted to expand his primary sources on Black history. "Jeunes Amis is not a **black** organization!" the curator was insulted. "Thommy Lafon [the organization's founder] was not **black**. I am not **black**. Thommy Lafon would rise up from his grave in sheer anger if he ever knew that you had called us **black**! You will have to look elsewhere to find **black** history!" He thereupon ejected the researcher from the premises.[69]

Mother Henriette's descendants and supporters have written letters to the Vatican as well as to local Church leaders, asking that the Church's huge multimedia publicity campaign be corrected to refer to the proposed saint as "Creole," "biracial," "mixed," or some other term closer to how the woman saw herself a century and a half ago.[70] The Church has refused to change its course, suggesting that any media alteration would antagonize U.S. Blacks, the market at which the canonization is targeted. The only detailed explanation issued by the Church sug-

---

[68] The Multiracial Activist, *The Misidentification of Mother Henriette Delille,* August [Electronic Magazine] (2002).

[69] Virginia R. Dominguez, *White by Definition: Social Classification in Creole Louisiana* (New Brunswick NJ, 1986), 163.

[70] Interracial Voice, *Mother Henriette Delille & The One-Drop Rule -- Alive and Well?,* January 1 [Electronic Magazine] (2003b); Interracial Voice, *To the Most Reverend Alfred C. Hughes,* January 1 [Electronic Magazine] (2003); Interracial Voice, *An Open Letter to the Leadership of the Catholic Church Regarding the Racial/Cultural Labeling of Mother Henriette Delille* [Electronic Magazine] (2003b); Interracial Voice, *An open letter to Most Reverend Alfred C. Hughes* [Electronic Magazine] (2003a).

gests that Mother Henriette's "current ancestry" need not be the same as her original ancestry.[71]

Nevertheless, that the one-drop rule is often enforced in today's United States does not necessarily confirm all of the scholarly opinions previously related. Academics are virtually unanimous that the one-drop rule is somehow connected to "racism" (defined as Whites mistreating Blacks). Some (Fields, Hickman) affirm that it is used today by "racist" Whites against Blacks. Others (D'Souza, Williamson, Waters, Davis, Lythcott-Haims, Hickman) say that it is used nowadays by Blacks to resist White "racism." Nevertheless, some court decisions that enforce the one-drop rule seem to lack any trace of "racism." Indeed, many lack any evidence of "racial" mistreatment of anyone by anyone.

In 1988, 39-year-old Mary Christine Walker, a Denver schoolteacher with fair complexion, green eyes, and light brown hair claimed on a job application to be Black. Her prospective employer obtained Ms. Walker's birth certificate, found her listed there as "White," and accused her of "lying to take advantage of minority-hiring policies." Walker promptly filed suit in State District Court. She claimed to be Black, despite her looks. She said that her parents (allegedly, an interracial couple) had listed her as White on her birth certificate so that their daughter could take advantage of her European appearance when she grew up. Noting that Ms. Walker had the support of the Black community, Judge John Brooks Jr. on September 6, 1989, ordered the state Department of Vital Statistics to issue the woman a new birth certificate.[72] In this case, a person of neither African appearance nor African-American ethnicity was ruled to be Black on the basis of a one-drop rule that was demanded by the individual and supported by local Black political leadership. It is hard to see any "racism" here, no matter how you define that slippery term.

---

[71] Ferreira (2003a).

[72] AP, "Rewriting Her Story," *The National Law Journal*, (Sept. 18 1989), 51.

The Scholarly Consensus is Unpersuasive

Ultimately, however, the consensus of scholarly conclusions is unpersuasive. It seems evident that many academics claim that the one-drop rule is hegemonic today, and that most see it as related to "racism." They claim that the one-drop rule is used by Whites to apply "racism," or by Blacks to resist "racism," or that it somehow serves both purposes at once. But it is possible that such pronouncements reflect nothing more than that American scholars are members of U.S. society and, like it or not, they cannot help but partake of American racialism. Apparently, the one-drop rule is part of American culture, and so nearly every political camp feels compelled to defend it.

Skepticism towards their conclusions is unavoidable when many scholars morally advocate the one-drop rule. A legal scholar suggests that Americans who "pass"[73] in defiance of the one-drop rule are guilty of "cultural genocide."[74] A historian sees "passing" as "a particularly ugly manifestation of [racism]."[75] Another legal scholar writes, "[The] one drop rule united [the Negro] race as a people in the fight against slavery, segregation, and racial injustice."[76] The sociologist author of an outstanding overview of the multiracial movement of the 1990s writes that Americans who "pass" represent "psychosocial pathology" and are "insidious toxins in the racial ecology," "fraudulent," and "racial thieves."[77]

Many American scholars who avoid expressing moral judgment cannot help but let slip subconscious support of the

---

[73] *Passing*: a White American is discovered to have a Black-identified parent.

[74] Neil Gotanda, "A Critique of 'Our Constitution is Color-Blind'," *Stanford Law Review*, 44 (no. 1, November 1991), 59-60.

[75] Barbara Fields, "Of Rogues and Geldings," *American Historical Review*, 108 (no. 5, December 2003), 1404.

[76] Christine Hickman, "The Devil and the One Drop Rule," *Michigan Law Review*, 95 (no. 5, March 1997), 1163.

[77] G. Reginald Daniel, *More than Black?: Multiracial Identity and the New Racial Order* (Philadelphia, 2002), 8, 83, 111.

American one-drop rule. A sociologist who collected evidence that many genetically biracial students self-identify as "White" reports his discovery with the following words: "There exists a growing proportion of the black population who no longer view themselves as black."[78] Read that last quotation again. Compare it to the hypothetical, "a growing proportion of the Republican Party no longer view themselves as Republicans." The researcher labels his subjects a "proportion of the black population" despite their refusal to see themselves thus. Although the topic is voluntary self-identity, the very phrase used, "a proportion of the black population," involuntarily assigns the subjects to a group. It is imposed by the researcher's own subconscious commitment to the one-drop rule. A legal scholar without psychological credentials reports that people of dual genetic heritage who do not identify as solely "Black" are "in denial," and suffer from psychosocial marginalization.[79] (In fact, psychological studies show that young adults who consider themselves biracial or multiracial are "generally well adjusted."[80]) A journalism professor, who is sympathetic to White subjects who have some Black ancestry, nevertheless describes their lives as "painful deceit-ridden contortions."[81] She also says that Eston Hemings's direct descendants "for the last couple of centuries" have merely "lived as white."[82] A philosophy professor discussing a White young man with invisible Black ancestry says, "it would be nice to think that Matthews's friends would have come around to accepting that he was black."[83] The point is that he was not Black. One of his parents self-identified as Black (as

---

[78] Brunsma (2002), 114.

[79] Bijan Gilanshah, "Multiracial Minorities: Erasing the Color Line," *Law and Inequality*, 12 (December 1993), 183, 190.

[80] See particularly Christine Hall (1980) and Alvin Pouissant (1987), as quoted in Maria P.P. Root, "Resolving 'Other' Status: Identity Development of Biracial Individuals," *Women and Therapy*, 9 (1990), 186.

[81] Brooke Kroeger, *Passing: When People Can't be Who They Are* (New York, 2003), 9.

[82] Ibid., 28.

[83] Ibid., 22.

Carol Channing's paternal grandparents did). An anthropologist suggested that White Americans who ignore traces of Black ancestry are "not firmly anchored emotionally...."[84] A prize-winning historian in discussing the rise of the one-drop rule in the Jim Crow South writes, "They began to look with great suspicion upon mulattoes who looked white..."[85]

The Future

Ultimately, the most persuasive evidence is first-hand evidence. Is U.S. belief in a one-drop rule of invisible Blackness becoming more widespread or is it declining? One way of measuring the tenacity of the one-drop-rule is by examining how Black/White interracial parents identify their children on the census "race" question. Such couples are not typical of most Americans. Nevertheless, if interracial parents accept the legitimacy of African-American ethnic self-identity while simultaneously rejecting the one-drop rule, you would expect half of their children to be identified as White and half as Black. That the children of Black/White interracial parents have been more often identified as Black than as White since 1880 demonstrates that the one-drop rule has been accepted for many decades. In fact, the fraction of such children labeled as unmixed White has fallen steadily from 50 percent in 1940 to 13 percent in 2000. This suggests that the one-drop rule continues to grow stronger among Black/White interracial parents. On the other hand, the fraction of such children labeled as unmixed Black dropped abruptly from 62 percent in 1990 to 31 percent in 2000. This suggests that it has recently become unfashionable to make first-generation biracial children deny their European ancestry. Whether this portends a crack in the one-drop rule remains to be seen.

Interracially married couples are not typical of most Americans. Indeed, the very definition of the U.S. color line is that it denotes membership in a strongly endogamous group. As

---

[84] Ibid., 15.

[85] Joel Williamson, *The Crucible of Race: Black/White Relations in the American South Since Emancipation* (New York, 1984), 465.

of the 2000 census, less than four percent of married Blacks had a White spouse, a much lower out-marriage rate than that of any other U.S. ethnic boundary. Black/White interracial couples represent the tiny fraction of Americans who are willing to defy convention; who withstand pressure from friends and families on both sides. One would expect such parents to be less likely than most Americans to use a one-drop rule, especially when assigning "racial" identity to their own children.

If interracial parents accept the legitimacy of African-American ethnic self-identity while simultaneously rejecting the one-drop rule, you would expect half of their children to be identified as White and half as Black. This is independent of where the endogamous color line happens to lie along the phenotype continuum. In times and places, like 1930 Virginia, where dark Mediterranean looks could label one as Black, couples might be recorded in the census as intermarried if one were merely too swarthy for acceptance as White. In times and places, like 1850 South Carolina, where well-to-do people of visibly part-African appearance were considered White, couples would be recorded as intermarried only if the darker were very African-looking indeed.[86] Regardless of social convention, the laws of genetics predict that half of their children would inherit an appearance between the parents, one fourth would look more European than both, and one-fourth would look more African than both.[87] Given that children are evaluated by the same color-line criterion as their parents, wherever the line happens to be located along the phenotype continuum, then half of the children will look as White or Whiter than the White parent and half will look as Black or Blacker than the Black parent.[88] In short, if there were no one-drop rule then one would expect half of such first-

---

[86] For details on antebellum South Carolina's darkward-shifted color line, see *Chapter 10. Barbadian South Carolina: A Class-Based Color Line.*

[87] Assuming that both parents are not homozygotic at the three-to-six pairs of loci governing skin tone. See *Chapter 3. The Heredity of "Racial" Traits.*

[88] For an introduction to the genetics of "racial" appearance, see Curt Stern, *Principles of Human Genetics*, 3d ed. (San Francisco, 1973), 443-52; or L. L. Cavalli-Sforza and W. F. Bodmer, *The Genetics of Human Populations* (Mineola NY, 1999), 527-31.

generation biracial children to be seen as White and half as Black.

That the children of Black/White interracial parents have been more often identified as Black than as White since 1880 demonstrates that the one-drop rule has been accepted for many decades. The following table shows, for each census since 1880, the percentage of first-generation biracial children who were recorded as White:

Table 1. First-Generation Biracial Children Recorded as White[89]

Year	Pct White
1880	28%
1890	22%
1900	17%
1910	27%
1920	41%
1930	46%
1940	50%
1950	39%
1960	37%
1970	34%
1980	28%
1990	25%
2000	13%

The chart on the next page, Figure 24, "White Children of B/W Intermarriages," shows that the fraction of such children labeled as only White has fallen steadily from 50 percent in 1940 to 13 percent in 2000. This suggests that the one-drop rule continues to grow ever stronger among Black/White interracial parents.

---

[89] For the methodology used in arriving at the data shown in Tables 1 and 2, and Figures 1, 2 and 3, see section "The Identity of First-Generation Biracial Children" in *Appendix A, Census Data Processing Methodology.*

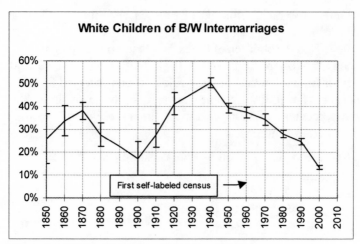

Figure 24. White Children of B/W Intermarriages

On the other hand, as shown in the chart of Figure 25, "Black Children of Interracial Marriages," the fraction of such children labeled as Black only (with no admixture) dropped abruptly from 62 percent in 1990 to 31 percent in 2000.

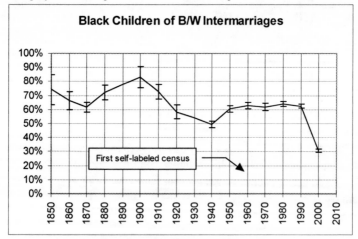

Figure 25. Black Children of B/W Intermarriages

That the fraction of White-labeled children and that of Black-labeled children have both fallen since 1990 indicates that, whereas the one-drop rule may continue in strength, discontinuity is weakening. Growing numbers of interracially married parents are rejecting the idea of having only two choices. Table 2, "First-Generation Biracial Children Recorded as Both or Neither" shows, for each census decade since 1960, the percentage of children whose parents rejected a binary choice, either writing in "multiracial," "biracial," "none-of-the-above," or by checking multiple boxes. In 1960, parents were not allowed to check off "other," nor to write something in. They had to pick one and only one of the given choices. In 1970, for the first time, they were allowed to choose "other." In that census, four percent of first-generation biracial children were reported as neither Black nor White. In 1980, this number had grown to eight percent, and many parents checked both boxes, despite this being explicitly forbidden by the instructions. By 1990, the number who rejected discontinuity had grown to thirteen percent. In 2000, for the first time, parents were allowed to check multiple boxes, and millions of parents jumped at the opportunity. In this census, well over half (56 percent) of first-generation biracial children were coded as belonging simultaneously to both "races."

Table 2. First-Generation Biracial Children Recorded as Both or Neither

Year	Pct Other
1960	0%
1970	4%
1980	8%
1990	13%
2000	56%

This suggests that it has recently become unfashionable to make first-generation biracial youngsters deny their European ancestry. Discontinuity seems to be losing its grip on the American psyche. On the other hand, whether the growing popularity of reporting such children to the census by checking off both boxes portends a crack in the one-drop rule, remains to be seen. As shown in Figure 26, "First-Generation Biracial Children's Identity," of the 44 percent of interracially married parents who check off only one box for their children, three times as many (31 percent) of these parents say that their kids are only Black, than those who say that their children are only White (13 percent).

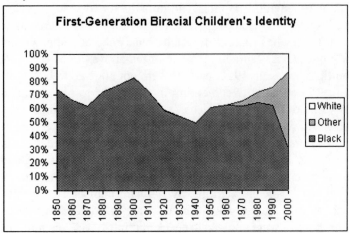

Figure 26. First-Generation Biracial Children's Identity

In short, there is little evidence that the U.S. endogamous color line itself is weakening significantly.[90] Nevertheless, the evidence of how interracial couples label their children for the census suggests that Blackness may be in the process of shifting more towards voluntary ethnic self-identity, rather than a mandatory involuntary membership in an endogamous group. At least this may be the case for people of only imperceptible or slight African ancestry. This may weaken the one-drop rule.

On the other hand, you can reap financial gain by "outing" as "Black" someone who is no longer alive to defend himself (Audubon, Broyard, the Healys, Davis) or herself (Phipps, Delille). Hence, authors will undoubtedly continue to pique reader interest with tales that so-and-so was actually Black and only pretended to be White. After all, the potential number of such revelations is vast. Every year, between 0.10 and 0.14 percent of formerly Black-labeled youngsters switch to calling themselves Hispanic or White after high school. This comes to between 35,000 and 50,000 individuals who switch "race" every

---

[90] See the topic "The Future" in *Chapter 6. Features of the Endogamous Color Line.*

year. It means that just over 2,000,000 White American adults alive today started life as Black children. Add up the numbers since 1850, and about 9,000,000 Americans took this step over the past century and a half. Their 74,000,000 White descendants, on average, have the genetic equivalent of one pureblooded African ancestor within the past 120 years.[91]

To recap: the U.S. endogamous color line originated in circa-1700 Virginia as a means of splitting potential servile insurrectionists. A century later, America's unique barrier to intermarriage was firmly in place in what had been the thirteen original colonies—from Massachusetts to Georgia. Today, the endogamous color line is unchanged with regards to either discontinuity or endogamy. In today's America there is no intermediate "Colored" or hybrid endogamous group. And in today's America, intermarriage between White endogamous group members and Black ones is an order of magnitude less frequent than between other ethnic groups in the United States or between people of European or African descent in other countries. In other ways, the endogamous color line has changed. The custom of European-looking children of Black parents being openly accepted into the White endogamous group vanished about fifty years ago, although it may be returning. A non-Hispanic today can seldom switch to the White side of the color line while publicly acknowledging parents who remain on the Black side. Eston Hemings would be pressured by society and its laws to remain Black for life in America today.[92] This particular change between 1800 and 2000 is shocking in its completeness. How did it come about? Did the one-drop rule of invisible Blackness start in one place? If so, where and when?

* * * * *

---

[91] See *Chapter 2. Afro-European Genetic Admixture in the United States, Chapter 3. The Heredity of "Racial" Traits, Chapter 4. The Perception of "Racial" Traits*, and *Chapter 5.The Rate of Black-to-White "Passing."*

[92] See the opening anecdote of *Chapter 9. How the Law Decided if You Were Black or White: The Early 1800s.*

This chapter defined the one-drop rule as hypodescent taken to absurd conclusion. It surveyed the writings of about two-dozen scholars to reveal a clear academic consensus that the one-drop rule is alive and well. It presented several examples of recent cases to show that the one-drop rule is routinely rejected, as well as other examples showing that it is equally often enforced. It explained that moral positioning and subconscious convictions make unsubstantiated assertions suspect. Finally, it examined census data on how interracial parents label their children to conclude that the one-drop rule may possibly become less fashionable, although advocating it will continue to be profitable.

Chapter 15.
The Invention of the One-Drop Rule in the 1830s North

Polly Gray was a fair-complexioned biracial woman from Hamilton County, Ohio. In November of 1829, she was tried for robbery and convicted due to the testimony of a Black witness for the prosecution. She appealed to the Supreme Court of Ohio on the grounds that she was White. Ohio statutes forbade Blacks from testifying against Whites, and yet she was convicted on Black testimony. Hence, she claimed, her conviction should be overturned.[1]

Her lawyer, Mr. Van Matre, argued that, despite Ms. Gray's slight African ancestry, she clearly looked more European than African. This meant that she was legally White by the rule of physical appearance in effect in Ohio at the time. The prosecutor, Mr. Wade, agreed that the rule of physical appearance was the only legal way of deciding which side of the endogamous color line someone was on. But he argued that state statutes referred to Negroes and Mulattos as separate cases. Hence, "White" in the written law, was limited only to those who were neither Mulatto nor Negro. And, since Ms. Gray, "appeared,

---

[1] 4 Ohio 353.

upon inspection... to be of a shade of color between the mulatto and white," she was not quite fair-complexioned enough to be considered White. Legally, the prosecutor insisted, she was a Mulatto and not White. Presumably, had Ms. Gray looked completely European and not been "a shade of color" darker than White, the prosecution would have agreed to void her conviction.

The Supreme Court agreed with both prosecution and defense that the rule of physical appearance was the only criterion for determining a person's endogamous group membership in Ohio. "We are unable to set out any other plain and obvious line or mark between the different races. Color alone is sufficient." The problem, in the judge's eye, was in deciding just where to draw the line. After deliberation, in January of 1831, the judge ruled, "We believe a man, of a race nearer white than a mulatto... should partake in the privileges of whites. We are of opinion that a party of such a blood is entitled to the privileges of whites, partly because we are unwilling to extend the disabilities of the statute further than its letter requires, and partly from the difficulty of defining and of ascertaining the degree of duskiness which renders a person liable to such disabilities."

This case, *Gray v. Ohio*, 1831, marks an important historical watershed. It was the last appeals case in the free states where all parties agreed that one of the traditional rules (physical appearance, blood fraction, or association) would determine which side of the endogamous color line you were on. It was the last appeals case in the free states where neither side argued that an invisible trace of African blood should be taken into account. Neither the lawyers, the judges, nor the convicted robber could have known that things would be different thereafter. From then on, some form of one-drop rule of invisible Blackness would be argued, unsuccessfully at first, in most "racial" identity cases heard in the North and later in the upper South. In less than a century, the one-drop rule would entirely supplant the rules of physical appearance, blood fraction, and association throughout the nation.

* * * * *

This chapter suggests, in five topics, that America's one-drop rule of invisible Blackness arose in the North between 1830 and 1840. *A Bidirectional Strategy* describes the analytic approach of bracketing the date by working forwards in time from the Revolution and backwards from Jim Crow. *Journals and Diaries* presents evidence from travelers' accounts and newspaper advertisements to show that descriptive terminology changed from "white" to "white-looking" during this period. *Literature and Drama* shows that "passing" literature, which depends upon the one-drop rule for intelligibility, first arose in this period. *Court Cases* discusses four pivotal court cases from before and after the emergence of the one-drop rule—two in Ohio and two cases in Kentucky. *Graphs and Charts* presents graphs of court decisions to show how criteria for determining whether you were White or Black changed over the past two centuries.

A Bidirectional Strategy

Anthropologically speaking, the notion of invisible Blackness—the idea that one can be a member of the U.S. Black endogamous group due to a trace of distant African ancestry—is a myth. In other words, it must have served some desirable social purpose or it would not have spread throughout the nation and been preserved to this day. But tracing the origins of the myth is as difficult as uncovering the origin of any other popular idea. The next few paragraphs sneak up on the idea from two directions: first, working forwards in time from the Revolution, and then working backwards from the Jim Crow era.

Working forwards in time from the formation of the Republic, we know that as of 1830, the one-drop rule (in the sense of an utterly European-looking person being seen as a member of the Black endogamous group due to an un-measurable trace of distant Black ancestry) had not yet been argued in an appeals court anywhere in the United States.[2] Furthermore, we know that

---

[2] See *Chapter 9. How the Law Decided if You Were Black or White: The Early 1800s.*

the farther south you look in the early antebellum period, the less familiar the terrain becomes. South Carolina had an extraordinarily permeable color line.[3] Alabama and Louisiana had two mildly endogamous color lines separating three groups.[4] And Florida lacked any endogamous color line at all.[5] Only the upper South and the North had an endogamous color line similar to today's—impermeable, based on hypodescent, and supported by a shared sense of ethnic self-identity.[6] And so, it seems reasonable to seek the birth of the one-drop rule and the notion of invisible Blackness, after 1830 and in the free states of the North.

Working backwards from the Jim Crow era, it is easy enough to identify when the first state legislated the one-drop rule of endogamous group membership as statutory law—it was 1910 Tennessee.[7] But the record shows that state legislatures did not take it upon themselves to invent such a rule. Statutes deciding which side of the endogamous color line you were on merely confirmed rules that had long been enforced as legal precedents. State appellate courts were the entities who had established the legal precedents.

Also, it is straightforward to work further backwards to find the first time that an appellate court upheld the one-drop rule of invisible Blackness—it was in the criminal prosecution of a marriage between a White woman and a Black man in 1880 Texas.[8] But, like state legislators, appeals judges themselves seldom invented new rules for society. They chose among arguments that had been presented at trial. And so the origin of the one-drop rule as an idea in the public mind must be sought in cases where the concept was argued in court, even though higher courts might have rejected it.

---

[3] *Chapter 10. Barbadian South Carolina: A Class-Based Color Line.*

[4] *Chapter 11. Antebellum Louisiana and Alabama: Two Color Lines, Three Endogamous Groups.*

[5] *Chapter 12. Spanish Florida: No Endogamous Color Line.*

[6] *Chapter 13. The Color Line Created African-American Ethnicity in the North.*

[7] Pauli Murray, ed. *States' Laws on Race and Color* (Athens, 1997), 428.

[8] *Moore v. State* 1880 Texas (7 Tex. Ct. App. 608).

Apparently, the first time in U.S. history that a lawyer argued the one-drop rule was in 1834 Ohio, in a school segregation case to which we shall return momentarily.[9] But even legal arguments cannot be the origin of the idea. Few lawyers can afford to present arguments that clash with social sensibilities. They must have gotten the idea from the greater society. In order to be argued in court, the one-drop rule must have been in the air at that time (the 1830s) and in that place (the North). And so, we must seek the birth of the one-drop rule in popular culture: in journals and diaries, in literature and drama. Then we shall return to court cases and to graphs and charts.

Journals and Diaries

Travelers' accounts illuminate the society of the time. Each account inadvertently reveals how the writer's mind worked. Since each writer was a member of the society of the time, their journals and diaries provide a glimpse of how people thought about the endogamous color line back then. Until the 1830s, such accounts invariably referred to "white" slaves in the American South. Before then, none used terms like "white-looking" slaves. But by 1840 travelers' accounts had shifted to the modern form of expression.

That "white-looking" is the current form of expression is indisputable. With one exception, every textbook or monograph, published since the turn of the twentieth century that the present author has uncovered, refers to "white-looking" slaves. No modern author can bring himself or herself to state the obvious fact that tens of thousands of White people (by the usage of the time) were enslaved in the antebellum South. Today's academic canon is that they were merely "white-looking"; they were not "really white" (whatever that means).[10]

---

[9] *Williams v. School District* 1834 Ohio (1 Wright 578); Helen Tunnicliff Catterall and James J. Hayden, *Judicial Cases Concerning American Slavery and The Negro* (New York, 1968), 5:4.

[10] The sole historiographic exception to currently mandatory academic doublespeak is the self-published monograph, Lawrence Raymond Tenzer, *The*

John Ferdinand Dalziel Smyth who toured the South in the 1770s wrote about "female slaves who are now become white by their mixture."[11] Jacques Pierre Brissot de Warville in 1788 reported a "white boy" in a Philadelphia school for Negro children.[12] Dr. Jesse Torrey in 1817 wrote about "a decently dressed white man" who was also a slave.[13] In 1839, reverend Francis Hawley of Connecticut wrote, "It is so common for the female slaves to have white children, that little or nothing is ever said about it."[14] No account before 1830 has yet turned up that employs modern ("white-looking") terminology.

The change in paradigm from "white" to "white-looking" apparently took less than a decade. In 1837, Captain Frederick Marryat wrote that "said boy is in a manner white, would be passed by and taken for a white man."[15] The following advertisements for runaways tell the story:

> $100 reward will be given for my man, Edmund Kenny. He has straight hair, and a complexion so white that it is believed a stranger would suppose there was no African blood in him. A short time since, he was in Norfolk with my boy Dick, and offered him for sale. He was apprehended but escaped under pretense of being a white man. — Anderson Bowles, *The Richmond Whig*, Va. Jan. 6, 1836.

> $10 reward for the apprehension of William Dubberly, a slave belonging to the estate of Sacker Dubberly, deceased.

Forgotten Cause of the Civil War: A New Look at the Slavery Issue (Mana-hawkin NJ, 1997).

[11] J.F.D. Smyth, *A Tour in the United States of America* (1784; reprint, NY, 1968), 2:181 as quoted in Tenzer (1997), 24.

[12] J.P. Brissot de Warville, *New Travels in the United States of America*, 1788, ed. and trans. Durand Echevarria and Mara Socenau Vamons (Cambridge, 1964), 217 as quoted in Tenzer (1997), 24.

[13] Jesse Torrey, American Slave Trade([1817] 1822; reprint, Westport, 1971), 24-25 as quoted in Tenzer (1997), 24.

[14] "Narrative and Testimony of Rev. Francis Hawley" in Theodore D. Weld, American Slavery as It Is: Testimony of a Thousand Witnesses (1839; reprint, NY, 1968), 97 as quoted in Tenzer (1997), 25-26.

[15] Frederick Marryat, *A Diary in America* (Paris, 1839), 250-51 as quoted in Tenzer (1997), 25.

He is about nineteen years old, quite white, and would not be readily taken for a slave. — John J. Lane, *The Newbern Spectator*, N.C., March 13, 1837.

Runaway from the subscriber, a bright slave named Sam; light sandy hair, blue eyes, ruddy complexion. He is so white as to pass easily for a white man. — Edwin Peck, Mobile Ala., April 22, 1837.

Runaway, a bright woman, named Julia, about twenty-five years old. She is white and very likely may attempt to pass for white. She is a good seamstress, dresses fine, and can read a little. $200 reward, if caught in any Free State and put into any good jail in Kentucky or Tennessee. — A.W. Johnson. *The Republican Banner* and *The Nashville Whig*, Tenn. July 14, 1840.

Runaway from me, a woman named Fanny. She is as white as most white women; with straight light hair and blue eyes, and can pass herself for a white woman. She is very intelligent; can read and write, and so forge passes for herself. She is very pious, prays a good deal, and was, as supposed, contented and happy. I will give $500 for her delivery to me. — John Balch, Tuscaloosa Alabama, May 20, 1845.

$25 REWARD. Ranaway from the plantation of Madame Duplantier, a bright boy named Ned, about thirty-five years old; speaks French and English. He may try to pass himself for a white man, as he is of a very clear color, and has sandy hair. — *The New Orleans Picayune*, Sept. 2, 1846.

Runaway from the subscriber, a very bright boy, twenty-two years old, named Wash. He might pass himself for a white man, as he is very bright, has sandy hair, blue eyes, and a fine set of teeth. — George O. Ragland, *The Chattanooga Gazette*, Tenn. Oct. 5, 1852.[16]

It seems that after 1840, with one class of exceptions, no slave was ever again reported as "white." They merely "looked white"

---

[16] The advertisements are as quoted in Tenzer (1997), 32. The ad for slave Ned who ran away from Madame Duplantier and "may try to pass himself for a white man" is particularly ironic. Mme. Duplantier was a wealthy slave-owning *gens de couleur libre,* a member of antebellum Louisiana's Colored endogamous group.

or "passed for white."[17] And so, judging by journals and diaries, the one-drop rule first arose in the United states between 1830 and 1840.

Literature and Drama

The one-drop rule first appeared in popular literature in novels and plays about "passing for white." This is because the concept of "passing for white" is an inseparable aspect of the one-drop rule. Cultures that lack a one-drop rule lack the idea of "passing for white." Indeed, as mentioned in the prior chapter, the very concept of "passing for white" is virtually unintelligible to people who were raised outside of the United States.[18]

For our purposes, "passing" literature refers to novels, plays, or short stories in which a European-looking character pretends to be a member of the White endogamous group but is "really" on the Black side of the color line. All three elements are essential: (1) Some African ancestry, (2) predominantly European appearance, and (3) pretense or concealment. Stories about European slaves were not uncommon, even before the Reformation. But unless the character actually has some recent African ancestry, such stories are not of interest here. Similarly, an African slave who wears a mask or otherwise disguises as European-looking in order escape captivity does not fall within our scope—only characters who look European. Finally, the tale of a European who is accepted without pretense or concealment as fully White, even though everyone around knows of the person's publicly acknowledged African ancestry is not a tale of passing in this context.[19]

---

[17] The exceptions were the polemical writings of Abolitionists, who as late as 1864, referred to European-looking slaves, especially children, as "white" in order to elicit sympathy for their plight. For several examples, see Tenzer (1997), starting at page 37.

[18] Hilary Beckles, "Black Men in White Skins: The Formation of a White Proletariat in West Indian Society," *The Journal of Imperial and Commonwealth History*, October (no. 15, 1986), 5-21.

[19] For instance, Alessandro de Medici, Queen Charlotte, Alexander Pushkin, Alexandre Dumas, and John James Audubon were not "passing" as defined

Passing literature can exist only within a readership market that accepts the one-drop rule. Cultures (such as Hispanic or Muslim societies), where a European-looking person with an African-looking grandparent is considered legitimately White, lack passing literature (as defined by the three above elements) because they lack a one-drop rule of invisible Blackness. We shall return to this point in the next chapter, when we contrast U.S. and Mexican cinematic adaptations of Fannie Hurst's novel, *Imitation of Life*. As exemplified above, the earliest non-fictional usage of the concept of passing, as defined by the above three elements (African ancestry, European appearance, pretense) was in advertisements for runaway slaves.

The earliest fictional use of the three-part concept was in the French novel *Marie; ou, L'Esclavage aux États-Unis* [*Marie; or, Slavery in the United States*] (Paris: 1835) by Gustave de Beaumont. It is apparently the first passing novel ever published.[20] Its narrator, Ludovic, falls in love with the title character, who turns out to have a touch of African ancestry through her Louisiana Colored Creole grandparent. The novel describes the "racial" intolerance of the North with such lines as:

> Public opinion, ordinarily so indulgent to fortune-seekers
> who conceal their names and previous lives, is pitiless in its
> search for proofs of African descent.... There is but one
> crime, of which the guilty bear everywhere the penalty and
> the infamy; it is that of belonging to a family reputed to be of
> color.—Though the color may be effaced, the stigma re-
> mains. It seems as if men could guess it, when they could no

---

here because there was no pretense or concealment of their African ancestry.

[20] An earlier example of "passing" in a different sense is *Bug-Jargal* (1826) by Victor Hugo, whose protagonist is an unscrupulous individual who "passes" as different races, nationalities, professions, and social classes as expediency dictates. It resembles the 2002 Dreamworks film "Catch Me if You Can," which was a remake of the 1961 film "The Great Imposter." The novel sheds no light on the U.S. one-drop rule.

longer see it. There is no asylum so secret, no retreat so secure as to conceal it.[21]

Marie is particularly interesting because the author does
not agree with his own characters. The characters are immersed
in a society that brutally enforces the one-drop rule. The author,
on the other hand, considers the notion to be an inexplicable
Americanism. *Marie*'s characters are portrayed as struggling for
acceptance, not as engaging in malicious pretense. The novel
was written by a Frenchman and published in France for a
French readership. Its tone is that of "look at the bizarre customs
of those strange Americans," rather than, "look at these people
pretending to be White."[22] Nevertheless, *Marie* is important to
this study because it is the first literary indication that a unique
and unprecedented social ideology, the one-drop rule, had recently arisen in the United States.

The first two American-written novels about passing in
the above sense are *Clotel; or, The President's Daughter: A Narrative of Slave Life in the United States* (1853) by William Wells
Brown and *The Garies and Their Friends* (1857) by Frank J.
Webb. William Wells Brown was a former slave and an established author who had published the autobiographical *Narrative
of William Wells Brown, a Fugitive Slave* in 1847. Frank J.
Webb, a freeborn African-American, was a newcomer to the
reading public. The two novels differ in several ways.

Clotel is about slavery. Its protagonist (Thomas Jefferson's slave daughter) escapes captivity, passes for White in the
North, but then returns to the South to rescue her own daughter
and dies in the attempt. Most of the novel does not focus upon
the pretense of Whiteness, but is instead a pastiche of slave tales
culled from the author's own experiences, hearsay, journalism,
and other fiction (including the acknowledged lifting of material

---

[21] Gustave de Beaumont, *Marie; or, Slavery in the United States*, trans.
Barbara Chapman (Stanford, 1958), 91-92.

[22] This interpretation is partly due to that Alexandre Dumas (père) was also
publishing in France at this time and was usually considered White despite
having a biracial father. (Although he was sometimes referred to as "Mulatto.")

from *The Quadroons*, an 1842 novel by Lydia Mary Child that is about miscegenation, not passing). *Clotel* lacks the unity customary to novels and seems disjointed to the modern reader. Nevertheless, it is the first known piece of literature depicting a society that considers Blackness to be an intangible trait. It is the first to portray people (both Black and White, it turns out) who believe that a European-looking person of undetectable African ancestry is a member of the Black endogamous group nonetheless. That the book was a success is persuasive evidence that most of its readers felt the same way.[23]

The Garies and Their Friends is about life in freedom in the North, not about slavery in the South. Although it abounds in sub-plots (more than are customary in most modern novels), it is more tightly written than Clotel and its sub-plots either illuminate or advance the main narrative. The tale focuses on passing by its title couple, and its sub-plots depict different forms of passing (accidental, deliberate, through ignorance, etc.).[24] Although it was published four years after *Clotel*, *The Garies and Their Friends* is credited by most scholars with inventing the literary theme of passing.[25]

Clotel and *The Garies and Their Friends* are similar in that they were the first successful novels published by African-Americans, and yet they are almost universally ignored in Black studies departments today. This is because their ideology is repellent to modern African-Americans. None of the characters who engage in passing in these two novels feels any guilt or remorse for the act. Some (usually delicate Victorian females like Clotel herself) sincerely want to be accepted as White. Others (usually defiant self-sacrificing Victorian men) consider it a justified deceit upon an unjust society. Modern critics see the characters' lack of guilt as a symptom of a "psychology of imitation and implied inferiority," and that it reveals the authors' "uncon-

---

[23] William Wells Brown, *Clotel, or, The President's Daughter: A Narrative of Slave Life in the United States* (London, 1853).

[24] Frank J. Webb, *The Garies and Their Friends* (London, 1857).

[25] Werner Sollors, *Neither Black Nor White Yet Both* (Cambridge, 1997), 499n53.

scious desire to be white" and "unabashed allegiance to Anglo-Saxon lineage." According to M. Giulia Fabi, the characters' lack of guilt "have had crippling repercussions on [the novels'] reception among scholars of African American literature to this day."[26]

And so, judging by literature and drama, the one-drop rule first arose in the United states in 1835, in Gustave de Beaumont's novel, *Marie; ou, L'Esclavage aux États-Unis.*

Court Cases

In May of 1834, Ohio residents Mr. and Mrs. Williams tried to enroll their five European-looking children in the District 6 public school. They were turned away because the law demanded racially segregated schools. Although the children's mother was White, the father admitted to having an imperceptible trace of Negro ancestry. The Williams couple sued the school board in *Williams v. School District*, 1834 Ohio.[27]

The trial went directly to the heart of the issue. Were the Williams children members of the Black endogamous group because their father had a slight degree of African ancestry? Or did they belong on the White side of the endogamous color line based upon their European appearance, blood fraction, and associations? Testimony was introduced in support of each definition. The school board proposed a one-drop rule of invisible Blackness. The children's records showed that they had African blood, they argued, and so they should be ruled to be Black even though they did not look it. The Williams family lawyer argued in favor of an appearance-based view of color line positioning. The children should be ruled White because, physically speaking, they "really were White," even though their father was not. The judge ruled in favor of the rule of physical appearance. The

---

[26] The quotations, along with a thorough literary analysis of both novels can be found in M. Giulia Fabi, *Passing and the Rise of the African American Novel* (Urbana, 2001), Chapter 1, "The Mark Without."

[27] Helen Tunnicliff Catterall and James J. Hayden, *Judicial Cases Concerning American Slavery and The Negro* (New York, 1968), 5:4.

children were White because they looked White. The court awarded damages to be paid to the Williams family and ordered the school board to admit their children.

In fact, the decision was far from inevitable, and the case could easily have gone either way. The judge explained that he ruled against the school board partly because they, "had the shabby meanness to ask from [Mr. Williams] his contribution of tax, and [then turn around and] exclude his children from the benefit of the schools he helped to support." Had the members of District 6 School Board had the sense to exempt the family from school taxes first, in order to exclude the children, as did the schools of the time in Connecticut,[28] the court would probably have ruled in their favor.

The defendants in this case argued that one could look European (as did the Williams children) yet be a member of the Black endogamous group nonetheless. As it turned out, the judge did not agree with the argument and he did not impose a one-drop rule. In fact, he explicitly ruled against such a thing. But the case is important because, as far as this study has been able to determine, *Williams v. School District* was the first time that a one-drop rule was seriously argued in a U.S. court of law.

Incredibly, this watershed case happened just three years after *Gray v. Ohio*, 1831, the robbery conviction case that opened this chapter. Recall that in *Gray v. Ohio*, the state prosecutor allowed a convicted felon to go free rather than argue that the female robber was "really" Black due to her acknowledged trace of African ancestry. Nevertheless, although the change was abrupt, there would be no turning back.

The same change happened in Kentucky, the slave state just across the Ohio River from free Ohio, only three years later. Polly McMinnis was a genetically European woman who won her freedom in the case of *Gentry v. McMinnis*, 1835 Kentucky.[29] She was born in Pennsylvania around 1786, probably to a mother who was a slave. Had Polly remained in Pennsylvania,

---

[28] See, for example, *Copp v. The Town of Norwich* 1855 Connecticut (24 Conn. 28).

[29] 33 Ky. 382.

she would have been a servant until reaching age 28 in 1814 and completely free thereafter. This is because, according to the Pennsylvania abolition statute of March 1, 1780:

> *Sec.* III. All persons... who *shall be* born within this state, shall not be deemed and considered as servants for life, *or slaves.* And all servitude for life, or *slavery of children*, in consequence of the slavery of their mothers... shall be, and hereby is, *utterly taken away, extinguished, and forever abolished.*

> *Sec.* IV. *Provided always*, that every negro and mulatto child, born within this state, after the passage of this act... who would, in case this act had not been made, have been born a... slave, shall be deemed to be [an involuntary servant]... until such child shall attain unto the age of twenty eight years....[30]

Instead, Polly was taken to Kentucky at age 11 and sold. Thirty-eight years later, she sued for her freedom. She was released because the slave-owner's case was weak and the above narrative was supported by evidence presented in court. The decision might have vanished historically had the slave-owner not appealed.

His appeal claimed that the trial judge had erred by instructing the jury as follows, "If upon their own view, they should be of the opinion that she was a white woman, they should find for her." The slave-owner's lawyer argued that that this instruction turned precedent on its head. Since he had proved that Polly was legitimately a slave by matrilineal descent, the jury lacked the authority to rule that she was White. Indeed, since her mother was a slave, her membership in the White endogamous group would be as irrelevant as was Eston Hemings's pre-manumission Whiteness.[31]

Chief Justice Robertson of the Supreme Court of Kentucky dismissed the argument thus:

> To a rational man... the best and highest proof of which any fact is susceptible, is the evidence of his own senses. This is

---

[30] 32 Ky. 432.

[31] See the opening anecdote of *Chapter 9. How the Law Decided if You Were Black or White: The Early 1800s.*

the ultimate test of truth, and is therefore the first principle in
the philosophy of evidence.... [Jurors] will not, they cannot—
and generally they ought not, to believe or accredit testimony
which contradicts the evidence of their senses, or subverts the
first principles of human belief.... A white person of unmixed
blood cannot be a slave.[32]

Justice Robertson freed Polly and went on to cite two Virginia
cases as precedent for the jury's right to determine endogamous
group membership (hence, slave status) by the rule of physical
appearance: *Hudgins v. Wrights*, 1806 and *Hook v. Nanny Pagee
and her Children*, 1811.[33]

At first glance, this case seems uninformative and typical
of others during the late antebellum upper South (Virginia, North
Carolina, Tennessee, Kentucky). It was about slavery, it tried to
decide the status of a person who was genetically European, and
no party involved suggested anything like a one-drop rule. In
fact, the slave-owner was willing to concede that Polly was
White in the then-common meaning of the term, which was
based on the rule of physical appearance. It may seem odd for
the judge to suggest that a person's looks did more than just lay
the burden of proof, that it could actually outweigh other evidence of slave status. But the oddness is illusory. The evidence
presented at trial was solid that Polly had been illegally taken
from a free state to a slave state in order to be sold. Indeed, just
four years later, in *Chancellor v. Milly*, 1839 Kentucky, the same
Court kept in bondage another genetically European woman who
had been a slave for forty years, ruling that her European looks
merely placed the burden of proof upon the slave-owner, who at
trial had not been given the opportunity to meet the burden.[34]

---

[32] 33 Ky. 382.

[33] Chief Justice Robertson erred. The two cited cases established only that a
person who was White by the rule of physical appearance did not have to
shoulder the *onus probandi* of *partus sequitur ventrem*. They did not hold
that a person who was White by the rule of physical appearance should be
freed from slavery despite being born of a slave mother. For the details of
these cases, see *Chapter 9. How the Law Decided if You Were Black or
White: The Early 1800s*.

[34] 39 Ky. 23.

What is important about the case is Justice Robertson's wording, "a white person... cannot be a slave." Compare it semantically to Justice Harper's words in *State v. Cantey*, 1835 South Carolina, "a slave cannot be a white man."[35] Each sentence describes a cause-and-effect relationship between the endogamous color line and slavery. To each writer, one is a fact of tangible reality, while the other is a social construct. Harper's words implied that slave status was real—you were either a slave or not. To Harper, which side of the endogamous color line you were on, was socially constructed to reflect that reality— slave status disqualified you from being accepted into the White side of the color line. Robertson's decision implies the reverse: that your endogamous group membership is the tangible reality—you are either White or Black. To Robertson, whether you were a slave reflected color line reality—Whiteness exempted you from being a slave. That many Americans today unthinkingly see Robertson's phrasing as correct and Harper's as a slip of the pen warns us that only one of these two opposing worldviews survives in today's United States. It also shows that, like Ohioans three years earlier, Kentuckians had begun to see endogamous group membership as something basic and immutable.

Gentry v. McMinnis documents the first time that endogamous group membership was seen in a U.S. court as being more real than matrilineal descent. That the endogamous color line had somehow become tangible reality is important. Despite African laborers being involuntarily transported in large numbers between 1500 and 1900—four million to the Indian Ocean, eight million to the Mediterranean basin, eleven million to the New World—the idea that the color line outweighed property rights arose nowhere else but in the United States.[36] Seeing the endogamous color line as real and immutable, rather than as merely an expedient socio-political intermarriage barrier, was

---

[35] Catterrall (1968), 2:358.

[36] Pier M. Larson, "Reconsidering Trauma, Identity, and the African Diaspora: Enslavement and Historical Memory in Nineteenth-Century Highland Madagascar," *William and Mary Quarterly*, 56 (no. 2, April 1999), 335-62.

still a long way from a one-drop rule of invisible Blackness. The first time that a Southern appeals court would uphold a one-drop rule of invisible Blackness was still two generations in the future.[37] And yet, while the idea of the endogamous color line as tangible reality was a long way from the concept of invisible Blackness, it was a step in that direction. The overall record of court cases shows why.

Graphs and Charts

Figure 27, "Percent of Cases per Decade Nationwide" depicts 214 appeals cases between 1770 and 1969 where court records documented the reasoning behind how the judges resolved an individual's endogamous group membership. The figure shows what fraction of cases in each decade used each of three rules: physical appearance, blood fraction, and a one-drop-rule of distant infinitesimal ancestry. (For convenience, cases that used the rule of association are included in the blood-fraction plots.)[38]

---

[37] It would be in a case to determine the validity of a marriage as regarding an inheritance: *Scott v. Raubb* 1892 Virginia (88 Va. 721).

[38] See Appendix B. Court Case Data Processing Methodology for details on how these cases were examined. See URL <http://backintyme.com/rawdata/courtcases.xls> for the program used to tabulate and graph the results.

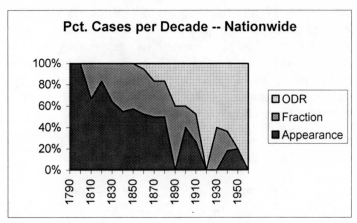

Figure 27. Percent of Cases per Decade Nationwide

The chart reveals that court cases underwent three phases over the past two centuries: a brief period when every case was claimed to have been decided by the rule of physical appearance, a longer period when the rule of blood fraction (and the rule of association) contended with the rule of physical appearance but never replaced it,[39] and a period lasting about a century when the one-drop rule of invisible Blackness emerged and gradually became more dominant until finally deciding every case.

Although the Figure 27, "Percentage of Cases per Decade Nationwide," accurately portrays the percentage of cases that used each of the three major rules for deciding which side of the endogamous color line you were on, the graph conceals the absolute numbers of cases. Another way of presenting the same information is depicted in the following figure. "Number of Cases per Decade – Nationwide" depicts the actual number of appeals cases heard broken down by the same criterion of color line determination. This figure reveals two important items of information that are not visible in the preceding chart.

---

[39] The reasons why different rules were applied at different times, along with each rule's strengths and weaknesses, can be found in *Chapter 9. How the Law Decided if You Were Black or White: The Early 1800s.*

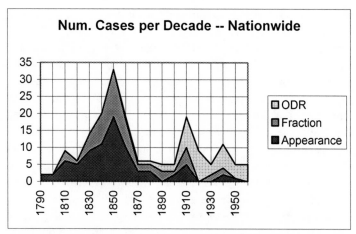

Figure 28. Number of Cases per Decade Nationwide

First, Figure 28 shows that the rise and eventual triumph of the one-drop rule took place during a century of gradual decline in the number of cases. The volume of color-line-determination cases appealed in the United States peaked at thirty-six cases in the decade of the 1850s, before the spread of the one-drop rule. The number of cases then declined in stages until, by 1960, they numbered only five per decade, all of which employed the one-drop rule. In short, the one-drop rule triumphed even as the number of cases fell to its lowest level since the 1850s' peak.[40]

Earlier, it was hypothesized that the volume of such cases indicates social uncertainty.[41] In times when the criteria for endogamous group membership were clearly understood and stable enough to be passed on from one generation to the next, people knew precisely what yardstick was used to position them with regards to the endogamous color line. With little element of uncertainty, few court cases would be litigated and even fewer ap-

---

[40] Since this study is limited to cases that were appealed, one might ask whether the measured rise and fall reflects the total number of cases or merely the number that were appealed. This is answered in *Appendix B. Court Case Data Processing Methodology.*

[41] See the topic "The National Color Line's Rise and Fall" in *Chapter 13. The Color Line Created African-American Ethnicity in the North.*

pealed. If this hypothesis is correct, then the gradual decline in the number of cases from 1850 to 1950 reveals that group membership determination gradually became more stable and less contested during that period. "Less contested" should not be interpreted to imply that people stopped contesting injustice or mistreatment of the Black endogamous group. The point is that people stopped contesting their socially assigned group membership itself.

Furthermore, it is not unreasonable to suggest that the one-drop rule may itself have contributed to this stability and lack of contestation. This is because the one-drop rule cannot be disputed. Once it becomes the criterion for determining endogamous group membership in court, *onus probandi* alone (where the burden of proof is laid) predetermines the outcome. Blood fraction can be disputed by presenting evidence of ancestry. Physical appearance can be disputed by introducing expert testimony, as in *State v. Asa Jacobs*, 1859 North Carolina or by letting the jury observe the subject, as in *Gentry vs. Polly McMinnis*, 1835 Kentucky.[42] But there is no way to dispute that someone may have an invisible trace of African ancestry in some unspecified distant past.[43]

The second item of information revealed by Figure 28 is that the number of cases (and, presumably, uncertainty as to where you were with regards to the endogamous color line) peaked three times. The first peak was in the decade of the Fugitive Slave Act. A free northerner was more likely to be taken into slavery if he or she was found to be Black. The second peak was in the 1910-19 decade, the nadir of the Jim Crow era by most measures. This was the decade when the one-drop rule was first adopted as state law. Tennessee led the parade by adopting a one-drop statute in 1910.[44] It was followed by Louisiana in the same year, Texas and Arkansas in 1911, Mississippi in 1917, North Carolina in 1923, Virginia in 1924, Alabama and Georgia

---

[42] 33 Ky. 382; 51 N.C. 284.

[43] One reason for the impossibility, of course, is that it is undisputed in paleoanthropology that genus *Homo* really did emerge in Africa.

[44] Pauli Murray, ed. *States' Laws on Race and Color* (Athens, 1997). 428.

in 1927, and Oklahoma in 1931.[45] During this same period, Florida, Indiana, Kentucky, Maryland, Missouri, Nebraska, North Dakota, and Utah retained their old blood fraction statutes *de juris* but amended these fractions (1/16, 1/32) to be equivalent to one-drop *de facto*.[46] One suspects that instability of color line positioning in this decade was caused by resistance to the initial introduction of the one-drop rule as statutory law.[47] The final peak was in the decade of the 1940s.

Another informative way of presenting the same data is by region. The four charts of Figure 29 display the number of cases per decade, broken down into the same three rules as before, but with one chart for each of four regions of the country. The chart labeled "Cases per Decade – North" includes court cases in the states of: Connecticut, Iowa, Illinois, Indiana, Kansas, Massachusetts, Maine, Michigan, New Jersey, New York, Ohio, Pennsylvania, and West Virginia (there were no cases in New Hampshire, Rhode Island, or Vermont). The chart titled "Cases per Decade – Upper South" includes: District of Columbia, Delaware, Kentucky, Maryland, Missouri, North Carolina, Tennessee, and Virginia. The chart labeled "Cases per Decade – Lower South" includes: Alabama, Arkansas, Florida, Georgia, Louisiana, Mississippi, and South Carolina. The final chart, labeled "Cases per Decade – West," includes all of the other states west of the Mississippi.

---

[45] Ibid., 173, 443, 37, 237, 330, 463, 22, 39, 358.

[46] Ibid., 77, 150, 164, 207, 254, 263, 459, .

[47] As of 1950, although each of the following states outlawed intermarriage and enforced at least some Jim Crow laws (such as school segregation), they either lacked statutory definitions of Black endogamous group membership or used older, more reasonable (1/4, 1/8) blood fraction or physical appearance rules: Arizona, California, Colorado, Delaware, District of Columbia, Idaho, Kansas. Montana, Nevada, New Mexico, Oregon, South Dakota, West Virginia, Wyoming, See Murray (1997), passim.

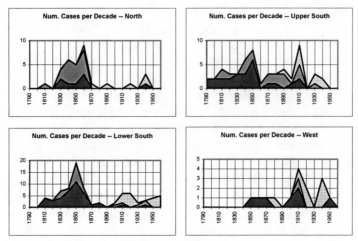

Figure 29: Number of Cases per Decade by Region

Two points are apparent in the charts by region. First, the one-drop rule determined court decisions earlier in the North than elsewhere, it appeared in the upper South about twenty years later, and it appeared in the lower South about ten years after that. The first cases that were decided on the basis of a one-drop rule took place in the North in the 1860s and 1870s. In the decades of the 1870s, 1890s, and 1920s, all of the cases in the north were based upon the one-drop rule. One-drop cases first began occurring in the upper South in the 1890s and did not become the sole method of determining endogamous group membership there until the 1940s. Finally, the first one-drop case in the lower South happened in the 1900s and one drop did not become the sole way of deciding cases there until the 1950s.

The second point apparent in the charts by region is that the three peaks of litigation manifested differently in each locale. Although all three of the eastern regions show the 1850s peak, coincident with the Fugitive Slave Act and the secession crisis, the Jim Crow peak of the 1910s is absent in the North but extremely prominent in the upper South. In fact, ten color line determination cases were held in the upper South between 1910 and 1919 but only eight took place there between 1850 and 1859. The western states had only one case or fewer per decade until the Jim Crow peak of the 1910s, which was extremely prominent. This is not surprising, since the west was not thickly populated until around the turn of the twentieth century. What may be unexpected is the peak of the 1940s, which was especially prominent in both the North and West.

Finally, it should be understood that the graphs of Figure 29 reflect only cases where appeals were actually decided on the basis of a one-drop rule. One could re-draw the graphs to show cases where trial courts reached a verdict based upon the one-drop rule, but the verdicts were overturned. As indicated in the following table, such an operation would shift all of the patterns to the left by two or three decades: 1840s North, 1860s upper South, 1880s lower South. Similarly, re-drawing the graphs to show the first cases when the one-drop rule was argued in court would shift the patterns earlier yet: 1830s North, 1850s upper South, 1870s lower South.

Table 3. The Spread of the One-Drop Rule

	North	U. South	L. South
First Argued in Court	1830s[48]	1850s[49]	1870s[50]
First Determined Verdict	1840s[51]	1870s[52]	1880s
First Affirmed on Appeal	1860s[53]	1890s[54]	1900s[55]
First Legislated	1910s	1910s	1910s

In other words, Table 3 shows that the slow North-to-South pattern of spread in the acceptance of the one-drop rule in court was superimposed upon the following four-step pattern common in every region throughout the nation. First, the one-drop rule was argued in court decades before it was accepted and led to verdicts. Second, trial verdicts based upon acceptance of the one-drop rule were overturned for decades before appeals courts came to accept it. Third, appeals courts were routinely (even exclusively) basing their decisions on the one-drop rule for decades before it was incorporated into statutory law. Finally, state legislatures throughout the United States bowed to what had already become customary and made the one-drop rule the law of the land.

* * * * *

---

[48] *Williams v. School District* 1834 Ohio, Catterall (1968) 5:4.

[49] *State v. Harris Melton & Ann Byrd* 1852 North Carolina (44 N.C. 49).

[50] *Walsh v. Lallande* 1873 Louisiana (25 La. Ann. 188).

[51] *Gordon v. Farrar* 1847 Michigan (2 Doug. 411).

[52] *Smith v. Allbright* 1873 Kentucky (6 Ky. Op. 376).

[53] *Draper v. Cambridge* 1863 Indiana, 20 Ind. 268. Unfortunately, this case is not as clear-cut in favor of the one-drop rule as one would like. It was about a child rejected from the all-White public schools of the time. The child's rejection was upheld on appeal (mandamus was not issued) on a technicality. In contrast, the first appellate decision in the North that indisputably upheld the one-drop rule was *Van Houten v. Morse* 1894 Massachusetts (162 Mass. 414), a breach of promise suit.

[54] *Scott v. Raubb* 1892 Virginia (88 Va. 721).

[55] *Succession of Fortier* 1899 Louisiana (51 La. Ann. 1562).

This chapter suggested that, far from being devised by slaveowners, America's one-drop rule of invisible Blackness arose in the North between 1830 and 1840 at the same time that African-American ethnicity was being invented. The chapter presented evidence from travelers' accounts and newspaper advertisements to show that descriptive terminology changed from "white" to "white-looking" during this period. It showed that literature hinging on the concept of "passing for White" first arose in this period. It discussed four pivotal court cases that bracketed the emergence of the one-drop rule in Ohio and Kentucky. It presented graphs of court decisions to show how criteria for determining whether you were White or Black changed over the past two centuries, and how the one-drop rule began in the North and spread southwards in a four-stage process. That the one-drop rule first arose in the free states in the 1830s will remain indisputable unless someone uncovers an example of the notion of invisible Blackness before 1830 anywhere, or in the South of the 1830s.

Chapter 16.
Why Did Northerners Invent a One-Drop Rule?

In 1835, Henry Bright, his wife, and their 3-year-old adopted daughter Elizabeth moved from Mobile Alabama to Cambridge Massachusetts. The toddler's biological mother had been one of the family's house-servants in Mobile—a slave. The deceased woman had apparently been of mixed ancestry. Had she been freed before her death, she might have become a member of Mobile's intermediate Colored group. Little Elizabeth could have been even lighter, of the appearance that Gulf Coast Americans considered White. The record does not show why the family moved to Massachusetts, but that Mrs. Bright had become an ardent abolitionist may have contributed to their relocation to a free state.[1]

Over the next two years, the Bright family learned that, to Massachusetts eyes, Elizabeth was on the Black side of the North's single impermeable color line. Family friends of their own White endogamous group understood the Brights' reasons for adopting the little girl, but court records invariably refer to her as non-White. Members of Massachusetts's Black commu-

---

[1] Helen Tunnicliff Catterall and James J. Hayden, *Judicial Cases Concerning American Slavery and The Negro* (New York, 1968), 4:501-5; Thatch. Cr. Cas. 488.

nity, on the other hand, had no doubts regarding Elizabeth's rightful place in society.

On September 17, 1837, when she was five years old, Elizabeth was kidnapped from her parents in Cambridge and taken to Boston by a Black couple. The Brights tracked down the kidnappers through an abolitionist friend. The kidnappers, named John and Sophia Robinson, claimed that they had merely rescued the child from the former slaveowners. Through the intermediary, the Brights pleaded for the return of their daughter. The Robinsons agreed to return Elizabeth to her parents if the Brights promised in writing not to sell her into slavery. The Brights wrote such a promise, but the child was not returned. The Brights then got the help of a "colored clergyman" named Snowden, who negotiated on their behalf. The Robinsons agreed to return Elizabeth if the Brights took out a $500 bond guaranteeing her freedom. The Brights took out such a bond, but the child was not returned. The Brights then enlisted several other abolitionists and Black leaders, who investigated and reported that Boston's Black community was united in support of the Robinsons' refusal to return the girl. But, they said that if the bond were increased to $1,000 (approximately $50,000 in today's money), the child might be returned. The Brights increased the bond to $1,000, but the child was not returned.

Belatedly realizing that the Robinsons had no intention of returning their daughter, the Brights took the kidnappers to court in *Commonwealth v. Robinson*, 1837 Massachusetts. The Robinsons testified that (1) they did not know the child's whereabouts and that (2) they would go to jail rather than return her to be raised by White people. How could a White family properly raise a Black child? Who would teach her African heritage? Who would even comb her hair, since White people do not know how to comb Black hair?[2] The court was unimpressed and ordered the defendants to produce the child on pain of imprisonment. They agreed, and the Brights went to the house indicated to retrieve their daughter.

---

[2] Among the reasons given in court for the kidnapping of Elizabeth Bright. Catterall (1968), 4:501-5, 503.

When the parents arrived at the agreed-upon transfer point, the terrified child ran into her mother's arms. Then, in what is arguably one of the most bizarre but informative scenes in the history of U.S. race relations, "five or six colored people" burst into the house. Armed men, apparently Black, forcibly tore the screaming child from her mother's arms and absconded with her again.

In the subsequent investigation, Black witnesses claimed to have no idea who the men were. When re-arrested on the kidnapping charge, the Robinsons denied any foreknowledge of the events. Unfortunately for the Robinsons, other Black witnesses swore that Boston's Black community would unite and fight rather than allow a Black child to be raised by White people. This led the jury to conclude that a conspiracy existed. The Robinsons were convicted of kidnapping, "that the defendants seized and confined and imprisoned a certain female child with intent to cause her to be secretly confined in this state against her will." They were sentenced to four months in the common jail.

The convicts immediately posted $2,000 bond ($100,000 in today's money), apparently collected from the Black community, and remained free while they appealed. Their conviction was upheld and they were ordered to serve their four-month sentences. They then offered to return the child in return for immunity for everyone involved in the conspiracy. On October 22, 1838, over thirteen months after she was taken, Elizabeth Bright was returned to her parents. *Commonwealth v. Robinson* was resolved in a deal that allowed all of the kidnappers to walk away.

*   *   *   *   *

The importance of *Commonwealth v. Robinson*, 1837 Massachusetts is that it shows coordinated action by a Black Yankee community to enforce something like a one-drop rule. Elizabeth Bright was not kidnapped because she was of one hundred percent African genetic admixture nor even because she was predominantly African—she was neither. She was kidnapped because Boston's African-American ethnic group saw her as one of them, due solely to her having a trace of known African ancestry.[3]

As explained in the previous chapter, the concept of invisible Blackness, the idea that you could be of European appearance but be ideologically Black in some way arose rather abruptly in the free states in the 1830s. The one-drop rule then spread slowly southwards and became the unwritten law of the land throughout the nation by the turn of the twentieth century. It became statutory in the 1910s and 1920s. This chapter addresses two questions. Why was the one-drop rule invented in the free states and not in the South? Why was it invented in the 1830s and not before nor after?

This chapter suggests a hypothesis in three topics. *A Watershed Event in Three Threads* explains that members of the White endogamous group suffered a wave of panic, fueled by sensationalist newspapers, that Blacks were secretly plotting to massacre Whites. *African-American Ethnic Solidarity Benefited* suggests that the one-drop rule was reinforced and encouraged by ethnic leaders seeking to strengthen group loyalties by strengthening group boundaries. *Other Voices* presents four objections to the hypothesis: The hypothesis suggests that Blacks and Whites cooperated in creating the one-drop rule. It denies that the one-drop rule increased slave assets held by planters. It ignores pre-1830 literature mentioning an indelible mark. It denies that Latin America has passing literature.

A Watershed Event in Three Threads

Between them, *Gray v. Ohio* and *Williams v. School District* marked the passing of an era. The two cases were only three years apart. What happened between 1831 and 1834 that led many members of mainstream northern society (the White endogamous group) to accept the concept that White-looking

---

[3] For an analysis of this phenomenon today, see Bartholet, "Where do Black Children Belong?: The Politics of Race Matching in Adoption," *University of Pennsylvania Law Review*, 139 (no. 5, May 1991), 1163-256.

Black people could exist? The transition was pivotal to the history of the one-drop rule.

To see its import, look again at the key phrase, "White-looking Black people." The phrase seems reasonable only because you are used to it. If someone said "tall-looking short people can exist" or "fat-looking thin people can exist," you would laugh at the silliness. But you do not laugh at the notion of "White-looking Black people," although a person from any other nation on earth would laugh. Why not? It is because at some point in America's past, membership in the Black endogamous group switched from reflecting appearance and blood fraction (recall that Eston Hemings was fully accepted as White in 1830) to reflecting ideology. To see this, compare the three phrases above with comparable ideological phrases: "Christian-looking Jews" or "American-looking communists." Suddenly, the phrase is not silly. The very earliest that anyone has been able to find this peculiar usage was shortly after 1831.

In those years, a wave of terror swept the nation, the fear that the Blacks were plotting to massacre all of the Whites. Three historical threads just happened to come together at this point in time: first, secret meetings of Black leaders; second, published calls for Black violence against Whites; third, a massacre of over 50 unarmed White women and children at the hands of U.S. Blacks. Together, the three threads created an atmosphere of suspicion and fear. Whites came to suspect that, among the Blacks who were secretly plotting to kill them, were some who looked just like their friends and neighbors. That is, some treacherous Blacks who looked White.

The first secret meeting of Black leaders was the one summoned by Richard Allen In September of 1830.[4] Allen contacted other leaders and forty delegates from Brooklyn, Rochester, Wilmington, Baltimore, and Boston met in secret for five days at Bethel Church, Philadelphia, that very month. No member of the White endogamous group was allowed inside. Despite the attempt at secrecy, the White press reported that a clandes-

---

[4] See the topic "The Integration versus Separatism Pendulum" in *Chapter 13. The Color Line Created African-American Ethnicity in the North.*

tine meeting of Black leaders had been held. The reality of the meeting's discussion would have been anticlimactic, had it been reported. As mentioned earlier, the agenda of the first meeting of what was to become the National Convention Movement actually focused upon two mundane topics. The first was support for Ohio refugees. The second was rejecting the American Colonization Society's plan to exile free Blacks to Africa. But imagined White fears trumped prosaic Black reality and White Americans became uneasy with the secrecy of it all.[5]

The published calls for Black violence against Whites appeared in a book by Boston haberdasher David Walker, titled *Appeal in Four Articles* (Boston, 1829).[6] According to Walker, members of the U.S. Black endogamous group were "the most degraded, wretched, and abject beings that ever lived since the world began.... Can our condition be any worse?" "They [Whites] are afraid to treat us worse, for they know well, the day they do it they are gone." "They [Whites] think nothing of murdering us... therefore, if there is an attempt by us, kill or be killed." Despite Walker's mysterious death after his book's publication (or perhaps because of it), it immediately went through three editions. Four states (Georgia, North Carolina, Mississippi, and Louisiana) ruled it seditious and demanded the author's arrest. Northern White abolitionists were horrified. Antislavery publisher Benjamin Lundy wrote, "A more bold, daring, inflammatory publication, perhaps, never issued from the press of any country. I can do no less than set the broadest seal of condemnation on it." Even William Lloyd Garrison deplored it as "most injudicious," although he also said that it held "many

---

[5] There are many excellent accounts of the rise and fall of the National Convention Movement. One that focuses on the exclusion of White observers (to say nothing White delegates) and consequent fear and suspicion among members of the White endogamous group is Elizabeth Rauh Bethel, *The Roots of African-American Identity* (New York, 1997), 83-34, 116, 124, 127-38.

[6] The impact of Walker's book on White fears is described in Leon F. Litwack, *North of Slavery: the Negro in the Free States, 1790-1860* (Chicago, 1961), 232-35.

valuable truths and seasonable warnings."[7] Valuable truths, however were not what some Americans sought. Walker's book raised the question in White minds of just what those secret Black meetings were all about.

The massacre of over 50 unarmed Whites at the hands of Blacks was led by Nat Turner in Southampton County, Virginia, on the night of August 21, 1831.[8] Reports of the event spread terror among White people across the country. That it was an insurrection employing bloody violence against their tormentors, by people who were kept in chains by equally bloody violence, seemed to escape White readers. That it was an unprovoked attack by Blacks against defenseless White women and children was clear to the same White readers. To many fearful Whites, Nat Turner's rebellion answered the question about what the secret meetings were about. Blacks, many Whites feared, were plotting another large-scale extermination of Whites, like the one that had taken place in El Cibao, Santo Domingo, in February of 1805 at the hands of Haitian Emperor Dessalines.[9]

It is hard to overstate the significance of the nationwide terror that followed the Nat Turner incident. White women and children had been slaughtered in the horrifying way: slashed and stabbed with knives, beheaded with axes, shot with crude guns. The victims included non-slaveowners as well as slaveowners, kind owners as well as cruel ones, women and children as well as men.[10] The victims had only one thing in common—they were White. As Joel Williamson put it, "The message of the slave insurrection was that when blacks rebelled, all Whites died."[11]

---

[7] As quoted in Litwack (1961), 234-35.

[8] The impact of Nat Turner's rebellion on White fears is described in Ira Berlin, *Slaves Without Masters: The Free Negro in the Antebellum South* (New York, 1974), 188-89.

[9] C. L. R. James, *The Black Jacobins: Toussaint L'Ouverture and the San Domingo Revolution*, 2d , rev. ed. (New York, 1989), 370.

[10] Herbert Aptheker, *American Negro Slave Revolts*, 6th ed. (New York, 1993), 298-300.

[11] Joel Williamson, *The Crucible of Race: Black/White Relations in the American South Since Emancipation* (New York, 1984), 15.

And so the three threads came together in late 1831: secret meetings called by Black leaders, meetings that were closed to non-Blacks, public calls for organized Black-on-White violence, and the reality of a massacre in Virginia. It was a tiny step for White mainstream society to suspect that "they" might be secretly among "us." Again, the mental image resonates with "Christian-looking Jews" or "American-looking communists," not with short-looking tall people or thin-looking fat people.

Black leaders tried to repair the damage that their closed-meeting policy had inadvertently caused. Although Richard Allen died before the second annual National Black Convention in 1831, his successor, Lewis Cook took the Convention podium to publicly deplore slave violence, saying that, "the free people of color have lived peaceably and quietly... and have never been the cause of any insurrectionary or tumultuous movements."[12]

Threats of White violence led organizers to move the third annual (1832) National Convention from Philadelphia's Benezet Hall to the First African Church.[13] Still trying to quench the blaze, Lewis Cook opened the Convention's doors to the public for the first time and explicitly invited "our white brethren" to attend as observers. White newspapers sent reporters, and some printed reassuring accounts, but it was too little too late.

Anti-Black feeling among Whites continued to deteriorate. Race riots and repressive legislation swept the North.[14] Over the next two decades, waves of legislation disfranchised Blacks throughout free states and slave states alike. New Jersey, Connecticut, and Pennsylvania quickly disfranchised their Black

---

[12] He apparently forgot about Denmark Vesey. The quotation is from Elizabeth Rauh Bethel, *The Roots of African-American Identity* (New York, 1997), 135.

[13] Bethel (1997), 135.

[14] Stephen B. Oates, *Our fiery trial : Abraham Lincoln, John Brown, and the Civil War era* (Amherst, 1979). For a detailed account of the anti-Black riots in Philadelphia in the decade after the Nat Turner, see Emma Jones Lapansky, "'Since They Got Those Separate Churches': Afro-Americans and Racism in Jacksonian Philadelphia," *American Quarterly*, 31 (no. 1, Spring 1980), 54-78. For a summary, see Litwack (1961), 75-92.

citizens.[15] Tennessee disfranchised its Black citizens in 1834 and North Carolina did the same in 1835.[16]

Disfranchisement via an early version of the one-drop rule was apparent in the case of *Hobbs v. Fogg*, 1837 Pennsylvania.[17] On October 13, 1835, a resident landowner in Luzerne County named William Fogg tried to vote in the Pennsylvania general election. He was turned away on the grounds that he descended from Negroes, and so was not entitled to vote. Fogg sued the election board for damages and won. He won because the judge found that: (1) Free Black and biracial Pennsylvanians had voted since the Revolution. (2) The statute in effect explicitly gave the vote to all freemen, without mentioning color or "race." And (3) the record of the legislative debates surrounding the statute,[18] revealed that the legislators had considered limiting the franchise only to Whites but had explicitly voted to make the law color-blind.

The board of electors appealed, and Fogg's victory was overturned. In July of 1837, Justice C. J. Gibson of the Supreme Court of Pennsylvania, Western District, Sunbury, said that allowing non-Whites to vote would violate a 1795 precedent (that Blacks could not vote), which he had heard about from his father. Justice Gibson could find no record of the case, but since his father's "remembrance of the decision is perfect and entitled to full confidence," the unrecorded precedent stood. The judge explained that Pennsylvania's explicitly color-blind constitution was actually intended to forbid Black voting. The letter of the law said "every *freeman* [emphasis Gibson's] of the age of twenty-one years, having *resided in the state* [ditto] two years before the election, and having within that time paid a state or county tax, shall enjoy the rights of an elector." Judge Gibson explained that the spirit of the law was that: (1) Negroes, by definition cannot "reside in the state" and (2) Negroes, by defini-

---

[15] Litwack (1961), 75-92.

[16] Ira Berlin, *Slaves Without Masters: The Free Negro in the Antebellum South* (New York, 1974), 190-92.

[17] 6 Watts 553.

[18] Pennsylvania Constitution of 1776, chapter II, section 6.

tion cannot be "freemen." He further explained that the legislature's explicitly voting forty years ago to strike the word "White" preceding "freeman" in the law meant that they considered the term redundant.

The point of this case is not to highlight Justice Gibson's disregard of both precedent and statute. As shown in the chapters on the antebellum lower South, judges everywhere often followed their own consciences.[19] And, in fact, in that very year of 1837, the Pennsylvania legislature clarified the situation by decreeing that no person of African descent would ever again be allowed to vote in Pennsylvania.[20] The point is that, until William Fogg admitted under oath in court that he descended from Negroes, the court records made no mention of the fact. The record does not state that the man looked more European than African, but one cannot help reaching this conclusion, given that he was compelled to admit African ancestry only under oath. Hence, *Hobbs v. Fogg*, 1837 Pennsylvania, may be the earliest documentary evidence of a decision in favor of something like a one-drop rule in a U.S. court of law.

The 1830s wave of terror and anti-Black reaction not only disfranchised Blacks, but racially segregated Northern public schools.[21] Public school segregation in the North at this time is exemplified by the case of *Crandall v. State*, 1834 Connecticut. An 1833 Connecticut statute forbade the teaching of Blacks from out of state. The reason, according to the act's preamble, was:

---

[19] See *Chapter 10. Barbadian South Carolina: A Class-Based Color Line, Chapter 11. Antebellum Louisiana and Alabama: Two Color Lines, Three Endogamous Groups,* and *Chapter 12. Spanish Florida: No Endogamous Color Line.*

[20] The legislature had recently received a strong "Pennsylvania Dutch" contingent. This ethnic group, formerly known as Germans, had been considered non-White until they managed to be accepted into American mainstream society. Their acceptance was accomplished, in part, by the time-honored technique of displaying public contempt for Blacks. See Noel Ignatiev, *How the Irish Became White* (New York, 1995), 76-77.

[21] Ibid., 113-52.

Whereas, attempts have been made to establish literary institutions in this state, for the instruction of coloured persons
belonging to other states and countries, which would tend to
the great increase of the coloured population of the state, and
thereby to the injury of the people....[22]

Prudence Crandall ran a boarding house. Among her
guests were Black students from out of state. Since these students attended a Connecticut school, Ms. Crandall was charged
and convicted of violating the new law. The Supreme Court of
Error of Connecticut, Windham (four justices presiding) overturned her conviction on the grounds that she was not operating
a school, but a boarding house, and boarding houses were not
illegal. Nevertheless, it is interesting that Connecticut evidently
enforced its law against teaching Blacks, even to the extent of
initially convicting a boarding-house owner who merely provided accommodations for out-of-state students. The school itself was shut down.[23] As contrast, consider that the harsh-
seeming South Carolina statute of 1740, criminalizing the teaching of slaves and free Blacks to read and write, was apparently
ignored. The very following year, 1741, saw the founding in
Charleston of South Carolina's first school for slaves and free
Blacks.[24]

During the 1830s, legislatures also imposed oppressive
anti-Black laws well beyond disfranchisement and school segregation. In 1832, Virginia legislature responded to the Nat Turner
incident by passing a series of laws placing free Blacks under
the same rules and regulations as slaves. Instead of paying fines
for minor infractions, for instance, free Blacks would thenceforth be publicly whipped.[25] Virginia also began strictly to enforce a previously ignored 1806 law that exiled former slaves

---

[22] 10 Conn. 339.

[23] Lerone Bennett Jr., *Before the Mayflower: A History of Black America*, 6th rev. ed. (New York, 1993), 457.

[24] Frank J. Klingberg, *An Appraisal of the Negro in Colonial South Carolina* (Philadelphia, 1975), 69-70.

[25] Joshua D. Rothman, *Notorious in the Neighborhood: Sex and Families Across the Color Line in Virginia, 1787-1861* (Chapel Hill, 2003), 210.

from the state.[26] No longer could the manumitted establish themselves as free Virginians.[27] This, incidentally, is why Eston Hemings and his family were forced to leave Charlottesville and move to Chillicothe, Ohio.[28] Religious freedom was also curtailed. South Carolina imposed such harsh restrictions upon Black worship services that the AME church was driven out of the state.[29]

The anti-Black wave of reaction of the 1830s was not limited to lawful oppression. According to Leon F. Litwack, "Between 1832 and 1849, Philadelphia mobs set off five major anti-Negro riots. In July, 1834, a white mob stormed though the Negro section, clubbed and stoned its victims, destroyed homes, churches, and meeting halls, forced hundreds to leave the city, and left many others homeless."[30] In 1835 New Hampshire, a mob harnessed a hundred yoke of oxen and dragged into a swamp a building used as a school for Black children. In 1837 Illinois, abolitionist publisher Elijah P. Lovejoy was killed by a mob while defending his printing press.[31]

Tens of thousands of American Blacks fled the United States. Within those two decades of the 1830s and 1840s, about twenty percent of the free members of America's Black endogamous group escaped to other countries. Thirteen thousand

---

[26] Va. Ch. 69, sec. 10, p. 97. See Rothman (2003), 43, 256n88.

[27] Annette Gordon-Reed, *Thomas Jefferson and Sally Hemings: An American Controversy* (Charlottesville, 1997), 15.

[28] See the opening anecdote of *Chapter 9. How the Law Decided if You Were Black or White: The Early 1800s.*

[29] Williamson (1984), 17.

[30] Litwack (1961), 100-1.

[31] Lerone Bennett Jr., *Before the Mayflower: A History of Black America*, 6th rev. ed. (New York, 1993), 458.

of them (like Hezekiah Grice[32]) went to Haiti. Sixty thousand went to Canada.[33]

In short, starting around 1830, terror produced reaction, which produced ostracism, which then produced otherness and fear in a vicious spiral. This study suggests that terror in the minds of mainstream America (the White endogamous group) is what led to the invention of the frightening notion of "White-looking Blacks." In other words, the 1830s wave of terror is what gave rise to One-Drop rule, which, as explained in the prior chapter, first arose during this period.

African-American Ethnic Solidarity Benefited

The terror of the 1830s eventually passed and life resumed its course. Had the notion of invisible Blackness arisen only within mainstream (White) popular culture, it might have faded out, along with the fears of massive uprisings and Black-on-White massacres. But by coincidence these were also the decades when Black Yankees invented African-American ethnicity.[34] And the idea that you could be a member of the African-American ethnic group, despite your European appearance, paralleled similar attitudes among German-Americans and Irish-Americans.

Ultimately, as suggested by Nathan Glazer in his essay "Universalization of Ethnicity" (1975), the growth of invented ethnicities was a reaction to the industrial revolution's urbaniza-

---

[32] The former ice dealer who persuaded Richard Allen to hold the first Convention. See the topic "The Integration versus Separatism Pendulum" in *Chapter 13. The Color Line Created African-American Ethnicity in the North.*

[33] Elizabeth Rauh Bethel, *The Roots of African-American Identity* (New York, 1997), 145.

[34] See *Chapter 13. The Color Line Created African-American Ethnicity in the North.*

tion, new occupations, mass education, and mass media.[35] The point is that U.S. ethnicities were and are distinguished by meticulously patrolled borders, rather than by significant difference in content.[36] And so, whatever made the border of African-American ethnicity more ideological and less substantive was likely to be adopted and incorporated in that particular ethnic canon.

Three pieces of evidence suggest that the notion of invisible Blackness was embraced by Blacks from its beginning because it benefited the invention of African-American ethnicity. First, separatist Afrocentrist Martin Delaney and integrationist patriot Frederick Douglass both supported a one-drop rule as enhancing African-American ethnic solidarity, even though they disagreed on nearly everything else. According to Judith Stein, in 1848, Frederick Douglass faced the challenge of mobilizing a Black Yankee (early African-American ethnic) community "who evidently did not identify with the slaves." He tried to create unity and purpose among them to fight slavery and to become abolitionists. He did this, according to Stein, "by asserting their oneness" with the slaves. "We are one people," Frederick Douglass affirmed, "one in general complexion, one in a common degradation, one in popular estimation."[37]

Second, court cases, like *Commonwealth v. Robinson*, 1837 Massachusetts, which opened this chapter, show Black Yankees adopting tactics (kidnapping an apparently European-looking five-year-old) which are intelligible only in the context of an internalized notion of invisible Blackness. Third, as pointed out earlier, members of the African-American ethnic group, not Whites, wrote the first American passing novels and plays.[38]

---

[35] Werner Sollors, *Theories of Ethnicity: A Classical Reader* (Washington Square NY, 1996), xvi.

[36] This is the consensus expressed by Gans, Glazer, Moynihan, Parsons, and Barth. For a useful survey, see Sollors (1996), xvi-xxi.

[37] Judith Stein, "Defining the Race 1890-1930," in *The Invention of Ethnicity*, ed. Werner Sollors (New York, 1989), 77-104, 77.

[38] See the topic "Literature and Drama" in *Chapter 15. The Invention of the One-Drop Rule in the 1830s North*.

Other Voices

As mentioned in the prior chapter, that the one-drop rule first arose in the free states in the 1830s will remain undisputed until someone uncovers an example of the notion of invisible Blackness anywhere before 1830 or in the South during the 1830s. Until then, the question is "why?" What gave rise to such a world-unique and counter-rational concept? The hypothesis presented above is that the one-drop rule arose in White society as a consequence of a nationwide wave of terror after secret meetings of Black leaders, calls for Black-on-White violence, and the Nat Turner incident. It also suggests that it arose in African-American society because leaders of the newly invented African-American ethnicity embraced it in the interests of it fostering solidarity, as evidenced by political rhetoric, passing novels, and court cases.

Four objections are sometimes raised against this hypothesis. It suggests that Blacks and Whites cooperated in creating the one-drop rule. It denies that the one-drop rule had anything to do with increasing the number of slave assets held by planters. It ignores pre-1830 literature mentioning an indelible mark. Finally, it denies that Latin America has passing literature.

It suggests that U.S. Blacks and Whites cooperated in creating the one-drop rule. Not deliberately, of course. It is simply that, among Whites, the notion of ideological or invisible Blackness was a fear-driven response to the terror of the 1830s. And it just so happened that, at roughly the same time, the same concept became useful to African-American political leaders in enhancing ethnic unity. This is objected to because the historiography of "race" in the United States has traditionally been the historiography of slavery. Ulrich Phillips argued that slavery civilized the savages and so benefited them in the long term. He claimed that kindly masters sheltered slave families, protected pregnant and nursing mothers, and discouraged sales that split families.[39] Responding to Phillips, historians of U.S. race rela-

---

[39] Ulrich Bonnell Phillips, *American Negro Slavery* (New York, 1918).

tions over the past century have developed two alternate interpretations of how slaves and their society reacted to their plight.

The first interpretation suggests that, because the under-
pinnings of African culture were destroyed during slavery,
American slaves lost family values and were infantilized. E.
Franklin Frazier argued that slavery cut Blacks off from their
cultural heritage.[40] It deprived fathers of authority and responsibility, led to matrifocal single-parent families, and resulted in a
people with chronic lack of individual impulse control. This resulted in Black inability to overcome poverty, even in regions
where post-slavery institutionalized racism was weak. Kenneth
Stampp detailed the horrors of human beings without rights being treated like livestock.[41] He agreed with Frazier that slavery
had led to matrifocal families and that frequent family separa-
tions led to social pathology. Stampp asserted that slavery's destruction of the Black family led to parental indifference and
sexual promiscuity. Daniel Moynihan and Stanley M. Elkins
dramatized the impact of slavery on the Black family by comparing the experience to Nazi concentration camps, leading to
victimization, infantilism, and destruction of culture.[42]

The opposite interpretation suggests that slavery was opposed and contested by the slaves who, far from being passive
victims, preserved a syncretic culture that enabled family values
to survive and flourish. Herbert Gutman and Jacqueline Jones
reacted against Frazier, Stampp, Moynihan, and Elkins. Gutman
asserted that, far from being passive victims, Black families resisted heroically.[43] Gutman and Jones claimed that, throughout
the south, most slaves lived in two-parent households. They af-

---

[40] Edward Franklin Frazier, *The Negro Family in the United States*, Rev.
and abridged ed. (Chicago, 1966).

[41] Kenneth M. Stampp, *The Peculiar Institution* (New York, 1953).

[42] Daniel Moynihan *"The Negro Family in America"* (1965); Stanley M.
Elkins, *Slavery: A Problem in American Institutional and Intellectual Life*,
3d , rev. ed. (Chicago, 1959).

[43] Herbert George Gutman, *The Black Family in Slavery and Freedom,
1750-1925* (New York, 1976a); Jacqueline Jones, *Labor of Love, Labor of
Sorrow: Black women, Work, and the Family From Slavery to the Present*
(New York, 1985).

firmed that Black families remained vigorous and preserved traditional African values despite slavery which, according to Gutman, was an oppressive circumstance similar to the exploitation of immigrant wage laborers. Eugene Genovese agreed with Gutman and Jones that slave families created "a world of their own" built on "life-affirming" African religion.[44] But he also acknowledged that, despite resistance, slave owners were firmly in command. He showed that slave tales of emasculated but brutal Black males, fatherless children, and wrecked families rested on irrefutable evidence.

This study does not examine these contending interpretations. They are mentioned only to note that both agree on one crucial point. Virtually every scholar of the history of the U.S. "race" notion (which is almost always interpreted as the history of slavery) agrees that antebellum Blacks and Whites were at odds. Conflict is the basic explanatory paradigm. Blacks resisted what Whites imposed, as Whites overcame Black resistance. As Barbara Fields puts it, "[Black] People no more fasten the stigma of race upon themselves than cattle sear the brand into their own flesh."[45] This book's hypothesis, in contrast, is that in the free states of the 1830s, Black Yankees were very proud indeed of their newly invented African-American ethnicity, and were thereby inadvertently complicit with White mainstream society in inventing and spreading the one-drop rule.

It denies that the one-drop rule had anything to do with increasing the number of slave assets held by planters. As mentioned earlier, many scholars assert, without evidence,

----

[44] Eugene D. Genovese, *Roll, Jordan, Roll: The World the Slaves Made* (New York, 1976).

[45] Barbara Fields, "Of Rogues and Geldings," *American Historical Review*, 108 (no. 5, December 2003), 1397-405, 1401; also, see Hickman's remark, "[Whites] fashioned [the one-drop rule] out of racism, malice, greed, lust, and ignorance.....," supra note 30 under topic "Many Scholars Believe the One-Drop Rule is Stronger Than Ever" in *Chapter 14. Features of Today's One-Drop Rule.*

that the one-drop rule was invented by slaveowners to increase their assets.[46]

> Children born of slaves and slave owners represented a blurring of the distinction between slave and free, between property and property owner. To deal with this problem, these children almost always were treated as black. Thus arose the "one drop" rule, which held that having a single black ancestor made a person black.[47]

> The [one-drop] rule also, conveniently, served to increase the number of slaves and exempted white landowners (particularly slaveholders) from the legal obligation of passing on an inheritance and other benefits of paternity to their multiracial offspring.[48]

> While whites publicly denounced miscegenation, white men practiced it with regularity by raping their female slaves (Blassingame 1972). The children of these unions, in accordance with the one-drop rule, were considered black and, therefore, assets for the slave master (Davis 1991). It was this economic incentive, grounded in white supremacist logic, that validated the one-drop rule as the definition of blackness in the plantation dominated South.[49]

This study, in contrast, presents evidence that the one-drop rule first appeared in the free states in the 1830s and in the South about a decade later. And it flatly states that no evidence yet uncovered connects it to slavery in any way.

It ignores pre-1830 literature mentioning an indelible mark. Admittedly, the first use of the term "one drop" in reference to African ancestry that this study has been able uncover

---

[46] See the historians listed in note 14 of *Chapter 9. How the Law Decided if You Were Black or White: The Early 1800s.*

[47] Steve Olson, *Mapping Human History: Discovering the Past Through Our Genes* (Boston, 2002), 60.

[48] G. Reginald Daniel, *More than Black?: Multiracial Identity and the New Racial Order* (Philadelphia, 2002), x.

[49] David L. Brunsma and Kerry Ann Rockquemore, "What Does 'Black' Mean? Exploring the Epistemological Stranglehold of Racial Categorization," *Critical Sociology*, 28 (no. 1/2, 2002), 101-21, 106-7.

predates 1830 by two years. A report of the Connecticut Colonization Society published the following paragraph in 1828:

> In every part of the United States there is a broad and impas-
> sible [sic] line of demarcation between every man who has
> *one drop of African blood* [emphasis mine] in his veins, and
> every other class in the community. The habits, the feelings,
> all the prejudices of society—prejudices which neither re-
> finement, nor argument, nor education, nor religion can itself
> subdue—mark the people of colour, whether bond or free, as
> the subjects of a degradation inevitable and incurable. The
> African in this country belongs by birth to the lowest station
> in society; and from that station he can never rise, be his tal-
> ent, his enterprise, his virtues what they may.[50]

This quotation seems to imply that the idea of invisible or ideologically based membership in the Black endogamous group
predates the watershed events in the early 1830s along the Ohio
River Valley, and may spring from late 1820s New England instead. But a closer reading of the Colonization Society report
shows that this is not the case. The report suggests that the reason why "prejudices of society" are so tenacious is because of
"the mark that nature has placed upon the Negro." The context
from which the above phrase was taken says that every man who
has one drop of African blood in his veins is marked by some
trace of African appearance. No matter how diluted the African
blood may be, a residue of visible evidence will always remain,
generation after generation. The folkloric belief in a physical
mark or stigma that remains visible despite infinite dilution of
Negro blood is not the subject of this study.[51]

   It denies that Latin America has passing literature. An
objection voiced by scholars of Latin America is that passing
literature, which this study claims is unique to the United States
because Latin American societies lack a one-drop rule, is in fact
popular in Latin American fiction. For example, the 1948 Mexi-

---

[50] *African Repository*, 4 (June 1928):118 as quoted in George M.
Fredrickson, *The Black Image in the White Mind: The Debate on Afro-
American Character and Destiny, 1817-1914* (New York, 1981a), 17.

[51] See the discussion of this folkloric belief under the topic "Definition" in
Chapter 14. Features of Today's One-Drop Rule.

can film "Angelitos Negros" is a remake of Fannie Hurst's passing novel *Imitation of Life*. Let us inspect this claim more
closely.

Recall that, as "passing" is defined above, pretense is an
essential element because it goes to the heart of the one-drop
rule—the belief that a European-looking person of negligible
African ancestry who denies being a member of the Black endogamous group is somehow deceiving society. The element of
pretense, of passing as White while "really being" Black may
seem a subtlety that is hard to detect.

Fannie Hurst's novel *Imitation of Life* has been filmed at
least three times. It was filmed twice in the United States, in
1934 with Claudette Colbert and again in 1959 with Lana
Turner. It was also filmed once in 1948 Mexico. The 1948
Mexican version more closely reflects pre-one-drop attitudes
that were common to the lower South (as explained in the prior
chapter), to Europe (as mentioned above), and to the North before 1829. The U.S. versions of the film, in contrast, reflect the
one-drop rule, which appeared in the North after 1830.

The film, "Angelitos Negros," was directed by Joselito
Rodriguez, starring Pedro Infante, Emilia Guiu, and Rita Montañer. The plot centers on a woman (Guiu), who does not know
that she is actually the daughter of the maid (Montañer), who is
visibly of part-African ancestry, and the wealthy European-
looking landowner. Born blonde, she is brought up as the patron's daughter and never told the truth. Infante plays a famous
(typically swarthy, Hispanic-looking) singer who marries her.
The crisis comes when their daughter is born with African features. She blames him and rejects the child. He raises the child
on his own with the help of an Afro-Cuban female friend. In the
end, the mother learns the truth of her own ancestry and the family is reconciled. According to Afro-Mexican director and
scriptwriter Rodriguez, whose own daughter plays the child, the
plot is based on the Fannie Hurst novel *Imitation of Life*.

Comparing *Angelitos Negros* with either U.S. version of
Imitation of Life reveals why "passing" novels are unintelligible
outside of the United States. In the American version of the
story, the crisis comes when the protagonist realizes that she is

"really Black." Although she initially denies her "heritage," (she looks completely European, after all), she eventually comes to understand that she must be true to her "race," and abandons her life as a White woman to live among Blacks. This, in the United States, is presumably a happier ending than "living a lie," as the character puts it.

In the Mexican version, no such issue ever arises. No one in the film is "really Black" or "really White." They are all Mexicans of varying degrees of genetic admixture. The crisis comes when a predominantly European-looking couple has a predominantly African-looking child. As explained earlier, something like this happens about once out of every eight thousand births in Spain and with slightly higher frequency in Mexico.[52] The plot plays out as a crisis of social status, not one of personal identity. The movie's theme, of course, is the colorism in Mexican society that makes a dark-complexioned child less welcome than a blonde, blue-eyed child. But no character ever questions his or her personal identity. They are all Mexicans. Everyone in the story knows and accepts that they are all of mixed heritage.

* * * * *

This chapter suggested a hypothesis for the origin of the one-drop rule in the 1830s free states. It proposed that members of the White endogamous group suffered a nationwide wave of terror that Blacks were secretly plotting to massacre Whites. At the same time, the one-drop rule was reinforced and encouraged by African-American ethnic leaders seeking to strengthen group loyalties. The chapter also presented four objections to the hypothesis.

---

[52] See the topic "How Many Black Children are Born into White Families?" in *Chapter 3. The Heredity of "Racial" Traits.*

Chapter 17.
The Antebellum South
Rejects the One-Drop Rule

James West, of Albemarle County Virginia, married
Susannah Harlow on August 28, 1794. Both are listed as White
on their marriage license, and both were accepted as White in
their community.[1] Despite their acceptance, it was common
knowledge in Charlottesville, which had an 1810 population of
just 260 residents, that James was the son of slaveowner Thomas
West and West's former Black slave, Priscilla.[2] Priscilla was a
quadroon[3] however, and so she bequeathed legal Whiteness to
her son in accordance with the Virginia law of 1785.[4]

James West's background paralleled that of his friend and
neighbor, Eston Hemings. Like Hemings, West's mother had
once been a slave and was on the Black side of America's en-

---

[1] Albemarle County Marriage Register, 1780-1868, August 29, 1794 as
cited in Joshua D. Rothman, *Notorious in the Neighborhood: Sex and Families Across the Color Line in Virginia, 1787-1861* (Chapel Hill, 2003),
262n36.

[2] See "Figure 1. Genealogy of the West-Isaacs-Hemings-Fossett Families"
in Rothman (2003), 54-55.

[3] Presumably, a person of one-fourth sub-Saharan genetic admixture.

[4] Paul Finkelman, "The Crime of Color," *Tulane Law Review*, 67 (no. 6,
1992), 2063-112, 2088, 2090.

dogamous color line. Like Hemings, West was accepted as socially White, along with his wife and children. In a lawsuit
(*Hays v. Hays*, 1836 Virginia), a West neighbor named Benjamin
Hays testified that the West children were "esteemed, received
and accepted as white men, were educated with white children
and required to perform and did perform Militia and other du-
ties, required only of white men, and allowed to intermarry
without objection on the score of blood, with white women."[5]

Another parallel is that both James West and Eston Hemings had siblings who were not accepted as White, despite the
blood fraction rule then in effect. In Hemings's case it was his
brother James Madison Hemings, who lived out his life on the
Black side of the endogamous color line. In West's case it was
his elder sister Nancy. Rather than bowing to social rejection,
however, Nancy and her husband fought back. He was a well-to-
do Jewish businessman named David Isaacs. In 1822, David and
Nancy Isaacs successfully defended themselves against a charge
of criminal intermarriage by proving, in a five-year battle
through the appellate system, that Nancy was legally White.[6] Of
course, we cannot know how much of Nancy West's social rejection in Charlottesville, in contrast to her brother James's acceptance, was due to her having a trace of African appearance (as
was the case with Jim-Mad Hemings) and how much was due
simply to her being a woman and married to a Jew.

The parallel between Charlottesville residents Eston Hemings and James West is imperfect. As mentioned earlier, Virginia
had responded to the Nat Turner incident of 1831 by ordering all
former slaves to leave the state.[7] Eston Hemings was forced to

---

[5] Albemarle County Ended Chancery Causes (Circuit Superior Court), case
#354, Library of Virginia, Richmond as cited in Rothman (2003), 262n37.

[6] Ibid., 59-67.

[7] Actually, the law (Va. ch. 69, sec. 10, p. 97) had been passed thirty years
earlier on January 25, 1806, but it was not seriously enforced until after the
Nat Turner incident. See Rothman (2003), 43, 256n88. Also see the topic
"A Watershed Event in Three Threads" in *Chapter 16. Why Did Northerners Invent a One-Drop Rule?*

move to Chillicothe Ohio because of this law.[8] James West was unaffected by it. Hemings was a former slave, having been manumitted by Thomas Jefferson's will. James West had been born free.

Curiously, despite David and Nancy Isaacs's court battle for Whiteness, their daughter, Julia Ann Isaacs (James West's niece), was socially accepted as White from birth like her cousins, the West children. When Julia Ann Isaacs grew up, she married Eston Hemings. She was with Eston, his mother Sally, and his brother Jim-Mad when the extended family had to leave Charlottesville Virginia for Chillicothe Ohio because her in-laws had once been slaves. She was still with him when the couple and their children moved to Wisconsin as members of the White endogamous group after changing their name to "Jefferson."[9]

* * * * *

This chapter suggests that between 1830 and slavery's end in 1865 the South was in transition. Early in this period, which side of the endogamous color line you were on depended on the rule of blood fraction as modified by the rule of physical appearance and the rule of association.[10] Eston Hemings, like his wife Julia Isaacs and her uncle James West, were accepted as White despite slight Black ancestry. But in the decades after 1830, after the North had accepted the notion of invisible Blackness, the idea spread southwards. Courts were at first willing to allow one-drop arguments to be made in court, but such arguments were not conclusive in reaching verdicts. Then after several years, verdicts began to be rendered based on invisible Blackness, although they were overturned. Later, appellate decisions

---

[8] Annette Gordon-Reed, *Thomas Jefferson and Sally Hemings: An American Controversy* (Charlottesville, 1997), 15. Hemings and his wife later changed their surname to "Jefferson" and moved to Wisconsin as a White family. See Rothman (2003), 86-87.

[9] Ibid., 86-87.

[10] See the topic "Physical Appearance, Blood Fraction, Association" in *Chapter 9. How the Law Decided if You Were Black or White: The Early 1800s.*

began to uphold such verdicts. Step by step, the one-drop rule spread deeper into the slave states. By 1865, the upper South had apparently become comfortable with a one-drop rule in practice, while still paying lip service to the old blood-fraction laws in theory.

This chapter presents its case in four topics. *Nat Turner Sealed Virginia's Color Line* explains why color-line determination became more important after 1830. *The Not-a-Negro Law* describes a moderately unsuccessful legislative attempt to enable respected citizens to avoid the oppressive anti-Black laws of the time. *Transitional Cases* reveals the inexorable north-to-south spread of the one-drop rule as reflected in appeals court cases. *Virginia Rejects the One-Drop Rule* describes the nation's first attempt to write a one-drop law. The attempt failed when it was realized that it would penalize elite Virginia families.

Nat Turner Sealed Virginia's Color Line

Like the Hemings family, the Wharton family of Stafford County, Virginia, was also ordered to leave the state after the Nat Turner incident. They were a large family, comprising William, Lemuel, Barney, Nancy, and Lewis. All had once been the property of deceased slaveowner John Cooke, and so they were subject to exile after 1832.[11] Like Eston Hemings, they had long been accepted as members of the White endogamous group. (James and Susannah West's family, who had also moved to the White side of the endogamous color line, did not fall under this law because they had been born free.)

Unlike the Hemings family, the Whartons apparently had influential friends. On March 9, 1833, fifty-one White men of

---

[11] As mentioned earlier, the Virginia legislature in 1832, responded to the Nat Turner incident by passing a series of laws placing free Blacks under the same rules and regulations as slaves. Instead of paying fines for minor infractions, for instance, free Blacks would thenceforth be publicly whipped. See Rothman (2003), 210. In addition, Virginia began strictly enforcing the 1806 law that had exiled former slaves. See Annette Gordon-Reed, *Thomas Jefferson and Sally Hemings: An American Controversy* (Charlottesville, 1997), 15.

Stafford County presented a signed petition to the state legislature, asking that the Whartons be exempted from the law exiling former slaves.[12] Their argument against exile was based on the Whartons' industrious contribution to the community. The part of the petition that asked them to be declared White was particularly persuasive. It was explicitly grounded upon all three of the traditional rules then in effect: blood fraction, physical appearance, and association.[13] First, that "more than three fourths of [the Whartons'] blood is derived from white ancestors." Second, that they looked completely European, being "all white persons in complexion." Finally, the petition explained that the Whartons saw themselves as White, had "no association with coloured persons," had married Whites, and "their partialities are decidedly for the whites."[14] The legislature agreed. They declared that the Whartons were "not negroes or mulattoes, but white persons, although remotely descended from a coloured woman."[15] They passed a special bill declaring the Whartons both White and not subject to exile.

Not all such petitioners were this fortunate. As is apparent in the following two graphs, between 20 percent and 40 percent of court cases during this period resulted in the individual being ruled to be on the Black side of the endogamous color line. The left graph shows the results of court determinations of endogamous group membership as percentages. The right graph depicts the same information as absolute numbers of rulings.

---

[12] Rothman (2003), 215.

[13] See the topic "Physical Appearance, Blood Fraction, Association" in *Chapter 9. How the Law Decided if You Were Black or White: The Early 1800s.*

[14] As quoted in Rothman (2003), 213.

[15] Journal of the House of Delegates, 1832-1833, March 9, 1833, p. 265 as quoted in Rothman (2003), 215.

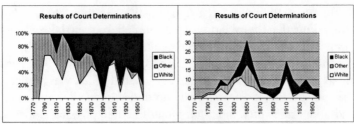

Figure 30. Results of Court Determinations

As mentioned earlier, court cases are somewhat self-selecting.[16] The ratio of cases where people were found to be White does not reflect the severity of the color line and tends to hover at 50 percent. That the fraction of cases ruling people to be White was in decline during the 1830-1850 period most likely means that a segment of the public had become uninformed as to the legal system's actual demands for awarding Whiteness. Either the courts had become stricter than many realized, or a segment of the public had become more accepting than the courts realized (most likely, the former). Either way, as the two graphs show, every late antebellum divergence from the 50-percent level was soon restored as either the public or the judges learned the new rules of the others' game.[17]

The Not-a-Negro Law

The harsh laws against free Blacks passed in 1832, coupled with the Whartons' success at being declared exempt, caused a sharp increase in the number of petitions to the Virginia legislature asking for exceptions similar to that of the Whartons.

---

[16] See *Chapter 9. How the Law Decided if You Were Black or White: The Early 1800s*, footnote 12. Also see *Appendix B. Court Case Data Processing Methodology*.

[17] For a contrasting view, that the relative preponderance of decisions one way or the other is significant to interpreting history, see Ariela J. Gross, "Litigating Whiteness: Trials of Racial Determination in the Nineteenth-Century South," *Yale Law Journal*, 108 (no. 1, 1998), 109-88, 122n32 or Donald Braman, "Of Race and Immutability," *UCLA Law Review*, 46 (1999), 1375-463, 1395n63.

In January of 1833, Virginia legislator John Murdaugh of Norfolk devised a solution. He introduced a bill, which became law, that exempted those "people of mixed blood, who are not negroes or mulattoes," from the anti-Black statutes and regulations if they obtained a local court certificate to that effect.[18]

Eventually referred to as the "Not-a-Negro" law, the statute seems meaningless on its face. This is because it explicitly applied only to people of less than 1/4 African ancestry. Anyone with one or more genetically African grandparents was legally defined as Negro or mulatto by the act of 1785, and so was not covered by the Not-a-Negro law's scope ("people of mixed blood, who are not negroes or mulattoes"). Hence, strictly speaking, it exempted from oppressive anti-Black laws only those individuals who were of such little African ancestry that they were already legally members of the White endogamous group and so exempt from all but the law of exile anyway. Could such a law help such people?[19]

Perhaps. As the situations of James Madison Hemings and Nancy West revealed, and as confirmed by the court case statistics presented above, there was a great difference between being legally White on the one hand, and being accepted as socially White by the political leaders of one's community on the other. Those individuals who were fully accepted as White by men whose opinions mattered in the halls of power—like James and Susannah West and their children, or the Whartons—needed no such a law to protect their social status, whatever their blood fraction. Some of the people potentially covered by the law were those of legally White blood fraction who, due to their slightly African appearance, could not achieve acceptance into White society. These were individuals like the 20-40 percent ruled to be Black in the two graphs above. But, due to the unwritten rule of physical appearance such people were consequently seen as "negroes or mulattoes" and so, catch-22, the law could not apply to

---

[18] Rothman (2003), 210-12.

[19] For a further discussion of the Not-a-Negro law in general, and of the Whartons in particular, see Walter Wadlington, "The Loving Case: Virginia's Anti-Miscegenation Statute in Historical Perspective," *Virginia Law Review*, 52 (no. 7, November 1966), 1189-223, 1196.

them either. In short, the Not-a-Negro" law was a well-intentioned gesture that apparently had little practical effect. It applied only to those who did not need its protection and excluded those who needed it most.

Some scholars suggest that the flaw in the Not-a-Negro law was that, although it declared that people who were legally White (by the 1785 blood fraction law) were exempt from the anti-Black laws, it did not declare them to be socially White. And this left them in a sort of legal limbo.[20] But this may be a merely theoretical quibble. It is exceedingly likely that by 1833, any law that declared a Virginian of slight African appearance to be socially White would have been ignored. Hence, it could never have passed the legislature. By 1833, the people of Virginia, like those of neighboring states, were being persuaded by a new way of seeing the endogamous color line, a southward-sweeping one-drop rule of invisible Blackness. Anyone with even rumored Black ancestry was starting to be seen as socially Black, despite appearance, regardless of blood fraction.

Transitional Cases

Four cases exemplify the southward spread of the one-drop rule of invisible Blackness. *State v. Harris Melton & Ann Byrd*, 1852 North Carolina was an anti-intermarriage case where the one-drop rule was argued but rejected on appeal. In the attempted-rape case, *State v. Anderson*, 1853 Missouri, one-drop was argued but rejected by the verdict. In *State v. William Chavers*, 1857 North Carolina the defendant was charged with owning a gun (like *State v. Whitmell Dempsey*, 1849 North Carolina[21]). The one-drop rule was argued and upheld by the verdict but overturned on appeal. Finally, in *State v. Asa Jacobs*, 1859 North Carolina (another weapons charge), the one-drop rule was argued, won at trial, and was upheld on appeal, but with a rheto-

---

[20] See, for example, Rothman (2003), 210-12.

[21] 31 N.C. 384. For details, under the topic "Physical Appearance, Blood Fraction, Association" in *Chapter 9. How the Law Decided if You Were Black or White: The Early 1800s.*

ric that denied invisible Blackness *de juris* while enforcing it *de facto*. Together, the four cases reveal increasing acceptance of a one-drop rule of invisible Blackness in the late antebellum upper South.

Harris Melton and Ann Byrd were an interracial couple in North Carolina who had wed despite the state anti-intermarriage statute of 1838. The law declared, "it shall not be lawful for any free negro or person of color to marry a white person; and any marriage hereafter solemnized or contracted between any free negro or free person of color and a white person, shall be null and void. All persons living together under such circumstances, as man and wife, are guilty of fornication and adultery." Fourteen years later, in *State v. Harris Melton & Ann Byrd*, 1852 North Carolina, the couple were indicted for fornication.[22] Ann was considered White, so the accusation hinged on Harris Melton's endogamous group membership.

The prosecution argued that, "the Act was general, prohibiting all mixtures of the white with the colored races, and it made no difference whether [Harris Melton's] blood was African or Indian, or in what degree, if there was any sensible taint of either—they were guilty." The defense insisted that, "unless the defendant Melton was within the fourth degree of negro or African blood, they could not be convicted." The jury was unable to reach agreement regarding the interpretation of the law.

Their confusion was due to a conflict between the statute under which the Meltons were indicted and an earlier statute. The law of 1836 had forbidden weddings (but not marriages) between White and Black, and had explicitly defined as "Black" anyone with one-eighth or more Negro blood. Although the 1836 law had punished, with a $100 fine, ministers and magistrates who performed such weddings, it did not declare such marriages void, nor did it punish interracial couples who married in defiance of the law (out of state, for example). In short, the old 1836 law was explicitly based upon the rule of blood fraction. The new 1838 law, in contrast, declared interracial marriages void and defined interracial couples as criminal fornicators, no matter

---

[22] 44 N.C. 49.

where they were wed. On the other hand, the new law did not specify which rule should be used to position someone on the Black side of the endogamous color line. Hence, the jury's confusion.

The jury returned two verdicts: guilty and not guilty. They found Melton to be partly Black, but were unable to say to what degree, since no evidence had been introduced as to blood fraction. They said that if they interpreted the new law as employing a one-drop rule, thereby applying to anyone with the slightest trace of African ancestry, then the defendants were guilty as charged. But if the jury interpreted the new law (which did not define Blackness) with the same one-eighth definition as the old law, then they found the couple to be not guilty. Judge Bailey ruled that, as a matter of law, the second interpretation was correct and released the couple. The prosecution appealed. North Carolina Supreme Court Justice C. J. Nash eventually affirmed the lower court's decision. He agreed with the trial judge that, by omitting a definition of Blackness in the new law, the legislature had intended to carry forward the old law's definition. *State v. Harris Melton & Ann Byrd*, 1852 North Carolina, is important because it was the first time that an appeals court in the South saw someone arguing in favor of a one-drop rule.[23]

In *State v. Anderson*, 1853 Missouri, a criminal court convicted an African-looking defendant of attempting to rape a European-looking victim.[24] Endogamous group membership was important because the sentence depended on it; Black-on-White attempted rape was punished by castration. The defendant appealed because no testimony had been offered at trial either that he was Black nor that the victim was White. The jury had evidently reached such a conclusion merely by observing the defendant and the victim in the courtroom. Anderson's lawyers argued that a one-drop rule of invisible Blackness should have been applied to the victim:

---

[23] The first such case anywhere in the United States happened eighteen years earlier in *Williams v. School District* 1834 Ohio, Catterall (1968), 5:4. For details, see the topic "Court Cases" in *Chapter 15.The Invention of the One-Drop Rule in the 1830s North.*

[24] 19 Mo. 241.

Under the statute, the question before the jury was not merely
one of color, but of race. Such questions are often of the
greatest difficulty, requiring for their solution scientific skill.
There are albinoes, mulattoes and quadroons, who excel
Caucasians in whiteness of skin. Yet, before the jury could
convict the defendant, it was necessary that they should find
that… the prosecutrix [was] a Caucasian. These facts they
could only find upon proof.[25]

The conviction was upheld by the state Supreme Court.
Reasoning that color and "race" were synonymous, two justices
ruled that the jury did not need testimony to determine what they
could see with their own eyes—that the victim was White. This
was the second time that the one-drop rule was argued south of
the Mason-Dixon line. As in North Carolina the previous year,
the one-drop rule was argued but rejected on appeal.

Four years later, in *State v. William Chavers*, 1857 North
Carolina, the defendant was indicted for carrying a shotgun, in
violation of section 66 of chapter 107 of the Revised Code then
in effect.[26] Although section 79 of the same chapter stated that
"all free persons descended from negro ancestors to the fourth
generation inclusive, though one ancestor of each generation
may have been a white person, shall be deemed free Negroes,"
thereby defining White as anyone with less than one-eighth Negro ancestry, the prosecution presented no evidence as to Chavers's degree of ancestry. Instead, they relied on testimony that
the defendant's father was a man of dark complexion and kinky
hair. The trial judge instructed the jury that the defendant was
Black within the spirit of the law. "Can it be then, that a remove
by one generation has the effect, in law, of turning a half negro
into a free white man in spite of the color of his skin or the kinking of his hair? It seems to me both unreasonable and absurd,
and therefore I cannot put such a construction upon the 79th section of the 107th chapter of the Act of Assembly, (Revised Code)
declaring who shall be deemed free negroes."[27]

---

[25] Idem.

[26] 50 N.C. 11.

[27] Idem.

William Chavers's conviction was overturned on appeal. For the third time, a one-drop rule of color-line determination was argued in a Southern court, in defiance of a statutory blood-fraction rule. As in the previous three cases, the rule of invisible Blackness was rejected at the appellate level.

Two years later, another North Carolinian of mixed ances-try was prosecuted for carrying a gun. *State v. Asa Jacobs*, 1859 North Carolina also saw the conviction of man for the crime of carrying a firearm—another shotgun, in this case.[28] The defen-dant claimed that he was White within the definition of the stat-ute. As in the previous three such cases, the North Carolina prosecutor did not try to prove the man's Blackness by comput-ing his blood fraction as required by the statutes. But this time they took a different approach. They called an expert witness—a forensic expert in the science of "race." The court accepted the witness, a Mr. Pritchett, as a forensic expert in color-line posi-tioning on the grounds that he owned slaves. Pritchett qualified himself as a forensic expert by testifying under oath:

> [T]hat he was a planter, an owner and manager of slaves, and had been for more than twelve years, that he had paid much attention to and had had much observation of the effects of the intermixture of negro or African blood with the white and Indian races, and that from such attention and observation, he was well satisfied that he could distinguish between the de-scendants of a negro and a white person, and the descendants of a negro and Indian; and further, that he could therefrom, also say whether a person was full African or negro, or had more or less than half negro or African blood in him, and whether the cross or intermixture was white or Indian blood.[29]

Once the court had accepted him as an expert witness, Pritchett turned his gaze upon Asa Jacobs and opined that the man had at least the statutory one-eighth African blood fraction in him. Without further ado, Jacobs was convicted and promptly ap-pealed.

---

[28] 51 N.C. 284.

[29] Idem.

The Supreme Court of North Carolina, Justice J. Battle presiding, filled several pages with its sole reason for upholding the conviction. Justice Battle explained (citing numerous precedents) that, since Blackstone's day, courts had accepted expert testimony in cases where special scientific training was necessary. Identifying the "true race" of someone who looked European was clearly beyond the skill of an ordinary layman, hence an expert had been needed and, "Pritchett, proved, in the present case, that he possessed the necessary qualification, to testify as such."[30]

Although *State v. Asa Jacobs* clearly came down in favor of invisible Blackness, it was still one step away from the eventual end-manifestation of the U.S. one-drop rule. The North Carolina statute then in effect defined someone with less than one full-blooded African great-grandparent as White, and the ruling paid lip service to this definition. In practice a one-drop rule had triumphed, but the prosecution's rhetoric was based on the defendant having a measurable fraction of recent African ancestry. They had simply interpreted the blood-fraction statute in the light of a physical appearance rule—a traditional approach.[31] That Asa Jacobs's Black physical appearance could be found only on the eye of the "expert witness" meant that the one-drop rule had been upheld *de facto* for the first time in a slave state's supreme court. And yet, by applying a rhetoric (specious though it may appear to modern eyes) that conservatively supported the traditional combination of written blood-fraction statute and unwritten rule of physical appearance, Justice Battle had preserved the older rules *de juris*. As we shall see later, the first time that an appeals court in the South openly and explicitly upheld the one-drop rule of invisible Blackness based on infinitesimal or mere rumored ancestry would be in the inheritance case, *Scott v. Raubb*, 1892 Virginia.[32]

---

[30] Idem.

[31] For details of this tradition, see the topic "Physical Appearance, Blood Fraction, Association" in *Chapter 9. How the Law Decided if You Were Black or White: The Early 1800s.*

[32] 88 Va. 721.

Virginia Rejects the One-Drop Rule

The clash between blood fraction and physical appearance rules and the Not-a-Negro Law continued to consume Virginia legislative time for another decade and a half. In 1849, the legislature widened the scope of the Not-a-Negro law to read that "any free person of mixed blood" could apply for a local court certificate that they were neither negroes nor mulattoes and so exempt from anti-Black laws.[33] This was apparently an attempt to broaden the law's scope to include those of ambiguous ancestry. But this change redirected John Murdaugh's original law to addressing merely whether people were subject to the anti-Black codes and away from considering whether they were White or not. The new law seemed to accomplish the worst of both alternatives. On the one hand, it was seen by European-looking Virginians of slight African ancestry as inadequately defending their rights to membership in the White endogamous group, as guaranteed by the 1785 blood-fraction law. On the other, it was seen by many ancestrally White Virginians as opening the door of Whiteness to African-looking people.

In December, 1853, delegate Travis H. Epes moved to solve the dilemma by adopting a true one-drop rule. He asked that Virginia change the definition of the endogamous color line to define as "Black" anyone "who may be known or proven to have negro blood in them." The public promptly chose sides in the ensuing debate over codifying the newfangled one-drop rule of invisible Blackness into written statutes.

A Richmond editor claimed in December of 1853 that Virginians wanted, "no such conflict between law and society" as in the 1785 blood-fraction law then in effect. "The present [1785 blood-fraction] law encourages amalgamation," he wrote. "The blood of the Caucasian cannot continue pure and undefiled while the law compels a fellowship with negroes."[34]

---

[33] Joshua D. Rothman, *Notorious in the Neighborhood: Sex and Families Across the Color Line in Virginia, 1787-1861* (Chapel Hill, 2003), 230.

[34] *Richmond Enquirer*, December 31, 1853 as quoted in Ira Berlin, *Slaves Without Masters: The Free Negro in the Antebellum South* (New York, 1974), 366.

The following week, a Charlottesville editor wrote, "What is a negro? White and black made a mulatto. Mulatto and white made a quadroon. Quadroon and white made a mustee. And, by law, mustee and white made a white." But, the editor continued, how could one make a white person out of a negro? If one looked closely, one could always detect "black and curly hair, nails dark and ill-shaped, feet badly formed, and much of the negroes [sic] propensities."[35]

In response, a person signing himself as "a lawyer" wrote that no law could ever make any practical difference in terms of social relations between the two endogamous groups. He pointed out that any rule of legal Whiteness was meaningless as long as social Whiteness was based upon having no visible Black ancestry:

> It is not likely that a person having the physical organization
> of the negro would gain admission to a fashionable party
> with or without his [Not-a-Negro law] certificate [regardless
> legal Whiteness], unless he should go without invitation to a
> mask-ball; and the exhibition of such a certificate would cer-
> tainly exclude or expel him thence. [36]

And the idea that a legal Whiteness definition based on blood fraction encouraged miscegenation was ludicrous:

> The process of *amalgamation* [emphasis in original] will not
> be more apt to be resorted to by any one because he knows
> that his progeny in the third, or even in the second genera-
> tion, may be able to get a certificate that they are not ne-
> groes.[37]

The most perceptive letter to the editor, however, was undoubtedly the one written a month later:

> [If a one-drop rule were adopted], I doubt not, if many who
> are reputed to be white, and are in fact so, do not in a very
> short time find themselves instead of being elevated, reduced

---

[35] *Richmond Enquirer*, January 3, 1854 as quoted in Berlin (1974), 365-56.

[36] *Richmond Enquirer*, January 3, 1854 as quoted in Rothman (2003), 236.

[37] Idem.

by the judgment of a court of competent jurisdiction, to the level of a free negro.[38]

This last letter effectively ended the debate. It finally dawned upon Virginia's legislators of 1853, that a strictly enforced one-drop rule would tar even the highest elite Tidewater families with the same brush. Epps's bill was quietly tabled and died when the session closed in March of 1854.[39]

As discussed later, this very point was echoed two generations later when South Carolina went through a similar debate, with a similar sudden realization and a similar result.[40] The one-drop rule can be accepted only by a public that is either: ignorantly confident that it has no African ancestry (as in the 1830s North), or one that has forgotten its own genealogy (as in the Jim Crow South). Virginians in 1854 well knew that they had grandparents who either had been, or had known someone who had been, accepted into the White side of the endogamous color line despite a touch of African ancestry. And so they could not bring themselves to pass such a law. Another three generations would have to pass before White Southerners forgot enough about their own heritage to swallow the one-drop rule.

* * * * *

This chapter explained why color line determination became more important after the Nat Turner incident. It described a moderately unsuccessful "Not-a-Negro Law" meant to help some Virginians avoid oppressive anti-Black laws. It revealed the steady north-to-south spread of the one-drop rule as reflected in appeals court cases. It described the nation's first attempt to write a one-drop law—an attempt that was abandoned when its consequences were grasped.

---

[38] *Richmond Enquirer*, February 24, 1854 as quoted in Rothman (2003), 230.

[39] Rothman (2003), 231.

[40] See the topic "South Carolina" in *Chapter 19. The One-Drop Rule in the Postbellum Lower South*.

Chapter 18.
The One-Drop Rule in
The Postbellum North and
Upper South

In 1893, Anna D. Van Houten of Seattle was divorced from her husband, moved to Boston and married Asa P. Morse. Mr. Morse soon learned that his new bride had a trace of African ancestry. He sought a divorce on the grounds that her neglecting to inform him of this fact before the nuptials constituted fraud and voided the marriage contract. In *Van Houten v. Morse*, 1894 Massachusetts, she counter-sued for breach of contract. At trial, the judge instructed the jury that, as a matter of law, Anna had been under no obligation to reveal everything in her past to her betrothed, and that mere reticence regarding her Black ancestry was not fraud. They pronounced a verdict in her favor.[1]

Asa Morse appealed on the grounds that the judge's instructions were improper. According to him, during their brief courtship Anna had described her parents to him as "both of the best white families in Charleston, South Carolina." She had shown him photographs of her parents, her sister, and her sister's children. Once having volunteered information about her parents, she was obligated to tell the whole story—that, although

---

[1] 162 Mass. 414.

they looked White, they were "really" Black. Her telling only part of the truth was fraudulent, he concluded.

On November 30, 1894, The Supreme Judicial Court of Massachusetts, justices Field, Allen, Morton, and Barker presiding, unanimously overturned the lower court's decision and dissolved the marriage.[2] Their ruling referred to Anna's family photographs, which had been introduced as evidence. According the justices, the photographs sustained Asa's claim of fraud precisely because they showed a typical European-looking family with no trace of African appearance.[3]

Van Houten v. Morse is of interest, not merely because it shows a one-drop rule being fully enforced at every judicial level in 1894 Massachusetts. By then, as previously shown, Northern courts had been exclusively following the one-drop rule for over two decades.[4] The case is interesting because both litigants were evidently telling the truth as they saw it. South Carolina, where Anna was from, would not abandon its class-based rule of endogamous color-line determination until the following year.[5] And even then, "Pitchfork" Ben Tillman's Re-

---

[2] The judges also gave other reasons for their decision. Anna had also neglected to tell her new husband that her previous husband had charged her with, "being a woman of violent and ungovernable temper, and of jealous, revengeful, and vicious disposition, and with having, within two weeks after their marriage, commenced a systematic course of violent, abusive, and cruel conduct towards him, which finally broke down his health, and compelled him to leave her; [that she had been charged] with assaulting him with a carving-knife, and with using profane epithets in regard to himself, his relatives and friends, and alleged numerous specific acts of violence and passion." Nevertheless, what interests this study is only Anna's invisible Blackness.

[3] Judging by the evidence presented in court, Anna's parents had less African genetic admixture than, say, Carol Channing. See Carol Channing, *Just Lucky I Guess: A Memoir of Sorts* (New York, 2002).

[4] See the figure "Number of Cases per Decade by Region" under the topic "Graphs and Charts" in *Chapter 15. The Invention of the One-Drop Rule in the 1830s North.*

[5] For the legal precedents that established a class-based color line in South Carolina, see the topic "The Rule of Socioeconomic Class" in *Chapter 10. Barbadian South Carolina: A Class-Based Color Line*, especially *State v. Cantey* 1835 South Carolina (2 Hill 614).

demptionist South Carolina Constitution of 1895 would adopt a one-eighth blood fraction, not one-drop. Hence, even after the adoption of a constitution that disenfranchised South Carolina's entire Black endogamous group, Anna's family would continue to vote as Whites back home in Charleston.[6] The case presents the curious spectacle of a genetically European woman who was legally Black in Boston, but whose parents were legally White in Charleston. This chapter and the next investigate how such a discrepancy came about.

* * * * *

This chapter presents two topics. *Three Midwest Cases* shows that in the immediate aftermath of the war, the midwestern states were still adjusting to the impact of the new one-drop rule. *Three Upper South Cases* discusses the pivotal watershed case that established the one-drop rule as the law of the land in court precedent.

Three Midwest Cases

Three cases illustrate the postbellum Midwest's increasing acceptance of the one-drop rule: *People v. Dean*, 1866 Michigan, *Monroe v. Collins*, 1867 (Term) Ohio, and *People v. Board of Registration*, 1868 Michigan. In the first, one-drop was the basis of the trial court's verdict, although overturned on appeal. In the second, the legislature attempted to make the one-drop rule statutory, but the state's highest court ruled the law unconstitutional. In the third, a court ordered a local election board to at least consider allowing someone of slight African appearance to vote if he qualified by blood fraction.

The year after the Civil War ended, William Dean was arrested for having voted in Michigan.[7] He had a trace of African ancestry (less than one-sixteenth, according to subsequent testi-

---

[6] See the topic "South Carolina" in *Chapter 19. The One-Drop Rule in the Postbellum Lower South.*

[7] 14 Mich. 406.

mony). The Michigan State Constitution restricted the franchise to White male citizens, but it did not specify just what was meant by the term "White." At Dean's trial, *People v. Dean*, 1866 Michigan, the state's Attorney-General A. Williams testified that Michigan law had always interpreted "White" as meaning a person with no trace of African ancestry at all, even if invisible. Williams said that:

> In making [jury] lists, the practice throughout the state has ever been to exclude therefrom all persons known to possess any negro or African blood in their veins. ... [P]ersons known to be at all affected by possessing negro or African blood, have never been enrolled as a part of the military force of the state.... [I]n taking the census... persons having even one-sixteenth part of negro or African blood in their veins, have always been enumerated as 'colored persons' and not as white.... [P]ersons belonging to the white race have not intermarried with those known to have any negro or African blood in their veins.... [P]ersons known to have more or less negro or African blood in their veins, have uniformly been excluded from ordinary social and familiar intercourse with white persons... [T]he prejudice which has existed in the minds of the white people of this state towards our colored population... has extended to all known to have any African blood in their veins. Hence, our legislation, wherever it has been prejudicial, on account of color, was so framed as to almost always bring within its purview all such persons. And the same is more or less true of the ruling class throughout the United States.[8]

Attorney-General Williams continued in this fashion for another dozen or so examples, claiming that the one-drop rule of invisible Blackness had always been in effect in Michigan and, indeed, had been followed in every state for many decades.[9] Counsel for the defense, Knight & Jennison, Larned & Hebden, and H. M. Cheever, argued that precedents existed, within Michigan

---

[8] Idem.

[9] Projecting current attitudes into the past was and still is common in court cases. Apparently, it was not enough to argue that a precedent-setting innovation was just or beneficial; one was also expected to argue that it had always been in effect, and so it was really not an innovation at all.

and without, for an interpretation that legislatures intended "White" to denote someone with less than fifty percent African ancestry. Dean was convicted and he appealed.

On May 1, 1866, the Supreme Court of Michigan was asked to rule on just how the word "White" in the Constitution was to be interpreted. On July 11, 1866, justices Campbell, Christiancy, Cooley, and Martin ruled that, "persons are white within the meaning of our constitution, in whom white blood so far preponderates that they have less than one-fourth of African blood; and that no other persons of African descent can be so regarded," thereby overturning Dean's conviction.[10]

George W. Collins was a student at Wilberforce University living in Xenia, Ohio, when he attempted to vote in the 1868 presidential election (when Illinois Republican Ulysses Grant defeated New York Democrat Horatio Seymour[11]). Collins was prevented from voting by elections supervisors who were obeying two recently passed laws that effectively disfranchised anyone with "a visible admixture of African blood." In *Monroe v. Collins*, 1867 (Term) Ohio, he sued the board of electors, won, and the board appealed. The Supreme Court of Ohio, justices Welch, Day, White, Brinkerhoff, and Scott presiding, ruled in favor of the college student and declared that the two laws in question were unconstitutional.[12]

What makes *Monroe v. Collins* interesting is that it reveals an unusual reversal in the roles of legislature and judiciary in mid-century Ohio. Apparently, the nationwide outcry at the ex-

---

[10] Justice Martin dissented, arguing that anyone with less than one-half African ancestry was legally White. This case is exhaustively analyzed in Michael A. Elliott, "Telling the Difference: Nineteenth-Century Legal Narratives of Racial Taxonomy," *Law and Social Inquiry*, (1999), 611-36, 617-26, who concludes that Chief Justice James V. Campbell personally advocated neither appearance nor blood fraction as criteria of endogamous group determination. According to Elliott, Campbell finally opted for a one-fourth blood-fraction rule only because it approximated the underlying reality of "race" (as Campbell perceived it) more closely than the appearance-based alternative.

[11] Seymour had become famous seven years earlier for his impulsive public reaction upon hearing news of the South's secession: "Good riddance!"

[12] 17 Ohio St. 665.

pulsion of 1200-2000 members of the Black endogamous group from their homes in 1829 Cincinnati had caused a minor back-lash among Ohio's more tolerant Whites.[13] In 1849, Ohio's legis-lature repealed many of the harsher features of the state's Black Laws.[14] Nevertheless, increasing tolerance of the Black endoga-mous group went hand-in-hand with increasingly harsh demands that the color line be enforced.[15] Despite midwestern lawmakers' repeated attempts to legislate a one-drop rule of invisible Black-ness after the 1831 Nat Turner incident,[16] the Ohio Supreme Court held to a blood-fraction rule for the next forty years. The state constitution declared that certain citizenship rights, such as voting, were restricted to members of the White endogamous group. The issue in *Monroe v. Collins* was: numerically speak-ing, what was the blood fraction to be?

The Ohio legislature had become increasingly responsive to what they perceived as voter demands for a stricter rule of color-line positioning. According to the lawmakers, the courts' blood-fraction rule of legal Whiteness resulted in many people of "visible African admixture" being allowed to vote, contrary to the sprit of the constitution. To overcome the courts, the legisla-ture passed two laws on April 16 and 17, 1868, titled "An Act to Preserve the Purity of Elections." Rather than attempting to openly contest the courts, the statutes were couched in terms that simply "regulated" the voting process. In reality, they flatly dis-

---

[13] For a summary of the 1829 Cincinnati incident, see under the topic "The Origins of African-American Ethnicity" in *Chapter 13. The Color Line Created African-American Ethnicity in the North.*

[14] For a reference to the 1849 repeal of the Black Codes, see V. Jacque Voegeli, *Free But Not Equal: The Midwest and the Negro During the Civil War* (Chicago, 1967), 1.

[15] Many today imagine that "racial" tolerance (in the sense of granting civil rights to the darkest of Afro-Americans) must always go hand-in-hand with a softening of the color line (in the sense of accepting intermarriage with the lighter ones). In fact, the opposite has often been the case, especially before the twentieth century.

[16] See, for example, *Williams v. School District*, 1834 Ohio, Catterall (1968), 5:4, discussed under topic "Court Cases" in *Chapter 15. The Inven-tion of the One-Drop Rule in the 1830s North.*

franchised anyone with any visible African traits. As John Little, the student's attorney put it, the statute ruled that:

> Any challenging party may ask other questions than those prescribed, and call any number of witnesses to prove *disqualification*, but the challenged person is not authorized to ask any question or to call any witnesses to prove *qualification*. Any sort of evidence is admitted to prove a man is black, but the person challenged is restricted to impossible evidence almost, and, in many cases, quite impossible, to prove he is white. Heavy penalties are visited upon persons for procuring the right to vote, against this law, but no penalty is prescribed for thwarting the right of visible admixture electors. Judges are severely punished for *receiving* votes not lawful, but no penalty is prescribed for *rejecting* lawful votes. It is made perjury to *procure* the right to vote by *false swearing*, but it is not made perjury to *defeat* the right by *false swearing*.[17]

The state's supreme court was not persuaded by the law. Their unanimous decision ruled that you were on the White side of the endogamous color line if you had a "preponderance of White blood" (less than half African ancestry). In Ohio, at least with regards to voting rights, the critical blood fraction became one-half. The court wrote that:

> What the legislature cannot do directly it cannot do by indirection. If it has no power expressly to deny or take away the right, it has none to define it away, or unreasonably to abridge or impede its enjoyment by laws professing to be merely remedial. ... It is not only true that the act is calculated to impair and defeat the exercise of the colored man's constitutional right to vote, but any candid man must admit that such *seems* to be its *leading*, nay its *only* object. It *seems* to be a studied and cunningly devised *scheme* to effect that single object, to the utmost that it could be effected, without *expressly* and *directly* violating the constitution of the State. ... We therefore hold the act of April 16, 1868, with the

---

[17] 17 Ohio St. 665.

clause in the subsequent law referred to, to be unconstitutional and void.[18]

The third appearance-versus-blood-fraction voting rights case in the postbellum Midwest appeared simultaneously in Michigan. In that same 1868 presidential election, a man recorded as O.S. Wood attempted to vote in Michigan and was rejected. Wood had evidence, in the form of birth records, that he had less than one-fourth Negro blood and so was on the White side of the endogamous color line in accordance with the ruling of *People v. Dean*, two years before (see above). But the Board of Registration took one look at him and refused even to examine his documents, "holding that he had more than one-fourth negro blood" as was plain by his appearance. Wood sued for a writ of mandamus, which the state supreme court granted in *People v. Board of Registration*, 1868 Michigan, ordering the board to examine the man's blood-fraction evidence.[19]

Three Upper South Cases

Northern attitudes towards the endogamous color line rolled over the South after the war. Those tasked with educating former slaves, and backed up by military occupation, joined civilians eager to profit by commercial reconstruction. One of the Northern attitudes brought South was the one-drop rule. Whites and Blacks alike carried it southwards. Its spread can be traced in the court cases of the time. Three cases reveal the gradual abandonment of both appearance and blood fraction as rules of endogamous group membership in the Reconstruction upper South, and their replacement by the one-drop rule. They are *Smith v. Allbright*, 1873 Kentucky, *McPherson v. Commonwealth*, 1877 Virginia, and *Scott v. Raubb*, 1892 Virginia. In the first two cases, the one-drop rule determined the initial verdict, although the decisions were not upheld on appeal. The third case

---

[18] Idem.

[19] 17 Mich. 427.

is the earliest on record anywhere in the South that finally established the one-drop rule was as legal precedent.

At the start of the 1872-73 school year, James Smith tried to enroll his children in the District 34 public school in Rockcastle County, Kentucky. Smith was an accepted member of the White endogamous group, and his children looked completely European, as did their parents and grandparents. The school board refused to admit the children because, according to three of its members, they had heard it told that the Smith children's maternal grandmother was the offspring of a marriage between a White woman and a man of mixed race. In other words, they alleged that a rumor said that the Smith children had a single great-grandparent with some Negro blood. In *Smith v. Allbright*, 1873 Kentucky, Smith sued to compel the school board to admit his children. The Garrard Circuit Court ruled in favor of the school board. The case was overturned by the Court of Appeals of Kentucky on January 21, 1873, on the grounds that documentary evidence had shown that the children's grandmother was considered White in the community, and that this was disputed only by improperly admitted hearsay evidence.[20]

In examining the case of *Smith v. Allbright*, it is important to recognize that such children would have been legally White by law, in every former slave state at the time. Reconstruction Virginia held that you were placed on the Black side of the endogamous color line if your Black blood fraction was 1/4 or more. Florida, Georgia, Missouri, Kentucky, Maryland, Mississippi, and North Carolina, relegated to Blackness anyone with 1/8 or more Black blood. South Carolina, Alabama, and Louisiana went only by appearance and socioeconomic class although, as we have seen, appearance also counted even in the blood-fraction states. The Smith children were alleged to have less than 1/8 blood fraction, they were of a middle-class family, they associated solely with Whites, and they looked fully European. As Judge Pryor of the Court of Appeals put it:

> The children were produced in court and are shown from
> their own appearance to be white children. The record shows

---

[20] 6 Ky. Op. 376.

> that they are white children, and there was no reason so far as
> appears from the facts proven for excluding them from the
> privileges of this common school.[21]

Nevertheless, the Kentucky circuit court ruled them to be Black
due to the one-drop rule of invisible Blackness. The appeals
court remanded the case because hearsay testimony had been
improperly admitted, and not because the allegation claimed insufficient blood fraction to make the children statutorily non-
White. As far as this study has been able to tell, this was the first
upper South case where the initial verdict was based on the one-
drop rule (in defiance of a blood-fraction statute, in fact), although it was remanded for retrial on appeal.

In 1877, Virginians George Stewart and Rowena McPherson were charged, tried, and convicted of living in illicit intercourse. At trial, the evidence presented for their intercourse was
that they were openly married and living together as a married
couple. The illicit nature of their relationship was due to the allegation that George was on the White side of the endogamous
color line and Rowena was on the Black side. Rowena's Black
endogamous group membership was allegedly based on her maternal grandmother, a "brown skin woman." The prosecution
agreed that her other three grandparents were on the White side
of the endogamous color line. But, since her "brown skin"
grandparent was legally Black, then Rowena was one-fourth
Black. Hence, according to Virginia's 1785 blood fraction statute, she was Black as well.[22]

The couple appealed their conviction to the Supreme
Court of Virginia in *McPherson v. Commonwealth*, 1877. In
March of 1877, Justices Moncure, Christian, Staples, and Burks
unanimously concluded that Rowena's "brown skin" grandmother must have had a faint trace of White blood in her. If she

---

[21] Idem.

[22] 69 Va. 939. The prosecution in this cased used the same nonsensical re-
cursive logic expressed by Justice Ruffin in *State v. Whitmell Dempsey* 1849
North Carolina (31 N.C. 384) and ridiculed by Justice Parson in *Thurman v.
State* 1850 Alabama (18 Ala. 276), both discussed under the topic "Physical
Appearance, Blood Fraction, Association" in *Chapter 9. How the Law De-
cided if You Were Black or White: The Early 1800s.*

had been a person of one hundred percent African genetic admixture, they reasoned, she would have been black-skinned, not brown. Consequently, they ruled that Rowena McPherson was White because, "less than one-fourth of her blood is negro blood. If it be but one drop less, she is not a negro."[23]

Prophetic words, "one drop." As far as anyone has been able to determine, this case was the first time that those words appeared in an appellate decision as a way of validly determining a person's endogamous group membership.[24] The irony is that they decided that a woman of Afro-European genetic admixture was White. Also, according to the record, *McPherson v. Commonwealth* was the last time that an upper South one-drop verdict would be overturned on appeal in order to uphold a blood-fraction statute.

The one-drop rule became the Upper South's standard fifteen years later, in *Scott v. Raubb*, 1892 Virginia. The case is important but complicated. It is important because it is the first upper South court case on record that was argued, decided, and upheld on appeal on the basis of a one-drop rule of invisible Blackness.[25] It was the first. The case is complicated because it entangles issues of slavery, manumission, emancipation, blood fraction, intermarriage, and inheritance.[26]

Jesse Scott was a freeborn member of antebellum Virginia's Black endogamous group, despite having less than the statutory one-fourth fraction of Negro ancestry. He owned slaves and farmland in Albemarle County. He worked the land with his sons Robert and James (also considered Black despite their less than one-fourth blood fraction). In 1861, as the Civil War was

---

[23] 69 Va. 939.

[24] Recall that the words "one drop," in the sense of Black ancestry, first appeared in an 1829 Colonization Society publication, referring to a visible mark that infallibly betrays Black blood (see under the topic "Other Voices" in *Chapter 16. Why Did Northerners Invent a One-Drop Rule?* The words first appeared in a court decision, as object of ridicule, in *Thurman v. State* 1850 Alabama (18 Ala. 276).

[25] The first in the North may have been the public school segregation case *Draper v. Cambridge*, 1863 Indiana, 20 Ind. 268.

[26] 88 Va. 721.

being fought nearby, Jesse assigned one of his female slaves, named Ann Settles, to household duty. Like her owners, Ann also had less than one-fourth "Negro blood." Young Master James and Ann promptly fell in love.

With his father's (her owner's) permission, the slave and the young master set up housekeeping as man and wife. The following year, as Lee was defeating McClellan in the Peninsula, the couple had a European-looking daughter whom they named Sarah E. Scott. Two years later, as Grant was defeating Lee at Petersburg, Ann died, leaving the toddler to be raised by her father. According to later testimony, "the child was retained in his house by James, and recognized as his child and reared to womanhood by him, and subsequently married a man named Raub [sic]."

When Jesse Scott died shortly after the war, his sons Robert and James split the farm between them and continued to work it. When James died intestate in 1888, his surviving brother, Robert, claimed James's half of the property in order to reunite the estate. Sarah E. Raubb, James's now-married daughter (Robert Scott's niece), contested this action, claiming her father's share of the farm as her own.

On October 19th, 1889, the Circuit Court of Albemarle County ruled in her favor and her uncle appealed the verdict. In order to make sense of the subsequent arguments, you must keep six points in mind. First, judging by the genetic testimony, everyone involved in this case had less than 25 percent African admixture; in other words, they probably all looked European.[27] Second, by the blood-fraction statute then in effect, every person involved was legally White. Third, everyone involved in the case self-identified socially as Black. Fourth, Sarah's mother, Ann, had been a slave before becoming the wife of Sarah's slave-owning father. Fifth, neither Ann's mid-war manumission, nor her marriage to James, had ever been formalized by paperwork. Sixth, a Reconstruction act decreed that emancipated slaves and previously manumitted free Blacks who had lived as husband

---

[27] At least as White as Dr. Shriver. See the photo in the topic "Admixture Scatter Diagrams" in *Chapter 2. Afro-European Genetic Admixture in the United States.*

and wife during slavery and continued to do so after the war, were to be considered legally married in every way. The case pivoted on the question of Sarah's legitimacy—were her parents ever legally married? One had been a slave, the other a slave-owner, both were socially Black but legally White, but were they married?

Sarah argued that, because her mother had been a slave and her father had been a free Black, their marriage had been legitimized by the Reconstruction act, despite the lack of wedding papers. Her Uncle Robert argued that the Reconstruction act did not apply because neither of Sarah's parents had ever been Black. They were both legally White, so they were never married, Sarah was illegitimate, and she could not inherit. Sarah countered that, although her mother was legally White, she had still been a slave thereby coming under the letter of the Reconstruction act. Her uncle countered that Ann had been a slave only until the instant when his father, old Jesse, had given his blessing to her marriage to James, back in 1861, and that thenceforth she had been *de facto* free despite the lack of manumission papers, so the Reconstruction act's slave clause did not apply either.

In 1892, four years after her father's death, the Supreme Court of Virginia, Justice Lacy presiding, ruled in Sarah's favor with an argument that was both fair to Sarah and apparently just, but that would echo down the subsequent decades as having opened a door. Justice Lacy ruled that, for the purposes of marriage and inheritance, Virginia law was thenceforth to be interpreted as meaning that anyone with any known Black ancestry would be considered Black, no matter how tiny their blood fraction was. Hence, Sarah's parents were both Black, thus they came under the Reconstruction act, and so Sarah was legitimate and could inherit. For the first time in history, a Southerner (Sarah Raubb) was ruled to fall on the Black side of the endogamous color line, despite appearance, despite blood fraction, despite socioeconomic class, solely because of invisible African ancestry. This watershed event happened in 1892. It happened at the request of the individual herself.

*   *   *   *   *

This chapter presented three postbellum court cases showing that midwestern states in the immediate postbellum period
were still adjusting to the impact of the new one-drop rule, followed by three southern cases that saw the establishment of the
one-drop rule as the court-precedent law of the land.

Chapter 19.
The One-Drop Rule Arrives in the Postbellum Lower South

Ten days after Florida seceded, the state's Senators David Levy Yulee, and Junior Senator Stephen Mallory (both born and raised in the British West Indies) walked out of the U.S. Capitol in Washington to lead the Confederacy in a war to preserve slavery. Eyewitness Virginia Clay-Compton wrote of the sad event in her diary:

> One by one, Senators Yulee, Mallory, Clay, Fitzpatrick and Jefferson Davis rose, the emotion of their brother senators and of us in the galleries increased, women grew hysterical and waved their handkerchiefs...men wept and embraced each other mournfully,... scarcely a member of that Senatorial body but was pale with the terrible significance of the hour.[1]

Throughout the United States, sons and husbands went to war. Like countless other American families, the Osbornes of St. Augustine were torn between loyalty to their state and to their country. The Osborne family was of Hispanic heritage, light-

---

[1] As quoted by Celeste H. Kavanaugh, *David Levy Yulee: A Man and His Vision* (Fernandina FL, 1995) 27.

brown complexion, and middle-class status. They were listed as members of the White endogamous group in the 1850 and 1860 censuses. The father, Samuel Osborne was a shipwright. His elder son, Sam Jr., was a journeyman in his father's trade. His younger son, Manuel, was an apprentice who drilled once a month with the local militia unit, the St. Augustine Grays. When war broke out, the Grays were activated into the Third Florida Infantry, Company "A," and young Manuel marched off as a White solder to fight for the Confederacy.

A few months later, in March of 1862, a U.S. Army regiment under General David Hunter landed in St. Augustine and recruited for the Union. Samuel and his elder son joined the fight to end slavery. To the Yankee eyes of the U.S. Army, the two Osborne men looked Black, despite the family's census records. And so, the Army shipped them to X Corps HQ in Hilton Head, South Carolina, for basic training.[2] They were posted to the First South Carolina Volunteer Infantry (later renamed the 33rd US Colored Troops), and served as Black soldiers until war's end.

The divided brothers and father never met in battle. All survived and they reconciled after the war. Manuel moved to Ft. Lauderdale, then retired back home to St. Augustine. All three men received military pensions; two from the U.S. Army, one from the former Confederate State of Florida. Manuel's name appears prominently in the town's muster roll of heroes who wore gray; the Confederacy saw him as White. His father and brother, who wore blue, only recently received recognition from the city; the Union saw them as Black. During Reconstruction, an avalanche of well-meaning Northerners buried Florida's lower South culture. The 1870 and 1880 censuses list the entire Osborne family as "Negroes."[3] Times were changing and the color line was shifting in the direction of the one-drop rule.

---

[2] For a similar account of differences in the perception of "racial" feature between Northerners and lower Southerners, see the diary of General Joshua Lawrence Chamberlain, of Little Round Top fame as mentioned under topic "A Permeable, Shifted Color Line" in *Chapter 10. Barbadian South Carolina: A Class-Based Color Line.*

[3] Most of the Osborne family's story is reported in Jaqueline K. Fretwell, *Civil War Times in St. Augustine* (St. Augustine, 1986), 96. Their census

*   *   *   *   *

This chapter presents three topics. *Florida and Georgia* shows two societies in transition. At mid-century, Florida was still in the process of adopting an endogamous color line. By Reconstruction, one was firmly in place and moving towards invisible Blackness. Similarly, the color line in Tidewater Georgia hardened between 1860 and 1880, but had not yet become a one-drop rule. *Louisiana* describes a post-war struggle between the old aristocracy, who strove unsuccessfully to preserve their biracial French culture and, on the other hand, an alliance of Yankee occupiers and Anglo-American Louisianans who crushed Colored Creole society out of existence by merging it with freed Blacks. *South Carolina* depicts a third society in transition. It describes the nation's second attempt to write a one-drop law. The second attempt, like the first in 1853 Virginia, failed when lawmakers realized that it would penalize elite White South Carolina families.

Florida and Georgia

Two biographical vignettes and a court case show that color-line attitudes in Florida and Georgia had also begun to change around mid-century. The court case is *Dillon v. Dillon*, 1878 Georgia. The biographical vignettes are about the two candidates for the U.S. Senate from Florida in 1845.

As discussed earlier, Andrew Jackson undermined Florida's biracial Spanish culture by flouting Article VI of the Adams-Oniz treaty that ceded Florida to the United States.[4] Some dark-complexioned members of Florida's genetically mixed population fled to Mexico or Cuba, some joined the maroons and became Seminoles, and others were accepted into main-

---

and tax records are available at the Research Library of the St. Augustine Historical Society.

[4] See the topic "Society Changed When the Americans Arrived" in *Chapter 12. Spanish Florida: No Endogamous Color Line.*

stream society as White Americans. Among those who successfully redefined themselves as White were both 1845 senatorial candidates, Joe Hernandez and David Levy.

José Mariano Hernandez's three plantations, San José, Malacompra, and Bella Vista, stretched along what is now Florida's highway A1A from Painter's Hill, just north of Flagler Beach, to Marineland.[5] His parents, Martin and Dorotea, had been among the original indentured servants of the New Smyrna Colony.[6] In September of 1822, President James Monroe appointed Hernandez as Florida's first territorial representative. He took his seat in the Seventeenth U.S. Congress at the age of thirty-five. In his six-month term, Hernandez accomplished two projects. First, he persuaded the president and Congress to repeal Jackson's discriminatory laws as they applied to light-complexioned Hispanic Floridians.[7] Second, he persuaded them to uphold Jackson's disfranchisement of free Blacks, Seminoles,

---

[5] Charlton W. Tebeau, *A History of Florida* (Coral Gables FL, 1971) 160, 163-64; Michael V. Gannon, ed. *The New History of Florida* (Gainesville, 1996) 210-11; Alfred J. Hanna, *A Prince in Their Midst: The Adventurous Life of Achille Murat on the American Frontier* (Norman OK, 1946) 82, 86.

[6] In 1768, several hundred bondsmen and women from the Balearic Islands, southern Italy, Sicily, Africa, and Greece had been brought to work indigo plantations in New Smyrna by Scotsman planter Andrew Turnbull. In a rare example of successful servile insurrection, they had fled the plantations during the chaos of the American Revolution and migrated to St. Augustine. By 1821, the "Minorcans" (as they are still called today, despite their genetic diversity) had become yeomen, shopkeepers, tradesmen, and professionals. A few, like Hernandez, had become wealthy planters. See Carita Doggett, *Dr. Andrew Turnbull and The New Smyrna Colony of Florida* (Eustis FL, 1919); United States Congress, *Biographical Directory of the United States Congress, 1774-1989* (Washington, 1989); Kathryn Hall Proby, *Audubon in Florida* (Coral Gables FL, 1974), 60; Daniel L. Schafer, "U.S. Territory and State," in *The New History of Florida*, ed. Michael V. Gannon (Gainesville, 1996), 207-30, 210-11; Philip D. Rasico, *The Minorcans of Florida: Their History, Language, and Culture* (New Smyrna Beach, 1990), 80; Alfred J. Hanna and Kathryn A. Hanna, *Florida's Golden Sands* (Indianapolis, 1950), 59; Alfred J. Hanna, *A Prince in Their Midst: The Adventurous Life of Achille Murat on the American Frontier* (Norman OK, 1946), 82.

[7] Kathryn Abbey Hanna, *Florida: Land of Change* (Chapel Hill, 1941), 146-47.

former slaves, and the descendants of runaways.[8] One might plausibly suspect that these were a *quid pro quo*. In order to save his own people, the Minorcans of St. Augustine, Hernandez may have thought it necessary to throw to the wolves those who were poorer and darker yet.

On February 19, 1823, Congressman Hernandez asked the chairman of the House Committee on Indian Affairs to remove the Seminoles to a reservation between Ocala and Tampa Bay.[9] He wrote that, consequent to their decimation by invading Americans from 1811 to 1818, the Seminoles "being thus broken up have continued ever since, without the least Kind of Spirit of industry or enterprize, [sic]—they could at one time have been considered as having arrived at the First Stage Civilization." But now, he concluded, they had degenerated to uselessness.[10] On February 21, Congress agreed and ordered the Seminoles to a reservation "south of Charlotte's River."[11] This resulted in the 1823 Treaty of Moultrie Creek, which ordered the Seminoles moved to a four-million-acre reservation between Ocala and Tampa, thus starting the chain of events that led to the Seminole trail of tears, over a decade later.[12]

In the fall of 1835, President Jackson ordered the U.S. Army to take the dark Seminoles into custody, return them to slavery, and deport the light-skinned ones to Oklahoma. The Seminoles did not accept their fate supinely. Jackson's order triggered what historian Larry Rivers calls "the largest slave rebellion in U.S. history."[13] Like other New World maroon communities, the Seminoles (a corruption of *cimarrones*, Spanish for

---

[8] John A Clegg, *The History of Flagler County* (Bunnell FL, 1976), 26 .

[9] George Klos, "Blacks and the Seminole Removal Debate," in *The African American Heritage of Florida*, ed. David R. Colburn and Jane L. Landers (Gainesville, 1995), 128-56, 153.

[10] John K. Mahon, *History of the Second Seminole War 1835-1842*, revised ed. (Gainesville, 1985), 30.

[11] Ibid., 39.

[12] Clegg (1976), 26.

[13] Larry Eugene Rivers, *Slavery in Florida: Territorial Days to Emancipation* (Gainesville, 2000), 13.

"runaways") are descendants of Europeans, Africans, and Native Americans who fled slavery generations ago. Culturally, they still consider themselves Native Americans and speak either Mikasuki or Muskogee.[14] On Christmas Day, Seminoles and their allies attacked San José, Malacompra, Bella Vista, and the other plantations owned by the anti-Seminole faction. Anglo-American militia under Hernandez (now a U.S. general) retaliated by attacking Bulowville, Carrickfergus, Rosetta and the other plantations owned by Seminole supporters.

The conflict became the longest, bloodiest, and costliest interracial war in U.S. history. It was waged, if any war can be said to have a single cause, in order to enforce the endogamous color line. In 1817 and again in 1823, the U.S. Army had offered peace if the Seminoles would give up their Negroes. Tribal leaders insisted that no Negroes lived among them—just dark Seminoles.[15] For ten years, U.S. troops pursued the Seminoles, trying to split Black from Indian in a culture that lacked the very concept of "race." As Major General Thomas Sidney Jesup wrote in 1836, "This... is a negro, not an Indian war."[16] In 1837, General Joe Hernandez thought he had won by capturing the enemy commanding general Asi-Yahola (nowadays known as "Osceola"), a man of Scottish descent. Hernandez had lured him into an ambush under a sham flag of truce.[17] But instead of surrendering, the Seminoles fought on. Seven years later, when Colonel William Worth finally announced that, "hostilities with the Indians within this Territory have ceased," two thousand U.S. soldiers and the same number of Seminole soldiers had lost their lives.[18] Dark-skinned families who had lived free for generations were "returned to slavery." Light-skinned Seminoles were deported to

---

[14] John K. Mahon and Brent R. Weisman, "Florida's Seminole and Miccosukee Peoples," in *The New History of Florida*, ed. Michael Gannon (Gainesville, 1996), 183-206.

[15] Kenneth W. Porter, *The Black Seminoles* (Gainesville, 1996) 19, 28.

[16] Ibid., 67.

[17] Ibid., 82-85.

[18] As quoted in Frank Laumer, *Dade's Last Command* (Gainesville, 1995), 241-43.

Oklahoma. A few hundred Seminole families refused to be torn apart, abandoned their homes and farms and fled deep into the Everglades.[19]

Throughout ten years of war, Hernandez demonstrated his loyalty and his adopted Anglo-American culture. By the time it was over, he had been fully accepted into the White side of the endogamous color line despite his parents' ancestry as members of the group once known as "Turnbull's niggers."[20] His sons went to the best private schools.[21] By 1845, he had become an influential Whig politician.

David Levy descended from Sephardic Jews in Africa. Centuries earlier, the Ladino-speaking Levy family had been expelled by Spain's Inquisition and joined the Sephardic Diaspora that enriched Mediterranean art, commerce, and politics for hundreds of years. They rose in Ottoman civil service. In 1776, Moses Levy's father, Jacob, was the *Yulee* of Morocco, the grand vizier or chief advisor to the king. A palace revolution drove the Levy family to flee to Gibraltar.[22] Young Moses sought his fortune in St. Thomas, Virgin Islands and married there. He entered a business partnership with another Sephardic Jew, Philip Benjamin. The Levy's son, David, was born in 1810. The Benjamin's son, Judah, was born the following year and the two boys became friends. Moses Levy moved to Cuba in 1816 and became wealthy as commissary supplies contractor to the Spanish Army in Havana. Anticipating Florida's transfer to the United States, he bought 60,000 acres of Florida land in 1818. He took up Florida residence in July 1821, thereby becoming a U.S. citizen. A few years later, David Levy was admitted to Harvard. His childhood friend, Judah Benjamin, simultaneously went to Yale.

---

[19] Idem.

[20] See the topic "Society Changed When the Americans Arrived" in *Chapter 12. Spanish Florida: No Endogamous Color Line*.

[21] See, for example, José Mariano Hernandez, "Hernandez to Hallowell," (1843).

[22] Daniel L. Schafer, "U.S. Territory and State," in *The New History of Florida*, ed. Michael V. Gannon (Gainesville, 1996), 207-30 221; Alfred J. Hanna and Kathryn A. Hanna, *Florida's Golden Sands* (Indianapolis, 1950) 130.

When David Levy graduated from college, he became a Presbyterian, a politician, and a businessman. He built a huge sugar cane plantation near Cedar Key and the county was named after him—Levy County. In 1841, he became Florida's territorial delegate to the US Congress, like Hernandez before him, and changed his surname by adopting his grandfather's old title, "Yulee." The arrival in Congress of a swarthy, multi-cultural, African Jew did not sit well with everyone. His election prompted New England's John Quincy Adams to sniff:

> Levy is said to be a Jew, and what will be, if true, a far more formidable disqualification, that he has a dash of African *blood* [italics mine] in him, which sub rosa, is the case with more than one member of the house.[23]

Adams's words reveal two points. First, Levy's "dash of African blood" was common knowledge. Second, since slight African ancestry was "the case with more than one member of the house," it was surely not a "formidable disqualification" in most people's minds. John Quincy Adams and other Northerners may have been horrified, but it was obviously not a problem with Levy's electorate or with other members of Congress from the lower South.

Levy served on the committee that wrote Florida's constitution. Together with Whig Governor Richard Keith Call, he spent the next five years leading the drive for Florida's statehood. In 1845, Congress accepted Florida as the twenty-seventh state (Iowa was the balancing free state). Levy (Democrat) and Hernandez (Whig) ran against each other for the state's first U.S. Senate seat.[24] Levy won and Hernandez retired to Cuba.[25]

Even at mid-century, as the upper South was in the process of considering the one-drop rule which had been invented in the North 20 years earlier, Florida was still struggling to imple-

---

[23] From Adams's famous diary, as quoted by Celeste H. Kavanaugh, *David Levy Yulee: A Man and His Vision* (Fernandina FL, 1995) 10.

[24] Alfred J. Hanna and Kathryn A. Hanna, *Florida's Golden Sands* (Indianapolis, 1950) 130.

[25] John K. Mahon, *History of the Second Seminole War 1835-1842*, revised ed. (Gainesville, 1985) 99.

ment the endogamous color line itself. The voters accepted both senatorial candidates as White even though both possessed widely known African ancestry.

The first stirrings of the one-drop rule in Florida appeared during Reconstruction when, as narrated in this chapter's opening anecdote, light-brown Hispanic soldiers who were White when they fought for the Confederacy, became re-defined as Black by occupying Northerners in the war's aftermath.

The hardening of the color line in late nineteenth-century Georgia is also evident. In 1877, Rachel Dillon (born Rachel Black) of Savannah divorced her husband of twenty years and sued for alimony and child support in *Dillon v. Dillon*, 1878 Georgia. According to the testimony of her neighbors, the Dillon couple and their children were well liked in the neighborhood. Until the sudden divorce, the marriage had been considered a model in the community.[26]

The community knew that Rachel had a touch of African ancestry, but they considered her White nonetheless. When they were newlyweds, Mr. Dillon had shown his love for his new bride by obtaining a special act from the Georgia general assembly publicly declaring that Rachel was legally positioned on the White side of the endogamous color line. Although late antebellum Georgia resembled North Carolina in having a one-eighth blood-fraction statute, attitudes towards color line permeability in mid-century Savannah resembled the class-based rules in nearby Charleston, South Carolina.[27] Nevertheless, Mr. Dillon had realized in the chaotic pre-war decade, that times were changing and the endogamous color line was hardening. He had ensured his bride's future social standing in December of 1857 by obtaining an act of the state legislature that declared:

---

[26] 60 Ga. 204.

[27] For the generational permeability of tidewater Georgia's color line, see Mark R. Schultz, "Interracial Kinship Ties and the Emergence of a Rural Black Middle Class," in *Georgia in Black and White: Explorations in the Race Relations of a Southern State, 1865-1950*, ed. John C. Inscoe` (Athens GA, 1994), 141-72.

Whereas doubts have existed whether [Rachel Black], of the county of Chatham, is entitled to the rights and privileges of citizenship; and whereas satisfactory proof has been furnished to establish her said rights and privileges; and whereas it is just and proper that said doubts should be forever removed: Be it enacted, that from and after the passage of this act, the said (naming her as before) and her children (naming them) be, and they are hereby, declared to be severally entitled to all and singular, the rights and privileges of citizens of Georgia, and to be fully capable, each or any of them, of inheriting, holding and receiving all manner of property, real or personal, by bequest, deed, or in any other manner whatever.[28]

The record is silent as to why Mrs. Dillon divorced her husband, much less why the divorce came after two decades of apparently happy marriage. His defense, however, must have stunned the community. He claimed that Rachel had been Black all along and that, per the state's anti-intermarriage law, they had never been legally married, and so he would pay neither alimony nor child support.

The jury was asked to decide on five questions of fact: First, did Mr. Dillon procure the act of the legislature asserting his bride's Whiteness? Second, was Rachel Dillon (the plaintiff) the same person as Rachel Black (named in the act)? Third, assuming that Rachel Dillon had less than the one-eighth statutory blood fraction, was she legally Mr. Dillon's wife? Fourth, did she in fact have less than the statutory one-eighth blood fraction? Fifth, if the Rachel were found to be non-White due to having more than the statutory one-eighth blood fraction, then was her marriage valid anyway?[29]

The jury quickly decided in the affirmative for every question but the fourth. The marriage was valid if she had less than one-eighth Negro blood, the marriage was also valid if she

---

[28] 60 Ga. 204.

[29] To a modern reader, point five seems to be a question of law, not fact, but this is the way that it was framed. Apparently, the distinction between issues of law (the judge's turf) versus fact (the jury's) was not always as clear-cut in the late nineteenth century as it is today.

had more than one-eighth Negro blood, and it was Mr. Dillon himself who had her Whiteness enacted by the legislature. But the jury could not reach a verdict on the fourth point (Rachel's actual blood fraction). They considered the question irrelevant in light of their findings on the other four. The court ordered the defendant to pay alimony and child support.

The lack of a jury decision on Mrs. Dillon's actual blood fraction was the basis for Mr. Dillon's appeal. In January of 1878, the Supreme Court of Georgia, Judge Bleckley presiding, upheld the decision with a pedagogical essay on the legal principle of *estoppel*, ruling that Mr. Dillon should never have been allowed to testify in court as to his wife's "race" because, twenty years earlier, he had sworn under oath that she was White. In sum, Mr. Dillon had correctly foreseen in 1857 that the color line would become harsher in coming decades. As it turned out, he was one of the first to try to take advantage of the new one-drop rule when his marriage collapsed.

Louisiana

As discussed earlier, mid-century Louisiana was also under pressure to change from Franco-American to Anglo-American customs, especially regarding the status of the in-between endogamous group, the Colored Creoles.[30] Slowly, the English-speaking immigrants had their way. They passed a succession of laws restricting the rights of free Blacks (limiting marriage, travel, firearms, property ownership, judicial standing, education, and so forth). In the early years, such anti-Black laws explicitly exempted the Colored endogamous group. By 1843, the Colored group was no longer named as legislative special case, but they still considered themselves exempt, and the courts still usually upheld their special status. Numerous court cases held that the Colored Creoles were not considered Black regard-

---

[30] See the topic "French-Speaking Louisiana" in *Chapter 11. Antebellum Louisiana and Alabama: Two Color Lines, Three Endogamous Groups.*

ing freedom papers, curfews, and the like.[31] But by the 1850s, the courts had begun to treat all but the wealthiest and most powerful Colored Creoles as free Blacks.[32]

The Colored Creole community began to split into two groups. Light-complexioned ones urged their darker relatives to emigrate. Those who were too dark to prosper under American rule (and who lacked the wealth to stay anyway) began to leave. Two groups went to Haiti shortly before 1850. In 1857, two shiploads went to Tampico. Another ship left for Vera Cruz a few months later. In one parish alone, the number of Colored Creoles too dark to pass into the White world fell from 351 in 1855, to 153 in 1860.[33]

In 1850, one Colored Creole in three owned at least $2,000 in real estate (about $100,000 in today's money).[34] But by 1860, only two groups of Colored Creoles remained. First, were those with such fair complexions that they were accepted as White, despite French accents. Pierre Gustave Toutant Beauregard was of this kind. Short, courtly and light-skinned, he was born in 1818 to a prosperous family of St. Bernard Parish.[35] Second, were those who were so wealthy that their darkness was politely ignored. Examples of this swarthy-but-rich kind included Aristide Mary, who owned real estate valued at $30,000 ($1,500,000 in today's money) and Antoine Dubuclet, a sugar planter with over 100 slaves who became state treasurer after the war.[36]

---

[31] Judith Kelleher Schafer, *Becoming Free, Remaining Free: Manumission and Enslavement in New Orleans, 1846-1862* (Baton Rouge, 2003), 97-98.

[32] Virginia Meacham Gould, "The Free Creoles of Color of the Antebellum Gulf Ports of Mobile and Pensacola: A Struggle for the Middle Ground," in *Creoles of Color of the Gulf South*, ed. James H. Dormon (Knoxville, 1996), 28-50, 44.

[33] Ibid., 45-46.

[34] Loren Schweninger, "Socioeconomic Dynamics among the Gulf Creoles," in *Creoles of Color of the Gulf South*, ed. James H. Dormon (Knoxville, 1996) 54.

[35] John S. Bowman, ed. *Who was Who in the Civil War* (New York, 1994), 21-22.

[36] Gould (1996), 28-50, 46.

At the war's outbreak, the Colored Creoles owned property worth $2 million ($100 million in today's money), and their working class still dominated such skilled crafts as bricklaying, cigarmaking, carpentry, and shoemaking.[37] When the shooting started, a substantial majority of Colored Creoles formed up their traditional militia units on behalf of the Confederacy.[38] Light complexioned ones were accepted. West Point graduate P.G.T. Beauregard of St. Bernard Parish became a Confederate general. But the Confederacy did not accept free Blacks in combat roles, so most Colored Creoles were turned away. Nevertheless, as in Brazil or Cuba today, money whitened. Even dark-complexioned Creoles could escape the free Black label if they had enough money. Jean-Baptiste Pierre-Auguste, Charles Lutz, and Leufroy Pierre-Auguste of St. Landry's Parish joined the Confederate army as combat soldiers. They saw action at Shiloh, Fredericksburg, and Vicksburg."[39]

As the war ground on to its conclusion, wealthy Colored Creoles adopted a certain noblesse oblige towards the Black freedmen. As officers, they had once commanded their own slaves in the state militia. Now they expected to resume a position of power. In 1864 they were horrified to learn that, far from granting them suffrage, the Union occupation forces under General Nathaniel Banks restricted their movement and civil rights, treating them as if they were freedmen themselves. In numbers, they dominated the New Orleans Equal Rights League of 1865, but found their political power hampered by the language barrier. English, it seems, had become the language of politics.[40]

The tension between the Colored Creoles and the Black freedmen became evident even as the war was ending. The Colored Creole-backed *New Orleans Tribune* supported the idea that the elite should lead and the freedmen should follow. The com-

---

[37] Eric Foner, *Reconstruction: America's Unfinished Revolution* (New York, 1988), 47.

[38] James G. Hollandsworth, *The Louisiana Native Guards: The Black Military Experience During the Civil War* (Baton Rouge, 1995), 1-20.

[39] Schweninger (1996), 60.

[40] Foner (1988), 64-65.

peting liberal newspaper, the *Black Republican*, editorialized that "We all know that not one in a hundred of our brethren on the plantations would ever receive his just earnings if the [Colored] planter were left to himself." During postwar Reconstruction, many Colored Creoles refused to send their children to school with former slaves. Although this may have been due to language difference, it exacerbated tension between them and the freedmen, and this led to a self-perceived distinction between Colored Creoles and freedmen politicians. During the Constitutional Convention, a freedman delegate vowed that he did not intend "to have the whip of slavery cracked over us by no [Colored] slaveholder's son."[41]

They joined a three-way struggle for power, trying to wrest political control from Black freedmen and Black Yankees. According to the *New Orleans Tribune*, they were subject to "innumerable petty antagonisms," and prey to scheming [Black Yankee] carpetbaggers who took "advantage of the apparent jealousy existing between free colored people and freedmen to assert political leadership among rural blacks." The *Tribune's* editor, spokesman of the "old free population" insisted that only the Colored Creoles had the education and breeding to rule. Reconstruction's shaky start and premature collapse in Louisiana was, in part, due to the Colored Creoles' difficulty in making common cause with the Black freedmen—a difficulty exacerbated by their French-English language barrier.[42]

The Colored Creoles did not gracefully join common cause with their former slaves—they were gradually pushed into it by Northern attitudes towards the color line. They found themselves compelled to defend newly won Black rights, like it or not. "The civil rights struggle was waged, for the most part, by the [Creole] elite. The issue had little meaning for the freedmen-

---

[41] Ibid., 65, 101, 113.

[42] Ibid., 306; John David Smith, *Black Voices From Reconstruction* (Gainesville, 1997), 93.

farmers whose life-style precluded dinner at hotels or first-class seats on trains."[43]

In 1864, General Nathaniel Banks of the occupying U.S. Army in New Orleans tried one last time to preserve the Jamaica-like class-based alliance between the White and Colored endogamous groups on the one hand, against the free Blacks and newly freed former slaves on the other. Lincoln had asked Banks to satisfy the Abolitionist Congress while at the same time cultivating a single color line (rather than Louisiana's traditional two lines) separating only two endogamous groups (rather than the traditional three). Banks secured the agreement of a Louisiana federal judge named Durrell to rule that anyone with "a major part of white blood, should possess all the rights of a white man."[44] But the attempt failed before the solidarity that was growing between former biracial slave-owners and their former slaves. "As far as the law is concerned," declared the *Mobile Nationalist*, "the [Colored] Creole and freedman stand upon the same level.... They must, in the future, rise or fall together."[45] Many dark-skinned freeborn Colored Creoles realized that their future was in the hands of Yankees, Black and White. They refused to dissociate themselves from the freedmen because the freedmen were the only source of political power still open to them. Banks's plan failed. As Banks put it, "a few men, who wanted to break the bundle of sticks without loosening the band, defeated [the plan]."[46]

The splitting of Louisiana's Colored Creole families into Black and White branches accelerated after the war. Ultimately, the problem was the evaporation of the Coloured/Black color line and the hardening of the White/Colored color line. It was

[43] Dorothy Sterling, ed. *The Trouble They Seen: The Story of Reconstruction in the Words of African Americans* (New York, 1994), 239; Foner (1988), 285.

[44] Nathaniel Prentiss Banks, "Report to the President," *Appletons Annual Cyclopaedia and Register of Important Events*, 1864, 480-1.

[45] As quoted in Foner (1988), 215.

[46] Ibid., 480. For a slightly garbled account of these events, see Lerone Bennett Jr., *Forced Into Glory: Abraham Lincoln's White Dream* (Chicago, 1999), 620.

becoming increasingly accepted among all English-speaking Americans, Yankees and Rebels alike, Blacks and Whites alike, that anyone of any discernable African descent was a member of the endogamous Black group.[47] (Contrast this with post-emancipation Jamaica, where the beleaguered White population allied with the Mulatto elite to keep down the free Blacks.) And so, Anglo-American attitudes forced light-complexioned Creoles to pass into the White world, like it or not. And dark-complexioned Creoles were pushed into the ranks of Black freedmen—again, like it or not. As Judith Schafer put it, "Little did they know that emancipation would lower their status, as whites increasingly lumped freed slaves and former free people of color together as one large and highly objectionable part of the state's population."[48]

Two cases show Louisiana in transition: *Walsh v. Lallande*, 1873 and *Succession of Fortier*, 1899. Charles Lallande was a member of Louisiana's Colored Creole endogamous group. His paternal grandparents were Spanish and Native American, his maternal grandparents were French and African, and all had been born free. He had homesteaded a tract of federally owned land in Pointe Coupee Parish, Louisiana on December 31, 1844 and had "been in quiet possession of the property" ever since. On November 14, 1860, an *ex parte* proceeding by the commissioner of the U.S. general land office ordered the cancellation of Lallande's homestead on the ground that he was a free Negro, and so could not be a citizen of the United States. The land was then awarded to a person on the White side of the White/Colored color line, William Walsh, who, in 1866, obtained a ruling from the U.S. Secretary of the Interior dispossessing Lallande on the same grounds. Lallande refused to vacate his homestead, Walsh sued and won a court order removing Lallande. The court grounded its decision on the U.S. Supreme Court ruling in *Scott v. Sandford*, 1857, that Negros could not be

---

[47] Adam Fairclough, *Race & Democracy: The Civil Rights Struggle in Louisiana, 1915-1972* (Athens, 1995), 5.

[48] Judith Kelleher Schafer, *Becoming Free, Remaining Free: Manumission and Enslavement in New Orleans, 1846-1862* (Baton Rouge, 2003), 165.

U.S. citizens.[49] Lallande appealed the order to the Louisiana Supreme Court in *Walsh v. Lallande*, 1873 Louisiana, justices Ludeling, Taliaferro, Wyly, and Morgan presiding.[50]

In March, 1873, the state supreme court overturned the lower court and awarded the property back to Charles Lallande. They ruled that *gens de couleur libre* had been citizens of Louisiana "in the full enjoyment of those rights [of citizenship]" since long before the Dred Scott case, which was inapplicable in any event. According to the Louisiana Supreme Court, the Dred Scott decision, "was that a negro of African descent, whose ancestors were of pure African blood, and were brought into this country and sold as negro slaves, was not a citizen." But, according to the Louisiana justices, Charles Lallande and those of his Colored Creole endogamous group were not "free Negroes." They were Colored, not Black, and so they were not subject to laws regarding free Negroes. In fact, the justices unanimously ruled, "by the treaty whereby Louisiana was acquired, the free colored inhabitants of Louisiana were admitted to citizenship of the United States." In an interesting moment of historical irony, Redemptionist Louisiana's highest court held that the Reconstruction federal government could not revoke a Colored person's citizenship. Curiously, everyone involved in the case— litigants as well as judges—pointedly ignored the fourteenth amendment to the U.S. Constitution, which had been ratified on July 9, 1868, guaranteeing national as well as state citizenship to all native-born residents.[51]

---

[49] 60 U.S. 393.

[50] 25 La. Ann. 188.

[51] To put this point in context, Louisiana at the time was in the throes of what can only be called an intrastate civil war. Even as the *Walsh v. Lallande* decision was being announced, The First Battle of the Cabildo (5 March 1873) was being fought, when all-White state troops loyal to Democrat governor-elect John McEnery were defeated by integrated soldiers of the Metropolitan Police, loyal to Republican governor-elect William Pitt Kellogg. One year later, The White League triumphed and captured the state when their all-White forces used artillery to crush the integrated state militia under former Confederate General James Longstreet in the Battle of Liberty Place (14 September 1874). Apparently, the federal Constitution was not in the forefront of Louisianians' minds at this time. For a summary of the mili-

The first lower South case arguably decided by the one-drop rule upheld on appeal happened twenty-six years later. It was the estate dispute, *Succession of Fortier*, 1899 Louisiana.[52] "Angela Fortier, widow of Placide Bienvenu, died in the city of New Orleans on the 8th of April, 1896." So begins the court record of a turn-of-the-twentieth-century case, which reveals that a one-drop rule was starting to be applied in New Orleans at that time. Angela was at least 80 years old when she died intestate and childless. But shortly after the Parish of New Orleans took possession of her estate, a niece named Delphine Fortier, who was at least 60 years old, appeared on the scene and claimed possession as Angela's sole surviving blood kin.

Testimony would show that, three years after the Louisiana Purchase, Jean Michel Fortier, an influential member of New Orleans's White endogamous group and director of the Bank of Louisiana established a *plaçage* relationship with Marguerette Henriette Milon, a woman of the Colored endogamous group.[53] They lived as husband and wife for thirty years, he dying in 1836 and she in 1838. They left a son, Edmond Gustave Fortier, who was accepted into the White side of the White/Colored color line and a daughter, Angela Fortier (the woman after whom this case is named), who lived her life as a member of the Colored group.

Edmond Gustave Fortier, like his father, also established a long-term monogamous *plaçage* relationship. He and Caroline Delzey, a Colored woman, lived as husband and wife for nearly forty years and had a daughter, Delphine (Angela's niece). In

---

tary events of these years, see Kimberly S. Hanger, *A Medley of Cultures: Louisiana History at the Cabildo* (New Orleans, 1996a), Chapter 9.

[52] 51 La. Ann. 1562.

[53] Although usually described as concubinage where White men took Colored mistresses, the custom of *plaçage* provided legally enforceable rights for the woman. It was unrelated to endogamous group membership *per se*, but is an aspect of the French upper class. As Susanne Heine puts it, "The latest public figure known to have pursued this way of living was the late Prime Minister, Mitterand, whose parallel family came to light only after his death." See Interracial Voice, *Politically Correct Revisionism: Or Why Mixed-Race Heroes Blacken Over Time*, March/April [Electronic Magazine] (2002).

1862, Edmond Gustave was on his deathbed. The priest who was summoned to administer the Sacrament of Extreme Unction said that Edmond's sins could not be absolved as long as he and Caroline remained unmarried in the eyes of the Church. Witnesses were assembled and the elderly couple was wed just hours before Gustave perished. Over thirty years later, their now-elderly daughter Delphine fought the Parish of New Orleans over her Aunt Angela's estate.

Everyone agreed that Delphine was the late Aunt Angela's next of kin. The issue was whether Delphine was legitimate. It seems that by 1862, when Delphine's dying father married her mother, it was illegal in Louisiana to marry across the Colored/White color line.[54] (It had been illegal since 1808 to marry across the Black/Colored color line.[55]) The state argued that, since Gustave was White and Caroline was Colored, the deathbed wedding was illegal, their daughter Delphine was illegitimate, and could not inherit her Colored Aunt Angela's estate. Delphine argued that her father had been White only by courtesy because his mother (Delphine's paternal grandmother) had been Colored. According to Delphine, when the deathbed wedding took place the entire Fortier family (except for long-departed bank director Jean Michel) had actually been Colored.[56]

On June 19, 1899, The Supreme Court of Louisiana, Justices Nicholls and Watkins presiding, ruled that Edmond Gustave had been Colored all along, despite his having lived his life as an accepted member of White society. The court ruled that the deathbed wedding was thus valid, and that Delphine could claim her aunt's estate. Neither appearance nor blood fraction was cited in making this determination. Appearance seems to have been disregarded because the entire family looked European, as far as anyone can tell from the testimony. Blood fraction seems to have been disregarded because Louisiana's Constitution of

---

[54] H. E. Sterkx, *The Free Negro in Ante-Bellum Louisiana* (Cranbury NJ, 1972), 285-315 passim.

[55] Louisiana Code of 1808, page 24, Article 8.

[56] Many witnesses phrased their testimony as if endogamous group membership were biologically determined, rather than socially assigned.

1892 had just changed the statutory definition from one-fourth (like Virginia) to one-eighth (like North Carolina) and, although Edmond Gustave was clearly White by either criterion, the point was never raised in court by either side.[57] Like *Scott v. Raubb*, 1892 Virginia, *Succession of Fortier*, 1899 Louisiana was apparently decided on the basis of the one-drop rule of invisible Blackness. And like *Scott v. Raubb* the one-drop rule was invoked at the request of the individual herself, wanting to be declared non-White so that she could inherit a non-White ancestor's estate.

South Carolina

At war's end, South Carolina's Mulatto elite quickly moved to seize power. Across the South, only one fourth of the delegates of Reconstruction constitutional conventions were of the Black endogamous group. In South Carolina they were in the majority—seventy-six out of 124.[58]

At first, they were decidedly ambiguous about the future role of freedmen, their former slaves and inferiors. The conflict was felt in all social institutions. In 1866, Rev. Henry M. Turner wrote about his parishioners, "the blacks were arrayed against the brown or mulattoes, and the mulattoes in turn against the blacks."[59] The educated Mulatto elite found freedmen's religious

---

[57] Some scholars suggest that a later case—*State v. Treadaway*, 1910 Louisiana, 126 La. 300—was more important in the rise of the one-drop rule. See, for example, *Luther Wright, Jr.*, "Who's Black, Who's White, and Who Cares: Reconceptualizing the United States's Definition of Race and Racial Classifications," *Vanderbilt Law Review*, 48 (no. 2, 1995), 513-70, 528-29 and Virginia R. Dominguez, *White by Definition: Social Classification in Creole Louisiana* (New Brunswick NJ, 1986), 30-33. For a contemporary account of Louisiana's switch from 1/4 to 1/8 blood fraction, see *Succession of Gabisso*, 1907 Louisiana, 119 La. 704.

[58] Thomas Holt, *Black Over White: Negro Political Leadership in South Carolina During Reconstruction* (Urbana, 1977), 57; Dorothy Sterling, ed. *The Trouble They Seen: The Story of Reconstruction in the Words of African Americans* (New York, 1994), 123.

[59] Eric Foner, *Reconstruction: America's Unfinished Revolution* (New York, 1988), 101.

practices alien and were appalled by the anti-intellectualism of freedmen leaders.[60] Although many welcomed slavery's end, most resented their loss of status and felt, correctly, that they were being submerged in a sea of freedmen. Most "avoided politics either because their business commitments took precedence, or so as not to jeopardize the personal connections with wealthy whites on which their economic standing depended."[61]

There were exceptional leaders, however, and their influence soon became decisive. Francis L. Cardozo, the son of a Jewish businessman and a free biracial mother, had attended the University of Glasgow and in 1865 took charge of the American Missionary Association's largest Charleston school. He made no distinction between freeborn and freed children and ridiculed the elitist idea that biracial children were more intelligent than African-looking ones. His influence was strong. Soon, the sons and daughters of elite South Carolina Mulatto families fanned out across the state to teach former slaves, a mission closed to the Louisiana Creoles, trapped behind their language barrier. Many South Carolina Mulattos then gained political power among working class freedmen and were elected as Constitutional Convention delegates and later as state legislators. Despite a few initial clashes between freedmen and the Mulatto elite, the latter soon came to throw their lot in with the former, as in Louisiana.[62]

Things were different for White planters, even those with slight African ancestry. Attitudes changed after Reconstruction, when South Carolina's color line hardened and its well-deserved reputation for color line permeability began to dwindle. By the custom of a dying past, such planters were still accepted as White. Then, South Carolina legislators explicitly debated the

---

[60] Ibid., 361.

[61] Leon F. Litwack, *Been in the Storm So Long: The Aftermath of Slavery* (New York, 1979), 513-14.

[62] Thomas Holt, *Black Over White: Negro Political Leadership in South Carolina During Reconstruction* (Urbana, 1977), 58; Joel Williamson, *After Slavery: The Negro in South Carolina During Reconstruction, 1861-77* (Chapel Hill, 1965), 313; Foner (1988), 102, 318-19; John David Smith, *Black Voices From Reconstruction* (Gainesville, 1997) 94, 109.

endogamous color line in the Constitutional Convention of 1895. The convention was called through the power and influence of "Pitchfork" Ben Tillman with the specific goal of disenfranchising South Carolina's entire Black endogamous group.[63] Among influential White delegates (including some of slight African ancestry) were: John Gay Evans, John Laurens Manning Irby, George Dionysius Tillman (Pitchfork Ben's brother), and John Pendleton Kennedy Bryan. Among the Black delegates (including some of significant European ancestry) were: Robert Smalls,[64] Thomas E. Miller, William J. Whipper, James Wigg, and Isiah R. Reed, from Beaufort; and Robert B, Anderson from Georgetown.[65]

The White delegates (including those with slight African ancestry) proposed to insert a prohibition of marriage across the Black/White color line into the new constitution.[66] Since the prohibition was ostensibly intended to protect "racial" purity, Robert Smalls proposed an amendment that any White person guilty of cohabiting with a Negro be barred from holding public office. The uproar that this caused prompted James Wigg to crow that, for once, "the coons had the dogs up a tree."[67] Smalls followed up by proposing that "all white men now cohabiting with Negro women be disbarred from voting in this convention." He was gaveled down when a White member replied that "if the

---

[63] George Brown Tindall, *South Carolina Negroes, 1877-1900* (Columbia, 1952), 81-91; Holt (1977), 220. "Pitchfork" Ben Tillman is probably best remembered as the politician who, upon hearing that President Roosevelt had dined with Booker T. Washington at the White House in October 1901, said, "Now we will have to kill a thousand niggers to get them back in their place."

[64] Smalls was a famous Civil War hero, best-known for having captured a Confederate ship in 1862 and delivering it to the U.S. Navy. A year later, he was commissioned a ship's captain in the U.S. Navy.

[65] Tindall (1952), 81.

[66] Ibid., 298.

[67] News and Courier, "The Miscegenation Matter," *The News and Courier*, Oct. 4 1895b, 1.

amendment should prevail... this convention would have to be adjourned *sine die* for lack of a quorum."[68]

Once the intermarriage prohibition was passed, a discussion ensued as to the definition of a "negro." The original committee had proposed a one-eighth blood-fraction rule, bringing South Carolina into line with North Carolina to the north and Georgia to the south. But now Mr. Johnstone, the young delegate from Newberry, proposed amending this to a one-drop rule of endogamous group membership. He proposed to forbid "marriage between a white person and a person having any negro blood at all in his or her veins." A hush settled over the White delegates and the Black delegates sat back to observe their discomfort.[69] It was an eerie re-play of the Virginia debates of 1853.[70]

"Pitchfork" Ben rose and tried to persuade Johnstone to withdraw his motion. Johnstone was adamant. Another delegate spoke quietly to Johnstone privately, to no avail. George Dionysius Tillman realized that such a definition would relocate many valued White citizens to the Black side of the endogamous color line. Perceiving the injustice of this proposal as well as its threat to White supremacy, and foreseeing that it could socially rip his state apart, he rose to his feet and gave the best-remembered speech of his political career:

> If the law is made as it now stands respectable families in Aiken, Barnwell, Colleton, and Orangeburg will be denied the right to intermarry among people with whom they are now associated and identified. At least one hundred families would be affected to my knowledge. They have sent good soldiers to the Confederate Army, and are now landowners and taxpayers. Those men served creditably, and it would be unjust and disgraceful to embarrass them in this way. It is a scientific fact that there is not one full-blooded Caucasian on

---

[68] Theodore D. Jervey, *The Slave Trade: Slavery and Color* (Columbia, 1925), 196-200.

[69] News and Courier, "The Miscegenation Matter," *The News and Courier*, Oct. 4 1895b, 1.

[70] See the topic "Virginia Rejects the One-Drop Rule" in *Chapter 17. The Antebellum South Rejects the One-Drop Rule.*

the floor of this convention. Every member has in him a certain mixture of... colored blood. The pure-blooded white has needed and received a certain infusion of darker blood to give him readiness and purpose. It would be a cruel injustice and the source of endless litigation, of scandal, horror, feud, and bloodshed to undertake to annul or forbid marriage for a remote, perhaps obsolete trace of Negro blood. The doors would be open to scandal, malice and greed; to statements on the witness stand that the father or grandfather or grandmother had said that A or B had Negro blood in their veins. Any man who is half a man would be ready to blow up half the world with dynamite to prevent or avenge attacks upon the honor of his mother in the legitimacy or purity of the blood of his father.[71]

The *Charleston News and Courier* reported the above speech under the headline "All Niggers, More or Less!" What is interesting to this study is that the Black delegates did not see the one-drop rule of invisible Blackness as a threat. By definition, such an endogamous group membership rule could affect only those who were middle class, looked European, and had no documented blood fraction. It was apparently a matter of indifference to the Black delegates—a White-on-White squabble. Only the White delegates saw it as a threat.

Two generations earlier, Virginia had gone through a similar debate, with a similar sudden realization, and a similar result.[72] One more generation would have to pass before White Southerners forgot enough about their own heritage to swallow the one-drop rule.

---

[71] The speech is quoted in Joel Williamson, *New People: Miscegenation and Mulattoes in the United States* (New York, 1980) 93; Lerone Bennett Jr., *Before the Mayflower: A History of Black America*, 6th rev. ed. (New York, 1993) 319; J.A. Rogers, *Sex and Race*, 3 vols. (St. Petersburg, Fla.: Helga M. Rogers, 1944) II:367-70; and Theodore D. Jervey, *The Slave Trade: Slavery and Color* (Columbia: The State Company, 1925) 199. See News and Courier, "All Niggers, More or Less!," *The News and Courier*, Oct. 17 1895a, 5 for the full-length original.

[72] See the topic "Virginia Rejects the One-Drop Rule" in *Chapter 17. The Antebellum South Rejects the One-Drop Rule.*

* * * * *

This chapter showed three societies in transition. At mid-century, Florida was still in the process of adopting an endogamous color line, but one was firmly in place and moving towards invisible Blackness by Reconstruction. The color line in Tidewater Georgia hardened between 1860 and 1880, but had not yet become a one-drop rule. *Louisiana* was the site of a struggle between the old aristocracy, who strove unsuccessfully to preserve their biracial French culture, and an alliance of Yankee occupiers and Anglo-American Louisianans who crushed Colored Creole society out of existence by merging it with freed Blacks. Finally, South Carolina lawmakers tried to write a one-drop law. This second attempt, like the first in 1853 Virginia, failed when the lawmakers realized that it would penalize elite White South Carolina families.

Chapter 20.
Jim Crow Triumph of the One-Drop Rule

In the 1913-1914 school year, three children, wards of G.W. Tucker, were expelled from the Dalcho, South Carolina, public school on the ground that their family surname (Kirby) was rumored to be of Croatan[1] origin. Tucker appealed to the state Board of Education and was turned down. He appealed to the South Carolina Supreme Court in *Tucker v. Blease*, 1914 South Carolina.[2]

Inspection of the record suggests that the case was not even arguable. The state's constitution was clear. As set by Ben Tillman's 1895 Constitutional Convention, it defined endogamous group membership via a one-eighth blood-fraction rule.[3] The school segregation statute was equally clear. It did not contain any rule determining whether a child was Black, but relied

---

[1] *Croatan* was the pre-1953 name of a maroon community centered in Robeson County, North Carolina. In 1953, the Croatans renamed themselves "Lumbee Indians." For details, see topic "The Maroon Escape Hatch" in *Chapter 5. The Rate of Black-to-White "Passing."* The most common Lumbee surnames are "Locklear" and "Goins."

[2] 97 S.C. 303.

[3] For details, see under the topic "South Carolina" in *Chapter 19. The One-Drop Rule in the Postbellum Lower South.*

on the constitution. The trial testimony was clear. No witness testified that the Kirby children had any Black ancestry at all, much less one-eighth.

The witnesses who wanted the children defined as Black argued only that the "Kirby" surname reminded people of the Croatans, a maroon community who were said to have Negro blood. They testified that all of the decent White people in Dalcho would withdraw their own children from public school, put them cruelly to work plowing the fields, and condemn them to illiteracy if the Kirby children were allowed to attend the White school.

On April 21 of 1914, Chief Justice Gary rendered a decision that consigned the Kirby children to the Black side of the endogamous color line. He apparently felt that he had no choice:

> While the testimony shows that the children are entitled to be classed as white, nevertheless the action of the board of trustees was neither capricious nor arbitrary.... The testimony also shows that the decided majority of the patrons would refuse to send their children to the Dalcho school if the Kirby children were allowed to continue in attendance. Tested by the maxim, "The greatest good to the largest number," it would seem to be far better that the children in question should be segregated than that the large majority of the children attending that school should be denied educational advantages.[4]

Although no allegation was ever made that the Kirby children were anything other than of pure European ancestry, South Carolina's highest court decreed them and their descendants to be Black by public demand.[5]

* * * * *

---

[4] 97 S.C. 303.

[5] For an antebellum case of a family legislatively decreed to be White by popular demand, see the case of the Whartons under the topic "Nat Turner Sealed Virginia's Color Line" in *Chapter 17. The Antebellum South Rejects the One-Drop Rule.*

The early decades of the twentieth century, especially the years from 1900 to 1919, saw the triumph of the one-drop rule throughout America. Americans of European appearance, culture, and genetic admixture had sometimes been assigned to the Black endogamous group in earlier decades. Indeed, the notion of invisible Blackness started in the North and worked its way into the upper South slave states during the crisis decade of the 1850s, spreading to the lower South after Reconstruction. But no prior progress can compare to the explosion in its court usage between 1900 and 1919. During these years, a dozen states adopted statutory endogamous group membership based on "one drop." A dozen other states retained blood fraction statutes *de jure* but amended them to such tiny fractions that they were one-drop *de facto*. In yet other states, judges and juries ignored their own states' statutes or constitutions in order to assign to the Black group anyone with relatives or social connections in the Black group.

As mentioned earlier, some use the term "one-drop rule" as synonymous with Marvin Harris's term "hypodescent," meaning that Americans of visible African admixture are considered Black, even if that admixture is less than 50 percent.[6] The present work focuses only upon the most extreme form of one-drop—the idea that Americans who look completely European, without even a hint of Africa, are still classified as members of the Black endogamous group. They are seen as unsuitable marriage partners by Whites but suitable by Blacks because of an invisible touch (one drop) of Black ancestry.

This chapter examines, in four topics, the events of those decades that gave rise to the notions of endogamous group membership that are still in force today. *Terminology Changed* shows that the word "Colored," no longer denoted an intermediate group in the Franco-American culture of the Gulf Coast but became a polite euphemism for any member of the Black endogamous group anywhere. *White Children Consigned to Blackness* shows that, by far, the strictest enforcement of the one-drop rule in these years was for school segregation, not intermarriage.

---

[6] See footnote 3 of *Chapter 1. Introduction.*

White Adults Challenged to Defend Their Whiteness offers a slight viewpoint shift to reveal that the one-drop rule did not affect Blacks at all—it targeted only Whites. *African-American Complicity* shows that far from resisting or challenging the one-drop rule, members of the African-American ethnic community, especially its leadership, embraced and enforced it from their side of the color line, as they had in the late antebellum North, as they continue to do today.

Terminology Changed

During this period, the word "Colored," as used in court, no longer denoted a member of the intermediate endogamous group within the Franco-American culture of the Gulf Coast. Instead, it became a polite euphemism for any member of the Black endogamous group anywhere. Three cases show the shift in word meaning: one in North Carolina, two in Louisiana.

Ferrall v. Ferrall, **1910 North Carolina.** In November of 1907, Frank S. Ferrall of Franklin County, North Carolina, filed for divorce from Susie Patterson Ferrall and refused to pay alimony or child support because he had recently learned that his wife "was and is of negro descent within the third generation." (The state constitution in effect, Part 1, Section 2083, forbade "All marriages between a white person and ... a person of negro or Indian descent to the third generation inclusive"—a one-eighth blood fraction rule.) Evidence presented at the trial of *Ferrall v. Ferrall*, 1910 North Carolina showed that Susie did in fact have a great-grandfather, named Julius Coley, who was of mixed ancestry. The trial centered on whether the one-eighth definition of "negro" meant that the great-grandfather in question had to be of one hundred percent African genetic admixture in order to consign Susie to the Black side of the endogamous color line or whether the great-grandfather's mixed ancestry sufficed. If the former, as in the case of *McPherson v. Commonwealth*, 1877 Virginia, then she was White.[7] If the latter recur-

---

[7] 69 Va. 939. See under the topic "Three Upper South Cases" in *Chapter 18. The One-Drop Rule in The Postbellum North and Upper South.*

sive definition applied, as in *State v. Whitmell Dempsey*, 1849 North Carolina, then she was Black.[8] The jury found that the woman was a member of the White endogamous group, but County Judge Cooke set aside the verdict and ruled to the contrary.

Susie Ferrall appealed and, on October 12 of 1910, the Supreme Court of North Carolina unanimously reversed the lower court's decision, Justices Hoke and Clark presiding.[9] Although the plaintiff had cited *State v. Treadaway*[10] in favor of one-drop, Justice Hoke stuck with the one-eighth blood fraction rule still in effect in North Carolina. His opinion cited several cases, including *State v. William Chavers*, 1857 North Carolina,[11] *McPherson v. Commonwealth*, 1877 Virginia, and *Wall v. Oyster*, 1910 District of Columbia,[12] to the effect that any blood fraction rule had to be based on the most recent ancestor of one hundred percent African genetic admixture, not on an ancestor with mixed blood. To do otherwise would be irresolvable. He also refuted the plaintiff's contention that what determined whether the great-grandfather, Julius Coley, was legally a Negro was his acceptance into society, stating:

> We may not approve the position earnestly insisted upon by plaintiff's counsel that the negro ancestor, whose blood must determine the issue, should be considered not a negro of pure African blood, but one who has his status as a negro ascertained and fixed by the recognition and general consensus of the community where his lot is cast. Such a position ignores the ordinary and usual acceptation of the words, "Of negro

---

[8] 31 N.C. 384. See under the topic "Physical Appearance, Blood Fraction, Association" in *Chapter 9. How the Law Decided if You Were Black or White: The Early 1800s.*

[9] 153 N.C. 174.

[10] 126 La. 300.

[11] 50 N.C. 11. See under the topic "Transitional Cases" in *Chapter 17. The Antebellum South Rejects the One-Drop Rule.*

[12] 36 App. D.C. 50. For details, see under the topic "White Children Consigned to Blackness," in this chapter.

descent to the third generation inclusive" [and] is contrary, as
stated, to a long line of authoritative precedents.[13]

In short, the rule of association did not trump the rule of blood
fraction in 1910 North Carolina. Interestingly, this was one of
the last color-line-determination cases ever held in the United
States that employed anything other than a one-drop rule (until
affirmative action litigation resurrected the rule of association).
Incidentally, assuming that her great-grandfather was of 50-50
Euro-African genetic admixture, Susie Ferrall had less of Africa
in her than do millions of White Americans.[14]

Lee v. New Orleans Great Northern RR, 1910 Louisiana. The earliest case explicitly to define "colored" as synonymous with "negro" was *Lee v. New Orleans Great Northern RR*,
1910 Louisiana. In 1909, a conductor of the New Orleans Great
Northern Railroad forcibly ejected two unaccompanied minors,
Edith and Belle Lee respectively 14 and 16 years old, from a
Whites-only railroad train eight miles before their destination
because he insisted that they were "colored." The girls' parents
sued for damages. They lost at trial and, on January 31 of 1910,
they lost on appeal to the Supreme Court of Louisiana.[15] In his
decision, Justice Land explained that times had changed. "One
hundred years ago, in the territory of Orleans, the term 'persons
of color' was used to designate people who were neither white
nor black," he wrote, citing *Adelle v. Beauregard*, 1810 Louisiana.[16] He acknowledged that, despite a brief interruption just
before the Civil War,[17] Colored/White intermarriage had been

---

[13] 153 N.C. 174.

[14] See *Chapter 2. Afro-European Genetic Admixture in the United States.*

[15] 125 La. 236.

[16] 1 Mart o.s. 183. See under the topic "French-Speaking Louisiana" in
*Chapter 11. Antebellum Louisiana and Alabama: Two Color Lines, Three
Endogamous Groups.* This was the case that established the Louisiana
precedent that members of the Colored endogamous group were not Black
in the eyes of the law, nor vice-versa.

[17] As presented under topic "Louisiana" in *Chapter 19. The One-Drop Rule
in the Postbellum Lower South,* the late antebellum enforcement of the letter
of Article 8 of the Louisiana Code of 1808 (enforcement demanded by Arti-

accepted in Louisiana since colonial times, "but by Act No. 54, p. 63, of 1894, marriages between white persons and persons of color were again prohibited. By Act No. 87 of 1908 concubinage between a person of the Caucasian or white race and a person of the negro or black race was made a felony."

He further explained that the transportation segregation statute, "Act No. 111 of 1890 draws a sharp line of distinction, without a margin, between the white and colored races in the matter of separate accommodations on railroad trains." Justice Land explained that:

> The [antebellum] lawmaker never applied the term "colored" to slaves, but since emancipation that term has been used as synonymous with negro. Among slaves the word "negro" or "nigger" was considered as a term of reproach, and they usually spoke of themselves as "colored." This nomenclature has survived, and has become a popular term, embracing all persons of negro blood.

Justice Land understood that, in order to sustain their case, the Lee children would have had to prove that they had no Negro ancestry at all, however distant. He understood that proving such a negative was impossible, but he wrote anyway:

> The petition charges the defendant company with the violation of a penal statute, and the burden of proof was on the plaintiff to establish the essential facts necessary for a recovery of the damages claimed, to wit, that his children belonged to the white race, and were unlawfully assigned to a coach or compartment set apart for colored persons. One who charges another with a culpable breach of duty must prove the fact, though it involves a negative.[18]

He concluded that whether the Lee children had one drop of Negro blood was solely a matter for the jury to decide, and that they had decided against the children. As precedent, he cited

---

cle 95 of the Code of 1825) led to Louisiana's first one-drop rule case, *Succession of Fortier*, 1899 Louisiana, 51 La. Ann. 1562.

[18] 125 La. 236.

White v. Tax Collector, 1836 South Carolina.[19] Incidentally, according to the record, both of the children's parents, Sam Lee and his wife, were White.

State v. Treadaway, 1910 Louisiana. Octave Treadaway of New Orleans and his plaçage mistress were charged with violating the law in *State v. Treadaway*, 1910 Louisiana. He was a member of the White endogamous group. She was a member of the intermediate Colored group. Two years earlier, in 1908, the State of Louisiana had adopted Act 87 declaring that:

> Concubinage between a person of the Caucasian or white race and a person of the negro or black race is hereby made a felony, and whoever shall be convicted thereof in any court of competent jurisdiction shall for each offense be sentenced to imprisonment at the discretion of the court for a term of not less than one month nor more than one year with or without hard labor.[20]

The couple was acquitted at trial on the grounds that the woman was Colored, and not "negro or black." The prosecutor appealed, saying that the words "colored" and "black" were synonyms. The woman admitted to being an octoroon,[21] so she was "black" by definition, he said.

In a decision handed down on April 25 of 1910, the Supreme Court of Louisiana upheld the acquittal. Justice Provosty wrote the opinion, which focused on the semantics of the statute. Did its words "negro or black" mean the same thing as "colored"? In answer, Justice Provosty cited approximately 213 pre-

---

[19] *White v. Tax Collector* 1836 South Carolina (3 Richardson 136), Catterall (1968) 2:400, was one of several antebellum South Carolina cases that decided whether someone with a touch of African ancestry had been accepted into South Carolina's White endogamous group by the rules of association and socioeconomic class. In *White v Tax Collector*, (as in *State v. Davis*, 1831 and *State v. Hanna,*, 1831, but in contrast to *State v. Cantey*, 1835, which went the other way), the South Carolina court decided that a person had not satisfied the rule of association despite passing the rule of socioeconomic class. For details, see the topic "The Rule of Socioeconomic Class" in *Chapter 10. Barbadian South Carolina: A Class-Based Color Line*.

[20] 126 La. 300.

[21] Presumably, someone of one-eight African genetic admixture.

vious court cases, 24 other states' statutory definitions (including North Carolina, Alabama, Florida, Maryland, South Carolina, Tennessee, Georgia, Mississippi, West Virginia, Virginia, Kentucky, Missouri, Arkansas, Texas, New York, Massachusetts, Indiana, Ohio, Arizona, Nebraska, Nevada, Illinois, Montana, Michigan), 7 dictionaries (including Webster's International, Century, A. & E. E. of Law, Webster's Thompson and Thompson, Standard), and 4 encyclopedias (Cyclopedia of Knowledge, Zell's Encyclopaedia, Britannica, Americanized Britannica) to conclude that nowhere in history had the word "colored" ever been used as synonym for "negro" or "black." He wrote, "The foregoing review ... suffices to show that the word "negro," very far from having been generally recognized and accepted as including within its meaning persons of mixed negro blood, has, on the contrary, never been so used...."[22]

After arguing from historical word usage, Justice Provosty turned to set theory:

> These decisions are authority that a negro is necessarily a person of color; but not that a person of color is necessarily a negro. There are no negroes who are not persons of color; but there are persons of color who are not negroes. The term "colored," [was invented] for the very purpose of having in the language a term including... both negroes and descendants of negroes; but the converse is not true. The word "negro" was never adopted into the language for the purpose of designating persons of mixed blood. ... Nor can there be, we think, any serious denial of the fact that in Louisiana, and, indeed, throughout the United States (except on the Pacific slope), the word "colored," when applied to race, has the definite and well-known meaning of a person having negro blood in his veins. We think, also, that any candid mind must admit that the word 'negro' of itself, unqualified, does not necessarily include within its meaning persons possessed of only an admixture of negro blood.... else, why should the word 'colored' have received such universal adoption as meaning persons of negro blood pure or mixed, if there was

---

[22] 126 La. 300.

already in the language a word expressing that meaning, and no special word was needed to express it?[23]

Having argued from set theory, Justice Provosty turned to refuting the prosecution's specific arguments. The prosecution argued that the statute must have been intended to cover people of mixed ancestry, since White/Black concubinage was "practically unknown." Provosty replied:

> That argument would have great weight if it did not... lose sight of... the history of the negro race in Louisiana, and the whole past legislation of the state on the subject of the sexual relations of the two races. [F]rom birth of the state up to the last session of the Legislature concubinage with even the pure-blooded negro was not forbidden,... and that from 1870 up to 1894 marriage with the pure-blooded negro was not only not forbidden, but was legal. ... Up to the session of 1908, [the legislature] had not deemed the time ripe for prohibiting concubinage even with the pure-blooded negro. [If] it deemed the time ripe in 1908 for prohibiting concubinage with the person of slight admixture of negro blood, no matter how slight the admixture, and has done so by this statute... it has certainly chosen to do it in most questionable form.... That our Legislature, which in the whole history of the state has not deemed it expedient to impose the slightest inhibition or penalty upon concubinage even with the pure-blooded negro... should all of a sudden... have awakened to the necessity of making concubinage even with persons barely exhibiting a trace of negro blood not only an offense and a crime, but a felony, is not a conclusion necessarily to be adopted.[24]

Justice Provosty concluded by observing that the original version of the 1908 statute, "as framed by its author and presented to the Legislature... contained the following clause: 'That a person who is as much as one thirty-second part negro shall be, for the purpose of this act, a person of the negro race.'" This clause was stricken out by the legislature before the law's passage. If the legislature had intended to redefine the word "colored" as synonymous with "negro" in defiance of ancient Lou-

---

[23] Idem.

[24] Idem.

isiana legal tradition and history, all they would have had to do was to have left that clause intact.[25]

The Treadaway couple were released. Within a month of the decision, the Louisiana legislature reconvened and amended the statute by re-inserting the stricken clause.[26] Louisiana's three-caste system was legislatively collapsed down to two groups separated by a single color line. The word "colored," once the designation for the lower South's middle group became synonymous with "Black" throughout the United States. Incidentally, if the woman really was an "octoroon," then she had less African admixture than do millions of White Americans.[27]

White Children Consigned to Blackness

According to Gunnar Myrdal, writing in 1944, "The ban on intermarriage has the highest place in the white man's rank order of social segregation and discrimination."[28] This may have been the case in 1944. But the evidence of court cases in the 1910-1919 period refutes this. In contrast to the findings of Myrdal and his team, the strictest enforcement of the one-drop rule during these years, by far, was for school segregation, not intermarriage.

***Eubank v. Boughton*, 1900 Virginia.** George Boughton of King and Queen County, Virginia, tried to register his son in the Stevensville District public school for the 1899-1900 school year. The School board refused to accept the child because:

> They were informed and believed that the child of petitioner is a negro, and to permit him to attend the school for white

---

[25] Idem.

[26] Virginia R. Dominguez, *White by Definition: Social Classification in Creole Louisiana* (New Brunswick NJ, 1986), 31-32.

[27] See *Chapter 2. Afro-European Genetic Admixture in the United States*.

[28] Gunnar Myrdal, Richard Mauritz Edvard Sterner, and Arnold Marshall Rose, *An American Dilemma: The Negro Problem and Modern Democracy* (New York, 1972), 606.

children would not only materially interfere with its prosperity and efficiency, but, in their judgment, would destroy it.[29]

Boughton sued for a writ of mandamus. He presented birth records to show that he, his wife, and their children had been members of the White endogamous group, as all of their ancestors had been for at least three generations. The Circuit Court ruled in his favor and issued a writ ordering the little boy to be admitted to the school for White children, stating that "it established the fact that petitioner's son 'has not one-fourth of negro blood in him,' and is, therefore, a white person." In *Eubank v. Boughton*, 1900 Virginia, the school board appealed the writ and, on July 5, 1900, the Supreme Court of Virginia, Justice P. Keith presiding, reversed the district court, withdrew the writ, and ordered the Boughtons to pay court costs. His written explanation stated that a district school board was outside of the scope of authority of the Circuit Court. Indeed, even the State Supreme Court lacked authority over a school board.

> Whether a child is white or colored is a fact to be determined by the [school] board, and involves the exercise of a judicial discretion on the part of the board which the courts cannot control.[30]

Note that, according to the documentary evidence presented, the Bougton children had no more African ancestry than do most White Americans.[31]

Gilliland v. Board of Education, **1906 North Carolina.** For the first seven days of the 1905-1906 school year, the Gilliland children attended the Avery's Creek Township, Buncombe County public school for children of the White endogamous group. They were then ejected by order of the school board on the grounds that one of their eight great-grandparents was rumored to have had a trace of Black ancestry. The Gillilands sued in *Gilliland v. Board of Education*, 1906 North Carolina and won a writ of mandamus. The school board ap-

---

[29] 98 Va. 499.

[30] Idem.

[31] See *Chapter 2. Afro-European Genetic Admixture in the United States.*

pealed on the grounds that opinion and hearsay testimony had been admitted at trial to the effect that the great-grandfather in question had been accepted into White society. The Supreme Court of North Carolina agreed that, "the cause was made to depend and did depend on that single question whether the plaintiffs were children of the white race pure and unmixed with any negro blood." Nevertheless, on March 22, 1906, Justice Hoke upheld the original verdict. His decision was based the jury's having reached a decision of fact, and that the testimony about the great-grandfather's membership in White society had been admissible.[32] Again, the only evidence of the children not being members of the White endogamous group was a rumor about a single great-grandparent being mixed. Even if accurate, the rumor would have made the children Whiter (in the sense of genetic admixture) than many if not most White Americans.[33]

Wall v. Oyster, 1910 District of Columbia. In September of 1910, the child Isabel I. Wall was expelled from the Brookland White School in Washington DC by the principal because she had "negro blood." Her parents appealed to the school board, to the Supreme Court of the District of Columbia, and finally to the District of Columbia Court of Appeals. While it was possible that the child may have had a distant touch of African ancestry through one great-grandparent, she, like her parents and grandparents before her was accepted as White in the community. They lost each time in *Wall v. Oyster*, 1910 District of Columbia. Although the statutes of the District of Columbia contained no definition of endogamous group membership, the courts decided on the basis of a one-drop rule. Each court agreed that, "There was to be observed of the child no physical characteristic which afforded ocular evidence suggestive of aught but the Caucasian." Nevertheless, the school segregation statute in effect prohibited "colored" children from attending White schools. And so, according to Chief Justice Shepard, presiding over the Court of Appeals, the children were "colored" and could not attend a White school. In explaining his decision, Shepard noted that

---

[32] 141 N.C. 482.

[33] See *Chapter 2. Afro-European Genetic Admixture in the United States.*

some states had recently enacted statutes defining "colored" as one with any Negro blood, however faint. Nevertheless, he did not rely on other states' laws. Instead, as precedents supporting his ruling, Justice Shepard cited two court cases—*Lee v. New Orleans Great Northern RR* and *State v. Treadaway* (both discussed above).[34] Again, even if the rumor about Isabel's great-grandparent had been accurate, the little girl would have been Whiter (in the sense of genetic admixture) than many if not most White Americans.[35]

Mullins v. Belcher, 1911 Kentucky. Early in the 1910-1911 school year, the children Troy and Loucreta Mullins were expelled from Public School No. 28 of Pike County Kentucky because they were said to be "colored." Section 187 of the Kentucky Constitution read, "... no distinction shall be made on account of race or color, and separate schools for white and colored children shall be maintained."[36] Their guardian challenged the school board in the Pike County Circuit Court, in the case *Mullins v. Belcher*, 1911 Kentucky, on the basis that the children were completely European in appearance and had been raised as members of White society. The county court found that the children had one-sixteenth of Negro blood and so upheld their expulsion. They appealed the decision. On March 9 of 1911, the Court of Appeals of Kentucky sustained their expulsion. Judge William Rogers Clay cited *State v. Treadaway*[37] to opine:

> [The] appellants are as fair as members of the white race, and there is nothing in their personal appearance to indicate the presence of negro blood. In our opinion, however, the question does not depend upon personal appearance. The color of the person may be one means of indicating the class to which he belongs, but the question in its final analysis depends upon whether or not the person has, or has not, an appreciable admixture of negro blood. ... As the makers of the Constitution did not undertake to define the words "colored chil-

---

[34] 36 App. D.C. 50.

[35] See *Chapter 2. Afro-European Genetic Admixture in the United States.*

[36] This sentence would probably fascinate a semanticist.

[37] 126 La. 300.

dren" as employed in section 187, we conclude that these words were used in their ordinary and general sense, and that they include all children wholly or in part of negro blood, or having any appreciable admixture thereof.[38]

Again, if the Mullins children truly were of one-sixteenth African genetic admixture, they would have been Whiter (in the sense of genetic admixture) than tens of millions of White Americans.[39]

***Cole v. District Board*, 1912 Oklahoma.** In the 1911-1912 school year, the children of Morton Cole were expelled from the all-White Public School No. 29 of McIntosh County, Oklahoma on the ground that they were "negroes." Cole sued for a writ of mandamus in *Cole v. District Board*, 1912 Oklahoma and lost in the District Court. He appealed and, on April 9 of 1912, Justice C. Ames of the Supreme Court of Oklahoma ordered a new trial.[40] His ruling was based on improperly excluded evidence. Testimony had been admitted to show that Cole associated with members of the Black endogamous group, but similar testimony showing association with members of the White group had been excluded. Two points make this case interesting. First, the term "Negro" is used instead of "colored" in its modern sense—that is, as anyone who is a member of the Black endogamous group, regardless of appearance. Contrast this with the terminology used in *State v. Treadaway*, 1910 Louisiana, *Wall v. Oyster*, 1910 District of Columbia, and *Mullins v. Belcher*, 1911 Kentucky, which held that "Negro" denoted African appearance and "colored" meant of mixed heritage. Second, Justice Ames cited eight prior cases setting the precedent that the rule of association alone, even without evidence of African ancestry, sufficed to define someone's position relative to the color line.[41] What is important about this case is that association alone

---

[38] 142 Ky. 673.

[39] See *Chapter 2. Afro-European Genetic Admixture in the United States.*

[40] 32 Okla. 692.

[41] The cases were: *Hopkins v. Bowers* 111 N.C. 175, *Bryan v. Walton* 20 Ga. 480, *White v. Clements* 39 Ga. 232, *State v. Patrick* 51 N.C. 308, *Nave's Adm'r v. Williams* 22 Ind. 368, *Chancellor v. Milly* 9 Dana 23, *Tucker v. State* 24 Ala. 77, and *Locklayer v. Locklayer* 139 Ala. 354.

was ruled sufficient to determine one's endogamous group; evidence of blood was not needed. As mentioned earlier, the rule of association is usually the principle rule used in affirmative action litigation today.[42] As in several of the preceding cases, the children were never even alleged to have Black ancestry. No one disputed that they were White, biologically speaking.

Johnson v. Board of Education, **1914 North Carolina.** In February of 1914, Mr. and Mrs. J.S. Johnson obtained a writ of mandamus in the Superior Court of Wilson County, North Carolina, ordering the School Board to admit their children into the school for children of the White endogamous group. The School Board appealed the order in *Johnson v. Board of Education*, 1914 North Carolina. Both parties admitted that Mr. Johnson was a member of the White endogamous group and had no trace of African ancestry. Both parties also admitted that the children's mother had a trace of distant African ancestry. She had been ruled a member of the White endogamous group, however, when the couple wed because she had less than the one-eighth blood fraction specified in the North Carolina Constitution. The problem was that a 1905 law forbade any child, "with negro blood in his veins, however remote the strain, from attending a school for the white race." Consequently, the case pivoted on whether a school segregation statute could override a color line definition explicit in the state's constitution.[43] In September of 1914, the Supreme Court of North Carolina reversed the order, citing as precedent *Ferrall v. Ferrall*, *Wall v. Oyster*, and *Tucker v. Blease*.[44] Justices Walker and Clark unanimously ruled that the

---

[42] See *Chapter 14. Features of Today's One-Drop Rule.*

[43] 166 N.C. 468.

[44] As described earlier in this chapter, *Ferrall v. Ferrall*, 153 N.C. 174, ruled Susie Patterson to be White based on blood fraction. In that decision, Justice Hoke mentioned the newly passed school segregation statute employing a one-drop rule and predicted that its constitutionality would soon be challenged. *Wall v. Oyster*, 36 App. D.C. 50, also described above, ruled District of Columbia children to be Black, as in Johnson v. Board, but there was no conflicting blood fraction statute or constitutional provision in effect in that case. Finally *Tucker v. Blease*, 97 S.C. 303, also described above, was the case that overturned centuries of South Carolina color-line permeability.

statute defining Blackness via a one-drop rule, for purposes of school attendance, did not conflict with a constitutional definition aimed at intermarriage. The writ of mandamus was nullified and the Johnson children were found to be on the Black side of the endogamous color line, despite both of their parents being legally White. Again, even accepting the opposition's testimony, the Johnson children were as White or Whiter (genetically speaking) than tens of millions of White Americans.[45]

***Medlin v. Board of Education*, 1914 North Carolina.** In the 1913-1914 school year, the children of J.R. Medlin were expelled from Public School No. 2, House's Creek Township, Wake County, North Carolina, on the ground that their mother, Nan Powers, was rumored to have had a grandmother of mixed ancestry. In *Medlin v. Board of Education*, 1914 North Carolina, the parents obtained a writ of mandamus after a county court trial characterized solely by hearsay. No witness offered documentation of the grandmother's ancestry. No witness had ever seen Mrs. Medlin's grandmother. Instead, every witness testified solely as to rumors that they had heard and whether, in the witness's opinion, the rumors had been started deliberately and with malicious intent. The jury found the Medlin children to be White and the school board appealed. On November 18, 1914, the Supreme Court of North Carolina upheld the lower court in a split decision. Chief Justice Clark wrote the ruling. The other two justices (Walker and Hoke) dissented. In essence, Justice Clark wrote a three-page explanation justifying his finding that the hearsay and innuendo offered by plaintiff's witnesses (that the rumor of a mixed grandmother was maliciously invented) were more persuasive than testimony for the defense. In his eyes, the children were members of the White endogamous group. Justices Walter and Hoke wrote a six-page dissent, finding that the hearsay and innuendo offered by defense's witnesses (that the rumor of a mixed grandmother was not malicious—it was invented out of civic duty) were more persuasive than testimony for the plaintiff. In their eyes, the children were members of the

---

[45] See *Chapter 2. Afro-European Genetic Admixture in the United States.*

Black endogamous group.[46] Interestingly, in this case Justice Hoke abandoned his reliance on the state constitution's blood-fraction definition, which he had held to four years earlier in *Ferrall v. Ferrall*, Instead, he went with the school-segregation statute's one-drop rule, following the precedent set by Justices Walker and Clark two months earlier in *Johnson v. Board of Education*.[47] Again, no one disputed that the Medlin children were genetically White.

  ***Moreau et al. v. Grandich et ux.*, 1917 Mississippi.** Late in 1916, the children of Antonio Grandich and his wife were expelled from the public school of Bay St. Louis, Hancock County, Mississippi because, according to the trustees, they were of the "colored race." Denying that they had any trace of African ancestry, the Grandich family applied for a writ of mandamus from the county circuit court. According to the trustees, a rumor had it that the children's great-grandmother, Christiana Jourdan, must have had Negro blood. This rumor was based on another rumor that two of Christiana's daughters had married members of the Black endogamous group, something which no White woman would have done had she been completely White. In short, the children were found to belong on the Black side of the color line because of the Blackness by association of two great-aunts from whom they did not descend. The writ was issued and the trustees appealed to the state Supreme Court of Mississippi in *Moreau et al. v. Grandich et ux.*, 1917.[48] On March, 1917, citing *Lee v. New Orleans Great Northern RR*, 1910 Louisiana and *Mullins v. Belcher*, 1911 Kentucky, Justice Ethridge overturned the county court's mandamus order and ruled against the Grandich children.[49] Again, no one disputed that the Grandich children were genetically White.

---

[46] 167 N.C. 239.

[47] *Ferrall v. Ferrall*, 153 N.C. 174, and *Johnson v. Board of Education* , 166 N.C. 468, are both described earlier in this chapter.

[48] 114 Miss. 560.

[49] *Lee v. New Orleans*, 125 La. 236, discussed earlier in this chapter, ruled that a Colored person had to ride in the Jim Crow car, despite the ancient Louisiana tradition that "Colored" denoted a third group with most of the rights of the White group. *Mullins v. Belcher*, 142 Ky. 673, also discussed

***Oberly v. School Board*, 1918 Louisiana.** The daughter of Mr. and Mrs. Oberly attended the Calcasieu Parish Public School from age 7 to 14, when she was expelled for being rumored to have invisible "negro blood." The parents sought a writ of mandamus from the local court, which was denied. They appealed to the Louisiana Supreme Court in *Oberly v. School Board*, 1918 Louisiana. On January 3 of 1918, Justice Provosty handed down the decision that:

> The case does not involve any pecuniary amount, and does not fall in any one of the classes of cases of which jurisdiction is given to this court irrespective of amount. This court, therefore, has no jurisdiction of it. ... Appeal dismissed.[50]

No testimony was offered that the Oberly girl was anything other than genetically White.

***State v. School District*, 1922 Arkansas.** In 1921, the three grandchildren of Ophelia James were expelled from Public School No. 16 in Montgomery County, Arkansas for having Black ancestry. Ophelia was the daughter of Maria Gocio, who admitted to a trace of Cherokee ancestry, and the school board held that Cherokees had Negro blood. The children's parents sought a mandamus order and were refused. They appealed and lost in *State v. School District*, 1922 Arkansas. The issue came down to which of two Arkansas statutes applied. Section 996, relating to the segregation of public transportation, defined "negro" as anyone "in whom there is a visible and distinct admixture of African blood." Section 2603, relating to concubinage, defined "colored" as "any person having any trace of negro blood, whether visible or not." Since the public school statute referred to the segregation of "negro" (rather than of "colored") children, the parents argued that Section 996 (defining "negro" by visible admixture) applied. On June 5, 1922, Justice Humphreys of the Supreme Court of Arkansas ruled that:

---

above, ruled that Kentucky would follow a one-drop rule because the state constitution did not define "colored."

[50] 142 La. 788.

> Petitioner's children in appearance, show no sign of negro
> blood, and, judged from their appearance alone, would pass
> for persons of pure Caucasian blood. ... [Nevertheless], the
> purpose and intent of the statute was to prevent social equal-
> ity or intermingling of the white and African races, thereby
> maintaining harmony and peace in the schools. As much con-
> fusion and disorder would result from admitting children in
> the white schools who have a trace of negro in them, though
> not disclosed by their appearance, as from admitting children
> who possess a visible and distinct admixture of African
> blood. We think the interpretation placed upon the statute by
> the [lower] court is correct. The language is broad, and has
> no relation to the degree in blood.[51]

In short, the three children were ruled to be Black solely because
one grandparent admitted to having Cherokee ancestry.

Someone might suspect that the foregoing twelve cases
(including *Tucker v. Blease*, 1914 South Carolina, which opened
the chapter) were selected from a larger set of cases in order to
include only those cases where courts consigned to Blackness
children who had no more African genetic admixture than the
typical White American and whose parents did not self-identify
as ethnically African-American. Someone might suspect that the
above account deliberately excluded cases where courts consigned to Blackness children who really did have more African
admixture than the typical White American, or whose families
really did self-identify as ethnically African-American.

Such suspicion would be inaccurate. The above account
lists every single appealed court case in the United States between 1900 and 1922 that involved schools where "racial identity" was at issue. Without exception, every such case adjudi-
cated the Blackness of children who, in plain factual reality—
assuming the accuracy of opposing testimony—were no Blacker
(neither genetically nor ethnically) than the typical White
American. Only two cases (Gilliland and Cole) ruled the children to be White. All the others flew in the face of factual reality
and banished the children and their future descendants to the
Black side of America's endogamous color line. To be sure,

---

[51] 154 Ark. 176.

some victims may actually have had a distant trace of African ancestry, as do one-third of White Americans. But if this made them Black, then it means that one-third of all White Americans were also Black and the question remains—why single these out?

White Adults Challenged to Defend Their Whiteness

Locklayer v. Locklayer, **1903 Alabama.** Jason Locklayer died in Lawrence county, Alabama, on November 29, 1887.[52] His widow, Nancy Locklayer, sued the executor of the estate to have $265.81 in personal property set aside from the bulk of the estate and awarded to her. The county probate court agreed with her and ordered the executor to comply. In *Locklayer v. Locklayer*, 1903 Alabama, the executor appealed on the grounds that Jason Locklayer, although he had lived his life as a member of the White endogamous group, had been accepted as White man for jury duty, and had affidavits attesting his Whiteness, was actually secretly a Negro by ancestry. The executor explained that, since the alleged widow was undoubtedly White, the marriage had never been valid and so she did not have any right to the $265.81. Witnesses were summoned and documents entered into evidence. Some claimed that they had heard that "[the deceased] did not have any African blood in his veins, but was of mixed blood, being part Indian, part Portuguese, and part Caucasian." Others testified that they had heard he had Negro ancestry. On November of 1903, Justice Tyson of the Supreme Court of Alabama ruled against Nancy Locklayer. He decided that the deceased had been a member of the Black endogamous group, that the widow was a member of the White endogamous group (although no evidence was ever presented one way or the other about her), and so their relationship "was clearly illegal and

---

[52] *Locklayer* or *Locklear* is one of the most common surnames within the Lumbee maroon community centered on Robeson County, North Carolina (called "Croatan" before 1953). For details, see topic "The Maroon Escape Hatch" in *Chapter 5. The Rate of Black-to-White "Passing."*

adulterous." Consequently, she had no claim on any part of the $265.81.[53]

Moon v. Children's Home, 1911 Virginia. In 1911, the Circuit Court of Albemarle County, Virginia, took twelve-year-old Madeline and ten-year old Ruby from the custody of their mother, Lucy Moon, and committed them to the Children's Home Society of Virginia. The reason was that when the girls' father died, leaving them and their mother destitute, Lucy remarried a man with known African ancestry. Lucy appealed the ruling and commitment order in the case of *Moon v. Children's Home*, 1911 Virginia. On November 16, 1911, the Supreme Court of Virginia ordered the children returned to their mother. According to Justice Buchanan, that although John Moon (the children's stepfather) had one-sixteenth "of colored blood in his veins," this fact alone did not make his White wife an unfit parent.[54] Since John had less than one-fourth blood fraction (the Virginia rule then in effect), he was "colored" but not legally a "Negro" or "Mulatto." Assuming the validity of the opposition's testimony, the stepfather was genetically Whiter than millions of White Americans. Also, the two children suffered the punishment, although neither was alleged to have any African ancestry at all.

Railroad Company v. Ritchel, 1912 Kentucky. On July 9 of 1910, Rella Ritchel, a 20-year-old schoolteacher who had immigrated with her parents from Russia at age nine, was forcibly and rudely ejected from a railroad car reserved for members of the White endogamous group by the train conductor. The man insisted that he could tell by her appearance that she was a member of the Black endogamous group. She sued the railroad and won $3750 in punitive damages in Bourbon County Circuit Court. In *Railroad Company v. Ritchel*, 1912 Kentucky, the rail-

---

[53] 139 Ala. 354.

[54] 112 Va. 737. The idea that intermarriage proves parental unfitness was eventually adopted by many states. A family friend of the present author is an elderly woman of Irish extraction and of the White endogamous group, whose two children were taken away by the state in 1943 Miami precisely because she married a man of the Black group after being widowed and left destitute.

road appealed on the grounds that the plaintiff was a Russian Jewess (a fact that Rella did not deny), and that this made her a member of the Black group ("colored," in the wording of the Kentucky law then in effect). On June 4, 1912, the Court of Appeals of Kentucky upheld the lower court. Judge William Rogers Clay (the same jurist as in *Mullins v. Belcher*, 1911 Kentucky) wrote that Jews were not colored under the law, "while she was a person of dark complexion and dark hair and eyes, her features were characteristic of the Jewish race, and bore no resemblance to those of a person of the colored race."[55] Even granting the accuracy of opposing testimony, Rella was genetically and ethnically "Whiter" than the typical White American.

***Duvigneaud v. Loquet et al.*, 1912 Louisiana.** Adelard Duvigneaud had died in New Orleans in 1873, leaving his wife, Marie Philomene Bechet, with lifetime use of their house. When she died in 1910, an inheritance dispute arose between Adelard's children and Marie Philomene's offspring by her second marriage. The pivotal claim on the part of the latter was that Adelard had not been completely White, but that Philomene had been. This would have made their marriage illegal and their children bastards incapable of inheriting. In the intervening years, new laws had done away with the traditional privileges of the Colored endogamous group. Colored-White intermarriage had been outlawed and public transportation segregated. More importantly, the determination of membership in the White endogamous group had become much stricter. Like George Tillman's "hundred families",[56] the very same man who was a member of the White community when alive in 1873 might well have been relegated to Blackness in 1912 after he was dead. In the event, the Civil District Court, Parish of Orleans, ruled in *Duvigneaud v. Loquet et al.*, 1912 Louisiana, that Abelarde had been White at the time and that the laws did not retroactively redefine him. The children of Marie Philomene's second marriage appealed. On October 21, 1912, the Supreme Court of Louisiana, Justice Land

---

[55] 148 Ky. 701.

[56] See under the topic "South Carolina" in *Chapter 19. The One-Drop Rule in the Postbellum Lower South.*

presiding, ruled entirely on the basis of witnesses' recollections of association and social acceptance that Abelard had been White (his brother had been a City Court judge), his marriage legal, and his children legitimate.[57]

Stewart v. Profit, 1912 Texas. A dispute over community property in 1912 Galveston, Texas, centered upon whether a woman could sell real estate without her husband's participation. The husband, Calvin Bell, was African in appearance and undisputedly on the Black side of the color line. But the woman, Katie Bell, looked so European that the couple had been convicted of criminal intermarriage. Calvin had to live in a house "several hundred yards away in the town of La Marque" in order to avoid further prosecution and the risk of being lynched. When Katie sold the property to Stewart, Calvin's interest came into question because, if she was a member of the White endogamous group, then their marriage was void but the title transfer was valid. On the other hand, if she were ruled to be on the Black side of the endogamous color line, then the marriage was valid but the property sale was not. Her endogamous group membership was determined at trial in *Stewart v. Profit*, 1912 Texas, and she was found to be White, despite the couple's prior conviction having been excluded as evidence. The ruling was upheld on appeal on March 9 and again on March 28, 1912 rehearing, by the Court of Civil Appeals of Galveston, Texas, Judge Robert G. Street presiding. The point of interest here is that, as in the simultaneous case, *Cole v. District Board*, the judge held that association alone sufficed to determine a person's endogamous group membership.[58]

Marre v. Marre, 1914 Missouri. Louis Marre and Agnes E. Nash were married in St. Louis, Missouri, on November 2, 1908. On March 15 of 1911 he obtained an annulment from the St. Louis City Circuit Court on the ground that Agnes had an unspecified trace of Negro blood. Agnes appealed in *Marre v. Marre*, 1914 Missouri. On June 20, 1914, the Court of Appeals of Missouri reversed the annulment. All of the evidence pre-

---

[57] 131 La. 568.

[58] 146 S.W. 563.

sented regarding Agnes's endogamous group membership was about her associations and those of her family. None of the testimony attempted to prove or disprove either her blood fraction or her appearance. According to the unanimous decision by Justices Reynolds, Nortoni, and Allen:

> The mother of defendant testified in the most positive terms that there was no negro blood in the family, in the veins of herself, her husband or her children; her family had lived in Kentucky and in Mexico; two or more of her daughters are married to white men; their associates are with white people, not with negroes, although they had a few friends who are negroes. One of her immediate ancestors was a Mexican.[59]

Although the court found that Black endogamous group membership had not been proven, the three justices agreed that appearance was unimportant; invisible Blackness is what determined group membership: "We must bear in mind that the prohibition of the statute is not against color, but blood, or race." Curiously, they cited *Gentry vs. Polly McMinnis*, 1835 Kentucky as precedent for this position when, in fact, that case had ruled precisely the opposite, "To a rational man... the best and highest proof of which any fact is susceptible, is the evidence of his own senses. ... A white person of unmixed blood cannot be a slave."[60]

***Neuberger v. Gelder*, 1916 Louisiana.** In *Neuberger v. Gelder*, 1916 Louisiana, a man tried to annul his marriage on the ground that he had discovered that his wife was colored. According to Justice Provosty of the Supreme Court of Louisiana (the same who wrote the ruling in *State v. Treadaway*, 1910):

> This is a suit in nullity of marriage, on the ground that the plaintiff is a white man and the defendant a colored woman. The defendant has always passed for a white person. She attended the public schools as such, and was married to plaintiff as such. Her father was unquestionably white, and was married to her mother. The preponderance of the evidence is

---

[59] 184 Mo. App. 198.

[60] 33 Ky. 382. See under the topic "Court Cases" in *Chapter 15. The Invention of the One-Drop Rule in The 1830s North.*

that her mother also passed for a white woman. Whether she was such really or not is left doubtful. The trial judge saw her on the witness stand, and saw and heard the other witnesses, and concluded that she was white. Judgment affirmed.[61]

***McGoodwin v. Shelby*, 1918 Kentucky.** According to Judge Sampson of the Marion County, Kentucky Circuit Court:

> In May, 1915, Miss Florrie Hood, a most eccentric and peculiar woman, died intestate, childless and unmarried, at her home in Lebanon, Kentucky, she being about seventy years of age, and the owner by inheritance of several houses and lots and some acreage property in the city of Lebanon, and quite an amount of personal property.... There were no close relatives living so far as known. Some very distant relatives... began to assert claim to the estate.... It was known, however, that one Thomas C. Shelby, a nephew of Miss Florrie Hood, had many years before left Marion county on account of trouble and had gone to Florida..., and had not been heard from since his departure, so far as the public was advised. Whether Thomas C. Shelby was living or dead, or if dead, had he left heirs, became a very important question in the settlement of the Hood estate because if he was living or had left heirs of his body, capable of inheriting from collateral kin, he or they were entitled to the entire estate of Miss Hood....[62]

After dispatching investigators throughout Florida and mailing 1,500 postcards to different post offices in search of Thomas Shelby or his descendants, the estate administrators located Shelby's widow and two minor children—sole heirs to the Hood fortune. The problem was that the widow (the mother of the heirs) "was the daughter of William Scott, and William Scott was the son of Joe Scott, and Joe Scott was [reputed to have been] a mulatto, so that the mother of the children of Thomas C. Shelby was not a pure-blooded white woman." This would make illegal their parents' marriage and render the children bastards incapable of inheriting. All of the claimants agreed that trying to settle such an issue by investigation would be unpredictable and

---

[61] 139 La. 758.

[62] 181 Ky. 230 .

risky to all. The late Miss Florrie had left enough to go around, so the claimants (including the children's court-appointed attorney) reached an out-of-court settlement to distribute the property among themselves. The case, *McGoodwin v. Shelby*, 1918 Kentucky, then wound its way through the Kentucky court system for the next three years. First, the original probate court disallowed the agreement as being unconscionable since the children could not possibly be considered anything but White, based on their great-grandparents, grandparents, and parents having always associated solely with White people. Then, the Kentucky Court of Appeals overruled the probate court on the ground that it was a valid choice by the children's attorney not to open that particular can or worms. Finally, on December 6, 1918, the Kentucky Court of Appeals overruled itself, upholding the out-of-court settlement but reducing the attorneys' fees extracted from Miss Florrie's estate. In the end, the Kentucky Court of Appeals, all justices sitting, ruled that:

> Under section 233 of the Kentucky Constitution all laws in force in Virginia on June 1, 1792... are in force within [Kentucky] unless they have been altered or repealed by the general assembly [and that] the Virginia act of 1785 declaring that a person having one-fourth part or more of negro blood shall be deemed a mulatto, is in force in Kentucky by virtue of section 233 of the Constitution.

Since the Shelby children undoubtedly had less than the specified fraction of "Negro" blood, even granting the allegations about their great-grandfather Joe Scott, they were legally White in Kentucky and could inherit. This case is the best example of the mismatch between color line criteria for school attendance and for other purposes. The Shelby children were White, as far as inheriting Miss Florrie's estate was concerned. But there is no doubt, judging by Kentucky Court of Appeals Judge William Rogers Clay's one-drop ruling in *Mullins v. Belcher*, 142 Ky. 673, seven years earlier, that the Shelby children would have been rejected from Kentucky's White schools despite their legal Whiteness.

***Reed v. State*, 1922 Alabama.** In 1921, Percy Reed was convicted by the Circuit Court of Washington County, Alabama, of the felony of marrying a White woman and was sentenced to an indeterminate term in the state penitentiary. Prosecution witnesses at his trial testified that he was Black but, when asked how they knew, they referred only to his swarthy (but not African) appearance. The jury found Reed guilty, despite the judge's instructions that the court "had ascertained that defendant is of Indian or Spanish origin."[63] When denied a new trial by the county court, Reed took his case, *Reed v. State*, 1922 Alabama, to the Alabama Court of Appeals. On January 10 of 1922, Justice Merritt ruled that, since the prosecution had offered no evidence that Reed was not Hispanic, the conviction was overturned.[64]

Rollins v. State, **1922 Alabama.** In 1921, a Jefferson County, Alabama, court convicted Jim and Edith Rollins of interracial sex. Rollins was an elderly African-looking businessman. Edith Labue was a European-looking woman from Sicily. Miscegenation was a serious crime at that place and time, punishable with a mandatory two to seven years in the state penitentiary for each party.[65] But it would have been hopeless to argue that Jim was not Black. His dark brown complexion had more of Africa than of Europe in it, and the state's one-drop "racial" definition was clear: "The word 'negro' means [anyone with] negro ancestors, without reference to or limit of time or number of generations."[66] The Rollins couple appealed their conviction in *Rollins v. State*, 1922 Alabama, presenting the state Court of Appeals with a problem. The court apparently did not want to lock up an elderly couple who were respected members of their community.[67] How could the court legitimately let the Rollins couple off the hook? The solution was elegantly simple. Alabama's definition effectively labeled as "Negro" every Mediter-

---

[63] How they had ascertained such a thing does not appear in the record.

[64] 18 Ala. App. 353.

[65] Pauli Murray, ed. *States' Laws on Race and Color* (Athens, 1997), 30.

[66] Ibid., 22.

[67] Alabama Court of Appeals Judge P.J. Bricken was also irritated that a city detective named Hubbard had persuaded the defendant to sign a confession by the unorthodox method of pushing the muzzle of a loaded revolver against Jim Rollins's head and threatening to blow his brains out.

ranean native from Athens to Gibraltar since ancient times. On January 17, 1922, Judge Bricken reasoned that no evidence suggested that Sicilians were White under the law. Hence, the couple had violated no statute, and their conviction was reversed.[68]

Some might suspect that the present author exposes the above history because he considers morally acceptable the mistreatment of people of mostly African ancestry or those who identify ethnically as African-American, and that he draws the line only at mistreatment of those who are considered White. Such suspicion would be incorrect. The Jim Crow era saw the cruelest wave of "racial" hatred that America has yet experienced. Millions of Americans of the Black endogamous group were disfranchised, killed, brutalized, and discouraged even from their children learning the three Rs. Mere words cannot describe the horror.[69] Even though only about 20,000 American citizens were murdered outright by the system—tortured to death in public rituals called "lynchings"[70]—the duration (half a century) and the number of people ultimately affected (ten million African Americans in 1920) is comparable to the Nazi holocaust. The Jim Crow system was morally reprehensible by any standard, whether evaluated in the light of Benthian Utilitarianism, Kantian categorical imperatives, or religious teachings. That most of its victims were of the Black endogamous group cannot justify it. That some of its victims were of the White endogamous group cannot make it any more or less reprehensible. Nevertheless, to repeat the disclaimer in this book's introduction, "This book does not address the morality of the U.S. system of two endogamous groups—whether any particular feature is 'good' or 'bad'."[71]

---

[68] 18 Ala. App. 354.

[69] Although one historian makes a great effort to describe it in Leon F. Litwack, *Trouble in Mind: Black Southerners in the Age of Jim Crow* (New York, 1998).

[70] According to the Tuskegee Institute, nearly 5,000 of these killings were extrajudicial.

[71] See below footnote 10 in *Chapter 1. Introduction.*

The above cases are important because they raise two historical questions that cry out for answers. First, why did 1900-1920 mainstream White society (via the courts) punish selected White Americans by decreeing them to be Black?[72] How were the victims of this deliberate judicial ostracism chosen? Second, why have American scholars turned their backs on such easily available court records and pretended to believe that the one-drop rule's victims merely "looked White," but that they were "really Black" in some metaphysical sense? The next chapter suggests possible answers.

African-American Complicity

Did many people of African-American ethnicity embrace and support the one-drop rule of invisible Blackness during the Jim Crow era, as they did in the 1830s?[73] As in the antebellum period, we must seek the answer in literature and in diaries, rather than in court cases. We have already seen that African-American delegates to "Pitchfork" Ben Tillman's 1895 South Carolina Constitutional Convention were apathetic towards the topic, in contrast to their strong participation in issues of marriage and voting rights.[74]

The number of "passing" novels written by African-Americans soared in the last quarter of the nineteenth century.[75] Although often set in the lower south, they were almost invaria-

---

[72] To be sure, some victims may actually have had recent African ancestry, as do one-third of White Americans. But if this made them Black, then it means that one-third of all White Americans were also Black and the question remains—why pick these out?

[73] The above words, "of African-American ethnicity," are meant to exclude the few remaining Colored Creoles of the Gulf Coast (who did not self-identify with Northern-born African-American ethnicity). As shown earlier, they tenaciously opposed the one-drop rule.

[74] See under the topic "South Carolina" in *Chapter 19. The One-Drop Rule in the Postbellum Lower South.*

[75] For a survey and a hypothesis explaining the suddenly increased popularity of this genre, see Kathleen Pfeiffer, *Race Passing and American Individualism* (Amherst, 2003), 1.

bly written by northerners and, in contrast to antebellum passing novels, they invariably portray endogamous-group switching as morally reprehensible. To be sure, some characters, such as Clare Kendry in Nella Larsen's *Passing*, seem comfortable with their position on the White side of America's endogamous color line, but in the end, they receive their comeuppance for their transgression. (Students love to debate whether, in *Passing*'s final dramatic scene, Clare accidentally fell to her death from the sixth-floor window, jumped in suicide, or was pushed by Irene Redfield, the heroine who refused to pass.)[76] As one scholar explains it, "Passing for white has long been viewed as an instance of racial self-hatred or disloyalty. It is predicated, so the argument goes, on renouncing blackness—an 'authentic' identity, in favor of whiteness, an 'opportunistic' one."[77]

On the other hand, class mobility and mobility among ethnic groups is a fundamental component of the "American Dream." If anything, the early twentieth century—the time of Horatio Alger stories and the assimilationist "melting pot" paradigm—saw heightened enthusiasm towards self-improvement. The notion of the "self-made man" was a fundamental component of the "American Dream." In point of fact, Americans born into the Black endogamous group were mobile. Black-to-White endogamous group mobility was and is a hallmark of American society. The step has been taken by one African-American youngster out of every thousand in every year of the nation's history.[78]

One would therefore expect critiques of the "passing" novel genre to notice that African-American authors' hostility to group switching actually denigrates acceptance and embraces intolerance. As one scholar puts it, "The paradoxical coexistence of the cult of the socialz upstart as 'self-made man' and the per-

---

[76] For a particularly deep analysis of this novel, including the suppressed homosexuality that gives it tension, see Pamela L. Caughie, *Passing and Pedagogy: The Dynamics of Responsibility* (Urbana, 1999), 124-43.

[77] Pfeiffer (2003), 2.

[78] See the topic "The Average Yearly Rate is Between 0.10 and 0.14 Percent" in *Chapter 5. The Rate of Black-to-White "Passing."*

manent racial identification and moral condemnation of the racial passer as 'imposter' constitutes the frame within which the phenomenon of passing took place."[79] The fact is that, since the Jim Crow era, scholarly interpretations have almost universally supported the African-American authorial consensus that switching from an African-American ethnic identity to, say Irish-American, Italian-American, or Hispanic, is akin to treason. As one exceptional analyst puts it, "Though assimilation is hardly an uncontested component of ethnic identity, the assimilated ethnic rarely faces the kind of hostility—either within the narrative itself or in the critical discourse surrounding it—faced by the passing character."[80]

First-hand accounts of educators in the South during this period abound with examples of the southward spread of the Northern one-drop rule custom. Northern traditions were imposed by well-intentioned immigrants. A White Northern schoolteacher of Southern Black children recorded a particularly poignant account in her 1910 diary:

> "The talented tenth" was, at birth, farther along than the others. It was lighter in color and had inherited land or education or money from white or free ancestors. It had the first higher education and produced most of the early professional men. ... They told me that their particular problem was being colored at all. Being too white themselves, they could not assimilate the lower class. They were the prestige pattern, but too high on the hill—a target for snipers. They suffered in conscience about trouble that could be hardly expressed. Those who came North were sometimes fair enough to pass, but "passing" was then regarded as treason to the race. I never knew anyone who did not think so.[81]

---

[79] Werner Sollors, *Neither Black Nor White Yet Both* (Cambridge, 1997), 250.

[80] Pfeiffer (2003), 4. Another exceptional analyst who sees this oddity is M. Giulia Fabi, *Passing and the Rise of the African American Novel* (Urbana, 2001).

[81] Lura Beam, *He Called Them by the Lightning: A Teacher's Odyssey in the Negro South, 1908-1919* (Indianapolis, 1967), 40-41.

As discussed earlier, Yankees of the newly invented African-American ethnicity were inadvertently complicit with White mainstream society in spreading the original one-drop rule in the 1830s.[82] Americans of the White endogamous group invented the one-drop rule in reaction to the fear that White-looking Blacks were secretly in their midst, plotting their murders as Nat Turner's followers had done. But Black Yankees soon internalized the idea. This should not surprise. When ethnicities form under a hegemonic mainstream society, they often adopt mainstream values. Today, for example, when people of any U.S. ethnicity are asked what makes their particular group unique and different from the "others," close family ties and respect for education always top the list. Every ethnicity claims to uniquely embrace these two values.[83] In fact, these values are internalized from the mainstream and contradicted by the historical record. (Immigrant Irish, for example, forbade their children to learn to read and write.[84])

Black Yankees absorbed the one-drop rule from the surrounding mainstream society. For Americans of the newly invented African-American ethnicity, it strengthened the border of ethnic solidarity by retaining within their ethnic community the European-looking offspring of mixed marriages—a century before Du Bois coined the term "talented tenth." As one educator of the time wrote in her diary, "the unwritten law was that Negroes should form a solid unit against the white man. ... Passing over to whites was regarded as betrayal."[85] This does not suggest that members of America's Black endogamous group were unanimous in supporting the one-drop rule, any more than Whites were. As the record shows, it was contested by many

---

[82] See the topics "African-American Ethnic Solidarity Benefited" and "Other Voices" in *Chapter 16. Why Did Northerners Invent a One-Drop Rule?*

[83] Mary C. Waters, *Black Identities: West Indian Immigrant Dreams and American Realities* (New York, 1999), 67.

[84] Oscar Handlin, *Boston's Immigrants, 1790-1880*, Rev. and enl. ed. (Cambridge MA, 1959), Chapter 5.

[85] Beam (1967), 51, 89.

individuals from both sides of the color line. Nevertheless, as the court cases also show, the fraction of Americans, Black and White, who advocated the one-drop rule increased dramatically during the early Jim Crow period.

The hatred and revulsion towards passing that was expressed by both Blacks and Whites of the early twentieth century (and expressed by most Blacks and Whites today, according to academic consensus[86]) is thought-provoking. One would think that color-line permeability would be embraced and encouraged by those wishing to oppose U.S. racialism. As one scholar puts it, "Understood in [the light of history], passing offers a problematic but potentially legitimate expression of American individualism, one that resists segregation's one-drop logic and thereby undermines America's consciously constructed ideology of racial difference."[87] Apparently, however, this was not (and is not) the case.

Both the White carpetbaggers and the African-American Yankees who went south after the war to teach and lead the freedmen carried the one-drop rule in their cultural baggage. The Northern Black-White cultural unanimity imposed the one-drop rule as a mandatory component of the new hegemony. Sometimes it was imposed gently, as in the literature of "passing" novels. Sometimes it was imposed brutally, as in the preceding court cases. Sometimes it was imposed on former slaves who welcomed it along with their first taste of freedom. Sometimes it was imposed against fierce cultural resistance by the biracial elite of the lower South, whose heritage and traditions stemmed from Barbados, France, or Spain, rather than from Boston, New York, or Philadelphia. But gently or brutally, against acceptance or resistance, it was imposed. It was not a conflict between Blacks and Whites. It was a conflict between the North's and upper South's worldview of a single harsh color line on the one

---

[86] For a survey of today's academic consensus, see the topic "Many Scholars Believe the One-Drop Rule is Stronger Than Ever" in *Chapter 14. Features of Today's One-Drop Rule.*

[87] Pfeiffer (2003), 2.

hand, against the lower South's permeable three-caste worldview on the other.

* * * * *

This chapter examined events of 1900-1919 that gave rise to the ideas of endogamous group membership that are still in force today. It showed that the word "Colored," no longer denoted an intermediate group in the Franco-American culture of the Gulf Coast but became a polite euphemism for any member of the Black endogamous group anywhere. It showed that the strictest enforcement of the one-drop rule in those years was for school segregation. It offered a viewpoint shift to reveal that the one-drop rule targeted only Whites, not Blacks. It showed that members of the African-American ethnic community, especially its leadership, embraced and enforced the one-drop rule within their constituencies.

Chapter 21.
Why Did One-Drop Become
Nationwide Tradition?

In 1910, the Rock Lick district of Buchanan County, Virginia, comprised little more than unpainted log cabins perched on steep hillsides about fifty miles north of Bristol, in the heart of the Cumberland Plateau. The first railroad spur into the county had been built two years earlier, and coal was replacing timber as the area's major product, just as timber had replaced sheep herding in the region after the Civil War. The Looney and Spencer clans of Rock Lick had been on friendly terms.

George Looney (35 years old) presided over a household consisting of his 39-year-old wife Patti, seven children ranging from newborn to 17 years of age, and his unmarried older brother, 44-year old Henderson Looney. The Looney clan had been in the area for generations, and many county residents were George Looney's distant kinfolk, including the local schoolmaster.[1]

The Spencer families were newcomers. Jordan Spencer and his wife Alafair had immigrated from Kentucky just before the turn of the century, bringing their two sons: George and

---

[1] 1910 census for Rock Lick magisterial district, Buchanan County, Virginia, 166A.

Jack.[2] By 1910, 30-year-old George Spencer had established his own household with his 30-year-old wife Arminda, three daughters and two sons, including seven-year-old Melvin, who attended the local school run by Looney's third cousin.[3] George Spencer's little brother, Jack, had also set up housekeeping, even though he was still in his late teens. Jack had just moved into a tiny cabin with his 15-year-old bride, Nancy.[4]

We shall probably never know why young, independent, married Jack Spencer killed middle-aged, dependent, bachelor Henderson Looney. Jack was never tried for murder, and he and Nancy continued to live in Rock Lick for decades thereafter.[5] Their son Dan was born in 1926.[6] Perhaps the killing of Henderson Looney was ruled to be an accident, or it might have been self-defense. In any event, the law did not prosecute Jack. This drove an enraged George Looney to take his frustrated revenge out on Jack's seven-year-old nephew, Melvin.

Looney traveled to Johnson County, Kentucky, whence Jordan Spencer had emigrated, and obtained affidavits from three men in their eighties, who claimed to remember Jordan Spencer's father (little Melvin's great-grandfather) as a red-headed man who might possibly have been rumored to have some Negro ancestry.[7] Armed with the three affidavits, Looney returned to Rock Lick and persuaded his schoolteacher cousin, Joseph McClanahan, to expel the third-grader from school without notifying his parents. They were denied opportunity to appeal the ruling that Melvin (and, presumably, the entire Spencer clan) was secretly Black.

Melvin's parents were unable to make any headway with the school. And so, in *Spencer v. Looney*, 1914 Virginia, they

---

[2] Ibid., 168A.

[3] Ibid., 165B.

[4] Idem.

[5] 1920 census for Rock Lick magisterial district, Buchanan County, Virginia, 12B.

[6] 1930 census for Knox, Buchanan County, Virginia, 19A.

[7] Daniel J. Sharfstein, "The Secret History of Race in the United States," *Yale Law Journal*, 112 (no. 6, 2003), 1473-509, 1475.

sued George Looney for slander and demanded $10,000 in damages.[8] Looney claimed the slander defense of truth.

At trial, the three old men from Kentucky waffled and wavered and avoided making any firm statement regarding the long-deceased Spencer's bloodline. When questioned by Looney's attorney, "Did you ever hear it reported that he had negro blood about him?" one of them replied "I might have heard it, and I might not."[9] Even the man hired by Looney as an expert in sniffing out "Negro blood" declared himself unable to do so and, when pressed, proceeded to identify several unrelated courtroom bystanders as secretly Black. By all three of the traditional rules—by appearance, by blood fraction, and by association—little Melvin was White. But the jury ruled the child to be Black anyway and found for defendant Looney.

The decision was overturned on the Spencers' appeal and the lawsuit was sent back for re-trial, but there is no record that it ever again came before a court. It is uncertain whether Melvin went back to the school in Rock Lick, but he did learn to read and write. Melvin was White in the eyes of Rock Lick's census takers before these events, and he continued to be recorded as census-White for the rest of his life. By the 1930 census, he was 26 years old, literate, and had set up housekeeping with his 21-year-old wife, Calla.[10]

* * * * *

As explained in the previous chapter, the one-drop rule triumphed and became accepted nationwide in the first three decades of the twentieth century. This chapter addresses the

---

[8] 116 Va. 767. Also, see Sharfstein (2003) for an excellent account of this case. Sharfstein differs from the above account only in interpretive slant. Sharfstein uses *Spencer v. Looney* to show that the one-drop rule (and "race" itself) was often contested before it became codified into statute in the wave of state laws that started in 1910. The above account, in contrast, shows that the one-drop rule was sometimes used for personal motives precisely because it could not be defended against.

[9] Sharfstein (2003), 1485.

[10] 1930 census for District 12, Rock Lick, Buchanan County, Virginia, 3B.

question, "Why did one-drop triumph at this time and not before nor after?"

It suggests a hypothesis in six topics. *The One-Drop Rule Punished Entire Families, not Just Individuals*, shows that, although the court cases dealt with individuals, entire families were actually punished. *The One-Drop Rule was Known to be Irrational*, presents evidence that one-drop trials were not searches for either factual accuracy or for moral justice. *The One-Drop Rule was Wielded Against Whites, not Against Blacks*, shows that the victims were White. To be sure, some victims may actually have had recent African ancestry, as do one-third of White Americans. But if this made them Black, then it means that one-third of all White Americans were also Black and the question remains—why pick these out? *Why Did it Happen*, surveys the literature for the causes of the Jim Crow wave of terror itself. *The One-Drop Rule Kept White Families in Line*, presents this study's hypothesis that one-drop was an instance of a well-studied phenomenon of group dynamics involving ideological self-preservation. *Other Voices*, offers an alternative explanation.

The One-Drop Rule Punished Entire Families, not Just Individuals

Despite contemporary rhetoric to the contrary, being ruled Black was a form of judicial punishment. The overt side of the question in early twentieth-century one-drop cases was "To which side of the U.S. endogamous color line should you be assigned?" But the question also had a covert aspect. The question was asked in the context of a land where, for at least two centuries, being relegated to the Black side of the endogamous color line meant loss of status, civil rights, and economic opportunity. And so, the covert aspect of the same question was "Should you be forcibly deprived of your social status, civil rights, and economic opportunity?"

Furthermore, the question had an explicit side and an implicit side. Explicitly, court rulings were only about the individuals before the bench. Implicitly, the consequences of being ruled Black were unbounded. Since Americans consider membership in the Black endogamous group to be hereditary, banishment to the Black side of the endogamous color line affected entire families—the victims' children and grandchildren, presumably for all eternity to come. Such old-testament-like eternal hereditary punishment is unique in the annals of American jurisprudence.

The One-Drop Rule was Known to be Irrational

The point of relating *Spencer v. Looney* is to exemplify, as is also evident in the cases of the prior chapter, that the one-drop rule was so arbitrary that it was often employed to satisfy personal self-interest. It will not do to say that the judges, juries and attorneys involved in one-drop cases sought the truth to the best of their ability. There is little evidence that they sought objective truth. First, there was no objective truth to be sought. Second, they knew that there was no objective truth to be sought. Instead, many if not most one-drop cases were simply contests of arbitrary power.

There is little evidence that they sought objective truth. If such decisions had been based upon factual reality—a search for truth—then testimony and judicial reasoning would have focused on the tangible, as in other decades. In the three centuries of British North American history that preceded the explosion in one-drop cases around 1900, courts had routinely tried to answer the question (both its explicit and implicit sides) by seeking facts in external reality. In *Flores v. State*, 1910 Texas, a court considered whether "hair was not kinky or nappy."[11] In *Bartelle v. United States*, 1908 Oklahoma, a court considered whether a person "had brown skin."[12] In *Daniel v. Guy*, 1861 Arkansas, a judge ruled that, "No one, who is familiar with the peculiar formation of the negro foot, can doubt, but that an inspection of that

---

[11] 60 Tex. Crim. 25.

[12] 2 Okla. Crim. 84.

member would ordinarily afford some indication of the race."[13] *In Rhinelander v. Rhinelander*, 1927 New York, an attorney instructed a young wife to remove her clothing so that the all-male jury could inspect the precise color of her nipples.[14] In *Estate of Monks*, 1941 California, a manicurist testified that, "the palms of her hands and her fingernails showed Negro blood in her."[15] Peculiar and misguided as some of these efforts may appear to modern eyes, the courts clearly sought to uncover tangible reality.

But in the three decades from 1900 to 1930, the question was more often addressed by rumor, innuendo, and hearsay. In *Tucker v. Blease*, 1914 South Carolina, the judge acquiesced to mob rule with the words, "The greatest good to the largest number."[16] In *Ferrall v. Ferrall*, 1910 North Carolina, the plaintiff argued for nonsensical recursion.[17] In *Eubank v. Boughton*, 1900 Virginia and in *Oberly v. School Board*, 1918 Louisiana, state supreme courts ruled that the judicial system was powerless to intervene.[18] In the other nine cases involving children (including the one that opens this chapter), no evidence was ever introduced about the individuals under scrutiny—it was solely hearsay about absent, usually deceased, ancestors.

There was no objective truth to be sought. When twentieth-century Americans redefined the color line as intangible or metaphysical, they abandoned any hope of assessing endogamous group membership rationally. North Americans, like all New World peoples are a genetic mix of the three great colonial demographic streams—Europe, Africa, and Native America. To be sure, North Americans are not as homogeneously admixed as, say, Argentineans because they have managed to preserve an endogamous enclave of distinctively part-African appearance,

---

[13] 23 Ark. 50.

[14] 245 N.Y. 510.

[15] 48 Cal. App. 2d 603.

[16] 97 S.C. 303.

[17] 153 N.C. 174.

[18] 98 Va. 499; 142 La. 788.

but they are admixed nonetheless. The search for White-looking Americans with invisible Black ancestry was doomed from the start because the objective reality is that the term, "White-looking Americans with invisible Black ancestry," fits all, most, or many White Americans, depending on how "White" and "Black" are defined. In the light of paleoanthropology, all members of the U.S. White endogamous group have distant African ancestry because the human species emerged in Africa and colonized the globe starting about 60 millennia ago. In the light of Mediterranean prehistory, most White Americans descend from peoples who migrated back and forth across the Mediterranean to repopulate Europe when the glaciers receded 15 millennia ago. In the light of admixture mapping, one-third of White Americans have measurable recent African ancestry within the past five centuries—the equivalent of one ancestor of one hundred percent African admixture within the past 115 years.[19] When it comes down to external reality, the one-drop cases were not analogous to seeking a needle in a haystack; they were seeking hay in a haystack while pretending that the stack contained something other than hay.

They well knew that there was no objective truth to be sought. A correspondent to the 1854 *Richmond Enquirer* wrote: "[If a one-drop rule were adopted], I doubt not, if many who are reputed to be white, and are in fact so, do not in a very short time find themselves instead of being elevated, reduced by the judgment of a court of competent jurisdiction, to the level of a free negro."[20] George Tillman orated in 1895, "If the law is made as it now stands respectable families in Aiken, Barnwell, Colleton, and Orangeburg will be denied the right to intermarry among people with whom they are now associated and identified."[21] Charles Chesnutt wrote, "As you have all the features of

---

[19] See under the topic "Admixture Scatter Diagrams" in *Chapter 2. Afro-European Genetic Admixture in the United States.*

[20] See under the topic "Virginia Rejects the One-Drop Rule" in *Chapter 17. The Antebellum South Rejects the One-Drop Rule.*

[21] See under the topic "South Carolina" in *Chapter 19. The One-Drop Rule Arrives in the Postbellum Lower South.*

a white man, you would, at least in South Carolina, have simply to assume the place and exercise the privileges of a white man."[22] Justice Clark of the Supreme Court of North Carolina wrote:

> If indeed, the plaintiff had discovered any minute strain of colored origin after the youth of his wife has been worn away for his pleasure and in his service, justice and generosity dictated that he keep to himself that of which the public was unaware... The plaintiff, if possessed of any sentiment of manhood, would have shielded his wife and children by removing to another locality or to a State where the fact, if known, would not be deemed a stigma.[23]

They knew. Independent approaches converge on 0.10 to 0.14 percent as the annual rate at which European-looking children born into the Black side of the U.S. endogamous color line have switched to the White side of the line in adulthood for the past three centuries.[24] Given the 9.7 million African-Americans recorded by the 1910 census, this means that 97,000-to-130,000 Black Americans became White in that decade. Even if the actual number during the Jim Crow wave of terror were less than one-tenth of this long-term average (9,000 individuals per decade, say), it would still mean that at least one thousand people successfully became White during this decade for every single "racial-determination" court case that was appealed. That this rate of color line permeability passed unnoticed by America's elite is untenable, given public statements like those quoted in the preceding paragraph.

The one-drop rule was irrational in the early twentieth century and its enforcers knew that it was irrational. One historian refers to this phenomenon as a wave of insanity—paranoia—that mysteriously swept over the South in those

---

[22] See under the topic "A Permeable, Shifted Color Line" in *Chapter 10. Barbadian South Carolina: A Class-Based Color Line.*

[23] See *Ferrall v. Ferrall*, 1910 North Carolina under the topic "Terminology Changed" in Chapter 20. *Jim Crow Triumph of the One-Drop Rule.*

[24] See *Chapter 5. The Rate of Black-to-White "Passing."*

years.[25] The oddity is that the one-drop is still irrational today and yet, as demonstrated earlier, it is still advocated by many American scholars today who also well know that it is irrational.[26]

The One-Drop Rule was Wielded Against Whites, not Against Blacks

An even greater oddity in the study of U.S. "race" relations is that many if not most American scholars see the triumph of the one-drop rule in the early twentieth century as an aspect of White-on-Black oppression. As demonstrated earlier, the consensus among today's scholars is that the one-drop rule was somehow an example of "racism" (Whites mistreating Blacks).[27] The one-drop rule is usually depicted as exemplifying White society's intolerance towards Americans of the Black endogamous group during the Jim Crow wave of terror. The accepted wisdom seems to be that the victims of the one-drop rule, like the victims of other Jim Crow intolerance, were members of the U.S. Black endogamous group and that the perpetrators were members of mainstream society—the U.S. White endogamous group. There is no question that the perpetrators were society's White elite; the one-drop rule was enforced by judicial means, after all. But why do most American scholars portray its victims as Black? Even Joel Williamson, who of all American scholars of the "race" notion may most clearly see the one-drop rule phenomenon as an example of mass paranoia, refers to its victims as "mulattoes who looked white."[28] The only definition of "mu-

---

[25] Joel Williamson, *The Crucible of Race: Black/White Relations in the American South Since Emancipation* (New York, 1984), 464-65, 467-68.

[26] See under the topic "Many Scholars Believe the One-Drop Rule is Stronger Than Ever" in *Chapter 14. Features of Today's One-Drop Rule.*

[27] See under the topics "Other Evidence Confirms the One-Drop Rule's Popularity," "Many Scholars Believe the One-Drop Rule is Stronger Than Ever," and "The Scholarly Consensus is Unpersuasive" in *Chapter 14. Features of Today's One-Drop Rule.*

[28] Williamson (1984), 465.

latto" that could make sense out of Williamson's phrase is as reference to voluntary membership in an ethnic community. But, as demonstrated above, the victims of the one-drop cases definitely did not voluntarily consider themselves "mulattoes."

Why do most American scholars portray the one-drop rule victims as Black? It cannot be because they looked even slightly African in appearance (dark skin tone, tightly-curled hair, etc.). The whole point of the one-drop court trials was to determine the endogamous group membership of people who looked utterly European. Had a victim of one of these irrational trials been of sub-Saharan phenotype, there would have been no trial. Indeed, the record of every one-drop trial stresses that the victims looked White.

Why do most American scholars portray the one-drop rule victims as Black? It cannot be because the victims self-identified as being of African-American ethnicity. Virtually all U.S. scholars claim that the one-drop rule is an example of U.S. "racism" (Whites mistreating Blacks). And yet, scholars who are (reluctantly) willing to express their own definition of who is Black, when pressed, usually use a voluntary ethnicity formulation such as "self-identity" or "racial identity."[29] But the victims of the one-drop trials vehemently denied any such self-identity. That their endogamous group membership was to be assigned involuntarily by a court was the whole point of the trials.

Why do most American scholars portray America's one-drop rule victims as Black? It cannot be because the victims had recent (albeit invisible) ancestry traceable to the U.S. Black endogamous group. In none of the court cases was any credible evidence presented of this. In most of the cases (in all of the school segregation cases), it was never even alleged. Furthermore, even if traceable ancestry had been alleged (which it was not) and proven (which it was not), it would have applied equally to one-third of America's Whites. Indeed, given that most of the cases were held in the South, it would have applied

---

[29] Personal experience of the present author in querying historians of "race relations" by email.

to an even greater fraction of the White witnesses, jurors, and judges in those very cases.

Why do most American scholars portray America's one-drop rule victims as Black? It cannot be because physical anthropology supports the idea of intangible "race." Even those few remaining anthropologists today who disagree with the American Anthropological Association's disavowing of the entire concept of "race" in 1998[30] also reject the one-drop notion of invisible Blackness.[31] Indeed, as early as 1911, anthropologists led by Franz Boas[32] had begun to doubt that any connection existed between physical appearance and cultural traits. For that matter, no scientist since Napoleonic times has ever embraced the notion of "racial membership" as something undetectable by definition.[33]

The fact is that, by any rational criterion, the one-drop rule victims were as thoroughly members of the U.S. White endogamous group as were any other Euro-Americans then or now. They looked European. They associated only with others on the White side of the endogamous U.S. color line. They were not shown (or, in many cases even alleged) to have recent Black ancestry. And they vehemently insisted that they were White. What conceivable rationale in the scholarly American mind today can portray them as somehow intangibly Black?

Why do so many American scholars today either believe that the one-drop rule is universally enforced or advocate that it should be enforced, or both? Why do most American scholars insist in the face of objective reality that the victims of the one-drop rule were Black? This work does not attempt to answer these two questions. Such an effort would take us into episte-

---

[30] See the Association's "Statement on 'Race'" at URL <http://www.aaanet.org/stmts/racepp.htm>.

[31] Nova: George W. Gill, *Does Race Exist?: An Proponent's Perspective* <http://www.pbs.org/wgbh/nova/first/gill.html> (2000).

[32] Franz Boas, *The Mind of Primitive Man* (New York, 1911).

[33] For a historical survey of anthropological views of "race," see George W. Stocking, *Race, Culture, and Evolution: Essays in the History of Anthropology* (New York,, 1968), 42-68.

mology and the psychopathology of master narratives, an area that is at best peripheral to the history of the one-drop rule.[34]

The two questions are presented here only to make a point. Neither of the two beliefs has any place in a search for the causes of the one-drop rule's triumph. Both must be shed. The counterfactual notion that the elite Whites who enforced the one-drop rule were motivated by a search for truth or justice, and the bizarre notion that their victims were somehow intangibly Black, both must be discarded if there is to be any hope of identifying the causes of the phenomenon.

Why Did it Happen?

In its most succinct form, the puzzle that the past presents to us is this: Why did American society banish many White families to Blackness? More precisely, why did U.S. courts in the first three decades of the twentieth century knowingly persecute entire families by banishing them from the White side of the endogamous color line to the Black side of the endogamous color line, thereby presumably depriving them and their descendants forever of status, civil rights, and economic opportunity.

The known facts are five: (1) the victims were banished from the White side of the U.S. endogamous color line to the Black side, (2) the victims were thereby punished by loss of rights and status, (3) the victims were entire families and their descendants, (4) the punishment was not the result of a rational search for factual justice, and (5) the persecution began around the turn of the twentieth century. One non-fact must be discarded as a distraction—that the victims really were members of the Black endogamous group in some metaphysical or intangible sense. To be sure, some victims may actually have had recent African ancestry, as do one-third of White Americans. But if this made them Black, then it means that one-third of all White Americans were also Black and the question remains—why pick these out?

---

[34] Indeed, merely asking the questions with some tenacity has resulted in the present author being accused of White supremacy and "racism."

The first component of the answer lies in the phenomenon's timing. It occurred as the Jim Crow wave of terror was
rising to its peak. It might have occurred earlier, but it did not.
One-drop statutes had been debated in 1854 Virginia and in 1895
South Carolina but had been defeated. Although Americans had
toyed with a one-drop rule for decades, and it had been invoked
in a few court cases in the 1890s, it did not triumph and become
a nationwide tradition until the Jim Crow wave of terror and oppression was underway. And so, the first step of the answer is
that the one-drop rule must have had some connection with Jim
Crowism. Given the timing of events, in fact, one may suspect
that the Jim Crow event somehow caused the triumph of the
one-drop rule.

That the Jim Crow wave of terror and oppression somehow caused the triumph of the one-drop rule opens a second
question, "What triggered the Jim Crow wave of terror and oppression?" To set the context, it may be useful to skim five national trends that coincided in this period. Jim Crow might have
been triggered, or at least worsened, by some combination of the
five: industrialization, consumerism, state activism, progressivism, and imperialism. Each trend could be traced at least back to
the early nineteenth century. And each advanced throughout the
nineteenth century with periods of stasis punctuated by surges of
change. But between 1880 and 1920, all five trends overlapped.
Their combined impact was significant.

Industrialization. The relocation and growth of factories
sprang from improved technologies for exploiting and distribut-
ing energy. Anthracite packed more power into a smaller pack-
age than water or animal muscle. Improved seaports allowed
energy-efficient propeller ships to replace paddle-wheelers. Railroads covered the nation. Macadamized roads allowed internal
combustion engines to reach every corner. Greatly improved
coal distribution allowed factories to relocate from millstreams
to be nearer their vendors, customers, and workers. Electric
power generation and distribution accelerated the trend to an
even higher level. Factory relocation led to dense urbanization.
Cities' expansion and the use of telephones accelerated business
cycles and fueled unprecedented production of goods. Rising

wealth attracted immigrants, whose men displaced wage-earning women, and whose wives and children added ethnic conflict to the stresses already besetting a nation that was changing faster than many people could adapt. The depression of 1893-1897 was caused by overproduction. Food and manufactured goods were both produced faster than they could be consumed. Society responded in three ways: consumerism, state activism, and imperialism.[35]

Consumerism. By competing among themselves for sales to the public, producers and merchants created a consumer culture. Mail order houses exploited communications and transportation technology, selling and shipping goods to the most remote communities. Urban department stores anticipated the modern mall in attracting browsers with restaurants, activities, and entertainment in the expectation that some would stop and shop. Advertising became an art form, developing product loyalty by persuading buyers that the particular brand advertised was the secret to upper middle-class status. Entertainment became more hectic as fickle vaudeville, with a different program of ten-minute acts each week, replaced the traditional minstrel shows whose traveling troupes could not incorporate novelty quickly enough.[36]

State Activism. Rising prosperity came with worsening inequality. Wealth concentration and income maldistribution both rose steadily during the period. Even as the increasingly well-off middle class established popular standards for style and consumption, the number of those without access to the nation's industrial bounty grew. The poor become steadily poorer and more populous. Urban labor conditions became unhealthful or dangerous, as even the children of immigrant families came to be exploited. Meanwhile, farming became more capital-intensive

---

[35] See Alfred Dupont Chandler, *The Visible Hand: The Managerial Revolution in American Business* (Cambridge MA, 1977); William Cronon, *Nature's Metropolis: Chicago and the Great West* (New York, 1991); Alan Trachtenberg and Eric Foner, *The Incorporation of America: Culture and Society in the Gilded Age*, 1st ed. (New York, 1982).

[36] See Roy Rosenzweig, *Eight Hours for What we Will: Workers and Leisure in an Industrial City, 1870-1920*, 1st pbk. ed. (Cambridge UK, 1985).

due to competitive need for advanced machinery, and so farmers were ever more vulnerable to losing everything during commodity price declines. As social stresses mounted and civil society seemed unable to fix itself, the state came to be seen as morally responsible for the welfare of the masses—a notion that would have puzzled antebellum politicians. Minor political parties with narrow reformist agenda proliferated and the major parties reacted by co-opting selected programs. Despite legislative efforts to ameliorate inequality and exploitation, the courts seemed to be in the thrall of corporations and the socio-economic elite. Laws meant to protect the powerless were interpreted so as to enhance the powerful. The 1875 federal civil rights act, which was meant to end "racial" discrimination, was first interpreted by courts as supporting corporations rather than individuals, and then ruled unconstitutional altogether. The Sherman anti-trust act, which was meant to break up monopolistic trusts and combinations, was interpreted by courts as outlawing organized labor action, while "trusts and combinations" simply renamed themselves "holding companies." The Fifteenth Amendment forbade states from restricting voting rights on account of "race," and so Jim Crow regulations throughout the South disfranchised Blacks using an assortment of discriminatory excuses. Despite a half-century of activism, only four states allowed White women to vote by 1900, and female suffrage by undeniable right seemed as remote as ever.[37]

Progressivism. The obvious need for social reform, coupled with the political system's apparent inability to respond effectively, sparked a national voluntary movement known as Progressivism. The Progressive movement is analytically challenging for two reasons. On the one hand, its advocates agreed that it was the duty of all good Americans to roll up their sleeves and

---

[37] See Herbert George Gutman, *Work, Culture, and Society in Industrializing America: Essays in American Working-Class and Social History*, 1st ed. (New York, 1976b); Ruth Birgitta Anderson Bordin, *Woman and Temperance: The Quest for Power and Liberty, 1873-1900* (Philadelphia, 1981); Lawrence Goodwyn, *Democratic Promise: The Populist Moment in America* (New York, 1976); Nell Irvin Painter, *Standing at Armageddon: The United States, 1877-1919*, 1st ed. (New York, 1987).

pitch in, in order to right wrongs, end injustices, reform society, end political and business corruption, and forge a new melting pot nation comprising every suitable race, creed, and color. On the other, they disagreed sharply about the details. Were the desperately poor the victims of cruel exploitation or of their own ignorance? Should social workers correct inequity by providing a welfare "safety-net," or by teaching their clients how to become good Americans? Was business corrupting politics or vice-versa? Could Italians and Greeks ever become White? What about Jews? For that matter, if any ethnic group could be embraced by America's expanding blanket of acceptance merely by adopting middle-class Protestantism and abandoning foreign ways, then what was to stop Blacks from become White? Progressives differed in the solutions that they advocated. More importantly, they differed in how they defined the problems to be solved. Self-labeled Progressives spanned the entire ideological spectrum, from nonjudgmental settlement houses and ethnic self-help societies at one end, to eugenicists and Klansmen at the other. WTCU suffragettes, fundamentalists, Populist Farmers, currency reformers, and public health activists fought for their aims somewhere in-between.

Imperialism. Apparently inspired by Ranke, the American Historical Association in the 1890s established the academic policy that loyalty to the nation should thenceforth define history teaching. In the same decade, the nation's most famous historian, F.J. Turner, taught that repeated settlement of new frontiers had made Americans into a uniquely adventurous, optimistic, and democratic race, but that the frontier was now closed; that Americans needed a new frontier if democracy were to survive. This suggestion coincided with Mahan's influential book on the importance of sea power, and so America belatedly joined the European scramble to acquire colonies. Americans became inspired by the vision: that the White Man's Burden was to occupy lands inhabited by their little brown brothers, and lift them out of the dust of ignorance into the light of Protestantism. Americans soon learned that there were not enough little brown brothers to go around, and so the nation fought a short, one-sided, splendid little war against a geriatric Spain to acquire some brown brothers of their own. They then fought a long, ugly war of mutually escalating atrocities to crush a Philippine Insurrection by brown folks who preferred to uplift themselves without help. By then, America had become such an important world power that it could not avoid involvement in the First World War.[38]

Ultimately, what drove all five changes was technology. The first half of the nineteenth century saw the culmination of the Enlightenment in a flood of scientific discoveries, ranging from the germ theory of disease to natural selection. The second half of the century saw this science turned into an avalanche of technology whose effects, direct and indirect, transformed the nation.

The plight of African-Americans epitomized the brutal inconsistency of the Gilded Age. Despite three centuries since colonization, America's odd endogamous color line had preserved two genetically separate populations. Other slaveowning countries had either absorbed their small African populations by genetic assimilation within a few generations (Spain, Portugal, Argentina, Mexico), or had quickly developed a unimodal genetic admixture distribution in lands where Africans had been a demographic majority (Morocco, Brazil, Puerto Rico).[39] Inspired by B.T. Washington's vision that successful Blacks who earned middle-class financial status would inevitably be granted social acceptance, thousands of Black professionals and entrepreneurs staked their careers and their lives on the New South. Thousands were then tortured to death in public rituals by a society whose vision of the problem to be solved was the precise opposite— that successful Blacks did not know their place. Driven out by Jim Crow and attracted by northern industrialists who wanted leverage against unions, Blacks began the Great Migration. This demographic mass movement from the rural South to the urban North created a Harlem Renaissance of music, art, and literature.

---

[38] See Walter LaFeber, *The New Empire: An Interpretation of American expansion, 1860-1898* (Ithaca, 1963); Emily S. Rosenberg and Eric Foner, *Spreading the American Dream: American Economic and Cultural Expansion, 1890-1945*, 1st ed. (New York, 1982).

[39] See under the topic "Admixture Scatter Diagrams" in Chapter 2. *Afro-European Genetic Admixture in the United States.*

It also spawned an endemic criminal caste among urban Blacks who, although used as pawns in management-versus-labor games, never received any real opportunity to work in factories.[40]

By 1920, America's fundamental paradox had taken its current shape. The nation's near-unlimited willingness to embrace immigrants, its reward of unmatched class mobility for those who have been accepted into the mainstream, coupled with the strange permanency of an endogamous color line that would permanently ostracize from the fruits of society an enclave comprising Americans of mainly African appearance.[41] The causes of Jim Crow have been discussed by numerous scholars.[42] It is not discussed here except to add two minor points that some scholars may have missed. First, it was a nationwide phenomenon, not a Southern one. Second, it may have been one of a cycle of plunges in "race" relations.

The Jim Crow event was a nationwide phenomenon, not a Southern one. Some scholars focus exclusively on the South to explain the Jim Crow event.[43] But this may be because they focus on the terrorizing and disfranchisement of African Ameri-

---

[40] See Alan Dawley, *Struggles for Justice: Social Responsibility and the Liberal State* (Cambridge MA, 1991); Roger Lane, *Roots of Violence in Black Philadelphia, 1860-1900* (Cambridge MA, 1986); Kenneth L. Kusmer, *A Ghetto Takes Shape: Black Cleveland, 1870-1930* (Urbana, 1976).

[41] See Gary Gerstle, *American Crucible: Race and Nation in the Twentieth Century* (Princeton, 2001).

[42] Three whom I have found to be especially perceptive are: C. Vann Woodward, *The Strange Career of Jim Crow*, 3d rev. ed. (New York, 1974); George M. Fredrickson, *The Black Image in the White Mind: The Debate on Afro-American Character and Destiny, 1817-1914* (New York, 1981a); and Stetson Kennedy, *Jim Crow Guide: The Way it Was* (Boca Raton FL, 1990).

[43] But for exceptions, who view it with nationwide scope, see Heather Cox Richardson, *The Death of Reconstruction: Race, Labor, and Politics in the Post-Civil War North, 1865-1901* (Cambridge MA, 2001); Michael Perman, *Struggle for Mastery: Disfranchisement in the South, 1888-1908* (Chapel Hill, 2001); and the first-hand account, William Archibald Dunning, *Essays on the Civil War and Reconstruction, and Related Topics* (New York, 1904).

cans, which were phenomena limited to the South. But if you step back and look only at the strength of the endogamous color line, the strictness with which it was enforced, you can get a broader picture. As mentioned earlier, socially coerced endogamy is ostracism that excludes the enclave group from the greater society. The following graph, "Intermarriage, North and South," plots the intermarriage rate at each census decade in two series: the black line tracks Black/White intermarriage in the former slave states. The grey line tracks intermarriage in those states of the Northeast and the Midwest that did not have slavery in 1861.

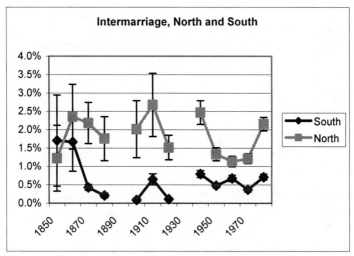

Figure 31. Intermarriage, North and South[44]

The chart shows that antebellum intermarriage was higher in the South than in the North. This is not surprising, given the color line's permeability in the lower South and its split nature along the Gulf coast. The chart shows that intermarriage had plunged to a negligible level in the South by 1880 and had virtually vanished in the South by 1900, reflecting the beginning of the Jim Crow period. But it also shows that intermarriage in the North fell by about one-third between 1869 and 1880. To be

---

[44] For the derivation of this chart, see under the topic "Intermarriage, North and South" in *Appendix A. Census Data Processing Methodology.*

sure, the confidence-interval error-bars are large here, reflecting the small sample size available in these census years, but the trend is unmistakable. Black families were increasingly segregated from the mainstream during the Jim Crow era, in the North well as the South.

The Jim Crow event may have been one of a cycle of plunges in "race" relations. This is pure speculation, but it may be worth investigating. Judging by contemporary documents, race-relations plunged in 1730s, the first generation after the endogamous color line was invented.[45] And, judging by contemporary documents, race-relations plunged again in the 1830s, consequent to the Nat Turner incident.[46] And, judging by intermarriage statistics, race-relations plunged again in the 1920s.[47] No evidence suggests that comparable plunges took place during the intervening years. Like economic cycles, each specific plunge can be explained by antecedent events, and yet our recognizing their once-a-century cyclical nature may yield broader insight.

The One-Drop Rule Kept White Families in Line

In any case, whatever the causes of the Jim Crow wave of terror and oppression, the timing linkage between Jim Crow and the triumph of the one-drop rule is unmistakable. After discarding the two popular but demonstrably counterfactual notions— that the elites who enforced one-drop sought truth or justice, and

---

[45] See under the topic, "It was a 'Divide and Conquer' Tactic" in *Chapter 8. Why Did Virginia's Rulers Invent a Color Line?*, especially Governor Gooch's letter to the Lords of Trade and Plantations.

[46] See under the topic "A Watershed Event in Three Threads" in *Chapter 16. Why Did Northerners Invent a One-Drop Rule?*, especially the accounts of the riots in the Boston, New York, Philadelphia, and Cincinnati.

[47] See the figure "Intermarriage, North and South," immediately above, or the figure "Black/White Intermarriage" under topic "Endogamy" in *Chapter 6. Features of the Endogamous Color Line.*

that their victims were somehow intangibly Black[48]—this study suggests that the one-drop rule emerged in order to keep otherwise compassionate White American families in line.

The triumph of the one-drop rule was a manifestation of the Jim Crow mentality of oppression and terror preserving itself from erosion. It is the same ideological self-preservation phenomenon that led lynch mobs to threaten "nigger-lovers" with the noose. It is the same ideological self-preservation phenomenon that leads packs of school bullies to ostracize any child who defends their victims. In the behavioral field of group dynamics, it is a well-known phenomenon that, when one group bullies another, members of the first group who refuse to participate in the bullying are exiled to the victimized group. According to Napier, "any member who does not adhere will be seen as a threat... and efforts will be made to induce him or her to return to the group procedures."[49] In order to be allowed to remain within the oppressing group, members must accept group norms.[50] Although minor exclusions may involve being left out of certain activities, the most severe punishment is that of "forced exile." This is a form of social death because the excluded person is cut off from the support, care and spiritual life of the... community.[51]

Ordinary folks are just not cruel enough to maintain such an oppressive system without coercion. Families make friends with other families. Businessmen make deals with other businessmen. Laborers organize with other laborers. And young people fall in love with other young people. Left to their own devices, ordinary people would have woven at least a partly colorblind network of such family alliances. If this had been al-

---

[48] To be sure, some victims may actually have had recent African ancestry, as do one-third of White Americans. But if this made them Black, then it means that one-third of all White Americans were also Black and the question remains—why pick these out?

[49] Rodney Napier and Matti K. Gershenfeld, *Groups: Theory and Experience*, 7th ed. (Boston, 2004).

[50] Susan Opotow, "Moral Exclusion and Injustice: An Introduction," *Journal of Social Issues*, 46 (no. 1, 1990), 1-20.

[51] Mircea Eliade and Charles J. Adams, eds. *The Encyclopedia of Religion* (New York, 1987);

lowed to happen, Jim Crow would have collapsed within a generation or two, just as prior waves of "racial" hatred had collapsed in 1765 and 1865.

And so, the purpose of the one-drop rule—the idea that a White family could be consigned to the Black side of the endogamous color line—was to keep otherwise compassionate Whites in line.[52] The previous chapter's account of the court cases of the time reveals the pattern. When a family's "racial" identity was to be decided, parades of prosecution witnesses testified, one by one, that a grandmother was once seen eating a meal with a Black tradesman, that an uncle was once seen shaking hands with a Black businessman, that a teenaged boy once schemed a silly prank with a Black youngster, that a great-aunt married a colored man. In every post-1900 appellate court case that this study has uncovered where a family's "racial" identity was resolved on the basis of the one-drop rule, the family in question was as genetically white as millions of other White Americans. They had simply made the terrible mistake of befriending Blacks at a family-to-family level.

"Who cares?" you ask, "surely judges and juries did not think that you can inherit African genes by eating, shaking hands, scheming a prank, or by a non-ancestral relative's actions." But the record makes it clear that the one-drop rule was never about biological ancestry.[53] It was always about family friendships and family alliances. Any White family who got too close to a Black family risked expulsion from the White endogamous group, along with their progeny, for all generations to come—a horrific fate, back then. If White families had been allowed to befriend Black families, the whole system of Jim Crow terror would have collapsed much sooner than it did. This does not suggest that some nefarious conspiracy plotted this solution to the problem of preserving Jim Crow. It is simply a routine and

---

[52] To be sure, some victims may actually have had recent African ancestry, as do one-third of White Americans. But if this made them Black, then it means that one-third of all White Americans were also Black and the question remains—why pick these out?

[53] See the immediately preceding note.

well-studied manifestation of group ideological self-preservation.

Far from being victimized by the phenomenon, African-American leaders were indifferent to one-drop laws and opposed to children of Blacks switching to adopt a White self-identity in adulthood. As mentioned earlier, Black leadership saw one-drop legislation as a White-on-White squabble.[54] And Black educators saw endogamous-group-switching as morally reprehensible because it weakened ethnic solidarity.[55] It appears that the White public knew that the purpose of the one-drop rule was to keep Whites from defending Blacks. At the same time, its purpose within the Black community was to define the borders of ethnic membership.

Other Voices

An alternative hypothesis to explain the triumph of the one-drop rule is that the Jim Crow wave of terror triggered the first great migration of the descendants of enslaved African-Americans to the northern industrial cities. The unskilled labor force in Southern agriculture comprised mainly Blacks. The northwards migration of Blacks reduced the availability of unskilled labor in the south and threatened agri-businesses (the plantations). Planters responded to the lack of labor by encouraging judges and legislators to shift the color line palewards, thereby increasing the size of the Black endogamous group and trapping numbers of poor Whites on the Black side of the endogamous color line.[56] This explanation is buttressed by the lack of commercial plantations in the Cumberland Plateau and the

---

[54] See the 1895 South Carolina Constitutional Convention described under topic "African-American Complicity" in *Chapter 20. Jim Crow Triumph of the One-Drop Rule.*

[55] See the discussion of "passing" and "passing novels" in the same place.

[56] This hypothesis was proposed to the OneDropRule discussion group in October, 2004, by John M. Hartley at URL <http://groups.yahoo.com/group/OneDropRule/message/7823>.

concurrent resistance to one-drop enforcement in that same region of the country.[57]

Others have questioned four points: whether one-drop enforcers were indifferent to biological ancestry, whether Blacks suffered as much as Whites from such enforcement, whether it was scientifically supported, and whether the enforcers deliberately conspired.[58]

This study concludes that enforcers were indifferent to biological ancestry because in the decade of peak enforcement, between 97,000 and 130,000 Americans redefined themselves as White (despite having at least one Black parent). But only a few dozen cases were prosecuted and appealed. Even if only one out of every hundred cases was appealed, this still means that the authorities selectively prosecuted only one such situation out of every several thousand. Their statements on record show that they knew they were prosecuting only a tiny chosen fraction of such cases. Admittedly, their public rhetoric was meant to arouse support by goading the public into hysteria (or "paranoia," as Joel Williamson puts it) over biological ancestry. But leaders' public rhetoric does not always match their actual agenda. This may have been such a case. The ignorant public was obsessed with biological ancestry. But the educated elite knew that White Southerners were actually mixed.

That Blacks suffered far more than Whites at the hand of Jim Crow is a given. Nothing here should give any other impression. Jim Crow (and its associated lynchings) was the inhumane oppression of a pariah caste (Blacks) by a ruling caste (Whites). Nevertheless, the cause-and-effect relationship between the hyper-enforcement of the endogamous color line during Jim Crow and the exiling of selected White families to Blackness is bidirectional. Such exile was a horrific fate only because Blacks were cruelly persecuted. Had this not been so, exile would have been a useless deterrent. Conclusion: the Jim Crow terror caused

---

[57] See the testimony by the old men from Kentucky in *Spencer v. Looney*, 1914 Virginia (116 Va. 767), the anecdote that opens this chapter.

[58] Arguments proposed by George Winkel on June 29, 2005, at URL < http://backintyme.com/ODR/viewtopic.php?p=2435>.

one-drop enforcement because it is what made the threat of exiling White families to Blackness viable. On the other hand, the Jim Crow terror would have ended sooner had compassionate White families not been cowed into submission by threat of exile. So in this sense, one-drop enforcement prolonged the Jim Crow terror.

Whether one-drop enforcement was scientifically supported is hard to say. The heyday of scientific racialism had already ended by 1890. Peer-reviewed anthropological journal articles during the Progressive era focused on the cultural (learned) determinants of group (class, caste, ethnicity, race) formation and denied biological determinism. One can trace the transition in George W. Stocking, *Race, Culture, and Evolution: Essays in the History of Anthropology* (New York, 1968). Indeed, today's grotesque mismatch between what scientists tell each other and what popularizers tell the public began with Franz Boas, *The Mind of Primitive Man* (New York, 1911) and the New York Times reviewer who said that the book was "the desperate attempt of a Jew to pass himself off as white." One wonders whether the 1910's faddish surge in public enthusiasm for bio-race was not in fact a cognitive dissonance reaction to the start of science's denial of the notion. Nevertheless, one cannot marshal evidence either way.

Finally, it is safe to say that White elites deliberately conspired to create and enforce the Jim Crow terror. One-drop enforcement exiling White families to Blackness was also consciously planned. But a historical work must also take a distant view that explains why such one-drop enforcement was concocted at that particular moment in history, and not earlier or later. Although society's elites choose policies to further their ends, there are vaster currents in human affairs that determine what those ends are, and what means are available at any specific moment. Hence, this work pegs one-drop enforcement to the Jim Crow terror and leave it to others (Williamson, Kennedy, Van Woodward, Berlin) to explain the Jim Crow terror.

* * * * *

This chapter suggested a hypothesis for the triumph of the one-drop rule in the first three decades of twentieth century. It showed that, although the court cases dealt with individuals, entire families were actually punished. It presented evidence that one-drop trials were not searches for either factual accuracy or for moral justice. It explained that the victims of the one-drop rule were White. To be sure, some victims may actually have had recent African ancestry, as do one-third of White Americans. But if this made them Black, then it means that one-third of all White Americans were also Black and the question remains—why pick these out? It outlined the causes of the Jim Crow wave of terror itself. It presented the hypothesis that one-drop was an instance of well-studied phenomenon of group dynamics involving ideological self-preservation. It also offered one alternative explanation.

In short, this study hypothesizes that the triumph of the one-drop rule kept otherwise compassionate White American families in line during the Jim Crow wave of terror. The phenomenon was nothing more than a manifestation of the ideological self-preservation of the Jim Crow mentality itself. This hypothesis will be disproved if evidence can be found that significant numbers of White families who defended or befriended Blacks being victimized by Jim Crow, were *not* challenged to prove their Whiteness.

Conclusion

This book used recent findings in molecular anthropology to explain that one-third of White Americans carry measurable recent African genetic admixture in their DNA, the equivalent of having a single ancestor of one hundred percent African admixture from around the year 1880. The physical features associated with African versus European ancestry in the U.S. culture are due to about a dozen genes. Such "racial" traits are so ephemeral that three generations of intermarriage suffice to erase all traces of them. The 0.7 percent average African admixture found in today's White Americans is the result of genes slowly leaking through the color line from Black to White. In every year that has passed since the 1691 invention of the endogamous color line, between 0.10 and 0.14 percent of the Black population on average switched self-identity from the Black side of the endogamous color line to the White side.

The book told the history of America's intermarriage barrier. The endogamous color line was invented in the late seventeenth-century Chesapeake to deter servile insurrection. It reinforced the aggressive ethnic voting blocs of the Jacksonian urban North. In the period between the invention of the color line and the Civil War, Americans in the North and the upper South gradually changed how they identified which side of the color line you were on. Throughout the eighteenth century, the primary criterion was your physical appearance. Although some colonies had blood-fraction laws, courts tended to rule that, if you looked European, then you belonged on the White side of the color line. During the nineteenth century, blood fraction as adjusted by association gradually became important additional criteria. By 1890 in the North and the upper South, if you had a Black grandparent and associated with Blacks, you were Black even if you looked European. The lower South was different.

Until Reconstruction, the lower South had very different color-line traditions. Louisiana and Alabama had two color lines separating three mildly endogamous groups: Black, White, and Colored. South Carolina had an extraordinarily permeable color line determined as much by class as by physical appearance. And Spanish Florida had no endogamous barrier at all. After Reconstruction, the nation as a whole adopted the impermeable single color line and the concept of African-American ethnicity that had been born in Boston, New York, and Philadelphia.

The book traced the origin and unfolding of the notion of invisible Blackness by examining travelers' accounts, diaries, fiction literature, advertisements for runaway slaves, and a database of 300 court cases held from 1770 to 1990 to resolve on which side of the color line you belonged. The notion of a "White-looking Black person," arose in the 1830s North after the Nat Turner incident. This "one-drop rule" then spread slowly through the South, reaching Louisiana shortly after 1900. It triumphed and became nationwide consensus in a series of court decisions that ostracized many White families to the Black side of the color line, apparently as punishment either for associating with or for defending Blacks during the Jim Crow wave of terror. Even in the nineteenth century or at the worst of Jim Crow, however, the one-drop rule was actively resisted by Louisiana Creoles, Florida Hispanics, South Carolina elite, and the maroon (triracial) communities of the Southeast (Melungeons, Lumbees, Redbones, etc.). It continues to be resisted today by Louisiana Creoles, Hispanics, maroon (triracial) communities, and recent West Indian immigrants.

Section IV.
Appendices

Appendix A
Census Data Processing Methodology

Census tables and figures in the text came from downloading and tabulating publicly available data from the Census Bureau of the U.S. Department of Commerce. The Census Bureau sells machine-readable public use microdata series (PUMS) files from each ten-year census. A consortium of colleges led by the University of Minnesota has consolidated these files from 1850 through 1990 into an online database of detailed census data called Integrated Public Use Microdata Series (IPUMS). The IPUMS database at web site www.ipums.org enables researchers to study detailed demographic data on individual citizens while at the same time keeping each person's identity secret. Online user manuals, data dictionaries, and query language guides at the IPUMS web site explain how to extract data samples.

Concerns as to the Accuracy of Census Racial Designation

It is straightforward to download and tabulate this data, and most of the information, such as age, sex, and family relationships among household members is unremarkable. But, regarding the racial identity of individuals, it is useful to recognize a difference between how census data was collected in the period 1850 through 1950 and the method used from 1960 to the present. (IPUMS information is not available before 1850 because prior federal censuses did not record data on individuals—just summaries of entire households.) From 1850 through 1950, census forms captured the opinions of census takers, who were expected to follow written instructions. But from 1960 onwards, heads of households themselves filled out the census forms, and so one assumes that post-1955 data reflects how Americans saw themselves. In the 2000 census, for example, the question was worded thus: "What is this person's race? Mark [X] one or more races to indicate what this person considers himself/herself to be."[1]

How census racial classification was determined raises three possible concerns. First, because post-1955 census forms were self-administered, non-head-of-household spouses and children may not have been encouraged to express their individual opinions regarding racial identity. Second, although pre-1955 census takers were sometimes instructed to ask subjects their racial identities and then to record whatever their answers,[2] it seems likely that on such a sensitive topic, some enumerators may have written whatever racial identities he or she perceived. Hence, whereas the post-1955 data may reflect self-identity (at least that of household heads), pre-1955 data may also partly reflect the opinion of White middle-class society (from which the census-takers were recruited). Finally, it is widely known that the poor or homeless can inadvertently be left uncounted in the federal census.

Although all three concerns may affect some studies, they are not significant to this text. Self-labeling might introduce bias is the form of differences in the perception of racial features between different classes, castes, or ethnic groups. Leaving some

---

[1] See the 2000 census form questions available at
http://www.ipums.org/usa/voliii/inst2000.html#P6.

[2] A compendium of the enumerators' instructions used in every census since 1850 is available at web site
http://www.ipums.org/usa/pdemographic/racea.html

of the poor uncounted could also bias the data towards middle class perceptions, as would inadvertently capturing the attitudes of the census enumerators. Nevertheless, no evidence was uncovered of systematic historical differences in the perception of racial features between classes or castes. On the contrary, as discussed in the text, English-speaking Americans, Black and White, rich and poor, seem remarkably unanimous regarding who is of which "race." There are differences in the perception of racial features between English-speaking Americans (Black or White) and Hispanics. Accordingly, Hispanics were excluded from many of the tabulations, as indicated in the detailed explanations, below.

Another, concern is that census racial designations are not accurate, but instead merely record what Americans wanted to believe about themselves. Four kinds of evidence are usually cited to show this apparent problem. First, the same individuals were often racially classified differently in different censuses (Eston Hemings, for instance, was recorded as White in 1830, and in the special Virginia census of 1833, but as Mulatto in 1840[3]). Second, the number of gradations of racial designation changed from census to census. Third, such race-relations indicators as the rates of intermarriage, race-switching at maturity, and childhood Whiteness (see definitions under "Census Data Dictionary," below) changed from census to census. Fourth, race-relations indicators often differ significantly from one state or region to the next, even within the same census period.

Rather than contesting the present text, these findings validate it. The foundation paradigm guiding and shaping this study is that the current position of the American Anthropological Association is correct, and that there is no physical reality underlying census racial classification.[4] In short, there is no

---

[3] For details on Eston Hemings, see Daniel P. Jordan, "Statement on the TJMF Research Committee Report on Thomas Jefferson and Sally Hemings," (2000), 54, 47.

[4] For the American Anthopological Association's plea to the Federal Government to discontinue the census "race" question once and for all, see http://www.aaanet.org/gvt/ombdraft.htm. For an overview of these issues,

"real" racial identity and census racial designation records only what Americans want to believe about themselves. This is its sole purpose.[5] That people are often racially classified differently in different censuses is the very phenomenon sought in measuring the permeability of the U.S. color line. That the number of gradations of racial designation changed from census to census measures the discontinuity of the color line—an important measure of its strength. That such race-relations indicators as the rates of intermarriage, race-switching, and childhood Whiteness change over the decades is important to the study of the unfolding of American racialism. And that race-relations indicators often differ from one state to the next, even within the same census period, offers the opportunity to see details in changes in the color line. For instance, a north-to-south temporal movement pattern in the invention of the one-drop rule suggests that America's unique notion of invisible Blackness originated early in the nineteenth century in the urban cities of the northeast, but did not find its full flowering in American law and culture until its spread to the Jim Crow South late in the century.

Exogamy of All U.S. Groups

Data on the exogamy of all U.S. "racial" groups was obtained by downloading a one-percent sample (about 745,000 records) of the 2000 census. Each record describes an individual, his or her relationship to the head of household, his or her "race," and whether he or she was Hispanic. The records were tabulated using the following logic: The entire household was skipped unless both the head-of-household and the spouse of the head-of-household were present in the household's census record. The household was skipped if both head-of-household and

---

see Bijan Gilanshah, "Multiracial Minorities: Erasing the Color Line," *Law and Inequality*, 12 (December 1993), 183.

[5] A survey of "racial" classification systems used in every census since 1850 is available at web site http://www.ipums.org/usa/pdemographic/racea.html. The survey opens by explaining that the Census Bureau considers "race" to have been a socio-political construct, not a scientific or anthropological one.

spouse were White. Each individual was assigned a group number in accordance with his or her answer to the census question (1=White, 2=Black, 3=Amerind, 4=Japanese, 5=Chinese, 6=Other Asian). Anyone who claimed to be Hispanic was coded with group number 7=Hispanic, regardless of how they answered the "race" question. Every non-skipped couple was counted as one marriage. If one spouse was of group 1 (White) and the other spouse was of any group other than White, the couple was counted as one exogamous marriage. Exogamy rate was computed as $C/(2*B-C)$, where C is the number of exogamous marriages and B is the number of marriages. There are two common ways of expressing exogamy mathematically. The first defines it as the fraction of married individuals who have an outgroup spouse. The second defines it as the number of exogamous marriages as a fraction of total group marriages (both endogamous and exogamous). A simple algebraic formula translates between these two definitions.[6] The present text uses the first definition. The ninety-fifth percentile confidence interval was computed as plus or minus $1.96*SQRT(D*(1-D)/(2*B))$, where D is the exogamy rate as computed above and B is the number of marriages. It reflects, to 95 percent certainty, the range within which reality must lie. The original downloaded intermarriage census data set, code book, SPSS parameters file, and the Excel spreadsheet that tabulates the results are all contained in a 3 MB compressed file, which may be downloaded from <http://backintyme.com/rawdata/allexogamy.zip>.

Black/White Intermarriage

Data on Black/White intermarriage was obtained by downloading a one-percent sample (well over two million records) covering all available census decades from 1850 through 2000. Each record describes an individual, his or her relationship to the head of household, his or her "race," and whether he or

---

[6] The formula may be found in Stephan Thernstrom, Ann Orlov, and Oscar Handlin, eds. *Harvard Encyclopedia of American Ethnic Groups* (Cambridge MA, 1980), 516.

she was Hispanic. The records were tabulated using the following logic: The entire household was skipped unless both the head-of-household and the spouse of the head-of-household were present in the household's census record. The household was skipped if either the head-of-household or spouse was Hispanic. The household was skipped if neither head nor spouse had a Black racial designation. The household was skipped if either the head or spouse had a racial designation of anything other than Black or White. Every non-skipped couple was counted as one marriage. If one spouse was racially labeled as White and the other as Black, the couple was counted as one interracial marriage. Exogamy rate was computed as $C/(2*B-C)$, where C is the number of interracial marriages and B is the number of marriages. The same definition of exogamy rate was used as in the previous item, "Exogamy of All U.S. Groups." The ninety-fifth percentile confidence interval was also computed as in the previous item. The original downloaded intermarriage census data set, code book, SPSS parameters file, and the Excel spreadsheet that tabulates the results are all contained in a 6MB compressed file, which may be downloaded from <http://backintyme.com/rawdata/intermarriage.zip>.

Intermarriage, North and South

Data on regional differences in the rise and fall of intermarriage during the period studied was obtained by downloading a one-percent sample (well over two million records) covering all available census decades from 1850 through 2000. Each record describes an individual, his or her relationship to the head of household, his or her "race," and whether he or she was Hispanic. The records were tabulated using the following logic: The entire household was skipped unless both the head-of-household and the spouse of the head-of-household were present in the household's census record. The household was skipped if either the head-of-household or spouse was Hispanic. The household was skipped if neither head nor spouse had a Black racial designation. The household was skipped if either the head or spouse had a racial designation of anything other than Black or White.

Every non-skipped couple was counted as one marriage. The couples were sorted into census regions. If one spouse was racially labeled as White and the other as Black, the couple was counted as one interracial marriage. Exogamy rate was computed as C/(2*B-C), where C is the number of interracial marriages and B is the number of marriages. The same definition of exogamy rate was used as in the previous item, "Exogamy of All U.S. Groups." The Region labeled "North" comprised the states coded with census region 1-29 (the Northeast and the Midwest). The Region labeled "South" comprised the states code with census regions 31-39 (states that had slavery as of 1861). Western states were not counted one way or the other. The ninety-fifth percentile confidence interval was also computed as in the previous item. The original downloaded intermarriage census data set, code book, SPSS parameters file, and the Excel spreadsheet that tabulates the results are all contained in a 6MB compressed file, which may be downloaded from <http://backintyme.com/rawdata/byregion.zip>.

First-Generation Biracial Children's Identity

Data on the racial identity of first-generation Black/White biracial children was obtained by downloading a one-percent sample (well over two million records) covering all available census decades from 1850 through 2000. Each record describes an individual, his or her "race," the "races" of each of his or her parents, and whether the individual was Hispanic. The records were tabulated using the following logic: An individual was skipped if he or she was Hispanic. An individual was skipped unless both of his or her biological parents were present in the household—step-parents were not considered as "parents" for this purpose. An individual was skipped unless one parent was encoded as Black and the other was encoded as White. Every non-skipped individual was counted as one first-generation biracial child. Every such child that was encoded as "White" was counted as one White-designated child. Every such child that was encoded as "Black" was counted as one Black-designated child. Every child that was encoded as other than Black or White, or that was not racially encoded at all, was counted as one other-designated child. The ninety-fifth percentile confidence interval was computed as explained under "Black/White Intermarriage," above. The original downloaded biracial children census data set, code book, SPSS parameters file, and the Excel spreadsheet that tabulates the results are all contained in a 7MB compressed file, which may be downloaded from <http://backintyme.com/rawdata/censuskids.zip>.

Appendix B.
Court Case Data
Processing Methodology

This project was based on a study of every available U.S. court case, from 1800 through 1980, where (1) a person's endogamous group membership was an issue to be judicially resolved and (2) the rational for the decision was written down. Data about each case was collected, inserted into a database, and analyzed. The database was then tabulated, sorted, and graphed. This appendix comprises a description of the methodologies used in: data collection (how the cases were collected) and data dictionary (the meaning of each data item in the resultant database). It concludes with a discussion of the validity or usefulness of the database in assessing how Americans in the past decided to which endogamous group someone belonged.

Court Case Data Collection

The data collection team comprised two individuals: the author and Mrs. Mary Lee Sweet. The latter is an experienced, Florida-certified librarian and media specialist who is also the author's wife. We collected court case data related to the determination of endogamous group membership or racial identity in five steps as follows.

Step 1. We identified two sources from which possible cases were to be drawn. The primary source was the set of state case reporters. The two advantages of this source are that it is limited to appealed cases and that it is searchable by computer. That it holds only appeals cases was advantageous because the goal of this project was to identify trends in the criteria used to identify a person's endogamous group membership. Specifically, we wanted to determine when the one-drop rule first arose and how quickly it displaced other criteria of membership determination. Unchallenged lower court cases are often decided by juries who do not produce records of why decisions were made—what yardstick they used to measure one's endogamous group membership—and so they would not help achieve the project goal. Appealed cases, on the other hand, are resolved by judges who traditionally write explanations justifying their rulings—the precise information that we seek. That case reporters are searchable by computer (via LexisNexis or WestLaw) made the project feasible in a reasonable length of time. We doubt that such a study drawing from many tens of thousands of cases would have been practical without computer technology. The drawback of this source is that some state reporters do not start until the mid-nineteenth century. The first volume of *South Carolina Reports*, for instance, begins in 1868. Such late-starting sources can provide no insight into cases during the early republic or antebellum times. Hence, a second data source was needed.

Our second source of potential court cases was the five-volume set, Helen Tunnicliff Catterall and James J. Hayden, *Judicial Cases Concerning American Slavery and The Negro* (New York: Octagon Books, 1968), written in 1926 under the sponsorship of the Department of Historical Research of the Carnegie Institute (Washington DC). This collection was created as an attempt to document "all the cases relating to slavery and the negro which have been found."[1] The principle advantage of this source is that it fills the antebellum gap in some state reporters, since it includes cases going back to England during the colonial

---

[1] Helen Tunnicliff Catterall and James J. Hayden, *Judicial Cases Concerning American Slavery and The Negro* (New York, 1968), v.

period. Catterall has two minor drawbacks. First, it includes a few cases where the decision criteria were not recorded. As explained below in Step 5, these cases were not included in the final tabulations and graphs. Second, Catterall is not available online and so it could not be searched electronically.

Step 2. From both collections, we identified those cases where someone's endogamous group membership was at issue. For Catterall, we made this determination by studying the text of every case in the collection's 2,899 pages. This yielded 115 cases from Catterall. To extract cases from LexisNexis, we devised computer search routines to uncover appropriate cases from the state reporters. After experimenting with various algorithms, we settled on the following simple search string applied to the entire text of each case record: "mulatto or 'mixed blood' or 'negro blood'." The search string was arrived at by sampling, so as to leave no case of interest uncollected while collecting false-positives at a ratio of no more than ten-to-one. In other words, applying this search string to the text of all cases in the Georgia reporters will uncover 51 cases. Of these cases, 43 false-positives do not deal with endogamous group membership (for example: "the victim was found in a pool of *mixed blood* and beer," or "*mixed blood* and semen were collected from the body"). Eight cases in fact do deal with the topic of interest. We found that widening the net by using a more inclusive search string uncovered no more than the same eight cases of interest while adding many more false positives. In the end, the automated search string that we devised uncovered about 3,000 cases. We manually reduced this set of 3,000 cases down to a subset by selecting just those cases where endogamous group membership was at issue. To minimize human error, both substeps, computer search and manual selection, were performed twice, once by each team member. (Mrs. Sweet worked her way through the state case reporters ascending alphabetically starting from Alabama, while the author started at West Virginia and worked backwards.) Whenever the set of cases selected for a state differed between researchers, the reason for the difference was identified, and a final decision made by the author based solely on whether the case addressed someone's racial designation or endogamous group membership. This yielded 253 cases from LexisNexis.

Step 3. We merged the 115 Catterall cases and the 253 state reporter cases into a single computer database with six data items per case: LexisNexis reference (where applicable), Catterall volume and page (where applicable), citation, state, year, and general comments or notes. See Data Dictionary, below, for detailed definitions of these items. Some cases had been appealed multiple times or re-heard in different venues, thus producing multiple records in either Catterall, the state reporters, or both. In such situations, we inserted multiple records into the database. This is because different hearings often employed different race-determination criteria and had different outcomes. On the other hand, whenever the exact same case appeared in both Catterall and in the state reporters, only one record was inserted into the database. This yielded a net total of 275 cases. This database resides in a Microsoft Excel file and is available for public download   from   URL <http://backintyme.com/rawdata/courtcases.xls>.

Step 4. Based upon a careful reading of the record of each of the 275 cases stored in the database, we encoded a seventh data item: its *reason*. That is, why a court trial was necessary to resolve a person's "race." The reasons for determining someone's "race" included the following: marriage, slavery, school, testimony, birth certificate, will, vote, tax, escape, libel, sentence, gun, covenant, segregation, affront, burial, custody, immigration, jury, office, pass, property, and registration. These are explained under Data Dictionary, below.

Step 5. Upon examining each case recorded in the database, we added five more data items. These comprised the court's ruling (whether the subject was found to be White or Black), and four criteria codes telling how the decision was arrived at: appearance, association, blood fraction, and one-drop rule. As described under Data Dictionary, below, the criteria codes were not mutually exclusive. Also, cases in the final database might have a ruling but lack criteria codes or vice versa. This is because in some cases, although the court record explains without ambiguity the criterion used for endogamous group membership determination, the final decision is unclear. Testimony, for instance, might have been taken to prove a subject's "race" based on birth records but then something else entirely caused the case to be dismissed or remanded, and so a endogamous group membership decision was never made. In such cases, although we assigned criteria codes to the database matching what was in the record, we left blank the court's ruling (White or Black). In other cases, although the final decision is clear, no rationale was ever recorded.[2] We left criteria codes blank in such cases. Although cases like these could not be tabulated, we left them in the database so that future researchers who may wish to study them, need not collect them again.

Court Case Data Dictionary

As mentioned, the court cases database is available for public download from URL <http://backintyme.com/rawdata/courtcases.xls>. Each row represents one case. The following list describes each data item (or column) in the database of court cases.

Citation. The shortest unique and unambiguous key needed to retrieve the case from the LexisNexis online "Get a Case" web page, using the "Citation" access method at URL http://web.lexis-nexis.com/universe. For example, "14 Mich. 406." For cases not found in the state reporters, this column was encoded "n/a."

Source. The volume and page number of the case in Catterall. For example, "C3:493" means volume 3, page 493. For cases not found in Catterall, this was left blank.

Title. The abbreviated case name as it appears in LexisNexis indices. For example, "People v. Dean."

Year. The year in which the case was decided. Notice that many cases involving slavery were not resolved until years after the Civil War, such as a railroad's liability for a slave's escape,

---

[2] See 213 La. 654, for example.

or damages for false imprisonment by someone claiming to have been illegally enslaved.

State. The state in which the case was resolved. Again, this may not have been the same state where the events at issue transpired, especially in rulings as to the legality of marriages.

Reason (abbrev. "why"). As mentioned above in Step 4, this data item encoded why a court trial was necessary to resolve a person's endogamous group membership. Specific data values are:

- Slavery – These were cases where someone's endogamous group membership was at issue in order to decide whether the individual was slave or free. In most states during the antebellum period, one's endogamous group membership determined which party in a civil suit for freedom from slavery had the burden of proof. If a woman, say, were ruled to be of the Black endogamous group, then she had to prove by the preponderance of evidence that her mother was legally free. If she were ruled to be White, then the burden of proof was on the alleged slaveholder to present a valid bill of sale. As explained in the text, an alleged slave might be found to be *physically* White (European-looking) by a court, but the slave-owner might then satisfy the burden of proof by presenting solid evidence of the alleged slave's matrilineal descent from a legally enslaved woman. In such cases, the individual was held to be legally a slave and this had the consequence that she was also ruled to be *legally* of the Black endogamous group, despite her physical appearance. This was because, by definition, no legally enslaved person could be deemed to be a member of the White endogamous group.[3] Judges often commented on the discrepancy between *physical* "race" and *legal* "race."[4] It confused many. In 1815, Thomas

---

[3] See, for example, "It is hardly necessary to say that a slave cannot be a white man." (State v. Cantey, 1835 South Carolina); 17 Tex. 211; 8 Rob. 527; or 39 Ky. 23. Note that this concept is different from "A white person... cannot be a slave" (33 Ky. 382).

[4] See, for example, 8 Rob. 527.

Jefferson wrote a letter to Francis Gray, painstakingly explaining why Eston Hemings (his son, as it turned out) was a Negro as long as he was legally enslaved but "if emancipated, he becomes a free *white* man [emphasis Jefferson's], and a citizen of the United States...."[5]

- Marriage – Such cases resolved endogamous group membership in order to decide if a marriage were legal (usually in probate cases), since most states at one time or another held "interracial" marriages to be void. (Indeed, this is the very definition of endogamous group.)

- School – These cases were held to determine whether a child was a member of the White endogamous group in order to be allowed to attend a White school, since most states at one time or another had segregated schools.

- Testimony – Such cases decided whether a person was a member of the White endogamous group in order to be allowed to testify in a case involving a White person, since most states at one time or another forbade testimony by Black endogamous group members in cases involving White persons.

- Birth Certificate – After Reconstruction, states began issuing birth certificates to document individuals' "racial identity." Had this system been more strictly enforced, it would have simplified Jim Crow segregation by giving streetcar conductors, say, a reliable way of sorting passengers into carriages separated by the endogamous color line. In contrast to apartheid South Africa, however (where everyone was required to carry racial identity cards), Americans never embraced such governmental intrusion into daily life. As it was, hotels, restaurants, streetcars, and railroads were often sued for erring either way (see below under Segregation). Where birth certificates were used (in Louisiana, for example), they became important because they could open the

---

[5] Joshua D. Rothman, *Notorious in the Neighborhood: Sex and Families Across the Color Line in Virginia, 1787-1861* (Chapel Hill, 2003), 47.

door to White privilege or slam it shut. But, unlike apartheid South Africa, which appointed local Race Classification Boards to make changes and corrections (South Africans were often classified differently from their siblings and parents, and some people changed more than once), no U.S. state ever implemented a routine way of correcting errors in endogamous group membership identification.[6] Hence, the only recourse to someone wanting a corrected birth certificate was to sue the state. Such cases are encoded thus.

- Will – Some states at one time or another forbade members of the Black endogamous group from bequeathing property and some forbade Blacks from inheriting, especially the Black offspring of White parents. Hence, litigation over an estate often required first resolving a potential heir's endogamous group membership.

- Vote – Most states, at one time or another, barred Black endogamous group members from voting. These cases determined whether a citizen was a member of the White endogamous group in order to be allowed to vote.

- Tax – Some states at times had special tax regulations for taxpayers who were members of the Black endogamous group. Free Blacks in South Carolina, for example, paid a capitation tax for which Whites were not liable. Similarly, "colored persons" (a synonym for "Black" in the northern states) were exempt from property tax in 1855 Connecticut by statute (the legislature apparently reasoned that they need not pay for White schools, which their children were not allowed to attend).[7] Hence, tax cases sometimes hinged on someone's endogamous group membership.

---

[6] F. James Davis, *Who is Black?: One Nation's Definition* (University Park PA, 1991), 67, 97.

[7] 24 Conn. 28.

- Escape – When runaways boarded long-distance public transportation (steamboats, trains) in order to escape slavery, courts held carriers liable unless they could demonstrate that the person in question was so European-looking that he or she could not reasonably have been spotted as a slave. Although the rhetoric of such cases often seemed to focus on appearance (European versus African) rather than on endogamous group membership, the effect was the same. In many states in the early antebellum period, an escapee who was ruled so European-looking that no one could be held responsible for his escape, was de facto free, and thereby legally of the White endogamous group by definition.

- Libel – Some states at times held it actionable to publicly call someone by an inaccurate endogamous group membership term. The defense in such cases often tried to convince the court that the epithet was accurate.

- Sentence – Some crimes (rape, larceny) in some states at times had different statutory sentences, depending upon the convict's endogamous group membership.

- Gun – Antebellum free Blacks were forbidden to carry firearms in many slave states. Hence, a defense against such a charge was that the defendant was legally a member of the White endogamous group.

- Covenant – As late as the 1950s, real estate throughout the nation often carried deeds entailed by covenants that forbade sale to members of the Black endogamous group. A family who could prove that they were members of the White group would be allowed to buy such property.

- Segregation – During Jim Crow segregation, common carriers and owners of public accommodations were required by law to split customers into two groups by the endogamous color line. When a streetcar conductor or restaurant host erred in implementing the law, a lawsuit often resulted. Such cases often hinged on the customer's endogamous group membership.

- Affront – Some antebellum states made it a criminal offense for a free member of the Black endogamous group to be disrespectful towards a White group member. Whether or not such a crime had been committed sometimes depended on resolving the defendant's endogamous group membership.

- Burial – Cemeteries in some Jim Crow states were segregated. Consequently, whether a deceased was to be buried in a White cemetery was sometimes decided by litigation.

- Custody – Child custody disputes in divorce proceedings sometimes depended on the endogamous group memberships of the two parents.

- Immigration – Several antebellum midwestern states barred immigration by free members of the Black endogamous group. A family would be allowed to homestead, for example, if they could prove their White group membership in a Missouri court.

- Jury – Jury duty was restricted to male members of the White endogamous group in many antebellum states and Southern Jim Crow states. A person ruled to be White could serve.

- Office – Even some post-bellum states that allowed members of the Black endogamous group to vote, did not allow them to hold public office. Officeholders thus challenged had to prove their White group membership in court.

- Pass – Most antebellum slave states required that Black endogamous group members outside of a plantation or place of business carry a pass allowing their movement. Patrols scoured the highways for offenders. A person would not be required to carry a pass if he could prove himself in court to be White.

- Property – Free members of the Black endogamous group in some antebellum slave states were not allowed to own certain kinds of personal property (such as stocks and bonds). One could meet a challenge of dispossession by proving oneself to be of the White endogamous group.

- Registration – Urban free members of the Black endogamous group in some antebellum slave states were required to register with local authorities periodically. Anyone who could prove White group membership was not required to register.

Ruling (abbrev. "w/b"). As mentioned above in Step 5, this data item encoded the substance of the court's endogamous group membership determination. Specific data values are:

- W – The subject was ruled to be of the White endogamous group.

- B – The subject was ruled to be of the Black endogamous group.

- C – The subject was ruled to be neither of the Black endogamous group nor of the White endogamous group, but of the Colored endogamous group. Such rulings often occurred during the period of three-caste systems of the lower South in colonial and antebellum Louisiana, South Carolina, former Spanish Florida, and parts of Alabama.

- I – The subject was ruled to be neither of the Black nor White endogamous groups, but Amerind.

- ? – Although the court established the rule to be used, no final determination appears in the record. Such cases were included in the tabulations.

- n/a – The court left no rationale on record for its decision. Such cases were excluded from the tabulations.

As mentioned above in Step 5, four criteria codes capture the court's reasoning as to the person's endogamous group membership. The four codes are not mutually exclusive and some cases were resolved based on two or more of the following criteria.

Appearance (abbrev. app). These were cases where the record shows that the decision hinged, at least partly, on the subject's physical appearance (in genetics, his *phenotype*). With a few exceptions, people of strongly African appearance were assigned to the Black endogamous group.[8] We marked a case as having been decided by *appearance* when the record showed exactly which aspect of the individual's looks was considered crucial. It might seem that complexion, hair curliness, nose width, lip thickness, and the like would be important but, in fact, some cases depended upon the shape of the jaw or of the foot, or on purple- or blue-colored marks on certain parts of the body. As shown in the text, having a European appearance was decisive during the early republic, fell in importance throughout the nineteenth century, and became irrelevant by the Jim Crow era. On the other hand, having an African appearance usually consigned one to the Black side of the endogamous color line.

Association (abbrev. ass). In these cases, the court decided a person's endogamous group membership based on his having been accepted into society on that side of the color line, and associated only with people on that side. Our findings corroborate those of Ariela J. Gross that this yardstick was surprisingly common, especially in the lower south.[9] It may seem odd that, in order to be allowed legally to exercise the privileges of White endogamous group membership, one had to demonstrate that one had already violated law and custom by exercising those very privileges, but such was often the case. In many cases, the actual evidence presented contradicted the judge's rhetoric. In other words, a judge might write that his ruling was based on blood fraction, but the details on file might show that little or no evidence was presented as to ancestral birth records. Instead, the actual evidence cited might have been about the performance of social roles, even though the rhetoric was about blood. We always tried to capture the actual basis for the decision rather than its rhetorical justification. Usually this was obvious. When in doubt, we recorded both the expressed rationale and what we perceived as the actual rationale.

---

[8] The exceptions, then as now, were mainly Hispanics and Muslims.

[9] Ariela J. Gross, "Litigating Whiteness: Trials of Racial Determination in the Nineteenth-Century South," *Yale Law Journal*, 108 (no. 1, 1998), 109-188.

Blood Fraction (abbrev. fra). In 1910, before Tennessee became the first state to adopt the one-drop rule as law, almost every state's statutes defined endogamous group membership as based on Afro-European blood fraction. At that time, Florida, Georgia, Indiana, Missouri, South Carolina, Kentucky, Maryland, Mississippi, North Carolina, Tennessee, and Texas defined a Black endogamous group member as one with one or more "negro" great-grandparents (1/8 or more Black). Alabama used a 1/32 rule. Nebraska, Oregon, Virginia, and Michigan used as 1/4 rule (one or more "negro" grandparents). Ohio ruled that someone was legally of the White endogamous group if they were mostly of European blood.[10] Where courts accepted testimony regarding the appearance, endogamous group membership, social circle, or continent of origin of ancestors in order to measure a subject's blood fraction, we encoded it with this criterion. As mentioned above, we tried to identify the actual rationale used and the criteria were not mutually exclusive.

One-drop rule (abbrev. odr). Starting in 1910, most states switched to a group membership criterion based on the likelihood that a person had any ancestor of the Black endogamous group, no matter how distant. Endogamous group membership thus became unrelated to appearance, association or blood fraction. Indeed, it became unrelated to anything tangible or provable—the one-drop rule. We encoded cases in the database as using the one-drop rule only when they matched all three of the following filters: first, when the court employed such terms as "any traceable (detectable, discernable, known) Negro blood"; second, when it was clear from the record that the subject's appearance was completely European; and third, when in order definitively to prove the subject's legal membership in the White endogamous group in accordance with the court's reasoning, one would have had to introduce ancestral records going back forever (an impossible task). The idea that someone can legally and involuntarily be a member of the Black endogamous group due to invisible ancestry is, of course, the central investi-

---

[10] Gilbert Thomas Stephenson, *Race Distinctions in American Law* (New York, 1910), 15.

gative issue of this project. Two points of jurisprudence are of interest in the application of the one-drop rule. The first is that, in such cases, courts were more willing to accept hearsay testimony than was usual in other kinds of cases. Third-hand testimony as to the appearance or group membership of a subject's long-dead ancestors was routinely admitted. The courts' justification was that group-defining documents (such as birth records) may have vanished or may have never been recorded. (As mentioned above under Birth Certificate, the custom of including a newborn's "race" on birth records was a late-nineteenth-century innovation.) The second peculiarity of one-drop application was that courts using this criterion for determining endogamous group membership seemed strangely arbitrary in assigning the burden of proof. In some cases it fell to the plaintiff or prosecution, in others to the defense. Furthermore, in cases where the burden of proof fell upon the side arguing for White membership, that side's case was doomed from the start. It is simply not possible to demonstrate the absence of Black ancestry in anyone, for all past eternity. And so, a criminal court judging an intermarriage case, for example, might accept as prima facie, prosecution evidence that a marriage existed and that the defendants were of opposite endogamous groups. This left it to the defense to prove that the allegedly Black spouse had no Black ancestry (an impossible task).[11] Alternatively, before accepting that the crime of miscegenation had even occurred, the court might demand that the prosecution prove the allegedly White spouse's membership in the White endogamous group by the same standard. Such a burden in effect made it impossible even to show that a crime had been committed.[12] Cases went both ways, and it is not clear from the record that anyone involved—judges, jurors, parties, or counsel—realized that the verdict was thus completely predetermined by judge's ruling on who would shoulder the burden of evidence.

---

[11] See, for example, 48 Cal. App. 2d 603.

[12] See, for example, 18 Ala. App. 354.

Validity of Appealed Court Cases

Are appealed court cases valid or even useful in assessing how Americans in the past decided to which endogamous group someone belonged? Five objections arise in considering court cases as evidence: Court cases do not reflect all of society; they reflect only the opinions of elite powerful males. Written decision rationales may deceive, either deliberately or subconsciously. As many as ten cases may have been decided for every one case that was appealed. The ratio of cases where people were found to be White may not reflect the severity of the color line. The number of cases per decade may not reflect the severity of the color line. Each of these objections is discussed below.

Court cases do not reflect all of society; they reflect only the opinions of elite powerful males. With regards to the subject of this study—how U.S. society assigned people to one side or the other of the endogamous color line—the opinions of the socially powerful are precisely the ones of interest. With a few exceptions, the elite are who make and enforce the rules of endogamous group membership. Even apparent exceptions, such as the 1965-75 violent expulsion of civil rights workers of Hispanic and mixed heritage from CORE by Floyd McKissick and from SNCC by Stokeley Carmichael because they were "not Black enough" demonstrate that the elite make the rules on both sides of the endogamous color line. Whether changes in the attitudes of the working class or the marginalized were swayed by the leadership of the elite, or whether they influenced the elite to change is not important to this study. The result, the law and its enforcement, is what is of interest.

Written decision rationales may deceive, either deliberately or subconsciously. It is understood that the reasoning expressed by a judge in any particular case may not reflect his actual motivation for deciding as he did. As explained in *Chapter 4. The Perception of "Racial" Traits*, people often do not realize why they perceive someone to be Black or White and are even more often unable to articulate their reasons intelligibly. Consequently, it is possible than many or perhaps even most of the reasons given in case records fail to accurately reflect the judges' true feelings. Nevertheless, they are important to this study precisely because this project investigates changing fashions in the rhetoric of endogamous group membership determination. Whether such rhetoric reflects innermost feelings is interesting, but not central to the thesis. The law and its enforcement depend on written records, however self-serving or rationalizing they may be.

As many as ten cases may have been decided for every one case that was appealed. Since this study is limited to cases that were appealed, one might ask whether the measured rise and fall of different criteria for deciding someone's endogamous group membership reflects the total number of cases or merely the number that were appealed. For example, does the abrupt drop from over 35 cases per decade in the 1850s to under 10 cases in the 1870s show an overall decline in color-line litigation, or just a drop in the fraction of cases that were appealed? Does the abrupt appearance of the ultimate one-drop rule (invisible Blackness) late in the period reflect a true innovation in social mores or does it merely show the first time that such a criterion was appealed? The answer seems to be that appeals cases are a valid sample and do substantially reflect the great number of non-appealed cases. Ariela Gross sampled number of cases and number of appeals for the early-to-mid nineteenth century and found that the fraction of cases appealed did not change. Furthermore, most states did not add intermediate courts, nor limited the number of appeals to their highest courts until the twentieth century.[13] There is no evidence of systematic difference between appealed and non-appealed cases.

The ratio of cases where people were found to be White does not reflect the severity of the color line. That, throughout he period, about half of the individuals were ruled to be White is to be expected. The essence of the adversarial court system is that both parties think they have a chance to win. "Chance," in this context, means that the potential value of an outcome favorable to the party, times the likelihood of prevail-

---

[13] Ariela J. Gross, "Litigating Whiteness: Trials of Racial Determination in the Nineteenth-Century South," *Yale Law Journal*, 108 (no. 1, 1998), 109-188, 178.

ing, matches or exceeds the effort (time, money, professional help) invested in litigation. Other things being equal, few people will spend a great deal on a court case that they know they must lose.[14] And so, the fraction of outcomes that go one way or the other may be expected to hover around fifty percent. It seems plausible that, if courts in any particular region or period leaned seriously towards finding people to be Black, then only the most European-looking individuals with the most unblemished pedigree would try to achieve freedom through such courts. On the other hand, it seems plausible that, if courts at a place and time were extraordinarily liberal in finding Whiteness in those brought before the bench, then only those slave owners with notarized bill of sale in hand would bother to litigate.[15]

The number of cases per decade also does not reflect the severity of the color line. The occurrence of an unusually large number of cases in any given region or during any given decade does not necessarily mean that the color line was shifted towards one end or the other of the skin-tone continuum, nor that it was more or less strictly enforced. As discussed in *Chapter 5.The Rate of Black-to-White "Passing,"* exogamy and color line permeability are more straightforward and reliable ways of measuring where the color line was positioned and how seriously it was taken by society. Instead, the volume of such cases suggests social uncertainty. At some places and times, the criteria for endogamous group membership were clearly understood and stable enough to be passed on from one generation to the next as part of childhood socialization. During such periods and regions, people knew precisely what yardstick was used. With little element of uncertainty, relatively few occasions would arise

---

[14] Some litigants are not motivated by hope of victory, of course. But, as Damon Runyon said, "The race might not always go to the weak, nor the battle to the strong, but that's the way to bet." Criminal cases are not exempt from commonsense reasonableness either. Few prosecutors can afford habitually to prosecute mainly unwinnable cases. And defendants are less likely to appeal a ruling on the admission of testimony, say, unless they think that they have at least some chance of reversal.

[15] See the statistical digression of Chapter 5 for a detailed discussion of this point.

when both of two contending parties would think that they could prevail in court. And so, few court cases would be litigated and even fewer appealed.

On the other hand, when society was in transition from one criterion to another, from appearance to blood fraction, say, or from blood fraction to the one-drop extreme of invisible Blackness, then rules were uncertain. Generation gaps appeared as those who had learned and internalized one set of rules in their youth were overtaken by a younger generation with a new outlook. Class gaps, gender gaps, and color line gaps might also open. Those of different social rank might apply different rules, men might differ from women, and Blacks might adopt or advocate a different yardstick than that used by Whites. Where people apply different rules to the same issue, each of two opposing parties can anticipate a favorable outcome. Where each side's risk/benefit assessment justified fighting it out, court cases soared.

And so, this study suggests that the large number of cases in the early nineteenth-century upper South indicate a system in transition. Similarly, the lack of cases in the lower South and in the North suggests that both of these regions had relatively stable rules of endogamous group membership. Indeed, it is not unreasonable to suggest that the one-drop extreme of invisible Blackness may itself have contributed to this stability and lack of contestation. This is because the invisible Blackness cannot be disputed. Once it becomes the criterion for determining endogamous group membership in court, *onus probandi* alone (where the burden of proof is laid) predetermines the outcome. Blood fraction can be disputed by presenting evidence of ancestry. Physical appearance can be disputed by introducing expert testimony, as in *State v. Asa Jacobs*, 1859 North Carolina or by letting the jury observe the subject, as in *Gentry vs. Polly McMinnis*, 1835 Kentucky.[16] But there is no way to dispute that someone may have a trace of African ancestry in some unspecified distant past.[17]

---

[16] 33 Ky. 382; 51 N.C. 284.

[17] One reason for the impossibility, of course, is that it is undisputed in paleoanthropology that genus *Homo* really did emerge in Africa.

Works Cited

Aboud, Frances E. *Children and Prejudice* Social psychology and society. New York: Blackwell, 1988.

Allen, Theodore. *The Invention of the White Race.* 2 vols. Haymarket series. London: Verso, 1994.

Andrews, George Reid. "Race Versus Class Association: The Afro-Argentines of Buenos Aires." *Journal of Latin American Studies (UK)* 11, no. 1 (1979): 19-39.

Andrews, George Reid. "Racial Inequality in Brazil and the United States: A Statistical Comparison." *Journal of Social History* 26, no. 2 (1992): 229-63.

Andrews, George Reid. *The Afro-Argentines of Buenos Aires, 1800-1900.* Madison: University of Wisconsin, 1980.

AP. "Rewriting Her Story." *The National Law Journal* (1989): 51.

AP. *'Black' Councilman Retains Seat.* AP Domestic News, May 9 1984a. Accessed June 19 2003.

AP. *City Council Recall Vote Hinges on Councilman's Race.* AP Domestic News, May 8 1984b. Accessed June 19 2003.

AP. *'Culturally Black' Councilman Defeated.* AP Domestic News, December 20 1984c. Accessed June 19 2003.

AP. *'Culturally Black' Councilman Keeps His Seat.* AP Domestic News, May 9 1984d. Accessed June 19 2003.

AP. *Defeated Councilman Says Winner Lied About Being Black.* AP Domestic News, March 10 1984e. Accessed June 19 2003.

Aptheker, Herbert. *American Negro Slave Revolts.* 6th ed. New York: International Publishers, 1993.

Asbury, Herbert. *The Gangs of New York: An Informal History of the Underworld.* 1st Paragon House ed. New York: Paragon House, 1990.

Aspinall, Peter J. "Collective Terminology to Describe the Minority Ethnic Population: The Persistence of Confusion and Ambiguity in Usage." *Sociology* 36, no. 4 (2002): 803-16.

Baldwin, James. *Nobody Knows My Name.* New York: Dell, 1962.

Ball, Bonnie. *The Melungeons: Notes on the Origin of a Race.* Johnson City TN: Overmountain, 1992.

Bamshad, Michael J., Stephen Wooding, W. Scott Watkins, Christopher T. Ostler, Mark A. Batzer, and Lynn B. Jorde. "Human Population Genetic Structure and Inference of Group Membership." *American Journal of Human Genetics* 72 (2003): 578-89.

Banks, Nathaniel Prentiss. "Report to the President." *Appletons Annual Cyclopaedia and Register of Important Events,* 1864 1864, 480-1.

Bartholet. "Where do Black Children Belong?: The Politics of Race Matching in Adoption." *University of Pennsylvania Law Review* 139, no. 5 (1991): 1163-1256.

Barton, Robert A. "Neocortex Size and Behavioural Ecology in Primates." *Proceedings of the Royal Society: Biological Sciences* 263, no. 1367 (1996): 173-77.

Bartram, William, and Mark Van Doren. *The Travels of William Bartram.* New York: Dover, 1928.

Batiza, Rodolfo. "The Influence of Spanish Law in Louisiana." *Tulane Law Review* 23 (1958): 29-34.

Batiza, Rodolfo. "The Louisiana Civil Code of 1808: Its Actual Sources and Present Relevance." *Tulane Law Review* 46 (1971): 4-31.

BBC. *Hidden Race Bias 'Drains Brain'.* BBC News, Nov. 17 2003. Accessed Nov. 17 2003. BBC Web Site.

Beale, Calvin. "American Triracial Isolates." *Eugenics Quarterly* 4, no. 4 (1957): 187-96.

Beam, Lura. *He Called Them by the Lightning: A Teacher's Odyssey in the Negro South, 1908-1919.* Indianapolis: Bobbs-Merrill, 1967.

Beaumont, Gustave de. *Marie; or, Slavery in the United States.* Translated by Barbara Chapman. Stanford: Stanford University, 1958.

Beckles, Hilary. "Black Men in White Skins: The Formation of a White Proletariat in West Indian Society." *The Journal of Imperial and Commonwealth History* October, no. 15 (1986): 5-21.

Beckles, Hilary. *A History of Barbados: From Amerindian Settlement to Nation-State.* Cambridge UK: Cambridge University, 1990.

Begley, Sharon. "The Roots of Hatred: Our brains are Programmed to Distrust Outsiders But are We Hard-Wired to Hate?" *AARP*, May-June 2004.

Bennett Jr., Lerone. *Before the Mayflower: A History of Black America.* 6th rev. ed. New York: Penguin, 1993.

Bennett Jr., Lerone. *Forced Into Glory: Abraham Lincoln's White Dream.* Chicago: Johnson, 1999.

Bennett Jr., Lerone. *The Shaping of Black America.* Chicago: Johnson, 1975.

Berlin, Ira. *Slaves Without Masters: The Free Negro in the Antebellum South.* New York: New Free Press, 1974.

Berry, Brewton. *Almost White.* New York: Macmillan, 1963.

Bertoni, Bernardo, Bruce Budowle, Monica Sans, Sara A. Barton, and Ranajit Chakraborty. "Admixture in Hispanics: Distribution of Ancestral Population Contributions in the Continental United States." *Human Biology* 75, no. 1 (2003): 1-11.

Bethel, Elizabeth Rauh. *The Roots of African-American Identity.* New York: St. Martin's, 1997.

Bieber, Judy. "Race, Resistance, and Regionalism: Perspectives from Brazil and Spanish America." *Latin American Research Review* 32, no. 3 (1997): 152-168.

Blakey, Michael L. "Scientific Racism and the Biological Concept of Race." *Literature and Psychology* 1999, no. 1/2 (1999): 29.

Blessing, Patrick J. "The Irish." In *Harvard Encyclopedia of American Ethnic Groups,* ed. Stephan Thernstrom and Oscar Handlin, 524-45. Cambridge MA: Harvard University, 1980.

Boas, Franz. *The Mind of Primitive Man.* New York: Macmillan, 1911.

Bohnenberger, Carl. "The Settlement of Charlotia (Rolles Town), 1765." *The Florida Historical Quarterly* 4, no. 1 (1925): 43-49.

Borah, Woodrow Wilson, and Sherburne Friend Cook. *The Aboriginal Population of Central Mexico on the Eve of the Spanish Conquest.* Berkeley: University of California, 1963.

Bordin, Ruth Birgitta Anderson. *Woman and Temperance: The Quest for Power and Liberty, 1873-1900.* Philadelphia: Temple University, 1981.

Bortolini, Maria Catira, Wilson Araujo da Silva Junior, Dinorah Castro de Guerra, Gabriela Remonatto, Rosana Mirandola, Maria H. Hutz, Tania A. Weimer, Maria Cristina B.O. Silva, Marco Antonio Zago, and Francisco Mauro Salzano. "African-Derived South American Populations: A History of Symmetrical and Asymmetrical Matings According to Sex Revealed by Bi- and Uni-parental Genetic Markers." *American Jornal of Human Biology* 11 (1999): 561-63.

Bosch, Elena, Francesc Calafell, Zoe H. Rosser, Soren Norby, Niels Lynnerup, Matthew E. Hurles, and Mark A. Jobling. "High Level of Male-Biased Scandinavian Admixture in Greenlandic Inuit Shown by Y-Chromosomal Analysis." *Human Genetics* 112 (2003): 353-63.

Bowman, John S., ed. *Who was Who in the Civil War.* New York: Crescent Books, 1994.

Bowser, Frederick P. "Colonial Spanish America." In *Neither Slave Nor Free: The Freedmen of African Descent in the Slave Societies of the New World,* ed. David W. Cohen and Jack P. Greene, 19-58. Baltimore: Johns Hopkins University, 1972.

Bowser, Frederick P. "The Free Person of Color in Mexico City and Lima: Manumission and Opportunity, 1580-1650."

In *Race and Slavery in the Western Hemisphere: Quantitative Studies*, ed. Stanley L. Engerman, Eugene D. Genovese, Alan H. Adamson, and Mathematical Social Science Board History Advisory Committee, 331-61. Princeton: Princeton University, 1975.

Boyd-Bowman, Peter. "Patterns of Spanish Emigration to the Indies until 1600." *Hispanic American Historical Review* 56, no. 4/November (1976): 580-604.

Brace, C. Loring. *Does Race Exist?: An Antagonist's Perspective*. Nova, 2000. Accessed November 2000. web page. Available from <http://www.pbs.org/wgbh/nova/first/brace.html>.

Braman, Donald. "Of Race and Immutability." *UCLA Law Review* 46 (1999): 1375-1463.

Breen, T. H., and Stephen Innes. *"Myne Owne Ground": Race and Freedom on Virginia's Eastern Shore, 1640-1676*. New York: Oxford University, 1980.

Brodkin Sacks, Karen. "How Did Jews Become White Folks?" In *Race*, ed. Steven Gregory and Roger Sanjek, 78-102. New Brunswick NJ: Rutgers University, 1994.

Brodkin, Karen. *How Jews Became White Folks and What That Says About Race in America*. New Brunswick NJ: Rutgers University, 1998.

Brown Jr., Canter. "Race Relations in Territorial Florida, 1821-1845." *Florida Historical Quarterly* 73, no. 3 (1995): 287-307.

Brown, Kathleen M. *Good Wives, Nasty Wenches, and Anxious Patriarchs: Gender, Race, and Power in Colonial Virginia*. Chapel Hill: University of North Carolina, 1996.

Brown, William Wells. *Clotel, or, The President's Daughter: A Narrative of Slave Life in the United States*. London: Partridge & Oakey, 1853.

Brunner, Borgna, ed. *Time Almanac: The Ultimate Worldwide Fact and Information Source*. Boston: Information Please LLC, 1999.

Brunsma, David L., and Kerry Ann Rockquemore. "What Does 'Black' Mean? Exploring the Epistemological Stranglehold of Racial Categorization." *Critical Sociology* 28, no. 1/2 (2002): 101-121.

Callahan, Jim. *Lest We Forget: The Melungeon Colony of Newman's Ridge*. Johnson City TN: Overmountain Press, 2000.

Cartmill, Matt. "The Status of the Race Concept in Physical Anthropology." *American Anthropologist* 100, no. 3 (1998): 651-60.

Catterall, Helen Tunnicliff, and James J. Hayden. *Judicial Cases Concerning American Slavery and The Negro*. New York: Octagon Books, 1968.

Caughie, Pamela L. *Passing and Pedagogy: The Dynamics of Responsibility*. Urbana: University of Illinois, 1999.

Cavalli-Sforza, L. L., and W. F. Bodmer. *The Genetics of Human Populations*. Mineola NY: Dover, 1999.

Cerda-Flores, Ricardo M., Maria C. Villalobos-Torres, Hugo A. Barrera-Saldana, Lizette M. Cortes-Prieto, Leticia O. Barajas, Fernando Rivas, Angel Carracedo, Yixi Zhong, Sara A. Barton, and Ranajit Chakraborty. "Genetic Admixture in Three Mexican Mestizo Populations Based D1S80 and HLA-DQA1 Loci." *American Journal of Human Biology* 14 (2002): 257-63.

Chamberlain, Joshua Lawrence. *The Passing of the Armies*. New York: G.P. Putnam's Sons, 1915.

Chandler, Alfred Dupont. *The Visible Hand: The Managerial Revolution in American Business*. Cambridge MA: Belknap, 1977.

Channing, Carol. *Just Lucky I Guess: A Memoir of Sorts*. New York: Simon & Schuster, 2002.

Chesnutt, Charles Waddell. *The House Behind the Cedars*. Boston: Houghton Mifflin, 1900.

Chicago, University of, ed. *The New Encyclopaedia Britannica*. Chicago: William Benton, 1974.

Clegg, John A. *The History of Flagler County*. Bunnell FL: Hall, 1976.

Cohen, David Steven. *The Ramapo Mountain People*. New Brunswick NJ: Rutgers University, 1974.

Collins, Francis. *The Human Genome Project And Beyond*. National Human Genome Research Institute (NIH), July 7 2001. Accessed July 7 2003. Lecture Transcript Web Site. Available from <http://www.genome.gov/10001292>.

Collins-Schramm, Heather E., Bill China, Darwin J. Operario, Lindsey A. Criswell, and Michael F. Seldin. "Markers Informative for Ancestry Demonstrate Consistent Megabase-Length Linkage Disequilibrium in the African American Population." *Human Genetics* 113 (2003): 211-19.

Collins-Schramm, Heather E., Rick A. Kittles, Darwin J. Operario, James L. Weber, Lindsey A. Criswell, Richard S. Cooper, and Michael F. Seldin. "Markers that Discriminate Between European and African Ancestry Show Limited Variation Within Africa." *Human Genetics* 111 (2002): 566-69.

Congress, United States. *Biographical Directory of the United States Congress, 1774-1989*. Washington: U.S. Government Printing Office, 1989.

Coon, Carleton Stevens. *The Origin of Races*. New York: Knopf, 1962.

Corte-Real, H.B., V.A. Macaulay, M.B. Richards, G. Hariti, M.S. Issad, A. Cambon-Thomsen A, S. Papiha, J. Bertranpetit, and B.C. Sykes BC. "Genetic Diversity in the Iberian Peninsula Determined from Mitochondrial Sequence Analysis." *Annals of Human Genetics* 60, no. 4 (1996): 331-50.

Cosmides, Lola, John Tooby, and Robert Kurzban. "Perceptions of Race." *Trends in Cognitive Sciences* 7, no. 4 (2003): 173-79.

Cox, Major W. "Alabama Quietly Ends Race Certification Policy." *Montgomery Advertiser*, May 1993.

Cromwell, Adelaide M. *The Other Brahmins: Boston's Black Upper Class, 1750-1950*. Fayetteville: University of Arkansas, 1994.

Cronon, William. *Nature's Metropolis: Chicago and the Great West*. New York: W.W. Norton, 1991.

Cross, William E. *Shades of Black: Diversity in African-American Identity*. Philadelphia: Temple University, 1991.

Daniel, G. Reginald. *More than Black?: Multiracial Identity and the New Racial Order*. Philadelphia: Temple University, 2002.

Davis, Adrienne D. "Identity Notes Part One: Playing in the Light." *American University Law Review* 45 (1996): 695-720.

Davis, David Brion. *The Problem of Slavery in Western Culture*. Ithaca: Cornell University, 1966.

Davis, F. James. *Who is Black?: One Nation's Definition*. University Park PA: State University of Pennsylvania, 1991.

Davis, Susan G. *Parades and Power: Street Theatre in Nineteenth-Century Philadelphia*. Philadelphia: Temple University, 1986.

Dawkins, Richard. *The Ancestor's Tale: A Pilgrimage to the Dawn of Evolution*. Boston: Houghton Mifflin, 2004.

Dawley, Alan. *Struggles for Justice: Social Responsibility and the Liberal State*. Cambridge MA: Harvard University, 1991.

Day, Caroline Bond, and Earnest Albert Hooton. *A Study of Some Negro-White Families in the United States*. Cambridge MA: Harvard University, 1932.

Degler, Carl N. *Neither Black nor White: Slavery and Race Relations in Brazil and the United States*. New York: Macmillan, 1971.

DeVries, James E. *Race and Kinship in a Midwestern town: The Black Experience in Monroe, Michigan, 1900-1915* Blacks in the New World. Urbana: University of Illinois, 1984.

Diaz del Castillo, Bernal, and J. M. Cohen. *The Conquest of New Spain* The Penguin classics, L123. Baltimore,: Penguin Books, 1963.

Dickerson, Debra J. *The End of Blackness: Returning the Souls of Black Folk to Their Rightful Owners*. 1st ed. New York: Pantheon, 2004.

Dinnerstein, Leonard, and David M. Reimers. *Ethnic Americans: A History of Immigration.* 4th ed. New York: Columbia University, 1999.

Doggett, Carita. *Dr. Andrew Turnbull and The New Smyrna Colony of Florida.* Eustis FL: Drew, 1919.

Dominguez Ortiz, Antonio. *La Sociedad Espanola en el Siglo XVIII* Monografias Historico-Sociales, v. 1. Madrid: Instituto Balmes de Sociologia Departamento de Historia Social Consejo Superior de Investigaciones Cientificas, 1955.

Dominguez, Virginia R. *White by Definition: Social Classification in Creole Louisiana.* New Brunswick NJ: Rutgers University, 1986.

Douglass, Frederick. *Narrative of the Life of Frederick Douglass, an American Slave,* ed. Benjamin Quarles. Cambridge MA: Belknap Press, 1960.

D'Souza, Dinesh. *The End of Racism.* New York: Free Press, 1995.

Dunning, William Archibald. *Essays on the Civil War and Reconstruction, and Related Topics.* New York: Macmillan, 1904.

Dupuy, R. Ernest, and Trevor N. Dupuy. *The Harper Encyclopedia of Military History.* 4 ed. New York: Harper Collins, 1993.

Eliade, Mircea, and Charles J. Adams, eds. *The Encyclopedia of Religion.* New York: Macmillan, 1987.

Elkins, Stanley M. "Slavery in Capitalist and Non-Capitalist Countries." In *Slavery in the New World: A Reader in Comparative History,* ed. Laura Foner and Eugene D. Genovese, 8-26. Englewood Cliffs NJ: Prentice-Hall, 1969.

Elkins, Stanley M. *Slavery: A Problem in American Institutional and Intellectual Life.* 3d , rev. ed. Chicago: University of Chicago Press, 1959.

Elliott, Michael A. "Telling the Difference: Nineteenth-Century Legal Narratives of Racial Taxonomy." *Law and Social Inquiry* (1999): 611-36.

Eltis, David. *The Rise of African Slavery in the Americas*. Cambridge UK: Cambridge University, 2000.

Fabi, M. Giulia. *Passing and the Rise of the African American Novel*. Urbana: University of Illinois, 2001.

Fairclough, Adam. *Race & Democracy: The Civil Rights Struggle in Louisiana, 1915-1972*. Athens: University of Georgia Press, 1995.

Feagin, Joe R. *Racist America: Roots, Current Realities, and Future Reparations*. New York: Routledge, 2000.

Fernandez, Jose R., Mark D. Shriver, T. Mark Beasley, Nashwa Rafla-Demetrious, Esteban Parra, Jeanine Albu, Barbara Nicklas, Alice S. Ryan, Paul M. McKeigue, Clive L. Hoggart, Roland L. Weinsier, and David B. Allison. "Association of African Genetic Admixture with Resting Metabolic Rate and Obesity Among Women." *Obesity Research* 11, no. 7 (2003): 904-11.

Ferreira, Marion L. *A Letter to the Pope and an Archbishop's Racist Reply*. January 1. Interracial Voice, 2003a. Accessed June 29 2003. Electronic Magazine. Available from <http://interracialvoice.com/marion2.html>.

Ferreira, Marion L. *Mother Henriette Delille & The One-Drop Rule -- Alive and Well?* January 1. Interracial Voice, 2003b. Accessed June 29 2003. Electronic Magazine. Available from <http://interracialvoice.com/marion.html>.

Ferreira, Marion L. *The Misidentification of Mother Henriette Delille*. August. The Multiracial Activist, 2002. Accessed June 29 2003. Electronic Magazine. Available from <http://www.multiracial.com/readers/ferreira.html>.

Ficker, Douglas J. "From Roberts to Plessy: Educational Segregation and the 'Separate but Equal' Doctrine." *Journal of Negro History* 84, no. 4 (1999): 301-14.

Fields, Barbara. "Of Rogues and Geldings." *American Historical Review* 108, no. 5 (2003): 1397-405.

Finkelman, Paul. "The Color of Law." *Northwestern University Law Review* 87, no. 3 (1993): 937-91.

Finkelman, Paul. "The Crime of Color." *Tulane Law Review* 67, no. 6 (1992): 2063-2112.

Fischer, David H. *Historians' Fallacies*. New York: Harper & Row, 1970.

Foner, Eric. *Reconstruction: America's Unfinished Revolution*. New York: Harper & Row, 1988.

Foner, Laura. "Free People of Color in Louisiana and St. Domingue: A Comparative Portrait of Two Three-Caste Societies." *Journal of Social History* 3, no. 4 (1970): 406-30.

Foner, Philip Sheldon. *Frederick Douglass, a Biography*. New York: Citadel, 1964.

Frankenberg, Ruth. *White Women, Race Matters: The Social Construction of Whiteness*. Minneapolis: University of Minnesota Press, 1993.

Franklin, John Hope. *From Slavery to Freedom*. [1st] ed. New York: A. A. Knopf, 1947.

Frazier, Edward Franklin. *The Negro Family in the United States*. Rev. and abridged ed. Chicago: University of Chicago, 1966.

Fredrickson, George M. *The Black Image in the White Mind: The Debate on Afro-American Character and Destiny, 1817-1914*. New York: Harper & Row, 1981a.

Fredrickson, George M. *White Supremacy: A Comparative Study in American and South African History*. New York: Oxford University, 1981b.

Freehling, William W. *The Road to Disunion: Secessionists at Bay 1776-1854*. New York: Oxford University, 1990.

Fretwell, Jaqueline K. *Civil War Times in St. Augustine*. St. Augustine: St. Augustine Historical Society, 1986.

Gannon, Michael V. *The Cross in the Sand*. Gainesville FL: University of Florida, 1965.

Gannon, Michael V., ed. *The New History of Florida*. Gainesville: University of Florida, 1996.

Gates, H.L. *Loose Canons: Notes on the Culture Wars*. New York: Oxford University, 1992.

Gates, Henry Louis. "The Passing of Anatole Broyard." In *Thirteen Ways of Looking at a Black man*, xxvi, 226. New York: Random House, 1997.

Genovese, Eugene D. "The Treatment of Slaves in Different Countries: Problems in the Application of the Comparative Method." In *Slavery in the New World: A Reader in Comparative History*, ed. Laura Foner and Eugene D. Genovese, 202-10. Englewood Cliffs NJ: Prentice-Hall, 1969.

Genovese, Eugene D. *Roll, Jordan, Roll: The World the Slaves Made*. New York: Vintage, 1976.

Gerber, David A. *The Making of an American Pluralism: Buffalo, New York, 1825-1860* Statue of Liberty--Ellis Island Centennial series. Urbana: University of Illinois, 1989.

Gerstle, Gary. *American Crucible: Race and Nation in the Twentieth Century*. Princeton: Princeton University, 2001.

Gilanshah, Bijan. "Multiracial Minorities: Erasing the Color Line." *Law and Inequality* 12 (1993): 183.

Gill, George W. *Does Race Exist?: An Proponent's Perspective*. Nova, 2000. Accessed November 2000. web page. Available from <http://www.pbs.org/wgbh/nova/first/gill.html>.

Gladwell, Malcolm. "Black Like Them." *The New Yorker*, April 29 1996.

Gleason, Phillip. "Minorities (Almost) All: The Minority Concept in American Social Thought." *American Quarterly* 43, no. 3 (1991): 392-424.

Goodman, Mary Ellen. *The Culture of Childhood: Child's-Eye Views of Society and Culture*. New York: Columbia University, 1970.

Goodwyn, Lawrence. *Democratic Promise: The Populist Moment in America*. New York: Oxford University, 1976.

Gordon, Milton M. *Assimilation in American Life: The Role of Race, Religion, and National Origins*. New York: Oxford University, 1964.

Gordon-Reed, Annette. *Thomas Jefferson and Sally Hemings: An American Controversy*. Charlottesville: University of Virginia, 1997.

Gorn, Elliott J. "'Good-Bye Boys, I Die a True American': Homicide, Nativism, and Working-Class Culture in Antebellum New York City." *The Journal of American History* 74, no. 2 (1987): 388-410.

Gossett, Thomas F. *Race: The History of an Idea in America.* New ed. Race and American culture. New York: Oxford University, 1997.

Gotanda, Neil. "A Critique of 'Our Constitution is Color-Blind'." *Stanford Law Review* 44, no. 1 (1991): 1-68.

Gould, Virginia Meacham. "The Free Creoles of Color of the Antebellum Gulf Ports of Mobile and Pensacola: A Struggle for the Middle Ground." In *Creoles of Color of the Gulf South*, ed. James H. Dormon, 28-50. Knoxville: University of Tennessee, 1996.

Graham, Lawrence. *Our Kind of People: Inside America's Black Upper Class.* New York: HarperCollins, 1999.

Graham, Thomas. *The Awakening of St. Augustine.* St. Augustine: St. Augustine Historical Society, 1978.

Graves, Rachel. "Forgotten Culture: Ignored by Society, Black Mexicans Deny Their History." *Houston Chronicle*, July 3 2004.

Gross, Ariela J. "Litigating Whiteness: Trials of Racial Determination in the Nineteenth-Century South." *Yale Law Journal* 108, no. 1 (1998): 109-188.

Gutman, Herbert George. *The Black Family in Slavery and Freedom, 1750-1925.* New York: Pantheon Books, 1976a.

Gutman, Herbert George. *Work, Culture, and Society in Industrializing America: Essays in American Working-Class and Social History.* 1st ed. New York: Knopf, 1976b.

Gwaltney, John Langston. *Drylongso: A Self Portrait of Black America.* New York: Random House, 1980.

Hacker, Andrew. *Two Nations: Black and White, Separate, Hostile, Unequal.* New York: Ballantine, 1995.

Hall, Gwendolyn Midlo. *Africans in Colonial Louisiana: The Development of Afro-Creole Culture in the Eighteenth Century.* Baton Rouge: Louisiana State University, 1992.

Hancock, Scott. "The Elusive Boundaries of Blackness: Identity Formation in Antebellum Boston." *Journal of Negro History* 84, no. 2 (1999): 115-29.

Handlin, Oscar, and Mary F. Handlin. "Origins of the Southern Labor System." *William and Mary Quarterly* 7, no. 2 (1950): 199-222.

Handlin, Oscar. *Boston's Immigrants, 1790-1880*. Rev. and enl. ed. Cambridge MA: Harvard University, 1959.

Haney-Lopez, Ian F. *White by Law: The Legal Construction of Race*. New York: New York University, 1996.

Hanger, Kimberly S. "Origins of New Orleans Free Creoles of Color." In *Creoles of Color of the Gulf South*, ed. James H. Dormon, 1-27. Knoxville: University of Tennessee, 1996b.

Hanger, Kimberly S. *A Medley of Cultures: Louisiana History at the Cabildo*. New Orleans: Louisiana Museum Foundation, 1996a.

Hanna, Alfred J. *A Prince in Their Midst: The Adventurous Life of Achille Murat on the American Frontier*. Norman OK: University of Oklahoma, 1946.

Hanna, Alfred J., and Kathryn A. Hanna. *Florida's Golden Sands*. Indianapolis: Bobbs-Merrill, 1950.

Hanna, Kathryn Abbey. *Florida: Land of Change*. Chapel Hill: University of North Carolina, 1941.

Hannaford, Ivan. *Race: The History of an Idea in the West*. Baltimore: Johns Hopkins University, 1996.

Harding, R.M., E. Healy, A.J. Ray, N.S. Ellis, N. Flanagan, C. Todd, C. Dixon, A. Sajantila, I.J. Jackson, M.A. Birch-Machin, and J.L. Rees. "Evidence for Variable Selective Pressures at MC1R." *Journal of Human Genetics* 66, no. 4 (2000): 1351.

Harris, Marvin. "The Myth of the Friendly Master." In *Slavery in the New World*, ed. Laura Foner and Eugene D. Genovese, 38-47. Englewood Cliffs NJ: Prentice-Hall, 1969.

Harris, Marvin. *Patterns of Race in the Americas*. Westport CT: Greenwood, 1964.

Harrison, G.A., and J.J.T. Owen. "Studies on the Inheritance of Human Skin Colour." *Ann. Human Genetics* 28 (1964): 27-37.

Haynes, Monica L. "Passing: How Posing as White Became a Choice for Many Black Americans." *Post-Gazette*, Oct. 26 2003, Lifstyle, 1.

Heine, Susanne M.J. *Politically Correct Revisionism: Or Why Mixed-Race Heroes Blacken Over Time*. March/April. Interracial Voice, 2002. Accessed January 7 2004. Electronic Magazine. Available from <http://interracialvoice.com/sheine7.html>.

Heine, Susanne M.J. *To the Most Reverend Alfred C. Hughes*. January 1. Interracial Voice, 2003. Accessed June 29 2003. Electronic Magazine. Available from <http://interracialvoice.com/sheine8.html>.

Heinegg, Paul. *Free African Americans of Maryland and Delaware from the Colonial Period to 1810*. Baltimore: Genealogy Publishing, 2000.

Hellwig, David J., ed. *African-American Reflections on Brazil's Racial Paradise*. Philadelphia: Temple University, 1992.

Hening, William Waller. *The Statutes at Large: Being a Collection of all the Laws of Virginia, from the First Session of the Legislature in the Year 1619*. Richmond [Va.]: Printed by and for Samuel Pleasants Junior printer to the Commonwealth, 1809.

Hernandez, Jose Mariano. "Hernandez to Hallowell." : The James S. Hallowell Collection of the Alexandria Library, 1843.

Hernandez, Peggy. *Firemen Who Claimed to be Black Lose Appeal*. The Boston Globe, July 26 1989. Accessed June 19 2003.

Hernandez, Peggy. *Two Fight Firing over Disputed Claim They are Black*. The Boston Globe, September 29 1988. Accessed June 19 2003.

Herskovits, Melville J. *The Anthropometry of the American Negro*. New York: Columbia University, 1930.

Hickman, Christine. "The Devil and the One Drop Rule." *Michigan Law Review* 95, no. 5 (1997): 1161-1265.

Higginbotham, Leon A., Jr., and Barbara K. Kopytoff. "Racial Purity and Interracial Sex in the Law of Colonial and Antebellum Virginia." *Georgetown Law Journal* 77, no. 6 (1989): 1967-2029.

Hill, Louise Biles. "George J. F. Clarke, 1774-1836." *The Florida Historical Quarterly* 21, no. 3 (1943): 197-253.

Hirschfeld, Lawrence A. "Do children have a theory of race?" *Cognition* 54, no. 2 (1995a): 209-52.

Hirschfeld, Lawrence A. "The Inheritability of Identity: Children's Understanding of the Cultural Biology of Race." *Child Development* 66, no. 5 (1995b): 1418-37.

Hirschfeld, Lawrence A. *Race in the Making: Cognition, Culture, and the Child's Construction of Human Kinds* Learning, development, and conceptual change. London: MIT Press, 1996.

Hodes, Martha Elizabeth. *White Women, Black Men: Illicit Sex in the Nineteenth-Century South*. New Haven: Yale University, 1997.

Hoetink, Harry. *Caribbean Race Relations: A Study of Two Variants*. London: Oxford University, 1971.

Hollandsworth, James G. *The Louisiana Native Guards: The Black Military Experience During the Civil War*. Baton Rouge: Louisiana State University, 1995.

Hollinger, David A. "Amalgamation and Hypodescent: The Question of Ethnoracial Mixture in the History of the United States." *American Historical Review* 108, no. 5 (2003): 1363-90.

Holmes, Robyn M. *How Young Children Perceive Race*. Thousand Oaks CA: Sage, 1995.

Holt, Thomas. *Black Over White: Negro Political Leadership in South Carolina During Reconstruction* Blacks in the New World. Urbana: University of Illinois, 1977.

Howe, William Wirt. "Roman and Civil Law in America." *Harvard Law Review* 16 (1903): 142-58.

Hyde, Lewis. *Trickster Makes This World: Mischief, Myth, and Art*. New York: North Point, 1998.

Ignatiev, Noel. *How the Irish Became White*. New York: Routledge, 1995.

Jacobson, Matthew Frye. *Whiteness of a Different Color: European Immigrants and the Alchemy of Race*. Cambridge: Harvard University, 1998.

James, C. L. R. *The Black Jacobins: Toussaint L'Ouverture and the San Domingo Revolution*. 2d , rev. ed. New York: Vintage Books, 1989.

Jefferson, Thomas, Andrew Adgate Lipscomb, Albert Ellery Bergh, and Richard Holland Johnston. *The Writings of Thomas Jefferson*. Washington DC: Thomas Jefferson Memorial Association, 1905.

Jervey, Theodore D. *The Slave Trade: Slavery and Color*. Columbia: The State Company, 1925.

Johnson, James Weldon. *Along This Way: The Autobiography of James Weldon Johnson*. New York: Da Capo, 1973.

Johnson, Michael P., and James L. Roark. *Black Masters: A Free Family of Color in the Old South*. 1st ed. New York: Norton, 1984.

Johnston, James Hugo. *Race Relations in Virginia & Miscegenation in the South, 1776-1860*. Amherst: University of Massachusetts, 1970.

Jones, Jacqueline. *Labor of Love, Labor of Sorrow: Black women, Work, and the Family From Slavery to the Present*. New York: Basic Books, 1985.

Jones, Kevin. "DNA Study Results." A paper delivered at the Fourth Union: A Melungeon Gathering, Kingsport TN, June 20 2000a.

Jones, Nicholas A., and Amy Symens Smith. *The Two or More Races Population: 2000*. Washington: U.S. Census Bureau, 2001. Census 2000 Brief, C2KBR/01-6.

Jones, Steve, Robert Martin, and David Pilbeam, eds. *The Cambridge Encyclopedia of Human Evolution*. Cambridge UK: Cambridge University, 1992.

Jones, Trina. "Shades of Brown: The Law of Skin Color." *Duke Law Journal* 49, no. 6 (2000b): 1487-1558.

Jordan, Daniel P. *Statement on the TJMF Research Committee Report on Thomas Jefferson and Sally Hemings*. : Thomas Jefferson Memorial Foundation, Inc., 2000.

Jordan, Winthrop D. "American Chiaroscuro: The Status and Definition of Mulattoes in the British Colonies." In *Slavery in the New World: A Reader in Comparative History*, ed. Laura Foner and Eugene D. Genovese, 189-201. Englewood Cliffs NJ: Prentice-Hall, 1969.

Jordan, Winthrop D. *The White Man's Burden: Historical Origins of Racism in the United States.* New York: Oxford University, 1974.

Jordan, Winthrop D. *White Over Black: American Attitudes Toward the Negro, 1550-1812.* Chapel Hill: University of North Carolina, 1968.

Kahane, P.P. *Ancient and Classical Art.* Vol. 1. 6 vols. 20,000 Years of World Painting, ed. Hans L. C. Jaffe. New York: Dell, 1967.

Kalla, A.K. "Inheritance of Skin Colour in Man." *Anthropologist* Special Volume (1968): 158-68.

Kanetsky, P.A., J. Swoyer, S. Panossian, R. Holmes, D. Guerry, and T.R. Rebbeck. "A Polymorphism in the Agouti Signaling Protein Gene is Associated with Human Pigmentation." *American Journal of Human Genetics* 70 (2002): 770-75.

Kaplan, Melanie D. G. "Different Strokes." *USA Weekend*, June 20-22 2003, 10.

Katz, Phyllis A. *Development of Children's Racial Awareness and Intergroup Attitudes.* Washington: National Institute of Education, 1981.

Kavanaugh, Celeste H. *David Levy Yulee: A Man and His Vision.* Fernandina FL: Amelia Island Museum of History, 1995.

Kayser, Manfred, Silke Brauer, Hiltrud Schadlich, Mechthild Prinz, Mark A. Batzer, Peter A. Zimmerman, B.A. Boatin, and Mark Stoneking. "Y Chromosome STR Haplotypes and the Genetic Structure of U.S. Populations of African, European and Hispanic Ancestry." *Genome Research* 13 (2003): 624-34.

Keen, Benjamin. *A History of Latin America.* 5th ed. Boston: Houghton Mifflin, 1996.

Kennedy, N. Brent. *The Melungeons, The Resurrection of a Proud People: An Untold Story of Ethnic Cleansing in America*. Macon: Mercer University, 1997.

Kennedy, Randall. "Interracial Intimacy." *Atlantic Monthly*, December 2002, 103-10.

Kennedy, Randall. *Interracial Intimacies: Sex, Marriage, Identity, and Adoption*. New York: Pantheon Books, 2003.

Kennedy, Stetson. *Jim Crow Guide: The Way it Was*. Boca Raton FL: Atlantic University, 1990.

Kingsley, Zephaniah. *Balancing Evils Judiciously: The Proslavery Writings of Zephaniah Kingsley* Florida History and Culture, ed. Daniel W. Stowell. Gainesville: University of Florida, 2000.

Kitano, Harry H. L., and Roger Daniels. *Asian Americans: Emerging Minorities*. 2nd ed. Englewood Cliffs: Prentice Hall, 1995.

Klein, A. Norman. "West African Unfree Labor Before and After the Rise of the Atlantic Slave Trade." In *Slavery in the New World: A Reader in Comparative History*, ed. Laura Foner and Eugene D. Genovese, 87-95. Englewood Cliffs NJ: Prentice-Hall, 1969a.

Klein, Herbert S. "Anglicanism, Catholicism, and the Negro Slave." In *Slavery in the New World: A Reader in Comparative History*, ed. Laura Foner and Eugene D. Genovese, 138-166. Englewood Cliffs NJ: Prentice-Hall, 1969b.

Klingberg, Frank J. *An Appraisal of the Negro in Colonial South Carolina*. Philadelphia: Porcupine, 1975.

Klos, George. "Blacks and the Seminole Removal Debate." In *The African American Heritage of Florida*, ed. David R. Colburn and Jane L. Landers, 128-56. Gainesville: University of Florida, 1995.

Knobel, Dale T. *Paddy and the Republic: Ethnicity and Nationality in Antebellum America*. 1st ed. Middletown CT: Wesleyan University, 1986.

Koger, Larry. *Black Slaveowners: Free Black Slave Masters in South Carolina, 1790-1860*. Jefferson NC: McFarland, 1985.

Kolchin, Peter. *American Slavery 1619-1877*. New York: Hill and Wang, 1993.

Kroeger, Brooke. *Passing: When People Can't be Who They Are*. New York: Public Affairs, 2003.

Kuhn, Thomas S. *The Structure of Scientific Revolutions*. Chicago: University of Chicago, 1962.

Kunkel, Paul A. "Modifications in Louisiana Negro Legal Status Under Louisisana Constitutions, 1812-1957." *Journal of Negro History* 44 (1959): 1-25.

Kurzban, Robert Owen. "The Social Psychophysics of Cooperation in Groups." Ph.D., University of California, 1998.

Kurzban, Robert, John Tooby, and Leda Cosmides. "Can Race be Erased? Coalitional Computation and Social Categorization." *Proceedings of the National Academy of Sciences* 98, no. 26 (2001): 15387-15392.

Kusmer, Kenneth L. *A Ghetto Takes Shape: Black Cleveland, 1870-1930*. Urbana: University of Illinois, 1976.

LaFeber, Walter. *The New Empire: An Interpretation of American expansion, 1860-1898*. Ithaca: Cornell University, 1963.

Landers, Jane G., ed. *Against the Odds: Free Blacks in the Slave Societies of the Americas*. London: Frank Cass, 1996.

Landers, Jane L. "Traditions of African American Freedom and Community in Spanish Colonial Florida." In *The African American Heritage of Florida*, ed. David R. Colburn and Jane L. Landers, 17-41. Gainesville: University of Florida, 1995.

Landers, Jane. *Black Society in Spanish Florida*. Chicago: University of Illinois, 1999.

Landry, Bart. *The New Black middle Class*. Berkeley: University of California, 1987.

Lane, Roger. *Roots of Violence in Black Philadelphia, 1860-1900*. Cambridge MA: Harvard University, 1986.

Lapansky, Emma Jones. "'Since They Got Those Separate Churches': Afro-Americans and Racism in Jacksonian Philadelphia." *American Quarterly* 31, no. 1 (1980): 54-78.

Larson, Pier M. "Reconsidering Trauma, Identity, and the African Diaspora: Enslavement and Historical Memory in Nineteenth-Century Highland Madagascar." *William and Mary Quarterly* 56, no. 2 (1999): 335-62.

Laumer, Frank. *Dade's Last Command*. Gainesville: University of Florida, 1995.

Levy, Leonard W., and Harlan B. Philips. "The Roberts Case: Source of the "Separate but Equal" Doctrine." *American Historical Review* 56, no. 3 (1951): 510-8.

Lieberman, Leonard, Rodney C. Kirk, and Alice Littlefield. "Perishing Paradigm: Race--1931-99." *American Anthropologist* 105, no. 1 (2003): 110-13.

Litwack, Leon F. *Been in the Storm So Long: The Aftermath of Slavery*. New York: Random House - Vintage, 1979.

Litwack, Leon F. *North of Slavery: the Negro in the Free States, 1790-1860*. Chicago: University of Chicago, 1961.

Litwack, Leon F. *Trouble in Mind: Black Southerners in the Age of Jim Crow*. New York: Vintage Books, 1998.

Loercher, Diana. "Black Art Exhibit." *The Ann Arbor News*, July 27 1977, B5.

Loewen, James W. *The Mississippi Chinese: Between Black and White* Harvard East Asian series, 63. Cambridge MA: Harvard University, 1971.

Love, Edgar F. "Marriage Patterns of Persons of African Descent in a Colonial Mexico City Parish." *Hispanic American Historical Review* 41, no. 1 (1971): 79-91.

Lowenthal, David. "Post-Emancipation Race Relations: Some Caribbean and American Perpectives." *Journal of Interamerican Studies and World Affairs* 13, no. 3/4 (1971): 367-77.

Lutz, Christopher. *Santiago de Guatemala, 1541-1773: City, Caste, and the Colonial Experience*. Norman: University of Oklahoma, 1994.

Lythcott-Haims, Julie C. "Where Do Mixed Babies Belong-Racial Classification in America and Its Implications for Transracial Adoption." *Harvard Civil Rights-Civil Liberties Law Review* 29 (1994): 531-58.

MacLeod, Murdo J. "Spain and America: The Atlantic Trade 1492-1720." In *The Cambridge History of Latin Amer-*

ica: Colonial Latin America, ed. Leslie Bethell, 1, 341-88. Cambridge UK: Cambridge University, 1984.

Mahon, John K. *History of the Second Seminole War 1835-1842.* revised ed. Gainesville: University of Florida, 1985.

Mahon, John K., and Brent R. Weisman. "Florida's Seminole and Miccosukee Peoples." In *The New History of Florida*, ed. Michael Gannon, 183-206. Gainesville: University of Florida, 1996.

Malcomson, Scott L. *One Drop of Blood: The American Misadventure of Race.* New York: Farrar Straus Giroux, 2000.

Martinez Alcubilla, Marcelo. *Codigos antiguos de Espana: coleccion completa de todos los codigos de Espana, desde el Fuero juzgo hasta la Novisima recopilacion, con un glosario de las principales voces anticuadas, notas, bindices parciales y un repertorio general alfabbetico de materias.* Madrid: Administracion J. Lopez Comancho Impresor, 1885.

Martinez Alier, Verena. *Marriage, Class and Colour in Nineteenth-Century Cuba: A Study of Racial Attitudes and Sexual Values in a Slave Society.* London: Cambridge University, 1974.

McNergney, Robert F., and Joanne M. Herbert. *Foundations of Education: The Challenge of Professional Practice.* 3rd ed. Boston: Allyn and Bacon, 2001.

McPherson, James A. *Battle Cry of Freedom: The Civil War Era.* New York: Ballantine, 1988.

Merriwether, D. Andrew, Sara Huston, Sudha Iyengar, Richard Hamman, Jill M. Norris, Susan M. Shetterly, M. Ilyas Kamboh, and Rpbert E. Ferrell. "Mitochondrial Versus Nuclear Admixture Estimates Demonstrate a Past History of Directional Mating." *American Journal of Physical Anthropology* 102 (1997): 153-59.

Miller, Kerby A. *Emigrants and Exiles: Ireland and the Irish Exodus to North America.* New York: Oxford University, 1985.

Mills, Donna Rachal. *Florida's First families: Translated Abstracts of pre-1821 Spanish Censuses.* Tuscaloosa, AL: Mills Historical Press, 1992.

Mills, Gary B. "Miscegenation and the Free Negro in Antebellum 'Anglo' Alabama: A Reexamination of Southern Race Relations." *Journal of American History* 68, no. 1 (1981): 16-34.

Mills, Gary B. *The Forgotten People: Cane River's Creoles of Color.* Baton Rouge: Louisiana State University, 1977.

Mintz, Sidney W. "Labor and Sugar in Puerto Rico and Jamaica, 1800-1850." In *Slavery in the New World: A Reader in Comparative History,* ed. Laura Foner and Eugene D. Genovese, 170-7. Englewood Cliffs NJ: Prentice-Hall, 1969.

Model, Suzanne, and Gene Fisher. "Unions Between Blacks and Whites: England and the U.S. Compared." *Ethnic and Racial Studies* 25, no. 5 (2002): 728-54.

Molnar, Stephen. *Human Variation: Races, Types, and Ethnic Groups.* 5th ed. Upper Saddle River NJ: Prentice Hall, 2002.

Morales Padron, Francisco. "La Vida Cotidiana en una Hacienda de Esclavos." *Revista del Instituto de Cultura Puertorriquena* 4, no. 10 (1961): 23-33.

Morgan, Edmund Sears. *American Slavery, American Freedom: The Ordeal of Colonial Virginia.* New York: Norton, 1975.

Morner, Magnus. *Race Mixture in the History of Latin America.* Boston: Little Brown, 1967.

Murray, Pauli, ed. *States' Laws on Race and Color.* Athens: University of Georgia, 1997.

Myrdal, Gunnar, Richard Mauritz Edvard Sterner, and Arnold Marshall Rose. *An American Dilemma: The Negro Problem and Modern Democracy.* New York: Pantheon Books, 1972.

Napier, Rodney, and Matti K. Gershenfeld. *Groups: Theory and Experience.* 7th ed. Boston: Houghton Mifflin, 2004.

Nash, Gary B. *Red, White, and Black: The Peoples of Early America.* 2nd ed. Englewood Cliffs NJ: Prentice-Hall, 1982.

News and Courier. "All Niggers, More or Less!" *The News and Courier,* Oct. 17 1895a, 5.

News and Courier. "The Miscegenation Matter." *The News and Courier*, Oct. 4 1895b, 1.

Oates, Stephen B. *Our fiery trial : Abraham Lincoln, John Brown, and the Civil War era.* Amherst: University of Massachusetts Press, 1979.

Olson, Steve. *Mapping Human History: Discovering the Past Through Our Genes.* Boston: Houghton Mifflin, 2002.

O'Neill, Tom. "Untouchables." *National Geographic*, June 2003, 2-31.

Opotow, Susan. "Moral Exclusion and Injustice: An Introduction." *Journal of Social Issues* 46, no. 1 (1990): 1-20.

Orfield, Gary, and Susan E. Eaton. *Dismantling Desegregation: The Quiet Reversal of Brown v. Board of Education.* New York: New Press, 1996.

O'Toole, James M. "Racial Identity and the Case of Captain Michael Healy, USRCS." *Prologue: Quarterly of the National Archives & Records Administration* 29, no. 3 (1997).

Painter, Nell Irvin. *Standing at Armageddon: The United States, 1877-1919.* 1st ed. New York: W.W. Norton, 1987.

Parra, E.J., R.A. Kittles, G. Argyropoulos, C.L. Pfaff, K. Hiester, C. Bonilla, N. Sylvester, D. Parrish-Gause, W.T. Garvey, L. Jin, P.M. McKeigue, M.L. Kamboh, R.E. Ferrell, W.S. Pollitzer, and M.D. Shriver. "Ancestral Proportions and Admixture Dynamics in Geographically Defined African Americans Living in South Carolina." *American Journal of Physical Anthropology* 114 (2001): 18-29.

Parra, Esteban J., Amy Marchini, Joshua Akey, Jeremy Martinson, Mark A. Batzer, Richard Cooper, Terrence Forester, David B. Allison, Ranjan Deka, Robert E. Ferrell, and Mark D. Shriver. "Estimating African American Admixture Proportions by Use of Population-Specific Alleles." *American Journal of Human Genetics* 63 (1998): 1839-51.

Pereira, L., M.J. Prata, and A. Amorim. "Diversity of mtDNA Lineages in Portugal: Not a Genetic Edge of European Variation." *Annals of Human Genetics* 64 (2000): 491-506.

Perman, Michael. *Struggle for Mastery: Disfranchisement in the South, 1888-1908*. Chapel Hill: University of North Carolina, 2001.

Pfaff, C.L., E.J. Parra, C. Bonilla, K. Hiester, P.M. McKeigue, M.I. Kamboh, R.G. Hutchinson, R.E. Ferrell, E. Boerwinkle, and M.D. Shriver. "Population Structure in Admixed Populations: Effect of Admixture Dynamics on the Pattern of Linkage Disequilibrium." *American Journal of Human Genetics* 68 (2001a): 198-207.

Pfaff, C.L., E.J. Parra, J. Ye, A. Massac, R.A. Kittles, and M.D. Shriver. "Using Estimates of Individual Admixture to Study the Genetics of Phenotypic Traits: Skin Pigmentation in African Americans." *American Journal of Human Genetics* 69, no. 4 (2001b): 410.

Pfeiffer, Kathleen. *Race Passing and American Individualism*. Amherst: University of Massachusetts, 2003.

Phillips, Ulrich Bonnell. *American Negro Slavery*. New York: D. Appleton, 1918.

Phinney, Jean S., and Mary Jane Rotheram. *Children's Ethnic Socialization: Pluralism and Development*. Beverly Hills: Sage, 1987.

Poitrineau, Abel. "Demography and the Political Destiny of Florida During the Second Spanish Period." *The Florida Historical Quarterly* 66, no. 4 April (1988): 420-443.

Polgreen, Lydia. "For Mixed-Race South Africans, Equity is Elusive." *The New York Times International*, July 27 2003, 3.

Pollitzer, William. "The Physical Anthropology and Genetics of Marginal People of the Southeastern United States." *American Anthropologist* 74, no. 3 (1972): 723-30.

Porter, Judith D. R. *Black Child, White Child: The Development of Racial Attitudes*. Cambridge MA: Harvard University, 1971.

Porter, Kenneth W. *The Black Seminoles*. Gainesville: University of Florida, 1996.

Powell, A.D. *Pissing on the Graves of Heroes*. May. Interracial Voice, 2003. Accessed June 29 2003. Electronic Maga-

zine. Available from
<http://interracialvoice.com/powell14.html>.

Powell, A.D. *When Are Irish-Americans Not Good Enough to Be
Irish-American?: 'Racial Kidnaping' and the Case of the
Healy Family.* November. Interracial Voice, 1998. Accessed June 29 2003. Electronic Magazine. Available
from <http://interracialvoice.com/powell8.html>.

Price, Richard. *Maroon Societies: Rebel Slave Communities in
the Americas.* [1st] ed. Garden City NY: Anchor Press,
1973.

Proby, Kathryn Hall. *Audubon in Florida.* Coral Gables FL: University of Miami, 1974.

Quarles, Benjamin. "Abolition's Different Drummer." In *The
Antislavery Vanguard: New Essays on the Abolitionists,*
ed. Martin B. Duberman, 130. Princeton: Princeton University, 1965.

Rana, B.K., D. Hewett-Emmett, B.H.J. Chang, L. Jin, N. Sam-
buughin, M. Lin, S. Watkins, B. Michael, L.B. Jorde, M.
Ramsay, R. Jenkins, and W.H. Li. "High Polymorphism
at the Human Melanocortin 1 Receptor Locus." *Genetics*
151, no. 4 (1999): 1547-48.

Rasico, Philip D. *The Minorcans of Florida: Their History, Language, and Culture.* New Smyrna Beach: Luthers, 1990.

Rebato, E., I. Salces, L. San Martin, J. Rosique, and C. Susanne.
"Sibling Correlations of Skin Pigmentation During
Growth." *Human Biology* 71, no. 2 (1999): 277-93.

Relethford, J.H., F.C. Lees, and P.J. Bayard. "Sex and Age Variation in the Skin Color of Irish Children." *Current Anthropology* 26, no. 3 (1985): 386-97.

Relethford, John. *Genetics and the Search for Modern Human
Origins.* New York: Wiley-Liss, 2001.

Richards, Martin, Chiara Rengo, Fulvio Cruciani, Fiona Gratrix,
James F. Wilson, Rosaria Scozzari, Vincent Macaulay,
and Antonio Torroni. "Extensive Female-Mediated Gene
Flow from Sub-Saharan Africa into Near Eastern Arab
Populations." *American Journal of Human Genetics* 72
(2003): 1058-64.

Richardson, Heather Cox. *The Death of Reconstruction: Race, Labor, and Politics in the Post-Civil War North, 1865-1901*. Cambridge MA: Harvard University, 2001.

Rivara, Frederick P., and Laurence Finberg. "Use of the Terms Race and Ethnicity." *Archives of Pediatrics & Adolescent Medicine* 155, no. 2 (2001): 119.

Rivers, Larry Eugene. *Slavery in Florida: Territorial Days to Emancipation*. Gainesville: University of Florida, 2000.

Robinson, Eugene. *Coal to Cream*. New York: The Free Press, 1999.

Rodas, Clemencia, Nancy Gelvez, and Genoveva Keyeux. "Mitochondrial DNA Studies Show Asymmetrical Amerindian Admixture in Afro-Colombian and Mestizo Populations." *Human Biology* 75, no. 1 (2003): 13-30.

Rodriguez, Clara E. "Challenging Racial Hegemony: Puerto Ricans in the United States." In *Race*, ed. Steven Gregory and Roger Sanjek, 131-45. New Brunswick NJ: Rutgers University, 1994.

Roediger, David R. *The Wages of Whiteness: Race and the Making of the American Working Class*. London: Verso, 1991.

Rogers, J.A. *Sex and Race*. 3 vols. St. Petersburg, Fla.: Helga M. Rogers, 1944.

Root, Maria P.P. "Resolving 'Other' Status: Identity Development of Biracial Individuals." *Women and Therapy* 9 (1990): 185-205.

Rosenberg, Emily S., and Eric Foner. *Spreading the American Dream: American Economic and Cultural Expansion, 1890-1945*. 1st ed. New York: Hill and Wang, 1982.

Rosenzweig, Roy. *Eight Hours for What we Will: Workers and Leisure in an Industrial City, 1870-1920*. 1st pbk. ed. Cambridge UK: Cambridge University, 1985.

Rothman, Joshua D. *Notorious in the Neighborhood: Sex and Families Across the Color Line in Virginia, 1787-1861*. Chapel Hill: University of North Carolina, 2003.

Rout, Leslie B. *The African Experience in Spanish America, 1502 to the Present Day* Cambridge Latin American studies ; 23. Cambridge UK: Cambridge University, 1976.

Russell, Kathy, Midge Wilson, and Ronald E. Hall. *The Color Complex: The Politics of Skin Color Among African Americans*. 1st ed. New York: Harcourt Brace Jovanovich, 1992.

Sagra, Ramón de la. *Historia Economico-Política y Estadística de la Isla de Cuba*. Havana: Arazoza y Soler, 1831.

Sailer, Steve. *Analysis: Race Now Not Black and White*. UPI, May 8 2002. Accessed May 8 2002.

Salazar, Lila E. *Love Child: A Genealogist's Guide to the Social History of Barbados*. St. Michael, Barbados: Family Find, 2000.

Sanjek, Roger. "Intermarriage and the Future of Races in the United States." In *Race*, ed. Steven Gregory and Roger Sanjek, 103-30. New Brunswick NJ: Rutgers University, 1994.

Sarpy, John O. *An open letter to Most Reverend Alfred C. Hughes*. Interracial Voice, 2003a. Accessed June 29 2003. Electronic Magazine. Available from <http://interracialvoice.com/sarpy.html>.

Sarpy, John O. *An Open Letter to the Leadership of the Catholic Church Regarding the Racial/Cultural Labeling of Mother Henriette Delille*. Interracial Voice, 2003b. Accessed June 29 2003. Electronic Magazine. Available from <http://interracialvoice.com/sarpy2.html>.

Schafer, Daniel L. "U.S. Territory and State." In *The New History of Florida*, ed. Michael V. Gannon, 207-30. Gainesville: University of Florida, 1996.

Schafer, Daniel L. *Anna Kingsley*. St. Augustine: St. Augustine Historical Society, 1994.

Schafer, Judith Kelleher. *Becoming Free, Remaining Free: Manumission and Enslavement in New Orleans, 1846-1862*. Baton Rouge: Louisiana State University, 2003.

Schultz, Mark R. "Interracial Kinship Ties and the Emergence of a Rural Black Middle Class." In *Georgia in Black and White: Explorations in the Race Relations of a Southern*

State, 1865-1950, ed. John C. Inscoe`, 141-72. Athens GA: University of Georgia, 1994.

Schweninger, Loren. "Socioeconomic Dynamics among the Gulf Creoles." In *Creoles of Color of the Gulf South*, ed. James H. Dormon. Knoxville: University of Tennessee, 1996.

Scioto Gazette. "A Sprig of Jefferson was Eston Hemings." *Scioto Gazette*, Aug. 1 1902.

Sharfstein, Daniel J. "The Secret History of Race in the United States." *Yale Law Journal* 112, no. 6 (2003): 1473-1509.

Shreeve, James. "Terms of Estrangement." *Discover*, November 1994, 56.

Shriver, Mark D., Esteban J. Parra, Sonia Dios, Carolina Bonilla, Heather Norton, Celina Jovel, Carrie Pfaff, Cecily Jones, Aisha Massac, Neil Cameron, Archie Baron, Tabitha Jackson, George Argyroupoulos, Li Jin, Clive J. Hoggart, Paul M. McKeigue, and Rick A. Kittles. "Skin Pigmentation, Biogeographical Ancestry, and Admixture Mapping." *Human Genetics* 112 (2003): 387-99.

Sider, Gerald M. *Lumbee Indian Histories: Race, Ethnicity, and Indian Identity in the Southern United States* Culture and class in anthropology and history ; v. 2. Cambridge UK: Cambridge University, 1993.

Sio, Arnold A. "Marginality and Free Coloured Identity in Caribbean Slave Society." In *Caribbean Slave Society and Economy: A Student Reader*, ed. Hilary Beckles and Verene Shepherd, 150-59. New York: New Press, 1991.

Skidmore, Thomas E. "Racial Mixture and Affirmative Action: The Cases of Brazil and the United States." *American Historical Review* 108, no. 5 (2003): 1391-6.

Smedley, Audrey. *Race in North America: Origin and Evolution of a Worldview*. 2nd ed. Boulder: Westview, 1999.

Smith, John David. *Black Voices From Reconstruction*. Gainesville: University of Florida, 1997.

Sollors, Werner. *Neither Black Nor White Yet Both*. Cambridge: Harvard university, 1997.

Sollors, Werner. *The Invention of Ethnicity*. New York: Oxford University, 1989.

Sollors, Werner. *Theories of Ethnicity: A Classical Reader.* Washington Square NY: New York University, 1996.

Southern, Eileen. *The Music of Black Americans: A History.* 2nd ed. New York: Norton, 1983.

Sowell, Thomas. *Ethnic America: A History.* New York: Basic Books, 1981.

Stampp, Kenneth M. *The Causes of the Civil War.* New York: Simon & Schuster, 1959.

Stampp, Kenneth M. *The Peculiar Institution.* New York: Vintage/ Random House, 1953.

Stein, Judith. "Defining the Race 1890-1930." In *The Invention of Ethnicity*, ed. Werner Sollors, 77-104. New York: Oxford University, 1989.

Stephenson, Gilbert Thomas. *Race Distinctions in American Law.* New York: AMS Press, 1910.

Sterkx, H. E. *The Free Negro in Ante-Bellum Louisiana.* Cranbury NJ: Associated University Presses, 1972.

Sterling, Dorothy, ed. *The Trouble They Seen: The Story of Reconstruction in the Words of African Americans.* New York: Da Capo, 1994.

Stern, C. "Model Estimates of the Frequency of White and Near-White Segregants in the American Negro." *Acta Genetica* 4 (1953): 281-98.

Stern, Curt. *Principles of Human Genetics.* 3d ed. San Francisco: W. H. Freeman, 1973.

Stocking, George W. *Race, Culture, and Evolution: Essays in the History of Anthropology.* New York,: Free Press, 1968.

Stone, Ferdinand. "The Law with a Difference and How it Came About." In *The Past as Prelude: New Orleans, 1718-1968*, ed. Hodding Carter, 42-70. New Orleans: Tulane University, 1968.

Stott, Richard Briggs. *Workers in the Metropolis: Class, Ethnicity, and Youth in Antebellum New York City.* Ithaca, N.Y.: Cornell University, 1990.

Stuckert, Robert S. "The African Ancestry of the White American Population." *Ohio Journal of Science* 55, no. May (1958): 155-60.

Sturm, Richard A., Neil F. Box, and Michele Ramsay. "Human Pigmentation Genetics: The Difference is Only Skin Deep." *BioEssays* 20 (1998): 712-21.

Sykes, Bryan. *The Seven Daughters of Eve.* 1st American ed. New York: Norton, 2001.

Takaki, Ronald T. *Iron Cages: Race and Culture in Nineteenth-Century America.* Revised ed. New York: Oxford University, 2000.

Tannenbaum, Frank. *Slave and Citizen, the Negro in the Americas.* Boston: Beacon Press, 1946.

Tebeau, Charlton W. *A History of Florida.* Coral Gables FL: University of Miami, 1971.

Tenzer, Lawrence Raymond. *The Forgotten Cause of the Civil War: A New Look at the Slavery Issue.* Manahawkin NJ: Scholars' Pub. House, 1997.

Thernstrom, Stephan, Ann Orlov, and Oscar Handlin, eds. *Harvard Encyclopedia of American Ethnic Groups.* Cambridge MA: Belknap, 1980.

Thomas, Hugh. *The Slave Trade: The Story of the Atlantic Slave Trade: 1440-1870.* New York: Simon and Schuster, 1997.

Thornton, John Kelly. *Africa and Africans in the Making of the Atlantic World, 1400-1800.* 2nd ed. New York: Cambridge University, 1998.

Tindall, George Brown. *South Carolina Negroes, 1877-1900.* Columbia: University of South Carolina, 1952.

Tocqueville, Alexis de. *Democracy in America.* New York: Harper & Row, 1966.

Trachtenberg, Alan, and Eric Foner. *The Incorporation of America: Culture and Society in the Gilded Age.* 1st ed. New York: Hill and Wang, 1982.

Trollope, Anthony, and Fred D'Aguiar. *The West Indies and the Spanish Main.* New York: Carroll & Graf, 1999.

Tucker, M. Belinda, and Claudia Mitchell-Kernan. "New Trends in Black American Interracial Marriage: The Social Structural Context." *Journal of Marriage and the Family* 52, no. 1 (1990): 209-218.

Ullman, Victor. *Martin R. Delany: The Beginnings of Black Nationalism*. Boston,: Beacon, 1971.

UPI. *Black or White? Race Becomes Political Issue*. UPI Domestic News, April 19 1984a. Accessed June 19 2003.

UPI. *Candidate's Race a Major Issue in Recall Election*. UPI Domestic News, May 8 1984b. Accessed June 19 2003.

UPI. *Green-Eyed 'Black' Man Wins Recall Election*. UPI Domestic News, May 9 1984c. Accessed June 19 2003.

UPI. *Race the Major Issue in Recall Election*. UPI Domestic News, May 8 1984d. Accessed June 19 2003.

Van Ausdale, Debra, and Joe R. Feagin. *The First R: How Children Learn Race and Racism*. Lanham MD: Rowman & Littlefield, 2001.

Voegeli, V. Jacque. *Free But Not Equal: The Midwest and the Negro During the Civil War*. Chicago: University of Chicago, 1967.

Wade, Peter. *Blackness and Race mixture: The Dynamics of Racial Identity in Colombia* Johns Hopkins Studies in Atlantic History and Culture. Baltimore: Johns Hopkins University, 1993.

Wadlington, Walter. "The Loving Case: Virginia's Anti-Miscegenation Statute in Historical Perspective." *Virginia Law Review* 52, no. 7 (1966): 1189-1223.

Walker, Peter. *Moral Choices: Memory, Desire, and Imagination in Nineteenth-Century American Abolition*. Baton Rouge: Louisiana State University, 1978.

Wang, Jinliang. "Maximum-Likelihood Estimation of Admixture Proportions From Genetic Data." *Genetics* 164 (2003): 747-65.

Ward, Geoffrey C. *Not for Ourselves Alone: The Story of Elizabeth Cady Stanton and Susan B. Anthony*. New York: Knopf, 1999.

Warren, Jonathan W., and France Winddance Twine. "White Americans, the New Minority?" *Journal of Black Studies* 28, no. 2 (1997): 200-218.

Waters, Mary C. *Black Identities: West Indian Immigrant Dreams and American Realities*. New York: Harvard University, 1999.

Waters, Mary C. *Ethnic Options: Choosing Identities in America.* Berkeley: University of California, 1990.

Watson, Graham. *Passing for White: A Study of Racial Assimilation in a South African School.* London: Tavistock, 1970.

Webb, Frank J. *The Garies and Their Friends.* London: Arno Press, 1857.

Wikramanayake, Marina. *A World in Shadow: The Free Black in Antebellum South Carolina* Tricentennial studies, no. 7. Columbia: University of South Carolina, 1973.

William Harlan Gilbert, Jr. "Memorandum Concerning the Characteristics of the Larger Mixed-Blood Racial Islands of the Eastern United States." *Social Forces* 24, no. 4 (1946): 438-47.

Williams, Richard. *Hierarchical Structures and Social Value: The Creation of Black and Irish Identities in the United States.* Cambridge UK: Cambridge University, 1990.

Williamson, Joel. *After Slavery: The Negro in South Carolina During Reconstruction, 1861-77.* Chapel Hill: University of North Carolina, 1965.

Williamson, Joel. *New People: Miscegenation and Mulattoes in the United States.* New York: Free Press, 1980.

Williamson, Joel. *The Crucible of Race: Black/White Relations in the American South Since Emancipation.* New York: Oxford University, 1984.

Winkler, Wayne. *Walking Toward the Sunset: The Melungeons of Appalachia.* 1st ed. Macon GA: Mercer University, 2004.

Wood, Peter H. *Black Majority: Negroes in Colonial South Carolina From 1670 Through the Stono Rebellion.* 1st ed. New York: Knopf, 1974.

Woodbury, Stephen A. *Culture, Human Capital, and the Earnings of West Indian Blacks.* : Upjohn Institute, 1993. Staff Working Paper.

Woodson, Carter G. "The Negroes of Cincinnati Prior to the Civil War." *The Journal of Negro History* 1, no. 1 (1916): 1-22.

Woodward, C. Vann. *The Strange Career of Jim Crow.* 3d rev. ed. New York: Oxford University, 1974.

Wright, Luther, Jr. "Who's Black, Who's White, and Who Cares: Reconceptualizing the United States's Definition of Race and Racial Classifications." *Vanderbilt Law Review* 48, no. 2 (1995): 513-70.

Xie, Yu, and Kimberly Goyette. "The Racial Identification of Biracial Children with One Asian Parent: Evidence from the 1990 Census." *Social Forces* 76, no. 2 (1997): 547-70.

Yanez, Barbara. "Taking a Closer Look at the 'One Drop Rule': An Interview with Frank Sweet." *Mulatto Nation Times*, July 2004.

Yiannopoulos, A. N. "The Early Sources of Louisiana Law: Critical Appraisal of a Controversy." In *An Uncommon Experience: Law and Judicial Institutions in Louisiana, 1803-2003*, ed. Judith Kelleher Schafer and Warren M. Billings, 93-108. Lafayette: University of Southwestern Louisiana, 1997.

Zack, Naomi. *Thinking About Race*. Belmont, CA: Wadsworth, 1998.

Index

𝔅𝔞𝔠𝔨𝔦𝔫𝔱𝔶𝔪𝔢

30 Medford Drive
Palm Coast FL 32137-2504
386-446-4909

To order extra copies of this book, visit
http://backintyme.com/ad230.htm

Our complete line of publications is at:
http://backintyme.com/publishing.htm

Printed in the United States
88704LV00002B/108/A